Key to Entries

☃ Children welcome (from age shown in brackets, if specified)

🅿 Off-street car parking (number of places shown in brackets)

⊁ No smoking

📺 Television (either in every room or in a TV lounge)

🛌 Pets accepted (by prior arrangement)

✗ Evening meal available (by prior arrangement)

Ⓥ Special diets catered for (by prior arrangement - please check with owner to see if your particular requirements are catered for)

🏭 Central heating throughout

♿ Suitable for disabled people (please check with owner to see what level of disability is

GW00497163

∦ Drying facili...

The location heading - every hamlet, village, town and city mentioned in this directory is represented on the local path map at the head of each chapter.

Use the National Grid reference with Ordnance Survey maps and any atlas that uses the National Grid. The letters refer to a 100 kilometre grid square. The first two numbers refer to a North/South grid line and the last two numbers refer to an East/West grid line. The grid reference indicates their intersection point.

Local pubs - these are the names of nearby pubs that serve food in the evening, as suggested by local B&Bs

Map reference (in the order that the location appears along the route).

Penny Hassett   12

National Grid Ref: PH2096.

🍴 🍺 Cat & Fiddle, The Bull

Distance from routes in miles

(On route) *The Old Rectory, Main Street, Penny Hassett, Borchester, Borsetshire, BC2 3QT.*
C18th former rectory, lovely garden.
Grades: ETB 2 Cr, Comm.
Tel: **01048 598464.** Mrs Smythe.
Rates fr: *£14.00*-**£16.00.**
Open: All Year
Beds: 1F 1D 1T
Baths: 1 Private 2 Shared
☃(4) 🅿(2) ⊁ 📺 🛌 ✗ 🏭 Ⓥ ♿ ❄ ⚓

The figure in *italics* is the lowest 1998 double or twin rate per person per night. The figure in **bold** is the lowest 1998 single rate. Some establishments do not accept single bookings.

Bedrooms
F = Family
D = Double
T = Twin
S = Single

Grades - the English, Scottish and Welsh Tourist Boards (**ETB**, **STB** and **WTB**) have the national Crown rating (**Cr**), in which the range of facilities and services an establishment provides is indicated by "Listed" or 1 to 5 Crowns in ascending order of merit. An optional quality grading, using the terms Approved (**Approv**), Commended (**Comm**), Highly Commended (**High Comm**) and De Luxe is also used. More details of the national Crown rating and the quality grading can be had from any Tourist Information Centre. The Automobile Association (**AA**) employs two grading systems: the one for hotels uses 1 to 5 Stars (**St**) in ascending order of merit; there is also a B&B rating that uses the letter **Q** (for quality) on a scale of 1 to 4; the highest have 4 Qs and a Selected award (**Select**). For more details, telephone the AA on 01256 20123. The Royal Automobile Club (**RAC**) also uses a Star (**St**) system for large hotels; small hotels and B&Bs obtain the ratings 'Acclaimed' (**Acclaim**) or 'Highly Acclaimed' (**High Acclaim**). For more details, telephone the RAC on 0181-686 0088.

CYCLEWAY COMPANION

EDITORS
TIM STILWELL, MARTIN DOWLING

STILWELL
Publishing Ltd

Distributed in Great Britain, Europe & the Commonwealth by Bailey Distribution Ltd, Learoyd Road, New Romney, Kent, TN28 8XU (Tel: 01797 366905) and available from all good bookshops. Distributed in North America by Seven Hills Book Distributors, 49 Central Ave, Cincinatti, Ohio 45202, USA (Tel: (513) 381 3881).

ISBN 1-900861-06-2.

Published by Stilwell Publishing Ltd, 59 Charlotte Road, Shoreditch, London, EC2A 3QT. Tel: 0171-739 7179. Fax: 0171-739 7191. E-mail: tim@stilwell.demon.co.uk

© Stilwell Publishing Ltd, March 1998 (unless otherwise stated).

All maps in this book have been copied from pre-1948 mapping showing the National Grid

Stilwell Publishing Ltd:
Editor: Tim Stilwell
Assistant Editors: Martin Dowling, Eleanor O'Kane

Design and Maps: Nigel Simpson
Cover Photograph by Jason Patient

Printed in the Channel Islands by the Guernsey Press Company, Guernsey, Channel Islands.

Contents

Introduction

Several years ago, my wife and I set out to walk one of Britain's National Trails, the North Downs Way over several weekends. Neither of us are born to camping, nor could we afford to stay in expensive hotels. We decided on B&Bs and found a problem straightaway. One could not find good value bed and breakfast accommodation along the route without going to a lot of trouble. Local libraries, directory enquiries, six different Tourist Information Centres and a large pile of brochures yielded nothing but a hotchpotch of B&B addresses, most of them miles out of our way. We abandoned the research and did the walk in one-day stretches, high-tailing it back to our London home each evening on the train.

The point is that we didn't really want to take the train back, especially when the time spent in waiting and travelling matched the time spent walking. A good weekend's walk would have been ideal, but we didn't know where to stay. The Law of Sod dictates that wherever you choose to finish your day's cycling, there is either nothing in sight or a large country house hotel charging £100 for a one night stay. The train proved the logical option.

We therefore went on to create and publish a book called the National Trail Companion which publishes accommodation details for footpaths in the order that they appear along a path. Three years later, this Cycleway Companion is arranged along similar lines – for cyclists travelling along recognised cycle routes.

Long distance cycleways have become very popular over the last 10 years. County councils in particular have seen cycleways as a means of promoting tourism in the further-flung parts of their county. The Sustrans initiative has used the leisure-based cycle route as a flagship for their more wide-reaching campaign for sustainable transport. The Cyclists' Touring Club has spruced up its image and begun to market its own routes on a broader basis. The travel pages of our weekend newspapers regularly feature cycle breaks at home and abroad. The popularity of mountain biking and off-road cycling is clear; they even have their own specialist magazines. All in all, there are three times as many people cycling for their holiday than there were 20 years ago.

So when a man from Cornwall telephoned us in April last year to ask us whether we could bring out an accommodation book that catered for cyclists rather than for walkers, we finally jumped at the challenge. He had been the umpteenth person to ask us such a question that year. Twelve months later, here is the result. 21 long distance cycle routes are featured in this book. They fall into three separate categories. The county cycleways are waymarked routes set up by the relevant county council. Only 9 counties and one National Park so far have had the imagination to set up their own cycleways. These routes are all waymarked except for those in Leicestershire (devised before the split with Rutland) and Essex.

The Sustrans routes are part of the widely-publicized National Cycle Network, supported by the Bristol-based Sustrans organisation. The National Cycle Network was one of the first projects to win financial backing from the Millennium Commission – a cool £42,500,000 up to the year 2000. Sustrans' objective is principally environmental: to create 7,000 miles of cycle routes with common standards in partnership with local government. The Sustrans routes shown here are conceived as leisure routes. In fact, Sustrans is at pains to point out that cycling is not just a leisure activity. It is a sustainable means of transport which does not rely on a finite resource – oil – and which produces no air pollution, no traffic jams, no billion-pound road schemes and no scrap disposal problems. In every sense, cycling costs less than motoring. Sustrans therefore has a loftier aim than happier holiday-making: it is to get us all out of automobiles and onto bicycles. This will not happen if there are no safe places to cycle – hence Sustrans' far-sighted and dedicated work in devising these routes. Sustrans also advise on and initiate civil engineering projects with local government to smooth the way further for the bicycle.

The Cyclists' Touring Club routes have been around for a long time – it's just that route guides are available only to CTC members. The appearance of four routes in this Stilwell's guide is therefore quite an achievement. We chose these in particular from a huge CTC list of routes. Each seemed to us to capture the spirit of a great cycling holiday in the UK – fantastic scenery, plenty of things to see and do and possibly just that bit more of a challenge in terms of ascent and descent. The CTC is in a superb position to provide just this, because it has so much experience in cycle touring in this country. These routes are real gems – our thanks go to Steve Swithin and the CTC for allowing us to promote them. Just buy into the club membership and you'll not only be able to get the guides to these routes but you'll also have access to hundreds of other holiday ideas.

The Cycleway Companion does not attempt to tell the reader where to turn left or right, how far it is to the next stop or the steepness of the hills. This we leave to the admirable maps and guides already on the market (each chapter introduction tells you where to get hold of these). Instead, this book offers logistical help – where to stay and where to find pubs that serve evening meals along each route. It's my contention that once you've done one long distance cycle route, you want to do another, perhaps over a series of weekends rather than in one fell swoop. Planning and plotting the accommodation for such a journey is usually a long-winded affair. You have to ring Tourist Information Centres, wait for their literature, and then match unknown place-names to your mapped route. With this Cycleway Companion you can happily work out where to stay without the hassle, leaving you longer to devise a more extensive itinerary en route.

All information published in these pages has been collected over one year and provided by the owners themselves. The vast majority offer bed and breakfast at well under £25 per person per night, which we consider near the limit a cyclist would wish to pay. The pink highlight boxes are advertisements. Once again, we should make it clear that inclusion in these pages does not imply personal recommendation – we have not visited them all, merely written to them or phoned them. A simple glance over the salient details on any page, however, and the reader will be his or her own guide.

Owners were asked to provide their lowest rates per person per night for the year in question. The rates are thus forecasts and are in any case always subject to fluctuation in demand. Of course, some information may already be out of date. Grades may go up or down, or be removed altogether. British Telecom may alter exchange numbers. Proprietors may decide on a whim to move out of the business altogether. That is why the Cycleway Companion has to be a yearbook; in general, though, the information published here will be accurate, pertinent and useful for a long time to come.

One of the most important considerations for any cyclist planning a night's rest at a hostel or B&B is 'how far off the route is it?' Our concern has been, of course, to research Youth Hostels and B&Bs that are at least close to a given route; the reader can gauge at a glance how far one village is from the route compared with another. The accommodation lists are published in the order in which they appear along the path. We have numbered the locations to make cross-referencing easier.

We have also included pubs and inns that serve food in the evenings. For many cyclists, the promise of an evening meal will be of prime importance in deciding where to stay. These pubs have been suggested as decent places to eat by the B&B owners themselves – we publish them here so that you know you'll have something to fall back on if that B&B doesn't serve dinner itself. The direction in which the locations are listed is determined by popular choice and not by personal preference. If you wish to cycle the C2C from East to West or the Lon Las Cymru from Holyhead to Cardiff, then you will simply have to flick backwards through the chapter's pages rather than forwards. As far as mapping is concerned, I have omitted giving Landranger map numbers, except in the introduction to each path. The Ordnance Survey's national grid references are more important; to this end we have indicated grid labels and lines at the edge of each map.

Throughout the book you will find boxes offering advice to cyclists staying at B&Bs. Some of you may think these a waste of time and in fact, they are partly a publishing trick. They fill space and tidy the page up. But we really have heard horror stories about all sorts of guests from B&B owners, mainly concerning disregard for other people's property. Much of this is done through thoughtlessness and not by intent. If a few words can remind someone of his or her obligations, then these boxes, however self-important, will have done the trick.

Tim Stilwell
Stoke Newington, March 1998

Cycleway Locations

STILWELL'S CYCLEWAY COMPANION

Sustrans Carlisle to Inverness

At 402 miles, this massive crossing of Scotland from south to north is the longest route featured in this book. The **Scottish National Cycle Route** is a section of the planned Inverness to Dover route, the backbone of the new UK National Cycle Network. It runs on traffic-free paths and traffic-calmed roads from the English border city of Carlisle through the western Lowlands and Galloway Forest Park to Ayr on the west coast before reaching Glasgow, Scotland's metropolis. The northern section of the way will take you down the north bank of the Clyde Estuary to Dumbarton and the southern shore of Loch Lomond before you strike out into the varied and truly breathtaking scenery of the Scottish Highlands, from Loch Venachar to Loch Tay and across the Drumochter Pass, continuing through Strathspey below the Cairngorms to Inverness on the Moray Firth. The route is signposted by blue direction signs with a cycle silhouette and the number 7 in a red rectangle.

The indispensable **official route map and guide** for the Scottish National Cycle Route, which includes listings of cycle repair/hire shops along the route, comes in two parts, *Carlisle to Glasgow* and *Glasgow to Inverness*, and is available from Sustrans, 35 King Street, Bristol BS1 4DZ, tel 0117-926 8893, fax 0117-929 4173, @ £5.99 each (+ £1.50 p&p for both together or either one).

Maps: Ordnance Survey 1:50,000 Landranger series: 26, 27, 35, 36, 42, 43, 51, 52, 57, 63, 64, 70, 76, 77, 83, 84, 85

Transport: Carlisle, Glasgow and Inverness are all main termini on the Intercity network. There are connections to numerous other places on or near the route.

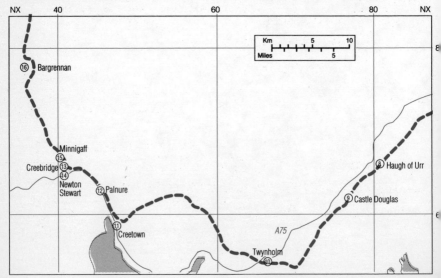

Carlisle   1

National Grid Ref: NY3955

¶⊙¶ ◀ Metal Bridge Inn

(▲ 0.25m) *University of Northumbria, The Old Brewery Residences, Bridge Lane, Caldewgate, Carlisle, Cumbria, CA2 5SR.*
Tel: **01228 597352. After 6pm: 01228 59486**
Under 18: £10.00 **Adults:** £10.00
Self-catering Facilities, Showers, Laundry Facilities
Accommodation in an award-winning conversion of the former Theakston's brewery. Single study bedrooms with shared kitchen and bathroom in flats for upto 7 people

(0.5m) *Howard Lodge, 90 Warwick Road, Carlisle, Cumbria, CA1 1JU.*
Actual grid ref: NY407558
Grades: ETB 1 Cr, Comm, AA 3 Q, Recomm
Tel: **01228 29842** Mr Hendrie.
Rates fr: *£15.00-£15.00*.
Open: All Year **Beds:** 2F 1D 2T 1S
Baths: 6 Ensuite 1 Shared
🛇 🅿 (6) 🗖 ⛷ ✕ 📖 Ⓥ
Large Victorian house on main road, 400 metres from city centre. Recently refurbished with ensuite facilities. Satellite TV and welcome tray in all rooms. Now with private parking

(0.5m) *Courtfield Guest House, 169 Warwick Road, Carlisle, Cumbria, CA1 1LP.*
Short walk to historic city centre. Close to M6, J43
Grades: ETB 3 Cr, High Comm
Tel: **01228 22767** Mrs Dawes.
Rates fr: *£17.50-£20.00*.
Open: All Year
Beds: 1F 2D 1T **Baths:** 4 Private
🛇 🅿 (4) 🗖 ⛷ ✕ 📖 Ⓥ

(0.25m) *Avondale, 3 St Aidans Road, Carlisle, Cumbria, CA1 1LT.*
Grades: ETB 2 Cr, High CommRAC Acclaim
Tel: **01228 23012** Mr & Mrs Hayes.
Rates fr: *£18.00-£20.00*.
Open: All Year (not Xmas)
Beds: 1D 2T
Baths: 1 Private 1 Shared
🅿 (3) 🗖 ✕ 📖 Ⓥ
Attractive, comfortable Edwardian house in a quiet position, convenient for M6 (J43), city centre & amenities. Spacious well-furnished rooms. Most hospitable. Private parking

(0.5m) *Chatsworth Guest House, 22 Chatsworth Square, Carlisle, Cumbria, CA1 1HF.*
Grade II Listed city centre house overlooking gardens. Close to bus stations, rail and all amenities
Grades: ETB 2 Cr, Comm
Tel: **01228 24023**
Mrs Irving.
Rates fr: *£14.00-£16.00*.
Open: All Year (not Xmas)
Beds: 2F 3T 2S
Baths: 2 Ensuite 1 Shared
🛇 (2) 🗖 ✕ 📖 ⚡

(0.25m) *Craighead, 6 Hartington Place, Carlisle, Cumbria, CA1 1HL.*
Actual grid ref: NY405559
Grades: ETB 2 Cr, Comm
Tel: **01228 596767** Mrs Smith.
Rates fr: *£15.50-£15.50*.
Open: All Year (not Xmas)
Beds: 1F 2D 1T 2S
Baths: 1 Ensuite 2 Shared
🛇 🗖 ⛷ 📖 Ⓥ ⚡
Grade II Listed spacious Victorian town house with comfortable rooms and original features. CTV, tea/coffee tray - all rooms. Minutes walk city centre, bus & rail station and all amenities. Friendly personal service

(0.25m) *Cornerways Guest House, 107 Warwick Road, Carlisle, Cumbria, CA1 1EA.*
Large Victorian town house
Grades: ETB 1 Cr, Comm
Tel: **01228 21733** Mrs Fisher.
Rates fr: *£13.00-£14.00*.
Open: All Year (not Xmas)
Beds: 1F 2D 4T 3S
Baths: 2 Ensuite 2 Shared
🛇 🅿 (5) 🗖 ⛷ ✕ 📖 Ⓥ ⬛

(On route) *East View Guest House, 110 Warwick Road, Carlisle, Cumbria, CA1 1JU.*
Actual grid ref: NY407560
A warm welcome assured at this Victorian family-run guesthouse
Grades: ETB 1 Cr, Comm
Tel: **01228 22112** (also fax no)
Mrs MacKin.
Rates fr: *£16.00-£18.00*.
Open: All Year **Beds:** 3F 3D 1T 1S
Baths: 8 Ensuite
🛇 🅿 (4) 🗖 📖 ⚡

(0.5m) *Langleigh House, 6 Howard Place, Carlisle, Cumbria, CA1 1HR.*
Comfortable home with Victorian furniture
Grades: ETB 2 Cr, High Comm, AA Listed
Tel: **01228 30440**
Rates fr: *£20.00-£25.00*.
Open: All Year
Beds: 3D **Baths:** 3 Ensuite
🛇 🅿 (10) 🗖 📖 ⛇ Ⓥ ⚡

(0.5m) *Marchmain Guest House, 151 Warwick Road, Carlisle, Cumbria, CA1 1LU.*
Comfortable accommodation with friendly atmosphere
Grades: ETB 1 Cr, Comm
Tel: **01228 29551** Mr Bertham.
Rates fr: *£16.00-£15.00*.
Open: All Year
Beds: 2F 2D 1T 1S
Baths: 1 Ensuite 2 Shared
🛇 ⅍ 🗖 ✕ 📖 Ⓥ

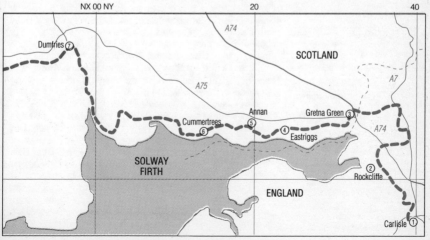

(0.5m) *7 Hether Drive, Lowry Hill, Carlisle, Cumbria, CA3 0ED*.
Bungalow ramped access. Wheel-in shower
Grades: ETB 1 Cr
Tel: 01228 27242
Mrs Young.
Rates fr: *£16.50*-**£18.50**.
Open: All Year
Beds: 1F 1D 1T
Baths: 2 Private 1 Shared
⌂ (0) 🅿 (2) ❑ ★ ▥ ⓺ ⓥ ✦

(0.5m) *Parkland Guest House, 136 Petteril Street, Carlisle, Cumbria, CA1 2AW*.
Good service guest house, Hadrian's Wall
Grades: ETB 3 Cr, Comm, AA 3 Q, Recomm
Tel: 01228 48331 (also fax no)
Mrs Murray.
Rates fr: *£15.00*-**£17.50**.
Open: All Year
Beds: 2F
⌂ 🅿 (3) ⚲ ❑ ★ ✗ ▥ ⓥ

(0.5m) *Howard House, 27 Howard Place, Carlisle, Cumbria, CA1 1HR*.
Elegant Victorian town house
Tel: 01228 29159 / 512550
Mrs Fisher.
Rates fr: *£15.00*-**£15.00**.
Open: All Year
Beds: 2F 3D 3T
Baths: 2 Private 2 Shared
⌂ ❑ ★ ✗ ▥ ⓥ 🖋 ✦

Rockcliffe 2

National Grid Ref: NY3561

(1m) *Metal Bridge House, Metal Bridge, Rockcliffe, Carlisle, Cumbria, CA6 4HG*.
In country, close to M6/74
Grades: ETB 1 Cr, Comm
Tel: 01228 74695
Mr Rae.
Rates fr: *£14.00*-**£18.00**.
Open: All Year
Beds: 1D 2T
Baths: 1 Shared
⌂ 🅿 (4) ❑ ★ ▥.

Gretna Green 3

National Grid Ref: NY3168
⑩ ⛊ Royal Stewart Motel, Solway Lodge Hotel

(On route) *Greenlaw Guest House, Gretna Green, Gretna, Dumfriesshire, CA6 5DU*.
Homely, comfortable, friendly guest house
Grades: STB 2 Cr, Approv, AA 2 Q, Recomm
Tel: 01461 338361
Ms Adams.
Rates fr: *£15.00*-**£17.00**.
Open: All Year (not Xmas)
Beds: 1F 4D 3T 2S
Baths: 1 Ensuite 1 Private 3 Shared
⌂ 🅿 (12) ❑ ★ ✗ ▥ 🖋 ✦

Eastriggs 4

National Grid Ref: NY2466

(On Route) *Stanfield Farm, Eastriggs, Annan, Dumfriesshire, DG12 6TF*.
C19th farmhouse within easy reach of three golf courses and Gretna Green
Grades: STB Listed, Comm
Tel: 01461 40367
Mrs Mallinson.
Rates fr: *£16.00*-**£16.00**.
Open: Easter to Oct
Beds: 1F 2D
Baths: 1 Private 1 Shared
⌂ 🅿 (3) ❑ ★ ▥ ⓥ

Annan 5

National Grid Ref: NY1966

(0.5m) *Ravenswood, St Johns Road, Annan, Dumfriesshire, DG12 6AW*.
Red sandstone villa. Family-run
Tel: 01461 202158
Mr James.
Rates fr: *£17.00*-**£18.50**.
Open: All Year
Beds: 3F 2D 1T 2S
Baths: 2 Shared
⌂ ❑ ★ ✗ ▥ ⓥ

(0.5m) *Corner House Hotel, 78 High Street, Annan, Dumfriesshire, DG12 6DL*.
Town centre budget hotel
Tel: 01461 202754
Rates fr: *£21.00*-**£24.00**.
Open: All Year
Beds: 3F 11D 16T 1S
Baths: 1 Ensuite 8 Shared
⌂ ❑ ★ ✗ ▥ ⓥ

(0.5m) *The Craig, 18 St Johns Road, Annan, Dumfriesshire, DG12 6AW*.
Friendly comfortable Victorian private house
Tel: 01461 204665 Mrs Anderson.
Rates fr: *£14.00*-**£14.00**.
Open: All Year (not Xmas)
Beds: 1F 2T 1S
Baths: 1 Shared
⌂ (6 months) ❑ ★ ▥ ✦

Cummertrees 6

National Grid Ref: NY1466
⑩ ⛊ Kirkland Hotel, Golf Hotel

(1m) *Huckledale Farm, Cummertrees, Annan, Dumfriesshire, DG12 5QA*.
Large well-appointed farmhouse
Grades: STB 2 Cr, Comm
Tel: 01461 700228 Mrs Forrest.
Rates fr: *£18.00*-**£22.00**.
Open: All Year (not Xmas)
Beds: 1F 1D 1T
Baths: 2 Ensuite 1 Private
⌂ 🅿 (6) ❑ ✗ ▥ ⓥ

Dumfries 7

National Grid Ref: NX9776
⑩ ⛊ The Swan, Station Hotel, Hill Hotel, Moreig Hotel

(0.5m) *Cairndoon, 14 Newall Terrace, Dumfries. DG1 1LW*.
Town centre, gracious, quiet home. Warm and friendly welcome
Tel: 01387 256991 Mrs Stevenson.
Rates fr: *£16.50*-**£16.50**.
Open: All Year **Beds:** 2F 1S
Baths: 1 Private 1 Shared
⌂ 🅿 (2) ❑ ▥ ⓥ 🖋 ✦

Carlisle to Dumfries

From the city centre of **Carlisle** (see the *Cumbria Cycleway*), the route proceeds to Rockcliffe on the Eden Estuary and Longtown on the Esk before crossing The Border to reach Gretna Green, the renowned border village whose Old Smithy was, during the eighteenth and nineteenth centuries, the site of numerous clandestine marriages of English people, in whose country marriage was the exclusive provenance of the Church. Heading west along the Solway Firth you reach **Annan** and then the village of Ruthwell, whose church houses a towering magnificently carved seventh-century cross. A little way further, Caerlaverock Castle is a beautiful thirteenth-century ruin built of pink stone, with a twin-towered gatehouse and surrounded by a moat. The nearby Wildfowl and Wetland Centre shelters bird species including the barnacle goose. Cycling up the beautiful Nith Estuary you reach the Queen of the South, **Dumfries**, much of which is built in the local red sandstone. Here behind the neoclassical columns of his mausoleum in St Michael's Churchyard lies Robert Burns, who lived in Dumfries for the last five years of his life. The Burns House has a collection of his paraphernalia and the Robert Burns Centre, located in a converted water mill, is a themed museum, with a cafe.

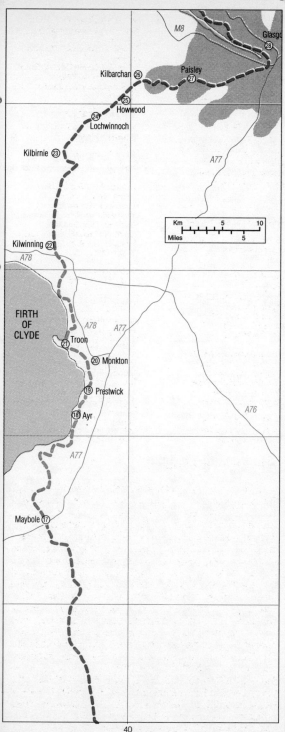

(0.5m) *4 Cassalands, Dumfries.*
DG2 7NS.
Large Victorian private house -
central
Tel: **01387 253701** Mrs Vaughan.
Rates fr: *£16.00-£16.00*.
Open: All Year (not Xmas)
Beds: 1D 1T 2S
Baths: 2 Shared
🐴 🅿 (6) ❏ ✕ ▥ ✦

(0.5m) *Shambellie View,*
Wellgreen, Glencaple Road,
Dumfries. DG1 4TD.
Modernised, centrally-heated villa
Grades: STB Listed, Comm
Tel: **01387 269331**
Mr & Mrs Burdekin.
Rates fr: *£14.50-£14.50*.
Open: All Year (not Xmas)
Beds: 1D 1T
Baths: 2 Shared
🐴 🅿 (3) ❏ 🛏 ✕ ▥ Ⓥ ♦ ✦

(0.5m) *Moreig Hotel, 67 Ann*
Road, Dumfries. DG1 3EG.
Elegant large sandstone licensed
hotel
Tel: **01387 255524** Mr Black.
Rates fr: *£22.50-£35.00*.
Open: All Year
Beds: 3F 3D 2S
Baths: 8 Ensuite
🐴 🅿 (20) ❏ 🛏 ✕ ▥ Ⓥ

(0.5m) *Lochenlee, 32 Ardwall*
Road, Dumfries. DG1 3AQ.
Quiet, warm, large Edwardian
house
Tel: **01387 265153** Mrs Porteous.
Rates fr: *£14.00-£13.00*.
Open: All Year
Beds: 2F 1S
Baths: 1 Shared
🐴 ⚲ ❏ ▥ Ⓥ

(0.5m) *Selmar, 41 Cardoness*
Street, Dumfries. DG1 3AL.
Small homely bed & breakfast
Tel: **01387 252095**
Mrs McKie.
Rates fr: *£13.50-£13.50*.
Open: All Year (not Xmas)
Beds: 1F 1T
Baths: 1 Shared
🐴 🛏 ✕ ▥ Ⓥ ♦ ✦

(0.5m) *Laurelbank Guest House,*
7 Laurieknowe, Dumfries. DG2 7AH.
Centrally situated, ensuite showers
Grades: STB 2 Cr, Comm
Tel: **01387 269388**
Rates fr: *£17.00-£24.00*.
Open: Mar to Nov
Beds: 1F 1D 2T
Baths: 1 Shared
🐴 🅿 (5) ⚲ ❏ ▥ Ⓥ

(0.5m) *The Knock Guest House, 1*
Lockerbie Road, Dumfries. DG1 3AP.
Large Victorian private house
Tel: **01387 253487**
Mr Sutherland.
Rates fr: *£14.00-£14.00*.
Open: All Year
Beds: 1F 1D 1T
🐴 (Any) 🅿 (1) ❏ 🛏 ✕ ▥ Ⓥ

40

(0.5m) *Inverallochy, 15 Lockerbie Road, Dumfries. DG1 3AP.*
Large semi-detached town house
Tel: **01387 267298**
Mrs Brown.
Rates fr: *£15.00-£16.00.*
Open: Easter to Oct
Beds: 1F 1T 2S
Baths: 1 Shared
🛇 **P** (3) ⌿ ⌷ ▥ **V**

Haugh of Urr 8

National Grid Ref: NX8066

📶 ◖ Laurie Arms

(0.25m) *Corbieton Cottage, Haugh of Urr, Castle Douglas, Kirkcudbrightshire, DG7 3JJ.*
Delightful country cottage, lovely views
Tel: **01556 660413**
Mr Jones.
Rates fr: *£15.00-£16.00.*
Open: All Year (not Xmas)
Beds: 1D 1T
Baths: 1 Shared
P (2) ⌿ ⌷ ✕ ▥

(0.25m) *Woodburn House, Haugh of Urr, Castle Douglas, Kirkcudbrightshire, DG7 3YB.*
Former C18th coaching inn
Grades: STB Listed, High Comm, AA 2 Cr
Tel: **01556 660217**
Mrs Wormald.
Rates fr: *£16.00-£19.00.*
Open: All Year
Beds: 1F 1D 1T
Baths: 1 Ensuite 2 Private
🛇 (0) **P** (6) ⌷ ✿ ✕ ▥ ⫽

Castle Douglas 9

National Grid Ref: NX7662

📶 ◖ Old Smugglers Inn, King's Arms, Douglas Arms, Market Inn, Laurie Arms

(0.25m) *Craigvar House, 60 St Andrew Street, Castle Douglas, Kirkcudbrightshire, DG7 1EN.*
Grades: STB 2 Cr, High Comm
Tel: **01556 503515**
Mrs Brierley.
Rates fr: *£20.00-£26.00.*
Open: Mar to Oct
Beds: 1D 1T
Baths: 2 Ensuite
P (1) ⌿ ⌷ ▥ **V**
Personally-run Georgian town house in a quiet area of this market town. A perfect base for walking, cycling, birdwatching, castles, gardens & non-smokers

---

Pay B&Bs by cash or cheque and be prepared to pay up front.

(0.25m) *Barrington House, 39 St Andrew Street, Castle Douglas, Kirkcudbrightshire, DG7 1EN.*
Grades: STB Listed, Comm, AA 3 Q
Tel: **01556 502601** Mrs Farley.
Rates fr: *£20.00-£22.00.*
Open: All Year **Beds:** 2D 1T
Baths: 2 Ensuite, 1 Private
🛇 (12) **P** (2) ⌿ ⌷ ✿ ✕ ▥ ⅁ **V** ⫽
Central Galloway market town. Many golf courses. Ideal for hill-walking, cycling, orienteering, fishing, bird-watching. Beautiful coastline. Numerous places of interest. Residents' lounge. Very warm welcome

(0.25m) *Kings Arms Hotel, Castle Douglas, Kirkcudbrightshire, DG7 1EL.*
Converted coaching inn
Grades: STB 4 Cr, Approv, AA 2 St, RAC 2 St
Tel: **01556 502626**
Mr Fulton.
Fax no: 01556 502097
Rates fr: *£25.00-£28.00.*
Open: All Year (not Xmas)
Beds: 2F 4D 4T 2S
Baths: 9 Ensuite 1 Private
🛇 **P** (15) ⌷ ✿ ✕ ▥ **V** ♦ ⫽

All cycleways are popular: you are well-advised to book ahead

---

Dumfries to Maybole

From Dumfries you head southwest through Haugh of Urr to reach **Castle Douglas** and nearby Threave Garden (National Trust for Scotland), with the sumptuous colours of its flowers and woodland, where there is also a restaurant. On to Tongland on the Dee and Gatehouse of Fleet, a pretty town in the lovely Fleet Valley. Nearby fifteenth-century Cardoness Castle is a typical Scottish tower house. From Gatehouse you head on to Creetown, where the River Cree flows into Wigtown Bay, before reaching Palnure on the edge of **Galloway Forest Park**, a beautiful 300-square-mile area of peaks in surroundings of forested hills and moorland with numerous lochs and a network of rivers. The Park's Kirroughtree Visitor Centre is nearby. Newton Stewart is a centre for salmon and trout fishing in the Cree; from here you follow the river upstream before heading into Glen Trool. Continuing through the Forest Park, the route wends its way over fairly gentle hills before a steeper climb and descent over Nick of the Balloch to the River Stinchar, and another climb to the summit below White Scaurins. You now descend steadily to reach Crosshill and **Maybole**. The climb out of Maybole yields splendid views out to sea – your first sight of the Firth of Clyde.

All rates are subject to alteration at the owners' discretion.

Twynholm 10

National Grid Ref: NX6654

📶 ◖ Star Hotel

(0.5m) *Glencroft, Twynholm, Kirkcudbright, Kirkcudbrightshire, DG6 4NT.*
Modern comfortable farmhouse near A75
Grades: STB 1 Cr, Comm
Tel: **01557 860252** Mrs Robson.
Rates fr: *£14.00-£14.00.*
Open: Easter to Oct
Beds: 1F 1D 1S
Baths: 2 Shared
🛇 (3) **P** ⌿ ✿ ✕ ▥ ⅁ **V** ⫽

Creetown 11

National Grid Ref: NX4758

(0.25m) *Marclaysean Guest House, 51 St John Street, Creetown, Newton Stewart, Wigtownshire, DG8 7JB.*
1889 local granite-built house
Grades: STB Listed, Comm
Tel: **01671 820319**
Mrs Seal Spiers.
Rates fr: *£18.00-£20.00.*
Open: Mar to Oct
Beds: 1D 1T 1S
Baths: 1 Private 1 Shared
🛇 ⌷ ✕ ▥ **V**

Palnure 12

National Grid Ref: NX4563

¶ Crown Hotel, Bruce Hotel

(On route) *The Stables Guest Tearoom*, Palnure, Newton Stewart, Wigtownshire, DG8 6JB.
Tea room. Bed and breakfast, comfortable home
Tel: **01671 404224** (also fax no)
Mrs Stables.
Rates fr: £17.00-£18.00.
Open: Mar to Nov
Beds: 2D 1T
Baths: 3 Ensuite
🛏 (1) 🅿 (8) 🗖 🛏 ✕ 🎟 & 🖾 🗎 ✦

Creebridge 13

National Grid Ref: NX4165

(On route) *Villa Cree*, Creebridge, Newton Stewart, Wigtownshire, DG8 6NR.
Peaceful riverside home, tiered gardens, ideally situated for fishing, touring
Tel: **01671 403914** Mr Rankin.
Rates fr: £15.00-£18.00.
Open: All Year (not Xmas)
Beds: 1T 2D 1S
Baths: 1 Ensuite 1 Private 1 Shared

(On route) *The Old Manse*, Creebridge, Newton Stewart, Wigtownshire, DG8 6PU.
Large Victorian manse of character
Tel: **01671 402901** Mrs McKay.
Rates fr: £15.00-£20.00.
Open: Apr to Oct
Beds: 1D 1T
Baths: 1 Ensuite 1 Private
🛏 (1) 🅿 (4) 🗖 🛏

Newton Stewart 14

National Grid Ref: NX4065

¶ Crown Hotel, Bruce Hotel

(▲ 0.5m) *Minnigaff Youth Hostel*, Newton Stewart, Wigtownshire, DG8 6PL.
Actual grid ref: NX411663
Tel: **01671 402211**
Under 18: £4.95 **Adults:** £6.10
Self-catering Facilities
Galloway Forest Park is nearby; fish in the River Cree; take a daytrip to the wild goat park and nature trails. The RSPB runs a reserve at Wood of Cree; scenic Glen Trool is nearby

(2m) *Carty Farm*, Newton Stewart, Wigtownshire, DG8 6AY.
Farmhouse, one mile Newton Stewart
Tel: **01671 402570**
Mrs Butcher.
Rates fr: £15.00-£15.00.
Open: All Year (not Xmas)
Beds: 1D 1T 1S
Baths: 1 Shared
🛏 🅿 (6) 🗖 🎟

(0.5m) *Palakona Guest House*, 30 Queen Street, Newton Stewart, Wigtownshire, DG8 6JL.
Centrally located, comfortable, homely
Tel: **01671 402323**
Mr Barlow.
Rates fr: £15.00-£15.00.
Open: All Year
Beds: 4F
Baths: 2 Shared
🛏 🅿 (3) 🗖 🛏 ✕ 🎟 🖾 🗎 ✦

Minnigaff 15

National Grid Ref: NX4166

¶ Cree Inn

(On route) *Flowerbank Guest House*, Minnigaff, Newton Stewart, Wigtownshire, DG8 6PJ.
Quiet C18th house. River setting
Grades: STB 2 Cr, Comm
Tel: **01671 402629**
Mrs Inker.
Rates fr: £16.50-£20.00.
Open: All Year (not Xmas)
Beds: 3F 2D 1T
Baths: 3 Ensuite 1 Private 2 Shared
🛏 🅿 (10) ⅃ 🗖 🛏 ✕ 🎟 🖾 🗎

Bargrennan 16

National Grid Ref: NX3576

(1.5m) *House O'Hill Hotel*, Bargrennan, Newton Stewart, Wigtownshire, DG8 6RN.
Actual grid ref: NX351769
Small, family-run C19th hotel
Grades: STB 3 Cr, Approv
Tel: **01671 840243** (also fax no)
Mrs Allwood.
Rates fr: £20.00-£23.00.
Open: All Year
Beds: 2F
Baths: 2 Private
🛏 🅿 🗖 🛏 ✕ 🎟 🖾 🗎 ✦

Maybole 17

National Grid Ref: NS2909

¶ Bruce Hotel, Welltrees Inn, Pippin's Hotel

(0.25m) *Homelea*, 62 Culzean Road, Maybole, Ayrshire, KA19 8AH.
Victorian villa near Culzean Castle, Burns Country & Turnberry golf courses
Grades: STB 3 Cr
Tel: **01655 882736** Mrs McKellar.
Fax no: 01655 883557
Rates fr: £15.00-£17.00.
Open: Mar to Oct
Beds: 1F 1D **Baths:** 2 Shared
🛏 🅿 ⅃ 🗖 🎟 🗎 ✦

The lowest *double* rate per person is shown in *italics*.

Ayr 18

National Grid Ref: NS3422

¶ Tam O'Shanter Inn, Kylestrome Hotel, Finlay's Bar, Burrofield's Bar, Carrick Lodge, Durward Hotel, Hollybush Inn

(▲ 0.5m) *Ayr Youth Hostel*, 5 Craigwell Road, Ayr. KA7 2XJ.
Actual grid ref: NS331211
Tel: **01292 262322**
Under 18: £6.50 **Adults:** £7.75
Self-catering Facilities, Family Bunk Rooms, Shop, Laundry Facilities
An excellent family base, with a barbecue, a 3-mile sandy beach and plenty to see nearby, including Burns Cottage, Culzean Castle and a Gold Cup racecourse

(0.5m) *Belmont Guest House*, 15 Park Circus, Ayr. KA7 2DJ.
Grades: STB 2 Cr, Approv
Tel: **01292 265588** Mr Hillhouse.
Fax no: 01292 290303
Rates fr: £17.50-£19.00.
Open: All Year (not Xmas)
Beds: 2F 2D 1T **Baths:** 5 Private
🛏 🅿 (5) 🗖 🛏 🎟 & 🖾 ✦
Warm, comfortable hospitality assured in this Victorian town house, situated in a quiet residential area within easy walking distance of the town centre and beach. Ground floor bedroom with ensuite available

(0.5m) *Deanbank*, 44 Ashgrove Street, Ayr. KA7 3BG.
Excellent highly commended B&B accommodation
Grades: STB 1 Cr, High Comm
Tel: **01292 263745** Ms Wilson.
Rates fr: £20.00-£20.00.
Open: All Year
Beds: 1F 1D **Baths:** 1 Shared
🛏 (1) 🅿 🗖 🛏 🎟 🖾

(0.5m) *Leslie Anne*, 13 Castlehill Road, Ayr. KA7 2HX.
Tel: **01292 265646** Mrs Hainey.
Rates fr: £20.00.
Open: All Year (not Xmas)
Beds: 1F 1D 1T
Baths: 3 Ensuite 1 Shared
🛏 🅿 (6) 🗖 🎟 🖾
Elegant town house. Beautiful, well-equipped bedrooms with antique, queen-size, brass beds, excellent breakfasts. Private parking. Ideally situated golf, touring, Glasgow and Prestwick airports

(0.5m) *Iona*, 27 St Leonards Road, Ayr. KA7 2PS.
Ideally situated for easy access to both town and countryside
Grades: STB 2 Cr, Comm
Tel: **01292 269541** (also fax no)
Mr & Mrs Gibson.
Rates fr: £16.00-£16.00.
Open: Feb to Nov
Beds: 1D 1T 2S
Baths: 2 Ensuite 1 Shared
🛏 🅿 (4) 🗖 🛏 ✕ 🎟 🖾

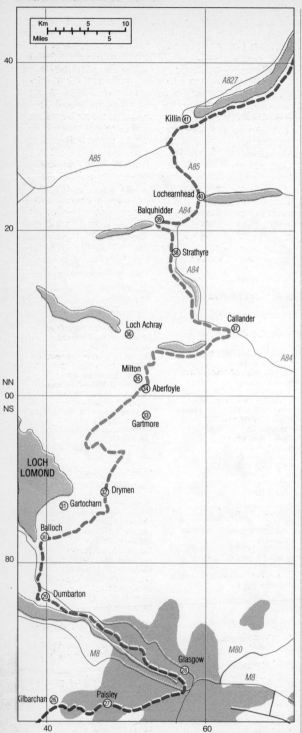

(0.5m) 9 Midton Road, Ayr.
KA7 2SE.
Close to town centre, beach, good
base for tourist exploration
Tel: 01292 288473 Mrs Horn.
Rates fr: *£14.00-£14.00*.
Open: All Year
Beds: 1F 1T 1S
Baths: 1 Shared
🛇 ❑ ⌂ ⛾ ▥.

**(0.5m) The Dunn Thing Guest
House, 13 Park Circus, Ayr.**
KA7 2DJ.
House in quiet tree-lined street near
shore front
Grades: STB 2 Cr, Approv
Tel: 01292 284531 Mrs Dunn.
Rates fr: *£18.00-£20.00*.
Open: All Year
Beds: 2D 1T **Baths:** 3 Ensuite
🛇 ❑ ⌂ ✗ ▥ ⛾ Ⓥ

**(0.5m) Windsor Hotel, 6 Alloway
Place, Ayr.** *KA7 2AA.*
Comfortable, private, family-run
hotel
Grades: STB 3 Cr, Comm
Tel: 01292 264689 Mrs Hamilton.
Rates fr: *£22.00-£22.00*.
Open: All Year (not Xmas)
Beds: 4F 3D 1T 2S
Baths: 7 Ensuite 1 Private
2 Shared
🛇 ❑ ⌂ ✗ ▥ ⛾ Ⓥ ▮

(0.5m) 13 Forest Way, Ayr. *KA7 3ST.*
Quiet bungalow in suburbs
Tel: 01292 267100 Ms Murdoch.
Rates fr: *£16.00-£18.00*.
Open: Easter to Nov
Beds: 1F 1D
Baths: 1 Shared
🛇 (3) ℗ (3) ❑ ⌂ ▥ ⛾

**(0.5m) Inverewe Guest House,
45 Bellevue Crescent, Ayr.** *KA7 2DP.*
Home form home. Central location
Tel: 01292 265989
Mr & Mrs Taylor.
Rates fr: *£15.00-£18.00*.
Open: All Year
Beds: 1F 2D 1T 1S
Baths: 2 Ensuite 1 Shared
🛇 ℗ (2) ❑ ⌂ ▥ Ⓥ

**(0.5m) Ferguslea, 98 New Road,
Ayr.** *KA8 8JG.*
Traditional Scottish hospitality
Grades: STB 2 Cr, Comm
Tel: 01292 268551 Mrs Campbell.
Rates fr: *£15.00-£15.00*.
Open: All Year
Beds: 2T 1S
Baths: 1 Private 2 Shared
🛇 ℗ (3) ❑ ⌂ ▥ Ⓥ

**(0.5m) Kingsley Guest House,
10 Alloway Place, Ayr.** *KA7 2AA.*
Family guest house, great value
Grades: STB 1 Cr, Approv
Tel: 01292 262853 Mrs Craig.
Rates fr: *£16.00-£17.50*.
Open: All Year
Beds: 3F 1D 2S
Baths: 2 Shared
🛇 ❑ ⌂ ✗ ▥ Ⓥ ▮ ✦

Maybole to Glasgow

Descending to reach the coast at Doonfoot, you cycle along the seafront of its sandy beach into **Ayr**, birthplace of Robert Burns. The old town nestles around the fifteenth - century auld brig over the River Ayr, which features in Burns' poem 'Twa Brigs'. St John's Tower is the remnant of a church where Cromwell had an armoury. Scotland's most important racecourse is on the north bank of the river. The next stretch along the coast is peppered with golf courses – the game originated in Scotland. After Prestwick you reach Troon, one of the locations of the British Open golf championship. The Scottish Maritime Museum is at Irvine; from here you head inland to Kilwinning and up the Garnock Valley to Kilbirnie, before turning east through Lochwinnoch, Kilbarchan and Johnstone to **Paisley**. The interior of the town's abbey,

which was originally founded in the twelfth century but overhauled in the Victorian era, is richly decorated. The stained glass dates from various periods. The Museum and Art Gallery has a large exhibition of shawls documenting the history of the famous Paisley Pattern, which was developed from Indian designs. At the Sma' Shot Cottages, a large themed exhibition recreates different aspects of life in the eighteenth and nineteenth centuries. From Paisley you weave your way mostly through urban sprawl, but pass close to Pollok Country Park, where the fantastic Burrel Collection, which includes Chinese porcelain, Egyptian antiquities, medieval tapestries and furniture, stained glass and a large collection of paintings among much else, is flooded with sunlight in its superb purpose-built gallery. Proceeding to the south bank of the Clyde, cross Bell's Bridge to reach the centre of Scotland's powerhouse and largest city, Glasgow.

(0.5m) *38 Forehill Road, Ayr.*
KA7 3DT.
Comfortable bungalow, homely atmosphere
Tel: **01292 286686**
Mrs Stewart.
Rates fr: *£14.50-£16.50.*
Open: All Year
Beds: 1F 1D 1T
Baths: 1 Shared
🛇 🅿 (3) 🖵 ✕ 🎟 &

(0.5m) *Kilkerran, 15 Prestwick Road, Ayr. KA8 8LD.*
Family-run guest house
Tel: **01292 266477**
Ms Ferguson.
Rates fr: *£14.00-£14.00.*
Open: All Year
Beds: 1F 1D 2T 1S
Baths: 2 Private 1 Shared
🛇 🅿 (5) 🖵 🖈 ✕ 🎟 & Ⓥ

(0.5m) *The Elms Court Hotel,*
Miller Road, Ayr. KA7 2AX.
Comfortable town centre hotel
Grades: STB 4 Cr, Comm,
AA 2 St
Tel: **01292 264191**
Mr & Mrs Gregor.
Fax no: 01292 610254
Rates fr: *£30.00-£30.00.*
Open: All Year
Beds: 3F 7D 6T 4S
Baths: 20 Private
🛇 🅿 ⅍ 🖵 🖈 ✕ 🎟 & Ⓥ 🛢 ✦

(0.5m) *Brookholm Guest House,*
15 Castlehill Road, Ayr. KA7 2HX.
Good service in beautiful Ayrshire
Tel: **01292 289510**
Mrs Morrison.
Rates fr: *£15.00-£15.00.*
Open: All Year
Beds: 1F 1D 1T
Baths: 2 Private 2 Shared
🛇 🅿 (6) 🖵 🖈 ✕ 🎟 Ⓥ

(0.5m) *23 Dalblair Road, Ayr.*
KA7 1UF.
Delightfully friendly boarding house
Tel: **01292 264798** Mr & Mrs Gambles.
Rates fr: *£17.50-£17.50.*
Open: All Year
Beds: 1D 1T 2S **Baths:** 2 Shared
🅿 🖵 🎟

(0.5m) *Eglington Guest House,*
23 Eglinton Terrace, Ayr. KA7 1JJ.
Listed Victorian terraced house
Grades: STB 1 Cr, Comm
Tel: **01292 264623**
Mrs & Mrs Clark.
Rates fr: *£15.00-£17.00.*
Open: All Year
Beds: 2F 1D 2T 1S
Baths: 2 Private 2 Shared
🛇 🖵 🖈 ✕ 🎟 Ⓥ

(0.5m) *26 Bellevue Crescent, Ayr.*
KA7 2DR.
Beautifully appointed Victorian terrace house
Tel: **01292 287329** Mrs McDonald.
Rates fr: *£18.00-£27.00.*
Open: All Year (not Xmas)
Beds: 3D 2T **Baths:** 5 Private
🛇 🅿 (2) ⅍ 🖵 🎟

Prestwick 19

National Grid Ref: NS3425
🍴 🍺 The Wheatsheaf, North Beach Hotel

(0.5m) *66 Adamton Road,*
Prestwick, Ayrshire, KA9 2HD.
Homely, quiet B&B
Tel: **01292 470399** Mrs Auld.
Rates fr: *£14.00-£14.00.*
Open: All Year
Beds: 1D 1T 1S **Baths:** 2 Shared
🛇 🅿 🖵 🎟

Monkton 20

National Grid Ref: NS3627

(1m) *Crookside Farm, Kerrix Road, Monkton, Prestwick, Ayrshire, KA9 2QU.*
Comfortable farmhouse central heating throughout, ideal for golfing, close to airport
Tel: **01563 830266** Mrs Gault.
Rates fr: *£12.00-£12.00.*
Open: All Year (not Xmas)
Beds: 1F 1D
Baths: 1 Shared
🛇 🅿 🖵 🖈 🎟 & Ⓥ

Troon 21

National Grid Ref: NS3230
🍴 🍺 Old Loans Inn, Ardneil Hotel

(0.5m) *The Cherries, 50 Ottoline Drive, Troon, Ayrshire, KA10 7AW.*
Beautiful home on golf course near beaches and restaurants
Grades: STB 2 Cr, Comm
Tel: **01292 313312** Mrs Tweedie.
Fax no: 01292 319007
Rates fr: *£17.00-£17.00.*
Open: All Year (not Xmas)
Beds: 1F 1T 1S
Baths: 1 Private 2 Shared
🛇 🅿 (5) ⅍ 🖵 🖈 🎟 Ⓥ ✦

(0.5m) *April Rose, 2 Golf Place, Troon, Ayrshire, KA10 6LA.*
In quiet cul-de-sac, near 3 golf courses, handy for airport / rail station
Grades: STB 2 Cr, Comm
Tel: **01292 315168** Mrs Bonner.
Rates fr: *£17.00-£20.00.*
Open: All Year
Beds: 1F 1T
Baths: 1 Ensuite 1 Private
🛇 🅿 ⅍ 🖵 🖈 🎟 Ⓥ ✦

(0.5m) *Kilmorack*, 87 Bentick Drive, Troon, Ayrshire, KA10 6HZ.
Comfortable Edwardian private house
Tel: **01292 311626**
Mrs McGeachin.
Rates fr: £18.00-£22.00.
Open: All Year (not Xmas)
Beds: 2D 1T
Baths: 3 Private
⛻ ▣ (2) ⊬ ⊡ ▥ Ⓥ

Kilwinning 22

National Grid Ref: NS3043
▮⊚ ◫ Blair Tavern, Ship Inn, Claremont Hotel

(3m) *Tarcoola*, Montgreenan, Kilwinning, Ayrshire, KA13 7QZ.
Tel: **01294 850379** Mrs Melville.
Fax no: 01294 850249
Rates fr: £15.00-£15.00.
Open: All Year
Beds: 1D 1S
Baths: 1 Shared
⛻ ▣ (3) ⊬ ⊡ ⊁ ▥ ⊬
Attractive country setting.
Convenient for Arran ferry, Ayrshire golf and Glasgow City attractions. Local pub food. Near A736 Irvine to Glasgow. Friendly welcome. Languages spoken

(1m) *Woodburn Cottage*, Woodwynd, Kilwinning, Ayrshire, KA13 7DD.
Delightful converted C19th farmhouse
Grades: STB Listed, Comm
Tel: **01294 551657**
Mrs Harris.
Fax no: 01294 558297
Rates fr: £16.50-£16.50.
Open: All Year (not Xmas)
Beds: 2T 1S
Baths: 2 Shared
⛻ ▣ (3) ⊬ ⊡ ▥ Ⓥ

(0.5m) *Claremont Guest House*, 27 Howgate, Kilwinning, Ayrshire, KA13 6EW.
Friendly family-run guesthouse, close to town centre & all public transport
Tel: **01294 553905** Mrs Filby.
Rates fr: £15.00-£15.00.
Open: All Year
Beds: 1F 1S **Baths:** 2 Shared
⛻ ▣ ⊡ ▥.

Kilbirnie 23

National Grid Ref: NS3154
▮⊚ ◫ Mossend Hotel

(0.5m) *Alpenrose*, 113 Herriot Avenue, Kilbirnie, Ayrshire, KA25 7JB.
Home from home Scottish villa
Tel: **01505 683122** Mrs Cameron.
Rates fr: £11.00-£11.00.
Open: All Year
Beds: 1D 1T 1S **Baths:** 1 Shared
⛻ ▣ (4) ⊡ ⊁ ⊠ ▥ ⅋ Ⓥ

Lochwinnoch 24

National Grid Ref: NS3559
▮⊚ ◫ Mossend Hotel, Gateside Inn

(0.25m) *East Lochhead*, Largs Road, Lochwinnoch, Renfrewshire, PA12 4DX.
Grades: STB 2 Cr, High Comm
Tel: **01505 842610** (also fax no)
Mrs Anderson.
Rates fr: £25.00-£35.00.
Open: All Year
Beds: 1F 1T
Baths: 1 Ensuite 1 Private
⛻ ▣ (6) ⊬ ⊡ ⊠ ▥ ⅋ Ⓥ
Country house in large garden with beautiful views over Barr Loch and the Renfrewshire Hills. Home-cooked dinners by request. Private off-road parking

(0.25m) *Springfield*, North Kerse, Lochwinnoch, Renfrewshire, PA12 4DT.
C17th modernised mill cottage, 15 mins Glasgow Airport
Grades: STB Listed, Comm
Tel: **01505 503690**
Mr & Mrs Rothney.
Rates fr: £16.00-£16.00.
Open: All Year
Beds: 1D 1T 1S
Baths: 2 Shared
⛻ ▣ (6) ⊡ ⊁ ⊠ ▥ Ⓥ ⅃ ⅋

Howwood 25

National Grid Ref: NS3960

(1m) *Howwood Inn*, Main Road, Howwood, Johnstone, Renfrewshire, PA9 1BQ.
Comfortable family run C18th coaching inn. Ideal touring base
Tel: **01505 703119** Mrs Donnelly.
Rates fr: £18.00-£18.00.
Open: All Year
Beds: 1F 1D 2T 1S
Baths: 2 Shared
⛻ ▣ (50) ⊡ ⊠ ▥ Ⓥ

Kilbarchan 26

National Grid Ref: NS4063
▮⊚ ◫ Trust Inn, Gryffe Arms

(1m) *Gladstone Farmhouse*, Burntshields Road, Kilbarchan, Johnstone, Renfrewshire, PA10 2PB.
Welcoming farmhouse ten minutes from airport
Grades: STB Listed, Comm
Tel: **01505 702579**
Mrs Douglas.
Rates fr: £15.00-£15.00.
Open: All Year
Beds: 1F 1D 1T
Baths: 1 Ensuite 1 Shared
⛻ ▣ (6) ⊡ ⊁ ⊠ ▥ & Ⓥ

Glasgow

The great city of **Glasgow** has long been Scotland's industrial hub, historically the centre of the European tobacco trade until shipbuilding and heavy industry took over. The city's Victorian civic architecture was built on wealth that flowed from industries whose employees were crammed into its notorious squalid and insanitary tenements. The grand public architecture of the eighteenth and nineteenth centuries includes the City Chambers, elegantly colonnaded Stirling's Library, Hutcheson's Hall with its white spire, designed by David Hamilton (now National Trust for Scotland) and Trades House, Glasgow's only surviving Robert Adam building, with a green dome and trade-inspired internal decoration. The earlier history of the city is reflected by Provand's Lordship, a fifteenth-century house (now a museum) and

thirteenth-century **St Mungo's Cathedral**. Close by, St Mungo's Museum of Religious Life and Art is an excellent display of the art of the world's religions. In addition to the Burrell Collection, Glasgow's many superb museums include the **Hunterian** (archaeology and Scottish art), **Kelvingrove Art Gallery** and **Museum** (Scottish and European art and Scottish natural history), the **Museum of Transport** (including bicycles, trains and trams) and the **People's Palace** (the city's social history). The considerable legacy of art nouveau architect and designer Charles Rennie Mackintosh includes the **Glasgow School of Art**, which demonstrates inside and out his concept of a building as total work of art, Queen's Cross Church and Scotland Street School. Mackintosh House, an impressive recreation of the interior of his home, is at the Hunterian.

Paisley   27

National Grid Ref: NS4863

(1m) *Myfarrclan Guest House*,
146 Corsebar Road, Paisley,
Renfrewshire, PA2 9NA.
Grades: STB 3 Cr, Deluxe
Tel: **0141 884 8285** (also fax no)
Mr & Mrs Farr.
Rates fr: £25.00-£35.00.
Open: All Year
Beds: 2D 1T
Baths: 2 Ensuite 1 Private
🛇 🅿 (2) ⌧ ❏ ✕ ▥ 🔥 Ⓥ ▐
Nestling in leafy suburb,
convenient for touring Loch
Lomond, Stirling and Islands.
(Tours [disabled] and itinaries
provided) Friendly relaxed
atmosphere - many extras. Lounge
/ garden conservatory

(1m) *Accara Guest House*,
75 Maxwellton Road, Paisley,
Renfrewshire, PA1 2RB.
Townhouse near Glasgow Airport
Grades: STB 1 Cr, Comm
Tel: **0141 887 7604**
Mrs Stevens.
Rates fr: £16.00-£16.00.
Open: All Year
Beds: 1F 1D 1T 1S
Baths: 2 Shared
🛇 ❏ ▥ Ⓥ

Glasgow   28

National Grid Ref: NS5965
🍴 🍺 Orchard Park Hotel,
Bellahouston Hotel, Garfield
House Hotel, Highlanders Park,
Pablo's, Dino's

(▲ 2m) *Glasgow Youth Hostel*,
7/8 Park Terrace, Glasgow. G3 6BY.
Actual grid ref: NS575662
Tel: **0141 332 3004**
Under 18: £9.95
Adults: £11.50
Evening Meals Available, Self-
catering Facilities, Family Bunk
Rooms, Shop, Laundry Facilities
Glasgow's alive. There are the dear
green places of the city parks, like
Kelvingrove. There's great shop-
ping, and things to see. A great
base too for touring the Trossachs,
the Clyde Coast and Loch Lomond

(2m) *Holly House*, 54 Ibrox
Terrace, Glasgow, G51 2TB.
Tel: **0141 427 5609 / 0850 223500**
(mobile)
Mr Divers.
Fax no: 0141 427 5608
Rates fr: £20.00-£25.00.
Open: All Year
Beds: 2F 2D 2T 2S
Baths: 5 Ensuite
🛇 (10) 🅿 (6) ❏ ▥.
Situated in an early Victorian
tree-lined terrace in the city centre,
near Glasgow Airport, Ibrox
Stadium, Burrel Gallery, 10
minutes to SECC. Family owned

(2m) *36 St Vincent Crescent*,
Glasgow. G3 8NG.
Grades: STB Listed, Comm
Tel: **0141 248 2086** (also fax no)
Mrs MacKay.
Rates fr: £27.50-£30.00.
Open: All Year (not Xmas)
Beds: 1T 4D
Baths: 2 Ensuite 1 Private
1 Shared
⌧ ❏ ▥.
Victorian house on the edge of the
city centre. Close to the SECC,
Kelvingrove Art Galley and the
best restaurant in town. All rooms
are individually decorated.
Continental breakfast only

(2m) *32 Riddrie Knowes*, Glasgow.
G33 2QH.
Large 1920s bungalow, easy
access. Self catering also available
Grades: STB 3 Cr, Comm
Tel: **0141 770 5213**
Mr Bain & Mr A E Mole.
Fax no: 0141 770 0955
Rates fr: £18.00-£18.00.
Open: All Year
Beds: 1D 1T
Baths: 2 Private
🛇 (3) 🅿 (2) ⌧ ❏ 🐾 ▥ 🔥 Ⓥ

(2m) *Kirkland House*, 42 St
Vincent Crescent, Glasgow. G3 8NG.
Grades: STB Listed, Comm
Tel: **0141 248 3458 / 427 5609**
Mrs Divers.
Fax no: 0141 221 5174 / 427 5608
Rates fr: £25.00-£25.00.
Open: Mar to Oct
Beds: 1F 2D 3T 2S
Baths: 6 Private 2 Shared
🛇 (1) ⌧ ❏ ▥.
City-centre guest house with
excellent rooms on beautiful
Victorian Crescent in Finnieston
(Glasgow's 'little Chelsea'). Short
walk to Scottish Exhibition Centre,
Museum-Art Gallery, Kelvingrove
Park and all West End facilities

(2m) *Park House*, 13 Victoria Park
Gardens South, Glasgow. G11 7BX.
Large Victorian private home
Grades: STB 3 Cr, High Comm
Tel: **0141 339 1559** (also fax no)
Mrs Hallam.
Rates fr: £25.00-£27.50.
Open: All Year
Beds: 2D 1T
🛇 🅿 (4) ❏ ✕ ▥ Ⓥ

All rooms full and
nowhere else to stay?
Ask the owner if
there's anywhere
nearby

(2m) *Lochgilvie House*,
117 Randolph Road, Broomhill,
Glasgow. G11 7DS.
Grades: STB Listed, Comm
Tel: **0141 357 1593** (also fax no)
Mrs Ogilvie.
Rates fr: £18.00-£20.00.
Open: All Year
Beds: 1F 1T 1D
Baths: 2 Shared
❏
Luxurious Victorian town house
situated in Glasgow's prestigious
West End, adjacent to rail station,
convenient for art galleries,
museums, International Airport,
eight minutes by train to city centre

(2m) *23 Dumbreck Road*,
Glasgow. G41 5LJ.
Large Victorian house, easy access
to motorways, city centre, airport
Grades: STB listed, Comm
Tel: **0141 427 1006** Mrs Sinclair.
Rates fr: £18.00-£20.00.
Open: Apr to Sep
Beds: 1D 1S
Baths: 2 Shared
🅿 (5) ❏ ✕ ▥ Ⓥ

(4m) *10 Forres Avenue, Giffnock*,
Glasgow. G45 6LJ.
Private house in quiet suburb
Grades: STB 1 Cr, Comm
Tel: **0141 638 5554, Mobile 0410**
864151 Mrs Davies.
Rates fr: £17.00-£17.00.
Open: All Year (not Xmas)
Beds: 2D
Baths: 1.5 Shared
🅿 (4) ❏ 🐾 ▥ Ⓥ

(6m) *21 West Avenue, Stepps*,
Glasgow. G33 6ES.
Conveniently located friendly
family home
Grades: STB 2 Cr, Comm
Tel: **0141 779 1990** Mrs Wells.
Fax no: 0141 779 1990
Rates fr: £20.00-£20.00.
Open: All Year
Beds: 1F 1D 1S
Baths: 2 Ensuite 1 Private
🛇 (Any) 🅿 (2) ⌧ ❏ ▥ Ⓥ

(2m) *The Terrace House Hotel*,
14 Belhaven Terrace, Glasgow.
G12 0TG.
Friendly family-run West End hotel
Grades: STB 3 Cr
Tel: **0141 337 3377** (also fax no)
Ms Black.
Rates fr: £29.00-£45.00.
Open: All Year
Beds: 4F 5D 3T 3S
Baths: 15 Private
🛇 ⌧ ❏ 🐾 ✕ ▥ Ⓥ ▐

(2m) *16 Bogton Avenue*, Glasgow.
G44 3JJ.
Red sandstone terraced private
house
Grades: STB 1 Cr, Comm
Tel: **0141 637 4402** Mrs Paterson.
Rates fr: £18.00-£18.00.
Open: All Year (not Xmas)
Beds: 1T 2S **Baths:** 2 Shared
🅿 (2) ⌧ ❏ ✕ ▥ Ⓥ ▐ ✦

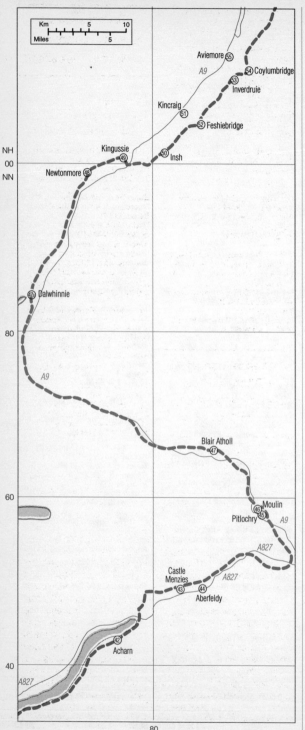

(2m) *Kelvingrove Hotel,*
944 Sauchiehall Street, Glasgow.
G3 7TH.
Centrally located family-run hotel
Grades: STB 2 Cr
Tel: **0141 339 5011** Mr Wills.
Fax no: 0141 339 6566
Rates fr: *£19.00-£22.00.*
Open: All Year
Beds: 4F 7D 5T 4S
Baths: 18 Private 1 Shared
⌂ �ＰＱ 🗠 ﹟ ✗ ▥, Ⅴ ▯

(2m) *4 Holyrood Crescent,*
Glasgow. G20 6HJ.
Large Victorian private town house
Grades: STB 1 Cr, Comm
Tel: **0141 334 8390** Mrs Adey.
Rates fr: *£15.00-£18.00.*
Open: Apr to Sep
Beds: 1F 1D 1T
Baths: 2 Shared
⌂ Ｑ ▥,

(2m) *Botanic Hotel,* 1 Alfred
Terrace, By 625 Gt Western Road,
Glasgow. G12 8RF.
Large Victorian private house
Grades: STB 2 Cr, High Comm,
AA 3 Q
Tel: **0141 339 6955** Mr Soldani.
Rates fr: *£21.00-£25.00.*
Open: All Year
Beds: 1F 4D 5T 1S
Baths: 7 Private 4 Shared
⌂ ＰＱ 🗠 ﹟ ✗ ▥, Ⅴ ▯

(2m) *Queens Park Hotel,* 10
Balvicar Drive, Glasgow. G42 8QT.
Friendly hotel with park view
Grades: STB 3 Cr, Approv
Tel: **0141 423 1123** Mrs Harte.
Fax no: 0141 423 4917
Rates fr: *£20.00-£30.00.*
Open: All Year
Beds: 5F 10D 15T 8S
⌂ Ｐ (6) Ｑ ﹟ ✗ ▥, Ⅴ

(2m) *Albion Hotel,* 405-407 North
Woodside Road, Glasgow. G20 6NN.
Ideal for seeing Glasgow
Tel: **0141 334 8159** (also fax no)
Mrs Doull.
Rates fr: *£25.00-£35.00.*
Open: All Year
Beds: 2F 6D 4T 4S
Baths: 16 Private
⌂ Ｐ (10) ✂ Ｑ ﹟ ✗ ▥, ⅙ Ⅴ

(2m) *Ambassador Hotel,* 7 Kelvin
Drive, Glasgow. G20 8QG.
Large Victorian private house
Grades: STB 3 Cr, Comm
Tel: **0141 946 1018** Mrs Hendry.
Rates fr: *£25.00-£35.00.*
Open: All Year
Beds: 4F 4D 3T 5S
Baths: 16 Private
⌂ Ｐ (12) ✂ Ｑ ﹟ ✗ ▥, ⅙ Ⅴ

The *lowest* **single**
rate *is shown in* **bold.**

Dumbarton 29

National Grid Ref: NS4075

⑩ ◀ Abbotsford Hotel

(0.5m) *Kilmalid House, 17 Glen Path, Dumbarton. G82 2QL.*
Large Victorian manse.
Overlooking castle
Tel: **01389 732030**
Mr & Mrs Muirhead.
Rates fr: £16.00-£16.00.
Open: All Year
Beds: 1F 2D 1S
Baths: 1 Shared
🛏 🅿 (12) 🗐 🕇 🎟, Ⅴ

(0.5m) *The Gable, 1 Sutherland Drive, Dumbarton. G82 3NT.*
Clean, comfortable, warm, friendly home
Tel: **01389 732223**
Mrs Larkin.
Rates fr: £15.00-£18.00.
Open: All Year
Beds: 1D 1T 1S
Baths: 1 Shared
🛏 🅿 (1) 🗐 🕇 ✕ 🎟, Ⅴ

Balloch 30

National Grid Ref: NS3982

⑩ ◀ Roundabout Inn, Balloch Hotel

(0.25m) *Glyndale, 6 McKenzie Drive, Balloch, Alexandria, Dunbartonshire, G83 8HL.*
Easy access of Loch Lomond, Glasgow Airport & public transport
Grades: STB Listed, Comm
Tel: **01389 758238**
Mrs Ross.
Rates fr: £15.50-£17.00.
Open: All Year
Beds: 1D 1T
Baths: 1 Shared
🛏 🅿 (2) 🗐 🕇 🎟, Ⅴ

(0.25m) *Kinnoul, Drymen Road, Balloch, Alexandria, Dunbartonshire, G83 8HS.*
Scottish hospitality guaranteed
Grades: STB 3 Cr, Comm
Tel: **01389 721116** (also fax no)
Mrs Elder.
Rates fr: £17.00-£25.00.
Open: All Year
Beds: 2F 2D 1T
Baths: 3 Ensuite 2 Private
🛏 🅿 (10) 🗐 🎟,

(0.25m) *Oakvale, Drymen Road, Balloch, Alexandria, Dunbartonshire, G83 8JY.*
Beautiful family home - pretty rooms
Tel: **01389 751615**
Mrs Feltham.
Rates fr: £16.00-£20.00.
Open: All Year
Beds: 2D 1T
Baths: 3 Ensuite
🛏 🅿 (4) 🗐 🎟,

(0.25m) *Gowanlea Guest House, Drymen Road, Balloch, Alexandria, Dunbartonshire, G83 8HS.*
Comfortable family-run guest house
Grades: STB 2 Cr, High Comm, AA 4 Q, Select
Tel: **01389 752456** Mrs Campbell.
Fax no: 01389 710543
Rates fr: £18.00-£22.00.
Open: All Year (not Xmas)
Beds: 2D 2T **Baths:** 4 Ensuite
🛏 🅿 (4) ✔ 🗐 🎟, Ⅴ

(0.25m) *Montrose Cottage, Ballagan, Balloch, Alexandria, Dunbartonshire, G83 8NB.*
Country cottage 1 mile outside Ballock
Tel: **01389 750194** Mrs Hendry.
Rates fr: £14.00-£14.00.
Open: All Year (not Xmas)
Beds: 1D 1T
🛏 🅿 (4) ✔ 🗐 🎟, Ⅴ

(0.25m) *Anchorage Guest House, Balloch Road, Balloch, Alexandria, Dunbartonshire, G83 8SS.*
Detached cottage
Tel: **01389 753336** Mr Bowman.
Rates fr: £15.00-£20.00.
Open: All Year
Beds: 1F 2D 2T **Baths:** 4 Private
🛏 🅿 (6) 🗐 🕇 🎟, ♿

Please respect a B&B's wishes regarding children, animals & smoking.

All cycleways are popular: you are well-advised to book ahead

---

Gartocharn 31

National Grid Ref: NS4286

⑩ ◀ Hungry Monk, Clachan Inn

(3m) *Ardoch Farm, Gartocharn, Loch Lomond, G83 8ND.*
Grades: STB 2 Cr, High Comm
Tel: **01389 830279** Mr Morgan.
Fax no: 01389 830623
Rates fr: £22.00-£28.00.
Open: All Year (not Xmas)
Beds: 2D 1T
Baths: 3 Ensuite
🛏 🅿 (5) ✔ 🗐 🎟, Ⅴ
Ardoch enjoys spectacular views of Loch Lomond peacefully surrounded by 130 acres. The house is newly renovated with pretty rooms, two with balconies, and luxury bathrooms

(2m) *Mardella Farm, Old School Road, Gartocharn, Loch Lomond, Alexandria, Dunbartonshire, G83 8SD.*
Actual grid ref: NS438864
Welcoming, happy atmosphere.
Ducks galore!
Grades: STB Listed, AA 4 Q, Select
Tel: **01389 830428**
Mrs MacDonell.
Rates fr: £18.50-£23.00.
Open: All Year **Beds:** 2F 1D
Baths: 1 Ensuite 1 Shared
🛏 🅿 (5) ✔ 🗐 🕇 ✕ 🎟, ✦

Glasgow to Loch Tay

Proceeding through the decaying shipyards of the north bank of the Clyde, you reach **Dumbarton** before heading north to Balloch Castle Country Park by Loch Lomond. Having left metropolitan Clydeside spectacularly behind, you continue to Drymen before cycling through Queen Elizabeth Forest Park, where be red deer, to reach Aberfoyle. Climbing northward you are in the heart of the Trossachs, a wild and wonderful region of craggy hills, forest and secluded waterfalls. Hugging the southern shore of Loch Venachar you arrive at **Callander**, a small town with excellent facilities, where the Rob Roy and Trossachs visitor centre introduces the region and offers an audiovisual presentation on its famous son, the most renowned of the MacGregors and hero of Sir Walter Scott's novel. From here you cycle along the west bank of Loch Lubnaig to reach Balquhidder at the eastern end of Loch Voil and Lochearnhead at the western end of Loch Earn. Climbing to the summit of Glen Ogle and descending to Lix Toll, you reach **Killin**, where the River Dochart cascades over the town's pretty waterfall into Loch Tay. The mountain **Ben Lawers** glowers across from the other side as you undertake the long ride down the southern shore of the loch.

Drymen 32

National Grid Ref: NS4788

|O| ◗ The Clachan, The Winnock, Old Mill

(1m) *East Drumquhassle Farm, Gartness Road, Drymen, Glasgow. G63 0DN.*
Actual grid ref: NS486872
Grades: STB 1 Cr, Comm
Tel: 01360 660893 Mrs Cross.
Rates fr: *£17.50-£20.00.*
Open: All Year
Beds: 1F 1D 1T
Baths: 1 Ensuite 1 Private
為 � (4) ⊬ ◻ ⼿ ✕ 皿. ⓥ ⿰ ⿰
Quiet comfortable, rural, beautiful views, home cooking, excellent touring base. Right on the West Highland Way

(0.25m) *Buchanan Arms Hotel, Main Street, Drymen, Glasgow. G63 0BG.*
Former coaching inn, luxury leisure club
Grades: STB 4 Cr, Comm, AA 3 St, RAC 3 St
Tel: 01360 660588
Mr Kernohan.
Rates fr: *£46.00-£46.00.*
Open: All Year
Beds: 3F 10D 30T 9S
Baths: 52 Ensuite
為 ⎡ (100) ◻ ⼿ ✕ 皿. ⓥ ⿰ ⿰

(0.25m) *Ceardach, Gartness Road, Drymen, Glasgow. G63 0BH.*
Converted 250-year-old smithy
Tel: 01360 660596 (also fax no)
Mrs Robb.
Rates fr: *£12.50-£15.00.*
Open: All Year (not Xmas)
Beds: 2D 1T
Baths: 1 Shared
為 (0) ⎡ (3) ◻ ⼿ 皿. ⿐ ⓥ ⿰ ⿰

(0.25m) *Winnock Hotel, The Square, Drymen, Glasgow. G63 0BL.*
C17th country inn
Grades: STB 4 Cr, Comm, AA 2 St, RAC 3 St
Tel: 01360 660245 Mr Warnes.
Rates fr: *£19.50-£32.00.*
Open: All Year
Beds: 6F 12D 16T 4S
Baths: 38 Private
為 ⎡ (60) ◻ ✕ 皿. ⓥ ⿰ ⿰

Gartmore 33

National Grid Ref: NS5297

|O| ◗ Black Bull

(4m) *Ardshiel, Main Street, Gartmore, Stirling. FK8 3RJ.*
Attractive old manse, friendly welcome
Tel: 01877 382457
Mrs Glasse-Davies.
Rates fr: *£14.50-£15.00.*
Open: All Year (not Xmas)
Beds: 1D
Baths: 1 Ensuite
為 ⎡ (1) ⊬ ◻ ⼿ 皿. ⓥ ⿰

Aberfoyle 34

National Grid Ref: NN5200

|O| ◗ Old Coach House Inn, Inverard Hotel

(0.25m) *Tigh na Cruinn, Manse Road, Aberfoyle, Stirling. FK8 3XF.*
Picturesque bungalow in woodland setting
Tel: 01877 382760 Mrs Marnie.
Rates fr: *£16.20-£20.00.*
Open: Easter to Oct
Beds: 2D
Baths: 1 Ensuite 1 Shared
為 ⎡ (3) ⊬ ◻ ⼿ 皿. ⓥ

(0.25m) *Mayfield, Main Street, Aberfoyle, Stirling. FK8 3UQ.*
Large Victorian private house in centre of Aberfoyle
Grades: STB Listed, Comm
Tel: 01877 382845 Mrs Oldham.
Rates fr: *£16.00-£16.00.*
Open: All Year (not Xmas)
Beds: 2D 1S
Baths: 3 Ensuite
為 ⎡ (4) ◻ ⼿ 皿. ⓥ

Milton 35

National Grid Ref: NN5001

|O| ◗ Byre Inn

(1m) *Creag Ard House B & B, Milton, Stirling. FK8 3TQ.*
Spectacular views, loch, mountains, forests
Grades: STB 2 Cr, Comm
Tel: 01877 382297
Mr Carter.
Rates fr: *£17.50-£20.00.*
Open: All Year
Beds: 3D 3T 1S
Baths: 4 Private 1 Shared
為 (1) ⎡ (10) ⼿ 皿. ⓥ

Loch Achray 36

National Grid Ref: NN5106

(5m) *Glenbruach Country House, Loch Achray, Trossachs, Callander, Perthshire, FK17 8HX.*
Tel: 01877 376216 (also fax no)
Mrs Lindsay.
Rates fr: *£22.00-£25.00.*
Open: All Year (not Xmas)
Beds: 2D 1T
Baths: 2 Ensuite 1 Private
為 (12) ⎡ (3) ◻ ⼿ ✕ 皿. ⿐
Unique country mansion in the heart of Rob Roy country. All rooms with Loch views. Interesting interior design and collections in this Scots-owned home

---

Pay B&Bs by cash or cheque and be prepared to pay up front.

All cycleways are popular: you are well-advised to book ahead

Callander 37

National Grid Ref: NN6307

|O| ◗ Myrtle Inn, Lade Inn, The Threshold, Argyll Inn, The Bridgend

(0.25m) *Roslin Cottage, Lagrannoch, Callander, Perthshire, FK17 8LE.*
Beautiful C18th stone cottage & garden on outskirts of town
Tel: 01877 330638 Mrs Ferguson.
Fax no: 01877 331448
Rates fr: *£15.50-£18.50.*
Open: All Year
Beds: 3D 1T 2S **Baths:** 1 Shared
為 ◻ ⼿ ✕ 皿. ⓥ ⿰

(On Route) *Craigroyston, 4 Bridge St, Callander, Perthshire, FK17 8AA.*
Circa 1745. Cycling, walking, fishing nearby. Central for touring
Tel: 01877 331395
Mr & Mrs MacLeod.
Rates fr: *£18.00-£20.00.*
Open: All Year
Beds: 1F 1D 1S
Baths: 3 Ensuite
為 ◻ ⼿ ✕ 皿. ⓥ

(0.25m) *Arden House Guest House, Bracklinn Road, Callander, Perthshire, FK17 8EQ.*
Peacefully situated with marvellous views
Grades: STB 3 Cr, High Comm
Tel: 01877 330235 (also fax no)
Mr McGregor.
Rates fr: *£21.00-£23.00.*
Open: Mar to Oct
Beds: 1F 2D 2T 1S
Baths: 6 Private
為 ⎡ (8) ⊬ ◻ ⼿ ✕ 皿. ⓥ

(0.25m) *Brook Linn Country House, Callander, Perthshire, FK17 8AU.*
Victorian house in elevated position
Grades: STB 3 Cr, High Comm
Tel: 01877 330103 (also fax no)
Mrs House.
Rates fr: *£20.00-£16.00.*
Open: Easter to Mid Nov
Beds: 2F 3D 1T 1S
Baths: 7 Private
為 (1) ⎡ (10) ⊬ ◻ ⼿ ✕ 皿. ⓥ ⿰

(0.25m) *Auchinlea, Ancaster Road, Callander, Perthshire, FK17 8EL.*
Quietly situated bungalow near town
Tel: 01877 330769 Mrs McKenzie.
Rates fr: *£15.00-£17.00.*
Open: All Year **Beds:** 1D 1T
為 ⎡ (1) ⊬ ◻ ⼿ 皿.

(0.25m) *East Mains House,*
Bridgend, Callander, Perthshire,
FK17 8AG.
C18th mansion house, mature
garden
Grades: STB 2 Cr, Comm
Tel: 01877 330535 (also fax no)
Mr & Mrs Thompson.
Rates fr: £18.00-£18.00.
Open: All Year
Beds: 1F 3D 1T
Baths: 4 Ensuite 1 Shared
🛇 🅿 (7) 🗲 ⏁ 🐾 ✕ ⏍ Ⓥ

(0.25m) *Lubnaig Hotel, Leny*
Feus, Callander, Perthshire,
FK17 8AS.
Luxury award-winning private
hotel
Grades: STB 2 St
Tel: 01877 330376 (also fax no)
Mr & Mrs Low.
Rates fr: £25.00-£30.00.
Open: Easter to Oct
Beds: 5D 5T
Baths: 10 Ensuite
🛇 (7) 🅿 (10) 🗖 🐾 ✕ ⏍ Ⓥ

(0.25m) *Teithside House,*
Bridgend, Callander, Perthshire,
FK17 8AF.
Scenically located, on riverbank
Tel: 01877 331333 Mrs Henderson.
Rates fr: £16.00-£16.00.
Open: All Year (not Xmas)
Beds: 2F 3D 1T
Baths: 2 Private 3 Shared
🛇 🅿 (6) 🗖 🐾 ⏍ Ⓥ

(0.25m) *9 Katrine Crescent,*
Callander, Perthshire, FK17 8JR.
Superior accommodation in
peaceful surroundings
Tel: 01877 330396 Mrs Milligan.
Rates fr: £17.00-£17.00.
Open: Easter to Oct
Beds: 1T **Baths:** 1 Ensuite
🅿 (1) 🗲 🗖 ⏍

Strathyre 38

National Grid Ref: NN5617
🍴 🍺 Strathyre Inn, Bell Shian
Hotel

(0.25m) *Ben Sheann Hotel,*
Strathyre, Callander, Perthshire,
FK18 8NA.
Old Victorian hotel, beautiful
Strathyre, Callander Trossachs
route
Tel: 01877 384609 (also fax no)
Mrs Hyde.
Rates fr: £19.50-£20.50.
Open: All Year
Beds: 3F 3D 2T 1S
Baths: 2 Ensuite 2 Shared
🛇 🅿 (15) 🗖 🐾 ✕ Ⓥ

All rates are subject
to alteration at the
owners' discretion.

(0.25m) *Coire Buidhe, Strathyre,*
Callander, Perthshire, FK18 8NA.
Former mill. Value for money
Grades: STB Listed, Approv
Tel: 01877 384288
Mr & Mrs Reid.
Rates fr: £14.00-£15.00.
Open: All Year (not Xmas)
Beds: 2F 2D 2T 2S
Baths: 1 Private 3 Shared
🛇 🅿 (6) 🗖 ⏍ Ⓥ ▮ ✦

(0.25m) *The Inn At Strathyre,*
Main Street, Strathyre, Callander,
Perthshire, FK18 8NA.
Comfortable friendly C18th inn
Grades: STB 3 Cr, Approv
Tel: 01877 384224
Mr La Piazza.
Fax no: 01877 384224 / 384344
Rates fr: £18.00-£25.00.
Open: All Year
Beds: 4D 3T
Baths: 7 Private
🛇 (5) 🅿 (15) 🗖 ✕ ⏍ Ⓥ ▮ ✦

Balquhidder 39

National Grid Ref: NN5320
🍴 🍺 Kingshouse Hotel

(0.25m) *Monachachyle Mhor,*
Hotel/farmhouse, Balquhidder,
Lochearnhead, Perthshire,
FK19 8PQ.
C18th restaurant in own 2000 acres
Grades: STB 4 St, High Comm
Tel: 01877 384622 Mrs Lewis.
Fax no: 01877 384305
Rates fr: £32.50-£42.50.
Open: All Year
Beds: 3D 2T 5D
Baths: 10 Ensuite
🅿 (12) 🗖 ✕ ⏍ Ⓥ ▮

(0.25m) *Calea Sona, Balquhidder,*
Lochearnhead, Perthshire, FK19 8NY.
Comfortable stone house,
wonderful views
Grades: STB 2 Cr, Comm
Tel: 01877 384260 (also fax no)
Mrs Blain.
Rates fr: £21.00-£25.00.
Open: All Year (not Xmas)
Beds: 1D 1T
Baths: 1 Ensuite 1 Private
🅿 (4) 🗖 ⏍ Ⓥ

Lochearnhead 40

National Grid Ref: NN5823
🍴 🍺 Clachan Cottage Bar

(0.25m) *Clachan Cottage Hotel,*
Lochside, Lochearnhead,
Perthshire, FK19 8PU.
Lochvies Restaurant - finest
Scottish cuisine
Grades: STB 3 Cr, Comm
Tel: 01567 830247 Mr Low.
Fax no: 01567 830300
Rates fr: £27.00-£27.00.
Open: Easter to Dec
Beds: 2F 10D 9T
Baths: 21 Private
🛇 🅿 (60) 🗖 🐾 ✕ ⏍ ♿ Ⓥ

Killin 41

National Grid Ref: NN5732
🍴 🍺 Bridge of Lochay Hotel

(▲ 0.25m) *Killin Youth Hostel,*
Killin, Perthshire, FK21 8TN.
Actual grid ref: NN569338
Tel: 01567 820546
Under 18: £4.85 **Adults:** £6.10
Self-catering Facilities, Shop
Picturesque Killin has the Falls of
Dochart, beautiful in fine weather
and impressive when in spate.
There are standing stones from the
Bronze Age, and the grave of
Fingal, the Celtic hero. The area
provides views of Ben Lawers and
Loch Tay and a wide range of
wildlife

(0.25m) *Falls of Dochart Cottage,*
Killin, Perthshire, FK21 8SW.
Tel: 01567 820363
Mr & Mrs Madd.
Rates fr: £15.00-£15.00.
Open: All Year (not Xmas)
Beds: 1T 1D 2S
Baths: 2 Shared
🅿 (4) 🗲 🗖 ✕ ⏍ Ⓥ
C17th cottage, overlooking the
falls and river - home cooking -
comfortable and friendly
atmosphere. Open all year: central
to magnificent mountain area -
renowned for hill walking

(0.25m) *Breadalbane House, Main*
Street, Killin, Perthshire, FK21 8UT.
Large converted bank, home from
home
Grades: STB 3 Cr, Comm
Tel: 01567 820386 Mrs Grant.
Rates fr: £18.00-£20.00.
Open: All Year (not Xmas)
Beds: 2F 2D 1T
Baths: 5 Ensuite
🛇 🅿 (6) 🗲 🗖 🐾 ✕ ⏍ ♿ Ⓥ

(0.25m) *Dalchenna, Craignavie*
Road, Killin, Perthshire, FK21 8SH.
Riverside view, edge of village
Tel: 01567 820281 Mrs Willison.
Rates fr: £14.00-£14.00.
Open: Jun to Sep
Beds: 1D 1S **Baths:** 1 Shared
🛇 🅿 🗲 🗖 ⏍ Ⓥ

Acharn 42

National Grid Ref: NN7543
🍴 🍺 Croft-Na-Caber Hotel

(On route) *Old School House,*
Acharn, Aberfeldy, Perthshire,
PH15 2HS.
Converted schoolhouse near Loch
Tay
Grades: STB 2 Cr, Comm
Tel: 01887 830307 (also fax no)
Mrs Brodie.
Rates fr: £18.00-£25.00.
Open: Easter to Oct
Beds: 2D 1T
Baths: 2 Ensuite 1 Shared
🛇 🅿 (10) 🗖 🐾 ⏍ Ⓥ

Castle Menzies 43

National Grid Ref: NN8349

🍴 🍺 Aileen Chraggan Hotel

(0.25m) *South Lodge, Castle Menzies, Aberfeldy, Perthshire, PH15 2JD.*
Comfortable, converted C18th lodge
Grades: STB Listed, High Comm
Tel: 01887 820115 Mrs Bolam.
Rates fr: *£16.00-£17.00.*
Open: All Year (not Xmas)
Beds: 1D 1T
Baths: 1 Ensuite 1 Private
🛏 🅿 (4) 🕭 ❌ 🖾 🖤 🖺 ✦

Aberfeldy 44

National Grid Ref: NN8549

🍴 🍺 Aileen Chraggan Hotel, Coshieville Hotel

(0.5m) *Handa, Taybridge Road, Aberfeldy, Perthshire, PH15 2BH.*
Large private house
Tel: 01887 820334
Mrs Bassett Smith.
Rates fr: *£16.00.* **Open:** All Year
Beds: 1D 1T **Baths:** 2 Private
🅿 🗆 🖾 🖤

(0.5m) *Tomvale, Tom of Cluny, Aberfeldy, Perthshire, PH15 2JT.*
Modern farmhouse
Grades: STB Listed, Approv
Tel: 01887 820171 Mrs Kennedy.
Rates fr: *£15.00-£16.00.*
Open: All Year (not Xmas/New Year)
Beds: 1F 1D **Baths:** 1 Shared
🛏 🅿 🗆 🐾 ❌ 🖾 🖤 ✦

(0.5m) *Callwood Cottage, Aberfeldy, Perthshire, PH15 2ND.*
Highland cottage in idyllic setting
Tel: 01887 830310 Mrs MacIntosh.
Rates fr: *£17.00-£25.00.*
Open: All Year (not Xmas/New Year)
Beds: 2D
Baths: 1 Ensuite 1 Private
🅿 (4) 🕭 🗆 ❌ 🖾 🖤 🖺

(0.5m) *Boisdale, Old Crieff Road, Aberfeldy, Perthshire, PH15 2DH.*
Welcoming, traditional bed & breakfast
Tel: 01887 820278
Mr & Mrs Steven.
Rates fr: *£15.00-£15.00.*
Open: Jun to Sep
Beds: 1D 1T **Baths:** 1 Shared
🛏 (14) 🅿 (3) 🖾 🖤 ✦

(0.5m) *2 Rannoch Road, Aberfeldy, Perthshire, PH15 2BU.*
Large modern bungalow, comfortable and friendly
Grades: STB Listed, Comm
Tel: 01887 820770 Mrs Ross.
Rates fr: *£15.00-£15.00.*
Open: Easter to Oct
Beds: 2D 1T **Baths:** 1 Shared
🅿 (4) 🗆 🖾

(0.5m) *Balnearn House, Aberfeldy, Perthshire, PH15 2BJ.*
Outstanding - not to be missed
Grades: STB 2 Cr, Comm
Tel: 01887 820431 Mr MacLaurin.
Rates fr: *£18.50-£22.50.*
Open: Easter to Oct
Beds: 1F 7D 2T
Baths: 8 Ensuite 2 Private
🛏 🅿 (30) 🗆 🐾 🖾 🖤

(0.5m) *Carn Dris, Aberfeldy, Perthshire, PH15 2LB.*
Large Edwardian private guest house
Tel: 01887 820250
Mrs Bell Campbell.
Rates fr: *£18.23-£18.23.*
Open: Mar to Oct
Beds: 2D 1T
Baths: 1 Private 1 Shared
🛏 (10) 🅿 (4) 🕭 🗆 🐾 🖾

(0.5m) *Dunolly House, Taybridge Drive, Aberfeldy, Perthshire, PH15 2BL.*
Spacious Victorian dwelling house
Tel: 01887 820298 Mr Hermiston.
Rates fr: *£14.00-£11.00.*
Open: All Year
Beds: 6F 6D 2T 1S
Baths: 3 Private 5 Shared
🛏 🅿 (15) 🗆 🐾 ❌ 🖾 🖤

Pitlochry 45

National Grid Ref: NN9458

🍴 🍺 Acarsaid Hotel, Pine Trees Hotel, Atholl Arms Hotel, Old Smithy, Old Armoury, Craigvrack Hotel, Moulin Inn, Ballinling Inn

(🔺0.5m) *Pitlochry Youth Hostel, Knockard Road, Pitlochry. PH16 5HJ.*
Actual grid ref: NN943584
Tel: 01796 472308
Under 18: £6.50 **Adults:** £7.75
Evening Meals Available, Self-catering Facilities, Family Bunk Rooms, Shop, Laundry Facilities
Pitlochry is a bustling small town at the very centre of Scotland. Scenic countryside ideal for climbing. The Festival Theatre is open May-October - outdoor shows all summer. The Highland Games are in September

(On route) *Poplars Hotel, 27 Lower Oakfield, Pitlochry, Perthshire, PH16 5DS.*
Grades: STB 3 Cr, Comm
Tel: 01796 472129 Ms Shepherd.
Rates fr: *£18.00-£19.00.*
Open: All Year
Beds: 3F 4D 4T
Baths: 11 Ensuite
🛏 🅿 (15) 🗆 🐾 ❌ 🖾 🖤
Impressive Victorian house set in a large garden, with spectacular views of the Tummel Valley, yet still within easy walking distance of the town centre

(0.5m) *Kinnaird House, Kirkmichael Road, Pitlochry, Perthshire, PH16 5JL.*
Spacious, comfortable, clean, quality accommodation in superb surroundings. Friendly and relaxing
Grades: STB 2 Cr, High Comm
Tel: 01796 472843
Mr & Mrs Norris.
Rates fr: *£20.00-£30.00.*
Open: All Year
Beds: 2D 1T **Baths:** 3 Private
🅿 (7) 🕭 🗆 🖾 🖤

Loch Tay to the Pass of Drumochter

From Kenmore at the northeastern end of Loch Tay you follow the River Tay to the sixteenth-century fortified tower house Castle Menzies, historic seat of the Menzies clan, and Aberfeldy, where the restored water mill dates from the early nineteenth century. From here you continue to **Pitlochry**. Here the Edradour Distillery is Scotland's smallest whisky distillery and the Pitlochry Festival Theatre stages a different play every night from May to October. By the hydroelectric power station is a fish ladder, by which the salmon can bypass the dam on the Tummel to reach their breeding grounds. A short way through the Tummel Forest Park, the spectacular Pass of Killiecrankie was the setting in 1689 for the Battle of Killiecrankie, a great Jacobite victory in the period when such things happened. A little further on is Blair Atholl, where there is a working water mill, and nearby Blair Castle, seat of the Dukes of Atholl. Over the long period since its foundation in the thirteenth century, this striking white fortress has undergone much alteration. It is the scene every May for the parade of the Atholl Highlanders, Britain's only legal private army. The route through Glen Garry culminates in a steady ascent to the **Pass of Drumochter.** This will test your stamina. There is no alternative to the A9 and there is only one hotel listed in this book - at Dalwhinnie.

(On route) *Westlands Of Pitlochry,*
160 Atholl Road, Pitlochry,
Perthshire, PH16 5AR.
Grades: STB 4 Cr, Comm
Tel: **01796 472266** Mr Mathieson.
Fax no: 01796 473994
Rates fr: *£25.50*-**£25.50**.
Open: All Year
Beds: 2F 6D 6T 1S
Baths: 15 Private
🛏 🅿 (30) 🛖 🛒 ✗ 📖 🔽 ▮
Beautifully presented stone-built
hotel run by resident owners
Andrew & Sue Mathieson. All
rooms have facilities. Cocktail bar
and restaurant have appealing
menus including vegetarian

(0.5m) *Grove Cottage, 10 Lower*
Oakfield, Pitlochry, Perthshire,
PH16 5DS.
Victorian house with lovely views
Tel: **01796 472374** Mrs Hawkes.
Rates fr: *£14.00*-**£15.00**.
Open: All Year
Beds: 1D 1T 2S
Baths: 2 Private 1 Shared
🅿 (4) 🛖 🛒 ✗ 📖 🔽

(0.5m) *Balrobin Hotel, Higher*
Oakfield, Pitlochry, Perthshire,
PH16 5HT.
Quality accommodation with
panoramic views at affordable
prices
Grades: STB 3 Cr, High Comm
Tel: **01796 472901** Mr Hohman.
Fax no: 01796 474200
Rates fr: *£25.00*-**£25.00**.
Open: Apr to Oct
Beds: 1F 12D 2T 1S
Baths: 16 Private
🛏 (10) 🅿 (16) 🛒 ✗ 📖 🔽 ▮

(0.5m) *Tigh-Na-Lnol, 11 West*
Moulin Road, Pitlochry,
Perthshire, PH16 5EA.
Modern bungalow in quiet village
Tel: **01796 482240** (also fax no)
Mrs Davidson.
Rates fr: *£13.00*-**£13.00**.
Open: All Year (not Xmas)
Beds: 1F 1T **Baths:** 1 Shared
🛏 🅿 (2) ✍ 🛖 🛒 📖 🔽 ▮ ✦

(0.5m) *8 Darach Road, Pitlochry,*
Perthshire, PH16 5HR.
Situated in quiet district
Tel: **01796 472074**
Mrs Weyda-Wernick.
Rates fr: *£12.50*-**£16.00**.
Open: All Year
Beds: 1D
Baths: 2 Shared
🛏 🅿 (3) 🛖 🛒 📖

(0.5m) *Lynedoch, 9 Lettoch*
Terrace, Pitlochry, Perthshire,
PH16 5BA.
Stone-built with adjoining annexe
Grades: STB Listed, Comm
Tel: **01796 472119**
Mrs Williamson.
Rates fr: *£15.00*-**£15.00**.
Open: Mar to Oct
Beds: 2D 1T **Baths:** 2 Shared
🛏 (3) ✍ 🛖 📖

(0.5m) *Carra Beag Guest House,*
16 Toberargan Road, Pitlochry,
Perthshire, PH16 5HG.
Comfortable, good food, lovely
view
Grades: STB Approv
Tel: **01796 472835**
Mr Stone.
Rates fr: *£16.00*-**£16.00**.
Open: All Year
Beds: 2F 4D 3T 3S
Baths: 9 Private 1 Shared
🛏 🅿 (15) ✍ 🛖 🛒 ✗ 📖 🔽 ▮ ✦

(0.5m) *Tigh-Na-Cloich Hotel,*
Larchwood Road, Pitlochry,
Perthshire, PH16 5AS.
Lovely Victorian house, friendly
informal atmosphere, comfortable,
licensed
Grades: STB 3 Cr, Comm
Tel: **01796 472216** (also fax no)
Mrs Hawley.
Rates fr: *£20.00*-**£18.00**.
Open: All Year
Beds: 1F 4D 5T 2S
Baths: 10 Ensuite 1 Shared
🛏 🅿 (12) ✍ 🛖 ✗ 📖 🔽 ▮ ✦

(0.5m) *Briar Cottage, Wellbrae,*
Pitlochry, Perthshire, PH16 5HH.
Bright modern house. Family-run.
Suitable for disabled
Tel: **01796 473678**
Mrs Scott.
Rates fr: *£14.50*-**£25.00**.
Open: Easter to Oct
Beds: 1D 2T
Baths: 2 Shared
🛏 🅿 (3) 🛖 📖 ♿ 🔽

(0.5m) *Tigh-Nan-Eilan,*
28 Tomcroy Terrace, Pitlochry,
Perthshire, PH16 5JA.
Rural setting with views to the hills
all around
Tel: **01796 473039** (also fax no)
Mrs Young.
Rates fr: *£15.00*-**£20.00**.
Open: Easter to Oct
Beds: 1D 1T
Baths: 1 Shared
🅿 (2) ✍ 🛖 📖 🔽

(0.5m) *Adderley Private Hotel,*
23 Toberargan Road, Pitlochry,
Perthshire, PH16 5HG.
A small family-run hotel
Grades: STB 3 Cr, Approv
Tel: **01796 472433**
Mr McGhie.
Rates fr: *£21.00*-**£21.00**.
Open: All Year (not Xmas)
Beds: 2F 3D 1T 1S
Baths: 7 Private
🛏 🅿 (8) 🛖 🛒 ✗ 📖 🔽 ▮ ✦

(0.5m) *Craigower Hotel,*
134-136 Atholl Road, Pitlochry,
Perthshire, PH16 5AB.
Vegetarian and excellent full menu
Tel: **01796 472590**
Rates fr: *£20.00*-**£20.00**.
Open: All Year
Beds: 2F 12D 7T 3S
Baths: 23 Ensuite
🛏 🅿 (15) 🛖 🛒 ✗ 📖 ♿ 🔽

The lowest *double* rate per
person is shown in *italics*.

Moulin   46

National Grid Ref: NN9459

(1.5m) *Craig Dubh Cottage,*
Manse Road, Moulin, Pitlochry,
Perthshire, PH16 5EP.
Tel: **01796 472058**
Mrs Bright.
Rates fr: *£14.00*-**£14.00**.
Open: Mid-April to mid-Oct
Beds: 1D 1T 2S
Baths: 1 Ensuite 1 Shared
🅿 (3) 🛖 🛒 📖 🔽
A family home where we welcome
B&B guests. One mile from the
town centre with a large garden, at
the end of a quiet lane

Blair Atholl   47

National Grid Ref: NN8765

🍴 🍺 Atholl Arms Hotel, Tilt Hotel

(0.25m) *Dalgreine, Off St Andrews*
Crescent, Blair Atholl, Pitlochry,
Perthshire, PH18 5SX.
Attractive comfortable guesthouse,
set in beautiful surroundings
Grades: STB 2 Cr, High Comm,
AA 4 Q, Select
Tel: **01796 481276**
Mrs Sherrington.
Rates fr: *£15.00*-**£15.00**.
Open: All Year
Beds: 1F 2D 2T 1S
Baths: 3 Private 1 Shared
🛏 🅿 (6) ✍ 🛖 🛒 ✗ 📖 🔽 ▮ ✦

(0.25m) *Lauchope House, The*
Terrace, Bridge Of Tilt, Blair
Atholl, Pitlochry, Perthshire,
PH18 5SX.
Situated in large garden. Superb
views. Near Blair Castle and
Pitlochry
Tel: **01796 481200**
Mrs McFarlane.
Rates fr: *£14.50*-**£14.50**.
Open: Easter to Oct
Beds: 1F 1D
Baths: 1 Private 1 Shared
🛏 🅿 (3) ✍ 🛖 📖

(0.25m) *Baile Na Bruaich, Glen*
Fender, Blair Atholl, Pitlochry,
Perthshire, PH18 5TU.
Family house, outstanding
mountain views
Tel: **01796 481329**
Mrs Thomson.
Rates fr: *£16.50*-**£16.50**.
Open: Easter to Oct
Beds: 1D 1T 1S
Baths: 1 Shared
🛏 (0) 🅿 (4) ✍ 🛖 🛒 ✗ 📖 ▮ ✦

Dalwhinnie 47a

National Grid Ref: NN6384

(0.5m) *Loch Ericht Hotel,*
Dalwhinnie, Inverness-shire,
PH19 1AE.
Family-run country hotel
Tel: **01528 522257**
Ms Sutherland.
Fax no: 01528 522270 /
01463 782531
Rates fr: *£25.00-£25.00.*
Open: Easter to Nov
Beds: 2F 10D 15T
Baths: 27 Private
🛏 🅿 🗔 🛏 🗙 🎞 ₺ ᗱ Ⅴ

Newtonmore 48

National Grid Ref: NN7199

🍴 🍺 Braeriach Hotel, Glen Hotel

(0.25m) *Woodcliffe, Laggan Road,*
Newtonmore, Inverness-shire,
PH20 1DG.
Comfortable, traditional stone villa
Grades: STB Listed, Comm
Tel: **01540 673839**
Mrs Morrison.
Rates fr: *£14.00-£14.00.*
Open: All Year (not Xmas)
Beds: 1F 1D
Baths: 1 Ensuite 1 Private
🛏 🅿 (6) 🗔 🛏 🎞 Ⅴ ₳ ✦

(0.25m) *Greenways, Golf Course*
Road, Newtonmore, Inverness-
shire, PH20 1AT.
Central stone house, overlooking
golf course
Grades: STB 1 Cr, Comm
Tel: **01540 673325** Mrs Muir.
Rates fr: *£13.00-£13.00.*
Open: All Year (not Xmas/New
Year)
Beds: 1D 1T 1S
Baths: 1 Shared
🛏 (12) 🅿 (6) 🗔 🎞 Ⅴ ₳ ✦

(0.25m) *Craigellachie House,*
Main Street, Newtonmore,
Inverness-shire, PH20 1DA.
Relaxed, comfortable, former
C19th inn
Grades: STB 1 Cr, Comm
Tel: **01540 673360** Mrs Main.
Rates fr: *£15.50-£16.50.*
Open: All Year (not Xmas)
Beds: 1F 1D
Baths: 1 Shared
🛏 🅿 (4) ⅙ 🗔 🛏 🎞 Ⅴ ₳ ✦

(0.25m) *Pines Hotel, Station Road,*
Newtonmore, Inverness-shire,
PH20 1AR.
Country house in large gardens
Tel: **01540 673271**
Mr & Mrs Raw.
Rates fr: *£23.50-£23.50.*
Open: Apr to Oct
Beds: 2D 3T 1S **Baths:** 6 Ensuite
🛏 (6) 🅿 (^) ⅙ 🗔 🗙 🎞 Ⅴ

Kingussie 49

National Grid Ref: NH7500
🍴 🍺 Scot House Hotel, Tipsy
Laird

(0.25m) *The Osprey Hotel,*
Kingussie, Inverness-shire,
PH21 1EN.
Grades: STB 3 Cr, Comm
Tel: **01540 661510** (also fax no)
Mr Burrow.
Rates fr: *£23.00-£23.00.*
Open: All Year
Beds: 3D 3T 2S
Baths: 6 Ensuite 2 Private
🛏 🅿 (8) 🗔 🛏 🗙 🎞 ₺ Ⅴ ₳ ✦
Small hotel in Area of Outstanding
Beauty, offering warm welcome,
ensuite accommodation and award-
winning food. Ideal base for
touring, walking, golf, fishing, etc

(On Route) *Bhuna Monadh,*
85 High Street, Kingussie,
Inverness-shire, PH21 1HX.
Recently refurbished Listed
building
Grades: STB 2 Cr, Comm
Tel: **01540 661186** / 0385 931345
Ms Gibson.
Rates fr: *£17.00-£17.00.*
Open: All Year
Beds: 1D 1T
Baths: 2 Ensuite
🛏 🅿 (5) ⅙ 🗔 🛏 🗙 🎞 Ⅴ ₳ ✦

(0.25m) *Glengarry, East Terrace,*
Kingussie, Inverness-shire, PH21 1JS.
Traditional stone villa, attractive
gardens, in quiet residential
location
Grades: STB 2 Cr, High Comm
Tel: **01540 661386** (also fax no)
Mr & Mrs Short.
Rates fr: *£17.00-£19.00.*
Open: All Year
Beds: 2D 2S
Baths: 1 Ensuite 1 Shared
🅿 (4) ⅙ 🗔 🗙 🎞

(0.25m) *St Helens, Ardbroilach*
Road, Kingussie, Inverness-shire,
PH21 1JX.
Elegant Victorian private house
with magnificent views over
Cairngorm Mountains
Grades: STB 2 Cr, High Comm
Tel: **01540 661430** Mrs Jarratt.
Rates fr: *£20.00-£38.00.*
Open: All Year
Beds: 2D 1T
Baths: 3 Private
🅿 (4) ⅙ 🗔 🎞 Ⅴ

(1m) *Ruthven Farmhouse,*
Kingussie, Inverness-shire,
PH21 1NR.
Spacious house in landscaped
grounds
Grades: STB Listed, 2 Cr, Crown
Tel: **01540 661226** Mrs Morris.
Rates fr: *£16.00-£16.50.*
Open: All Year
Beds: 2D 1T **Baths:** 3 Private
🛏 (10) 🅿 (7) 🗔 🎞 Ⅴ ₳

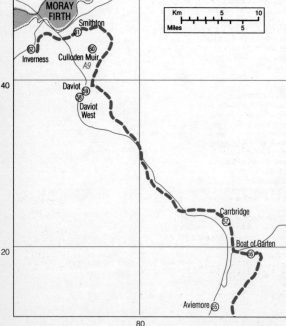

80

The Pass of Drumochter to Inverness

The way through Glen Truim leads to **Newtonmore** and **Kingussie**, where Ruthven Barracks was built in the early eighteenth century by the ascendant royal family to suppress the Jacobites. From here you head on through Strathspey, haven of ospreys and salmon, past Loch Insh to **Inverdruie** near Aviemore, and on to **Boat of Garten**; before turning west and then north to Carrbridge, and on to Slochd Summit. After descending to Tomatin across the River Findhorn you proceed to **Culloden**. Here in 1746 the last battle fought anywhere in Britain finally crushed the Jacobite rebellion, leading to the flight of Prince Charles Edward Stuart and the mass murder and pillage of the Highland Clearances. Before you reach the town the Culloden Visitor Centre, at the site of the battle, offers an audiovisual presentation. It is but a short way to **Inverness**, capital of the Highlands, where the route ends on the west bank of the River Ness. In front of the Victorian castle, built on the site of the earlier edifice razed by the Jacobites, stands a statue of Flora MacDonald, the local heroine who helped 'Bonnie' Prince Charles Edward Stuart escape from Benbecula to Skye after Culloden. The Museum and Art Gallery has displays of local interest; and Balnain House, a museum of Highland music, is well worth a visit. To the south of town, the northern section of Thomas Telford's Caledonian Canal leads into Loch Ness. To the north, you can take a cruise around the Moray Firth to spot seals and perhaps dolphins traversing the bay.

(0.25m) *Arden House,*
Newtonmore Road, Kingussie,
Inverness-shire, PH21 1HE.
Comfortable Scottish Victorian villa
Grades: STB 1 Cr, Comm
Tel: 01540 661369 (also fax no)
Mrs Spry.
Rates fr: *£17.00*-**£17.00**.
Open: All Year (not Xmas)
Beds: 1F 3D 1T 1S
Baths: 1 Ensuite 2 Shared
🅿 ⅋ 🗇 ✕ 📖 ⅏ Ⓥ

(0.25m) *Greystones, Acres Road,*
Kingussie, Inverness-shire,
PH21 1LA.
Secluded Victorian family home
Grades: STB Listed, Comm
Tel: 01540 661052
Mr & Mrs Johnstone.
Fax no: 01540 662162
Rates fr: *£16.00*-**£16.00**.
Open: All Year
Beds: 1F 1D 1T
Baths: 2 Shared
🐾 (1mth) 🅿 (6) ⅋ 🗇 🛏 ✕ 📖 Ⓥ ⅋

Insh   50

National Grid Ref: NH8101
🍴 🍺 The Boathouse

(On route) *Bothan Airigh, Insh,*
Kingussie, Inverness-shire,
PH21 1NU.
Newly-built croft-type detached house & gardens
Tel: 01540 661051 Mrs McAdam.
Rates fr: *£13.50*-**£13.50**.
Open: All Year
Beds: 1F 1D 1T **Baths:** 2 Shared
🐾 🅿 (6) ⅋ 🗇 ✕ 📖 Ⓥ

The lowest *double* rate per person is shown in *italics*.

The *lowest* **single** rate *is shown in* **bold**.

Kincraig   51

National Grid Ref: NH8305
🍴 🍺 Kith and Kin Inn, Ossian Hotel

(1m) *Braeriach Guest House,*
Kincraig, Kingussie, Inverness-
shire, PH21 1QA.
River and mountain views, extremely comfortable
Grades: STB 3 Cr, Comm
Tel: 01540 651369 Mrs Johnson.
Rates fr: *£18.00*-**£18.00**.
Open: All Year
Beds: 1F 2D 1T
Baths: 4 Ensuite
🐾 🅿 (4) 🗇 🛏 ✕ 📖 Ⓥ ⅋

(1m) *Kirkbeag, Milehead,*
Kincraig, Kingussie, Inverness-
shire, PH21 1ND.
Converted C19th church, quiet location
Grades: STB Listed, Comm
Tel: 01540 651298 Mrs Paisley.
Rates fr: *£15.00*-**£19.00**.
Open: All Year
Beds: 1D 1T
Baths: 2 Shared
🐾 🅿 (6) 🗇 ✕ 📖 Ⓥ ⅋

(1m) *Grampian View, Kincraig,*
Kingussie, Inverness-shire,
PH21 1NA.
Elegant well-maintained Victorian house
Grades: STB 2 Cr, Comm
Tel: 01540 651383 Mrs Neck.
Rates fr: *£17.00*-**£17.00**.
Open: All Year
Beds: 2D 2T 1S
Baths: 5 Private
🐾 🅿 (5) 🗇 🛏 📖 Ⓥ ⅋ ⅋

(1m) *Ossian Hotel, Kincraig,*
Kingussie, Inverness-shire,
PH21 1QD.
Family -run hotel in beautiful village
Grades: STB 4 Cr, Comm
Tel: 01540 651242
Mrs Rainbow.
Fax no: 01540 651633
Rates fr: *£18.50*-**£18.50**.
Open: Feb to Dec
Beds: 2F 3D 2T 2S
Baths: 9 Private
🐾 🅿 (20) ⅋ 🗇 🛏 ✕ 📖 Ⓥ ⅋ ⅋

Feshiebridge   52

National Grid Ref: NH8504
🍴 🍺 Loch Insh Watersports, Ossian Hotel

(On route) *Balcraggan House,*
Feshiebridge, Kincraig, Kingussie,
Inverness-shire, PH21 1NG.
Wonderful setting where wildlife, walks and cycle routes abound
Tel: 01540 651488
Mrs Gillies.
Rates fr: *£25.00*-**£25.00**.
Open: All Year
Beds: 1D 1T
Baths: 2 Ensuite
🐾 (10) 🅿 (2) ⅋ 🗇 ✕ 📖 Ⓥ

(0.25m) *March House Guest*
House, Feshiebridge, Kincraig,
Kingussie, Inverness-shire,
PH21 1NG.
Outstanding location, delicious fresh food
Grades: STB 3 Cr, High Comm
Tel: 01540 651388 (also fax no)
Mrs Hayes.
Rates fr: *£18.00*-**£20.00**.
Open: Dec to Oct
Beds: 1F 2D 3T
Baths: 5 Ensuite 1 Private
🐾 🅿 (8) 🛏 ✕ 📖 Ⓥ ⅋ ⅋

Inverdruie 53

National Grid Ref: NH9011

⊯ 🍴 Invergarry Hotel, Glengarry
Castle Hotel, Lock Inn

(0.25m) *Port Macdonell,*
Inverdruie, Aviemore, Inverness-
shire, PH35 4HL.
Beautiful 1864 cottage, renovated
to a high standard. On A82
Tel: **01809 501262**
Mrs Service.
Rates fr: *£16.00*-**£25.00**.
Open: Jan to Dec
Beds: 1F 1T
Baths: 2 Ensuite 1 Private
ॐ (5) 🅿 (6) ⅙⬜📺 🎥 🛢

Coylumbridge 54

National Grid Ref: NH9110

⊯ 🍴 Bridge Inn, Cairgorm Hotel

(On route) *Avalon, Coylumbridge,*
Aviemore, Inverness-shire,
PH22 1RD.
Modern country setting, wonderful
walks
Tel: **01479 810158**
Mrs McCombie.
Rates fr: *£17.00*-**£17.00**.
Open: All Year
Beds: 1D 1T
Baths: 2 Ensuite
ॐ (2) 🅿 (3) ⅙⬜🎠📺 🎥 🛢 ⚡

Aviemore 55

National Grid Ref: NH8912

⊯ 🍴 Cairngorm Hotel, Old Bridge
Inn, Winking Owl

(▲2m) *Aviemore Youth Hostel,*
25 Grampian Road, Aviemore,
Inverness-shire,
Actual grid ref: NH893119
Tel: **01479 810345**
Under 18: £7.10
Adults: £8.60
Self-catering Facilities, Family
Bunk Rooms, Shop, Laundry
Facilities
Set in birch woodlands next to a
nature reserve, an ideal base for
you to explore the beauty of
Strathspey

(2m) *Ravenscraig Guest House,*
Aviemore, Inverness-shire, PH22 1RP.
Grades: STB 2 Cr, Comm
Tel: **01479 810278**
Mr Thompson.
Rates fr: *£20.00*-**£20.00**.
Open: All Year
Beds: 2F 5D 4T 1S
Baths: 12 Ensuite
ॐ 🅿 (14) ⬜🎠📺 🎥 🛢 ⚡
Comfortable rooms and excellent
breakfasts make Ravenscraig "the
place to stay in Strathspey". Our
central location makes Aviemore a
super location for touring the
Highlands

(2m) *A`anside Guest House, Off*
Grampian Road, Aviemore,
Inverness-shire, PH22 1QD.
Beautiful views, spacious gardens,
lochside beach only three miles
away
Grades: STB 2 Cr, Comm
Tel: **01479 810871** Mrs Roberts.
Rates fr: *£17.00*-**£22.00**.
Open: All Year
Beds: 2F 4D 1T 1S
Baths: 6 Ensuite 2 Shared
ॐ 🅿 (8) ⬜📺 🎥

(2m) *Kinapol Guest House,*
Dalfaber Road, Aviemore,
Inverness-shire, PH22 1PY.
Friendly, modern, quiet, central,
mountain views, riverside walks,
bike hire
Grades: STB 1 Cr, Comm
Tel: **01479 810513** (also fax no)
Mr & Mrs Hall.
Rates fr: *£14.00*-**£16.00**.
Open: All Year
Beds: 2F 3D
Baths: 2 Shared
ॐ 🅿 (4) ⬜📺 🎥 🛢 ⚡

(2m) *Richeldis, 21 Muirton,*
Aviemore, Inverness-shire, PH22 1SF.
Modern, detached bungalow in
village
Grades: STB Listed, Comm
Tel: **01479 811074**
Mrs Edmondson.
Rates fr: *£14.00*-**£15.00**.
Open: All Year
Beds: 3T
Baths: 1 Shared
ॐ 🅿 (4) ⅙⬜📺 🎥

(2m) *Alt-na-Craig House,*
131 Grampian Road, Aviemore,
Inverness-shire, PH22 1RL.
Victorian house - restaurant, bars,
garden
Tel: **01479 810378** Mrs Whelan.
Fax no: 01479 812121
Rates fr: *£18.00*-**£18.00**.
Open: All Year
Beds: 2F 6D 4T
Baths: 7 Ensuite 2 Shared
ॐ 🅿 (12) ⬜🎠🗙📺 🎥

(2m) *Waverley, 35 Strathspey*
Avenue, Aviemore, Inverness-shire,
PH22 1SN.
Modern comfortable bungalow
Tel: **01479 811226** Mrs Fraser.
Rates fr: *£15.00*-**£16.00**.
Open: All Year (not Xmas)
Beds: 1D 1T
Baths: 1 Ensuite 1 Private
ॐ (8) ⅙⬜📺 🎥 ⚡

(2m) *Ardlogie Guest House,*
Dalfaber Road, Aviemore,
Inverness-shire, PH22 1PU.
Quiet street. Views to Cairngorms
Grades: STB Listed, Comm
Tel: **01479 810747**
Rates fr: *£18.00*.
Open: All Year
Beds: 4D 1T
Baths: 4 Ensuite 1 Private
🅿 (3) 🎠📺.

(2m) *Lynwilg House, Aviemore,*
Inverness-shire, PH22 1PZ.
Spacious, award-winning 1920s
country house
Grades: STB 3 Cr, High Comm
Tel: **01479 811685** (also fax no)
Mrs Cleary.
Rates fr: *£28.00*-**£30.00**.
Open: Jan to Oct
Beds: 2D 1T 1S
Baths: 3 Ensuite 1 Private
ॐ (10) 🅿 (10) ⅙⬜🗙📺 🎥 🛢 ⚡

(2m) *Sonas, 19 Muirton, Aviemore,*
Inverness-shire, PH22 1SF.
Ideally situated to explore
Highlands/ski
Tel: **01479 810409** Mrs Clark.
Rates fr: *£14.00*-**£17.50**.
Open: All Year (not Xmas)
Beds: 2D 1T **Baths:** 2 Shared
ॐ (10) 🅿 (3) ⅙⬜🎠📺 🎥

Boat of Garten 56

National Grid Ref: NH9418

⊯ 🍴 Boat Hotel, Craigard Hotel,
The Heatherbank

(0.25m) *Heathbank - The*
Victorian House, Drumuillie Road,
Boat of Garten, Inverness-shire,
PH24 3BD.
Grades: STB 3 Cr, High Comm
Tel: **01479 831234** Mr Burge.
Rates fr: *£25.00*-**£30.00**.
Open: March to Oct & New Year
Beds: 1F 4D 2T
Baths: 7 Ensuite
ॐ (12) 🅿 (8) ⅙⬜🗙📺 🎥 🛢 ⚡
Beautiful, charactreful, full of
curiosities. Some four poster bed-
rooms, even a sunken bathroom!
Imaginative, individual chef
(Association Culinaire Francaise,
Taste of Scotland) cooks from the
heart! Rather intriguing - a special
house!

(5m) *Mullingarroch Croft, Boat of*
Garten, Inverness-shire, PH24 3BY.
Excellent area for fishing, walking,
golf and bird watching
Tel: **01479 831645** Mrs Grant.
Rates fr: *£15.50*-**£15.50**.
Open: Apr to Oct
Beds: 2D 1S **Baths:** 1 Shared
ॐ 🅿 (3) ⬜📺.

(On route) *The Old Ferrymans*
House, Boat of Garten, Inverness-
shire, PH24 3BY.
Tel: **01479 831370** (also fax no)
Ms Matthews.
Rates fr: *£18.00*-**£18.00**.
Open: All Year (not Xmas/New
Year)
Beds: 1T 1D 2S
Baths: 2 Shared
ॐ 🅿 (4) ⅙🎠🗙📺 🎥 🛢 ⚡
Which? recommended. Sitting
room with woodstove, books, no
TV, garden, substantial and/or
healthy breakfasts, Meals with
smoked salmon, venison etc. RSPB
Reserve 0.5 mile. Golf across river

(0.25m) *Locheil, Boat of Garten,
Inverness-shire, PH24 3BX*.
Small friendly B & B
Grades: STB 1 Cr, Comm
Tel: 01479 831603
Mrs Davison.
Rates fr: *£15.00-£15.00*.
Open: All Year
Beds: 1D 1T 2S
Baths: 1 Shared
🛇 🅿 (5) 🖵 ✕ 🎹 🛢 ✦

(0.25m) *Glen Sanda, Street Of
Kincardine, Boat of Garten,
Inverness-shire, PH24 3BY*.
Modern bungalow with view
Grades: STB 2 Cr, High Comm
Tel: 01479 831494 Mrs Lyons.
Rates fr: *£17.50-£17.50*.
Open: All Year
Beds: 2D 1T
Baths: 3 Private
🅿 (3) ⚡ 🖵 🎹 🛢

(0.25m) *Ryvoan Guest House,
Kinchurdy Road, Boat of Garten,
Inverness-shire, PH24 3BP*.
Beautifully furnished Victorian
house in wooded gardens with red
squirrels
Grades: STB 3 Cr, High Comm,
AA 4 Q, Select
Tel: 01479 831654
Mr & Mrs Whiston.
Rates fr: *£18.00-£18.00*.
Open: All Year
Beds: 2D 1T
Baths: 2 Ensuite 1 Shared
🅿 (6) ⚡ 🖵 ✕ 🎹 🛢 🛢 ✦

Carrbridge 57
National Grid Ref: NH9022
🍴 🍺 Cairn Hotel, Rowanlea Bar

(0.25m) *Cairn Hotel, Main Road,
Carrbridge, Inverness-shire,
PH23 3AS*.
Grades: STB 3 Cr, Comm
Tel: 01479 841212 Mr Kirk.
Fax no: 01479 841362
Rates fr: *£17.00-£17.00*.
Open: All Year (not Xmas)
Beds: 2F 2D 1T 2S
Baths: 4 Ensuite 1 Shared
🛇 🅿 (20) 🖵 ✕
Enjoy log fires, real ale, malt
whiskies, affordable food and
weekend entertainment in this
family-owned village centre hotel.
Reductions for children and longer
stays

(On route) *Craigellachie House,
Main Street, Carrbridge,
Inverness-shire, PH23 3AS*.
Non-smoking, Victorian house,
village centre, Many attractions
close by
Grades: STB 2 Cr, Comm
Tel: 01479 841641 Mrs Pedersen.
Rates fr: *£15.00-£15.00*.
Open: All Year
Beds: 2F 2D 2T 1S
Baths: 3 Private 2 Shared
🛇 🅿 (8) ⚡ 🖵 ✕ 🎹 �finV 🛢 ✦

(0.25m) *Carrmoor Guest House,
Carr Road, Carrbridge, Inverness-
shire, PH23 3AD*.
Licensed, family-run, warm
welcome
Grades: STB 3 Cr, Comm
Tel: 01479 841244 (also fax no)
Mrs Stitt.
Rates fr: *£18.00-£20.00*.
Open: All Year
Beds: 1F 3D 2T
Baths: 6 Ensuite
🛇 🅿 (6) 🖵 🍴 ✕ 🎹 �finV 🛢 ✦

(0.25m) *Cruachan, Carrbridge,
Inverness-shire, PH23 3AA*.
Modern bungalow
Grades: STB 2 Cr, Comm
Tel: 01479 841609 Mrs Campbell.
Rates fr: *£13.00-£14.00*.
Open: All Year
Beds: 1T 1S 1D **Baths:** 1 Private
🛇 (12) 🅿 (5) 🖵 🍴 🎹 ♿ �finV

(0.25m) *Mariner Guest House,
Station Road, Carrbridge,
Inverness-shire, PH23 3AN*.
Modern, comfortable, friendly.
Quiet area
Tel: 01479 841331 Mrs Handley.
Rates fr: *£18.00-£21.00*.
Open: Dec to Oct
Beds: 2F 2D 2T
Baths: 6 Private 1 Shared
🛇 (2) 🅿 (6) 🖵 🍴 ✕ 🎹

Daviot West 58
National Grid Ref: NH7239

(2m) *Crofthill, Daviot West,
Inverness. IV1 2XQ*.
Modern rural family home
Tel: 01463 772230 Mrs Lees.
Rates fr: *£16.00-£20.00*.
Open: Easter to Sep
Beds: 1D 1T
Baths: 2 Ensuite
🛇 🅿 (4) ⚡ 🖵 🍴 🎹 �finV

Daviot 59
National Grid Ref: NH7138
🍴 🍺 Deerstalker, Tomasin Inn

(1m) *Glenashdale, Daviot,
Inverness. IV1 2EP*.
Warm welcome assured. No
smoking
Grades: STB 2 Cr, High Comm
Tel: 01463 772221 Mrs Kinnear.
Rates fr: *£20.00-£25.00*.
Open: All Year
Beds: 1D 1T 1F 1S
Baths: 4 Private
(4) ⚡ 🖵 ✕ 🎹 ♿ �finV

**Bringing children with
you? Always ask for
any special rates.**

(1m) *Torguish House, Daviot,
Inverness. IV1 2XQ*.
Torguish: Former manse set in
quiet rural area
Tel: 01463 772208
Mr & Mrs Allan.
Fax no: 01463 772308
Rates fr: *£16.00-£20.00*.
Open: All Year
Beds: 3F 3D 2T
Baths: 5 Ensuite 1 Private
2 Shared
🛇 🅿 (20) 🖵 🍴 🎹 �finV

Culloden Muir 60
National Grid Ref: NH7345
🍴 🍺 Culloden Moor Inn

(3m) *Westhill House, Westhill,
Culloden Muir, Inverness. IV1 2BP*.
Grades: STB 1 Cr, Comm
Tel: 01463 793225 Mrs Honnor.
Fax no: 01667 454509
Rates fr: *£18.00-£18.00*.
Open: Mar to Oct
Beds: 1F 1T 1S
Baths: 2 Ensuite 1 Shared
🛇 🅿 (4) ⚡ 🖵 🍴 🎹 ♿ �finV
Spacious, comfortable family home
amidst trees, wildlife and with glo-
rious views. One mile Culloden
Battlefield, three miles Inverness.
Perfect centre for touring
Highlands

Smithton 61
National Grid Ref: NH7145

(On route) *3a Resaurie, Smithton,
Inverness. IV1 2NH*.
Grades: STB 2 Cr, Comm
Tel: 01463 791714 Mrs Mansfield.
Rates fr: *£15.00-£15.00*.
Open: All Year (not Xmas)
Beds: 2D 1T
Baths: 1 Ensuite 1 Shared
🛇 🅿 (3) ⚡ 🖵 🍴 ✕ 🎹 �finV 🛢 ✦
Quiet residential area. 3 miles east
of Inverness. Adjacent to farmland.
Views to Moray Firth and Ross-
shire Hills. Home baking. High tea.
Evening meals

**The Grid Reference
beneath the location
heading is for the
village or town - *not*
for individual houses,
which are shown
(where supplied) in
each entry itself.**

Inverness 62

National Grid Ref: NH6645

|⚫| 🍴 Craigmonie Hotel, The Waterside, The Waterfront, Findlay's, Loch Ness House Hotel, Mairten Lodge, Heathmount Hotel, The Harlequin, Johnny Foxes, Dores Inn

(▲ 0.5m) *Inverness Milburn Youth Hostel, Victoria Drive, Inverness. IV2 3BQ.*
Actual grid ref: NH667449
Tel: **01463 231771**
Under 18: £9.95 **Adults:** £11.50
Evening Meals Available, Self-catering Facilities, Family Bunk Rooms, Laundry Facilities
OPENING EASTER 1998. Brand new hostel situated close to the town centre and all its amenities, the shops, cafes and the lively Eden Court Theatre. The gateway to the Highlands

(0.5m) *Hawthorn Lodge House, 15 Fairfield Road, Inverness. IV3 5QA.*
Grades: STB Listed, Comm
Tel: **01463 715516** Mrs Davidson.
Fax no: 01463 221578
Rates fr: £18.00-£18.00.
Open: All Year
Beds: 1F 1T 1D
Baths: 1 Ensuite
🛏 🅿 (6) 🔲 🛍 & ☑ 🛊 ✦
Hawthorn Lodge is only 5 minutes' walk from town centre / train station. 2 minutes' walk from the River Ness. Accepts all major credit cards

(0.5m) *Clach Mhuilinn, 7 Harris Road, Inverness. IV2 3LS.*
Immaculate luxury accommodation. Non-smoking. Delicious breakfasts overlooking garden. Residential area
Grades: STB 2 Cr, High Comm, AA 4 Q
Tel: **01463 237059**
Mrs Elmslie.
Fax no: 01463 242092
Rates fr: £23.00-£23.00.
Open: Mar to Nov
Beds: 1D 1T 1S
Baths: 3 Ensuite
🅿 (3) 🗡 🔲 🛍 ☑

(0.5m) *St Anns House, 37 Harowden Road, Inverness. IV3 5QN.*
Grades: STB 2 Cr, Comm, AA 3 Q, Recommended, RAC Acclaimed
Tel: **01463 236157** (also fax no)
Rates fr: £22.00-£19.50.
Open: Feb to Oct
Beds: 1F 2D 2T 1S
Baths: 5 Ensuite 1 Private
🛏 🅿 (4) 🔲 🛍 ☑
Friendly, small, clean, family-run hotel, 10 minutes' walk from town centre, bus and rail stations. Restricted licence. Guest lounge. Lovely gardens. Brochure available

(0.5m) *The Borve, 9 Old Edinburgh Road, Inverness. IV2 3HF.*
Grades: STB Listed, High Comm, AA 4 Q
Tel: **01463 234728** Mrs White.
Fax no: 01463 711017
Rates fr: £20.00-£22.00.
Open: All Year (not Xmas)
Beds: 1F 2T 2D
Baths: 2 Ensuite 2 Shared
🛏 🅿 (4) 🗡 🔲 🛍 ☑ 🛊 ✦
Situated in a quiet residential area and only 2 minutes from the castle and River Ness, this listed Victorian town house has recently been refurbished to the highest standards. Genuine Highland hospitality guaranteed

(0.5m) *Druidh's Burn House, Old Edinburgh Road South, Inverness. IV1 2AA.*
Very comfortable, large rooms, quiet, two miles form town centre
Grades: STB 4 St
Tel: **01463 718573** Mr Smith.
Rates fr: £19.00-£35.00.
Open: All Year (not Xmas)
Beds: 1T 2D
Baths: 3 Ensuite
🛏 🅿 (4) 🗡 🔲 🛍 ✦

(0.5m) *Strathmhor Guest House, 99 Kenneth Street, Inverness. IV3 5QQ.*
Grades: STB 2 Cr
Tel: **01463 235397**
Mr & Mrs Reid.
Rates fr: £15.00-£18.00.
Open: All Year
Beds: 2F 1D 1T 1S
Baths: 2 Ensuite 2 Shared
🛏 🅿 (6) 🔲 🛍.
Warm welcome awaits at refurbished Victorian home. Comfortable bedrooms and guest lounge. Short walk into town. Theatres, restaurants, leisure centre, golf course and fishing nearby

(0.5m) *Crown Hotel, 19 Ardconnel Street, Inverness. IV2 3EU.*
Clean, warm, friendly. Excellent breakfast, four minutes from the station
Grades: STB 2 Cr, Comm
Tel: **01463 231135** (also fax no)
Rates fr: £16.00-£18.00.
Open: All Year (not Xmas)
Beds: 2F 2D 1T 2S
Baths: 3 Private 2 Shared
🛏 🔲 🛍 ☑

(0.5m) *Torridon Guest House, 59 Kenneth Street, Inverness. IV3 5PZ.*
Grades: STB 2 Cr, Comm
Tel: **01463 236449** (also fax no)
Mrs Stenhouse.
Rates fr: £15.00-£18.00.
Open: All Year **Beds:** 3F
Baths: 2 Ensuite 1 Private
🛏 (5) 🅿 (4) 🔲 🛍 ☑ 🛊
Comfortable, family-run house, 5 minutes from town centre, good food, good beds, and a warm welcome assured

(2m) *Taransay, Lower Muckovie Farm, Inverness. IV1 2BB.*
Actual grid ref: NH705435
Grades: STB 2 Cr, Comm
Tel: **01463 231880** (also fax no)
Mrs Munro.
Rates fr: £18.00-£25.00.
Open: All Year (not Xmas)
Beds: 1D/F
Baths: 1 Ensuite 1 Private
🛏 🅿 (3) 🗡 🔲 🛊 🛍.
Taransay is a beautifully situated spacious bungalow on quiet dairy farm 2 miles south of Inverness near Drumossie Hotel (B9177) & Culloden Battlefield. Magnificent views

(0.5m) *Tanera, 8 Fairfield Road, Inverness. IV3 5QA.*
Warm, comfortable, friendly family house, close to town and all amenities
Tel: **01463 230037** (also fax no)
Mrs Geddes.
Rates fr: £16.00-£20.00.
Open: All Year (not Xmas)
Beds: 2D 1T
Baths: 2 Ensuite 1 Private 1 Shared
🛏 (10) 🅿 (3) 🔲 🗡 🛍 ☑ ✦

(0.5m) *Kendon, 9 Old Mill Lane, Inverness. IV2 3XP.*
Grades: STB 2 Cr, Comm
Tel: **01463 238215**
Mrs Kennedy.
Rates fr: £19.00.
Open: Mar to Nov
Beds: 2D 1T
Baths: 3 Ensuite
🅿 (4) 🗡 🔲 🛍 ☑ 🛊
Family bungalow in peaceful location with large garden and private parking. All rooms ensuite with TV and tea/coffee facilities. Totally non-smoking. Excellent restaurants nearby

(0.5m) *Laggan View, Ness Castle Fishings, Dores Road, Inverness. IV1 2DH.*
Attractive house in rural setting. Walks by river, through woods
Grades: STB 3 Cr, Comm
Tel: **01463 235996**
Fax no: 01463 711552
Rates fr: £18.00-£20.00.
Open: All Year
Beds: 1F 1D 1T
Baths: 2 Ensuite 1 Private
🛏 🅿 (4) 🔲 🗡 ✕ 🛍 ☑

(0.5m) *Abb Cottage, 11 Douglas Row, Inverness. IV1 1RE.*
Central, quiet, riverside listed terraced cottage. Easy access public transport
Tel: **01463 233486**
Miss Storrar.
Rates fr: £15.00-£20.00.
Open: Mar to Dec
Beds: 3T
Baths: 1 Shared
🛏 (12) 🗡 ✕ 🛍 & ☑

(0.5m) *Winmar House Hotel,*
Kenneth Street, Inverness. IV3 5QG.
Family-run, ideal touring base.
Good Scottish breakfasts. Ample
parking
Grades: STB 2 Cr, Comm
Tel: **01463 239328** (also fax no)
Mrs Maclellan.
Rates fr: *£15.00-£20.00.*
Open: All Year (not Xmas)
Beds: 4F 3D 2T 1S
Baths: 4 Ensuite 3 Private
2 Shared
⋟ 🅿 (10) 🖵 🛏 🎹 & Ⅴ

(0.5m) *68 Lochalsh Road,*
Inverness. IV3 6HW.
Family-run, 10 mins' walk town
centre. Ideal for Loch Ness. See
dolphins in the Moray Firth
Grades: STB Listed, Comm
Tel: **01463 223020** (also fax no)
Mrs Matheson.
Rates fr: *£14.00-£16.00.*
Open: All Year (not Xmas)
Beds: 1F 1D 1T 2S
Baths: 2 Ensuite 3 Shared
⋟ (5) ⊬🖵🎹.

(0.5m) *1 Caulfield Park,*
Inverness. IV1 2GB.
Modern detached villa in quiet
location. Non-smoking throughout
Grades: STB 2 Cr, High Comm
Tel: **01463 792882** Mrs MacCuish.
Rates fr: *£16.00.*
Open: May to Sep **Beds:** 1D 1T
Baths: 1 Ensuite 1 Shared
🅿 (2) ⊬🖵 🎹. Ⅴ

(0.5m) *Hebrides, 120a*
Glenurquhart Rd, Inverness. IV3 5TD.
Non-smoking guest house with
parking
Grades: STB High Comm
Tel: **01463 220062** Mrs MacDonald
Rates fr: *£18.00.* **Open:** All Year
Beds: 2D **Baths:** 1 Private
🅿 (3) ⊬🖵 🎹. Ⅴ 🎄 ✦

(0.5m) *Inverglen Guest House, 7*
Abertarff Road, Inverness. IV2 3NW.
Comfortable Victorian villa. Warm
welcome
Grades: STB 2 St, Comm
Tel: **01463 237610**
Rates fr: *£22.00.* **Open:** All Year
Beds: 2F 1T 2D **Baths:** 5 Private
⋟ 🅿 (6) ⊬🖵 🎹. Ⅴ 🎄 ✦

(0.5m) *East Dene, 6 Ballifeary*
Road, Inverness. IV3 5PJ.
Near Eden Court Theatre
Grades: STB 3 Cr, High Comm
Tel: **01463 232976** (also fax no)
Mrs Greig.
Rates fr: *£16.00-£29.00.*
Open: All Year
Beds: 3D 1T
Baths: 3 Ensuite
🅿 (4) 🖵 🛏 ✕ 🎹. Ⅴ

(0.5m) *Ivybank Guest House,*
28 Old Edinburgh Road, Inverness.
IV2 3HJ.
Delightful Georgian house with
tower
Grades: STB 2 Cr, High Comm
Tel: **01463 232796** (also fax no)
Mrs Cameron.
Rates fr: *£20.00-£25.00.*
Open: All Year
Beds: 3D 2T 1S
Baths: 3 Private 1 Shared
⋟ 🅿 (6) ⊬🖵 🛏 🎹. Ⅴ 🎄 ✦

Sustrans Hull to Harwich

The **Hull to Harwich Cycle Route** is a section of the new National Cycle Network, running on traffic-free paths and traffic-calmed roads between the Continental ferry ports of Hull in the East Riding of Yorkshire and Harwich in the northeastern corner of Essex. 370 miles long, it links the towns of Lincoln and Boston in Lincolnshire, Wisbech in Cambridgeshire and King's Lynn, Fakenham and Norwich in Norfolk with Beccles, Woodbridge and Ipswich in Suffolk and Colchester in Essex. The flat landscape of the Eastern counties yields long views and makes excellent cycling country: the only up-and-down of any degree (and this undemanding) comes in the route through the northern reaches of the Lincolnshire Wolds. The route is clearly signposted by blue direction signs with a cycle silhouette and the number 1 in a red rectangle.

The indispensable **official route map and guide** for the route comes in two parts, *Hull to Fakenham* and *Fakenham to Harwich*, and is available from Sustrans, 35 King Street, Bristol BS1 4DZ, tel 0117-926 8893, fax 0117-929 4173, @ £5.99 each (+ £1.50 p&p for both together or either one).

Maps: Ordnance Survey 1:50,000 Landranger series: 107, 112, 113, 121, 122, 131, 132, 133, 134, 155, 156, 168, 169

Trains: Hull, King's Lynn, Norwich, Ipswich, Colchester and Harwich are all main line termini; there are connecting services to many other places on or near the route.

Hull to Market Rasen

Kingston-upon-Hull is the major port of the Humber, the great deepwater estuary of England's East Coast. The poet Philip Larkin said the only good thing about the place is that it is 'very nice and flat for cycling'. For your purposes, that's a recommendation. The Streetlife Transport Museum may be of interest, as it has a recreation of a bicycle repair workshop from the early days of the beautiful machine. Of more general interest are the Town Docks Museum, the Ferens Art Gallery and the birthplace of William Wilberforce, who achieved the abolition of slavery in Britain. From the docks you head west, staying close to the river, to Hessle, where you join the Humber Bridge cyclepath to cross the resplendent Humber Bridge. The longest suspension bridge in the world, it was completed in 1981. The best view of the bridge is from the waterside at Barton-upon-Humber, on the other side. From Barton you head south, and into the Lincolnshire Wolds. From here it's a brief climb and then descent to Walesby, before you head down to the small market town of **Market Rasen**.

Hull   1

National Grid Ref: TA0929

(1m) *Town House, 102 Sunny Bank, Spring Bank West, Hull.* HU3 1LF.
Guest house, quiet location
Tel: **01482 446177**
Mr Hogg.
Rates fr: *£14.00*-**£15.00**.
Open: All Year
Beds: 1D 2T 4S
Baths: 1 Shared
🛏 (8) 🛋 🛏 📺

(1m) *Marlborough Hotel, 232 Spring Bank, Hull.* HU3 1LU.
Family run near city centre
Tel: **01482 224479** Mr Stonehouse.
Rates fr: *£13.00*-**£15.00**.
Open: All Year
Beds: 3F 2D 5T 6S
Baths: 3 Shared
🛏 🅿 (10) 🛋 🛏 ✗ 📺

The lowest *double* rate per person is shown in *italics*.

The *lowest* **single** rate is shown in **bold**.

(2m) *Beck House Hotel, 628 Beverley High Road, Hull.* HU6 7LL.
Elegant, Victorian town house hotel
Tel: **01482 445468** Mrs Aylwin.
Rates fr: *£19.00*-**£19.00**.
Open: All Year
Beds: 1F 3D 6S   Baths: 6 Private
🛏 🅿 (8) 🛋 📺

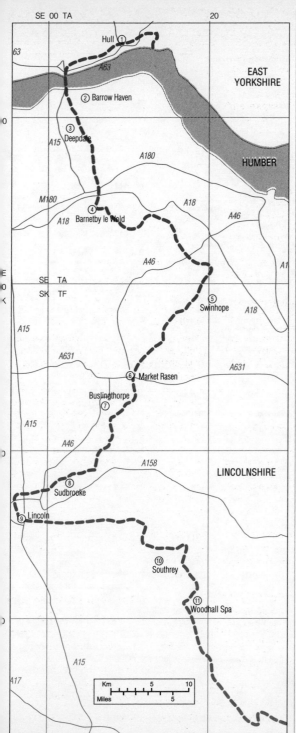

Barrow Haven   2

National Grid Ref: TA0622

¶●¶ ◀ Barrow Haven Inn

(2m) *Castle House, Barrow Haven,
Barton-upon-Humber, Lincs,
DN19 7EY.*
C18th farmhouse near Norman
castle
Tel: **01469 530040**
Mrs Rawlings.
Rates fr: *£12.50-£12.50.*
Open: All Year (not Xmas)
Beds: 1D 2S
Baths: 1 Shared
🛏 🅿 (2) ⬜ ▥

Deepdale   3

National Grid Ref: TA0418

(1m) *West Wold Farmhouse,
Deepdale, Barton-upon-Humber.
DN18 6ED.*
C19th comfortable family
farmhouse
Tel: **01652 633293**
Mrs Atkin.
Rates fr: *£16.00-£16.00.*
Open: All Year
Beds: 1D 1T
Baths: 1 Private 1 Shared
🛏 🅿 (All) ⿻ ⬜ ⼞ ✕ ▥ Ⓥ 🗎 ⼢

Barnetby le Wold   4

National Grid Ref: TA0509

(0.5m) *Holcombe Guest House,
34 Victoria Road, Barnetby le
Wold, Lincs, DN38 6JR.*
Actual grid ref: TA059097
Very comfortable, modern, guest
house
Grades: ETB 3 Cr, Comm
Tel: **01850 764002**
Mrs Vora.
Rates fr: *£15.00-£17.50.*
Open: All Year
Beds: 2F 1D 2T 6S
Baths: 4 Private 2 Shared
🛏 🅿 (7) ⬜ ⼞ ✕ ▥ ⼕ Ⓥ 🗎 ⼢

Swinhope   5

National Grid Ref: TF2196

(5m) *Hoe Hill, Swinhope,
Binbrook, Market Rasen. LN8 6HX.*
Actual grid ref: TF210950
Grades: ETB 2 Cr, High Comm
Tel: **01472 398206**
Rates fr: *£18.00-£20.00.*
Open: Feb to Dec
Beds: 1T 2D 1S
Baths: 1 Ensuite 2 Shared
🛏 (5) 🅿 (10) ⬜ ✕ ▥ Ⓥ 🗎 ⼢
In the Lincolnshire wolds. Be
pampered. Good food, spacious,
pretty bedrooms, open fires, large
garden, fresh flowers, good books,
safe parking - a gentle, peaceful
experience

Market Rasen 6

National Grid Ref: TF1089

🍴 🍺 White Swan

(0.5m) *The Waveney Guest House,* Willingham Road, Market Rasen, Lincs, LN8 3DN.
Family size Tudor-style cottage
Tel: **01673 843236**
Mrs Dawson-Margrave.
Rates fr: *£15.00-£17.00.*
Open: All Year
Beds: 1F 2T **Baths:** 3 Private
🛏 🅿 (6) ⚡ 🏠 🛏 ✗ 🛏 Ⅵ ⓐ ✦

Buslingthorpe 7

National Grid Ref: TF0885

🍴 🍺 White Hart

(1m) *East Farm House,* Middle Rasen Road, Buslingthorpe, Market Rasen, Lincs, LN3 5AQ.
Spacious C18th house overlooking farmland
Grades: ETB 2 Cr, High Comm
Tel: **01673 842283** Mrs Grant.
Rates fr: *£19.00-£21.00.*
Open: All Year
Beds: 1D 1T **Baths:** 2 Private
🛏 (5) 🅿 (5) ⚡ 🏠 🛏 ✗ 🛏 Ⅵ ✦

Sudbrooke 8

National Grid Ref: TF0376

🍴 🍺 Bottle & Glass, White Hart

(1m) *Westwood House,* Wragby Road, Sudbrooke, Lincoln, Lincs, LN2 2QU.
Spacious luxury accommodation, lovely gardens
Tel: **01522 751903** (also fax no)
Mrs Weaver.
Rates fr: *£17.50-£20.00.*
Open: All Year (not Xmas)
Beds: 1D 1T
Baths: 1 Shared
🛏 (12) 🅿 (6) ⚡ 🏠 🛏 Ⅵ ✦

Lincoln 9

National Grid Ref: SK9771

🍴 🍺 Lord Tennyson, Sun Inn, The Barge, Royal William

(🔺 1m) *Lincoln Youth Hostel,* 77 South Park, Lincoln. LN5 8ES.
Actual grid ref: SK980700
Warden: Ms H Yardley.
Tel: **01522 522076**
Under 18: £5.95
Adults: £8.80
Evening Meals Available (7pm), Family Bunk Rooms, Television, Showers, Shop
Victorian villa in a quiet road opposite South Common open parkland

---

(On route) *Ridgeways Guest House,* 243 Burton Road, Lincoln. LN1 3UB.
Actual grid ref: SK972727
Tel: **01522 546878** (also fax no)
Mr Barnes.
Rates fr: *£17.50-£20.00.*
Open: All Year
Beds: 2F 1D 1T
Baths: 3 Ensuite 1 Private
🛏 🅿 (4) ⚡ 🏠 🛏 🛏 Ⅵ ⓐ
Situated uphill within easy walking distance to the historic heart of Lincoln's cathedral, castle, Lawn Conference Centre. Also uphill Lincoln's shops, pubs and restaurants. Private car park and garden for guests' use. Credit cards accepted

---

(0.75m) *Newport Guest House,* 26-28 Newport, Lincoln. LN1 3DF.
Victorian house only four minutes' walk from cathedral and castle
Tel: **01522 528590**
Fax no: 01522 524868
Rates fr: *£16.00-£16.00.*
Open: All Year
Beds: 1F 4T 1D 1S
Baths: 2 Shared
🛏 🅿 (4) ⚡ 🏠 🛏 🛏 Ⅵ ⓐ ✦

(1m) *The Old Rectory,* 19 Newport, Lincoln. LN1 3DQ.
Large Edwardian house near cathedral, castle and old English inns
Tel: **01522 514774** Mr Downes.
Rates fr: *£17.50-£19.00.*
Open: All Year (not Xmas)
Beds: 1F 3D 1T 1S
Baths: 4 Private 1 Shared
🛏 🅿 (8) ⚡ 🏠 🛏 Ⅵ

(1m) *10 Neustadt Court,* Danes Terrace, Lincoln. LN2 1PG.
In the heart of the city
Tel: **01522 531831** Mr Tod.
Rates fr: *£15.00-£20.00.*
Open: All Year (not Xmas)
Beds: 1T
🛏 (3) 🅿 (1) ⚡ 🏠 🛏 Ⅵ

(1m) *Westlyn House,* 67 Carholme Road, Lincoln. LN1 1RT.
Victorian town house with garden
Tel: **01522 537468** (also fax no)
Mrs Kaye.
Rates fr: *£17.00-£18.00.*
Open: All Year (not Xmas)
Beds: 1F 2T 1D 1S
Baths: 3 Shared
🛏 🅿 (3) ⚡ 🏠 🛏 🛏 Ⅵ ⓐ

(1m) *Edward King House,* The Old Palace, Minster Yard, Lincoln. LN2 1PU.
By Cathedral and Old Palace
Tel: **01522 528778** Rev Adkins.
Fax no: 01522 527308
Rates fr: *£18.00-£18.50.*
Open: All Year (not Xmas)
Beds: 1F 11T 5S **Baths:** 7 Shared
🛏 🅿 (12) ⚡ 🏠 🛏 Ⅵ ⓐ

(1m) *Admiral Guest House,* 16 Nelson Street, Lincoln. LN1 1PJ.
Old-type Nelson's cottages
Tel: **01522 544467** Mr Robertson.
Rates fr: *£13.00-£13.00.*
Open: All Year
Beds: 4F 2D 1T 2S
Baths: 6 Private 2 Shared
🛏 🅿 🏠 🛏 ✗ 🛏 Ⅵ ⓐ ✦

Market Rasen to Boston

From Market Rasen it's a leisurely jaunt through a series of Lincolnshire villages to **Lincoln**. Here you can find the largest collection of bicycles in Britain at the National Cycle Museum. The massive cathedral, whose three towers dominate the flat landscape for miles around, originated in the Norman period, but was ruined by an earthquake in the twelfth century. The reconstruction dates from the Early English period of the Gothic age. Most noteworthy is the intricate narrative carving of the frieze on the west front. Lincoln Castle also dates from the Norman period, and houses one of only four existing original copies of the Magna Carta; but from 1787 until 1878 it was used as the city jail.

The pews in the prison chapel resemble coffins – a reminder of the era's not-so-progressive attitudes towards criminal justice. The route through southern Lincolnshire brings you to Tattershall Bridge, close to Tattershall Castle, an early brick building put up in the fifteenth century, with late Gothic fireplaces and tapestries. With the Boston Stump, the 288-foot tower of the church of St Botolph (nicknamed from its lack of a spire), rising ahead, you cycle on to *St Botolph's Town*. **Boston**, standing close to where the Witham flows into The Wash, was the starting point for the first abortive voyage of the Pilgrim Fathers, who were imprisoned in the Guildhall, now a museum. The link remains strong with the town's greater namesake in Massachussetts.

(1m) *Mayfield Guest House, 213 Yarborough Road, Lincoln.* LN1 3NQ.
Comfortable, convenient for tourist attractions
Grades: ETB 2 Cr, Comm
Tel: **01522 533732** (also fax no)
Mr Benson.
Rates fr: *£17.50*-**£17.00**.
Open: All Year (not Xmas)
Beds: 2F 1D 1T 1S
Baths: 4 Ensuite 1 Private
☎ (5) ▣ (5) ⌿ ☐ ⅏ Ⅵ ⓐ ✦

Southrey 10

National Grid Ref: TF1366
†⊙† ◖ Riverside Inn

(1m) *Riverside Inn, Ferry Road, Southrey, Lincoln.* LN3 5TA.
Peaceful country inn by river
Tel: **01526 398374**
Mrs Walley.
Rates fr: *£15.00*-**£18.00**.
Open: All Year
Beds: 1F
Baths: 1 Shared
☎ ▣ (10) ☐ ⵏ ✗ ⅏ Ⅵ ⓐ ✦

Woodhall Spa 11

National Grid Ref: TF1963
†⊙† ◖ The Mall, Abbey Lodge

(0.5m) *Claremont Guest House, 9-11 Witham Road, Woodhall Spa, Lincs,* LN10 6RW.
Homely unspoilt Victorian guest house, garden available. Compere welcome
Grades: ETB 2 Cr
Tel: **01526 352000**
Mrs Brennan.
Rates fr: *£15.00*-**£15.00**.
Open: All Year
Beds: 2F 3D 2T 2S
Baths: 2 Ensuite 2 Shared
☎ ▣ (4) ☐ ⵏ ✗ Ⅵ ✦

(0.5m) *Pitchaway Guest House, The Broadway, Woodhall Spa, Lincs,* LN10 6SQ.
Friendly family-run guest house
Grades: ETB 2 Cr
Tel: **01526 352969**
Miss Leggate.
Rates fr: *£15.00*-**£15.00**.
Open: All Year
Beds: 2F 1D 2T 2S
Baths: 2 Private 2 Shared
☎ (1) ▣ (10) ⌿ ☐ ✗ ⅏ Ⅵ ⓐ ✦

(0.5m) *Dower House Hotel, Manor Estate, Woodhall Spa, Lincs,* LN10 6PY.
Large Victorian dower house
Tel: **01526 352588** Mr Plumb.
Rates fr: *£32.00*-**£42.00**.
Open: All Year
Beds: 1F 6T
Baths: 6 Private 1 Shared
☎ ▣ (40) ☐ ⵏ ✗ ⅏ Ⅵ ⓐ ✦

Boston 12

National Grid Ref: TF3344
†⊙† ◖ White Hart, Four Crossroads Inn, Red Cow

(On route) *Lochiel Guest House, 69 Horncastle Road, Boston, Lincs,* PE21 9HY.
Comfortable, friendly, picturesque waterside setting
Grades: ETB Listed
Tel: **01205 363628** Mrs Lynch.
Rates fr: *£17.00*-**£18.00**.
Open: All Year (not Xmas)
Beds: 1D 1T 1S
Baths: 1 Private 1 Shared
☎ (2) ▣ (3) ⌿ ☐ ⅏ Ⅵ ⓐ

(0.5m) *Bramley House, 267 Sleaford Road, Boston, Lincs,* PE21 7PQ.
Comfortable former farmhouse; large garden and good value
Grades: ETB Listed, Comm
Tel: **01205 354538** (also fax no)
Mrs Tilke.
Rates fr: *£16.50*-**£19.50**.
Open: All Year (not Xmas)
Beds: 4D 2T 4S
Baths: 3 Ensuite 2 Shared
▣ (15) ⌿ ☐ ✗ ⅏ ⓖ Ⅵ

(0.5m) *The Chestnuts, 117 London Road, Boston, Lincs,* PE21 7EZ.
Late Victorian three-storey house
Grades: ETB 2 Cr Comm
Tel: **01205 354435**
Mrs Clarke.
Rates fr: *£16.00*-**£18.00**.
Open: All Year
Beds: 1D 2T
Baths: 3 Private
☎ (5) ▣ (5) ⌿ ☐ ⅏ Ⅵ

(0.5m) *90 Pilleys Lane, Boston, Lincs,* PE21 9RB.
Modern, large, comfortable bungalow
Tel: **01205 360723** Mrs Claridge.
Rates fr: *£14.00*-**£15.00**.
Open: All Year
Beds: 1F
☎ (1month) ▣ (4) ⌿ ☐ ✗ ⅏ ⓖ

(0.5m) *Park Lea Guest House, 85 Norfolk Street, Boston, Lincs,* PE21 6PE.
Comfortable accommodation, friendly service
Tel: **01205 356309** Mrs Cockburn.
Rates fr: *£15.00*-**£17.00**.
Open: All Year
Beds: 4F 1T
Baths: 3 Private
☎ ▣ (5) ☐ ⵏ ✗ ⅏ Ⅵ

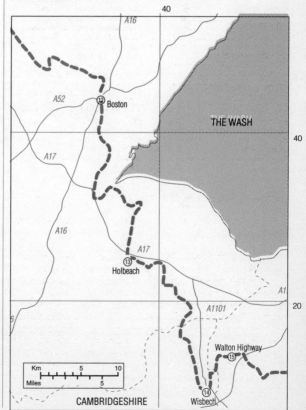

Holbeach 13

National Grid Ref: TF3625

🍴 🍺 Bull's Neck, Crown Hotel, Black Bull

(0.25m) *Cackle Hill House, Cackle Hill Lane, Holbeach, Spalding, Lincs, PE12 8BS.*
Modern comfortable farmhouse. Rural position
Grades: ETB 2 Cr, High Comm
Tel: **01406 426721**
Mrs Biggadike.
Fax no: 01406 424659
Rates fr: *£20.00-£22.00.*
Open: All Year (not Xmas)
Beds: 1D 2T
Baths: 2 Ensuite 1 Private
🛏 (10) 🅿 (5) ⅍ 🖵 ✕ 🎱.

(0.25m) *Barrington House, Barrington Gate, Holbeach, Spalding, Lincs, PE12 7LB.*
Spacious Georgian house, near town centre
Grades: ETB 2 Cr, Comm
Tel: **01406 425178 / 520320**
Mrs Symonds.
Fax no: 01406 425178
Rates fr: *£17.50-£20.00.*
Open: All Year
Beds: 2D 1T 1S
Baths: 2 Ensuite 2 Private
🛏 🅿 (5) 🖵 🍴 🎱.

Wisbech 14

National Grid Ref: TF4609

🍴 🍺 The Blackfriars, Red Lion

(0.5m) *Algethi Guest House, 136 Lynn Road, Wisbech, Cambs, PE13 3DP.*
Friendly-run guesthouse near town centre and river
Tel: **01945 582278** Mrs McManus.
Fax no: 01945 466456
Rates fr: *£14.00-£14.00.*
Open: All Year
Beds: 2F 1D 2S **Baths:** 2 Private
🛏 🅿 (5) 🖵 🍴 ✕ 🎱 ⅍ 🆅 ♿ ∥

(0.5m) *Ravenscourt, 138 Lynn Road, Wisbech, Cambs, PE13 3DP.*
Edwardian house, original features located walking distance from town centre
Tel: **01945 585052** (also fax no)
Mr Parish.
Rates fr: *£15.00-£17.50.*
Open: All Year
Beds: 2F 1D 1T 1S
Baths: 4 Private
🛏 🅿 ⅍ 🖵 🎱 🆅 ♿ ∥

(0.5m) *Deben Guest House, 146 Lynn Rd, Wisbech, Cambs, PE13 3DP.*
Edwardian house, friendly atmosphere
Tel: **01945 583121** Mr Potter.
Rates fr: *£14.00-£14.00.*
Open: All Year
Beds: 1F 1D 1T 2S
🛏 🅿 (6) 🖵 ✕ 🎱 🆅

(0.5m) *Holly Gap, Mill Tree Lane, Wisbech, Cambs, PE13 4TR.*
Rural farm bungalow with horses
Grades: ETB Listed
Tel: **01945 463119**
Mrs Fountain-Hoare.
Rates fr: *£15.00-£16.50.*
Open: All Year (not Xmas)
Beds: 1D 1T
Baths: 1 Shared
🛏 🅿 (5) ⅍ 🖵 🍴 🎱 ♿

Walton Highway 15

National Grid Ref: TF4912

🍴 🍺 King of Hearts

(0.5m) *Homeleigh Guest House, Lynn Road, Walton Highway, Wisbech, Cambs, PE14 7DE.*
Large Victorian private house
Tel: **01945 582356** Mrs Wiseman.
Fax no: 01945 587006
Rates fr: *£18.00-£18.00.*
Open: All Year
Beds: 2D 2T 2S
Baths: 6 Ensuite
🛏 🅿 (10) 🖵 🍴 ✕ 🎱 ♿ 🆅 ♿ ∥

> All cycleways are popular: you are well-advised to book ahead

King's Lynn 16

National Grid Ref: TF6120

|○| ◀ The Wild Fowler, Lord Kelvin

(▲ 0.5m) *King's Lynn Youth Hostel, Thoresby College, College Lane, King's Lynn, Norfolk, PE30 1JB.*
Actual grid ref: TF616199
Tel: 01553 772461
Under 18: £5.40 **Adults:** £8.00
Self-catering Facilities, Showers
Traditional hostel in a wing of the 500-year-old Chantry college building in the historic part of King's Lynn. Discover heritage buildings and museums and other attractions in the varied West Norfolk countryside

(0.5m) *Guanock Hotel, Southgates, London Road, King's Lynn, Norfolk, PE30 5JG.*
Grades: ETB Listed, AA Listed, RAC Listed
Tel: 01553 772959 (also fax no)
Mr Parchment.
Rates fr: *£17.00*-**£21.00**.
Open: All Year
Beds: 5F 4D 3T 5S
Baths: 5 Shared
🛏 (1) 🅿 (12) 🗖✗▥.Ⅴ▐
Warm friendly hotel noted for cleanliness and good food. Close to town centre and all industrial estates, adjacent to historic Southgates, near Sandringham House

(0.5m) *Havana Guest House, 117 Gaywood Road, King's Lynn, Norfolk, PE30 2PU.*
Large Victorian house, comfortable, well-appointed bedrooms, ample parking
Grades: ETB 2 Cr, Comm, AA 3 Q, RAC Acclaim
Tel: 01553 772 331 Mrs Breed.
Rates fr: *£15.00*-**£17.00**.
Open: All Year (not Xmas)
Beds: 1F 2D 3T 1S
Baths: 4 Private 1 Shared
🛏 (2) 🅿 (8) ⚄🗖▥.Ⅴ▐

(0.5m) *Maranatha Guest House, 115 Gaywood Road, King's Lynn, Norfolk, PE30 2PU.*
Large Victorian guesthouse with garden, parking
Grades: ETB 2 Cr, Approv
Tel: 01553 774596 Mr Bastone.
Rates fr: *£14.00*-**£17.00**.
Open: All Year
Beds: 2F 2D 2T 3S
Baths: 2 Ensuite 1 Private
🛏 🅿 (8) 🗖★✗▥.Ⅴ

(0.5m) *Flints Hotel, 73 Norfolk St, King's Lynn, Norfolk, PE30 1AD.*
Modern hotel
Grades: ETB Listed, Approv
Tel: 01553 769400 Mr Flint.
Rates fr: *£18.00*-**£18.00**.
Open: All Year
Beds: 1F 1D 1T 1S
🛏 (1) 🅿 (7) 🗖✗▥.Ⅴ

Boston to Beccles

Now you strike out southwards across the Fens, the low-lying country of southern Lincolnshire and northern Cambridgeshire which, before it was drained in the seventeenth century by Dutchmen, was inhospitable marshland. After crossing the River Welland at Fosdyke Bridge, it's over three marshes to Holbeach, before crossing into Cambridgeshire at Tydd St Giles and proceeding to **Wisbech** on the River Nene, the 'capital of the fens'. Here the Fenland Museum sports, among other things, a reconstructed Victorian post office. Leaving Wisbech to the north you come into Norfolk and head eastwards. After crossing the River Great Ouse at Wiggenhall St Germans, you cycle into **King's Lynn**, and on to Castle Rising and Sandringham. (See under *CTC Circular Tour of East Anglia*.) From here it's on to Ringstead, not far from the spectacular cliffs of Hunstanton, then Burnham Market, birthplace of Admiral Nelson (with three pubs carrying his worthy name), before you reach the market town of **Fakenham**. The route now takes you along the line of the River Wensum to the attractive village of Reepham, with its Georgian and half-timbered houses and the redbrick Old Brewery House, and on to **Norwich**. (See under *CTC Circular Tour of East Anglia*.) Having cycled through the city centre, you cross the River Yare and skirt the Norfolk Broads as far as Loddon, before heading south to the banks of the Waveney, which you follow downstream until the route enters Suffolk at **Beccles**.

(0.5m) *Fairlight Lodge, 79 Goodwins Road, King's Lynn, Norfolk, PE30 5PE.*
Lovely Victorian home, warm welcome
Grades: ETB 2 Cr, High Comm, AA 4 Q
Tel: 01553 762234 Mrs Rowe.
Fax no: 01553 770280
Rates fr: *£16.00*-**£20.00**.
Open: All Year (not Xmas)
Beds: 2D 3T 2S
Baths: 4 Ensuite 2 Shared
🛏 🅿 (6) 🗖★▥.Ⅴ

Dersingham 17

National Grid Ref: TF6830

|○| ◀ The Feather's

(0.5m) *Meadow Vale, 63 Manor Road, Dersingham, Kings Lynn, Norfolk, PE31 6LH.*
Modern comfortable house, friendly atmosphere
Grades: ETB Listed, Comm
Tel: 01485 540769 Mrs Williams.
Rates fr: *£15.00*-**£15.00**.
Open: Easter to Oct
Beds: 1D 1T 1S **Baths:** 1 Shared
🛏 (8) 🅿 (4) ⚄🗖▥.

(0.5m) *The White House, 44 Hunstanton Road, Dersingham, Kings Lynn, Norfolk, PE31 6HQ.*
Comfortable, warm welcome, good breakfast
Tel: 01485 541895 Ms Nightingale.
Rates fr: *£15.50*-**£15.50**.
Open: All Year **Beds:** 2D 2T 1S
Baths: 1 Private 2 Shared
🛏 🅿 (5) 🗖★▥.&Ⅴ

Sedgeford 18

National Grid Ref: TF7136

|○| ◀ King William

(0.25m) *Dove Hill Cottage, Cole Green, Sedgeford, Hunstanton, Norfolk, PE36 5LS.*
Actual grid ref: TF714365
Family house in conservation area
Tel: 01485 571642 Mrs Lyle.
Rates fr: *£16.00*-**£16.00**.
Open: All Year (not Xmas)
Beds: 1F 1T
Baths: 1 Shared
🅿 (4) 🗖★▥.Ⅴ▐✦

Old Hunstanton 19

National Grid Ref: TF6842

(2m) *Lakeside, Waterworks Road, Old Hunstanton, Norfolk, PE36 6JE.*
Converted waterworks, overlooking private lake
Grades: ETB 3 Cr
Tel: 01485 533763 Mr Diamant.
Rates fr: *£18.00*-**£17.50**.
Open: All Year
Beds: 3D 1T 2S
Baths: 4 Private 1 Shared
🛏 (13) 🅿 (10) 🗖✗▥.Ⅴ▐

Pay B&Bs by cash or cheque and be prepared to pay up front.

Hunstanton 20

National Grid Ref: TF6740

🍽️ 🍺 Golden Lion, Ancient Mariner Inn

(▲ 3m) *Hunstanton Youth Hostel, 15 Avenue Road, Hunstanton, Norfolk, PE36 5BW.*
Actual grid ref: TF674406
Warden: Ms S Haworth.
Tel: **01485 532061**
Under 18: £5.95 **Adults:** £8.80
Evening Meals Available (7pm),
Family Bunk Rooms, Television,
Showers, Shop
Victorian carrstone house in sea-side resort with Blue Flag beach, famous for birdwatching and ecology studies

(3m) *Caltofts, 15 Austin Street, Hunstanton, Norfolk, PE36 6AJ.*
Guest house situated in quiet road,
2 mins sea and shops
Tel: **01485 533759**
Mr & Mrs Vass.
Rates fr: *£16.00*-**£16.00**.
Open: All Year
Beds: 2F 2D 1T 1S
Baths: 2 Private 1 Shared
🛏️ 🅿️ (3) ⅍ 🗢 🗙 ⅏.

(3m) *Sutton House Hotel, 24 Northgate, Hunstanton, Norfolk, PE36 6AP.*
Edwardian house near town/sea
Tel: **01485 532552** (also fax no)
Mr Emsden.
Rates fr: *£20.00*-**£25.00**.
Open: All Year
Beds: 2F 4D 2T
Baths: 8 Private
🛏️ (1) 🅿️ (6) 🗢 🗙 ⅏. 🔟 🍴 ⚡

(3m) *Rosamaly Guest House, 14 Glebe Avenue, Hunstanton, Norfolk, PE36 6BS.*
Relaxed, comfortable, warm friendly guest house
Grades: ETB Listed, Approv
Tel: **01485 534187** Mrs Duff Dick.
Rates fr: *£16.00*-**£16.00**.
Open: All Year
Beds: 2F 1D 1T 1S
Baths: 2 Shared
🛏️ 🗢 🗙 ⅏. 🔟

(3m) *Kiama Cottage, 23 Austin Street, Hunstanton, Norfolk, PE36 6AN.*
Friendly small family guest house
Grades: ETB 2 Cr, Comm
Tel: **01485 533615**
Mr & Mrs Flowerdew.
Rates fr: *£16.00*-**£19.00**.
Open: Easter to Oct
Beds: 1F 2D 1T
Baths: 4 Private
🛏️ 🅿️ (1) 🗢 🗙 ⅏. 🔟 🍴 ⚡

(3m) *Burleigh Hotel, 7 Cliff Terrace, Hunstanton, Norfolk, PE36 6DY.*
Home-from-home, friendly atmosphere
Grades: ETB 3 Cr, Comm
Tel: **01485 533080**
Mr & Mrs Abos.
Rates fr: *£21.00*-**£23.00**.
Open: All Year
Beds: 4F 4D 2T 1S
Baths: 9 Ensuite 2 Private
🛏️ (5) 🗢 🗙 ⅏. 🔟 🍴 ⚡

(3m) *Deepdene Hotel & Leisure Club, 29 Avenue Road, Hunstanton, Norfolk, PE36 5BW.*
Large Victorian house
Tel: **01485 532460** Mrs Brunt.
Rates fr: *£25.00*-**£25.00**.
Open: All Year
Beds: 3F 3D 3S
Baths: 1 Private
🛏️ 🅿️ (6) 🗢 🗙 ⅏. 🔟

Thornham 21

National Grid Ref: TF7343

🍽️ 🍺 King's Head, Chequers Inn

(2m) *The Chequers, High Street, Thornham, Hunstanton, Norfolk, PE36 6LY.*
C18th freehouse close to sea and
RSPB, good food, real ales, warm
welcome
Tel: **01485 512229**
Rates fr: *£25.00*-**£25.00**.
Open: All Year
Beds: 2D 1S
Baths: 3 Ensuite
🅿️ (35) ⅍ 🗢 🗙 ⅏. 🔟

(2m) *Ilex Cottage, High Street, Thornham, Hunstanton, Norfolk, PE36 6QY.*
Fully modernised old style property
Tel: **01485 512310** Miss Leary.
Rates fr: *£17.50*-**£20.00**.
Open: All Year
Beds: 1D 2T
Baths: 2 Private 1 Shared
🛏️ (8) 🅿️ (5) ⅍ 🗢 🛏️ 🗙 ⅏. 🔟 🍴 ⚡

(2m) *Orchard House, Thornham, Hunstanton, Norfolk, PE36 6LY.*
Tucked away in centre of
picturesque village
Grades: ETB 2 Cr, Comm
Tel: **01485 512259** Mrs Rutland.
Rates fr: *£18.50*-**£30.00**.
Open: All Year (not Xmas Day)
Beds: 1D 2T
Baths: 2 Ensuite 1 Shared
🛏️ (8) 🅿️ (4) ⅍ 🗢 ⅏. 🔟 🍴 ⚡

(2m) *Kings Head Hotel, High Street, Thornham, Hunstanton, Norfolk, PE36 6LY.*
C16th inn, open log fires
Tel: **01485 512213** Mrs John.
Rates fr: *£18.00*-**£18.00**.
Open: All Year (not Xmas)
Beds: 2D 1T
Baths: 1 Shared
🛏️ 🅿️ ⅍ 🗢 🗙 ⅏. 🍴 ⚡

(2m) *Rush Meadow, Main Road, Thornham, Hunstanton, Norfolk, PE36 6LZ.*
Comfortable home, marsh/sea views
Tel: **01485 512372** Mr Wyett.
Rates fr: *£20.00*-**£30.00**.
Open: All Year (not Xmas)
Beds: 1F 1D
Baths: 1 Ensuite 1 Private
🛏️ 🅿️ (5) ⅍ 🗢 🛏️ ⅏. 🔟

Choseley 22

National Grid Ref: TF7540

(0.5m) *Choseley Farmhouse, Choseley, Docking, Kings Lynn, Norfolk, PE31 6LZ.*
Actual grid ref: TF755408
C16th Listed farmhouse with
Tudor chimneys
Tel: **01485 512331**
Major & Mrs Hutchinson.
Rates fr: *£15.00*-**£15.00**.
Open: Easter to Oct
Beds: 1D 1T
Baths: 1 Shared
🅿️ (6) ⚡

Brancaster 23

National Grid Ref: TF7743

🍽️ 🍺 Ship Hotel

(2m) *The Old Bakery, Main Road, Brancaster, Kings Lynn, Norfolk, PE31 8AZ.*
Delightful converted old bakery
and cottage set in grounds of one
acre
Tel: **01485 210501**
Mrs Townshend.
Rates fr: *£18.00*-**£22.50**.
Open: All Year (not Xmas)
Beds: 1F 2D 1S
Baths: 2 Ensuite 2 Shared
🛏️ 🅿️ (3) 🗢 ⅏. 🍴 ⚡

Burnham Market 24

National Grid Ref: TF8342

🍽️ 🍺 Hoste Arms, The Fishes

(On route) *Millwood, Herrings Lane, Burnham Market, Kings Lynn, Norfolk, PE31 8DW.*
Actual grid ref: TF8343
Peaceful, luxurious, coastal country
house
Grades: ETB Listed, High Comm
Tel: **01328 730152** Mrs Leftley.
Fax no: 01328 730158
Rates fr: *£25.00*-**£30.00**.
Open: All Year (not Xmas)
Beds: 1D 1T
Baths: 2 Ensuite
🛏️ (8) 🅿️ (4) ⅍ 🗢 🛏️ ⅏.

The lowest *double* rate per person is shown in *italics*.

The lowest *single* rate *is shown in* **bold.**

Burnham Overy 25

National Grid Ref: TF8442

🍴 🍺 The Hero

(0.5m) Ostrich House, *Burnham Overy, Kings Lynn, Norfolk, PE31 8HU.*
Actual grid ref: TF842429
300-year-old Listed end-of-terrace cottage
Grades: ETB Listed
Tel: **01328 738517**
Mrs O'Connor.
Rates fr: *£16.00-£16.00.*
Open: All Year (not Xmas)
Beds: 1D 1T 1S
Baths: 2 Shared
🅿 (3) 🛏 🛏 🕯 ∗

Burnham Overy Staithe 26

National Grid Ref: TF8444

(1.5m) Domville Guest House, *Glebe Lane, Burnham Overy Staithe, Kings Lynn, Norfolk, PE31 8JQ.*
Quietly situated, family-run guest house
Grades: ETB 1 Cr, Comm
Tel: **01328 738298**
Mr & Mrs Smith.
Rates fr: *£17.00-£17.00.*
Open: All Year (not Xmas)
Beds: 2D 2T 4S
Baths: 2 Private 2 Shared
🛏 (6) 🅿 (10) 🗲 🛏 ✗ V 🕯 ∗

Wells-next-the-Sea 27

National Grid Ref: TF9143

🍴 🍺 Lifeboat Inn, Three Horseshoes, Crown Hotel

(1.5m) The Cobblers Guest House, *Standard Road, Wells-next-the-Sea, Norfolk, NR23 1JU.*
Actual grid ref: TF918435
Tel: **01328 710155** (also fax no)
Mr & Mrs Stew.
Rates fr: *£13.00-£17.00.*
Open: All Year
Beds: 2F 1T 3D 2S
Baths: 3 Ensuite 2 Shared
🛏 (5) 🅿 (8) 🛏 ✗ 🛏 V 🕯
Family-run guest house set close to the harbour in Wells. Comfortable guest lounge and conservatory. Private, secluded garden and off-street parking

(1.5m) Mill House, *Northfield Lane, Wells-next-the-Sea, Norfolk, NR23 1JZ.*
Actual grid ref: TF918435
Mill House: a former mill-owner's house in secluded gardens
Tel: **01328 710739**
Mr Downey.
Rates fr: *£17.00-£17.50.*
Open: All Year
Beds: 1F 3D 2T 2S
Baths: 6 Ensuite 2 Private
🛏 (8) 🅿 (10) 🛏 🛏 ✗ 🛏 ⅙ ∗

(1.5m) The Warren, *Warham Road, Wells-next-the-Sea, Norfolk, NR23 1NE.*
Comfortable bungalow in quiet location. 10 minutes' walk from all amenities
Grades: ETB Listed
Tel: **01328 710273** Mrs Wickens.
Rates fr: *£18.00-£20.00.*
Open: All Year (not Xmas)
Beds: 1D 1T
Baths: 1 Ensuite 1 Private
🅿 (2) 🗲 🛏 🛏 🛏 V

(1.5m) The Normans Guest House, *Invaders Court, Standard Road, Wells-next-the-Sea, Norfolk, NR23 1JW.*
Actual grid ref: TF917435
Elegant Georgian house within courtyard. Some rooms overlook saltmarshes
Tel: **01328 710657**
Mrs MacDonald.
Fax no: 01328 710468
Rates fr: *£23.50-£30.00.*
Open: All Year (not Xmas)
Beds: 6D 1T
Baths: 7 Ensuite
🅿 (10) 🗲 🛏 🛏 ∗

(1.5m) St Heliers Guest House, *Station Road, Wells-next-the-Sea, Norfolk, NR23 1EA.*
Large Georgian house, centrally located
Tel: **01328 710361** (also fax no)
Mrs Kerr.
Rates fr: *£16.00-£20.00.*
Open: All Year
Beds: 1F 1D 1T
Baths: 2 Shared
🅿 (5) 🗲 🛏 🛏 V 🕯 ∗

(1.5m) East House, *East Quay, Wells-next-the-Sea, Norfolk, NR23 1LE.*
Actual grid ref: TF921437
Old house overlooking coastal marsh
Tel: **01328 710408** Mrs Scott.
Rates fr: *£20.00-£25.00.*
Open: All Year (not Xmas)
Beds: 2T **Baths:** 2 Ensuite
🛏 (7) 🅿 (2) 🛏 🛏 ∗

(1.5m) Greengates, *Stiffkey Road, Wells-next-the-Sea, Norfolk, NR23 1QB.*
Actual grid ref: TF9243
Cottage with views over marshes
Tel: **01328 711040** Mrs Jarvis.
Rates fr: *£16.00-£20.00.*
Open: All Year (not Xmas)
Beds: 1T 1D **Baths:** 2 Private
🅿 (2) 🛏 🛏

(1.5m) Brooklands, *31 Burnt Street, Wells-next-the-Sea, Norfolk, NR23 1HP.*
Charming beamed 200-year-old house
Tel: **01328 710768** Mrs Wykes.
Rates fr: *£15.00-£18.00.*
Open: Apr to Oct
Beds: 1F 1D **Baths:** 1 Shared
🛏 (7) 🅿 (2) 🗲 🛏 🛏 🛏

(1.5m) Eastdene Guest House, *Northfield Lane, Wells-next-the-Sea, Norfolk, NR23 1LH.*
Comfortable guest house
Tel: **01328 710381** Mrs Court.
Rates fr: *£18.00-£20.00.*
Open: All Year
Beds: 1D 2T 1S
Baths: 3 Private 1 Shared
🛏 (9) 🅿 (5) 🗲 🛏 ✗ 🛏 V 🕯 ∗

(1.5m) Hideaway, *Red Lion Yard, Wells-next-the-Sea, Norfolk, NR23 1AX.*
Actual grid ref: TF924344
Annexe on to private house
Grades: ETB 2 Cr, Comm
Tel: **01328 710524**
Miss Higgs.
Rates fr: *£17.00-£20.00.*
Open: Jan to Nov
Beds: 1D 2T
Baths: 3 Ensuite
🅿 (3) 🛏 ✗ 🛏 V 🕯 ∗

(1.5m) West End House, *Dogger Lane, Wells-next-the-Sea, Norfolk, NR23 1BE.*
Small friendly guest house
Tel: **01328 711190**
Mr Cox.
Rates fr: *£14.00-£14.00.*
Open: All Year
Beds: 1F 1T 1D 1S
Baths: 2 Shared
🛏 🅿 (4) 🛏 ✗ 🛏 V

Warham 28

National Grid Ref: TF9441

(1.5m) The Three Horseshoes / The Old Post Office, *69 Bridge Street, Warham, Wells-next-the-Sea, Norfolk, NR23 1NL.*
Dream country cottage
Tel: **01328 710547**
Mr Salmon.
Rates fr: *£20.00-£20.00.*
Open: All Year (not Xmas)
Beds: 3D 1S
Baths: 1 Private 1 Shared
🛏 (14) 🅿 (20) 🛏 🛏 ✗ 🛏 V 🕯 ∗

Wighton 29

National Grid Ref: TF9439

🍴 🍺 Sandpiper Inn

(On route) The Carpenters' Arms, *57 High Street, Wighton, Wells-next-the-Sea, Norfolk, NR23 1PF.*
Actual grid ref: TF942397
Tel: **01328 820752**
Mrs Marsh.
Rates fr: *£17.50-£25.00.*
Open: All Year
Beds: 1D 2T
Baths: 1 Shared
🛏 (7) 🅿 (30) 🛏 🛏 ✗ 🛏 V 🕯
This traditional village inn set in the River Stiffkey valley offers peace and quiet along with delicious home-cooked food and excellent ales

Walsingham 30

National Grid Ref: TF9437

¶ol ■ White Horse

(0.25m) *St Davids House, Friday Market, Walsingham, Norfolk, NR22 6BY.*
Tudor house in medieval village, five miles from coast
Grades: ETB 2 Cr, Approv
Tel: 01328 820633 Mrs Renshaw.
Rates fr: *£18.00-£18.00.*
Open: All Year **Beds:** 3F 1D 1T
Baths: 1 Ensuite 2 Shared
ॐ ○ ♌ ☆ ✕ Ⅵ 🖢 ⊀

(On route) *Knights Gate Guest House, Knights Street, Little Walsingham, Walsingham, Norfolk, NR22 6DA.*
Actual grid ref: TF935368
Walsingham - 'England's Nazareth', More than 500,000 visit every year. Unspoilt Norfolk coast 5 miles
Tel: 01328 820200 Mrs Brooks.
Rates fr: *£22.00-£27.00.*
Open: All Year (not Xmas)
Beds: 3T **Baths:** 3 Private
ॐ ☐ (6) ☐ Ⅲ. Ⅵ

(0.25m) *Vicarage Cottage, Great Walsingham, Walsingham, Norfolk, NR22 6DS.*
Historic house in historic village
Tel: 01328 820381 Mrs Dyson.
Rates fr: *£21.00-£25.00.*
Open: Easter to Oct
Beds: 1F **Baths:** 1 Ensuite
ॐ ☐ ⊬ ☐ Ⅲ. ♿

(0.25m) *The Old Bakehouse, 33 High Street, Walsingham, Norfolk, NR22 6BZ.*
Restaurant with rooms. Small, friendly
Tel: 01328 820454 Mrs Padley.
Rates fr: *£20.00-£25.00.*
Open: All Year (not Xmas)
Beds: 2D 1T
Baths: 1 Private 1 Shared
ॐ ○ ☆ ✕ Ⅲ. Ⅵ

(0.25m) *Foundry Farm House, Hindringham Road, Walsingham, Norfolk, NR22 6DR.*
Modern, comfortable farmhouse
Tel: 01328 820316 Mr Fox.
Rates fr: *£17.00-£15.00.*
Open: Easter to Nov
Beds: 2T 2S
Baths: 2 Shared
ॐ ☐ (4) ☐ ✕ Ⅲ. Ⅵ 🖢 ⊀

(0.25m) *Orchard Cottage, Wighton Road, Walsingham, Norfolk, NR22 6DP.*
Modern cottage with stunning views
Tel: 01328 820740 Mrs Beavis.
Rates fr: *£17.75-£20.00.*
Open: Easter to Oct
Beds: 1D 1T
Baths: 2 Shared
ॐ ☐ ⊬ ☐ Ⅲ.

East Barsham 31

National Grid Ref: TF9133

¶ol ■ White Horse Inn

(0.5m) *White Horse Inn, Fakenham Road, East Barsham, Fakenham, Norfolk, NR21 0LH.*
Grades: ETB 3 Cr
Tel: 01328 820645 (also fax no)
Mrs Baines.
Rates fr: *£24.00-£30.00.*
Open: All Year
Beds: 1F 3T
Baths: 3 Private
ॐ ☐ (50) ⊬ ○ ☆ Ⅲ. Ⅵ
Cosy inn with inglenook fireplace, in village 8 miles from coast, golf, racecourse

(0.25m) *Fieldview, West Barsham Road, East Barsham, Fakenham, Norfolk, NR21 0AR.*
Central, comfortable, modern flint house
Tel: 01328 820083 Mrs Batty.
Rates fr: *£20.00-£20.00.*
Open: All Year **Beds:** 2D 3T
Baths: 1 Ensuite 2 Shared
ॐ (8) ☐ (5) ⊬ ☐ Ⅲ. Ⅵ

Great Ryburgh 32

National Grid Ref: TF9527

(1m) *Highfield Farm, Great Ryburgh, Fakenham, Norfolk, NR21 7AL.*
Beautiful large farmhouse, peaceful location
Tel: 01328 829249 Mrs Savory.
Rates fr: *£16.00-£21.00.*
Open: All Year (not Xmas)
Beds: 1D 2T **Baths:** 1 Ensuite
ॐ (12) ☐ (10) ⊬ ☐ ✕ Ⅲ.

Felthorpe 33

National Grid Ref: TG1618

¶ol ■ Marsham Arms, The Ratcatchers, Yeast & Feast

(1.5m) *Spinney Ridge, Hall Lane, Felthorpe, Norwich. NR10 4BX.*
Tel: 01603 754833
Mr & Mrs Thompson.
Rates fr: *£17.00-£15.00.*
Open: All Year (not Xmas)
Beds: 1F 1D 1T 1S
Baths: 2 Private 2 Shared
ॐ (5) ☐ (4) ⊬ ☐ Ⅲ.
Charactered, warm and friendly house in quiet setting, just off the A1149, centres us for Norwich, North Norfolk and the Broads. Convenient to recommended restaurants

(2m) *Lodge Farmhouse, The St, Felthorpe, Norwich. NR10 4BY.*
Comfortable accommodation, friendly service
Tel: 01603 754896 Mrs Howe.
Rates fr: *£14.00-£14.00.*
Open: All Year (not Xmas)
Beds: 1D 1T **ॐ ☐ (4) ⊬ ☐ Ⅲ. Ⅵ**

(1.5m) *Flitcham Cottage, Fir Covert Road, Felthorpe, Norwich. NR10 4DT.*
Well-appointed converted farm cottage
Grades: ETB Listed, Comm
Tel: 01603 867493 Mr Smith.
Rates fr: *£15.00-£15.00.*
Open: All Year (not Xmas)
Beds: 2D 1T **Baths:** 1 Shared
ॐ ☐ (9) ⊬ ☐ Ⅲ. Ⅵ 🖢 ⊀

Norwich 34

National Grid Ref: TG2308

¶ol ■ King's Head, Coach & Horses, The Pickwick, The Black Horse, The Mitre

(▲ 0.5m) *Norwich Youth Hostel, 112 Turner Road, Norwich, Norfolk, NR2 4HB.*
Actual grid ref: TG213095
Tel: 01603 627647
Under 18: £5.95 **Adults:** £8.80
Evening Meals Available (6.30-7.15pm), Self-catering Facilities, Television, Showers
In quiet suburban street outside the city centre, a good place for exploring Norwich. Within easy reach of East Anglian countryside, from seaside to the Broads

(1m) *Earlham Guest House, 147 Earlham Road, Norwich. NR2 3RG.*
Grades: ETB 2 Cr, Comm, AA 3 Q
Tel: 01603 454169 (also fax no)
Mr & Mrs Wright.
Rates fr: *£17.00-£20.00.*
Open: All Year
Beds: 2F 1T 2D 2S
Baths: 2 Ensuite 2 Shared
ॐ ⊬ ☐ Ⅲ. Ⅵ
Susan and Derek Wright offer welcoming and friendly hospitality with comfortable and modern facilities close historic Norwich centre and University. Non-smoking. Visa, Mastercard

(1m) *Chiltern House, 2 Trafford Road, Norwich. NR1 2QW.*
Good home cooking. 5 minutes city centre. Celia & Ken Harrison welcome you all year round
Grades: ETB Listed
Tel: 01603 663033 Mrs Harrison.
Rates fr: *£17.00-£17.00.*
Open: All Year **Beds:** 1F 1D 5S
Baths: 1 Ensuite 1 Shared
ॐ ☐ ✕ Ⅲ. ♿ Ⅵ

(1m) *Edmar Lodge, 64 Earlham Road, Norwich. NR2 3DF.*
A real home from home. Come and be spoilt!
Grades: ETB 2 Cr, Comm
Tel: 01603 615599 Mrs Lovatt.
Fax no: 01603 632977
Rates fr: *£16.50-£23.00.*
Open: All Year
Beds: 2F 1D 1T 1S
Baths: 3 Private 2 Shared
ॐ ☐ (6) ☐ Ⅲ. Ⅵ

(1m) *Trebeigh House, 16 Brabazon Road, Hellesdon, Norwich. NR6 6SY.*
Friendly comfortable, quiet private house. Convenient airport and tourist attractions
Tel: **01603 429056** Mrs Jope.
Fax no: 01603 414247
Rates fr: *£16.00-*£17.00.
Open: All Year (not Xmas)
Beds: 1D 1T **Baths:** 1 Shared
🛏 🅿 (2) ½ 🗆 �🖂 🗓 ⓥ ⓘ

(1m) *Rosedale, 145 Earlham Road, Norwich. NR2 3RG.*
Comfortable, friendly, family guest house
Grades: ETB Listed, Approv
Tel: **01603 453743**
Mrs Curtis.
Fax no: 01603 408473
Rates fr: *£16.50-*£16.00.
Open: All Year (not Xmas)
Beds: 1F 1D 3T 3S
Baths: 2 Shared
🛏 (4) 🅿 (1) 🗆 �🖂 ⓥ

(1m) *Alpha Hotel, 82 Unthank Road, Norwich. NR2 2RW.*
Comfortable Victorian rectory with character
Grades: ETB 2 Cr
Tel: **01603 621105** (also fax no)
Mr Downton.
Rates fr: *£20.00-*£22.00.
Open: All Year (not Xmas)
Beds: 6D 6T 9S
Baths: 10 Ensuite 4 Shared
🛏 (10) 🅿 (16) ½ 🗆 �🖂

(1m) *The Sycamores, 59 Aylsham Road, Norwich. NR3 2HF.*
Comfortable, modern, private house
Grades: ETB Listed, Comm
Tel: **01603 665798**
Mrs Adams.
Rates fr: *£16.00-*£16.00.
Open: Mar to Dec
Beds: 1F 1D
Baths: 1 Ensuite 1 Private
🛏 (3) 🅿 (2) ½ 🗆 �🖂 ⓥ

(1m) *Butterfield Hotel, 4 Stracey Road, Norwich. NR1 1EZ.*
Large Victorian private house
Grades: ETB Listed
Tel: **01603 661008 / 624041**
Rates fr: *£34.00-*£17.00.
Open: All Year (not Xmas)
Beds: 4F 4D 4S
Baths: 4 Ensuite 2 Shared
🛏 🅿 🗆 ⋔ ✕ �🖂 &

(1m) *30 St Stephens Road, Norwich. NR1 3RA.*
Beautifully restored Victorian Listed house
Tel: **01603 760238** Mrs Middleton.
Rates fr: *£15.00-*£22.00.
Open: All Year (not Xmas)
Beds: 2D **Baths:** 1 Shared
🛏 🅿 (1) ½ 🗆 �🖂

The lowest *double* rate per person is shown in *italics*.

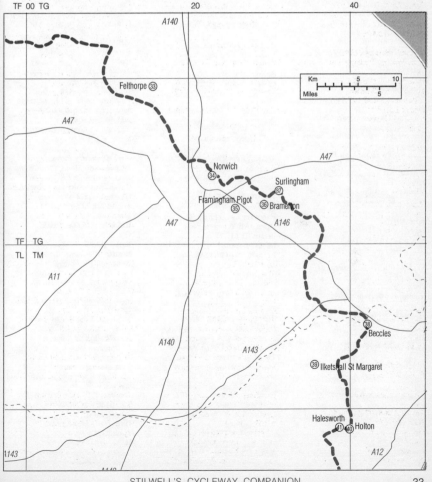

Framingham Pigot   35

National Grid Ref: TG2703
🍴 🍺 Railway Tavern, The Gull

(2m) *The Old Rectory, Rectory
Lane, Framingham Pigot, Norwich.
NR14 7QQ.*
Friendly comfortable Victorian
Rectory. Large garden. 10 mins
Norwich centre
Grades: ETB Listed
Tel: 01508 493082 Mrs Thurman.
Rates fr: *£19.00-£19.00.*
Open: All Year (not Xmas)
Beds: 1F 1D 1T
Baths: 2 Ensuite 1 Shared
🛏 🖭 (6) ⅍ ♛ 🖵 📖 ⬩

Bramerton   36

National Grid Ref: TG2905
🍴 🍺 Woods End Tavern

(0.5m) *Rolling Acre, Woods End,
Bramerton, Norwich. NR14 7ED.*
Comfortable period country house.
Quiet, fine view
Tel: 01508 538529 Mrs Barton.
Rates fr: *£17.50-£19.00.*
Open: All Year **Beds:** 1F 1D
Baths: 1 Ensuite 1 Shared
🛏 (12) 🖭 (6) 🖵 ♛ 📖 Ⅴ

Surlingham   37

National Grid Ref: TG3106
🍴 🍺 Goldham Hall, Ferry House

(0.25m) *The Hermitage, Chapel
Loke, Surlingham, Norwich. NR14 7AQ.*
Peaceful C18th beautiful country
home
Tel: 01508 538431 Mr Pinder.
Rates fr: *£17.00-£18.00.*
Open: All Year (not Xmas)
Beds: 1D 1T 1S
Baths: 1 Ensuite 1 Shared
🛏 (12) 🖭 (8) 🖵 ♛ 📖 Ⅴ ⬩

Beccles   38

National Grid Ref: TM4289
🍴 🍺 Bear and Bells, The Horseshoe

(0.5m) *Catherine House, 2
Ringsfield Road, Beccles, Suffolk,
NR34 9PQ.*
Comfortable family home,
excellent facilities
Grades: ETB 2 Cr, Comm
Tel: 01502 716428 Mrs Renilson.
Rates fr: *£16.50-£16.50.*
Open: All Year **Beds:** 1F 1D 1S
Baths: 1 Ensuite 1 Shared
🛏 🖭 (5) 🖵 ✗ 📖 Ⅴ ⬩

(0.5m) *St Peters House, Old
Market, Beccles, Suffolk, NR34 9AP.*
Converted fisherman's chapel.
Gothic style
Tel: 01502 713203 (also fax no)
Mrs Broome.
Rates fr: *£20.00-£25.00.*
Open: All Year
Beds: 1D 1T 1S **Baths:** 1 Shared
🛏 (1) 🖭 (4) 🖵 ♛ ✗ 📖 Ⅴ 🛆

Ilketshall St Margaret 39

National Grid Ref: TM3585
🍴 🍺 Rumburgh Buck

(4m) *Shoo-Devil Farmhouse,
Ilketshall St Margaret, Bungay,
Suffolk, NR35 1QU.*
Comfortable, secluded thatched
C16th farmhouse
Grades: ETB 2 Cr, Comm
Tel: 01986 781303
Mrs Lewis.
Rates fr: *£17.50-£20.00.*
Open: Easter to Oct
Beds: 1D 1T
Baths: 2 Ensuite
🖭 (6) ⅍ 🖵 ✗ 📖 Ⅴ

Holton   40

National Grid Ref: TM4077

(0.25m) *Gavelcroft, Harrisons
Lane, Holton, Halesworth, Suffolk,
IP19 8LY.*
Listed C16th farmhouse in tranquil
surroundings
Tel: 01986 873117
Mrs Hart.
Rates fr: *£18.00-£22.00.*
Open: All Year (not Xmas)
Beds: 1F 1T
Baths: 2 Private
🛏 🖭 (8) ⅍ 🖵 ♛ ✗ 📖 ⬩ Ⅴ

Halesworth   41

National Grid Ref: TM3877
🍴 🍺 Queen's Head

(0.25m) *Fen Way, School Lane,
Halesworth, Suffolk, IP19 8BW.*
Bungalow set in peaceful meadow-
land
Tel: 01986 873574
Mrs George.
Rates fr: *£14.00-£16.00.*
Open: All Year
Beds: 2D 1T
Baths: 1 Shared
🛏 (5) 🖭 (5) ⅍ 🖵 ✗ 📖

Sibton   42

National Grid Ref: TM3669

(0.5m) *Sibton White Horse,
Halesworth Road, Sibton,
Saxmundham, Suffolk, IP17 2JJ.*
Grades: ETB Listed, Approv
Tel: 01728 660337
Mr Waddingham.
Rates fr: *£17.00-£20.00.*
Open: All Year
Beds: 3D 2T 3S
Baths: 7 Ensuite 1 Private
🛏 🖭 (60) ♛ ✗ 📖 ⬩ Ⅴ 🛆
C16th inn with large secluded
grounds. Eight rooms in separate
modern accommodation (all with
private facilities), play area,
reastaurant and bar menu

Badingham   43

National Grid Ref: TM3068
🍴 🍺 White Horse, Queen's Head

(1m) *Colston Hall, Badingham,
Woodbridge, Suffolk, IP13 8LB.*
C16th farmhouse, wonderful
setting, quiet
Grades: ETB 2 Cr, Comm
Tel: 01728 638375 (also fax no)
Mrs Bellefontaine.
Rates fr: *£20.00-£30.00.*
Open: All Year (not Xmas)
Beds: 1F 1D 1T
Baths: 3 Private
🛏 🖭 (Many) ⅍ 🖵 ♛ 📖 ⬩ Ⅴ 🛆

Framlingham   44

National Grid Ref: TM2863
🍴 🍺 Queen's Head, The Crown,
White Horse

(On Route) *Shimmens Pightle,
Dennington Road, Framlingham,
Woodbridge, Suffolk, IP13 9JT.*
Grades: ETB Listed, Comm
Tel: 01728 724036
Mrs Collett.
Rates fr: *£19.00-£21.00.*
Open: All Year (not Xmas)
Beds: 1F 1D 1T
Baths: 1 Shared
🛏 (6) 🖭 (5) ⅍ 🖵 📖 ⬩ Ⅴ
Comfortable family home set in an
acre of landscaped garden, over-
looking fields. Ground floor rooms
with wash basins. Local cured
bacon & home preserves

(1m) *Boundary Farm, Off
Saxmundham Road, Framlingham,
Woodbridge, Suffolk, IP13 9NU.*
C17th farmhouse, open countryside
Grades: ETB 1 Cr, Comm
Tel: 01728 723401
Mrs Cook.
Rates fr: *£16.00-£20.00.*
Open: All Year
Beds: 2D 1T
Baths: 1 Private 2 Shared
🛏 🖭 (8) 🖵 ✗ 📖 Ⅴ 🛆 ⬩

Dallinghoo   45

National Grid Ref: TM2655
🍴 🍺 Three Tuns, The Castle

(On Route) *Old Rectory,
Dallinghoo, Woodbridge, Suffolk,
IP13 0LA.*
Restful rural retreat, regularly
revisited. Guest rooms have
southerly views
Grades: ETB Listed, Comm
Tel: 01473 737700
Mrs Quinlan.
Rates fr: *£15.00.*
Open: All Year (not Xmas)
Beds: 1D 1T
Baths: 1 Private 1 Shared
🛏 🖭 (6) ⅍ 📖 Ⅴ

Bredfield 46

National Grid Ref: TM2652

(0.5m) *Moat Farmhouse,
Dallinghoo Road, Bredfield,
Woodbridge, Suffolk, IP13 6BD.*
Converted farm building. Self-
contained
Grades: ETB Listed, Comm
Tel: 01473 737475 Mrs Downing.
Rates fr: *£16.00-£16.00*.
Open: Mar to Oct
Beds: 1D 1T **Baths:** 1 Shared
⌂ (1) 🅿 (4) ⚡🖂 🖾.

Woodbridge 47

National Grid Ref: TM2649

🍴 🍺 The Crown, Cherry Tree

(0.25m) *19 Saxon Way, Bury Hill,
Woodbridge, Suffolk, IP12 1LG.*
Wooded location (one third to
Oxfam)
Tel: 01394 387931 Mrs Mummery.
Rates fr: *£15.00-£15.00*.
Open: All Year
Beds: 1T **Baths:** 1 Private
⌂ 🅿 (2) 🖂 🖾.

(0.25m) *Fen House, Fen Walk,
Woodbridge, Suffolk, IP12 4BG.*
Comfortable house (one third to
Oxfam)
Tel: 01394 387343 Mrs Thubron.
Rates fr: *£16.00-£15.00*.
Open: All Year
Beds: 1T 1S **Baths:** 1 Shared
⌂ 🅿 (4) ⚡🖂 🖿 🖾. 🆅 ⚘

Ipswich 48

National Grid Ref: TM1644

🍴 🍺 Westerfield Swan, The
Greyhound, The Ram, White Horse

(2m) *Orwell View, 24 Vermont
Road, Ipswich, Suffolk, IP4 2SR.*
Peaceful, close to centre, easy
parking
Tel: 01473 211451 Mrs Carroll.
Rates fr: *£12.50-£12.50*.
Open: All Year (not Xmas)
Beds: 1T 1S **Baths:** 1 Shared
🅿 (4) 🖂🖿🗙🖾. 🆅 ⛽

(2m) *Maple House, 114 Westerfield
Rd, Ipswich, Suffolk, IP4 2XW.*
Attractive private house near park
Tel: 01473 253797 Mrs Seal.
Rates fr: *£25.00-£15.00*.
Open: All Year (not Xmas)
Beds: 1D 1S **Baths:** 1 Shared
🅿 (3) ⚡🖂🖿🗙🖾. ⚒ ⚘

(2m) *107 Hatfield Road, Ipswich,
Suffolk, IP3 9AG.*
Large Victorian guest house,
modern facilities
Tel: 01473 723172 Mrs Debenham.
Fax no: 01473 270876
Rates fr: *£14.00-£15.00*.
Open: All Year **Beds:** 1D 2T
Baths: 1 Private 2 Shared
⌂ 🅿 🖂🖿🗙🖾. ⚒ 🆅

(2m) *Craigerne, Cauldwell
Avenue, Ipswich, Suffolk, IP4 4DZ.*
Tastefully restored Victorian,
gardens, parking
Tel: 01473 718200
Mrs Krotunas.
Rates fr: *£15.00-£15.00*.
Open: All Year (not Xmas)
Beds: 1D 1T 3S
Baths: 3 Ensuite 1 Shared
🅿 (10) 🖂🗙 🖾. 🆅

(2m) *Lochiel Guest House, 216
Felixstowe Road, Ipswich, Suffolk,
IP3 9AE.*
Large Victorian detached house
Tel: 01473 727775 Mrs McEvoy.
Rates fr: *£14.00-£14.00*.
Open: All Year
Beds: 1F 1D 3T 4S
Baths: 3 Private
⌂ 🅿 🖂🖿🗙 🖾.

(2m) *Mount Pleasant, 103
Anglesea Road, Ipswich, Suffolk,
IP1 3PJ.*
Tranquil, elegant Victorian town
house
Tel: 01473 251601
Rates fr: *£21.00-£27.00*.
Open: All Year (not Xmas)
Beds: 2D 1T 1S
Baths: 3 Ensuite 1 Private
⌂ (8) 🅿 (4) 🖂 🖾.

(2m) *Bridge Guest House,
4 Ancaster Road, Ipswich, Suffolk,
IP1 9AA.*
Family-run guest house, close town
centre
Tel: 01473 601760
Mr Pelletier.
Rates fr: *£14.00-£18.00*.
Open: All Year
Beds: 3F 6D 7S
Baths: 5 Private 3 Shared
⌂ 🅿 (12) 🖂🖿 🖾. 🆅

Kersey 49

National Grid Ref: TM0044

(2m) *Red House Farm, Kersey,
Ipswich, Suffolk, IP7 6EY.*
Comfortable farmhouse (c.1840)
Tel: 01787 210245 Mrs Alleston.
Rates fr: *£18.00-£20.00*.
Open: All Year
Beds: 1D 1T
Baths: 1 Private 1 Shared
🅿 (4) 🖂🖿🗙🖾. 🆅

Hadleigh 50

National Grid Ref: TM0242

🍴 🍺 Marquis of Cornwallis

(On route) *Frenchs Farm, Pond
Hall Road, Hadleigh, Ipswich,
Suffolk, IP7 5PQ.*
Large period country house.
Magnificent grounds. Extensive
horse riding facilities
Grades: ETB 2 Cr, Comm
Tel: 01473 824215 Mrs Stringer.
Rates fr: *£19.00-£20.00*.
Open: All Year
Beds: 2F 4D 1T 1S
Baths: 1 Private
⌂ 🅿 (30) 🖂🖿🗙 🖾.

Upper Layham 51

National Grid Ref: TM0340

(1m) *Marquis Of Cornwallis,
Upper Layham, Ipswich, Suffolk,
IP7 5JZ.*
Heavily beamed old country inn
Grades: ETB 2 Cr, Comm
Tel: 01473 822051 (also fax no)
Mr Abbott.
Rates fr: *£20.50-£29.00*.
Open: All Year **Beds:** 3D
Baths: 1 Private 2 Ensuite
⌂ 🅿 (22) 🖂🖿🗙 🆅

Halesworth to Dedham Vale

The way through the gently sloping rich farmland of Suffolk brings you to the market town of **Halesworth** and then the village of Peasenhall before you reach **Framlingham,** whose twelfth-century castle has a continuous curtain wall, from which there are fine views of the small town. From here it's on to the attractive town of **Woodbridge**, before you pass through the northwestern outskirts of **Ipswich**, Suffolk's county town. Ipswich Museum contains replicas of the Roman Mildenhall Treasure and the Sutton Hoo ship burial, both important local archaeological finds (the originals are in the British Museum in London), local studies exhibitions and anthropological galleries on Africa, Asia and the Americas. Christchurch Mansion is a Tudor house with substantial collections of Gainsborough and Constable, both local painters. The town's other celebrated Tudor building is the 'ancient house', faced with an outstanding seventeenth-century example of pargeting (sculpted plaster-work). Leaving town to the west, you go on to Whatfield and turn south through **Hadleigh**, before reaching **Stratford St Mary** in Constable's **Dedham Vale.**

Shelley   52

National Grid Ref: TM0338

(1.5m) *Spider Hall, Lower Raydon, Shelley, Ipswich, Suffolk, IP7 5QN.*
Lovely Grade II Listed C15th farmhouse
Grades: ETB Listed
Tel: **01473 822585** Mrs Pyman.
Fax no: 01473 824820
Rates fr: *£18.00-£18.00.*
Open: All Year (not Xmas)
Beds: 1D 1T **Baths:** 1 Shared
🛇 🅿 (6) 🗖 ⚲ ⛵ ⅢⅢ. Ⅴ

Higham   53

National Grid Ref: TM0335

(0.5m) *The Bauble, Higham, Colchester, Essex, CO7 6LA.*
Actual grid ref: TM031354
Peaceful old country home
Grades: ETB 2 Cr, High Comm, AA 4 Q, Recomm
Tel: **01206 337254** Mrs Watkins.
Fax no: 01206 337263
Rates fr: *£20.00-£22.00.*
Open: All Year
Beds: 2T 1S **Baths:** 3 Ensuite
🛇 (12) 🅿 (5) ⅙ 🗖 ⅢⅢ. Ⅴ 🛆 ⚡

Stratford St Mary   54

National Grid Ref: TM0434

🍴 🍺 Marlborough Head, Sun Hotel, The Swan, Black Horse

(0.25m) *Teazles, Stratford St Mary, Colchester, Essex, CO7 6LU.*
Comfortable old merchant weaver's house
Tel: **01206 323148** Mrs Clover.
Rates fr: *£18.00-£18.00.*
Open: All Year
Beds: 1F 1D 1T 1S
Baths: 1 Ensuite 1 Shared
🛇 🅿 ⅙ 🗖 ⚲ ⅢⅢ. Ⅴ 🛆 ⚡

All cycleways are popular: you are well-advised to book ahead

---

Pay B&Bs by cash or cheque and be prepared to pay up front.

Dedham   55

National Grid Ref: TM0533

🍴 🍺 The Anchor, Marlborough Head, The Sun

(2m) *Mays Barn Farm, Mays Lane, Dedham, Colchester, Essex, CO7 6EW.*
Actual grid ref: TM0531
Secluded, comfortable old farmhouse
Grades: ETB 2 Cr, High Comm
Tel: **01206 323191** Mrs Freeman.
Rates fr: *£19.00-£22.00.*
Open: All Year (not Xmas)
Beds: 1D 1T
Baths: 2 Private
🛇 (12) 🅿 (4) ⅙ 🗖 ⅢⅢ. Ⅴ

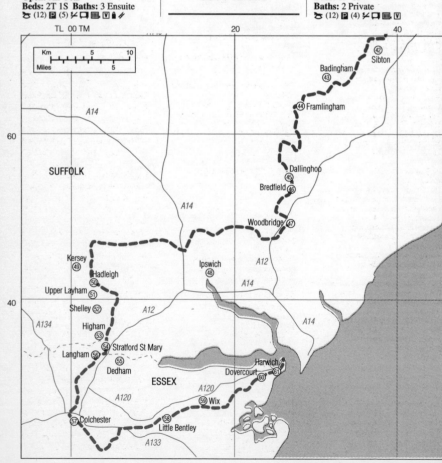

Langham 56

National Grid Ref: TM0233

|O| ◫ Shepherd & Dog

(1m) *Oak Apple Farm, Greyhound Hill, Langham, Colchester, Essex, CO4 5QF.*
Actual grid ref: TM023320
Comfortable farmhouse with large attractive garden
Grades: ETB Listed
Tel: 01206 272234 Mrs Helliwell.
Rates fr: *£18.50-£19.00.*
Open: All Year (not Xmas)
Beds: 2T 1S **Baths:** 1 Shared
ᵇ P (6) ◫ ▥ Ⓥ ▮ ✦

Colchester 57

National Grid Ref: TL9925

|O| ◫ The Forresters, Rovers Tye, Siege House

(0.5m) *The Red House, 29 Wimpole Rd, Colchester, Essex, CO1 2DL.*
Elegant, comfortable Victorian house. Short walk to town centre and stations
Tel: 01206 509005 Mrs Harrington.
Rates fr: *£18.00-£20.00.*
Open: All Year
Beds: 1T 2D **Baths:** 3 Ensuite
ᵇ (2) ✍ ◻ ✗ ▥ Ⓥ ▮

(0.5m) *St John's Guest House, 330 Ipswich Road, Colchester, Essex, CO4 4ET.*
Well situated close to town
Grades: ETB Listed
Tel: 01206 852288 Mrs Knight.
Rates fr: *£17.00-£25.00.*
Open: All Year **Beds:** 1F 1D 2T 1S
Baths: 2 Ensuite 1 Shared
ᵇ P (10) ✍ ◻ ▥ Ⓥ

(0.5m) *The Old Manse, 15 Roman Road, Colchester, Essex, CO1 1UR.*
Quiet town centre location beside Castle Park. 3 minutes walk to town
Grades: ETB Listed, AA 2 Q
Tel: 01206 545154 Ms Anderson.
Rates fr: *£18.00-£25.00.*
Open: All Year (not Xmas)
Beds: 1D 1T
Baths: 1 Private 2 Shared
ᵇ (3) P (1) ✍ ◻ ▥ Ⓥ

(0.5m) *Globe Hotel, 71 North Station Rd, Colchester, Essex, CO1 1RQ.*
Recently modernised Victorian pub/hotel
Tel: 01206 573881 Mr Higgins.
Rates fr: *£25.00-£30.00.*
Open: All Year **Beds:** 3F 3D 3T 3S
Baths: 12 Private
ᵇ P ◻ ✗ ▥ Ⓥ

(0.5m) *The Vines, 42 Military Road, Colchester, Essex, CO1 2AN.*
Large Georgian private house
Grades: ETB Listed
Tel: 01206 767301
Rates fr: *£16.50-£19.00.*
Open: All Year **Beds:** 1D 1T
Baths: 1 Ensuite 1 Private
ᵇ (0) P (1) ✍ ◻ ▥

Little Bentley 58

National Grid Ref: TM1125

(On route) *Bentley Manor, Little Bentley, Colchester, Essex, CO7 8SE.*
C16th manor house
Tel: 01206 250622 Mrs Dyson.
Rates fr: *£17.00-£20.00.*
Open: All Year (not Xmas)
Beds: 1F 1D 1T
ᵇ P ✍ ◻ ▥

Wix 59

National Grid Ref: TM1628

|O| ◫ Village Maid

(2m) *Dairy House Farm, Bradfield Road, Wix, Manningtree, Essex, CO11 2SR.*
Spacious, quality rural accommodation. A really relaxing place to stay
Grades: ETB 2 Cr, High Comm
Tel: 01255 870322 Mrs Whitworth.
Fax no: 01255 870186
Rates fr: *£17.00-£22.00.*
Open: All Year (not Xmas)
Beds: 1D 2T
Baths: 2 Ensuite 1 Private
ᵇ (10) P (10) ◻ ▥ Ⓥ ▮

(2m) *New Farm House, Spinnells Lane, Wix, Manningtree, Essex, CO11 2UJ.*
Country guesthouse with warmest welcome
Grades: ETB 3 Cr, Comm
Tel: 01255 870365 Mrs Mitchell.
Fax no: 01255 870837
Rates fr: *£21.00-£22.00.*
Open: All Year
Beds: 5F 1D 3T 3S
Baths: 7 Private 1 Shared
ᵇ P (20) ◻ ⊩ ✗ ▥ ⅋ Ⓥ ▮ ✦

Dovercourt 60

National Grid Ref: TM2531

(0.5m) *154 Fronks Road, Dovercourt, Harwich, Essex, CO12 4EF.*
Detached house in tree-lined boulevard
Tel: 01255 503081 (also fax no)
Mrs Cullen.
Rates fr: *£13.00-£15.00.*
Open: Dec to Jan
Beds: 1F 1T
Baths: 1 Shared
ᵇ P (4) ✍ ◻ ▥

(0.5m) *Swyncombe Guest House, 19 Cliff Road, Dovercourt, Harwich, Essex, CO12 3PP.*
Warm family-run guest house
Tel: 01255 551245
Mr Cheney.
Rates fr: *£14.00-£14.00.*
Open: All Year (not Xmas)
Beds: 1F 1D 1S
Baths: 2 Shared
ᵇ P ◻ ⊩ ✗ ▥ Ⓥ

Harwich 61

National Grid Ref: TM2431

|O| ◫ The Billy

(0.25m) *Reids of Harwich, 3 West Street, Harwich, Essex, CO12 3DA.*
Spacious Victorian property - historic location
Tel: 01255 506796
Mr Reid.
Rates fr: *£16.00-£16.00.*
Open: April to Oct
Beds: 1D 1T 1S
Baths: 2 Shared
ᵇ (12) ◻ ▥ Ⓥ ▮ ✦

(0.25m) *Queens Hotel, 119 High Street, Dovercourt, Harwich, Essex, CO12 3AP.*
Public house/hotel
Grades: ETB 1 Cr, Approv
Tel: 01255 502634
Mrs Skinner.
Rates fr: *£15.00-£15.00.*
Open: All Year
Beds: 1F 4T 2S
Baths: 2 Shared
ᵇ P (15) ◻ ✗ ▥

Colchester to Harwich

Crossing the River Stour into Essex, continue into **Colchester**, the oldest town in Britain. *Camulodunum* was the first capital of Roman Britain, and there are remains of the Roman walls. The town was sacked by Queen Boudicca ('Boadicea') of the Iceni tribe after the Romans killed her husband and raped her daughters. The honey-coloured Norman castle keep, the biggest in Europe, was built on the foundations of a Roman temple, and now houses a museum with Roman mosaics and statues. There is a museum of social history in the Saxon Holy Trinity Church. Also worth visiting is the Dutch Quarter, established by Flemish refugee weavers in the sixteenth century, which has tall Dutch-style houses. The route out of town goes to Wivenhoe, from where the final stretch leads to **Harwich**. The Harwich Redoubt, a circular fort currently undergoing restoration, was built against a feared invasion by Napoleon.

Sustrans Lon Las Cymru

The **Welsh National Cycle Route** is a section of the new UK National Cycle Network, running on traffic-free paths and traffic-calmed roads across the full length of Wales from the southeastern coast to the ferry port of Holyhead at the northwest of the Isle of Anglesey. It will take you through the full range of the Principality's breathtaking landscape, including two National Parks, the Brecon Beacons in the south and Snowdonia in the north. Much of the route is through sparsely populated regions. You should be prepared for a fair amount of climbing, particularly in the northern reaches, but don't let this put you off – Sustrans have designed the route with novice cyclists in mind. You can start at Cardiff, or at Chepstow on the English border; there are western and eastern alternative routes for most of the way, meeting and parting twice before meeting again for the final stretch from Porthmadog to Holyhead. The maximum distance is 288 miles; most of the route is signposted by blue direction signs with a cycle silhouette and the number 8 in a red rectangle.

The indispensable **official route map and guide** in English and Welsh for the Welsh National Cycle Route, which includes listings of cycle repair/hire shops along the route, comes in two parts, *Lon Las Cymru: Chepstow & Cardiff to Builth Wells* and *Lon Las Cymru: Builth Wells to Holyhead*, and is available from

Sustrans, 35 King Street, Bristol BS1 4DZ, tel 0117-926 8893, fax 0117-929 4173, @ £5.99 each (+ £1.50 p&p for both together or either one).

Maps: Ordnance Survey 1:50,000 Landranger series: 114, 123, 124, 135, 136, 147, 160, 161, 171, 172

Transport: Cardiff, Bangor and Holyhead are all main line rail termini; Chepstow is a stop on the line between Cardiff and Gloucester; there are connections to many other places on or near the route. Holyhead is a major ferry port to Ireland, serving Dublin and Dun Laoghaire.

Cardiff   1

National Grid Ref: ST1677

|●| ◄ Halfway Hotel, Poachers' Lodge, Clifton Hotel

(**▲** 2m) *Cardiff Youth Hostel, 2 Wedal Road, Roath Park, Cardiff. CF2 5PG.*
Actual grid ref: ST185788
Warden: Ms H Davis.
Tel: **01222 462303**
Under 18: £6.55 **Adults:** £9.75
Evening Meals Available (7pm), Family Bunk Rooms, Shop, Security Lockers, Parking, Laundry Facilities
Conveniently located hostel near the city centre and Roath Park lake, with cycling & sailing facilities

---

The lowest *double* rate per person is shown in *italics*.

(2m) *Rambler Court Hotel, 188 Cathedral Road, Pontcanna, Cardiff, S Glam, CF1 9JE.*
Grades: WTB 1 Cr, Comm
Tel: **01222 221187** (also fax no)
Ms Oxley & L Cronin.
Rates fr: *£14.00*-**£16.00.**
Open: All Year
Beds: 4F 3T 2S
Baths: 4 Private 2 Shared
㕔 🄿 ♥ 📖 & Ⅴ ⊁
Friendly family-run hotel, ideally situated in a tree-lined conservation area, 10 minutes' walk to the city centre. Good local restaurants & pubs

(2m) *Wynford Hotel, Clare Street, Cardiff, S Glam, CF1 8SD.*
Privately owned, city centre hotel
Grades: WTB 2 Cr, Comm
Tel: **01222 371983** Mr Popham.
Fax no: 01222 340477
Rates fr: *£24.00*-**£25.00.**
Open: All Year (not Xmas)
Beds: 3F 4D 11T 2S
Baths: 18 Private 2 Shared
㕔 🄿 (15) 🗀 ✗ 📖 Ⅴ ⓘ ⊁

(2m) *Tanes Hotel, 148 Newport Road, Roath, Cardiff, S Glam, CF2 1DJ.*
Hotel in Cardiff. Good service
Tel: **01222 491755 / 493898**
Mrs Mladenovic.
Fax no: 01222 491755
Rates fr: *£16.00*-**£18.00.**
Open: All Year (not Xmas)
Beds: 4F 3D 6T 9S
Baths: 3 Private 5 Shared
㕔 (4) 🄿 (10) ⊁ 🗀 ✗ 📖 &

(2m) *Annedd Lon Guest House, 157-159 Cathedral Road, Cardiff, S Glam, CF1 9PL.*
Large Victorian private house
Tel: **01222 223349**
Mrs Tucker.
Fax no: 01222 640885
Rates fr: *£18.00*-**£18.00.**
Open: All Year except Xmas to New Year
Beds: 1F 1D 1T 1S
Baths: 2 Ensuite 2 Shared
㕔 🄿 ⊁ 🗀 📖 Ⅴ

(2m) *Austins, 11 Coldstream Terrace, Cardiff, S Glam, CF1 8LJ.*
Small, friendly, city centre hotel
Grades: WTB 2 Cr, Comm
Tel: 01222 377148 Mr Hopkins.
Fax no: 01222 377158
Rates fr: £15.00-£16.00.
Open: All Year
Beds: 1F 5T 5S
Baths: 4 Private 2 Shared
⌂ ⌷ ⛥ ▥.

(2m) *Hotel Metropole, 175 Newport Road, Roath, Cardiff, S Glam, CF2 1AH.*
Large Victorian private hotel
Grades: WTB 1 Cr
Tel: 01222 464642 Mrs Bear.
Rates fr: £13.00-£14.00.
Open: All Year (not Xmas)
Beds: 2D 2T 6S
Baths: 3 Shared
Ⓟ (10) ⌷ ▥.

(2m) *Clayton Hotel, 65 Stacey Road, Roath, Cardiff, S Glam, CF2 1DS.*
Excellent family-run homely hotel
Tel: 01222 492345
Mr Milliner.
Rates fr: £14.00-£14.00.
Open: All Year (not Xmas)
Beds: 1F 2D 3T 4S
Baths: 4 Private 1 Shared
⌂ (3) Ⓟ (6) ⌿ ⌷ ✗ ▥. Ⓥ

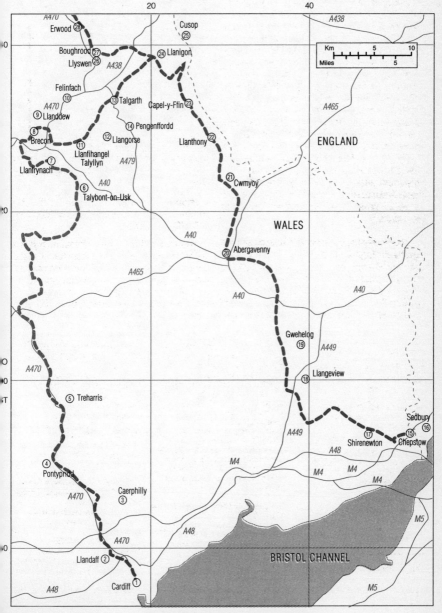

The Routes

The **western route** runs from **Cardiff** up the River Taff through the industrial heartland of South Wales to Pontypridd, Abercynon and Merthyr Tydfil, before wending through the beautiful wooded valleys below the Brecon Beacons range itself, within the **Brecon Beacons National Park**, to Brecon, where it turns east to join the other route close to the River Wye. From **Chepstow**, at the mouth of the Wye, the **eastern route** turns west to the River Usk, which it follows upstream to Usk before heading on to **Abergavenny**, where it enters the Brecon Beacons National Park to follow the River Honddu up the idyllic Vale of Ewyas to its source in the Black Mountains range, passing below Offa's Dyke and the border for much of the way until the two routes converge. After the stretch through the beautiful Wye Valley as far as **Builth Wells**, the route parts again as it heads into Mid Wales: the eastern way pursues the Wye Valley to Newbridge-on-Wye, Rhayader and Llangurig before turning eastwards to Llanidloes. The western section of this part of the route is unsignposted and tough going – only for experienced cyclists, preferably on a mountain bike: after **Llanwrtyd Wells** you take the Abergwysyn Pass up the 'Devil's Staircase' through dense forest, to reach the valley of the Towi with its breathtaking scenery. After following the Towi to its source you proceed to Devil's Bridge.

The two routes pass either side of the peak of **Plynlimon Fawr** in the Cambrian Mountains before they converge again at **Machynlleth**, where you cross the River Dovey into **Snowonia National Park**. The western alternative turns west to Tywyn on the coast before heading north and crossing the Barmouth viaduct bridge into **Barmouth**. From here you continue to Dyffryn Ardudwy and Llanbedr, and proceed to the toll bridge over the River Dwyryd into Penrhyndeudraeth, and on to Garreg, where the routes finally join. The eastern route from Machynlleth goes to Corris, and continues, with the majestic mass of Cader Idris towering away to the left, to **Dolgellau**. From here you cycle through the lovely Coed-y-Brenin Forest Park, in the heart of southern Snowdonia, and on to Trawsfynydd, Gellilydan and Maentwrog on the Dwyryd before reaching Garreg. The final stretch of the way proceeds through **Porthmadog** and around the western side of the Snowdon massif to Caernarfon and Bangor; having crossed the great Menai Suspension Bridge, you traverse the southern side of Anglesey, an island scattered with the remains of ancient Celtic settlements, to reach **Holyhead**.

(2m) *Domus Guest House,* 201 Newport Road, Roath, Cardiff, S Glam, CF2 1AJ.
Clean, friendly, family-run guest house. **Grades:** AA 2 St
Tel: **01222 473311** Mrs Barrett.
Rates fr: £18.00-**£18.00**.
Open: All Year (not Xmas)
Beds: 1F 3D 3T 2S
Baths: 2 Private 2 Shared
🛇 🄿 (10) 🛏 ✕ 🎢.

(2m) *Preste Garden Hotel,* 181 Cathedral Road, Pontcanna, Cardiff, S Glam, CF1 9PN.
Modernised, comfortable, ex-Norwegian Consulate
Tel: **01222 228607** Mr Nicholls.
Rates fr: £15.00-**£18.00**.
Open: All Year (not Xmas)
Beds: 1F 3D 3T 3S
Baths: 10 Private
🛇 🄿 (2) 🛏 🎢. 🆅 ▮

(2m) *Bon Maison Guest House,* 39 Plasturton Gardens, Pontcanna, Cardiff, S Glam, CF1 9HG.
Large Victorian house
Tel: **01222 383660** Mrs George.
Rates fr: £15.00-**£17.00**.
Open: All Year (not Xmas)
Beds: 1F 2D 1T
Baths: 2 Private 2 Shared
🛇 🛏 🎢. 🆅

Llandaff　　　　2

National Grid Ref: ST1577
🍴 🍺 Churchill's, Plymouth Arms

(0.5m) *Plas-Y-Bryn,* 93 Fairwater Road, Llandaff, Cardiff, S Glam, CF5 2LG.
Comfortable Edwardian semi on outskirts
Grades: WTB Listed, High Comm
Tel: **01222 561717** Mrs Lougher.
Rates fr: £17.00-**£17.50**.
Open: All Year
Beds: 2T 1S **Baths:** 1 Shared
🛇 ⅟ 🛏 🎢.

Caerphilly　　　　3

National Grid Ref: ST1586
🍴 🍺 Traveller's Rest, The Moat, Black Cock

(3m) *Watford Fach,* Watford Rd, Caerphilly, Mid Glam, CF83 1NE.
C17th farmhouse (longhouse)
Tel: **01222 851500**
Mr & Mrs Fahey.
Fax no: 01222 865021
Rates fr: £18.00-**£16.00**.
Open: All Year (not Xmas)
Beds: 2D 1T 2S
Baths: 5 Ensuite 3 Shared
🛇 🄿 (9) ⅟ 🛏 🎢. 🆅

(3m) *Dugann,* Springfield Bungalow, Rudry Road, Caerphilly, Mid Glam, CF83 3DW.
Lovely bungalow, lawned gardens, quiet
Grades: WTB Listed, Comm
Tel: **01222 866607** Mrs Powell.
Rates fr: £16.00-**£20.00**.
Open: All Year
Beds: 1F 1D
Baths: 1 Private
🛇 🄿 (4) 🛏 ✕ 🎢. 🆅

Pontypridd　　　　4

National Grid Ref: ST0789
🍴 🍺 The Stables, John & Maria's

(1m) *Market Tavern Hotel,* Market Street, Pontypridd, Mid Glam, CF37 2ST.
Tel: **01443 485331** Mrs Wallace.
Fax no: 01443 406784
Rates fr: £14.00-**£24.00**.
Open: All Year (not Xmas)
Beds: 2D 6T 3S
Baths: 11 Private
🛇 🄿 🎢. 🆅
Fully refurbished hotel with delightfully decorated ensuite bedrooms, function/breakfast room and two bars serving wide range of food and ale

Treharris 5

National Grid Ref: ST1097

¶ ⌖ Railway Inn, Cross Inn

(1m) *Fairmead, 24 Gelligaer Road, Treharris, Nelson, Mid Glam, CF46 6DN.*
A small family run quiet haven, offering a warm welcome
Grades: WTB 3 Cr, High Comm
Tel: 01443 411174 (also fax no)
Mrs Kedward.
Rates fr: *£25.00*-**£25.00**.
Open: All Year
Beds: 2D 1T
Baths: 2 Private 1 Shared
🛏 🅿 (5) ⅍ 🗅 ⌘ ✕ 🎟 🄥 🝙 ⚡

Talybont-on-Usk 6

National Grid Ref: SO1122

¶ ⌖ Traveller's Rest

(1m) *Llanddety Hall Farm, Talybont-on-Usk, Brecon, Powys, LD3 7YR.*
C17th Listed country house
Grades: WTB 3 Cr, High Comm, AA 4 Q, Select
Tel: 01874 676415
Mrs Atkins.
Rates fr: *£18.00*-**£21.00**.
Open: Mar to Dec
Beds: 2D 1T
Baths: 2 Ensuite 1 Private
🛏 (10) 🅿 (5) ⅍ 🗅 ✕ 🎟 🄥

Llanfrynach 7

National Grid Ref: SO0725

¶ ⌖ White Swan

(On route) *Llanbrynean Farm, Llanfrynach, Brecon, Powys, LD3 7BQ.*
Beautiful countryside, traditional family farmhouse, ideal location for Brecon Beacons
Tel: 01874 665222 Mrs Harpur.
Rates fr: *£16.50*-**£17.00**.
Open: Feb to Nov
Beds: 1F 1D 1T
Baths: 2 Private 1 Shared
🛏 🅿 🗅 ⌘ 🎟 🄥 🝙 ⚡

Brecon 8

National Grid Ref: SO0428

¶ ⌖ Three Horseshoes Inn, The Clarence, George Hotel, Red Lion

(▲ 0.5m) *Ty'n-y-Caeau Youth Hostel, Groesffordd, Brecon, Powys, LD3 7SW.*
Actual grid ref: SO074288
Tel: 01874 665270
Under 18: £5.40
Adults: £8.00
Evening Meals Available (6.30pm), Self-catering Facilities, Television, Showers
This old farmhouse is a good base for the Brecon Beacons National Park. Nature reserves are close by

(0.5m) *Beacons Guest House, 16 Bridge Street, Brecon, Powys, LD8 8AH.*
Grades: WTB 3 Cr, High Comm
Tel: 01874 623339 (also fax no)
Mr & Mrs Jackson.
Rates fr: *£18.00*-**£20.00**.
Open: All Year (not Xmas)
Beds: 4F 4D 3T 1S
Baths: 9 Private 3 Shared
🛏 🅿 (12) 🗅 ⌘ ✕ 🎟 ⅍ 🄥 🝙 ⚡
Georgian guest house of great character with excellent restaurant. Delightful, well-equipped bedrooms, cosy cellar bar, car park and lock-up. Centrally located for National Park

(0.5m) *Cambridge House, St David Street, Llanfaes, Brecon, Powys, LD3 8BB.*
Family-run. Off main road. Superb breakfasts. Evening meals. Friendly
Grades: WTB 1 Cr, High Comm
Tel: 01874 624699 Mr Lomas.
Rates fr: *£15.00*-**£16.00**.
Open: All Year
Beds: 2D 1T 1S
Baths: 1 Private 1 Shared
🛏 🅿 (4) ⅍ 🗅 ⌘ ✕ 🎟 🄥

The lowest *double* rate per person is shown in *italics*.

Cardiff to Brecon

Cardiff, the national capital, was in the past important for its docks, which shipped out coal from the South Wales mines. With the decline of the docks, Cardiff Bay is now undergoing extensive redevelopment, including the construction of a barrage to create a giant freshwater marina. There is a visitors' centre, built into a hollow tube that overlooks the bay, which has displays on the various projects underway. Also at Cardiff Bay is the Welsh Industrial and Maritime Museum, with prominence given to mining and to the railways. Other museums in and around Cardiff are the National Museum of Wales, including the natural history of Wales and a sizeable art collection, which includes Italian and Flemish Renaissance paintings, Impressionism, and sculpture; and the fantastic Welsh Folk Museum at St Fagan's, just west of town. This is a large site with reconstructed buildings, of all sorts and various periods, from all over the country. Other attractions are Cardiff Castle, an amalgam of Norman motte and bailey with an extensive Victorian Neo-Gothic fantasy by William Burges; and Llandaff Cathedral, originally twelfth century but with substantial nineteenth-century restoration, including work by prominent Pre-Raphaelites.

On the route just north of Cardiff, **Castell Coch** is a Victorian medieval fantasy also by William Burges, constructed out of a thirteenth-century ruined fortress.

At **Pontypridd** you can find the Pontypridd Historical and Cultural Centre, dedicated to life in the Valleys.

At **Aberfan**, stop to visit the Memorial Gardens dedicated to the 116 children who died when a slag heap collapsed onto their school in 1966.

Merthyr Tydfil has another Neo-Gothic castle, Cyfartha, a gallery of Welsh modern art and a museum which records the harsh conditions of nineteenth-century industrial life, the Ynysfach Engine House.

Every self-respecting Celtic nation produces whisky. If you've only heard of the Scotch and Irish varieties, you will be surprised to find the Welsh Whisky Visitor Centre at **Brecon**. The town also offers the Brecknock Museum, a document of past life in the region, and an intriguing cathedral, originally Norman but restored in the Victorian era.

(1m) *Flag & Castle Guest House,* 11 Orchard Street, Llanfaes, Brecon, Powys, LD3 8AN.
Convenient town/National Park amenities, near Taff Trail. Parking
Grades: WTB 2 Cr, Comm
Tel: 01874 625860
Mrs Jones.
Rates fr: £16.00-£17.50.
Open: All Year
Beds: 1F 2D 1T 2S
Baths: 1 Private 2 Shared
🛇 🅿 🖵 ⊩ 🛏 🎹 🆅

(0.5m) *Tir Bach Guest House,* 13 Alexandra Road, Brecon, Powys, LD3 7PD.
Panoramic view of Brecon Beacons. Quiet road near town centre
Grades: WTB 1 Cr, Comm
Tel: 01874 624551
Rates fr: £14.00-£15.00.
Open: All Year (not Xmas)
Beds: 1F 1T 1D
Baths: 1 Shared
🛇 🖵 🛏 🎹

(0.5m) *Paris Guest House,* 28 The Watton, Brecon, Powys, LD3 7EF.
Family-run C17th guest house
Grades: WTB 1 Cr
Tel: 01874 624205 Mrs Haines.
Rates fr: £15.00-£15.00.
Open: All Year (not Xmas)
Beds: 1F 1D 1T 1S
🛇 ⊬ 🖵 🛏 🎹 🛡 ⊬

(0.5m) *Lansdowne Hotel,* 39 The Watton, Brecon, Powys, LD3 7EG.
Family-run hotel close to all amenities
Grades: WTB 3 Cr, AA 1 St
Tel: 01874 623321 Mr Nancarrow.
Rates fr: £23.50-£27.50.
Open: All Year
Beds: 2F 4D 2T 2S
Baths: 8 Private 1 Shared
🅿 (7) 🖵 ✕ 🎹 🆅 🛡 ⊬

(0.5m) *Glanyrafon,* 1 The Promenade, Kensington, Brecon, Powys, LD3 9AY.
Elegant Edwardian house, quiet riverbank position
Grades: WTB 1 Cr, High Comm
Tel: 01874 623302 Mrs Roberts.
Rates fr: £15.00-£18.00.
Open: Easter to Oct
Beds: 2D 1T
Baths: 2 Shared
🛇 (10) 🅿 (3) ⊬ 🖵 🎹 🆅 🛡 ⊬

(0.5m) *Brynfedwen Farm,* Trallong Common, Brecon, Sennybridge, Brecon, Powys, LD3 8HW.
Welsh farmhouse in National Park
Grades: WTB 3 Cr, High Comm, AA 4 Q
Tel: 01874 636505 (also fax no)
Mrs Adams.
Rates fr: £18.00-£20.00.
Open: All Year (not Xmas)
Beds: 2D 1T
Baths: 3 Ensuite
🛇 🅿 (3) ⊬ 🖵 ✕ 🎹 ♿ 🛡 ⊬

Llanddew 9

National Grid Ref: SO0530

🍴 🍺 George Hotel

(1m) *The Old Rectory, Llanddew,* Brecon, Powys, LD3 9SS.
Peacefully situated Victorian private house
Grades: WTB 2 Cr, High Comm, RAC High Acclaim
Tel: 01874 622058 Mrs Williams.
Rates fr: £18.00-£24.00.
Open: All Year (not Xmas)
Beds: 1F 1D 1T
Baths: 2 Ensuite 1 Private
🅿 (10) ⊬ 🖵 🎹

Felinfach 10

National Grid Ref: SO0933

🍴 🍺 Old Mill

(3m) *The Old Mill, Felinfach,* Brecon, Powys, LD3 0UB.
C16th converted corn mill, within easy reach of Beacons Beacons
Grades: WTB 2 Cr, High Comm
Tel: 01874 625385 Mrs Boxhall.
Rates fr: £15.00-£18.00.
Open: Feb to Oct
Beds: 1D 2T
Baths: 2 Ensuite 1 Private
🛇 🅿 🖵 🎹 🆅

Llanfihangel Talyllyn 11

National Grid Ref: SO1128

(On route) *Glynderi, Llanfihangel Talyllyn, Brecon, Powys, LD3 7SY.*
Large Regency house in 3 acres mature gardens
Tel: 01874 658263 Ms Copping.
Fax no: 01874 658363
Rates fr: £18.00-£18.00.
Open: All Year (not Xmas)
Beds: 2D 1T
Baths: 3 Ensuite
🛇 🅿 (4) 🖵 🛏 ✕ 🎹 🆅

Llangorse 12

National Grid Ref: SO1327

🍴 🍺 Red Lion, Castle Inn

(1.5m) *Trewalter House,* Llangorse, Brecon, Powys, LD3 0PS.
Friendly, peaceful, views, good food
Grades: WTB 3 Cr, High Comm
Tel: 01874 658442 (also fax no)
Mrs Abbott.
Rates fr: £22.00-£27.00.
Open: All Year (not Xmas)
Beds: 2D 1T
Baths: 3 Private
🛇 🅿 🖵 ✕ 🎹 🛡 ⊬

The *lowest* single rate *is shown* in bold.

(1.5m) *Red Lion Hotel,* Llangorse, Brecon, Powys, LD3 7TY.
Friendly C18th village inn
Grades: WTB 3 Cr, Comm
Tel: 01874 658238 Mrs Rosier.
Fax no: 01874 658595
Rates fr: £20.00-£25.00.
Open: All Year
Beds: 1F 5D 3T 1S
Baths: 5 Private 5 Shared
🛇 🅿 (20) 🖵 🎹 🆅 🛡

Talgarth 13

National Grid Ref: SO1533

🍴 🍺 Masons' Arms Hotel, Castle Inn

(0.25m) *Craigend, The Bank,* Talgarth, Brecon, Powys, LD3 0BN.
Victorian village house - Brecon Beacons National Park
Grades: WTB Listed, Comm
Tel: 01874 711084 Ms Price.
Rates fr: £15.00-£16.00.
Open: All Year (not Xmas)
Beds: 2D 1T
Baths: 1 Ensuite 1 Shared
🛇 🅿 (5) ⊬ 🖵 🎹

(0.25m) *Castle Inn, Pengenffordd,* Talgarth, Brecon, Powys, LD3 0EP.
Actual grid ref: SO174296
Traditional rural inn
Tel: 01874 711353 Mr Mountjoy.
Rates fr: £18.00-£18.00.
Open: All Year
Beds: 1F 2D 1T 1S
Baths: 2 Private 1 Shared
🛇 🅿 (50) 🖵 ✕ 🎹 🆅 🛡

Pengenffordd 14

National Grid Ref: SO1730

(3m) *Cwmfforest Guest House,* Pengenffordd, Talgarth, Brecon, Powys, LD3 0EU.
Actual grid ref: SO183292
Idyllic sheltered location close to highest Black Mountains peaks. Traditional farmhouse
Grades: WTB 2 Cr
Tel: 01874 711398 Mrs Turner.
Fax no: 01874 711122
Rates fr: £20.00-£20.00.
Open: All Year **Beds:** 2T 2S
Baths: 2 Ensuite 1 Shared
🅿 (10) ⊬ 🖵 ✕ 🆅 🛡 ⊬

Chepstow 15

National Grid Ref: ST5393

🍴 🍺 Grape Escape, Live and Let Live

(0.5m) *Lower Hardwick House,* Mount Pleasant, Chepstow, Monmouthshire, NP6 5PT.
Spacious rooms, Georgian house set in acre of beautiful gardens
Tel: 01291 622162 Mrs Grassby.
Rates fr: £15.00-£18.00.
Open: All Year
Beds: 2F 1D 1T 1S
Baths: 2 Private 2 Shared
🛇 🅿 (12) 🖵 🛏 🎹 🛡

(0.5m) *Langcroft, 71 St Kingsmark Avenue, Chepstow, Monmouthshire, NP6 5LY.*
Actual grid ref: ST529938
Modern family friendly home
Grades: WTB Listed
Tel: 01291 625569 (also fax no)
Mrs Langdale.
Rates fr: *£15.00-£15.00.*
Open: All Year
Beds: 1D 1T 1S
Baths: 1 Shared
🛏 🅿 (2) ☐ ⌂ 🎴 🛏 ♿ ✧

(0.5m) *Cobweb Cottage, Belle Vue Place, Streep Street, Chepstow, Monmouthshire, NP6 5PL.*
Quiet, secluded, comfortable
period cottage
Tel: 01291 626643 Mrs Warren.
Rates fr: *£16.50-£18.00.*
Open: All Year (not Xmas)
Beds: 1D 1T
Baths: 1 Shared
🛏 (5) 🅿 (6) ⌂ ☐ 🎴 🎴

Sedbury 16

National Grid Ref: ST5493

(1m) *Upper Sedbury House, Sedbury Lane, Sedbury, Chepstow, Newport, Monmouthshire, NP6 7HN.*
Actual grid ref: ST547943
200-year-old superior country
house
Grades: ETB 2 Cr
Tel: 01291 627173 Mrs Potts.
Rates fr: *£16.50-£18.50.*
Open: All Year (not Xmas)
Beds: 1F 1D 1T
Baths: 1 Private 1 Shared
🛏 🅿 (10 cars) ☐ 🎴 ✕ 🎴 ♿ ✧

Shirenewton 17

National Grid Ref: ST4793
🍴 🍺 Tredegar Arms

(0.25m) *Parsons Grove, Earlswood, Shirenewton, Chepstow, Monmouthshire, NP6 6RD.*
Top-quality accommodation,
country house
Grades: WTB 2 Cr, High Comm
Tel: 01291 641382 (also fax no)
Mrs Powell.
Rates fr: *£17.00-£25.00.*
Open: All Year (not Xmas)
Beds: 2F
Baths: 2 Ensuite
🛏 🅿 (10) ☐ 🎴 🎴 ♿

Pay B&Bs by
cash or cheque and
be prepared to
pay up front.

Llangeview 18

National Grid Ref: SO3900

(0.5m) *The Rat Trap, Chepstow Road, Llangeview, Usk, Monmouthshire, NP5 1EY.*
Grades: WTB 3 Cr, High Comm
Tel: 01291 673288
Mr & Mrs Rabaiotti.
Fax no: 01291 673305
Rates fr: *£25.00-£42.50.*
Open: All Year
Beds: 1F 5D 4T 3S
Baths: 13 Private
🛏 🅿 (40) ☐ ✕ 🎴 ♿ 🖁
All rooms ensuite, TV, telephone,
tea/coffee etc. Olde worlde charm
& service with high standards.
Renowned for the choice &
excellence of our food

Gwehelog 19

National Grid Ref: SO3804
🍴 🍺 Hall Inn

(2m) *Oak Farm, Gwehelog, Usk, Monmouthshire, NP5 1RB.*
Comfortable self contained cottage
Tel: 01291 672830 Mrs Dean.
Fax no: 01291 673569
Rates fr: *£18.00-£18.00.*
Open: All Year (not Xmas)
Beds: 1F **Baths:** 1 Private
🛏 🅿 🎴 ✕ 🎴 ✧

All cycleways are
popular: you are well-
advised to book ahead

Abergavenny 20

National Grid Ref: SO2914
🍴 🍺 King's Arms, Walnut Tree
Inn, Canbrett Inn

(0.5m) *Ty`r Morwydd House, Pen-y-Pound, Abergavenny, Monmouthshire, NP7 5UD.*
Actual grid ref: SO297147
Grades: WTB Listed, Approv
Tel: 01873 855959
Mrs Senior.
Fax no: 01873 855443
Rates fr: *£14.60-£14.60.*
Open: All Year (not Xmas)
Beds: 19T 31S
Baths: 19 Shared
🛏 🅿 (30) ⌂ ☐ 🎴 🎴 🖁 ♿ ✧
Affordable superior hostel
accommodation for groups in
extended Georgian town house.
Quality catering, lounges, work-
rooms, residential licence. Leisure,
courses, conferences, etc.
Environmental courses a speciality

(0.25m) *Tyn-y-bryn, Deriside, Abergavenny, Monmouthshire, NP7 7HT.*
Actual grid ref: SO301165
Magnificent views, a homely
atmosphere. Comfortable accom-
modation & warm welcome
Grades: WTB 3 Cr, Comm
Tel: 01873 856682 (also fax no)
Ms Belcham.
Rates fr: *£20.00-£25.00.*
Open: Easter to Nov
Beds: 1F 1T 1D
Baths: 2 Ensuite
🅿 (6) ☐ 🎴 ✕ 🎴 🖁 ♿ ✧

Chepstow to Llanidloes

Chepstow Castle, built in the twelfth century, was the first stone castle in Britain. Its strategic location on a cliff overlooking the Wye, with a panorama of the area around the border, lends it considerable drama.

After flying to Scotland in 1941, Rudolf Hess was imprisoned in **Abergavenny** – Spandau was definitely a considerable comedown. The main attraction today is the Museum of Childhood and the Home, which has a haunted doll's house (*sic*). The restored eleventh-century castle keep hosts a museum of local history.

Llanthony Priory in the Vale of Ewyas is a romantic ruin in an unworldly setting. An Augustine foundation dating from the twelfth century, the ruined arches frame the mountains to create a picture of tranquillity.

Rhayader is an attractive town with eighteenth-century coaching inns.

At picturesque **Llanidloes** there is a rare free-standing Tudor market hall and an interesting museum, as well as a church with a hammerbeam roof dating from the fifteenth century.

Sustrans Lon Las Cymru

(0.5m) *Pentre House, Brecon Road, Abergavenny, Monmouthshire, NP7 7EW.*
Actual grid ref: SO283151
Pretty, small, Georgian country house in wonderful gardens
Grades: WTB 1 Cr, Comm
Tel: **01873 853435** (also fax no)
Mrs Reardon-Smith.
Rates fr: *£15.00-£18.00.*
Open: All Year
Beds: 1F 2D **Baths:** 2 Shared
ॐ ▣ (6) ☐ ⚲ ✗ ▥ Ⅵ ▒ ⚡

(0.5m) *The Guest House, Mansel Rest, 2 Oxford Street, Abergavenny, Monmouthshire, NP7 5RP.*
Licensed restaurant, central to town
Grades: WTB 1 Cr
Tel: **01873 854823**
Mrs Cook.
Rates fr: *£16.00-£18.50.*
Open: All Year
Beds: 3F 5D 5T 2S
Baths: 3 Shared
ॐ ▣ (10) ☐ ✗ ▥ Ⅵ ▒

All rooms full and nowhere else to stay? Ask the owner if there's anywhere nearby

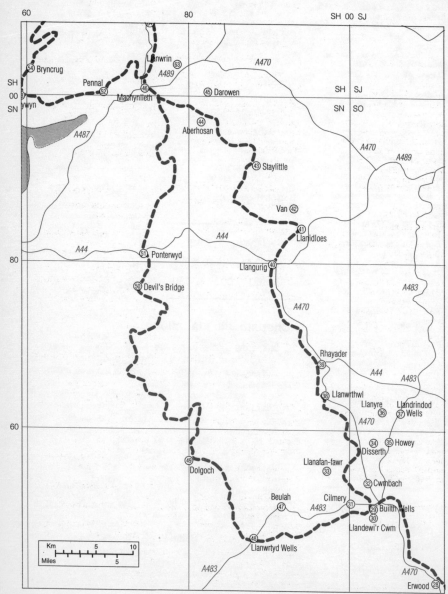

STILWELL'S CYCLEWAY COMPANION

Cwmyoy 21

National Grid Ref: SO2923

🍴 🍺 Skirrid Inn

(1m) *Gaer Farm, Cwmyoy,
Abergavenny, Monmouthshire,
NP7 7NE.*
Actual grid ref: SO298219
Peaceful farm. Rare breed animals
Grades: WTB 2 Cr, Comm
Tel: 01873 890345 Mrs Judd.
Rates fr: *£18.00*-**£20.00**.
Open: All Year (not Xmas)
Beds: 1D 1T
Baths: 2 Ensuite
🛏 (10) 🅿 (4) ⚡🛒 🏇 🛀 🎿🔒⚡

Llanthony 22

National Grid Ref: SO2827

🍴 🍺 Half Moon

(0.25m) *The Half Moon,
Llanthony, Abergavenny,
Monmouthshire, NP7 7NN.*
Actual grid ref: SO286278
Small, friendly country hotel
Tel: 01873 890611 Mrs Smith.
Rates fr: *£17.50*-**£20.00**.
Open: All Year (not Xmas)
Beds: 1F 4D 2T
Baths: 2 Shared
🛏 🅿 (5) 🏇 🛀 🛒 ⚡🔒🎿

Capel-y-Ffin 23

National Grid Ref: SO2531

(⛰ 0.25m) *Capel-y-Ffin Youth
Hostel, Capel-y-Ffin,
Abergavenny, Monmouthshire,
NP7 7NP.*
Actual grid ref: SO250328
Warden: Ms D Evans.
Tel: 01873 890650
Under 18: £4.45 **Adults:** £6.50
Evening Meals Available (7.30pm),
Showers, Central Heating, Shop,
No Smoking
*Old hill farm set in 40-acre
grounds on mountainside in Brecon
Beacons National Park*

(0.25m) *The Grange, Capel-y-Ffin,
Abergavenny. NP7 7NP.*
Actual grid ref: SO251315
Small Victorian family guest house
Grades: WTB 1 Cr
Tel: 01873 890215 Mrs Griffiths.
Rates fr: *£22.00*-**£22.00**.
Open: Easter to Nov
Beds: 3F 1D 3T 1S
Baths: 3 Shared 1 Ensuite
🛏 (8) 🅿 (10) 🛒 🏇 🛀 🛀 🎿 ⚡🔒🎿

The lowest *double*

rate per person is

shown in *italics*.

Llanigon 24

National Grid Ref: SO2139

🍴 🍺 Swan Hotel, Old Black Lion,
Hollybush Inn

(1.5m) *Lynwood, Llanigon, Hay-
on-Wye, Hereford. HR3 5PU.*
Modern bungalow. pleasantly
situated
Tel: 01497 820716 Mrs Davies.
Rates fr: *£15.00*-**£15.00**.
Open: Easter to Oct
Beds: 1D 1T 1S **Baths:** 1 Shared
🛏 🅿 (4) 🛒 🏇 🛀

Cusop 25

National Grid Ref: SO2341

🍴 🍺 Swan Hotel, Old Black Lion

(2m) *Fernleigh, Hardwick Road,
Cusop, Hay-on-Wye, Hereford.
HR3 5QX.*
Large Victorian private house
Tel: 01497 820459 Mr Hughes.
Rates fr: *£14.00*-**£18.00**.
Open: Easter to Oct
Beds: 2D 1T **Baths:** 1 Shared
🅿 🎿 🛒 🛀 ⓥ 🔒

Llyswen 26

National Grid Ref: SO1337

🍴 🍺 Griffin Inn, Bridge End Inn

(0.5m) *Lower Rhydness
Bungalow, Llyswen, Brecon,
Powys, LD3 0AZ.*
Very comfortable bungalow, 150
acre farm
Tel: 01874 754264 Mrs Williams.
Rates fr: *£15.00*-**£15.00**.
Open: Easter to Dec
Beds: 1D 1T 1S **Baths:** 1 Shared
🛏 🅿 (3) 🛒 🏇 ✗ 🛀

Boughrood 27

National Grid Ref: SO1339

🍴 🍺 Bridgend Inn, Griffin Inn

(On route) *Balangia, Station Road,
Boughrood, Brecon, Powys,
LD3 0YF.*
Small house near River Wye
Tel: 01874 754453 Mrs Brown.
Rates fr: *£14.00*-**£14.00**.
Open: Easter to Sep
Beds: 1D 1T 1S **Baths:** 1 Shared
🛏 🅿 🛒 ✗ 🛀 & ⓥ 🔒 🎿

(On route) *Upper Middle Road,
Boughrood, Brecon, Powys,
LD3 0BX.*
Actual grid ref: SO140392
Quietly situated smallholding.
Mountain views
Grades: WTB 2 Cr, Comm
Tel: 01874 754407 Mrs Kelleher.
Rates fr: *£15.00*-**£15.00**.
Open: All Year (not Xmas)
Beds: 1D 1T 1S
Baths: 1 Shared 1 Ensuite
🛏 🅿 (3) ⚡🛒 🏇 🛀 ⓥ 🔒 🎿

Erwood 28

National Grid Ref: SO0942

🍴 🍺 Erwood Inn, Wheelwrights'
Arms

(1m) *Orchard Cottage, Erwood,
Builth Wells, Powys, LD2 3EZ.*
C18th tastefully modernised Welsh
stone cottage. Gardens
overlooking river
Grades: WTB 2 Cr, High Comm
Tel: 01982 560600
Mr & Mrs Prior.
Rates fr: *£16.50*-**£21.00**.
Open: All Year
Beds: 1F 1D 1T
Baths: 1 Private 1 Shared
🛏 🅿 (5) ⚡🛒 🏇 🛀 ✗ 🛀 ⓥ

(1m) *The Old Vicarage, Erwood,
Builth Wells, Powys, LD2 3DZ.*
Spacious Edwardian former
vicarage
Grades: WTB 1 Cr, Comm
Tel: 01982 560680 Mrs Williams.
Rates fr: *£14.00*-**£14.00**.
Open: All Year
Beds: 1F 1D 1T 1S
Baths: 1 Shared
🛏 🅿 🛒 🏇 ✗ 🛀 ⓥ 🔒 🎿

Builth Wells 29

National Grid Ref: SO0350

🍴 🍺 Llanelwedd Arms,
Greyhound Hotel

(1m) *Dollynwydd Farm, Builth
Wells, Powys, LD2 3RZ.*
C17th farmhouse. Situated beneath
the Eppynt Hills
Grades: WTB 2 Cr
Tel: 01982 553660 Mrs Williams.
Rates fr: *£16.00*-**£16.00**.
Open: All Year (not Xmas)
Beds: 1D 2T
Baths: 1 Ensuite 1 Private
1 Shared
🛏 (12) 🅿 🛒 ✗ 🛀 ⓥ 🔒 🎿

(0.25m) *The Owls, 40 High Street,
Builth Wells, Powys, LD2 3AB.*
Actual grid ref: SO041510
Family-run licensed guest house
Grades: WTB 3 Cr, Comm
Tel: 01982 552518
Mrs Turner.
Fax no: 01982 553867
Rates fr: *£16.50*-**£14.00**.
Open: All Year
Beds: 1F 3D 1T 1S
Baths: 4 Ensuite 2 Shared
🛏 🅿 (8) 🛒 🛀 ⓥ 🔒 🎿

(0.25m) *Woodlands, Hay Road,
Builth Wells, Powys, LD2 3BP.*
Edwardian house in woodland
setting
Tel: 01982 552354 (also fax no)
Mrs Nicholls.
Rates fr: *£20.00*-**£25.00**.
Open: All Year (not Xmas)
Beds: 5T
Baths: 5 Ensuite
🅿 (4) ⚡🛒 🛀 &

(0.25m) *Bron Wye, Church Street,*
Builth Wells, Powys, LD2 3BS.
Large Victorian semi-detached
house
Grades: WTB 3 Cr, Comm
Tel: 01982 553587
Mr & Mrs Wiltshire.
Rates fr: *£16.00*-**£16.00**.
Open: All Year
Beds: 1F 2D 1T 1S
Baths: 5 Private
ॐ ▣ ⅋ ⌷ ⊁ ✕ ▥ ▯ ⬩ ⅌

Llanddewi'r Cwm   30

National Grid Ref: SO0348

(1.5m) *Newhall, Llanddewi'r Cwm,*
Builth Wells, Powys, LD2 3RX.
Grades: WTB 3 Cr, High Comm
Tel: 01982 552483 Mrs James.
Rates fr: *£18.00*-**£18.00**.
Open: All Year (not Xmas)
Beds: 1F 3D 1T
Baths: 3 Private 2 Shared
ॐ ▣ (6) ⌷ ✕ ▥ ▢
Farmhouse overlooking Wye
Valley comfortable accom-
modation, ensuite rooms. Good
home cooking, parking, lock up
cycle shed, 1 1/2 miles from Builth
Wells on B4520

Cilmery   31

National Grid Ref: SO0051

†⊙† ◧ Prince Llewelyn Inn

(2m) *Llewelyn Leisure Park,*
Cilmery, Builth Wells, Powys,
LD2 3NU.
Jacuzzi, snooker, self-catering
available. Discounts for 2 nights
and over
Tel: 01982 552838 (also fax no)
Mr Johnson.
Rates fr: *£24.00*-**£20.00**.
Open: All Year
Beds: 2F 1S
Baths: 1 Shared 1 Ensuite
ॐ ▣ (7) ⌷ ⊁ ▥ ⬩ ▢

Cwmbach   32

National Grid Ref: SO0254

(2m) *Rhydfelin, Cwmbach, Builth*
Wells, Powys, LD2 3RT.
1725 stone-built farmhouse &
restaurant
Grades: WTB Listed, High Comm
Tel: 01982 552493
Rates fr: *£17.50*-**£25.00**.
Open: All Year (not Xmas)
Beds: 1F 1T 2D
Baths: 1Ensuite 1 Private
ॐ ▣ (14) ⅋ ⌷ ⊁ ✕ ▥ ▢ ⬩

The *lowest* **single**

rate *is* shown in **bold**.

Llanafan-fawr   33

National Grid Ref: SN9655

(3m) *Gwern-Y-Mynach, Llanafan-*
fawr, Builth Wells, Powys, LD2 3PN.
Mixed sheep & dairy farm
Tel: 01597 860256 Mrs Davies.
Rates fr: *£12.00*-**£12.00**.
Open: All Year
Beds: 1F 1S
Baths: 1 Private 1 Shared
ॐ ⌷ ⊁ ✕ ▥.

Disserth   34

National Grid Ref: SO0358

†⊙† ◧ Drovers' Arms

(1.5m) *Disserth Mill, Disserth,*
Builth Wells, Powys, LD2 3TN.
A sun trap by stream
Grades: WTB Listed
Tel: 01982 553217 Mrs Worts.
Rates fr: *£15.00*-**£18.00**.
Open: Easter to Oct
Beds: 2D 1T
Baths: 1 Shared
ॐ ▣ (4) ⌷ ⊁ ✕ ▥ ⬩ ⅌

Howey   35

National Grid Ref: SO0558

(4m) *Brynhir Farm, Chapel Road,*
Howey, Llandrindod Wells, Powys,
LD1 5PB.
Grades: WTB 3 Cr, High Comm,
AA 4 Q, Select
Tel: 01597 822425 Mrs Nixon.
Rates fr: *£18.00*-**£20.00**.
Open: All Year
Beds: 2D 3T 1S
Baths: 6 Ensuite
ॐ ▣ (10) ⅋ ⌷ ⊁ ✕ ▥ ▢
C17th peacefully situated luxury
farmhouse in acres of grounds. Ideal
for walkers. Edge Kite Country.
Large ensuite rooms, CTV, radio.
Golf 1 mile, working farm

(4m) *Holly Farm, Howey,*
Llandrindod Wells, Powys, LD1 5PP.
Comfortable old farmhouse
Grades: WTB Listed, High Comm
Tel: 01597 822402 Mrs Jones.
Rates fr: *£17.00*-**£20.00**.
Open: Easter to Nov
Beds: 1F 1D 1T
Baths: 3 Private
ॐ ▣ (6) ⌷ ✕ ▥ ▢

(4m) *Three Wells Farm, Chapel*
Road, Howey, Llandrindod Wells,
Powys, LD1 5PB.
Licensed farm guest house which
overlooks a fishing lake in
beautiful countryside
Grades: WTB 4 Cr, High Comm,
AA 4 Q, Select, RAC High
Acclaim
Tel: 01597 824427 Mr Bufton.
Rates fr: *£18.00*-**£18.00**.
Open: All Year (not Xmas)
Beds: 1F 6D 6T 1S
Baths: 14 Private
ॐ (10) ▣ (20) ⅋ ⌷ ⊁ ✕ ▥ ▢ ⬩ ⅌

(3m) *Corven Hall, Howey,*
Llandrindod Wells, Powys, LD1 5RE.
Large Victorian country house
Grades: WTB 3 Cr, High Comm
Tel: 01597 823368
Mrs Prince.
Rates fr: *£16.50*-**£22.50**.
Open: All Year (not Xmas)
Beds: 6F 2D 2T
Baths: 8 Private 3 Shared
ॐ (3 months) ▣ (12) ⅋ ⌷ ⊁ ✕ ▥
⅊ ▢ ⬩ ⅌

Llanyre   36

National Grid Ref: SO0462

†⊙† ◧ Bell Country Inn

(2.5m) *Highbury Farm, Llanyre,*
Llandrindod Wells, Powys, LD1 6EA.
Peaceful spacious Victorian farm-
house nestling among tall trees.
Excellent food
Grades: WTB 2 Cr, High Comm
Tel: 01597 822716 (also fax no)
Mrs Evans.
Rates fr: *£16.00*-**£18.00**.
Open: Easter to Oct
Beds: 1F 1D 1T
Baths: 1 Private 1 Shared
ॐ ▣ (3) ⌷ ✕ ▥ ▢

Llandrindod Wells   37

National Grid Ref: SO0561

†⊙† ◧ Llanerch Inn, The Drovers

(4m) *Drovers Arms, Llandrindod*
Wells, Powys, LD1 5PT.
Superb village inn, great food, own
beer. Taste of Wales
Grades: WTB 2 Cr, Comm
Tel: 01597 822508 Mrs Day.
Fax no: 01597 822711
Rates fr: *£18.00*-**£22.00**.
Open: All Year (not Xmas)
Beds: 1D 1T
Baths: 1 Private
ॐ (8) ▣ (2) ⌷ ✕ ▥ ▢ ⬩ ⅌

(4m) *Llanerch Inn, Llanerch Lane,*
Llandrindod Wells, Powys, LD1 6BG.
C16th inn with relaxed atmosphere
Grades: WTB 4 Cr, High Comm
Tel: 01597 822086 Mr Leach.
Fax no: 01597 824618
Rates fr: *£25.00*-**£25.00**.
Open: All Year
Beds: 2F 5D 3T 2S
Baths: 11 Ensuite 1 Private
ॐ ▣ (50) ⌷ ⊁ ✕ ▥ ▢ ⬩ ⅌

(4m) *Griffin Lodge Hotel, Temple*
Street, Llandrindod Wells, Powys,
LD1 5HF.
Friendly, comfortable, licensed
Victorian hotel
Grades: WTB Listed, 3 Cr, High
Comm
Tel: 01597 822432 Mrs Jones. .
Fax no: 01597 825196
Rates fr: *£19.00*-**£22.00**.
Open: All Year (not Xmas)
Beds: 4D 4T
Baths: 5 Private 3 Shared
ॐ ▣ (8) ⌷ ⊁ ✕ ▥ ▢ ⬩ ⅌

(4m) *The Cottage, Llandrindod Wells, Powys, LD1 5EY.*
Unusual Edwardian (Arts/Crafts) residence. Central location. Superb base for touring
Grades: WTB 2 Cr, Comm
Tel: 01597 825435 Mr Taylor.
Rates fr: *£15.00-£17.00.*
Open: All Year (not Xmas)
Beds: 1F 2D 4T 1S
Baths: 4 Ensuite 1 Shared
🛏 🖵 🎹 ⓥ

(4m) *Greylands, High Street, Llandrindod Wells, Powys, LD1 6AG.*
Victorian spa town guesthouse surrounded by beautiful hills
Grades: WTB 3 Cr, Comm
Tel: 01597 822253
Mr MacDonald.
Rates fr: *£14.00-£15.00.*
Open: All Year
Beds: 1F 2D 1T 3S
Baths: 4 Private 1 Shared
🛏 🖵 🖵 🎋 ✕ 🎹 ⓥ 🛆 ✦

(4m) *Hillyers Guest, Tremont Road, Llandrindod Wells, Powys, LD1 5EB.*
Comfortable modernised Edwardian home
Grades: WTB 2 Cr, Comm
Tel: 01597 822345 Mr Kelsey.
Rates fr: *£14.00-£14.00.*
Open: All Year
Beds: 1F 1D 2T 2S
Baths: 1 Private 2 Shared
🛏 (10) 🅿 (4) 🖵 🎋 ✕ 🎹 ⓥ

(4m) *Rhydithon, Dyffryn Road, Llandrindod Wells, Powys, LD1 6AN.*
Family guesthouse, close to amenities
Tel: 01597 822624 Mrs Jones.
Rates fr: *£15.00-£15.00.*
Open: All Year (not Xmas)
Beds: 1D 1T 2S
Baths: 1 Shared
🛏 🖵 🎋 ✕ 🎹 ⓥ

Llanwrthwl   38

National Grid Ref: SN9763
🍴 🍺 Vulcan Arms

(1m) *Dyffryn Farm, Llanwrthwl, Llandrindod Wells, Powys, LD1 6NU.*
Actual grid ref: SN972645
Peaceful, spacious C17th stone farmhouse
Tel: 01597 811017 Mrs Tyler.
Rates fr: *£20.50-£20.50.*
Open: Mid-Mar to Oct
Beds: 2D 1T
Baths: 1 Ensuite 1 Shared
1 Private
🛏 (15) 🅿 (6) ⊬ 🖵 ✕ 🛆 ✦

Pay B&Bs by cash or cheque and be prepared to pay up front.

All rates are subject to alteration at the owners' discretion.

Rhayader   39

National Grid Ref: SN9768
🍴 🍺 Crown Inn, The Triangle, The Bear, The Sun

(0.5m) *Brynteg, East Street, Rhayader, Powys, LD6 5EA.*
Actual grid ref: SN972682
Comfortable Edwardian guest house
Grades: WTB 2 Cr, Comm
Tel: 01597 810052 Mrs Lawrence.
Rates fr: *£15.00-£15.00.*
Open: All Year (not Xmas)
Beds: 2D 1T 1S
Baths: 4 Private
🛏 🅿 (4) 🖵 ✕ 🎹 🛆

(0.5m) *Beili Neuadd, Rhayader, Powys, LD6 5NS.*
Actual grid ref: SN994698
Secluded position with stunning views
Grades: WTB 3 Cr, High Comm
Tel: 01597 810211 (also fax no)
Mrs Edwards.
Rates fr: *£18.00-£18.50.*
Open: All Year (not Xmas)
Beds: 2D 1T
Baths: 2 Ensuite 2 Private
🛏 (8) 🅿 🖵 🎋 ✕ 🎹 ⓥ 🛆 ✦

(0.5m) *Liverpool House, East House, Rhayader, Powys, LD6 5EA.*
Large pleasant guest house, private car park
Grades: WTB 2 Cr, Comm
Tel: 01597 810706 Mrs Griffiths.
Fax no: 01597 810356
Rates fr: *£14.00-£15.00.*
Open: All Year **Beds:** 2F 5D 1S
Baths: 7 Ensuite 1 Shared
🛏 🅿 (6) 🖵 🎋 🎹 ⓥ 🛆

(1m) *Gigrin Farm, Rhayader, Powys, LD6 5BL.*
Actual grid ref: SN980677
Cosy, C17th Welsh farmhouse
Grades: WTB Listed
Tel: 01597 810243
Mrs Powell. Fax no: 01597 810357
Rates fr: *£15.00-£16.00.*
Open: All Year (not Xmas)
Beds: 2D
Baths: 1 Shared Ensuite
🛏 (5) 🅿 (3) ⊬ 🖵 ✕ 🎹

(1m) *Downfield Farm, Rhayader, Powys, LD6 5PA.*
Friendly farmhouse
Grades: WTB 1 Cr, Comm
Tel: 01597 810394 Mrs Price.
Rates fr: *£14.00-£15.00.*
Open: Feb to Oct
Beds: 2D 1T **Baths:** 2 Shared
🛏 🅿 (10) 🖵 🎋 🎹 ✦

Llangurig   40

National Grid Ref: SN9079
🍴 🍺 Black Lion, Blue Bell

(0.25m) *The Old Vicarage Guest House, Llangurig, Llanidloes, Powys, SY18 6RN.*
Tel: 01686 440280 (also fax no)
Rates fr: *£18.00-£25.00.*
Open: Mar to Oct
Beds: 2F 1D 1T **Baths:** 4 Ensuite
🛏 (5) 🅿 (6) 🖵 🎋 ✕ 🎹
Charming Victorian vicarage in rural setting close to Elan Valley and Plynlimon Hills. Peaceful location. All rooms ensuite. Pets welcome. Ample car parking

---

Western Route to Machynlleth

Llanwrtyd Wells is a pretty spa town, developed in the eighteenth century around the sulphur spring named Ffynon Droellwyd. Mr Green at The Neuadd Arms is the organiser of the world famous 'Man v. Horse' race.

Strata Florida Abbey is the very impressive ruin of a twelfth-century Cistercian foundation. Although a victim of the Dissolution, there is a fair amount to see, including a great Norman arch at the western end.

At **Devil's Bridge** three stone bridges, the earliest reputedly built by the Knights Templars, are set against the stunning backdrop of the Mynach Falls.

It was at **Machynlleth** in 1404 that Owain Glyndwr, leader of the resistance to English rule, summoned a parliament and proclaimed himself Prince of Wales. The Parliament House contains themed displays. The town also hosts the Celtica exhibition, with a reconstructioin Celtic settlement and audio-visual displays. The Y Tabernacl building houses a cultural centre which includes the Wales Museum of Modern Art.

Llanidloes 41

National Grid Ref: SN9584

(1m) *Lloyds, Cambrian Place, Llanidloes, Powys, SY18 6BX.*
Actual grid ref: SN955844
Quiet, Victorian town-centre hotel, welcoming cyclists, walkers and tourists
Grades: WTB 2 Cr, Comm
Tel: 01686 412284 Mr Lines.
Fax no: 01686 412666
Rates fr: *£18.00*-**£16.50**.
Open: All Year
Beds: 2D 3T 4S
Baths: 6 Private 1 Shared
🛇 🖵 ✕ 📖 💟 👜 ⚡

(2m) *Dol-Llys Farm, Trefeglwys Road, Llanidloes, Powys, SY18 6JA.*
Actual grid ref: SN9686
C17th farmhouse
Grades: WTB 2 Cr, High Comm, RAC Listed
Tel: 01686 412694 Mr Evans.
Rates fr: *£15.00*-**£17.00**.
Open: All Year (not Xmas)
Beds: 2D 1T **Baths:** 3 Private
🖵 📖 👜

(1m) *Gorphwysfa Guest House, Westgate Street, Llanidloes, Powys, SY18 6HL.*
Large Victorian house & garden
Grades: WTB 2 Cr
Tel: 01686 413356
Mrs Lines.
Rates fr: *£12.50*-**£12.50**.
Open: All Year
Beds: 1F 1D 1T 1S
Baths: 2 Shared
🛇 (1yr) 🅿 (5) ✕ 🖵 🛏 ✕ 📖 💟 👜

Van 42

National Grid Ref: SN9587

(4m) *Esgairmaen, Van, Llanidloes, Powys, SY18 6NT.*
Actual grid ref: SN925904
Modern comfortable farmhouse
Tel: 01686 430272
Mrs Rees.
Rates fr: *£17.00*-**£17.00**.
Open: Easter to Oct
Beds: 1F 1D
Baths: 1 Private 1 Shared
🛇 🅿 ✕ 🖵 ✕ 📖 👜 ⚡

Staylittle 43

National Grid Ref: SN8892

🍴 🍺 Star Inn

(1m) *Maesmedrisiol Farm, Staylittle, Llanbrynmair, Powys, SY19 7BN.*
Actual grid ref: SN8894
Friendly, comfortable, stone-built farmhouse
Tel: 01650 521494 Mrs Anwyl.
Rates fr: *£14.00*-**£14.00**.
Open: All Year (not Xmas)
Beds: 2F 2D 1T 2S
Baths: 1 Private
🛇 (1) 🅿 (8) 🖵 📖 💟 👜 ⚡

Aberhosan 44

National Grid Ref: SN8097

(0.5m) *Bacheiddon Farm, Aberhosan, Machynlleth, Powys, SY20 8SG.*
Modern, comfortable farmhouse, lovely scenery
Grades: WTB 2 Cr
Tel: 01654 702229
Mrs Lewis.
Rates fr: *£17.00*-**£20.00**.
Open:
Beds: 3D
Baths: 3 Private
🛇 🅿 🖵

Darowen 45

National Grid Ref: SH8201

(4m) *Cefn Farm, Darowen, Machynlleth, Powys, SY20 8NS.*
Quiet, comfortable, modernised old farmhouse
Grades: WTB 2 Cr
Tel: 01650 511336
Mr Lloyd.
Rates fr: *£15.00*-**£15.00**.
Open: All Year (not Xmas)
Beds: 1F
Baths: 1 Private
🛇 🅿 (3) ✕ 🖵 🛏 📖 💟

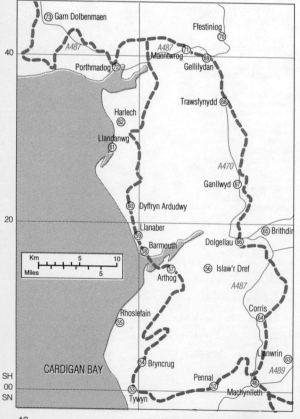

The Grid Reference beneath the location heading is for the village or town - *not* for individual houses, which are shown (where supplied) in each entry itself.

Machynlleth 46

National Grid Ref: SH7400

🍴 ◀ White Lion, Black Lion, Glyndwr Hotel, White Horse, The Wynnstay, Skinner's

(3m) **Talbontdrain**, Uwchygarreg, Machynlleth, Powys, SY20 8RR.
Actual grid ref: SH777959
Remote, comfortable farmhouse, excellent food, pianola, log fire, special holidays
Tel: **01654 702192**
Ms Matthews.
Rates fr: £17.00-£14.00.
Open: All Year (not Xmas)
Beds: 1D 1T 2S
Baths: 1 Private 1 Shared
🛇 🅿 (5) ⊬ � ✗ ▥ ▣ ✦

(0.5m) **Pendre Guest House**, Maengwym Street, Machynlleth, Powys, SY20 8EF.
Actual grid ref: SH748007
Georgian house, in historic market, Machynlleth, warm friendly atmosphere
Tel: **01654 702088**
Ms Petrie.
Rates fr: £16.50-£24.00.
Open: All Year (not Xmas)
Beds: 2F 1D 1T
Baths: 2 Private 2 Shared
🛇 🅿 (3) ▢ ♠ ▥ ▣ ✦

(0.5m) **The Glyndwr Hotel**, Doll Street, Machynlleth, Powys, SY20 8BQ.
Small family-run hotel
Tel: **01654 703989**
Mrs Duckett.
Rates fr: £16.00-£16.00.
Open: All Year
Beds: 1F 1D 1T
Baths: 2 Shared
🛇 🅿 ▢ ✗ ▥ ▣ ✦

(0.5m) **Awelon**, Heol Powys, Machynlleth, Powys, SY20 8AY.
Small comfortable private house
Grades: WTB Listed, Comm
Tel: **01654 702047**
Ms Williams.
Rates fr: £14.50-£15.00.
Open: All Year (not Xmas)
Beds: 1F 1T 1S
Baths: 1 Shared
🛇 (2) ♠ ▥ ▣ ✦

(0.5m) **Wynnstay Arms Hotel**, Maengwyn Street, Machynlleth, Powys, SY20 8AE.
Tastefully refurbished C18th coaching inn at the heart of historic market town
Grades: WTB 4 Cr, Comm, AA 2 St, RAC 2 St
Tel: **01654 702941**
Mr Healing.
Fax no: 01654 703884
Rates fr: £22.50-£25.00.
Open: All Year
Beds: 1F 11D 5T 6S
Baths: 23 Ensuite
🛇 🅿 (36) ⊬ ▢ ♠ ✗ ▥ ▣ ✦

(0.5m) **Dyfi Forester Inn**, 4 Doll Street, Machynlleth, Powys, SY20 8BQ.
Friendly town pub
Tel: **01654 702004** Mr Davies.
Rates fr: £15.00-£15.00.
Open: All Year (not Xmas)
Beds: 1F 1D 1S
Baths: 2 Shared
🛇 (12) 🅿 (15) ✗ ▣ ▣ ✦

(0.5m) **Maenllwyd**, Newtown Road, Machynlleth, Powys, SY20 8EY.
Large Victorian house
Grades: WTB 3 Cr, High Comm, AA 3 Q
Tel: **01654 702928** (also fax no)
Mr Vince.
Rates fr: £17.50-£23.00.
Open: All Year (not Xmas)
Beds: 2F 4D 2T
Baths: 6 Ensuite
🛇 🅿 (10) ⊬ ▢ ♠ ✗ ▥ ▣ ✦

Beulah 47

National Grid Ref: SN9251

🍴 ◀ Trout Inn

(3m) **Trout Inn**, Beulah, Llanwrtyd Wells, Powys, LD5 4UU.
Superb ensuite accommodation.
Home cooked food
Tel: **01591 620235** Ms Green.
Rates fr: £25.00-£30.00.
Open: All Year (not Xmas)
Beds: 1F 2D 2T
Baths: 5 Ensuite
🛇 (12) 🅿 (30) ⊬ ▢ ♠ ✗ ▥ ▣

Llanwrtyd Wells 48

National Grid Ref: SN8746

🍴 ◀ Stonecroft Inn

(0.25m) **Stonecroft Hostel**, Dolecoed Road, Llanwrtyd Wells, Powys, LD5 4RA.
Grades: WTB Listed, Approv
Tel: **01591 610327** Mr Lutman.
Fax no: 01591 610304
Rates fr: £9.00-£10.50.
Open: All Year
Beds: 15F 1T 2S
Baths: 6 Shared
🛇 🅿 (10) ▢ ♠ ✗ ▥ & ▣
Welcoming, friendly, highly recommended Aussie-owned self-catering accom. Real beds, no bunks, riverside garden. Fabulous Stonecroft Inn adjoins, CAMRA Good Beer Guide, live music

All rooms full and nowhere else to stay? Ask the owner if there's anywhere nearby

(0.25m) **Neuadd Arms Hotel**, The Square, Llanwrtyd Wells, Powys, LD5 4RB.
Half-Georgian, half-Victorian hotel
Grades: WTB 2 Cr, RAC 1 St
Tel: **01591 610236** Mr Green.
Rates fr: £20.00-£20.00.
Open: All Year
Beds: 1F 5D 6T 8S
Baths: 11 Private 4 Shared
🛇 🅿 (10) ⊬ ▢ ♠ ✗ ▥ ▣ ✦

(0.25m) **Cerdyn Villa**, Llanwrtyd Wells, Powys, LD5 4RS.
Peaceful, comfortable Victorian family house
Grades: WTB 2 Cr
Tel: **01591 610635** Ms Lomax.
Rates fr: £16.00.
Open: All Year **Beds:** 1F 1D 2T
Baths: 2 Private 2 Shared
🛇 🅿 (6) ▢ ♠ ✗ ▥ ▣ ▣

(0.25m) **Carlton House Hotel**, Dolycoed Road, Llanwrtyd Wells, Powys, LD5 4SN.
Bow windowed Edwardian villa
Tel: **01591 610248** Dr Gilchrist.
Fax no: 01591 610242
Rates fr: £23.00-£33.00.
Open: All Year (not Xmas)
Beds: 2F 2D 1T **Baths:** 5 Private
🛇 ▢ ♠ ✗ ▥ ▣

Dolgoch 49

National Grid Ref: SN8056

(▲0.25m) **Dolgoch Youth Hostel**, Dolgoch, Tregaron, Cardiganshire, SY25 6NR.
Actual grid ref: SH806561
Tel: **01974 298680**
Under 18: £4.00 **Adults:** £5.85
Self-catering Facilities, Showers, Shop
Remote farmhouse in the wild and lonely Tywi Valley providing simple yet spacious mountain hut type accommodation. No electricity. Open fire, gas lighting. Twm Shon Cattis Cave and Llyn Brianne Reservoir nearby

Devil's Bridge 50

National Grid Ref: SN7376

🍴 ◀ Hafway Inn

(On route) **Mount Pleasant**, Devil's Bridge, Aberystwyth, Ceredigion, SY23 4QY.
Actual grid ref: SN736769
Grades: WTB 3 Cr, High Comm
Tel: **01970 890219**
Mr & Mrs Connell.
Rates fr: £19.00-£24.00.
Open: All Year **Beds:** 2D 2T
Baths: 3 Ensuite 1 Private
🛇 (12) 🅿 (4) ⊬ ▢ ✗ ▥ ▣ ▣ ✦
Set amid beautiful countryside, ideal for touring, our guests have written: "super welcome", "very comfortable", "excellent food", "wonderful", "simply the best". Visit and see why

The lowest *double* rate per person is shown in *italics*.

(1m) *Erwbarfe Farm, Devil's Bridge, Aberystwyth, Ceredigion, SY23 3JR.*
Large welcoming comfortable farmhouse
Tel: **01970 890251** Mrs Lewis.
Rates fr: *£16.00*-**£25.00**.
Open: Apr to Sep
Beds: 1F 1D
Baths: 1S
🛏 🅿 (4) 🗗 🗙 ▥ Ⅴ ⓐ

Ponterwyd 51

National Grid Ref: SN7480

(0.25m) *Dyffryn Castell Hotel, Ponterwyd, Devils Bridge, Aberystwyth, Ceredigion, SY23 3LB.*
Actual grid ref: SN773817
Grades: WTB 3 Cr, Comm
Tel: **01970 890237** (also fax no)
Mrs Buntin.
Rates fr: *£20.00*-**£22.00**.
Open: All Year (not Xmas)
Beds: 6F 2D 1T
Baths: 6 Ensuite 1 Shared
🛏 🅿 (60) 🗗 ⵏ 🗙 ▥ Ⅴ ⓐ ✦
This family-run old coaching inn, situated in the tranquil Cambrian Mountains offers excellent food, real ale and comfortable ensuite accommodation and a homely Welsh welcome

Western Route through Snowdonia

From **Tywyn** you can take a steam train on the Talyllyn Railway to Abergynolwyn.
Barmouth is a pleasant seaside resort where you can find the Ty Gwyn Museum, a museum on the Tudors.
Harlech Castle is a World Heritage Site with a spectacular clifftop location overlooking the sea. Built by Edward I at the time of the conquest of Wales in the late thirteenth century, it was taken by Owain Glyndwr in 1404. The future Henry VII was besieged here for seven years during the Wars of the Roses. The most impressive feature is the gatehouse, with its two huge half-round towers.

Pennal 52

National Grid Ref: SH6900

(1m) *Gogarth Hall Farm, Pennal, Machynlleth, Powys, SY20 9LB.*
Enchanting farmhouse with panoramic views
Grades: WTB 3 Cr, High Comm
Tel: **01654 791235** (also fax no)
Mrs Breese.
Rates fr: *£12.50*-**£16.00**.
Open: All Year
Beds: 1F 1D
Baths: 2 Ensuite 1 Private
🛏 🅿 (6) 🗗 🗙 ▥ Ⅴ

Tywyn 53

National Grid Ref: SH5800
🍴 🍺 Peniarth Arms

(1m) *Hendy Farm, Tywyn. LL36 9RU.*
Large comfortable farmhouse near town
Grades: WTB 2 Cr, High Comm
Tel: **01654 710457**
Mrs Lloyd-Jones.
Rates fr: *£16.00*-**£19.50**.
Open: Apr-Oct
Beds: 2D 1T
Baths: 2 Ensuite 1 Private
🛏 ⵏ 🗗 ⵏ ▥ Ⅴ

(1m) *The Arthur Hotel, 6 Marine Parade, Tywyn. LL36 0DE.*
Comfortable family hotel, facing sea
Grades: WTB 3 Cr, Comm
Tel: **01654 712146** Mr Harrison.
Rates fr: *£21.00*-**£24.00**.
Open: Feb to Dec
Beds: 3D 3T 2S
Baths: 8 Private
🛏 🅿 ⵏ 🗗 🗙 ▥ Ⅴ

Bryncrug 54

National Grid Ref: SH6003

(1m) *Cynfal Farm, Bryncrug, Tywyn. LL36 9RB.*
Mixed working farm, magnificently situated with panoramic views
Grades: WTB 2 Cr, High Comm
Tel: **01654 711703** Mrs Evans.
Rates fr: *£16.00*-**£17.00**.
Open: All Year (not Xmas)
Beds: 2D 1T
Baths: 2 Ensuite 1 Private
🛏 (1) 🅿 (3) ⵏ 🗗 ▥

Rhoslefain 55

National Grid Ref: SH5705

(2m) *Bodowen, Rhoslefain, Tywyn. LL36 9SF.*
Old stone house, beautiful views
Grades: WTB 1 Cr, High Comm
Tel: **01654 710996** Mrs Bowles.
Rates fr: *£14.00*-**£18.00**.
Open: Easter to Oct
Beds: 1D 1T
Baths: 1 Shared
🛏 (5) 🅿 (2) ⵏ 🗗 ▥ Ⅴ ✦

The *lowest* **single** rate *is shown in* **bold**.

Islaw'r Dref 56

National Grid Ref: SH6815

(🔺 2m) *Kings (Dolgellau) Youth Hostel, Islaw'r Dref, Penmaenpool, Dolgellau, Gwynedd, LL40 1TB.*
Actual grid ref: SH683161
Warden: Mr I Macaerwright & Ms A Scott.
Tel: **01341 422392**
Under 18: £4.95 Adults: £7.20
Evening Meals Available (7pm), Self-catering Facilities, Grounds Available for Games, Shop, Parking, Camping Facilities
Traditional hostel set in idyllic wooded valley, with magnificent views up to Cader Idris and Rhinog mountain ranges

Arthog 57

National Grid Ref: SH6414
🍴 🍺 Fairbourne Hotel, The Ponderosa

(On route) *Graig Wen Guest House, Arthog. LL39 1BQ.*
Grades: WTB 3 Cr, Comm
Tel: **01341 250900 / 01341 250482**
Mrs Ameson.
Fax no: 01341 250482
Rates fr: *£15.50*-**£18.50**.
Open: All Year (not Xmas)
Beds: 1F 3D 2T 1S
Baths: 3 Ensuite 2 Shared
🛏 🅿 (20) 🗗 🗙 ▥ & Ⅴ ⓐ ✦
Situated in 42 acres woodland & pasture reaching down to Mawddach estuary. Ideal for walkers, mountain climbers & bird watchers. Disabled bedrooms available. Beaches, lakes, Cader Mountain nearby

(On route) *Cyfannedd Uchaf Guest House, Arthog. LL39 1LX.*
Actual grid ref: SH635127
We offer peace and tranquillity
Grades: WTB 1 Cr, High Comm
Tel: **01341 250526** Mrs Tovey.
Rates fr: *£17.00*-**£17.00**.
Open: May to Sep
Beds: 2D 1T
Baths: 1 Ensuite 1 Shared
🛏 (14) 🅿 (4) ⵏ 🗙 ▥ ⓐ ✦

All cycleways are popular: you are well-advised to book ahead

Barmouth 58

National Grid Ref: SH6115

🍴 🍺 Last Inn

(0.25m) *Bryn Melyn Hotel,*
Panorama Road, Barmouth.
LL42 1DQ.
Actual grid ref: SH620158
Delightful small hotel, informal
atmosphere, in idyllic position on
mountainside with stunning views
of river, mountains & sea. Ideal for
exploring all of Snowdonia
Grades: WTB 3 Cr, High Comm
Tel: **01341 280556**
Mr Clay. Fax no: 01341 280276
Rates fr: £29.00-**£35.00.**
Open: Feb to Nov
Beds: 2F 4D 3T
Baths: 9 Ensuite
🛇 (5) 🅿 (9) 🖵 🏋 🗙 🎟 ☑ ♿ ♦

(On Route) *The Gables, Fford*
Mynach, Barmouth, Gwynedd,
LL42 1RL.
Victorian house of character.
Lovely position near mountains.
Friendly atmosphere
Grades: WTB 2 Cr, Comm
Tel: **01341 280553**
Mr & Mrs Lewis.
Rates fr: £16.00-**£18.00.**
Open: Mar to Nov
Beds: 1F 2D 1S
Baths: 2 Ensuite 1 Shared
🛇 🅿 (5) 🏋 🖵 🏋 🗙 🎟 ♿ ♦

(0.25m) *The Sandpiper, 7 Marine*
Parade, Barmouth. LL42 1NA.
Sea front guest house
Grades: WTB 2 Cr, High Comm
Tel: **01341 280318**
Mr & Mrs Palmer.
Rates fr: £13.50-**£14.50.**
Open: Easter to Oct
Beds: 4F 5D 2S
Baths: 6 Private 3 Shared
🛇 🅿 🖵 🎟 ♿

(0.25m) *Tal-Y-Don Hotel, High*
Street, Barmouth. LL42 1DL.
Spacious rooms, good breakfasts &
welcoming
Tel: **01341 280508**
Mrs Davies.
Rates fr: £13.00-**£20.00.**
Open: All Year (not Xmas)
Beds: 3F 4D 3T
Baths: 4 Ensuite 2 Shared
🛇 🅿 🏋 🖵 🗙 🎟 ☑ ♿

(0.25m) *Wavecrest Hotel, 8*
Marine Parade, Barmouth.
LL42 1NA.
Actual grid ref: SH609160
Sea front, licensed traditional hotel
Grades: WTB 3 Cr, High Comm,
AA 2 St
Tel: **01341 280330** (also fax no)
Mr & Mrs Jarman.
Rates fr: £16.00-**£16.00.**
Open: Easter to Dec
Beds: 4F 4D 2S
Baths: 7 Private 2 Shared
🛇 🅿 (2) 🏋 🖵 🗙 🎟 ☑ ♦

(0.25m) *Lawrenny Lodge Hotel,*
Barmouth. LL42 1SU.
Family-run hotel, quiet location
Grades: WTB 3 Cr, Comm
Tel: **01341 280466**
Mr Barber.
Rates fr: £18.00-**£18.00.**
Open: Mar to Dec
Beds: 1F 4D 2T 1S
Baths: 7 Ensuite 1 Shared
🛇 🅿 (9) 🖵 🏋 🗙 🎟 ☑ ♦

Llanaber 59

National Grid Ref: SH6017

(On route) *Fronoleu Hall,*
Llanaber Road, Llanaber,
Barmouth. LL42 1YT.
Well-appointed coastal private
house
Tel: **01341 280491**
Mrs Amison.
Rates fr: £15.00-**£16.00.**
Open: Easter to Oct
Beds: 1F 2D 1T 1S
Baths: 2 Ensuite 3 Shared
🛇 🅿 (8) 🖵 🏋 🗙 🎟 ☑ ♦

Dyffryn Ardudwy 60

National Grid Ref: SH6022

(1m) *Ystumgwern Hall Farm,*
Dyffryn Ardudwy. LL44 2DD.
C16th luxury farmhouse, barn
conversion
Grades: WTB 2 Cr, Deluxe
Tel: **01341 247249**
Mrs Williams.
Fax no: 01341 247171
Rates fr: £18.00-**£20.00.**
Open: All Year
Beds: 4F 1D 1T 1S
Baths: 7 Ensuite
🛇 🅿 🖵 🏋 🎟 ♿ ☑

(0.25m) *Byrdir, Dyffryn Ardudwy.*
LL44 2EA.
Traditional Welsh stone farmhouse
Tel: **01341 247200**
Mrs Jones.
Rates fr: £19.00-**£19.00.**
Open: Easter to Sep
Beds: 2F 2D 1T 1S
Baths: 4 Ensuite 1 Private
🛇 🅿 (14) ♿ 🖵 🗙 🎟 ☑

Llandanwg 61

National Grid Ref: SH5628

🍴 🍺 Llanbeds, Victorian Inn

(2m) *Glan-Y-Gors, Llandanwg,*
Harlech. LL46 2SD.
Comfortable guest house near
beach
Grades: WTB 1 Cr, High Comm
Tel: **01341 241410**
Mrs Evans.
Rates fr: £14.00-**£14.50.**
Open: All Year
Beds: 1F 1D 1T
Baths: 1 Shared
🛇 🅿 (6) 🖵 🏋 🗙 🎟 ☑ ♦ ♦

Eastern Route through Snowdonia

On the eastern route out of
Machynlleth, the **Centre for
Alternative Technology** is a
self-sufficient community
started in the 1970s on the
site of a disused slate quarry,
where you can see renew-
able energy generation
(wind, water and solar power)
in action, as well as organic
gardens and numerous other
attractions.

Dolgellau was the site of a
Quaker community; entry to
the Quaker Heritage Centre is
free. To the north of town, the
Gwynfynydd Gold Centre and
Mine is the only working gold
mine open to the public.

Harlech 62

National Grid Ref: SH5831

(1m) *Tyddyn Y Gwynt, Harlech.*
LL46 2TH.
Central for beach & countryside
Grades: WTB 1 Cr, Comm
Tel: **01766 780298** Mrs Jones.
Rates fr: £15.00-**£15.00.**
Open: All Year
Beds: 1F 1T
Baths: 1 Shared
🛇 🅿 (6) 🖵 🏋 🎟 ♦ ♦

(1m) *Castle Cottage Hotel, Pen*
Llech, Harlech. LL46 2YL.
Comfortable C16th hotel
Grades: WTB 3 Cr, High Comm
Tel: **01766 780479** (also fax no)
Mr Roberts.
Rates fr: £28.00-**£20.00.**
Open: All Year (closed 3 wks in
Feb)
Beds: 3D 1T 2S
Baths: 4 Private 2 Shared
🛇 ♿ 🖵 🏋 🗙 🎟 ☑ ♦

(1m) *Lion Hotel, Harlech. LL46 2SG.*
2 bars & restaurant. Double rooms
ensuite
Grades: WTB 3 Cr, Comm
Tel: **01766 780731** Mr Morris.
Rates fr: £18.00-**£20.00.**
Open: All Year
Beds: 4D 1T 1S **Baths:** 5 Private
🅿 (3) 🖵 🏋 🗙 🎟 ♦

All rates are subject

to alteration at the

owners' discretion.

Llanwrin   63

National Grid Ref: SH7803

🍴 🍺 Black Lion

(3m) *Mathafarn, Llanwrin, Machynlleth, Powys, SY20 8QJ.*
Elegant country farmhouse
Grades: WTB 2 Cr, High Comm
Tel: 01650 511226 Mrs Hughes.
Rates fr: *£17.00-£17.00.*
Open: All Year (not Xmas)
Beds: 1D 1T 1S
Baths: 1 Private 1 Shared
🛏 🅿 🗆 ⊁ 🖿 🛈 ⌁

Corris   64

National Grid Ref: SH7507

(▲ 0.25m) *Corris Youth Hostel, Old School, Old Road, Corris, Machynlleth, Powys, SY20 9QT.*
Actual grid ref: SH753080
Tel: 01654 761686
Under 18: £5.40 **Adults:** £8.00
Evening Meals Available, Self-catering Facilities, Family Bunk Rooms, Central Heating, Security Lockers, Parking, Laundry Facilities, No Smoking
Picturesque former village school, recently renovated, with panoramic views of Corris

Brithdir   65

National Grid Ref: SH7618

🍴 🍺 Cross Foxes

(2m) *Llwyn Talcen, Brithdir, Dolgellau. LL40 2RY.*
Country house in rhododendron gardens. Marvellous views. Mountains on doorstep
Grades: WTB WTB Welcome Home Comm
Tel: 01341 450276
Mrs Griffiths.
Rates fr: *£16.00-£16.00.*
Open: All Year
Beds: 2D 1S
Baths: 1 Ensuite 1 Shared
🛏 🅿 (5) ⊬ 🗆 ⊁ ✕ 🖿 🛈 Ⓥ ⌁

(2m) *Y Goedlan, Brithdir, Dolgellau. LL40 2RN.*
Victorian vicarage in peaceful countryside. Spacious bedrooms. Hearty breakfast
Grades: WTB 1 Cr, Comm
Tel: 01341 423131 (also fax no)
Mrs Evans.
Rates fr: *£15.50-£17.50.*
Open: Feb to Nov
Beds: 1F 1D 1T
Baths: 1 Shared
🛏 (4) 🅿 (3) 🗆 🖿 Ⓥ

Dolgellau   66

National Grid Ref: SH7217

🍴 🍺 Cross Foxes Inn, Dylanwad Da, The George, Royal Ship, Ivy House

(On route) *Dolygader Guest House, Barmouth Road, Dolgellau. LL40 2YT.*
Convenient for golfing, fishing, cycling, pony trekking
Tel: 01341 422379 Mrs Davies.
Rates fr: *£15.00-£15.00.*
Open: All Year
Beds: 2D 1T
Baths: 1 Shared
🛏 (4) 🅿 🗆 ✕ 🖿 Ⓥ

(0.25m) *Ivy House, Finsbury Square, Dolgellau. LL40 1RF.*
Attractive country town guest house, licensed restaurant, good homemade food
Grades: WTB 3 Cr, Comm
Tel: 01341 422535 Mrs Bamford.
Fax no: 01341 422689
Rates fr: *£18.00-£20.00.*
Open: All Year
Beds: 1F 3D 2T
Baths: 3 Private 3 Shared
🛏 🗆 ⊁ ✕ 🖿 Ⓥ 🛈

(0.5m) *Esgair Wen Newydd, Garreg Feurig, Llanfachreth Road, Dolgellau. LL40 2YA.*
Bungalow, mountain views, very quiet. Friendly relaxed atmosphere. High standards
Grades: WTB 1 Cr, High Comm
Tel: 01341 423952 Mrs Westwood.
Rates fr: *£17.50-£19.50.*
Open: All Year (not Xmas)
Beds: 2D 1T **Baths:** 1 Shared
🛏 (3) 🅿 (3) ⊬ 🗆 ✕ 🖿 Ⓥ 🛈 ⌁

(3m) *Arosfyr Farm, Penycefn Road, Dolgellau. LL40 2YP.*
Homely farmhouse, own free-range eggs. Safe bicycle housing
Grades: WTB Listed, Approv
Tel: 01341 422355 Mr Skeel Jones.
Rates fr: *£15.00-£18.00.*
Open: All Year (not Xmas)
Beds: 1F 1D 1T **Baths:** 2 Shared
🛏 🅿 🗆 🖿 ⌁

(0.25m) *Bryn Rodyn Guest House, Maescaled, Dolgellau. LL40 1UG.*
Secluded C17th Welsh longhouse
Grades: WTB 1 Cr, Comm
Tel: 01341 423470 Mr Jones.
Rates fr: *£16.00-£20.00.*
Open: All Year
Beds: 1D 2T **Baths:** 1 Shared
🛏 🅿 (4) ⊬ 🗆 🖿 Ⓥ 🛈 ⌁

40

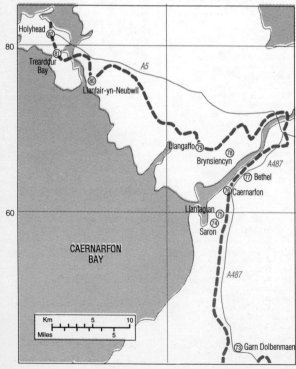

Holyhead
82
80
81
Treaddur Bay
A5
80
Llanfair-yn-Neubwll
Llangaffo 79
78
Brynsiencyn
A487
77 Bethel
76 Caernarfon
Llantaglan
60
75
Saron
CAERNARFON BAY
A487
Km 5 10
Miles 5
73 Garn Dolbenmaen

Planning a longer stay? Always ask for any special rates.

Porthmadog to Holyhead

From **Porthmadog** you can take the spectacular norrow-gauge Ffestiniog Railway to Blaenau Ffestiniog, up the route between the old slate mines and the coast. A detour to the southeast of town will bring you to the famous Italianate fantasy village of **Portmeirion**, assembled in the 1920s by Sir Clough Williams-Ellis out of buildings in a myriad styles brought here from different parts of Britain, and elsewhere.

Thirteenth-century **Criccieth** Castle was ruined by Owain Glyndwr in 1404. The ruins yield views across Cardigan Bay to Harlech.

The superlatively well-preserved **Caernarfon** Castle, with its polygonal towers, was built to be the royal seat in conquered Wales by Edward I. It was the scene in 1969 for a made-to-order pseudo-medieval ceremony marking Prince Charles' investiture as Prince of Wales.

At **Bangor**, the cathedral contains the famous sixteenth-century wooden carving, the Mostyn Christ. The main building of the university mirrors the design of the cathedral; the museum and art gallery has a Welsh national flavour; and the renovated Victorian pier gives excellent views of the Menai Suspension Bridge, built by Thomas Telford in 1826.

The reason for the fame of **Llanfairpwllgwyngyllgogerychwyrndrobwll-llantisiliogogogoch** should be self-evident even if this is the first you've ever heard of the place.

Plas Newydd, just beyond Llanfairetc, is an eighteenth-century house in the Gothic style – a rare thing. Designed by James Wyatt, the interior is eclectic; and there is a huge mural by Whistler. The grounds, which include a fine spring garden, yield splendid views to Snowdonia.

If the cycle route has failed to expend all your energy reserves, you can climb the 700-foot Holyhead mountain above **Holyhead**; at the top you will find a large Iron Age hill fort, Caer y Tawr. Below the mountain at South Stack, the Ellin's Tower Seabird Centre offers observation of the abundant bird life on the cliffs.

(2m) *Glyn Farm House,* Dolgellau. LL40 1YA.
Farmhouse overlooking picturesque Mawddach Estuary
Grades: WTB 2 Cr
Tel: **01341 422286** (also fax no)
Mrs Price.
Rates fr: *£14.50*-**£17.50**.
Open: Easter to Nov
Beds: 3D 1T 1S
Baths: 1 Private 1 Shared
🛏 🅿 (6) 🖵 🏠 ▥ Ⓥ

(2m) *Gwanas Farm,* Dolgellau. LL40 2SH.
Spacious Georgian farmhouse, sheep farm
Grades: WTB 1 Cr, Comm
Tel: **01341 422624** (also fax no)
Mrs Evans.
Rates fr: *£15.00*-**£17.00**.
Open: All Year (not Xmas)
Beds: 1F 1D 1T
Baths: 2 Shared
🛏 🅿 (8) 🖵 ▥ Ⓥ ✦

(2m) *Penbryn Croft,* Cader Road, Dolgellau. LL40 1RN.
Residence of historical interest
Tel: **01341 422815** Mrs Jones.
Rates fr: *£15.00*-**£18.00**.
Open: All Year (not Xmas)
Beds: 3D 3T
🛏 ⼂ 🖵 ✕ Ⓥ 🛉 ✦

Bringing children with you? Always ask for any special rates.

The lowest *double* rate per person is shown in *italics*.

Ganllwyd   67

National Grid Ref: SH7223

(0.5m) *Tyn Y Groes Hotel,* Ganllwyd, Dolgellau. LL40 2NH.
Former C16th coaching inn
Grades: WTB 3 Cr, RAC Acclaim
Tel: **01341 440275**
Mr & Mrs Ruthwell.
Rates fr: *£21.50*-**£21.00**.
Open: All Year
Beds: 1F 4D 1T 2S
Baths: 8 Private
🛏 (9) 🅿 ⼂ 🖵 🏠 ✕ ▥ Ⓥ 🛉

Trawsfynydd   68

National Grid Ref: SH7035

(1m) *Old Mill Farm House,* Fron Oleu, Trawsfynydd, Blaenau Ffestiniog. LL41 4UN.
Actual grid ref: SH7135
Olde Worlde charm, Wonderful scenery, friendly animals, large good breakfasts
Grades: WTB 2 Cr
Tel: **01766 540397** (also fax no)
Mr & Mrs Ramsay.
Rates fr: *£19.00*-**£20.00**.
Open: Easter to Oct
Beds: 3F 2D 2T   Baths: 7 Ensuite
🛏 🅿 (10) 🖵 🏠 ▥ 🛔 Ⓥ 🛉

(1m) *Bryn Celynog Farm,* Cwmprysor, Trawsfynydd, Blaenau Ffestiniog. LL41 4TR.
Actual grid ref: SH744354
Homely accomodation on working farm
Grades: WTB 2 Cr, High Comm
Tel: **01766 540378** (also fax no)
Mrs Hughes.
Rates fr: *£17.50*-**£20.00**.
Open: All Year
Beds: 1F 1D 1T
Baths: 1 Ensuite 1 Shared
🛏 🅿 (4) 🖵 🏠 ✕ ▥ Ⓥ 🛉 ✦

Gellilydan   69

National Grid Ref: SH6839
🍽 🍷 Bryn Arms

(1m) *Tyddyn Du Farm,* Gellilydan, Blaenau Ffestiniog. LL41 4RB.
Actual grid ref: SH691398
Enchanting C17th farmhouse, delicious cooking
Grades: WTB 3 Cr, Comm
Tel: **01766 590281**
Mrs Williams.
Rates fr: *£17.50*.
Open: All Year (not Xmas)
Beds: 1F 2D 1T 1S
Baths: 3 Private 2 Shared
🛏 🅿 (8) 🖵 🏠 ✕ ▥ Ⓥ 🛉 ✦

The lowest single rate is shown in bold.

(0.25m) *Gwynfryn, Gellilydan, Blaenau Ffestiniog*. *LL41 4EA*.
Actual grid ref: SH685398
Detached comfortable, clean, quiet period house
Grades: WTB 1 Cr, Comm
Tel: **01766 590225** Mrs Jones.
Rates fr: *£13.00-£13.00*.
Open: All Year (not Xmas)
Beds: 1F 1D 1S **Baths:** 1 Shared
🛇 🅿 ⊬ ✕ 📖 Ⓥ 🛭 ⌀

Ffestiniog   70
National Grid Ref: SH7041

🍴 🍺 The Grapes, Penwern, Llan

(3m) *Morannedd Guest House, Blaenau Road, Ffestiniog, Blaenau Ffestiniog*. *LL41 4LG*.
Comfortable guest house with mountain views
Grades: WTB 3 Cr, Comm
Tel: **01766 762734** (also fax no)
Mrs Lethbridge.
Rates fr: *£18.00-£17.00*.
Open: All Year
Beds: 2D 2T 1S
Baths: 4 Private 1 Shared
🛇 (10) 🅿 (4) ⊬ 🗆 🛏 ✕ 📖 Ⓥ 🛭

(3m) *Tyddyn Pant Glas, Ffestiniog, Blaenau Ffestiniog*. *LL41 4PU*.
Actual grid ref: SH709413
Self-contained annexe - superb views: excellent centre for all attractions
Grades: WTB 1 Cr, Comm
Tel: **01766 762442**
Mrs Langdale-Pope.
Rates fr: *£17.50-£20.00*.
Open: All Year (not Xmas)
Beds: 1D **Baths:** 1 Ensuite
🅿 ⊬ 🗆 📖

(2.5m) *Ty Clwb, The Square, Ffestiniog, Blaenau Ffestiniog*. *LL41 4LS*.
Actual grid ref: SH700418
Quality accommodation in peaceful village. All bedrooms have mountain views
Grades: WTB 2 Cr, High Comm
Tel: **01766 762658** Mrs Mobbs.
Rates fr: *£17.00-£20.00*.
Open: All Year (not Xmas)
Beds: 2D 1T **Baths:** 3 Private
🛇 ⊬ 🗆 🛏 📖 Ⓥ

Maentwrog   71
National Grid Ref: SH6640

🍴 🍺 Grapes Hotel

(0.25m) *The Old Rectory Hotel, Maentwrog, Blaenau Ffestiniog*. *LL41 4HN*.
Main house / budget annex, 3 acre garden. Informal, peaceful
Tel: **01766 590305** Ms Herbert.
Rates fr: *£18.00-£25.00*.
Open: All Year (not Xmas)
Beds: 3F 6D 2T 1S
Baths: 12 Private
🛇 🅿 🗆 🛏 ✕ 📖 Ⓥ 🛭 ⌀

Porthmadog   72
National Grid Ref: SH5638

🍴 🍺 Newborough Bach, The Ship

(0.25m) *Guest House, 5 Glaslyn Street, Porthmadog*. *LL49 9EG*.
Close to railway station and all amenities. Cleanliness guaranteed
Grades: WTB 1 Cr
Tel: **01766 514461**
Rates fr: *£15.00*.
Open: All Year (not Xmas)
Beds: 1F 1T 1D
Baths: 1Private 1 Shared
🛇 🗆 🛏 📖

(0.25m) *35 Madog Street, Porthmadog*. *LL49 9BU*.
Modern terraced house
Tel: **01766 512843**
Mrs Skellern.
Rates fr: *£12.50-£12.50*.
Open: All Year (not Xmas)
Beds: 1F 1D 1T 1S
Baths: 2 Shared
🛇 (3) 🗆 🛏 📖 Ⓥ

Garn Dolbenmaen   73
National Grid Ref: SH4944

🍴 🍺 The Goat, Bryncir

(2m) *Cefn Uchaf Farm Guest House, Garn Dolbenmaen, Porthmadog*. *LL51 9PJ*.
Comfortable, large farm guest house
Grades: WTB 3 Cr, High Comm
Tel: **01766 530239**
Mr & Mrs Easton.
Rates fr: *£18.50-£23.50*.
Open: Mar to Nov
Beds: 5F 1D 2T
Baths: 3 Private 2 Shared
🛇 🅿 (20) 🗆 🛏 ✕ 📖 Ⓥ

Saron   74
National Grid Ref: SH4658

🍴 🍺 Newborough Arms

(2m) *Pengwern Farm, Saron, Llanwnda, Caernarfon*. *LL54 5UH*.
Charming spacious farmhouse of character
Grades: WTB 3 Cr, De Luxe
Tel: **01286 831500 / 0378 411780**
Mr & Mrs Rowlands.
Fax no: 01286 831500
Rates fr: *£20.00-£25.00*.
Open: Feb to Nov
Beds: 1F 2D 1T
Baths: 3 Private
🛇 🅿 (3) ⊬ 🗆 🛏 ✕ 📖 Ⓥ

Bringing children with you? Always ask for any special rates.

Llanfaglan   75
National Grid Ref: SH4760

🍴 🍺 Harp Inn

(2m) *The White House, Llanfaglan, Caernarfon*. *LL54 5RA*.
Quiet, isolated country house. Magnificent views to mountains and sea
Grades: WTB 2 Cr, High Comm
Tel: **01286 673003**
Mr Bayles.
Rates fr: *£18.00-£22.00*.
Open: Mar to Nov
Beds: 2D 3T
Baths: 3 Ensuite 2 Private
🛇 🅿 (8) 🗆 🛏 📖

Caernarfon   76
National Grid Ref: SH4862

🍴 🍺 Newborough Arms, Prince of Wales, Black Boy, Ship & Castle

(0.25m) *Princes Of Wales Hotel, Bangor Street, Caernarfon*. *LL55 1AR*.
Centrally located, perfect stop-over en route for Irish Superfast, Irish ferries & Snowdonia
Grades: WTB 3 Cr, Comm
Tel: **01286 673367**
Ms Parry.
Fax no: 01286 676610
Rates fr: *£18.50-£18.50*.
Open: All Year
Beds: 3F 8D 6T 4S
Baths: 19 Private 2 Shared
🛇 (1) 🅿 (6) 🗆 🛏 ✕ 📖 Ⓥ 🛭 ⌀

(1m) *Cae Garw, Cadnant Valley Caravan Park, Llanberis Road, Caernarfon*. *LL55 2DF*.
Clean, comfortable house, entrance caravan park, short walk Caernarfon
Tel: **01286 673196**
Mrs Noon.
Rates fr: *£15.00-£15.00*.
Open: Mar to Nov
Beds: 1D 1T
Baths: 1 Shared
🅿 (4) 🗆 📖

Bethel   77
National Grid Ref: SH5265

🍴 🍺 Y Bedol

(1m) *Arosfa, Bethel, Caernarfon*. *LL55 1UN*.
Comfortable private house, mountain views
Grades: WTB Listed
Tel: **01248 671249**
Mrs Giblin.
Rates fr: *£13.00-£13.00*.
Open: All Year
Beds: 1F 1D 1T
Baths: 1 Shared
🛇 (1) 🅿 (5) 🗆 🛏 📖

Brynsiencyn 78

National Grid Ref: SH4867

|●| ◀ Penrhos Arms

(1.5m) *Fron Guest House, Brynsiencyn, Llanfairpwllgwyngyll, Anglesey, LL61 6TX.*
Traditional high class farmhouse accommodation
Grades: WTB 2 Cr, High Comm
Tel: 01248 430310 Mr Geldard.
Rates fr: *£14.50-£16.00.*
Open: All Year (not Xmas)
Beds: 3D
Baths: 1 Private 1 Shared
🅿 (4) 🛌 ⬛ ⊞.

Llangaffo 79

National Grid Ref: SH4468

(0.25m) *Plas Llangaffo, Llangaffo, Gaerwen, Anglesey, LL60 6LR.*
Quiet, comfortable farmhouse accommodation
Grades: WTB Listed
Tel: 01248 440452 Mrs Lamb.
Rates fr: *£14.50-£15.00.*
Open: All Year
Beds: 1F 2D 2T **Baths:** 2 Shared
🛏 🅿 (8) ⬛ 🛌 🍴 ✕ ⊞. & Ⓥ ⬛ ✦

Please don't camp on *anyone's* land without first obtaining their permission.

All rates are subject to alteration at the owners' discretion.

Llanfair-yn-Neubwll 80

National Grid Ref: SH3076

|●| ◀ Valley Hotel, Bull Hotel

(0.25m) *Ty Gwrthyn, Llanfair-yn-Neubwll, Holyhead, Anglesey, LL65 3LD.*
Country guest house. Sea views
Grades: WTB 2 Cr, Comm
Tel: 01407 741025
Mrs Montgomery Croft.
Rates fr: *£16.00-£20.00.*
Open: All Year
Beds: 1F 1D 2T
Baths: 3 Ensuite
🅿 (8) ⬛ 🍴 ⊞. &

Trearddur Bay 81

National Grid Ref: SH2578

|●| ◀ Trearddur Bay Hotel, Beach Hotel

(0.5m) *Moranedd Guest House, Trearddur Road, Trearddur Bay, Holyhead, Anglesey, LL65 2UE.*
Large comfortable house near sea
Grades: WTB Listed, RAC Listed
Tel: 01407 860324 Mrs Wathan.
Rates fr: *£14.00-£14.00.*
Open: All Year
Beds: 2F 3T 1S **Baths:** 2 Shared
🛏 🅿 ⊞.

Holyhead 82

National Grid Ref: SH2482

|●| ◀ Victoria Inn, Boat House Hotel

(0.5m) *Hendre, Porth Y Felin Road, Holyhead, Anglesey, LL65 1AH.*
Luxury accommodation opposite park. Beautiful views. 3 mins ferry terminal
Grades: WTB 3 Cr, Deluxe
Tel: 01407 762929 (also fax no)
Rates fr: *£20.00-£20.00.*
Open: All Year (not Xmas)
Beds: 2D 1T
Baths: 3 Private
🛏 🅿 (6) ⬛ ✕ ⊞. Ⓥ ⬛

(0.5m) *Roselea, 26 Holborn Road, Holyhead, Anglesey, LL65 2AT.*
Homely guest house 2 mins ferry, beaches, golf course & sailing. Guaranteed hospitality
Grades: WTB Listed, High Comm
Tel: 01407 764391 (also fax no)
Mrs Foxley.
Rates fr: *£14.00-£18.00.*
Open: All Year (not Xmas)
Beds: 1F 1D 1T
Baths: 1 Shared
🛏 🛌 ⬛ ✕ ⊞. Ⓥ ⬛

(0.5m) *Wavecrest, 93 Newry Road, Holyhead, Anglesey, LL65 1HU.*
Ideal for Ferry - open 24 hours
Grades: WTB 3 Cr, Comm
Tel: 01407 763637 (also fax no)
Mr Hiltunen.
Rates fr: *£14.00-£14.00.*
Open: All Year (not Xmas)
Beds: 3F 1T
Baths: 2 Private 2 Shared
🛏 🅿 ⬛ 🛌 🍴 ✕ ⊞.

Sustrans Sea to Sea

The **Sea to Sea** cycle route is both a section of the new National Cycle Network and an award-winning leisure route. 140 miles long, it starts on the Cumbrian west coast at Workington or Whitehaven, proceeds through the northern Lake District via Keswick to Penrith, and continues through eastern Cumbria to Allenheads in Northumberland; and then through the north of County Durham to Consett, from where it heads either to Newcastle and Tynemouth or to Sunderland. The route is clearly signposted by blue direction signs bearing a cycle silhouette and the legend 'C2C'.

The indispensable **official route map and guide** for the Sea to Sea cycle route is available from Sustrans, 35 King Street, Bristol BS1 4DZ, tel 0117-926 8893, fax 0117-929 4173, @ £5.99 (+ £1.50 p&p).

Maps: Ordnance Survey 1:50,000 Landranger series: 86, 87, 88, 89, 90, 91; and for the Penrith-Carlisle link, 85

Trains: The Intercity west coast main line goes to Carlisle, from where you can connect to Workington, Whitehaven or Penrith; or to Langwathby via the famous scenic Leeds-Settle-Carlisle Railway. The Intercity east coast main line goes to Newcastle, from where you can connect to Tynemouth or Sunderland.

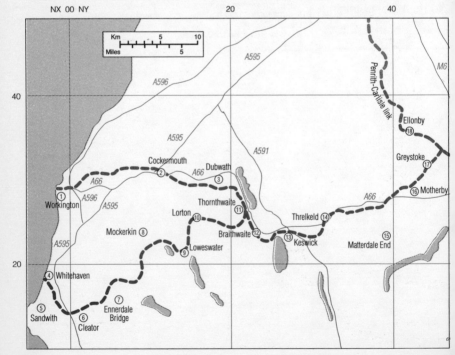

Workington or Whitehaven to Braithwaite

From the mid-nineteenth to mid-twentieth century, **Workington** was a major centre of the iron and steel industry, its particular success due to the fact that Henry Bessemer's steelmaking process depended on a supply of phosphorous free ores, in which this area is rich. The Helena Thompson Museum houses a display of costumes and embroidery. The first stretch of the way takes you up the Derwent Valley to Cockermouth, where the Wordsworth House is the birthplace of the region's most famous son. Elsewhere, the Printing House offers a myriad different types of printing press, and you can tour Jenning's Brewery on the banks of the Cocker. From here you head into the **Lake District National Park**, and on to Wythorp Woods, where you cycle down the west bank of **Bassenthwaite Lake**, with the imposing mass of **Skiddaw** towering above the opposite side, and on to Braithwaite. **Whitehaven** lies to the north of St Bees Head, a Heritage Coast with sandstone cliffs and nature reserves for the important bird life it supports. The town has been through a number of incarnations - harbour for St Bees Priory, major tobacco port, during which time the many Georgian buildings went up, and then coal and shipbuilding centre. The initial stage of the southern route takes you east by way of Cleator Moor to Kirkland, from where you ascend to the edge of the National Park. Here you ride northwards to the northwestern end of **Loweswater**, where you cycle down the northeast bank and then downstream alongside the River Cocker to Low Lorton, from where you ascend into Whinlatter Forest and then descend (steeply) to Thornthwaite, where you turn south to **Braithwaite**.

Workington 1

National Grid Ref: NX9927

▢▢ Traveller's Rest, Miners' Arms

(1.5m) *The Boston, 1 St Michael's Road, Workington, Cumbria,* CA14 3EZ.
Small guest house with big reputation. Ideal Lakes and sea
Grades: ETB Listed
Tel: **01900 603435** Mrs A Clarke.
Rates fr: *£12.50-£16.00.*
Open: All Year
Beds: 1F 1D 2T 2S
Baths: 1 Private 1 Shared
▢ ▢ (3) ▢ ▢ ▢

(On route) *Sandmans Guest House, 123 John Street, Workington, Cumbria,* CA14 3DD.
Small, friendly guest house, home from home; easy access to Lakes
Tel: **01900 605763** Mrs McKenna.
Rates fr: *£12.50-£15.00.*
Open: All Year
Beds: 1F 3T **Baths:** 1 Shared
▢ (3) ▢ ▢ ▢

(2m) *The Briery, Stainburn Road, Stainburn, Workington, Cumbria,* CA14 4UJ.
Friendly, family-run hotel
Tel: **01900 603395** Mr Lavelle.
Rates fr: *£15.00-£20.00.*
Open: All Year **Beds:** 4T 1S
▢ ▢ (60) ▢ ▢ ▢ ▢ ▢ ▢

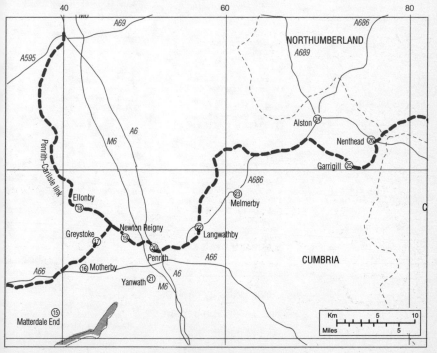

Cockermouth 2

National Grid Ref: NY1230

¹⁰¹ ◖ Black Bull, Brown Cow, Bitter End, Old Post House

(▲ 0.25m) *Cockermouth Youth Hostel, Double Mills, Cockermouth, Cumbria, CA13 0DS.*
Actual grid ref: NY118298
Tel: **01900 822561**
Under 18: £4.95
Adults: £7.20
Evening Meals Available (7pm), Self-catering Facilities, Showers
Simple accommodation in restored C17th watermill, convenient for northern and western fells and Cumbrian coastline

(0.25m) *The Castlegate Guest House, 6 Castlegate, Cockermouth, Cumbria, CA13 9EU.*
Tel: **01900 826749**
Miss Adams.
Rates fr: *£17.50-£20.00.*
Open: All Year
Beds: 2F 4D 1T
Baths: 4 Ensuite 2 Shared
🛏 ⌷ ⻗ 📖 ⒱ ▮ ✦
Grade II Listed Georgian town house, within short distance of unspoilt lakes. Expert advice on walks and tours. Popular with walkers and cyclists. Pets welcome

(0.25m) *Stanger Farm, Cockermouth, Cumbria, CA13 9TS.*
Homely working farm, magnificent scenery. Fishing, walks and huge breakfasts
Grades: ETB 1 Cr, Comm
Tel: **01900 824222**
Mrs Heslop.
Rates fr: *£16.50-£17.00.*
Open: All Year (not Xmas)
Beds: 1D 1T
Baths: 1 Shared
🛏 🄿 (4) ⌷ ✕ 📖 ⒱

(0.25m) *Emoh Ruo, 2 Willow Lane, Cockermouth, Cumbria, CA13 9DP.*
Family home - friendly atmosphere
Grades: ETB Listed
Tel: **01900 822951**
Mrs Grace.
Rates fr: *£14.00-£14.00.*
Open: All Year (not Xmas)
Beds: 2D 1S
Baths: 1 Shared
🛏 (3) 🄿 (2) ⼦ ⌷ 📖 ⒱

(0.25m) *Globe Hotel, Main Street, Cockermouth, Cumbria, CA13 9LE.*
C18 comfortable hotel
Grades: ETB 4 Cr, RAC 2 St
Tel: **01900 822126**
Miss Greening.
Rates fr: *£24.00-£25.00.*
Open: All Year (not Xmas)
Beds: 1F 11D 8T 5S
Baths: 20 Private 4 Shared
🛏 🄿 (10) ⌷ ⻗ ✕ 📖 ⒱

(0.25m) *Albany House, Wordsworth Terrace, Cockermouth, Cumbria, CA13 9AH.*
Friendly, comfortable Victorian guest house
Grades: ETB Listed
Tel: **01900 825630** Mr Nichol.
Rates fr: *£16.00-£16.00.*
Open: All Year
Beds: 1F 1D 1T 1S
Baths: 1 Private 1 Shared
🛏 ⼦ ⌷ ⻗ 📖 ⒱ ▮ ✦

Dubwath 3

National Grid Ref: NY1931

(1.5m) *Link House, Dubwath, Bassenthwaite Lake, Cockermouth, Cumbria, CA13 9YD.*
Grades: ETB 3 Cr, Comm, AA 4 Q, Select
Tel: **017687 76291** Mr Tuppen.
Fax no: 017687 76670
Rates fr: *£26.00-£26.00.*
Open: Feb to Nov
Beds: 1F 3D 2T 2S
Baths: 8 Ensuite
🛏 (7) 🄿 (10) ⌷ ✕ 📖 ⧠ ⒱ ▮
Family-run with excellent reputation for imaginative home cooking and inexpensive wine list. Friendly and relaxed atmosphere. Stunning scenery in quieter area. Leisure club membership

Whitehaven 4

National Grid Ref: NX9718

(1m) *Corkickle Guest House, 1 Corkickle, Whitehaven, Cumbria, CA28 8AA.*
Superb Georgian house. Residential licence
Grades: ETB 3 Cr, Comm
Tel: **01946 692073** (also fax no)
Mrs Pearson.
Rates fr: *£22.00-£24.50.*
Open: All Year (not Xmas/New Year)
Beds: 2D 2T 2S
Baths: 5 Ensuite 1 Private
🄿 (2) ⼦ ⌷ ⻗ ✕ 📖 ⒱ ▮ ✦

(0.5m) *The Cross Georgian Guest House, Sneckyeat Road, Hensingham, Whitehaven, Cumbria, CA28 8JQ.*
In private ground, spectacular views
Tel: **01946 63716** Mrs Bailey.
Rates fr: *£15.00-£15.00.*
Open: All Year
Beds: 2T 2S
Baths: 2 Private 1 Shared
🛏 🄿 (8) ⌷ ⻗ ✕ 📖 ⒱ ▮

Pay B&Bs by cash or cheque and be prepared to pay up front.

Sandwith 5

National Grid Ref: NX9614

¹⁰¹ ◖ Dog & Partridge, Lowther Arms

(▲ 3m) *Tarn Flatt Camping Barn, Tarnflat Hall, Sandwith, Whitehaven, Cumbria*
Actual grid ref: NX947146
Adults: £3.35+
Situated on St Bees Head overlooking Scottish coastline and the Isle of Man. RSPB seabird reserve and lighthouse nearby. ADVANCE BOOKING ESSENTIAL

(2m) *Aikbank Cottage, Sandwith, Whitehaven, Cumbria, CA28 9UG.*
Actual grid ref: NX964148
C17th Cottage and Post Office
Tel: **01946 695771** Mrs Urwin.
Rates fr: *£15.00-£15.00.*
Open: All Year (not Xmas)
Beds: 1D 1S **Baths:** 1 Shared
🛏 🄿 (2) ⌷ ⻗ ✕ 📖 ⒱ ▮ ✦

Cleator 6

National Grid Ref: NY0113

¹⁰¹ ◖ Grove Court Hotel

(1m) *Inglenook Cottage, 37 Main Street, Cleator, Cumbria, CA23 3BU.*
Modernised clean, comfortable cottage. Every facility
Tel: **01946 813156** Mrs Bradshaw.
Rates fr: *£14.50-£14.50.*
Open: All Year (not Xmas)
Beds: 1D 1T 1S **Baths:** 1 Shared
🛏 🄿 (2) ⌷ ⻗ 📖 ▮ ✦

Ennerdale Bridge 7

National Grid Ref: NY0715

(1.5m) *The Shepherds Arms Hotel, Ennerdale Bridge, Cleator, Cumbria, CA23 3AR.*
Grades: ETB 3 Cr, Comm
Tel: **01946 861249** (also fax no)
Mr Stanfield.
Rates fr: *£26.00-£26.00.*
Open: All Year **Beds:** 3D 4T 1S
Baths: 6 Ensuite 2 Private
🛏 🄿 (6) ⌷ ⻗ ✕ 📖 ⒱ ▮ ✦
A small friendly hotel, in the Lake District National Park, now under new management and completely refurbished, real ales, restaurant, bar meals, open fires

Mockerkin 8

National Grid Ref: NY0923

(▲ On route) *Swallow Camping Barn, Waterend, Mockerkin, Cockermouth, Cumbria*
Actual grid ref: NY116226
Adults: £3.35+
In picturesque valley of Loweswater, on a 200-acre working farm. Permits for fishing and boat hire on Loweswater available. ADVANCE BOOKING ESSENTIAL

Loweswater 9

National Grid Ref: NY1420

⊪ ⊠ Kirkstile, Wheatsheaf

(1m) *Brook Farm, Loweswater, Cockermouth, Cumbria, CA13 0RP.*
Quiet comfortable farmhouse, working farm
Grades: ETB 1 Cr, Comm
Tel: 01900 85606 (also fax no)
Mrs Hayton.
Rates fr: *£18.00-£18.00.*
Open: May to Oct
Beds: 1F 1D
Baths: 1 Shared
⌂ ⊠ (3) ⌁ ⊟ ⊠ ✕ ⓘ ⚡

Lorton 10

National Grid Ref: NY1525

⊪ ⊠ Wheatsheaf Inn

(0.5m) *Owl Brook, Whinlatter Pass, High Lorton, Lorton, Cockermouth, Cumbria, CA13 9TX.*
Attractive greenslate bungalow
Tel: **01900 85333**
Mrs Roberts.
Rates fr: *£16.50-£16.50.*
Open: All Year
Beds: 3D
Baths: 1 Shared
⌂ (3) ⊠ (3) ⌁ ⊟ ⊩ ✕ ⊞ ⊠

(0.25m) *Meadow Bank, High Lorton, Lorton, Cockermouth, Cumbria, CA13 9UG.*
Modern comfortable private house
Tel: **01900 85315**
Mrs Edmunds.
Rates fr: *£15.00-£16.00.*
Open: All Year (not Xmas)
Beds: 1T 2D
Baths: 1 Shared
⌂ (4) ⊠ (3) ⌁ ⊟ ⊞ ⊠ ⓘ ⚡

(0.25m) *The Old Vicarage, Church Lane, Lorton, Cockermouth, Cumbria, CA13 9UN.*
Victorian house in wooded grounds
Tel: **01900 85656**
Mrs Dobbie.
Rates fr: *£19.00-£19.00.*
Open: All Year
Beds: 2D 1T
Baths: 2 Private 1 Shared
⌂ (12) ⊠ (6) ⊟ ⊞ ⓘ ⚡

Thornthwaite 11

National Grid Ref: NY2225

⊪ ⊠ Swan Hotel

(On route) *Swan Hotel, Thornthwaite, Keswick, Cumbria, CA12 5SQ.*
Former C17th coaching inn
Tel: **017687 78256**
Mr & Mrs Harrison.
Rates fr: *£23.70-£23.70.*
Open: Easter to Nov
Beds: 7D 4T 2S
Baths: 9 Private 2 Shared
⌂ ⊠ ⊟ ⊩ ✕ ⊠

(0.25m) *Jenkin Hill Cottage, Thornthwaite, Keswick, Cumbria, CA12 5SG.*
Highly Commended country establishment
Grades: ETB Listed, High Comm
Tel: **017687 78443** Mr McMullan.
Rates fr: *£18.00-£26.00.*
Open: All Year (not Xmas)
Beds: 2D 1T
Baths: 3 Private
⌂ (13) ⊠ (5) ⌁ ⊟ ⊞ ⊠

Braithwaite 12

National Grid Ref: NY2323

⊪ ⊠ Middle Ruddings Hotel, Coledale Inn

(0.5m) *Cottage In The Wood Hotel, Whinlatter Pass, Braithwaite, Keswick, Cumbria, CA12 5TW.*
Tel: **017687 78409** Mrs Littlefair.
Rates fr: *£25.50-£25.50.*
Open: Mar to Nov
Beds: 6D 1T
Baths: 7 Private
⌂ (5) ⊠ (15) ⌁ ⊩ ✕ ⊞ ⊠ ⚡
Superb location in the Whinlatter Forest Park. Wonderful views. Excellent home cooking in idyllic surroundings. Log fires. Very well appointed bedrooms. 2 four poster rooms

(On route) *Kendoon, Braithwaite, Keswick, Cumbria, CA12 5RY.*
Panoramic views. Good food and drying facilities. Lockable bicycle shed. Tel. in advance outside school holidays
Grades: ETB Listed, Approv
Tel: **017687 78430**
Mrs Jackson.
Rates fr: *£13.50-£14.50.*
Open: All Year (not Xmas)
Beds: 1D 2T
Baths: 2 Shared
⌂ ⊠ (3) ⌁ ⊟ ⊩ ✕ ⊞ ⊠ ⓘ ⚡

(0.25m) *Coledale Inn, Braithwaite, Keswick, Cumbria, CA12 5TN.*
Large Georgian/Victorian family inn. Superb mountain views. Real ales
Grades: ETB 3 Cr, Comm
Tel: **017687 78272** Mr Mawdsley.
Rates fr: *£25.00-£20.00.*
Open: All Year
Beds: 4F 6D 1T 1S
Baths: 12 Private
⌂ ⊠ (15) ⊟ ⊩ ✕ ⊞ ⓘ ⚡

(0.25m) *Thelmlea Country Guest House, Braithwaite, Keswick, Cumbria, CA12 5TD.*
Country house in picturesque Lakeland village
Grades: ETB 3 Cr
Tel: **017687 78305** Mrs Robinson.
Rates fr: *£16.00-£16.00.*
Open: All Year
Beds: 2D 1T
Baths: 3 Ensuite
⌂ (2) ⊠ (8) ⊟ ⊩ ⊞ ⊠ ⓘ ⚡

Keswick 13

National Grid Ref: NY2623

⊪ ⊠ Four in Hand, Skiddaw Hotel, Dog & Gun, Golden Lion, Oddfellows Arms, Lakes Inn

(▲ 0.5m) *Keswick Youth Hostel, Station Road, Keswick, Cumbria, CA12 5LH.*
Actual grid ref: NY267235
Warden: Mr C Williams & Ms H Swatton.
Tel: **017687 72484**
Under 18: £6.55 **Adults:** £9.75
Evening Meals Available (7pm), Family Bunk Rooms, Games Room, Grounds Available for Games, Showers, Central Heating, Parking, Laundry Facilities
Standing above the River Greta, this hostel is ideally placed in Keswick - the northern hub of the Lake District - for superb views across the park to Skiddaw

(On route) *Easedale Hotel, Southey Street, Keswick, Cumbria, CA12 4EG.*
Grades: AA 2 Q
Tel: **017687 72710**
Mr Barraclough.
Fax no: **017687 71127**
Rates fr: *£15.00-£15.00.*
Open: All Year
Beds: 3F4D 2T 1S
Baths: 3 Private 2 Shared
⌂ ⊟ ✕ ⊞ ⊠
Owner-managed, hotel with emphasis on comfort, cleanliness. Good food and warm welcome. Close to town centre, yet easy access to walking routes

(0.5m) *Glaramara Guest House, 9 Acorn Street, Keswick, Cumbria, CA12 4EA.*
Actual grid ref: NY269232
Cosy family B&B. Good food, central, bike hire, C2C transport/storage
Tel: **017687 73216 / 75255**
Mrs Harbage (BHSII).
Fax no: 017687 73216
Rates fr: *£15.00-£15.00.*
Open: All Year
Beds: 2F 1D 1T 1S
Baths: 2 Private 2 Shared
⌂ ⊠ (3) ⌁ ⊟ ⊩ ⊞ ⊠ ⓘ

(0.5m) *The Paddock Guest House, Wordsworth Street, Keswick, Cumbria, CA12 4HU.*
Grades: ETB 2 Cr, Comm
Tel: **017687 72510**
Rates fr: *£16.00-£18.00.*
Open: All Year (not Xmas)
Beds: 1F 1T 4D
Baths: 3 Ensuite 3 Shared
⌂ ⊠ (5) ⊟ ⊩ ⊞ ⊠ ⓘ ⚡
Charming and friendly guesthouse offering comfortable bed and breakfast quietly yet conveniently situated close to 2 beautiful parks, lake and town centre

Braithwaite to Penrith

Two miles beyond **Braithwaite** you come to Portinscale, a village fringed by woodland on the banks of **Derwent Water**. From Nichol End, just off your road into the village, there is a boat service on this attractive lake. From Portinscale the route takes you into **Keswick**, the principal (and very popular) town of the northern Lake District. The town has been a major tourist centre since Victorian times, and its buildings date mostly from this period. Attractions include the Cumberland Pencil Museum, harking back to the days when Borrowdale graphite was the draughtsman's favourite substance; the *Beatrix Potter's Lake District* multimedia experience; and the Museum and Art Gallery, most notable for its manuscript collection featuring Wordsworth, Southey et al. Your road east from Keswick takes you (steeply) past Castlerigg Stone Circle, a neolithic site whose fantastic location sets it apart from those in Wiltshire. From here it's on to Threlkeld, below **Blencathra**, and then Troutbeck, before leaving the National Park and heading on to Greystoke and Little Blencow. From here you can make a detour to Hutton-in-the-Forest, a magnificent house built around a thirteenth-century tower, with an attractive eighteenth-century walled garden. From Little Blencow you come to **Penrith**, an attractive old town built of red sandstone, as is its ruined fourteenth-century castle. From Penrith there is a link route via Skelton, Stockdalewath on the Roe Beck and Dalston in the Caldew Valley to **Carlisle**, where you can join the *Sustrans Carlisle-Inverness* route.

(0.5m) *Dalkeith House,*
1 Leonards Street, Keswick,
Cumbria, CA12 4EJ.
Tel: **017687 72696** (also fax no)
Mr & Mrs Marsden.
Rates fr: £16.00-**£16.00**.
Open: All Year (not Xmas/New Year)
Beds: 4D 2T 1S
Baths: 4 Ensuite 1 Shared
🛏 🏠 🗙 🎤 🛍 ☑ ♦ ⚡
Comfortable Victorian guest house close to walking routes, park, shops and the Lake. You are assured a warm, friendly welcome and excellent home cooked food

(0.5m) *Century House, 17 Church Street, Keswick, Cumbria, CA12 4DT.*
Spotless Victorian Guesthouse, offering friendly but unobtrusive hospitality, sumptuous breakfasts
Tel: **017687 72843** North.
Rates fr: £16.50-**£20.00**.
Open: All Year (not Xmas)
Beds: 1F 1T 3D **Baths:** 4 Ensuite
🛏 🏠 🛍 ☑ ♦ ⚡

(0.5m) *Goodwin House, 29 Southey Street, Keswick, Cumbria, CA12 4EE.*
Warm, comfortable and friendly guesthouse, close to all amenities
Grades: AA 4 Q
Tel: **017687 74634** Mr Smith.
Rates fr: £18.00-**£20.00**.
Open: All Year (not Xmas)
Beds: 5D 1S **Baths:** 6 Ensuite
🛒 🏠 🛍 ⚡

(0.5m) *Chaucer House Hotel,*
Ambleside Road, Keswick,
Cumbria, CA12 4DR.
Actual grid ref: NY268232
Grades: ETB 3 Cr, High Comm
Tel: **017687 72318** Mr Pechartscheck.
Rates fr: £29.00-**£29.00**.
Open: Feb to Nov
Beds: 4F 14D 10T 7S
Baths: 32 Private 2 Shared
🛏 🏠 (27) 🗙 🎤 🛍 🍴 ☑ ♦ ⚡
Victorian House hotel close to town centre and lake. Comfortable, homely, warm & friendly atmosphere. Good food to suit all appetites. Four poster. Lift. Free midweek golf, drying room, lock-up bike store

(0.5m) *Portland House, 19 Leonard Street, Keswick, Cumbria, CA12 4EL.*
Comfortable and quiet Edwardian house, short walk from town centre
Grades: ETB Listed, Comm
Tel: **017687 74230**
Rates fr: £18.50-**£28.50**.
Open: All Year (not Xmas)
Beds: 1F 1T 2D 1S
Baths: 5 Ensuite
🛒 (3) 🏠 (3) 🏠 🎤 🛍 🍴 ☑

The lowest *double* rate per person is shown in *italics*.

(0.5m) *Langdale, 14 Leonard Street, Keswick, Cumbria, CA12 4EL.*
Tel: **017687 73977**
Mrs Vickers.
Rates fr: £15.50.
Open: All Year (not Xmas)
Beds: 1T 2D
Baths: 2 Ensuite 1 Shared
🛒 🏠 🛍 ☑
Victorian townhouse, quietly situated, convenient for town, lakes and fells. Cleanliness and good food in comfortable surroundings. Our extensive continental-style breakfast is a speciality

(0.25m) *Cumbria Hotel, 1 Derwentwater PlaceAmbleside Road, Keswick, Cumbria, CA12 4DR.*
Actual grid ref: NY268232
Quiet convenient location, secure cycle storage. So good you'll return!
Grades: ETB 2 Cr, Comm
Tel: **017687 73171** (also fax no)
Mr Colam.
Rates fr: £18.00-**£18.00**.
Open: Feb to Nov
Beds: 1F 3D 1T 3S
Baths: 4 Ensuite 2 Shared
🛒 🏠 (7) 🏠 🎤 🗙 🛍 ☑ ♦ ⚡

(0.5m) *Latrigg House, St Herbert Street, Keswick, Cumbria, CA12 4DF.*
Actual grid ref: NY270233
Quiet, convenient, friendly Victorian house. Excellent home cooking
Grades: ETB 2 Cr, Approv
Tel: **017687 73068**
Mr & Mrs Townsend.
Fax no: 017687 72801
Rates fr: £14.00-**£14.00**.
Open: All Year
Beds: 2F 1D 2T 1S
Baths: 3 Private 1 Shared
🛒 🏠 (1) 🛒 🏠 🗙 🛍 ☑ ♦ ⚡

(0.5m) *Clarence House, 14 Eskin Street, Keswick, Cumbria, CA12 4DQ.*
Superb ensuite accommodation where comfort and cleanliness are guaranteed
Grades: ETB 3 Cr, Comm
Tel: **017687 73186** (also fax no)
Mrs Raine.
Rates fr: £19.00-**£19.00**.
Open: All Year (not Xmas)
Beds: 1F 4D 3T 1S
Baths: 9 Private
🛒 (5) 🛒 🏠 🗙 🛍 ♦ ⚡

(On route) *Dolly Waggon Guest House, 17 Helvellyn Street, Keswick, Cumbria, CA12 4EN.*
Actual grid ref: NY269233
Friendly 'home from home' guest house. Walkers welcome. Own keys
Grades: ETB 2 Cr, Approv
Tel: **017687 73593**
Mrs Osborn.
Rates fr: £19.00-**£19.00**.
Open: All Year
Beds: 1F 4D 1T
Baths: 6 Private
🛒 (7) 🛒 🏠 🛍 ☑ ♦ ⚡

(0.5m) *Melbreak House,*
29 Church Strett, Keswick,
Cumbria, CA12 4DX.
Close to town centre. Arrive a
guest - leave as a friend
Tel: **017687 73398**
Mr & Mrs Hardman.
Rates fr: *£17.00-£17.00*.
Open: All Year
Beds: 3F 6D 1T 1S
Baths: 10 Ensuite
ॐ ⊭ ❑ ★ ✕ 🕮 🖤 ⊀

(0.5m) *Derwentdale Guest Hotel, 8*
Blencathra Street, Keswick,
Cumbria, CA12 4HU.
Friendly, family-run guest house
close to lake and parks
Grades: ETB Listed, Comm
Tel: **017687 74187** Mrs Riding.
Rates fr: *£15.00-£15.50*.
Open: All Year
Beds: 3D 1T 2S
Baths: 3 Ensuite
ॐ (10) ⊭ ❑ ✕ 🕮 🖤 ⬛

(0.25m) *Beckside, 5 Wordsworth*
Street, Keswick, Cumbria, CA12 4HU.
Actual grid ref: NY270235
Quality Ensuite accommodation.
Hearty breakfasts. Close to all
amenities
Grades: ETB 2 Cr, AA 3 Q,
RAC High Acclaim
Tel: **017687 73093**
Mr & Mrs Helling.
Rates fr: *£18.00-£22.00*.
Open: All Year
Beds: 3D 1T
Baths: 4 Private
ॐ ⊭ ❑ ✕ 🕮 🖤 ⬛ ⊀

Threlkeld   14

National Grid Ref: NY3125

(1m) *Scales Farm, Threlkeld,*
Keswick, Cumbria, CA12 4SY.
Picturesque, accessible, comfort-
able & welcoming
Grades: ETB 3 Cr, High Comm
Tel: **017687 79660** Mr Appleton.
Rates fr: *£21.00-£26.00*.
Open: All Year (not Xmas)
Beds: 1F 3D 1T
Baths: 5 Ensuite
ॐ 🅿 (6) ❑ ★ 🕮

Matterdale End   15

National Grid Ref: NY3824

🍴 🍺 Troutbeck Inn, Royal
Dockray

(3m) *Low Birch Close, Matterdale,*
Matterdale End, Penrith, Cumbria,
CA11 0RZ.
Comfortable, 'home from home'
farmhouse
Tel: **017684 83812**
Mrs Edmondson.
Rates fr: *£15.00-£15.00*.
Open: All Year
Beds: 2D
Baths: 1 Shared
ॐ 🅿 (3) ❑ ★ 🕮 🖤 ⬛ ⊀

Motherby   16

National Grid Ref: NY4228

🍴 🍺 Herdwick Inn

(1.5m) *Motherby House,*
Motherby, Penrith, Cumbria,
CA11 0RJ.
Homely, and muddy boots
welcome
Tel: **017684 83368**
Fax no: 01768 899501
Rates fr: *£15.50-£15.50*.
Open: All Year (not Xmas)
Beds: 2F
Baths: 2 Shared
ॐ 🅿 (4) ✕ 🕮 🖤 ⬛ ⊀

Greystoke   17

National Grid Ref: NY4430

🍴 🍺 Clickham Inn

(0.25m) *Lattendales Farm,*
Greystoke, Penrith, Cumbria,
CA11 0UE.
Comfortable C17th farmhouse
Tel: **017684 83474**
Mrs Ashburner.
Rates fr: *£15.00-£15.50*.
Open: Mar to Oct
Beds: 2D 1T
Baths: 1 Shared
ॐ (1) 🅿 (4) ⊭ ❑ ★ 🕮

Ellonby   18

National Grid Ref: NY4235

🍴 🍺 Dog & Gun

(2.5m) *Greenfields, Ellonby,*
Penrith, Cumbria, CA11 9SJ.
Highly commended comfortable
home. Easy access Northern Lakes,
Scottish Border
Grades: ETB Listed, High Comm
Tel: **01768 484671**
Mrs Green.
Rates fr: *£18.00-£18.00*.
Open: March to Oct
Beds: 2D 1S
Baths: 1 Shared
ॐ (8) 🅿 (3) ⊭ ❑ ✕ 🕮 🖤

Newton Reigny   19

National Grid Ref: NY4731

🍴 🍺 The Sun Inn

(0.5m) *Croft House, Newton*
Reigny, Penrith, Cumbria, CA11 0AY.
Georgian family house, 8 acres,
horses, ducks, hens; overlooking
Lakeland Fells
Grades: ETB 2 Cr, Comm
Tel: **01768 865535**
Mr Farncombe.
Fax no: 01768 865435
Rates fr: *£18.00-£25.00*.
Open: Easter to Oct
Beds: 1F 3D 1S
Baths: 2 Ensuite 1 Private
ॐ 🅿 (8) ⊭ ❑ 🕮 🖤

(On route) *The Sun Inn, Newton*
Reigny, Penrith, Cumbria, CA11 0AP.
Traditional village inn adjacent M6
Tel: **01768 867055** Mr Watts.
Rates fr: *£20.00-£18.00*.
Open: All Year
Beds: 2D 1T 1S
Baths: 2 Ensuite 2 Shared
ॐ 🅿 ⊭ ❑ ✕ 🕮 🖤

Penrith   20

National Grid Ref: NY5130

🍴 🍺 Two Lions, Royal Hotel,
Lowther Arms, Cross Keys, Dog &
Duck, Beacon Inn

(On route) *Norcroft Guest House,*
Graham Street, Penrith, Cumbria,
CA11 9LQ.
Grades: ETB 3 Cr, Comm
Tel: **01768 862365** (also fax no)
Mr Bray.
Rates fr: *£16.00-£21.50*.
Open: All Year (not Xmas)
Beds: 2F 2D 4T 1S
Baths: 6 Ensuite 1 Shared
ॐ 🅿 (7) ❑ ✕ 🕮 🖤
A special welcome awaits you in
our charming Victorian house.
Large comfortable ensuite bed-
rooms with colour TV, beverage
making facilities, spacious dining
room. Secure parking

(On route) *Albany House, 5*
Portland Place, Penrith, Cumbria,
CA11 7QN.
Friendly, comfortable Victorian
house. Good breakfast. 5 mins,
town centre
Grades: ETB Listed, Comm
Tel: **01768 863072** Mrs Blundell.
Rates fr: *£16.50-£20.00*.
Open: All Year
Beds: 4F 1D
Baths: 1 Private 2 Shared
ॐ 🅿 (1) ❑ 🕮 🖤

(On route) *The Friarage,*
Friargate, Penrith, Cumbria,
CA11 7XR.
Clean, comfortable historical
house. Ideal North/South,
East/West travellers
Tel: **01768 863635**
Mrs Clark.
Rates fr: *£15.00-£17.00*.
Open: Easter to Sept
Beds: 1D 1T 1S
Baths: 2 Shared
ॐ 🅿 (3) ❑ ★ 🕮 🖤 ⊀

(On route) *Grosvenor House,*
3 Lonsdale Terrace, Meeting
House Lane, Penrith, Cumbria,
CA11 7TS.
Large, comfortable terraced house;
good base for touring Lake District
Tel: **01768 863813**
Mrs Fitzpatrick.
Rates fr: *£14.00-£20.00*.
Open: Mar to Nov
Beds: 1D 1T
Baths: 1 Shared
ॐ ⊭ ❑ ★ 🖤 ⬛

Penrith to Consett

The route out of **Penrith** heads northeastwards to **Langwathby** in the Eden Valley, and on to **Little Salkeld**. Close to here stand Long Meg and Her Daughters, a late neolithic stone circle - Long Meg herself stands 18 feet high and is named from her eerily humanoid profile. From here you head onto Viol Moor, from where you make the climb to **Hartside**, where there is a cafe during the summer months with a spectacular panorama. There is a great deal of up-and-down in the route through the Pennines, which takes you to **Garrigill** on the River South Tyne, on to **Nenthead** and up to Black Hill on the county boundary, the highest point on the route. From here you descend through Northumberland over Coalcleugh Moor and Allendale Common to **Allenheads**. Now you enter County Durham and follow the Rookhope Burn stream down to **Rookhope**, from where there is a brief steep climb to the start of the Waskerley Way, a reclaimed railway path, which you follow down to **Consett**.

(0.5m) *Greystones, Brent Road,
Penrith, Cumbria, CA11 8AN.*
Small, friendly, comfortable.
Convenient M6
Tel: **01768 867340** Mrs Martin.
Rates fr: £16.00-£16.00.
Open: All Year
Beds: 1D 1T 1S **Baths:** 2S
⏰ 🅿 (3) ⅍ ⛴ 🛏 📺

(0.5m) *Corner House, 36 Victoria
Road, Penrith, Cumbria, CA11 8HR.*
Relaxed, comfortable, homely
atmosphere
Tel: **01768 863566** Miss Robinson.
Rates fr: £15.00-£20.00.
Open: Mar to Nov
Beds: 2D 1T **Baths:** 1 Shared
⏰ 🅿 (3) ⛴ 🛏 ✕ 🛏 📺

(0.5m) *Barco House, Carleton
Road, Penrith, Cumbria, CA11 8LR.*
Victorian house with parking
Tel: **01768 863176** Mrs Stockdale.
Rates fr: £16.00-£18.00.
Open: All Year
Beds: 2F 1T
⏰ 🅿 (8) ⅍ 🛏 ✕ 🛏 📺

(0.5m) *Beacon Bank Hotel,
Beacon Edge, Penrith, Cumbria,
CA11 7BD.*
Beautiful sandstone private hotel,
quiet
Grades: ETB 4 Cr, High Comm
Tel: **01768 862633** Mrs Black.
Rates fr: £20.00-£29.00.
Open: All Year
Beds: 2F 2D 2T 2S
Baths: 8 Private
⏰ 🅿 (10) ⅍ ⛴ ✕ 🛏 📺

Yanwath 21

National Grid Ref: NY5128
🍽 🍺 Gate Inn

(2m) *Gate Farm, Yanwath,
Penrith, Cumbria, CA10 2LF.*
Comfortable C17th farmhouse.
Good food
Tel: **01768 864459**
Mr & Mrs Donnelly.
Rates fr: £16.00-£16.00.
Open: All Year
Beds: 1F 2D 1T
Baths: 1 Ensuite
⏰ (0) 🅿 (10) ⅍ ⛴ ✕ 🛏 ♿ 📺

Langwathby 22

National Grid Ref: NY5733
🍽 🍺 Shepherds Inn

(0.25m) *Langstanes, Culgaith
Road, Langwathby, Penrith,
Cumbria, CA10 1NA.*
Actual grid ref: NY573336
Tel: **01768 881004** (also fax no)
Mr Granett.
Rates fr: £16.00-£16.00.
Open: All Year (not Xmas)
Beds: 1T 2D
Baths: 3 Ensuite
🅿 (3) ⛴ 🛏 📺 ♿ ⅍
Cumbrian sandstone house on edge
of quiet village. All rooms centrally
heated with beverage-making
facilities & colour TV

Melmerby 23

National Grid Ref: NY6137

(3m) *Gale Hall Farm, Melmerby,
Penrith, Cumbria, CA10 1HN.*
Large comfortable farmhouse near
Pennines and Lake District
Tel: **01768 881254**
Mrs Toppin.
Rates fr: £15.00-£15.00.
Open: Jun to Nov
Beds: 1F 1D 1S
Baths: 1 Shared
⏰ 🅿 (3) ⛴ 🛏 📺

Alston 24

National Grid Ref: NY7146
🍽 🍺 Blue Bell Inn, Angel Inn,
Turk's Head

(▲ 2m) *Alston Youth Hostel, The
Firs, Alston, Cumbria, CA9 3RW.*
Actual grid ref: NY717461
Warden: Mr R Richardson.
Tel: **01434 381509**
Under 18: £5.40
Adults: £8.00
Evening Meals Available (7pm),
Family Bunk Rooms, Showers,
Shop
*Purpose-built hostel overlooking
River South Tyne, on outskirts of
Alston, the highest market town in
England*

(2m) *Blue Bell Inn, Townfoot,
Alston, Cumbria, CA9 3RN.*
Tel: **01434 381566**
Rates fr: £14.00-£14.00.
Open: All Year (not Xmas)
Beds: 1T 3D 1S
Baths: 1 Shared
⏰ 🅿 (8) ⛴ 🛏 🛏 ♿ ◈
Bluebell Inn. At foot of town.
Alston ideal for walkers, cyclists
alike. Early C17th Inn. Many
original beams. Ask to see the
stone arch behind the bar

(0.75m) *Bridge End Farm, Alston,
Cumbria, CA9 3BJ.*
C18th farmhouse. Home cooking.
Generous breakfast. Warm
welcome awaits
Tel: **01434 381261** Mrs Williams.
Rates fr: £15.50-£17.50.
Open: All Year **Beds:** 2D 1T
Baths: 1 Private 1 Shared
⏰ (1) 🅿 (4) ⅍ ⛴ 🛏 ✕ 🛏 📺 ♿ ⅍

(On route) *Nentholme, The Butts,
Alston, Cumbria, CA9 3JQ.*
Actual grid ref: NY719467
Quiet location, 1 min walk from
town. Cycle hire, repairs on
C2C/Pennine Way route
Grades: ETB 2 Cr, Comm
Tel: **01434 381523** (also fax no)
Mrs Thompson.
Rates fr: £15.00-£20.00.
Open: All Year
Beds: 1F 2D 3T 1S
Baths: 2 Ensuite 1 Private
⏰ 🅿 (6) ⅍ ⛴ 🛏 ✕ 🛏 📺 ♿ ⅍

80

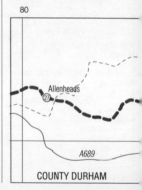

(2m) *Harbut Law, Brampton Road, Alston, Cumbria, CA9 3BD*.
Actual grid ref: NY708471
Large Victorian former farmhouse
Tel: **01434 381950** Mrs Younger.
Rates fr: *£14.00-£14.00*.
Open: All Year **Beds:** 2D 1T
Baths: 1 Private 2 Shared
☼ ▣ (5) ▢ ▥ Ⓥ ⋔ ✦

(2m) *Middle Bayles Farm, Penrith Road, Alston, Cumbria, CA9 3BS*.
Actual grid ref: NY747408
Former C18th country hunting lodge
Grades: ETB 2 Cr, Comm
Tel: **01434 381383** Mrs Dent.
Rates fr: *£16.00-£19.00*.
Open: All Year (not Xmas)
Beds: 1F 1D 1T **Baths:** 2 Private
☼ ▣ (4) ✂ ▢ ✕ ▥ Ⓥ ⋔

Garrigill 25

National Grid Ref: NY7441
†●† ◗ George & Dragon

(On route) *Ivy House Farm, Garrigill, Alston, Cumbria, CA9 3DU*.
Actual grid ref: NY744414
Historic C17th farmhouse high in unspoilt North Pennines, perfect for walking. **Grades:** AA 2 Q
Tel: **01434 382501** (also fax no)
Mrs Wells.
Rates fr: *£15.00-£15.00*.
Open: All Year (not Xmas)
Beds: 1F 1D 1T 2S
Baths: 1 Shared
☼ ▣ (10) ✂ ▢ ⋔ ✕ ▥ Ⓥ ⋔ ✦

(On route) *The Post Office, Garrigill, Alston, Cumbria, CA9 3DS*.
C17th village post office
Tel: **01434 381257**
Mrs Bramwell.
Rates fr: *£14.00-£14.00*.
Open: Easter to Oct
Beds: 2D 1T 1S
Baths: 1 Shared
☼ ▣ ✂ ▢ ⋔ ▥ Ⓥ ⋔ ✦

Nenthead 26

National Grid Ref: NY7843
†●† ◗ Miners' Arms, Crown Inn

(0.25m) *Cherry Tree, Nenthead, Alston, Cumbria, CA9 3PD*.
Stone-built farm cottages with modern amenities
Tel: **01434 381434**
Mrs Sherlock.
Rates fr: *£15.00-£15.00*.
Open: All Year (not Xmas)
Beds: 2F 2D 1T
☼ (13) ▣ (6) ▢ ✕ ▥ ⋔ ✦

(0.25m) *The Miners Arms, Nenthead, Alston, Cumbria, CA9 3PF*.
Homely family pub
Tel: **01434 381427** Miss Clark.
Rates fr: *£15.00-£15.00*.
Open: All Year
Beds: 1F 1D 1T
Baths: 1 Shared
☼ ▣ ✂ ▢ ⋔ ✕ ▥ Ⓥ

Allenheads 27

National Grid Ref: NY8545

(On route) *The Allenheads Inn, Allenheads, Hexham, Northd, NE47 9HJ*.
Eccentric, entertaining and high standards
Tel: **01434 685200** Mrs Stenson.
Rates fr: *£21.50-£21.50*.
Open: All Year
Beds: 5D 3T **Baths:** 8 Private
▣ (10) ▢ ⋔ ✕ ▥ Ⓥ ⋔

Stanhope 28

National Grid Ref: NY9939
†●† ◗ Queen's Head, Stanhope Old Hall

(2m) *Redlodge Cottage, 2 Market Place, Stanhope, Bishop Auckland, Co Durham, DL13 2UN*.
Well-appointed guest house
Tel: **01388 527851**
Mr & Mrs Hamilton.
Rates fr: *£17.00-£22.50*.
Open: All Year **Beds:** 2F 1D 1T
Baths: 1 Private 1 Shared
☼ ▣ (2) ▢ ⋔ ▥ Ⓥ ✦

The *lowest* **single** rate *is shown in* **bold.**

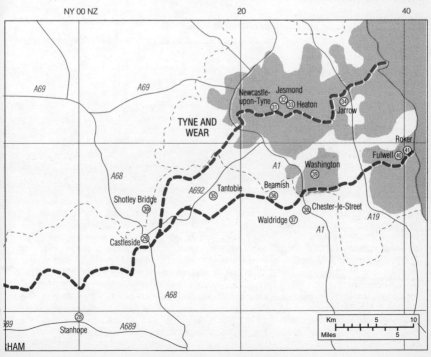

Castleside   29
National Grid Ref: NZ0848

(0.25m) *Bee Cottage Farm,*
Castleside, Consett, Co Durham,
DH8 9HW.
Actual grid ref: NZ070453
Lovely views, peaceful walks,
ideally situated Durham, Beamish
Museum, Metrocentre
Grades: ETB 2 Cr, High Comm
Tel: 01207 508224 Mrs Lawson.
Rates fr: *£22.00-£25.00.*
Open: All Year
Beds: 4F 3D 2T 1S
Baths: 5 Ensuite 2 Shared
🛇 🅿 (20) 🗇 ⊁ ⊓ ⭗ ✕ ▥ ♥ Ⓥ ▮

(1m) *Castlenook Guest House,*
18 Front Street, Castleside,
Consett, Co Durham, DH8 9AR.
C16th hostelry, castleside village
centre
Tel: 01207 506634 Mrs Stafford.
Rates fr: *£15.00-£20.00.*
Open: All Year (not Xmas)
Beds: 1D 2T 1S   **Baths:** 3 Private
🛇 🅿 (5) 🗇 ⊓ ▥ Ⓥ

Shotley Bridge   30
National Grid Ref: NZ0852

(0.5m) *Crown & Crossed Swords*
Hotel, Shotley Bridge, Consett,
Co Durham, DH8 0NH.
Historical country hotel
Tel: 01207 502006 Mrs Suddick.
Rates fr: *£18.00-£23.00.*
Open: All Year
Beds: 1F 4D 4T 1S
Baths: 4 Private 2 Shared
🛇 🅿 (40) 🗇 ⊓ ✕ ▥ Ⓥ

Newcastle-upon-Tyne   31
National Grid Ref: NZ2564

⋔ ◨ Prince of Wales

(▲ 1m) *Newcastle upon Tyne*
Youth Hostel, 107 Jesmond Road,
Newcastle-upon-Tyne. NE2 1NJ.
Actual grid ref: NZ257656
Warden: Mr L Heslop.
Tel: 0191 281 2570
Under 18: £5.95 **Adults:** £8.80
Evening Meals Available (7pm),
Self-catering Facilities, Family
Bunk Rooms, Games Room, Shop,
Parking
A large town house conveniently
located for the centre of this
vibrant city, the regional capital of
the North East

(1m) *Chirton House Hotel,*
46 Clifton Road, Newcastle-upon-
Tyne. NE4 6SH.
Large Victorian private house
Grades: ETB 3 Cr
Tel: 0191 273 0407 Mr Hagerty.
Rates fr: *£17.50-£25.00.*
Open: All Year
Beds: 3F 2D 3T 3S
Baths: 5 Ensuite 2 Shared
🛇 🅿 🗇 ⊓ ✕ ▥ Ⓥ ⊀

> Please respect
> a B&B's wishes
> regarding children,
> animals & smoking.

Jesmond   32
National Grid Ref: NZ2566

(2m) *Dene Hotel, 38-42 Grosvenor*
Road, Jesmond, Newcastle-upon-
Tyne. NE2 2RP.
Situated in quiet area of Jesmond,
only 4 minutes city centre,
University & shopping
Grades: ETB 3 Cr, Comm
Tel: 0191 281 1502 Mr Venayak.
Fax no: 0191 281 8110
Rates fr: *£23.75-£25.50.*
Open: All Year
Beds: 3F 5D 3T 12S
Baths: 11 Ensuite 12 Private
🛇 🅿 🗇 ✕ ▥ ⬛ Ⓥ ▮ ⊀

(2m) *Hansen Hotel, 131 Sandyford*
Road, Jesmond, Newcastle-upon-
Tyne. NE2 1QR.
Homely family business near town
Tel: 0191 281 0289 Miss Hansen.
Rates fr: *£17.00-£18.00.*
Open: All Year (not Xmas)
Beds: 2F 1T 8S   **Baths:** 4 Shared
🛇 ⊁ 🗇 ▥ Ⓥ

Heaton   33
National Grid Ref: NZ2766

⋔ ◨ Corner House

(2m) *Holly Guesthouse, 188*
Heaton Park Road, Heaton,
Newcastle-upon-Tyne. NE6 5AP.
Comfortable family-run guest
house. **Grades:** ETB Listed
Tel: 0191 265 6933
Mrs Richardson.
Rates fr: *£16.00-£16.50.*
Open: All Year
Beds: 1F 1T 1S   **Baths:** 1 Shared
🛇 (3) 🗇 ▥ Ⓥ ▮

Consett to Tynemonth or Sunderland

From Consett the northern route passes close to the impressively complete Derwentcote Steel Furnace (just beyond **Hamsterley**), a remnant of the Industrial Revolution; and follows the Derwent to the Tyne, which it crosses into **Newcastle**. The capital of the Northeast was built on coal and shipbuilding, rising to a position of importance in the nineteenth century. Sights from the earlier centuries of the city's history include the twelfth-century castle from which it gets its name, and the cathedral, notable for its fifteenth-century lantern tower. The Laing Gallery is the region's foremost art gallery, including a major display of British art. Newcastle's material icon is the Tyne Bridge, the great steel arch whose famous daughter spans Sydney Harbour. You get a view of the bridge to your left as the cycle route crosses the Tyne into Gateshead over the Swing Bridge. From here you head east to **Jarrow**, famed for the 1936 hunger march, where you cross the Tyne again through the pedestrian tunnel, and reach the North Sea at **Tynemouth**

The southern route out of Consett takes you to **Stanley**, and the Beamish Museum beyond. This is a large open-air re-creation of early twentieth-century life in the region, including tours of a reopened drift mine, a period High Street, a train station and a farmyard with rare old breeds of cattle and sheep. The Consett and Sunderland Railway Path takes you to **Chester-le-Street** and **Washington**, where the Old Hall was the ancestral home of the family of the eponymous founder of a certain country. There is also an Arts Centre; and the Washington Wildfowl and Wetlands Centre is east of town. The cycle route east crosses the River Wear over a footbridge to the village of Cox Green and leads into **Sunderland**, another old shipbuilding town. Here you cross back over the Wear into Monkwearmouth, and reach the North Sea by Roker Pier.

Jarrow 34

National Grid Ref: NZ3465

⦿ ◖ Lord Nelson

(0.5m) *148 Bede Burn Road,*
Jarrow, Tyne & Wear, NE32 5AX.
Guest house in famous Jarrow
Tel: **0191 428 4794**
Mr Kelly.
Rates fr: £14.00-£14.00.
Open: All Year
Beds: 1F 1T 1S 1D
Baths: 1Shared
◻ ▥

Tantobie 35

National Grid Ref: NZ1754

(2m) *Oak Tree Inn, Tantobie,*
Stanley, Co Durham, DH9 9RF.
Victorian inn with good restaurant
Grades: ETB 3 Cr
Tel: **01207 235445**
Mr & Mrs Plych.
Rates fr: £23.00-£23.00.
Open: All Year
Beds: 3D 1T 1S
Baths: 5 Ensuite 1 Shared
❧ (2) ▣ (12) ◻ ☏ ✕ ▥ ㊓ Ⓥ ▮

Beamish 36

National Grid Ref: NZ2253

⦿ ◖ Beamish Mary Inn

(0.25m) *No Place House, Beamish,*
Stanley, Co Durham, DH9 0QH.
Converted co-operative store, half
a mile from Beamish Museum
Grades: ETB 2 Cr, Comm
Tel: **0191 370 0891**
Mr & Mrs Wood.
Rates fr: £17.00-£17.00.
Open: All Year
Beds: 2D 1T
Baths: 2 Ensuite 1 Shared
❧ (3) ▣ (5) ◻ ☏ ▥ Ⓥ

Waldridge 37

National Grid Ref: NZ2550

⦿ ◖ Waldridge Tavern, Chester
Moor

(2m) *Waldridge Fell House,*
Waldridge Lane, Waldridge,
Chester-le-Street, Co Durham,
DH2 3RY.
Converted village chapel with
panoramic views and country
walks. Private parking
Grades: ETB 2 Cr, High Comm
Tel: **0191 389 1908** Mrs Sharratt.
Rates fr: £19.00-£23.00.
Open: All Year (not Xmas)
Beds: 5F
Baths: 1 Private 1 Shared
❧ ▣ (8) ◻ ☏ ▥ ㊓ Ⓥ

Chester-le-Street 38

National Grid Ref: NZ2751

⦿ ◖ Chester Moor, Waldridge
Tavern

(1.5m) *16 St Cuthberts Avenue,*
Holmlands Park, Chester-le-Street,
Co Durham, DH3 3PS.
Private house near Lumley Castle.
Extremely close to cricket grounds
Tel: **0191 387 3071** Mrs McCann.
Rates fr: £34.00-£17.00.
Open: All Year (not Xmas)
Beds: 1D 1S
Baths: 1 Shared
❧ (8) ▣ (2) ◻ ✕ ▥

The lowest *double*

rate per person is

shown in *italics*.

Washington 39

National Grid Ref: NZ3157

⦿ ◖ Cross Keys

(1.5m) *Village Farmhouse, Village*
Lane, Washington, Tyne & Wear,
NE38 7HS.
Actual grid ref: NZ311564
Full English breakfasts. Central
location. Ideal base for business
and touring
Grades: ETB 3 Cr, Comm
Tel: **0191 415 3355** (also fax no)
Mr Bloss.
Rates fr: £20.00-£25.00.
Open: All Year
Beds: 3F 4D 1T 2S
Baths: 4 Ensuite 1 Private 2 Shared
❧ ▣ (10) ◻ ☏ ✕ ▥ ㊓ Ⓥ ▮ ✦

Fulwell 40

National Grid Ref: NZ3957

⦿ ◖ New Derby

(2m) *Bed & Breakfast Stop,*
183 Newcastle Road, Fulwell,
Sunderland, Tyne & Wear, SR5 1NR.
Tudor-style, semi-detached
Grades: ETB 1 Cr, Comm
Tel: **0191 548 2291** Mrs Starr.
Rates fr: £13.00-£15.00.
Open: All Year
Beds: 1F 1T 1S **Baths:** 1 Shared
❧ (3) ▣ (3) ⅍ ◻ ✕ ▥

Roker 41

National Grid Ref: NZ4059

(1m) *8 St Georges Terrace, Roker,*
Sunderland, Tyne & Wear, SR6 9LX.
Small, friendly family-run guest
house. **Grades:** ETB 1 Cr
Tel: **0191 567 2438** Mr Dawson.
Rates fr: £15.00-£15.00.
Open: All Year
Beds: 4F 1D 1T 1S
Baths: 2 Private 5 Shared
❧ ▣ (3) ◻ ✕ ▥ Ⓥ

Sustrans West Country Way

The **West Country Way** is a recently-opened section of the new National Cycle Network, running on traffic-free paths and traffic-calmed roads from Padstow in Cornwall to Bristol, linking many historic towns in Devon and Somerset and passing through a great deal of this beautiful region's varied countryside, from the open heather-clad elevations of Bodmin Moor and Exmoor to the lowland of the Somerset Levels with its network of canals, which abruptly gives rise to the Mendip Hills. The route is clearly signposted by blue direction signs with a cycle silhouette and the number 3 in a red rectangle. The total distance is 230 miles.

The indispensable **official route map and guide** for the West Country Way is available from Sustrans, 35 King Street, Bristol BS1 4DZ, tel 0117-926 8893, fax 0117-929 4173, @ £5.99 (+ £1.50 p&p).

Maps: Ordnance Survey 1:50,000 Landranger series: 172, 180, 181, 182, 190, 193, 200, 201

Trains: Bristol and Bath are main termini on the Intercity network; Bodmin, Tiverton, Taunton and Bridgwater are main line stations, as is Exeter, from where you can connect to Barnstaple.

Padstow to Camelford

The typical pretty Cornish fishing port of **Padstow** sits enclosed from the Atlantic Ocean by the Camel Estuary. Here you will find the fifteenth-century Church of St Petroc, the Celtic monk who founded the town in the sixth century. The route takes you up the estuary to Wadebridge and then follows the river upstream. From the village of **Dunmere** you can make a detour into Bodmin, the historic county town. Here you will find *another* Church of St Petroc, with an elaborate twelfth-century carved font, and Bodmin Jail, a notorious nineteenth-century death row. Bodmin Town Museum covers archaeology of the town as well as Bodmin Moor. From Dunmere the route follows the Camel Trail through Dunmere Wood before turning off to **Blisland**. Here you head north along quiet roads through the western reaches of **Bodmin Moor**, passing close to remains of some of the Bronze Age settlements which are scattered over the moor. As you near the Camelford turning, you can see rising away to your right Rough Tor, the moor's second highest peak, one of the eroded granite outcrops which make the landscape of Bodmin Moor and Dartmoor so dramatic. There is a designated detour to Camelford, one of the many sole authentic locations of King Arthur's court of Camelot.

Padstow   **1**

National Grid Ref: SW9175

¶⊚ ▣ London Inn, Old Custom House, Golden Lion

(0.25m) *Rosehill, High Street, Padstow, Cornwall, PL28 8BB.*
House where Charles Dickens stayed. Elevated, peaceful, old town location
Tel: **01841 532761** (also fax no) Mrs Meyer.
Rates fr: *£16.00*-**£16.00.**
Open: All Year
Beds: 1T 1D **Baths:** 1 Shared
♿ ▣ ⓥ

(0.25m) *Khandalla, Sarahs Lane, Padstow, Cornwall, PL28 8.*
Large Victorian private house
Grades: ETB Listed
Tel: **01841 532961** Mrs Hair.
Rates fr: *£17.50*-**£18.00.**
Open: All Year
Beds: 1F 1D 1S
Baths: 2 Ensuite 1 Shared
♿ ▣ (3) ⠀ ⠀ ♿ ▥ ⓥ

The lowest *double* rate per

person is shown in *italics.*

The *lowest* **single**

rate *is shown in* **bold.**

(0.25m) *Newlands Hotel, Trevone Bay, Padstow, Cornwall, PL28 8QJ.*
Small licensed hotel
Grades: AA 3 Q, Recomm
Tel: **01841 520469** Mrs Philpott.
Rates fr: *£20.00*-**£18.00.**
Open: All Year
Beds: 1F 6D 3T 1S
Baths: 9 Private 1 Shared
♿ ▣ (15) ⠀ ⠀ ✗ ▥ ⓥ ▮ ⠀

(0.25m) *Cross House Hotel,*
Church Street, Padstow, Cornwall,
PL28 8BG.
Comfortable, friendly, family-run
hotel
Tel: **01841 532391** Miss Gidlow.
Rates fr: *£22.00-£30.00*.
Open: All Year **Beds:** 1F 5D 1T
Baths: 4 Ensuite 3 Shared
☎ (5) ₽ (4) ⌷ ⌷ ⌷ ✕ ⫼ ⫿ ⚿

St Issey 2

National Grid Ref: SW9271

(2m) *Trevorrick Farm, St Issey,*
Wadebridge, Cornwall, PL27 7QH.
Most comfortable, scenically
located farmhouse
Grades: ETB 2 Cr, Comm
Tel: **01841 540574** Mr Mealing.
Rates fr: *£17.50-£17.50*.
Open: All Year
Beds: 2D 1T **Baths:** 3 Ensuite
☎ ₽ (10) ⌷ ⌷ ⌷ ✕ ⫼ ⫿ ⚿

Wadebridge 3

National Grid Ref: SW9872

(0.25m) *Little Pound, Bodieve,*
Wadebridge, Cornwall, PL27 6EG.
Peaceful hamlet, terraced gardens
Tel: **01208 814449** Mrs Crook.
Rates fr: *£15.00-£15.00*.
Open: All Year (not Xmas)
Beds: 1F 1D 1S **Baths:** 1 Private
☎ (3) ₽ (4) ⌷ ⌷ ⫼

(0.25m) *Trevanion House,*
Trevanion Road, Wadebridge,
Cornwall, PL27 7JY.
C18th farmhouse - disabled
welcomed
Tel: **01208 814903** Mrs Todd.
Fax no: 01208 816268
Rates fr: *£17.00-£18.00*.
Open: Mar to Jan
Beds: 7T 4S
Baths: 9 Private 2 Shared
☎ (5) ₽ (8) ⌷ ⌷ ✕ ⫼ ⚿ ⫿ ⚿

Tresinney 4

National Grid Ref: SX1081
⫿⚿ ⚿ Masons Arms

(1m) *Higher Trezion, Tresinney,*
Advent, Camelford, Cornwall,
PL32 9QW.
Modern comfortable farmhouse
Tel: **01840 213761**
Mr & Mrs Wood.
Rates fr: *£14.00-£14.00*.
Open: All Year **Beds:** 1D 1T
Baths: 1 Private 1 Shared
⌷ ⫼ ⚿

Pay B&Bs by cash or
cheque and be prepared
to pay up front.

Camelford 5

National Grid Ref: SX1083
⫿⚿ ⚿ Masons Arms, Darlington
Hotel

(1.5m) *Silvermoon, Lane End,*
Camelford, Cornwall, PL32 9LE.
Ensuite, quietly situated, good
walking. Drying room, cycle park,
garden
Tel: **01840 213736** (also fax no)
Mrs Metters.
Rates fr: *£16.00-£15.00*.
Open: All Year
Beds: 2D 1T **Baths:** 3 Ensuite
☎ ₽ (4) ⌷ ⌷ ⌷ ✕ ⫼ ⚿ ⫿ ⚿

(1.5m) *Masons Arms, Market*
Place, Camelford, Cornwall,
PL32 9PD.
Charming C18th public house
Tel: **01840 213309** Mr Connolly.
Rates fr: *£15.00-£15.00*.
Open: All Year
Beds: 1F 2D 1T 2S
Baths: 2 Shared
☎ ₽ (2) ⌷ ⌷ ✕ ⫼ ⫿

(1.5m) *Trenarth, Victoria Road,*
Camelford, Cornwall, PL32.
Share my country home in friendly
comfort. Enjoy beaches, rugged
coast, moors
Tel: **01840 213289** Mrs Hopkins.
Rates fr: *£13.50-£13.50*.
Open: Easter to Oct
Beds: 1F 1D 1T
☎ ₽ (4) ⌷ ⌷ ⌷ ⫼ ⫿

Camelford to Exmoor

The route now leads to the coast at Millook, where there is some steep up-and-down cycling over the clifftops before the descent to Widemouth Bay with its wonderful sandy beach, and the ride into **Bude**, a noted surfing centre. From here you strike out eastwards through Marhamchurch and come into Devon, arriving at the village of Bridgerule on the Tamar. Then it's on to Sheepwash in the Torridge Valley, where you turn north. The way now runs along a former railway line - this stretch is shared with the Tarka Trail, named after Henry Williamson's classic 1927 novel, *Tarka the Otter* - to **Bideford**, on the Torridge Estuary. Here you will find a fourteenth-century bridge and a statue commemorating Charles Kingsley, who wrote the historical romance *Westward Ho!*, set in the town (the eponymous nearby coastal resort was named after the book). Now it's down the Torridge Estuary and up the Taw Estuary to Barnstaple, where John Gay, who wrote *The Beggar's Opera*, went to school at St Anne's Chapel, which can be visited. Then you head inland and on to Bratton Fleming, from where it's a climb into **Exmoor National Park.** The route ascends swiftly to Mole's Chamber, atop the lonely high grass and heather plateau, before turning southeastwards along a particularly stupendous section of road which runs along the Devon-Somerset border. You would be very lucky to see some of Exmoor's indigenous red deer, the largest wild animal native to England; the magnificent views, however, are guaranteed.

(2m) *Carcade Farm, Camelford, Cornwall, PL32 9XG.*
250-year-old comfortable farmhouse
Tel: **01840 212288** Mrs Stiles.
Rates fr: *£15.00*-**£15.00**.
Open: All Year
Beds: 1F 1D 1T 1S
⏁ �ⓟ (4) ⊬ ✕ 🎟️

(1.5m) *Countryman Hotel,*
7 Victoria Road, Camelford,
Cornwall, PL32 9XA.
Small friendly family-run hotel
Tel: **01840 212250**
Mr & Mrs Reeve.
Rates fr: *£15.00*-**£15.00**.
Open: All Year
Beds: 2F 5D 2T 2S
Baths: 4 Private 2 Shared
⏁ ⓟ (12) ⊔ ⊬ ✕ 🎟️ Ⓥ

Dizzard   6

National Grid Ref: SX1698

(On route) *Penrose, Dizzard, St Gennys, Bude, Cornwall, EX23 0NX.*
Cosy, comfortable, clean in NT
Tel: **01840 230318** Mrs Joyner.
Rates fr: *£17.00*-**£17.00**.
Open: All Year **Beds:** 3D
Baths: 2 Private 1 Shared
⏁ (3) ⓟ (6) ⊬ ⊔ ⊬ ✕ 🎟️ Ⓥ ▮

The lowest *double* rate per person is shown in *italics*.

Widemouth Bay   7

National Grid Ref: SS2002
🍴 🍺 Brocksmoor Hotel, Bay View Inn

(0.25m) *The Bay View Inn, Widemouth Bay, Bude, Cornwall, EX23 0AW.*
Actual grid ref: SS201028
Family freehouse pub, overlooking sea and sandy beaches (Real Ale)
Grades: ETB Listed
Tel: **01288 361273** (also fax no)
Mr Gooder.
Rates fr: *£13.00*-**£13.00**.
Open: All Year
Beds: 3F 3D 1T 2S
Baths: 4 Private 2 Shared
⏁ ⓟ (30) ⊔ ⊬ ✕ 🎟️ Ⓥ ▮

(0.5m) *Penhalt Farm, Widemouth Bay, Bude, Cornwall, EX23 0.*
Panoramic sea views, comfortable, welcoming
Tel: **01288 361210** Mrs Marks.
Rates fr: *£13.00*-**£15.00**.
Open: Sep to Jun
Beds: 1F 1T 1D **Baths:** 2 Shared
⏁ ⓟ ⊔ ⊬ 🎟️ Ⓥ ⊬

(0.25m) *Seaspray, 1 The Crescent, Widemouth Bay, Bude, Cornwall, EX23 0AD.*
Uninterrupted views of sea & cliffs
Tel: **01288 361459**
Mr & Mrs Golby-Green.
Rates fr: *£14.00*-**£15.00**.
Open: All Year
Beds: 2D 1T **Baths:** 3 Ensuite
ⓟ (4) ⊬ ⊔ 🎟️ Ⓥ ⊬

Bude   8

National Grid Ref: SS2106
🍴 🍺 The Crooklets, Preston Gate

(0.5m) *Mornish Hotel, 20 Summerleaze Crescent, Bude, Cornwall, EX23 8HJ.*
Actual grid ref: SS221140
On coastal path overlooking Summerleaze Beach, River Neet and Bude Canal. Member Les Routiers
Tel: **01288 352972** (also fax no)
Mr Hilder.
Rates fr: *£18.95*-**£18.95**.
Open: Mar to Nov
Beds: 3F 5D 2T
Baths: 10 Ensuite
⏁ ⓟ (4) ⊔ ⊬ ✕ 🎟️ Ⓥ ▮ ⊬

(0.5m) *Marhamrise Guest House, 50 Kings Hill, Bude, Cornwall, EX23 8QH.*
Comfortable house with beautiful views
Tel: **01288 354713**
Mrs Thornton.
Rates fr: *£15.00*-**£15.00**.
Open: Easter to Oct
Beds: 2D 2S
Baths: 1 Shared
⏁ (3) ⓟ (3) ⊔ ✕ 🎟️ ⅙ Ⓥ ▮ ⊬

(0.5m) *Kisauni, 4 Downs View, Bude, Cornwall, EX23 8.*
Bright, airy Victorian house. Romantic four poster bed
Tel: **01288 352653**
Mrs Kimpton.
Rates fr: *£13.00*-**£13.00**.
Open: All Year (not Xmas)
Beds: 2F 3D 1T 1S
Baths: 1 Ensuite 2 Shared
⏁ ⓟ (5) ⊔ ⊬ ✕ ⅙ Ⓥ ⊬

(0.5m) *Surfside, 19 Downs View, Bude, Cornwall, EX23 8RF.*
Warm friendly clean guest house
Tel: **01288 355637**
Mr & Mrs Constable.
Rates fr: *£13.00*-**£14.00**.
Open: Easter to Nov
Beds: 4F 4T 2S
ⓟ (3) ⊔ 🎟️

Crooklets   9

National Grid Ref: SS2006
🍴 🍺 The Crooklets

(1m) *Inn On The Green, Crooklets Beach, Crooklets, Bude, Cornwall, EX23 8NF.*
Comfortable family hotel, good food
Grades: ETB 3 Cr, Comm
Tel: **01288 356013** (also fax no)
Mr Bellward.
Rates fr: *£16.00*-**£16.00**.
Open: All Year (not Xmas)
Beds: 2F 6D 9T 3S
Baths: 16 Ensuite 3 Shared
⏁ (1) ⓟ (6) ⊔ ⊬ ✕ 🎟️ Ⓥ ▮ ⊬

Marhamchurch 10

National Grid Ref: SS2203

¶⦅ Bullers Arms

(1m) *Cann Orchard*,
*Marhamchurch, Stratton, Bude,
Cornwall, EX23 9TD.*
Actual grid ref: SS231047
Old country house, stunning
gardens and orchard
Tel: **01288 352098**
Mr Crocker.
Rates fr: *£16.00-*£20.00.
Open: Easter to Dec
Beds: 2D 1T
Baths: 2 Ensuite 1 Shared
♿ (5) ℗ (4) ⊬⊐ ∉

Holsworthy 11

National Grid Ref: SS3403

(1.5m) *Leworthy Farm*,
Holsworthy, Devon, EX22 6SJ.
Friendly, hospitable farmhouse
Tel: **01409 253488**
Mr & Mrs Cornish.
Fax no: 01409 254671
Rates fr: *£16.50-*£16.50.
Open: All Year
Beds: 4F 2D 1T 2S
Baths: 3 Private 2 Shared
♿ ℗ (20) ⊐✕ Ⓥ

Clawton 12

National Grid Ref: SX3599

¶⦅ Village Inn

(3m) *Claw House*, *Clawton,
Holsworthy, Devon, EX22 6QJ.*
Grades: ETB 1 Cr
Tel: **01409 253930**
Mrs Wallis.
Rates fr: *£18.00-*£16.00.
Open: All Year
Beds: 1T 1D 1S
Baths: 1 Ensuite 1 Shared
♿ (6) ℗⊬⊐✕ⅢⓋⅰ∉
Our lovely Georgian farmhouse has
spacious, comfortable rooms with
every consideration taken into
account. Pretty Devon village, with
fishing and golf nearby

(3m) *Court Barn Country Hotel*,
*Clawton, Holsworthy, Devon,
EX22 6PS.*
Large manor house in 5 acres
Grades: ETB 4 Cr, High Comm,
AA 2 St, RAC 2 St
Tel: **01409 271219**
Rates fr: *£30.00-*£35.00.
Open: All Year
Beds: 1F 3T 3D 1S
Baths: 8 Ensuite
♿ ℗ (16) ⊐✕ⅢⅢ⅃Ⓥ

Merton 13

National Grid Ref: SS5212

¶⦅ Bull & Dragon

(▲2m) *Great Potheridge
Camping Barn*, *Great Potheridge,
Merton, Okehampton, Devon*
Actual grid ref: SS513146
Adults: £3.35+
Camping Facilities
*Located at an outdoor Education
Centre, this barn provides excellent
bunk-house accommodation with
outdoor activities available.*
*ADVANCE BOOKING
ESSENTIAL*

(2m) *Richmond House*, *New Road
(A386), Merton, Okehampton,
Devon, EX20 3EG.*
We like to make everyone happy
and comfortable. Easy reach moors
and beach
Tel: **01805 603258** Mrs Wickett.
Rates fr: *£15.00-*£15.00.
Open: All Year (not Xmas)
Beds: 2F 2D 1S **Baths:** 1 Shared
♿ (5) ℗ (8) ⊐ℏⅰ∉

The *lowest* **single**
rate *is shown in* **bold.**

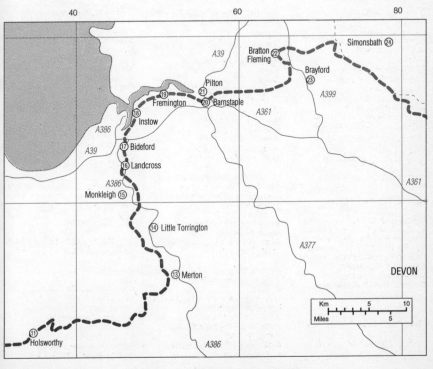

Little Torrington 14

National Grid Ref: SS4916

(0.5m) *Smytham Manor, Little Torrington, Torrington, Devon, EX38 8PU.*
Direct access to Tarka Trail
Tel: **01805 622110**
Mrs Crowe.
Rates fr: *£14.00-£14.00.*
Open: Easter to Oct
Beds: 1F 3D 3T
Baths: 5 Private 1 Shared
> 🖺 (10) 🗗 🛏 ✕ ▥ Ⅴ

Monkleigh 15

National Grid Ref: SS4520

(1.5m) *Petticombe Manor, Monkleigh, Bideford, Devon, EX39.*
Large manor, 35 acres parkland
Tel: **01237 475605**
Mr Wilson.
Rates fr: *£22.50.*
Open: All Year
Beds: 1F 2D
Baths: 3 Shared
> 🖺 🗗 🛏 ✕ ▥ Ⅴ

Landcross 16

National Grid Ref: SS4623

🍴 🍺 Tanton's Hotel

(On route) *Sunset Hotel, Landcross, Bideford, Devon, EX39 5JA.*
Actual grid ref: SS461239
Grades: ETB 3 Cr, Comm, AA 3 Q
Tel: **01237 472962**
Mrs Lamb.
Rates fr: *£23.00-£35.00.*
Open: Feb to Nov
Beds: 2F 2D 2T
Baths: 4 Private
🖺 (8) ⌁ 🗗 ✕ ▥ Ⅴ ▮ ⌁
Somewhere SPECIAL. Small country hotel, quiet peaceful location, overlooking spectacular scenery and Tarka Trail. Highly recommended quality accommodation. Superb food, everything homemade, special diets. Non-smoking establishment

Bideford 17

National Grid Ref: SS4526

(0.5m) *Ellerton, Glenburnie Road, Bideford, Devon, EX39 2LW.*
Warm welcome in family home on town outskirts. Breakfast menu
Tel: **01237 473352**
Mrs Garnsey.
Rates fr: *£15.00-£15.00.*
Open: All Year
Beds: 1D 2T
Baths: 2 Shared
> ⌁ 🗗 🛏 ▥ & Ⅴ ▮ ⌁

Instow 18

National Grid Ref: SS4730

🍴 🍺 Quay Inn, The Boathouse, Wayfarer Inn

(▲ 0.5m) *Instow Youth Hostel, Worlington House, New Road, Instow, Bideford, Devon, EX39 4LW.*
Actual grid ref: SS482303
Warden: Mr D Stuart.
Tel: **01271 860394**
Under 18: £5.95 **Adults:** £8.80
Evening Meals Available (7pm), Family Bunk Rooms, Television, Showers, Shop
Large Victorian country house with fine views across the Torridge Estuary

(0.25m) *Pilton Cottage, Victoria Terrace, Marine Parade, Instow, Bideford, Devon, EX39 4JW.*
Victorian house, beautiful estuary view, yards from sandy beach
Tel: **01271 860202**
Mr & Mrs Gardner.
Rates fr: *£17.50-£18.50.*
Open: Easter to Oct
Beds: 1F 2D 1T 1S
Baths: 1 Private 1 Shared
🖺 (3) ⌁ 🗗 ▮ ⌁

Fremington 19

National Grid Ref: SS5132

🍴 🍺 New Inn

(1m) *Oakwood, 34 Yelland Road, Fremington, Barnstaple, Devon, EX31 3DS.*
Run like a family home - very friendly
Tel: **01271 73884** Mrs George.
Rates fr: *£11.50-£11.50.*
Open: All Year
Beds: 1F 2D **Baths:** 1 Shared
> 🖺 (3) 🗗 ✕ ▥ ▮ ⌁

Barnstaple 20

National Grid Ref: SS5633

🍴 🍺 Windsor Arms, Ring O' Bells, Pyne Arms

(0.5m) *Crossways, Braunton Road, Barnstaple, Devon, EX31 1JY.*
Actual grid ref: SS555333
Detached house - town centre 150 yds
Tel: **01271 79120** Mr & Mrs Capp.
Rates fr: *£14.00-£16.00.*
Open: All Year (not Xmas)
Beds: 1F 1D 1T
Baths: 2 Private 1 Shared
> 🖺 (6) ⌁ 🗗 ▥ ▮ ⌁

All cycleways are popular: you are well-advised to book ahead

All rates are subject to alteration at the owners' discretion.

(0.5m) *West View, Pilton Causeway, Barnstaple, Devon, EX32 7AA.*
Modernised Victorian property overlooking park
Tel: **01271 42079** (also fax no)
Mrs Rostock.
Rates fr: *£17.00-£17.00.*
Open: All Year
Beds: 3F 3D 10T 7S
Baths: 5 Ensuite 7 Shared
> 🖺 (15) 🗗 🛏 ✕ ▥ Ⅴ ▮ ⌁

(0.5m) *Mount Sandford, Mount Sandford Road, Barnstaple, Devon, EX32 0HL.*
Lovely Georgian house. Beautiful gardens
Tel: **01271 42354** Mrs White.
Rates fr: *£18.00-£17.50.*
Open: All Year
Beds: 1F 1D 1T **Baths:** 3 Ensuite
> (3) 🖺 (3) ⌁ 🗗 ▥

Pilton 21

National Grid Ref: SS5534

🍴 🍺 Windsor Arms

(1m) *Bradiford Cottage, Halls Mill Lane, Pilton, Barnstaple, Devon, EX31 4DP.*
Actual grid ref: SS551345
Grades: ETB 1 Cr, Comm
Tel: **01271 345039** (also fax no)
Mrs Hare.
Rates fr: *£15.00-£15.00.*
Open: All Year (not Xmas/New Year)
Beds: 1D 1T 2S **Baths:** 1 Shared
> (8) 🖺 (4) ⌁ 🗗 ▥ ▮ ⌁
Family-run C17th cottage. Tranquil surroundings. Ideally placed for exploring Atlantic Coast and Exmoor. Outstanding welcome; lovely rooms, every home comfort, use of swimming pool

Bratton Fleming 22

National Grid Ref: SS6437

🍴 🍺 Black Venus

(On route) *Haxton Down Farm, Bratton Fleming, Barnstaple, Devon, EX32 7JL.*
Peaceful, working farm, comfortable and welcoming, central position, dinner available
Grades: ETB 2 Cr, Comm
Tel: **01598 710275** Mrs Burge.
Rates fr: *£16.00-£15.00.*
Open: Apr to Oct
Beds: 1F 1D
Baths: 1 Ensuite 1 Private
> 🖺 (3) 🗗 🛏 ✕ ▥ Ⅴ

Brayford 23

National Grid Ref: SS6634

iol ⊈ Black Venus, Poltimore Arms

(0.5m) *Rockley Farmhouse, Brayford, Barnstaple, Devon, EX32 7QR.*
Actual grid ref: SS704383
Delightful old farmhouse with stream-bordered garden. Farmyard friends
Grades: ETB Listed, High Comm
Tel: 01598 710429 Mrs Dover.
Rates fr: *£17.50-£17.50.*
Open: All Year **Beds:** 2D 1T
Baths: 1 Ensuite 1 Shared
ᄀ 🅿 🗲 🗖 🗙 🎟 🖤 🔌 ✧

Simonsbath 24

National Grid Ref: SS7739

(3m) *Moorland Cottage, Simonsbath, Minehead, Somerset, TA24 7LQ.*
Actual grid ref: SS735401
Comfortable renovated character farm cottage
Tel: 01643 831458 Mrs Pile.
Rates fr: *£15.00-£15.00.*
Open: All Year (not Xmas)
Beds: 1D 2S **Baths:** 1 Private
ᄀ 🅿 (4) 🗲 🗖 🔌 🗙 🎟 🖤 🔌 ✧

Hawkridge 25

National Grid Ref: SS8530

(2m) *Tarr Steps Hotel, Hawkridge, Dulverton, Somerset, TA22 9PY.*
Superbly situated country house hotel
Tel: 01643 851293 Ms Blackmore.
Fax no: 01643 851218
Rates fr: *£30.00-£40.00.*
Open: All Year
Beds: 6D 4T 2S
Baths: 8 Ensuite 1 Private 2 Shared
ᄀ 🅿 (20) 🔌 🗙 🎟 & 🖤 🔌 ✧

Hinam 26

National Grid Ref: SS8829

(2m) *Scatterbrook Farm, Hinam, Dulverton, Somerset, TA22 9QQ.*
Working farm, beautiful countryside
Grades: ETB Listed, Approv
Tel: 01398 323857
Ms Aldridge.
Rates fr: *£12.50-£15.00.*
Open: All Year
Beds: 2D 1T
Baths: 1 Ensuite
ᄀ 🅿 (4) 🗖 🔌 🗙 🎟 & 🖤 🔌 ✧

Dulverton 27

National Grid Ref: SS9128

iol ⊈ Tarr Farm Inn, The Bridge, Lion Hotel, White Horse

(▲ 2m) *Northcombe Camping Barn, Northcombe, Dulverton, Somerset*
Actual grid ref: SS916292
Adults: £3.35+
Self-catering Facilities, Showers, Camping Facilities
Beautifully converted windmill.
ADVANCE BOOKING ESSENTIAL

(2m) *Highercombe Farm, Dulverton, Somerset, TA22 9PT.*
Tel: 01398 323616 (also fax no)
Mrs Humphrey.
Rates fr: *£19.50-£22.00.*
Open: Mar to Nov
Beds: 2D 1T
Baths: 3 Ensuite
ᄀ (6) 🅿 🗖 🔌 🗙 🎟 🖤 🔌 ✧
On the edge of expansive moorland, you will find our welcome farmhouse home with rooms overlooking our 450 acres. Situated in the Exmoor National Park - 3 miles from Dulverton

(2m) *Springfield Farm, Ashwick Lane, Dulverton, Somerset, TA22 9QD.*
Comfortable farmhouse accommodation. Good food
Grades: ETB 2 Cr, Comm
Tel: 01398 323722 Mrs Vellacott.
Rates fr: *£17.50-£22.00.*
Open: Easter to Nov
Beds: 2D 1T
Baths: 2 Ensuite 1 Private
ᄀ 🅿 🗲 🗖 🔌 🗙 🎟 🖤 ✧

(0.25m) *Town Mills, Dulverton, Somerset, TA22 9HB.*
C19th mill house
Grades: ETB 2 Cr, High Comm
Tel: 01398 323124
Mrs Buckingham.
Rates fr: *£17.50-£21.00.*
Open: All Year
Beds: 4D 1T
Baths: 3 Private 2 Shared
ᄀ 🅿 (5) 🗖 🎟 🖤

Cove 28

National Grid Ref: SS9519

iol ⊈ Trout Inn, The Seahorse, The Anchor

(1.5m) *Hill Cottage, Cove, Tiverton, Devon, EX16 7RN.*
Calm, cosy, comfortable country cottage. Rest assured. We guarantee it
Tel: 01884 256978 Mrs Harris.
Rates fr: *£18.00-£18.00.*
Open: All Year (not Xmas)
Beds: 1D 1T **Baths:** 1 Shared
🅿 (2) 🗲 🗖 🗙 🎟

Planning a longer stay? Always ask for any special rates.

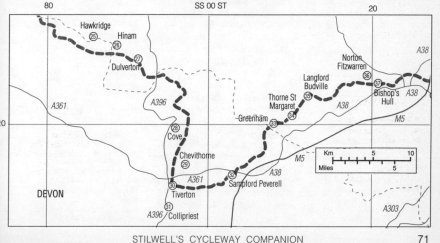

80　　　　　　SS 00 ST　　　　　　20

Chevithorne 29

National Grid Ref: SS9715

¶ ◖ Sea Horse

(On route) *Landrake Farm,*
Chevithorne, Tiverton, Devon,
EX16 7QN.
Working farm within easy reach of
moors and coasts
Grades: ETB Listed, Approv
Tel: 01398 331221 Mrs Kerslake.
Rates fr: *£15.00-£15.00.*
Open: Mar to Oct
Beds: 1F 1D 1T
Baths: 1 Shared
♿ 🅿 (4) ⛽ 🕇 ✕

Tiverton 30

National Grid Ref: SS9512

¶ ◖ Trout Inn, The Seahorse, The
Anchor

(0.5m) *Angel Guest House,*
13 St Peter Street, Tiverton, Devon,
EX16 6NU.
Comfortable Georgian house in
town centre. Colour TVs in rooms,
cycle shed. Ideal touring centre
Grades: ETB 2 Cr, Approv
Tel: 01884 253392 (also fax no)
Mr & Mrs Evans.
Rates fr: *£16.00-£16.00.*
Open: All Year
Beds: 2F 3D 1T 1S
Baths: 3 Private 2 Shared
♿ 🅿 (4) ⛽ 🕇 🛏 ▥ ✦

Bringing children with
you? Always ask for
any special rates.

Exmoor to Bridgwater

You eventually descend (steeply) to **Dulverton**, a pretty village where the National Park Visitors' Centre is located. From here you head down the Barle Valley to Brushford, where you leave Exmoor and head on to Morebath and Bampton. Cycling south from here you pass near to Knightshayes Court, a Victorian Gothic house with gardens divided into formal sections themed by scent or colour, before reaching **Tiverton**. The route now strikes out east along the Grand Western Canal, through Halberton and Sampford Peverell, crossing into Somerset and heading on to the county town, **Taunton**, in the heart of cider country. Taunton Castle was the scene of two fatal trials, that of the royal pretender Perkin Warbeck at the end of the fifteenth century; and the 'bloody assizes' of 1685, where the infamous Judge Jeffries ordered the executions of the Duke of Monmouth and his followers, who had attempted to seize the throne of England from James II. From Taunton you head northwards to **Bridgwater**, close to where the battle of Sedgemoor, fought in 1685, brought the Monmouth Rebellion to an end.

(0.5m) *Bridge Guest House,*
23 Angel Hill, Tiverton, Devon,
EX16 6PE.
Imposing Victorian riverside town
house
Grades: ETB 3 Cr, Comm,
AA 3 Q, Recomm, RAC Acclaim
Tel: 01884 252804
Ms Coxall.
Rates fr: *£17.50-£18.50.*
Open: All Year
Beds: 2F 2D 1T 4S
Baths: 5 Ensuite 2 Shared
♿ 🅿 (6) ⛽ 🕇 ✕ ▥ ⛽ ✦

(1m) *Lodge Hill Farm*
Guesthouse, Ashley, Tiverton,
Devon, EX16 5PA.
Log fire, good parking, tranquil
setting
Grades: ETB 2 Cr, Comm,
AA 1 Q, RAC Listed
Tel: 01884 252907
Mr & Mrs Reader.
Fax no: 01884 242090
Rates fr: *£17.00-£18.00.*
Open: All Year
Beds: 2F 2D 2T 2S
Baths: 7 Ensuite
🅿 (14) ⛽ ✕ ▥ ▥

Collipriest 31

National Grid Ref: SS9511

(2m) *Little Holwell, Collipriest,*
Tiverton, Devon, EX16 4PT.
A warm welcome awaits you in our
home, set in rolling hills in the
beautiful Exe Valley, 1.5 miles
south of Tiverton
Tel: 01884 257590 (also fax no)
Mrs Hill-King.
Rates fr: *£16.00-£16.00.*
Open: All Year (not Xmas)
Beds: 1F 2D
Baths: 1 Ensuite 1 Shared
🅿 (6) ⛽ ✕ ▥

Sampford Peverell 32

National Grid Ref: ST0314

¶ ◖ Globe Inn, Merriemead Hotel

(On route) *Challis, 12 Lower*
Town, Sampford Peverell, Tiverton,
Devon, EX16 7BJ.
Superb accommodation. Village
centre, beautiful gardens leading to
Grand Western Canal
Tel: 01884 820620
Mrs Isaac.
Rates fr: *£16.00-£17.50.*
Open: All Year (not Xmas)
Beds: 1D 1T 1S
Baths: 1 Ensuite 2 Shared
♿ 🅿 (6) ⛽ ⛽ 🕇 ▥

Greenham 33

National Grid Ref: ST0720

¶ ◖ Globe Inn

(On route) *Greenham Hall,*
Greenham, Wellington, Somerset,
TA21 0JJ.
Large turreted Victorian family
home, surrounded by beautiful
garden in rural location
Grades: ETB Listed, Approv
Tel: 01823 672603
Mrs Ayre.
Fax no: 01823 672307
Rates fr: *£19.00-£25.00.*
Open: All Year
Beds: 2F 3D 2T
Baths: 3 Ensuite 1 Private
3 Shared
♿ 🅿 (10) ⛽ 🕇 ▥ ▥ ✦

Thorne St Margaret 34

National Grid Ref: ST0921

(On route) *Thorne Manor, Thorne*
St Margaret, Wellington, Somerset,
TA21 0EQ.
Jacobean manor house
Tel: 01823 672954
Mrs Hasell.
Rates fr: *£18.00-£20.00.*
Open: Easter to Oct
Beds: 1F
♿ 🅿 (2) ⛽ ⛽

Langford Budville 35

National Grid Ref: ST1122

(0.25m) *Orchard Haven, Langford*
Budville, Wellington, Somerset,
TA21 0QZ.
Country house in lovely peaceful
location
Tel: 01823 672116
Mrs Perry Jones.
Rates fr: *£18.00-£21.00.*
Open: Easter to Oct
Beds: 2D
Baths: 1 Shared
♿ (5) 🅿 (4) ⛽ ⛽ ▥

Norton Fitzwarren   36

National Grid Ref: ST1925
¶ ♥ Cross Keys

(2m) *Old Manor Farmhouse,*
Norton Fitzwarren, Taunton,
Somerset, TA2 6RZ.
Modernised former Edwardian
farmhouse
Grades: ETB 3 Cr, Comm,
AA 3 Q, RAC Acclaim
Tel: 01823 289801 (also fax no)
Mr & Mrs Foley.
Rates fr: *£23.00-£34.00.*
Open: All Year (not Xmas)
Beds: 4D 2T 1S
Baths: 7 Ensuite
⚡ (1) 🅿 (12) ⚡□✕▥Ⅴ ⚡

Bishop's Hull   37

National Grid Ref: ST2024
¶ ♥ Old Inn, The Cavalier

(On route) *Hillview Guest House,*
Bishop's Hull, Taunton, Somerset,
TA1 5EG.
Spacious accommodation, warm &
friendly atmosphere, in attractive
village near Taunton
Grades: ETB Listed, Approv
Tel: 01823 275510 Mr Morgan.
Rates fr: *£17.50-£17.50.*
Open: All Year (not Xmas)
Beds: 2F 1D 1T 1S
Baths: 2 Ensuite 1 Shared
⚡ 🅿 (5) ⚡□✕▥

(0.25m) *Old Inn, Bishop's Hull,*
Taunton, Somerset, TA1 5EG.
C16th country inn in quiet village
Tel: 01823 284728 Mrs Redrup.
Rates fr: *£17.00-£17.00.*
Open: All Year (not Xmas)
Beds: 3F 4T 2S
Baths: 1 Private 2 Shared
🅿 (20) □✕▥Ⅴ

The lowest *double* rate per person is shown in *italics.*

Henlade   38

National Grid Ref: ST2623

(1m) *The Barn, Henlade, Taunton,*
Somerset, TA3 5NB.
Delightful character barn
conversion
Tel: 01823 442531
Mr & Mrs Harrison.
Rates fr: *£18.00-£27.00.*
Open: All Year (not Xmas)
Beds: 3D
Baths: 3 Ensuite
⚡🅿⚡□✕✕▥&Ⅴ

North Petherton   39

National Grid Ref: ST2832

(4m) *Lower Clavelshay Farm,*
North Petherton, Bridgwater,
Somerset, TA6 6PJ.
Actual grid ref: ST255310
Grades: ETB Listed, Approv
Tel: 01278 662347 Mrs Milverton.
Rates fr: *£15.00-£18.00.*
Open: All Year (not Xmas)
Beds: 1F 2D
Baths: 1 Ensuite 1 Shared
⚡🅿⚡□✕✕▥Ⅴ♣⚡
C17th farmhouse in beautiful
peaceful valley on Quantock Hills.
Warm welcome, friendly atmos-
phere, Excellent food. Ideal for
Quantocks. Exmoor, Somerset
Levels. Close Hestercombe
Gardens

(0.75m) *Quantock View House,*
Bridgwater Road, North Petherton,
Bridgwater, Somerset, TA6 6PR.
Actual grid ref: ST301342
Central for Cheddar, Wells,
Glastonbury, the Quantocks and
the sea
Grades: ETB 2 Cr, Approv
Tel: 01278 663309
Mr & Mrs George.
Rates fr: *£15.00-£15.00.*
Open: All Year
Beds: 2F 1T 1D
Baths: 3 Ensuite 1 Private
⚡🅿 (6) ⚡□✕✕✕▥Ⅴ♣⚡

Bridgwater   40

National Grid Ref: ST3037
¶ ♥ Malt Shovel, Hope Inn, The
Waterloo, King's Head, Crossways
Inn, Scarlet Pimpernel

(1m) *The Acorns, 61 Taunton Rd,*
Bridgwater, Somerset, TA6 3LP.
Tel: 01278 445577
Rates fr: *£15.00-£15.00.*
Open: All Year (not Xmas)
Beds: 3F 2D 5T 3S
Baths: 5 Ensuite 3 Shared
⚡🅿 (15) □✕▥ ⚡
Large Victorian house overlooking
the Bridgewater and Taunton
Canal, views to the Quantock Hills,
1.5 miles M5 motorway. Ideal for
touring Somerset and Devon

(1m) *Admirals Rest Guest House,*
5 Taunton Road, Bridgwater,
Somerset, TA6 3LW.
Elegant Victorian house, centrally
situated. Secure cycle park and
carpark
Grades: ETB 2 Cr, Comm
Tel: 01278 458580 Mrs Parker.
Rates fr: *£16.00-£18.00.*
Open: All Year **Beds:** 2F 1D 1T
Baths: 3 Ensuite 1 Private
⚡🅿 (5) □✕▥Ⅴ

(2m) *Cokerhurst Farm, 87*
Wembdon Hill, Bridgwater,
Somerset, TA6 7QA.
Friendly, comfortable, peaceful,
pleasant outlook
Grades: ETB 2 Cr, High Comm
Tel: 01278 422330 / 0850 692065
Mr & Mrs Chappell.
Rates fr: *£17.00-£17.00.*
Open: All Year
Beds: 1F 1D 1T
Baths: 1 Private 1 Shared
⚡🅿 (62) ⚡□▥♣⚡

(1m) *Chinar Guest House,*
17 Oakfield Road, Bridgwater,
Somerset, TA6 7LX.
Good beds, imaginative breakfasts,
peaceful
Grades: ETB Listed, AA 3 Q,
Recomm
Tel: 01278 458639 Mr & Mrs Bret.
Rates fr: *£19.00-£18.00.*
Open: All Year (not Xmas)
Beds: 1D 1S **Baths:** 2 Ensuite
⚡ (6) 🅿 (2) □✕▥Ⅴ⚡

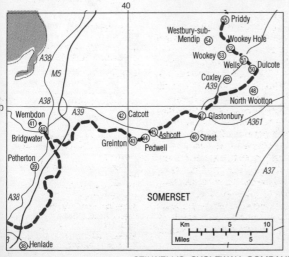

Bridgwater to the Mendips

From here it's east to **Glastonbury**, a small town more redolent with mythology of various kinds than anywhere in England. The towering ruins of the Benedictine abbey are all that remains of one of Britain's earliest Christian foundations. According to legend it was founded by Christ himself, brought here as a child by Joseph of Arimathea, who later returned with the Holy Grail and stuck his staff into the ground, which sprouted spontaneously into a thorn tree. The Glastonbury Thorn, in the abbey grounds, is descended from that original. Nearby Glastonbury Tor is said to be the Isle of Avalon, where King Arthur was brought after being mortally wounded in battle - the tomb of Arthur and Guinevere lies in the abbey grounds. Allegedly. From Glastonbury the route passes through the pancake-flat Somerset Levels to **Wells**, where stands one of England's most magnificent cathedrals, renowned for the ornately carved west front. Northwest of Wells you come to **Wookey Hole**, a striking group of caves, before ascending onto the limestone ridge of the Mendip Hills; after cycling along the ridge as far as **Charterhouse** you turn east to **East Harptree** and **Hinton Blewett**.

Wembdon   41

National Grid Ref: ST2837
¶⚫ Malt Shovel

(3m) *Wembdon Farm, Hollow Lane, Wembdon, Bridgwater, Somerset, TA5 2BD.*
Actual grid ref: ST281381
Grades: ETB 2 Cr, High Comm
Tel: **01278 453097** Mrs Rowe.
Fax no: 01278 445856
Rates fr: £18.00-£22.00.
Open: All Year (not Xmas)
Beds: 1T 2D
Baths: 2 Ensuite 1 Private
ﾋ (12) ᴾ (3) ⚡◻▥Ⅴ⚡
Enjoy a refreshing and memorable stay at our elegant yet homely farmhouse where comfort is assured. Guests' own lounge and dining room for superb breakfasts

Catcott   42

National Grid Ref: ST3939
¶⚫ King William Inn

(1m) *Pear Tree, 16 Manor Rd, Catcott, Bridgwater, Somerset, TA7 9HF.*
Comfortable touring base for Somerset
Tel: **01278 722390** Mrs Hill.
Rates fr: £15.00-£15.00.
Open: Easter to Nov
Beds: 1D 1T **Baths:** 1 Shared
ᴾ (2) ⚡◻▥Ⅴ⚫

Greinton   43

National Grid Ref: ST4136
¶⚫ Red Tile

(On route) *Greinton House, Greinton, Bridgwater, Somerset, TA7 9BW.*
Beautiful Listed old rectory
Tel: **01458 210307** Mrs Tingey.
Rates fr: £15.00-£20.00.
Open: All Year
Beds: 2D 1T **Baths:** 3 Private
ﾋ (10) ᴾ (4) ⚡◻▥

Pedwell   44

National Grid Ref: ST4236
¶⚫ Ring O' Bells

(On route) *Barncroft, 20a Taunton Road, Pedwell, Street, Somerset, TA7 9BG.*
Converted stone barn, very quiet
Tel: **01458 210294** Mrs Pitman.
Rates fr: £14.50-£15.50.
Open: All Year
Beds: 2D 1T **Baths:** 1 Shared
ﾋ (5) ᴾ (4) ⚡◻⋔▥Ⅴ

Ashcott   45

National Grid Ref: ST4337

(On route) *Little Whitley, Stagman Lane, Ashcott, Bridgwater, Somerset, TA7 9QW.*
Tel: **01458 210050** (also fax no)
Mrs Frampton.
Rates fr: £12.50-£12.50.
Open: All Year
Beds: 1F 1D
Baths: 1 Shared
ﾋ ᴾ (4) ⚡◻⋔✕▥Ⅴ
Secluded modern farmhouse. Large garden and goat enclosure. Small real ale brewery on site. Comfortable rooms and hearty breakfasts. Near Glastonbury, Somerset Levels, Clarks Village

Street   46

National Grid Ref: ST4836
¶⚫ Pipers' Inn

(▲ 3m) *Street Youth Hostel, The Chalet, Ivythorn Hill, Street, Somerset, BA16 0TZ.*
Actual grid ref: ST480345
Tel: **01458 442961**
Under 18: £5.40 **Adults:** £8.00
Self-catering Facilities, Showers, Camping Facilities
Former holiday home for workers at Clarks' shoemakers, this traditional hostel is a Swiss-style chalet overlooking Glastonbury Tor

(4m) *Marshalls Elm Farm, Street, Somerset, BA16 0TZ.*
Comfortable, 450-year-old characterful farmhouse
Tel: **01458 442878** Mrs Tucker.
Rates fr: £14.50-£15.00.
Open: All Year (not Xmas)
Beds: 1D 1T
Baths: 1 Shared
ﾋ ᴾ ⚡◻

Glastonbury   47

National Grid Ref: ST5039
¶⚫ The Lion, Mitre Inn, George & Pilgrim, Kingsdown Inn, Queen's Arms, Rose & Portcullis

(1m) *Meadow Barn, Middlewick Farm, Wick Lane, Glastonbury, Somerset, BA6 8JW.*
Grades: ETB 2 Cr, Comm
Tel: **01458 832351** (also fax no)
Mrs Coles.
Rates fr: £18.50-£23.50.
Open: All Year (not Xmas)
Beds: 1F 2D
Baths: 1 Ensuite 3 Private
ﾋ ᴾ ◻✕▥⚫Ⅴ⚡
Ground floor accommodation in coverted barn. Olde Worlde charm with country style decor with indoor swimming pool. Set in cottage gardens and apple orchards

(6m) *Lottisham Manor, Glastonbury, Somerset, BA6 8PF.*
C16th manor house. Lovely garden. Hard tennis court. Perfect peace
Tel: **01458 850205**
Mrs Barker-Harland.
Rates fr: £15.00-£17.50.
Open: All Year
Beds: 1D 1T 1S
Baths: 2 Shared
ﾋ ᴾ (8) ◻▥Ⅴ

The *lowest* **single** rate *is shown in* **bold.**

(0.5m) *The Who'd A Thought It Inn*, 17 Northload Street, Glastonbury, Somerset, BA6 9JJ.
Tel: **01458 834460** Mrs Ayres.
Fax no: 01458 831039
Rates fr: *£24.50-£29.50*.
Open: All Year (not Xmas)
Beds: 2T 2D 1S **Baths:** 5 Ensuite
ॐ (10) ☐ ✕ ▥ ⓥ
Town centre inn with an amazing collection of memorabilia and local artefacts 2 minutes' walk from Abbey ruins, 10 minutes walk from the Tor

(0.5m) *Shambhala Healing Centre*, Coursing Batch, Glastonbury, Somerset, BA6 8BH.
Beautiful house on sacred site on side of the Tor. Healing, massage, great vegetarian food
Tel: **01458 833081**
Fax no: 01458 831797
Rates fr: *£27.50-£27.50*.
Open: All Year
Beds: 3D 1S **Baths:** 3 Shared
ॐ ☐ ✕ ☐ ✕ ▥ ⓥ

(0.5m) *Blake House, 3 Bove Town*, Glastonbury, Somerset, BA6 8JE.
Actual grid ref: ST503390
Tel: **01458 831680** Mrs Hankins.
Rates fr: *£16.00-£16.00*.
Open: All Year (not Xmas)
Beds: 1D 1T **Baths:** 2 Ensuite
☐ ✕ ☐ ▥
Welcome to our Grade II Listed C17th stone house. Two minutes to town centre. Vegetarians welcome. Easy walking distance to Abbey, Tor and Chalice Well

(0.5m) *Pippin, 4 Ridgeway Gardens, Glastonbury, Somerset, BA6 8ER*.
Comfort, value for money in peaceful home opposite Chalice Hill
Grades: ETB Listed, Approv
Tel: **01458 834262** Mrs Slater.
Rates fr: *£13.50-£13.50*.
Open: All Year (not Xmas)
Beds: 1D 1T **Baths:** 1 Shared
ॐ ☐ (1) ☐ ▥ ⓥ ✦

(0.5m) *191a Wells Road*, Glastonbury, Somerset, BA6 9AW.
Ground floor detached cottage, 1.5 miles from High Street
Tel: **01458 834733** Mrs Bressey.
Rates fr: *£12.00-£12.00*.
Open: All Year (not Xmas)
Beds: 1T
Baths: 1Shared
☐ (1)

(0.5m) *Little Orchard*, Ashwell Lane, Glastonbury, Somerset, BA6 8BG.
Panoramic views over the Vale of Avalon
Grades: ETB Listed, Comm
Tel: **01458 831620** Mrs Gifford.
Rates fr: *£15.00-£17.50*.
Open: All Year
Beds: 1F 1D 1T 1S
Baths: 1 Shared
ॐ ☐ ☐ ✦ ▥ ⓥ

(0.5m) *Waterfall Cottage, 20 Old Wells Road, Glastonbury, Somerset, BA6 8ED*.
C17th cottage - healing/aromatherapy available
Tel: **01458 831707**
Mr Caswell.
Rates fr: *£14.50-£14.50*.
Open: All Year
Beds: 2T 1S
Baths: 1 Shared
☐ (2) ✕ ▥ ⓥ ✦

(0.5m) *46 High Street*, Glastonbury, Somerset, BA6 9DX.
Good centre for touring Somerset
Tel: **01458 832214**
Mr & Mrs Allen.
Rates fr: *£17.50-£20.00*.
Open: All Year
Beds: 1D 1T
Baths: 2 Private
ॐ (1) ☐ ☐ ✦ ⓥ

North Wootton 48

National Grid Ref: ST5641

⑩ ◧ Crossways Inn

(1m) *Riverside Grange*, Tanyard Lane, North Wootton, Wells, Somerset, BA4 4AE.
Converted tannery on river's edge
Grades: ETB 1 Cr, High Comm
Tel: **01749 890761**
Mrs English.
Rates fr: *£17.50-£22.00*.
Open: All Year (not Xmas)
Beds: 1D 1T
Baths: 2 Private
ॐ ☐ (3) ☐ ✦ ▥

Coxley 49

National Grid Ref: ST5343

(2m) *Home Farm, Stoppers Lane, Upper Coxley, Coxley, Wells, Somerset, BA5 1QS*.
Old cider house, converted pre-war
Grades: ETB 2 Cr, AA 2 Q
Tel: **01749 672434**
Ms Higgs.
Rates fr: *£18.50-£18.50*.
Open: All Year (not Xmas)
Beds: 2F 2D 2T 1S
Baths: 2 Ensuite 1 Private 4 Shared
ॐ (10) ☐ (7) ☐ ✦ ▥

(2m) *Hollow Tree Farm*, Launcherley, Coxley, Wells, Somerset, BA5 1QJ.
Modern, comfortable farm bungalow
Tel: **01749 673715**
Mrs Coombes.
Rates fr: *£14.00-£15.00*.
Open: Easter to Oct
Beds: 1F 1D
Baths: 1 Shared
ॐ (5) ☐ (5) ☐ ▥ ⓖ

Dulcote 50

National Grid Ref: ST5644

(On route) *Manor Farm, Dulcote, Wells, Somerset, BA5 3PZ*.
Actual grid ref: ST563447
Tel: **01749 672125** Ms Bufton.
Rates fr: *£18.50-£18.50*.
Open: All Year
Beds: 1T 2D 1S
Baths: 2 Ensuite 1 Private 1 Shared
ॐ ☐ (6) ✕ ☐ ▥ ⓖ ⓥ ⓘ ✦
Perfect rural peace, with magnificent views of Wells Cathedral across the fields. The Garden Suite with inglenook is lovely and Rosalind's animals - sheep, goats, chickens and cats - a delight

Wells 51

National Grid Ref: ST5445

⑩ ◧ Burcitt Inn, New Inn, Fountain Inn, City Arms, Miners Arms, New Inn

(0.75m) *Milton Manor Farm, Old Bristol Road, Upper Milton, Wells, Somerset, BA5 3AH*.
Listed Elizabethan manor house, Grade Two Star, with lovely view
Grades: ETB 1 Cr, Comm, AA 3 Q
Tel: **01749 673394** Mrs Gould.
Rates fr: *£15.50-£17.50*.
Open: All Year (not Xmas)
Beds: 1F 1D 1T **Baths:** 1 Shared
ॐ ☐ (4) ✕ ☐ ▥

(On route) *Bekynton House, 7 St Thomas Street, Wells, Somerset, BA5 2UU*.
Three minutes from cathedral, a few more to city restaurants
Grades: ETB 2 Cr, Comm, AA 4 Q, RAC Acclaimed
Tel: **01749 672222** (also fax no)
Mr & Mrs Gripper.
Rates fr: *£21.50-£28.00*.
Open: All Year (not Xmas)
Beds: 1F 3D 2T **Baths:** 6 Private
ॐ (5) ☐ (6) ✕ ☐ ▥ ⓥ

(0.5m) *17 Priory Road, Wells, Somerset, BA5 1SU*.
Large Victorian house. Homemade bread
Tel: **01749 677300** Mrs Winter.
Rates fr: *£15.00-£15.00*.
Open: All Year (not Xmas)
Beds: 3F 3S **Baths:** 2 Shared
ॐ ☐ (5) ✕ ☐ ▥ ⓥ

(0.5m) *The Old Poor House, 7a St Andrew Street, Wells, Somerset, BA5 2UW*.
Hospitable household, every comfort, Close to Cathedral, Bishop's Palace, Wookey Hole, Bath
Tel: **01749 675052** Ms Wood.
Rates fr: *£19.00-£19.00*.
Open: All Year (not Xmas)
Beds: 2D 2S **Baths:** 1 Shared
✦ ▥ ⓥ ✦

(0.5m) *30 Mary Road, Wells, Somerset, BA5 2NF*.
Small, friendly family home
Tel: **01749 674031** (also fax no)
Mrs Bailey.
Rates fr: *£15.00*-**£15.00**.
Open: Feb to Nov
Beds: 2D 2S
Baths: 1 Shared
🛇 (3) 🅿 (7) 🖵 🎟 Ⓥ ⓘ

(0.5m) *Cadgwith House, Hawkers Lane, Wells, Somerset, BA5 3JH*.
Spacious, friendly family home
Tel: **01749 677799**
Mrs Pletts.
Rates fr: *£15.00*-**£17.00**.
Open: All Year
Beds: 1F 1D 1T 1S
Baths: 2 Private 1 Shared
🛇 🅿 🖵 🎟 🎟 Ⓥ

(1m) *Carmen, Bath Road, Wells, Somerset, BA5 3LQ*.
Friendly comfortable house near centre
Tel: **01749 677331**
Mrs Parker.
Rates fr: *£16.00*.
Open: All Year (not Xmas)
Beds: 1T
Baths: 2 Ensuite
🅿 (2) ⅍ 🖵 🎟 Ⓥ

(1m) *Birdwood House, Bath Road, Wells, Somerset, BA5 3DH*.
Actual grid ref: ST571468
Large Victorian private house on B3139
Grades: ETB Listed
Tel: **01749 679250**
Mrs Crane.
Rates fr: *£16.00*-**£16.00**.
Open: All Year
Beds: 1D 1T
Baths: 1 Shared
🛇 🅿 (4) ⅍ 🖵 🎟 Ⓥ ⓘ ✦

Wookey Hole 52

National Grid Ref: ST5347

🍴 🍺 Ring O'Bells, The Pheasant

(0.5m) *Ganymede, Hurst Batch, Wookey Hole, Wells, Somerset, BA5 1BE*.
Comfortable stone cottage
Tel: **01749 677250** Mrs Baddeley.
Rates fr: *£13.00*-**£13.00**.
Open: Jan to Nov
Beds: 3D
Baths: 1 Ensuite 1 Shared
🛇 (8) 🅿 (2) ⅍ 🖵 🎟

(0.25m) *Whitegate Cottage, Milton Lane, Wookey Hole, Wells, Somerset, BA5 1DG*.
Large country cottage on farmland
Tel: **01749 675326** Mr & Mrs Lee.
Rates fr: *£12.50*-**£15.00**.
Open: All Year
Beds: 2D 1S
🅿 (4) 🖵 🎟 🎟

Wookey 53

National Grid Ref: ST5145

🍴 🍺 Burcitt Inn

(1.5m) *Burcott Mill Guest House, Burcott, Wookey, Wells, Somerset, BA5 1NJ*.
Actual grid ref: ST522456
Comfortable rooms next to working watermill twixt Mendips and Wetlands
Grades: ETB 2 Cr, Comm
Tel: **01749 673118** (also fax no)
Mr & Mrs Grimstead.
Rates fr: *£17.00*-**£20.00**.
Open: All Year
Beds: 2F 2D 2T 1S
Baths: 7 Private
🛇 🅿 (20) 🖵 🎟 🎟 ♿ Ⓥ ⓘ

(2m) *Cross Farm, Yarley, Wookey, Wells, Somerset, BA5 1PA*.
Comfortable, well-furnished C15th Somerset longhouse
Tel: **01749 678925**
Mr & Mrs Alcock.
Rates fr: *£13.50*-**£15.00**.
Open: Easter to Nov
Beds: 1F 2D
Baths: 1 Private 1 Shared
🅿 (6) 🖵 🎟 🎟 Ⓥ

Westbury-sub-Mendip 54

National Grid Ref: ST5048

🍴 🍺 Westbury Inn, The Lamb

(1.5m) *Box Tree House, Westbury-sub-Mendip, Wells, Somerset, BA5 1HA*.
Delightful converted C17th farmhouse
Grades: AA 4 Q
Tel: **01749 870777** Mrs White.
Rates fr: *£18.00*-**£20.00**.
Open: All Year
Beds: 1F 1D 1T
Baths: 1 Ensuite 2 Private
🛇 🅿 (4) 🖵 🎟 Ⓥ

Priddy 55

National Grid Ref: ST5251

🍴 🍺 Miners' Arms, New Inn

(0.5m) *Highcroft, Wells Road, Priddy, Wells, Somerset, BA5 3AU*.
Comfortable spacious modern country house, walking, touring, fishing. Wells, Cheddar, Bath
Grades: ETB 2 Cr, Comm
Tel: **01749 673446** Mrs Hares.
Rates fr: *£18.00*-**£18.00**.
Open: Mar to Nov
Beds: 1F 1D 1T 1S
Baths: 2 Ensuite
🛇 🅿 ⅍ 🖵 🎟 Ⓥ

(On route) *The Miners Arms, Priddy, Wells, Somerset, BA5 3DB*.
Situated in the heart of the beautiful Mendip Hills, fresh food
Tel: **01749 870217**
Mr & Mrs Reynolds.
Rates fr: *£22.00*-**£32.00**.
Open: All Year (not Xmas)
Beds: 1F 1D 1T
Baths: 3 Ensuite
🛇 🅿 (30) 🖵 🎟 ✕ 🎟 Ⓥ ✦

Charterhouse-on-Mendip 56

National Grid Ref: ST5055

🍴 🍺 New Inn

(1m) *Warren Farm, Charterhouse-on-Mendip, Blagdon, Bristol. BS18 6XR*.
1,000 acre sheep farm
Tel: **01761 462674** Mrs Small.
Rates fr: *£16.00*-**£16.00**.
Open: All Year (not Xmas)
Beds: 1F 1D 1S **Baths:** 1 Shared
🛇 🅿 ⅍ 🖵 🎟 Ⓥ ✦

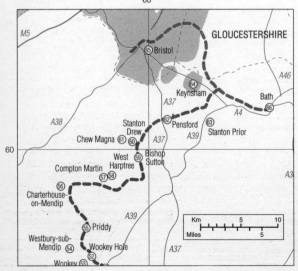

Compton Martin 57

National Grid Ref: ST5457

🍴 🍺 King's Arms

(8m) *Herons Green Farm,
Compton Martin, Bristol. BS18 6NL.*
Pretty farmhouse in peaceful
surroundings. Ideal for visiting
Bath, Wells, etc
Tel: **01275 333372** Mrs Hasell.
Fax no: 01275 333041
Rates fr: *£17.50-£20.00.*
Open: Mar to Oct
Beds: 1F 1D
Baths: 1 Shared
🛇 🅿 (3) ⅍ ❑ 🐾 🛏.

West Harptree 58

National Grid Ref: ST5656

(1m) *Vicarage Lawns, Bristol
Road, West Harptree, Bristol,
Somerset, BS18 6HF.*
In Mendip Hills village. In an acre
of walled garden
Grades: ETB 2 Cr
Tel: **01761 221668** Mrs Rowell.
Rates fr: *£16.00-£18.00.*
Open: All Year
Beds: 1F 2D 2T
Baths: 3 Private 1 Shared
🅿 (8) ⅍ ❑ ✗ 🛏. Ⓥ ⬥ ✦

**All cycleways are
popular: you are
well-advised to
book ahead**

Bishop Sutton 59

National Grid Ref: ST5859

🍴 🍺 Red Lion

(On route) *Centaur, Ham Lane,
Bishop Sutton, Bristol. BS18 4TZ.*
Grades: ETB 2 Cr, Comm
Tel: **01275 332321** Mrs Warden.
Rates fr: *£16.00-£16.50.*
Open: All Year (not Xmas)
Beds: 1F 1T
Baths: 1 Private 1 Shared
🛇 🅿 (4) ❑ 🛏. Ⓥ ⬥ ✦
Comfortable family house in
peaceful Chew Valley. Close to
lake for fishing, sailing & bird
watching. Within easy reach of
Bristol, Bath, Wells & Cheddar

Stanton Drew 60

National Grid Ref: ST5963

🍴 🍺 The Wheatsheaf, Druid's Arms

(0.5m) *Auden House, Stanton
Drew, Bristol. BS18 4DS.*
Large modern house in quiet
village. Off-street parking, fishing
nearby
Tel: **01275 332232** Mrs Smart.
Rates fr: *£12.50-£12.50.*
Open: All Year (not Xmas)
Beds: 2F 1D 1T 1S
Baths: 1 Ensuite, 1 Shared
🛇 🅿 (6) ⅍ ❑ 🐾 ✗ 🛏. Ⓥ ⬥ ✦

(1m) *Valley Farm, Sandy Lane,
Stanton Drew, Bristol. BS18 4EL.*
Modern farmhouse, quiet location,
old village
Tel: **01275 332723** Mrs Keel.
Rates fr: *£15.00-£20.00.*
Open: All Year (not Xmas)
Beds: 1F **Baths:** 2 Ensuite
🛇 🅿 (3) ⅍ ❑ 🛏. Ⓥ

Chew Magna 61

National Grid Ref: ST5763

🍴 🍺 Queens Arms, Stoke Inn

(2m) *Woodbarn Farm, Denny
Lane, Chew Magna, Bristol.
BS18 8SZ.*
Farmhouse B&B near Chew Valley
Lake, Bath, Wells
Grades: ETB 2 Cr, Comm
Tel: **01275 332599** (also fax no)
Mrs Hasell.
Rates fr: *£18.00-£20.00.*
Open: Mar to Dec
Beds: 1F 1D
Baths: 2 Ensuite
🛇 (3) 🅿 (6) ⅍ ❑ 🛏. Ⓥ ⬥ ✦

Pensford 62

National Grid Ref: ST6263

(0.25m) *The Hollies Guest House,
Pensford Hill, Pensford, Bristol.
BS18 4AA.*
Large old Victorian private bakery
Tel: **01761 490456**
Mr & Mrs Jones.
Rates fr: *£10.00-£12.00.*
Open: All Year
Beds: 1F 1T
Baths: 2 Shared
🛇 🅿 (3) ⅍ ❑ 🐾 🛏.

**Many rates vary
according to season -
the lowest only are
shown here**

Bristol (see over for Bath)

The rest of the way takes you through the hilly country of North Somerset to Saltford, where you join the Bristol and Bath Railway Path and turn towards **Bristol**, the capital city of the West Country. A county in its own right from 1373 until 1974, this status was withdrawn with the creation of the short-lived County of Avon, and reinstated in 1996. Before the rapid industrial development of the Midlands and North of England during the nineteenth century, Bristol was England's second city. It was from here that John Cabot made the first European voyage to North America, setting foot on Newfoundland in 1497 - the Cabot Tower in Brandon Hill Park gives panoramic views in all directions. St Mary Redcliffe, Elizabeth I's favourite church, is an outstanding perpendicular-style edifice with a famous nineteenth-century spire. In the seventeenth and eighteenth centuries the city's shady wealth came from the slave trade, as the principal port shipping West African captives to America before this mantle of shame passed to Liverpool. Bristol is most notable for the engineering achievements of Isambard Kingdom Brunel, whose original railway line from London Paddington still operates into Temple Meads Station - the terminus is a surviving Brunel design. Brunel was also responsible for the SS Great Britain, the first large iron passenger ship in the world, which stands in the dry dock; and outstandingly the Clifton Suspension Bridge, magnificently spanning the Avon Gorge west of town. Nowadays the city has a thriving black community; the St Paul's Carnival in early July is Bristol's answer to London's Notting Hill Carnival. The redeveloped quayside has two Arts Centres, the Watershed and the Arnolfini.

Bath

From Saltford an alternative route takes you to the small and lovely city of **Bath**, a World Heritage Site which boasts the stately Georgian houses of the Royal Crescent, the fifteenth-century perpendicular Bath Abbey, with its airy stone vault, and the Roman baths, still fed by a hot spring, covered by a Victorian pillared complex. Part of the Roman complex was a temple to Sulis Minerva, a deity combined from the Roman Minerva and Sul, the local Celtic god of the spa.

Stanton Prior 63

National Grid Ref: ST6762

🍴 🍺 The Wheatsheaf

(2m) *Poplar Farm, Stanton Prior, Bath. BA2 9HX.*
Spacious C17th farmhouse. Family-run farm. Idyllic village setting
Grades: ETB Listed, Comm
Tel: 01761 470382 (also fax no) Mrs Hardwick.
Rates fr: *£17.00-£18.00.*
Open: All Year (not Xmas)
Beds: 1F 1D 1T
Baths: 2 Private 1 Shared
🛏 (3) 🅿 (4) ⊁ 🗢 🛒 📺 ✓

Keynsham 64

National Grid Ref: ST6568

🍴 🍺 The Talbot

(2m) *Fiorita, 91 Bath Road, Keynsham, Bristol. BS18 1SR.*
Warm welcome, comfortable family home
Tel: 0117 986 3738 Mrs Poulter.
Rates fr: *£13.50-£15.00.*
Open: All Year (not Xmas)
Beds: 1D 1T
Baths: 1 Shared
🛏 🅿 (4) 🗢 🛒 ⓘ

All details shown
are as supplied
by B&B owners in
Autumn 1997.

Bristol 65

National Grid Ref: ST6075

🍴 🍺 Prince of Wales, Engineers' Arms

(▲ 1m) *Bristol International Youth Hostel, Hayman House, 14 Narrow Quay, Bristol. BS1 4QA.*
Actual grid ref: ST586725
Tel: 0117 922 1659
Under 18: £8.00
Adults: £11.65
Evening Meals Available (6-7.30pm), Self-catering Facilities, Television, Games Room, Showers, Shop, Laundry Facilities *With views over the waterways, this hostel has been sympathetically and imaginatively restored to create a relaxing yet cosmopolitan atmosphere*

(1m) *Arches Hotel, 132 Cotham Brow, Bristol. BS6 6AE.*
Friendly, private, non-smoking, city centre hotel
Grades: ETB 1 Cr, Comm
Tel: 0117 924 7398 (also fax no) Mr Lambert.
Rates fr: *£19.75-£22.50.*
Open: All Year (not Xmas)
Beds: 2F 4D 1T 3S
Baths: 2 Private 2 Shared
🛏 ⊁ 🗢 🍴 📺 ✓

(1m) *Norfolk House, 577 Gloucester Road, Horfield, Bristol. BS7 0BW.*
Actual grid ref: ST596774
Pleasant Victorian house overlooking park
Grades: ETB 1 Cr
Tel: 0117 951 3191
Mr Thomas.
Rates fr: *£16.00-£18.00.*
Open: All Year (not Xmas)
Beds: 2D 1T
Baths: 1 Ensuite 2 Shared
🛏 ⊁ 🗢 ✗ 🛒 ⓘ

(1m) *Alcove Guest House, 508-510 Fishponds Road, Bristol. BS16 3DT.*
Easy access, M32 half mile
Tel: 0117 965 3886 (also fax no)
Mr & Mrs Newman.
Rates fr: *£20.00-£20.00.*
Open: All Year
Beds: 2F 3D 3T 1S
Baths: 4 Private 4 Shared
🛏 (1) 🅿 (8) 🗢 🍴 🛒 ♿ 📺

(1m) *Camden Hotel, 129 Coronation Road, Southville, Bristol. BS3 1RE.*
Small licensed hotel, convenient city centre
Tel: 0117 923 1062
Mr East.
Rates fr: *£15.50-£18.00.*
Open: All Year
Beds: 2F 2D 3T 3S
Baths: 2 Private 3 Shared
🛏 🅿 (4) 🗢 🍴 ✗ 🛒 📺

(1m) *Downs View Guest House, 38 Upper Belgrave Road, Clifton, Bristol. BS8 2XN.*
Large Victorian house, centrally situated
Tel: 0117 973 7046 Ms Cox.
Rates fr: *£20.00-£24.00.*
Open: All Year
Beds: 1F 5D 2T 4S
Baths: 4 Private 2 Shared
🛏 (2) 🗢 🛒 📺

(1m) *Thornbury House, 80 Chesterfield Road, St Andrews, Bristol. BS6 5DR.*
Excellent hospitality - large Victorian house
Tel: 0117 924 5654 Mrs Smith.
Rates fr: *£20.00-£20.00.*
Open: All Year
Beds: 1D 1T
Baths: 2 Ensuite
🅿 (2) ⊁ 🗢 🛒 📺

Bath 66

National Grid Ref: ST7464

🍴 🍺 The Bear, Old Crown, Devonshire Arms, Park Tavern, The Huntsman, Royal Oak

(▲ 0.5m) *Bath Youth Hostel, Bathwick Hill, Bath, North East Somerset, BA2 6JZ.*
Actual grid ref: ST766644
Warden: Mr R Newsun.
Tel: 01225 465674
Under 18: £6.55 **Adults:** £9.75 (5.30-7.30pm), Family Bunk Rooms, Television, Games Room, Showers, Shop, Security Lockers *Handsome Italianate mansion, set in beautiful, secluded gardens, with views of historic city and surrounding hills*

(0.5m) *Wentworth House Hotel, 106 Bloomfield Road, Bath. BA2 2AP.*
Grades: ETB 2 Cr, Comm, AA 4 Q, RAC High Acclaim
Tel: 01225 339193
Mrs Kitching.
Fax no: 01225 310460
Rates fr: *£25.00-£38.00.*
Open: All Year (not Xmas)
Beds: 2F 8 D 5T
Baths: 13 Ensuite 2 Private
🛏 (5) 🅿 (20) 🗢 🍴 🛒 📺 ⓘ
Elegant Victorian mansion in secluded gardens with views from rear. Quietly situated, with free car park. Walking distance Bath - the Georgian city. Delicious breakfasts

(0.5m) *Kinlet Guest House, 99 Wellsway, Bath. BA2 4RA.*
Actual grid ref: ST745636
Home from Home. Friendly, comfortable, easy walk into the city
Grades: ETB 1 Cr, Comm
Tel: 01225 420268 (also fax no)
Mrs Bennett.
Rates fr: *£18.00-£18.00.*
Open: All Year
Beds: 1F 1D 1S
🛏 ⊁ 🗢 🛒 ⓘ ✓

(On route) *14 Raby Place,*
Bathwick Hill, Bath. BA2 4EH.
Grades: ETB 1 Cr, Comm
Tel: **01225 465120** Mrs Guy.
Fax no: 01225 465283
Rates fr: *£22.00*-**£20.00**.
Open: All Year
Beds: 1F 2D 2T
Baths: 4 Private
🛏 🕭 🖵 🏠 🖿 ▣
Charming Georgian terraced house.
Fresh fruit salads, organic eggs,
granary bread and bacon - if you
want it! - are all provided for
breakfast

(0.5m) *Dene Villa, 5 Newbridge*
Hill, Bath. BA1 3PW.
Victorian family-run guest house
Grades: ETB 2 Cr, Comm
Tel: **01225 427676** (also fax no)
Mrs Surry.
Rates fr: *£20.00*-**£16.00**.
Open: All Year
Beds: 1F 1D 1S
Baths: 3 Ensuite
🛏 (3) ▣ (4) 🖵 🖿 ▣ 🕭

(0.5m) *Sarnia, 19 Combe Park,*
Weston, Bath. BA1 3NR.
Actual grid ref: ST730656
Grades: AA 4 Q, Select
Tel: **01225 424159**
Mr & Mrs Fradley.
Rates fr: *£22.50*-**£25.00**.
Open: All Year (not Xmas/New
Year)
Beds: 1F 1D 1T
Baths: 2 Ensuite 1 Private
🛏 ▣ (3) 🕭 🖵 🖿 ▣ ♿ 🕭
Superb bed & breakfast in large
Victorian home. Spacious
bedrooms, comfortable lounge,
secluded gardens. English,
Continental and vegetarian
breakfasts. 1.5 miles from city
centre. Warm welcome, friendly
atmosphere

(0.5m) *14 Dunsford Place,*
Bathwick Hill, Bath. BA2 6HF.
Actual grid ref: ST759651
Comfortable home within 15 min-
utes' walk of Bath's city centre
Grades: ETB 2 Cr, Comm
Tel: **01225 464134**
Mrs Smith.
Rates fr: *£21.00*-**£35.00**.
Open: All Year (not Xmas)
Beds: 1D 1T
Baths: 2 Private
🕭 🖵 🖿.

(0.5m) *The Terrace Guest House,*
3 Pulteney Terrace, Bath. BA2 4HJ.
Small house close to city centre
Tel: **01225 316578**
Mrs Gould.
Rates fr: *£16.00*-**£20.00**.
Open: All Year (not Xmas)
Beds: 1F 1D 1S
Baths: 2 Shared
🛏 (6) 🖵 🖿. ▣ 🕭

(0.5m) *Wellsway Guest House,*
51 Wellsway, Bath. BA2 4RS.
Walking distance to city. Clean,
comfortable
Tel: **01225 423434**
Mrs Strong.
Rates fr: *£14.00*-**£19.00**.
Open: All Year
Beds: 1F 1D 1T 1S
Baths: 1 Shared
🛏 ▣ (2) 🖵 🏠 🖿. ▣

(0.25m) *Flaxley Villa, 9*
Newbridge Hill, Bath. BA1 3PW.
Flaxley Villa is a Victorian house
on the west side of Bath in residen-
tial area
Tel: **01225 313237** Mrs Cooper.
Rates fr: *£18.00*-**£18.00**.
Open: All Year
Beds: 1F 2D
Baths: 3 Private
🛏 (1) ▣ (5) 🖵 🖿. ▣

(0.5m) *Bailbrook Lodge, 35-37*
London Road West, Bath. BA1 7HZ.
Imposing Georgian house, restau-
rant overlooks lawns, close for M4
Tel: **01225 859090** (also fax no)
Mrs Addison.
Rates fr: *£26.00*-**£35.00**.
Open: All Year (not Xmas)
Beds: 4F 4D 4T
Baths: 12 Ensuite
🛏 ▣ (14) 🖵 🗙 🖿. ▣

(0.5m) *Fyfield, Ralph Allen Drive,*
Combe Down, Bath. BA2 5AE.
Attractive comfortable 1950s
house, large garden, 1.5 miles from
city centre
Tel: **01225 833561** Mrs Waterman.
Rates fr: *£18.00*-**£18.00**.
Open: All Year (not Xmas)
Beds: 1D 1T 1S
Baths: 1 Shared
🛏 ▣ (4) 🖵 🖿. ▣

(0.5m) *Ashley House, 8 Pulteney*
Gardens, Bath. BA2 4HG.
Actual grid ref: ST757646
Conveniently located quiet
Victorian house
Grades: ETB 1 Cr
Tel: **01225 425027**
Mrs Pharo.
Rates fr: *£16.00*-**£23.00**.
Open: All Year
Beds: 2F 2D 1T 3S
Baths: 5 Private 2 Shared
🛏 🕭 🖿. ▣ 🖢

The lowest *double*

rate per person is

shown in *italics*.

Round Berkshire Cycle Route

The **Round Berkshire Cycle Route** is a 140-mile circular route around the county of Berkshire, which has been deliberately routed along minor roads wherever possible. It starts and finishes in Reading, and runs anticlockwise around the whole of the county.

A detailed **guide leaflet** to the route is available free from Babtie Group, Shire Hall, Shinfield Park, Reading RG2 9XG, tel 0118-923 4603. The route is signposted by blue direction signs with a cycle silhouette on a green outline map of Berkshire.

Maps: Ordnance Survey 1:50,000 Landranger series: 174, 175

Trains: Reading, Maidenhead and Slough (from where there is a connection to Windsor) are on the main line out of London. There are connections to Newbury, Hungerford, Bracknell and many other places on or near the route.

Reading to Tidmarsh

Reading, the county town of Berkshire, lies where the River Kennet joins the Thames, and is economically one of the most important towns of the Thames Valley. It is largely nineteenth-century redbrick, and has a thriving commercial town centre. In medieval times there was a Benedictine abbey, founded in the twelfth century, of which a few ruins remain. The town also has a good museum, which houses the finds from the Roman town at Silchester in Hampshire, and a good theatre, the Hexagon. This is where Oscar Wilde spent two years in prison, after which he wrote the *Ballad of Reading Gaol.* Cycling west from the south bank of the Thames at Caversham Bridge, you leave town after Tilehurst station, and reach the village of **Tidmarsh.** A short detour north at this point leads to the small Thameside town of **Pangbourne**, used by the artist Ernest Shepard as the setting for his illustrations to *The Wind in the Willows*, whose author, Kenneth Grahame, lived here.

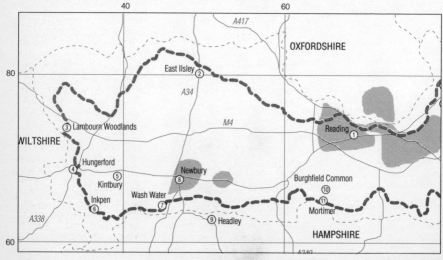

Reading 1

National Grid Ref: SU7173

¶❮ ◈ Mansion House, Gardeners' Arms, Horse & Jockey, Greyhound, Grouse & Claret

(0.5m) *Dittisham Guest House, 63 Tilehurst Road, Reading, Berks, RG3 2JL.*
Renovated Edwardian house. Ensuite rooms, carpark, close to centre
Grades: ETB Listed, Comm
Tel: **0118 956 9483**
Mr Harding.
Rates fr: *£17.50-£20.00.*
Open: All Year
Beds: 1F 1D 3S
Baths: 5 Ensuite
Ⓢ ₽ ▢ Ⅲ. ✦

(0.5m) *The Berkeley Guest House, 32 Berkeley Avenue, Reading, Berks, RG1 6JE.*
Friendly family-run home near town centre. We cater for diabetics. All mod cons every room
Tel: **0118 959 5699 / 0118 961 0329**
Mr Hubbard.
Rates fr: *£17.00-£20.00.*
Open: All Year
Beds: 2F 3T
Baths: 2 Ensuite 2 Shared
Ⓢ ₽ (6) ✂ ▢ ♁ Ⅲ. Ⓥ ♦ ✦

(0.5m) *10 Greystoke Road, Caversham, Reading, Berks, RG4 5EL.*
Family home in private road
Grades: ETB Listed, Comm
Tel: **0118 947 5784**
Mrs Tyler.
Rates fr: *£17.00-£18.00.*
Open: All Year (not Xmas)
Beds: 1D 2S
Baths: 2 Shared
₽ (1) ✂ ▢ Ⅲ.

East Ilsley 2

National Grid Ref: SU4981

¶❮ ◈ The Swan

(On route) *The Swan, East Ilsley, Newbury, Berks, RG20 7LF.*
C16th coaching inn, good food
Tel: **01635 281238** Mrs Connolly.
Fax no: 01635 281791
Rates fr: *£25.00-£34.00.*
Open: All Year **Beds:** 3F 4D 2T 3S
Baths: 8 Private 2 Shared
Ⓢ ₽ (24) ✂ ▢ ♁ ✗ Ⅲ. Ⓥ ♦

Lambourn Woodlands 3

National Grid Ref: SU3175

¶❮ ◈ Hare & Hounds

(0.5m) *Lodge Down, Lambourn Woodlands, Hungerford, Berks, RG17 7BJ.*
Country house in lovely grounds with luxury accommodation with ensuite bathrooms
Grades: ETB 2 Cr, Comm
Tel: **01672 540304** (also fax no)
Mrs Cook.
Rates fr: *£20.00-£20.00.*
Open: All Year
Beds: 1F 2D 2T **Baths:** 3 Ensuite
Ⓢ ₽ (6) ▢ Ⅲ. ♦ ✦

Hungerford 4

National Grid Ref: SU3368

¶❮ ◈ John O'Gaunt

(On route) *Wynbush, 135 Priory Road, Hungerford, Berks, RG17 0AP.*
Detached house, large garden, quiet. 3 miles M4
Tel: **01488 682045** Mrs Simmonds.
Rates fr: *£14.00-£16.00.*
Open: All Year
Beds: 1D 1S **Baths:** 1 Shared
Ⓢ ₽ (3) ✂ ▢ Ⅲ. Ⓥ

Kintbury 5

National Grid Ref: SU3866

¶❮ ◈ Crown & Garter

(3m) *The Forbury, Crossways, Kintbury, Hungerford, Berks, RG17 9SU.*
Extended C17th cottage
Tel: **01488 658377**
Mr Cubitt.
Rates fr: *£19.00-£19.50.*
Open: All Year (not Xmas)
Beds: 1D 1T 1S
Baths: 1 Private 1 Shared
Ⓢ ₽ ▢ ♁ ✗ Ⅲ. Ⓥ

Tidmarsh to Hungerford

After Tidmarsh you pass into the **North Wessex Downs** with the villages of Upper Basildon and Aldworth, where you will find the Four Points pub, from where you can head onto an alternative route along **the Ridgeway**, an ancient path along which lie numerous Iron Age forts. Near the point where you join the Ridgeway is the site of the Battle of Ashdown. In 871, Aethelred I of Wessex won a resounding victory in his campaign against the invasion of England by the Danes – only to be crushed by them at Merton (now in South London) shortly afterwards. After Aldworth you come to Compton, East and West Ilsley and Farnborough, and then down off the downs to the village of **Great Shefford** on the banks of the River Lambourn, which you follow upstream to **Lambourn** town, Berkshire's horseracing centre. After Lambourn it's south until you hit Ermine Street, the lesser of two Roman roads of that name, which runs from Silchester to Gloucester. After a brief stretch you turn right, cross the M4 and head on to **Hungerford**, on the River Kennet. At the Wharf you can view the **Kennet and Avon Canal**, constructed in 1774 and recently restored.

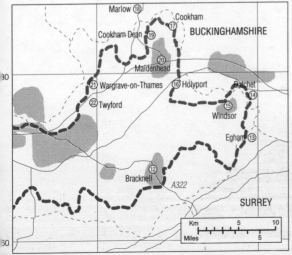

Hungerford to Finchampstead Ridges

Heading across Hungerford Common, the route takes you to the foot of **Walbury Hill**, the highest chalk hill in England. If you fancy a challenge, the view from the top is worth the climb, along quiet lanes. Otherwise, the route takes you around the hill and then eastwards on to **Newbury**, site of two battles in the Civil War, one of which (1643) is commemorated by the Falkland Memorial, close to the route on the way into town. The next stretch takes in two sites of legendary importance to the anti-nuclear movement, **Greenham Common**, just outside Newbury, former site of American Cruise Missiles and the resultant women's peace camp during the 1980s, and **Aldermaston**, site of the Atomic Weapons Research Establishment and of annual CND marches in the 1950s and 60s. Then it's into the coniferous woodland around Mortimer. A short detour over the Hampshire boundary takes you to the site of the Roman town of Calleva Atrebatum, at **Silchester**. This was the capital of the Atrebates tribe in the third and fourth centuries, and the site includes the walls, still upto 13 feet high in places, an amphitheatre, the foundations of a forum and the earliest known Christian church in Britain. After Mortimer it's across the Rivers Loddon and Blackwater near to Swallowfield Park, a seventeenth-century country house, and on to Wellingtonia Avenue, from where you can take a short detour to the viewpoint over the Blackwater Valley at Finchampstead Ridges.

Inkpen   6

National Grid Ref: SU3764

(On route) *Beacon House, Bell Lane, Upper Green, Inkpen, Hungerford, Berks, RG17 9QJ.*
Actual grid ref: SU368634
A warm welcome 60 miles west of London. 1930s country house
Tel: **01488 668640** Mr & Mrs Cave.
Rates fr: *£16.00*-**£16.00**.
Open: All Year
Beds: 1T 2S
Baths: 2 Shared
ॐ (7) ▤ ◻ ★ ✕ Ⅲ. Ⅴ ♠ ⚡

Wash Water   7

National Grid Ref: SU4563

(1m) *Cherry Tree Farm, Horris Hill, Wash Water, Newbury, Berks, RG20 9DQ.*
Country cottage, beautiful quiet location
Tel: **01635 44789**
Mrs Morris.
Rates fr: *£17.00*-**£17.00**.
Open: All Year (not Xmas)
Beds: 1T 1S
ॐ ▤ (6) ⠶ ◻ Ⅲ.

Newbury   8

National Grid Ref: SU4767

†●↑ ◖ Robin Hood, Red Lion, The Bunk

(2m) *15 Shaw Road, Newbury, Berks, RG14 1HG.*
Late-Georgian private house near town centre, rail and canal
Tel: **01635 44962**
Mrs Curtis.
Rates fr: *£16.00*-**£16.00**.
Open: All Year
Beds: 1D 1T
Baths: 1 Shared (for guests only)
ॐ ▤ ⠶ ◻ Ⅲ.

(2m) *Tonayne House, Oxford Road, Donnington, Newbury, Berks, RG14 2JD.*
Lovely red-brick Georgian private house
Tel: **01635 523138**
Mrs Ritchie.
Rates fr: *£17.00*-**£20.00**.
Open: All Year (not Xmas)
Beds: 1F 1T 1S
Baths: 1 Ensuite 1 Shared
ॐ ▤ (4) ⠶ ◻ ★ ✕ Ⅲ. Ⅴ ♠ ⚡

(2m) *Mousefield Farm, Long Lane, Shaw, Newbury, Berks, RG14 2TG.*
C17th comfortable, hospitable farm house
Grades: ETB Listed
Tel: **01635 40333**
Mrs Houghton.
Rates fr: *£18.00*-**£20.00**.
Open: All Year (not Xmas)
Beds: 1F 2T 2S
Baths: 3 Shared
ॐ ▤ (10) ◻ ★ Ⅲ. Ⅴ ♠ ⚡

Headley   9

National Grid Ref: SU5162

†●↑ ◖ The Harrow

(2m) *Denland, Thornford Road, Headley, Thatcham, Berks, RG19 8AD.*
Bungalow, each bedroom private entrance. Secure parking, pub meals
Tel: **01635 268465** Mr Tipple.
Rates fr: *£19.00*-**£19.00**.
Open: All Year
Beds: 1T 1S
Baths: 1 Shared
ॐ ▤ (5) ⠶ ◻ ★ Ⅲ. &

The lowest *double* rate per person is shown in *italics*.

The *lowest* **single** rate *is shown in* **bold.**

Burghfield Common   10

National Grid Ref: SU6566

†●↑ ◖ Hatch Gate

(2m) *Highwoods, Burghfield Common, Reading, Berks, RG7 3BG.*
Fine Victorian house in extensive grounds
Tel: **0118 983 2320** Mrs Steeds.
Fax no: 0118 983 1070
Rates fr: *£21.00*-**£19.00**.
Open: All Year
Beds: 1D 1S
Baths: 1 Ensuite 1 Shared
ॐ ▤ (6) ◻ Ⅲ.

(2m) *Firlands, Burghfield Common, Reading, Berks, RG7 3JN.*
Comfortable Victorian farmhouse in woods
Tel: **0118 983 2414** Mrs Stuckey.
Rates fr: *£17.00*-**£17.00**.
Open: All Year (not Xmas)
Beds: 2D
Baths: 1 Shared
ॐ ▤ ◻ Ⅲ.

Mortimer   11

National Grid Ref: SU6564

†●↑ ◖ Red Lion, Turners Arms

(On route) *35 The Avenue, Mortimer, Reading, Berks, RG7 3QU.*
Comfortable detached house, in quiet location
Tel: **0118 933 3166** Mrs Keast.
Rates fr: *£15.00*-**£15.00**.
Open: All Year
Beds: 1D 1T 1S
Baths: 1 Shared
ॐ (2) ▤ (8) ◻ ★ ✕ Ⅲ. & Ⅴ ⚡

All rates are subject to alteration at the owners' discretion.

Bracknell 12

National Grid Ref: SU8668

¶❙ ◨ Downshire Arms

(2m) *53 Swaledale, Wildridings, Bracknell, Berks, RG12 7ET.*
Near station, M3, M4 & shops
Tel: **01344 421247** Mrs Webber.
Rates fr: *£19.00*-**£20.00.**
Open: All Year (not Xmas)
Beds: 1T 1S
▣ (2) ⵉ ▢ ⃞,

Egham 13

National Grid Ref: TQ0071

¶❙ ◨ Happy Man, The Beehive

(1m) *The Old Parsonage, 2 Parsonage Road, Englefield Green, Egham, Surrey, TW20 0JW.*
Georgian parsonage, old-fashioned gardens
Tel: **01784 436706** (also fax no)
Mr & Mrs Clark.
Rates fr: *£25.00*-**£25.00.**
Open: All Year (not Xmas)
Beds: 1F 1D 1T 1S
Baths: 2 Ensuite 1 Private 1 Shared
▱ ▣ (3) ⵉ ▢ ★ ✕ ⃞, & ▯

(1m) *Beau Villa, 44 Grange Road, Egham, Surrey, TW20 9QP.*
Friendly, clean, comfortable family house
Tel: **01784 435115**
Mrs Wilding.
Rates fr: *£17.00*-**£20.00.**
Open: All Year (not Xmas)
Beds: 1D 1S
Baths: 1 Ensuite
▱ (14) ▣ (4) ▢ ⃞,

Datchet 14

National Grid Ref: SU9877

¶❙ ◨ Royal Stag

(0.25m) *The Chimneys, 55 London Road, Datchet, Windsor, Slough, Berks, SL3 9JY.*
Conveniently located, near Windsor, Heathrow, M4/M25 motorways
Tel: **01753 580401**
Mrs Greenham.
Fax no: 01753 540233
Rates fr: *£20.00*-**£28.50.**
Open: All Year
Beds: 1F 2D 1T
Baths: 2 Private
▱ ▣ ⵉ ▢ ⃞, ▯ ✦

Windsor 15

National Grid Ref: SU9676

¶❙ ◨ Royal Oak, Vansittart Arms, Windsor Lad, Nag's Head, Red Lion, The Trooper, Bexley Arms, Royal Stag

(▲ 0.5m) *Windsor Youth Hostel, Edgeworth House, Mill Lane, Windsor, Berkshire, SL4 5JE.*
Actual grid ref: SU955770
Warden: Mr C Thomas.
Tel: **01753 861710**
Under 18: £6.55
Adults: £9.75
Evening Meals Available (7pm),
Family Bunk Rooms, Games Room, Showers, Shop
Queen Anne residence in the old Clewer village quarter of historic Windsor

(0.5m) *62 Queens Road, Windsor, Berks, SL4 3BH.*
Excellent reputation, quiet, convenient, ground floor rooms. Largest family room available
Tel: **01753 866036** (also fax no)
Mrs Hughes.
Rates fr: *£18.00*-**£20.00.**
Open: All Year
Beds: 1F 1T **Baths:** 2 Private
▱ ▣ ⵉ ▢ ⃞, & ▯

All rates are subject to alteration at the owners' discretion.

All paths are popular: you are well-advised to book ahead

(0.5m) *Elansey, 65 Clifton Rise, Windsor, Berks, SL4 5SX.*
Modern comfortable house, patio, garden
Tel: **01753 864438** Mrs Forbutt.
Rates fr: *£18.00*-**£20.00.**
Open: All Year (not Xmas)
Beds: 1D 1T 1S
Baths: 1 Ensuite 1 Shared
▣ (2) ▢ ⃞, ▯

(0.5m) *Tanglewood, Oakley Green, Windsor, Berks, SL4 4PZ.*
Rural area, beautiful garden. Very quiet
Grades: ETB Listed, High Comm
Tel: **01753 860034** (also fax no)
Mrs Salter.
Rates fr: *£21.00*-**£27.00.**
Open: May to Sep
Beds: 2T 1S **Baths:** 1 Shared
▱ ▣ (4) ⵉ ▢ ⃞, ▯

(0.5m) *Suffolk Lock, 4 Bolton Avenue, Windsor, Berks, SL4 3AT.*
Large Victorian family guest house
Grades: ETB 2 Cr
Tel: **01753 864186** Mrs Jackson.
Fax no: 01753 862640
Rates fr: *£28.00*-**£49.00.**
Open: All Year
Beds: 1D 1T 1S **Baths:** 3 Ensuite
▱ ▣ (4) ▢ ★ ⃞, ▯ ▮ ✦

Finchampstead Ridges to Windsor

Cycling northeast you go around the southern perimeter of Bracknell, via Caesar's Camp, an Iron Age hill fort in Bracknell Forest, and then through woodland and parkland and across the Virginia Water beechlands into **Windsor Great Park**, a large tract of formal parkland replete with grazing deer. The route takes you through the Savill Gardens, and a short detour will bring you to the viewpoint at Snow Hill, by the 'Copper Horse' statue of George III. North of the Great Park you arrive at Old Windsor, from where a short detour east into Surrey will take you to **Runnymede**, the riverside meadow where in 1215 King John relinquished the absolute power of the monarchy with his signature on the Magna Carta. Here also stands the memorial to John F Kennedy. Sticking to the route, you hit the Thames at Datchet, and cycle along the north bank to **Eton**, where you can visit the red-brick Tudor buildings of *that* school, and then cross the river into **Windsor**. This town is dominated by the renowned castle, now restored after the great fire of 1992, whose most notable features are St George's Chapel, one of the most impressive examples of the Perpendicular style in England, and the State Apartments, which house, among other treasures, a large collection of pictures, including a tryptych of Charles I by Van Dyck and works by Canaletto, Holbein, Rubens, Rembrandt, Reynolds and Hogarth, as well as drawings by Leonardo and Michaelangelo.

(0.5m) *Halycon House,*
131 Clarence Road, Windsor,
Berks, SL4 5AR.
Large comfortable home, off-street
parking
Grades: ETB 2 Cr, Comm
Tel: 01753 863262 (also fax no)
Mr Golec.
Rates fr: £25.00-£43.00.
Open: All Year
Beds: 2D 1T
Baths: 3 Private
🛇 🅿 (5) ⊬ 🗗 🞹 Ⅴ

(0.5m) *2 Benning Close, St*
Leonards Park, Windsor, Berks,
SL4 4YS.
Modern detached large private
house
Tel: 01753 852294 Mrs Hume.
Rates fr: £18.00-£18.00.
Open: All Year
Beds: 1F 1D **Baths:** 2 Shared
🛇 🅿 (2) ⊬ 🗗 🞹 ᘓ Ⅴ

(0.5m) *77 Whitehorse Road,*
Windsor, Berks, SL4 4PG.
Modern, comfortable private house
Tel: 01753 866803 Mrs Andrews.
Rates fr: £18.00-£22.00.
Open: All Year (not Xmas)
Beds: 3D **Baths:** 2 Shared
🛇 (5) 🅿 (3) ⊬ 🗗 🞹

(0.5m) *Rocking Horse House,*
88 St Leonards Road, Windsor,
Berks, SL4 3DA.
Centrally situated, elegant
Victorian villa
Tel: 01753 853984 (also fax no)
Mr & Mrs Stanton.
Rates fr: £18.00-£30.00.
Open: All Year (not Xmas)
Beds: 2D 1T
Baths: 1 Private 2 Shared
🛇 (3) ⊬ 🗗 🞹 Ⅴ ✦

(0.5m) *62 Testwood Road,*
Windsor, Berks, SL4 5RW.
Modern semi in pleasant
surroundings
Tel: 01753 862409 (also fax no)
Ms Smits.
Rates fr: £18.00-£20.00.
Open: All Year
Beds: 1F 1D 1T 1S
Baths: 1 Private 1 Shared
🛇 (16) 🅿 (2) ⊬ 🗗 🞹 ✕ 🞹 Ⅴ

Holyport 16

National Grid Ref: SU8977

(1m) *Moor Farm, Holyport,*
Maidenhead, Berks, SL6 2HY.
Medieval manor with holiday
cottages
Grades: ETB 2 Cr, High Comm
Tel: 01628 633761 (also fax no)
Mrs Reynolds.
Rates fr: £22.00-£40.00.
Open: All Year
Beds: 1D 2T
Baths: 3 Private
🛇 🅿 (3) ⊬ 🗗 🞹

Cookham 17

National Grid Ref: SU8985

🍽 🍺 The Spencer

(0.5m) *Wylie Cottage, School*
Lane, Cookham, Maidenhead,
Berks, SL6 9QJ.
Actual grid ref: SU897851
Comfortable family home in
village
Grades: ETB Listed Comm
Tel: 01628 520106 (also fax no)
Mrs Crowe.
Rates fr: £20.00-£22.00.
Open: All Year (not Xmas)
Beds: 1D 1T **Baths:** 1 Shared
🛇 🅿 (2) ⊬ 🗗 🞹 ✦

(0.5m) *Koala, Vivien Close,*
Cookham, Maidenhead, Berks,
SL6 9DQ.
Actual grid ref: SU885845
Modern comfortable family home
Tel: 01628 523031
Mrs Gibbings.
Rates fr: £14.00-£15.00.
Open: All Year
Beds: 1F 1S **Baths:** 2 Shared
🛇 (3) 🅿 (3) ⊬ 🗗 🞹 Ⅴ ▪

Marlow 18

National Grid Ref: SU8586

🍽 🍺 Royal Oak, Bank of England,
The Three Horseshoes, Osbourne
Arms, The Pegasus, The Plough,
Hand Flowers, Hare & Hounds

(2m) *Sneppen House, Henley*
Road, Marlow, Bucks, SL7 2DF.
Within walking distance of town
centre and river. Good breakfast
Grades: ETB Listed, High Comm
Tel: 01628 485227
Mr Norris.
Rates fr: £20.00-£22.00.
Open: All Year
Beds: 1T 1D
Baths: 1 Shared
🛇 (2) 🅿 (4) 🗗 🞹

(2m) *Acha Pani, Bovingdon*
Green, Marlow, Bucks, SL7 2JL.
Actual grid ref: SU836869
Modern private house, quiet garden
Grades: ETB Listed, Comm
Tel: 01628 483435 (also fax no)
Mrs Cowling.
Rates fr: £17.00-£17.00.
Open: All Year
Beds: 1D 1T 1S
Baths: 1 Private 1 Shared
🛇 (10) 🅿 (3) 🗗 🞹 ✕ 🞹 Ⅴ ▪ ✦

(2m) *5 Pound Lane, Marlow,*
Bucks, SL7 2AE.
Actual grid ref: SU848861
Comfortable house, close to river
Grades: ETB Listed, Comm
Tel: 01628 482649 Mrs Bendall.
Rates fr: £17.50-£25.00.
Open: All Year (not Xmas)
Beds: 1D 1T **Baths:** 1 Shared
🛇 🅿 (2) ⊬ 🗗 🞹 Ⅴ ▪ ✦

(2m) *Sunnyside, Munday Dean,*
Marlow, Bucks, SL7 3BU.
Comfortable, friendly family home
Grades: ETB 1 Cr, Comm
Tel: 01628 485701
Mrs O'Connor.
Rates fr: £14.50-£16.00.
Open: All Year
Beds: 2D 1T
🅿 (5) ⊬ 🗗 🞹 Ⅴ

(2m) *29 Oaktree Road, Marlow,*
Bucks, SL7 3ED.
Comfortable, detached family
home
Tel: 01628 472145
Mr Lasenby.
Rates fr: £16.50-£18.00.
Open: All Year
Beds: 2T
Baths: 2 Private
🅿 (2) ⊬ 🗗 🞹 🞹

(2m) *The Venture, Munday Dean*
Lane, Marlow, Bucks, SL7 3BU.
Home from home. Quiet location
Tel: 01628 472195 Mrs Whittle.
Rates fr: £15.00-£20.00.
Open: All Year
Beds: 2D
Baths: 1 Shared
🛇 (10) 🅿 (4) ⊬ 🗗 🞹 Ⅴ

(2m) *50a New Road, Marlow*
Bottom, Marlow, Bucks, SL7 3NW.
Modern chalet-style house. Two
miles Thames
Grades: ETB Listed
Tel: 01628 472666 Mrs Parsons.
Rates fr: £19.00-£20.00.
Open: All Year
Beds: 1D 1T 1S **Baths:** 3 Shared
🅿 (4) ⊬ 🗗 🞹 Ⅴ

(2m) *Merrie Hollow, Seymour*
Court Hill, Marlow, Bucks, SL7 3DE.
Actual grid ref: SU840889
Secluded quiet country cottage
Grades: ETB Listed, Comm
Tel: 01628 485663 Mr Wells.
Rates fr: £17.50-£20.00.
Open: All Year
Beds: 1D 1T **Baths:** 1 Shared
🛇 🅿 (4) ⊬ 🗗 🞹 Ⅴ ✦

Cookham Dean 19

National Grid Ref: SU8684

🍽 🍺 Chequers, The Jolly Farmer,
Tom Cabin

(0.5m) *Primrose Hill, Bradcutts*
Lane, Cookham Dean,
Maidenhead, Berks, SL6 9TL.
Actual grid ref: SU879862
Rural location, convenient
Legoland, Windsor, Oxford,
excellent London train service
Grades: ETB Listed, High Comm
Tel: 01628 528179 Mrs Benson.
Rates fr: £18.00-£18.00.
Open: All Year (not Xmas)
Beds: 1F 1S
Baths: 1 Shared
🛇 🅿 (3) ⊬ 🗗 🞹 Ⅴ ▪ ✦

Windsor to Reading

At **Maidenhead**, the 128-foot brick arches - the largest in the world - of the railway bridge show that Brunel could do both kinds of bridge, Bristol's suspension bridge at Clifton being his famous example of the other kind. **Cookham** was home to the Artist Stanley Spencer, whose painting of Cookham Bridge is in London's Tate Gallery. The village has a gallery of his work, as well as a slightly odd fifteenth-century church tower with both a clock and a sundial. The viewpoint at Winter Hill yields a panorama onto the Chilterns in Buckinghamshire. The final stretch of the route takes you through some lovely Thames Valley countryside, and then by way of **Wargrave** and **Twyford** back into Reading.

(0.5m) *Cartlands Cottage, King's Lane, Cookham Dean, Maidenhead, Berks, SL6 9AY.*
Guest room, self-contained garden, rural, quiet
Grades: ETB 1 Cr, Approv
Tel: **01628 482196**
Mr & Mrs Parkes.
Rates fr: £22.00-**£23.50**.
Open: All Year
Beds: 1F **Baths:** 1 Private
🖚 🅿 (2) 🖵 📖 Ⅴ

Maidenhead 20

National Grid Ref: SU8781

🍽 🍺 Boulter's Lock Inn, Thames Hotel, Kingswood Hotel, Windsor Castle

(1m) *Laburnham Guest House, 31 Laburnham Road, Maidenhead, Berks, SL6 4DB.*
Actual grid ref: SU881808
Fine Edwardian house, near town centre, station and M4 motorway
Tel: **01628 676748** (also fax no)
Mrs Stevens.
Rates fr: £21.00-**£28.00**.
Open: All Year (not Xmas)
Beds: 1F 2D 1T 1S
Baths: 5 Private
🖚 🅿 (4) 🖊 🖵 📖 Ⅴ

(1m) *Sheephouse Manor, Sheephouse Road, Maidenhead, Berks, SL6 8HJ.*
Actual grid ref: SU8878
Charming C16th farmhouse
Grades: ETB 2 Cr, Comm
Tel: **01628 776902**
Mrs Street.
Fax no: 01628 25138
Rates fr: £22.50-**£33.00**.
Open: All Year (not Xmas)
Beds: 2D 1T 2S
Baths: 5 Private
🖚 (5) 🅿 (6) 🖵 🛉 📖 Ⅴ

(1m) *Clifton Guest House, 21 Craufurd Rise, Maidenhead, Berks, SL6 7LR.*
Family-run, evening meals, fully licensed.
Grades: ETB 3 Cr
Tel: **01628 623572** (also fax no)
Mr Arora.
Rates fr: £28.00-**£45.00**.
Open: All Year
Beds: 2F 4D 7T 3S
Baths: 7 Ensuite 3 Shared
🖚 (1) 🅿 (11) 🖵 ✗ 📖 ⚐ Ⅴ

(1m) *Copperfields Guest House, 54 Bath Road, Maidenhead, Berks, SL6 4JY.*
Comfortable, clean and caring accommodation
Tel: **01628 674941**
Mrs Lindsay.
Rates fr: £22.00-**£28.00**.
Open: All Year
Beds: 2F 2D 2T 1S
Baths: 3 Private
🖚 🅿 (5) 🖵 🛉 📖

(1m) *4 Gables Close, Off Ray Lea Road, Maidenhead, Berks, SL6 8QD.*
Modern comfortable house in quiet close
Tel: **01628 639630**
Mrs Blight.
Rates fr: £17.00-**£17.00**.
Open: All Year
Beds: 1D 1S
Baths: 1 Shared
🖚 🅿 (2) 🖵 ✗ 📖 Ⅴ ⚐

The Grid Reference beneath the location heading is for the village or town - *not* for individual houses, which are shown (where supplied) in each entry itself.

All rooms full and nowhere else to stay? Ask the owner if there's anywhere nearby

Wargrave-on-Thames 21

National Grid Ref: SU7978

🍽 🍺 The Bull

(0.25m) *Windy Brow, 204 Victoria Road, Wargrave-on-Thames, Reading, Berks, RG10 8AJ.*
Large Victorian house overlooking fields.
Grades: ETB Listed
Tel: **0118 940 3336**
Mrs Carver.
Rates fr: £20.00-**£25.00**.
Open: All Year
Beds: 1F 3D 3T 2S
Baths: 1 Private 2 Shared
🖚 🅿 (6) 🖊 🖵 🛉 📖 ⚐ Ⅴ

Twyford 22

National Grid Ref: SU7975

🍽 🍺 Queen Victoria, The Bull

(0.5m) *Chesham House, 79 Wargrave Road, Twyford, Reading, Berks, RG10 9PE.*
Ensuite, beverage facilities, television, refrigerator
Grades: ETB 2 Cr, High Comm
Tel: **0118 932 0428**
Mr & Mrs Ferguson.
Rates fr: £19.00-**£24.00**.
Open: All Year (not Xmas)
Beds: 1D 1T
Baths: 2 Private
🖚 🅿 (6) 🖵 📖 ⚐

(0.5m) *Copper Beeches, Bath Road, Kiln Green, Twyford, Reading, Berks, RG10 9UT.*
Quiet house, large garden. Close to M4/M40 Heathrow. London 1/2 hour by train
Tel: **0118 940 2929** (also fax no)
Mrs Gorecki.
Rates fr: £19.00-**£25.00**.
Open: All Year
Beds: 1F 1T 1D 1S
Baths: 1 Ensuite 2 Shared
🖚 🅿 (14) 🖵 📖 ⚐ ⚐

Cheshire Cycleway

The 135-mile **Cheshire Cycleway** takes you through the whole range of the county's scenery, from plain and parkland to the edge of the Pennine moors, and also gives a taste of Cheshire's urban landscape: the circular route has the historic towns of Chester and Macclesfield at either pole, and is sprinkled with castles and country houses.

A detailed **guide leaflet** to the cycleway route, which includes a list of cycle repair/hire shops on or near to the route, is available from Cheshire County Council, Tourism and Marketing Unit, Goldsmith House, Hamilton Place, Chester CH1 1SE, tel 01244 603107, @ 60p (+20p p&p). The route is signposted by blue Cheshire Cycleway direction signs with a cycle silhouette, only in a clockwise direction as described above.

Maps: Ordnance Survey 1:50,000 Landranger series: 117, 118.

Major **railway** termini along the route are Chester, Crewe, Macclesfield and Wilmslow, north east of Knutsford. Many other places are

served by local trains.

If you would like advice or help with planning the cycleway, **Byways Bike Breaks** specialise in cycling holidays in Cheshire. They can be contacted at 25 Mayville Road, Liverpool L18 0HG, tel 0151-722 8050.

Chester

The route begins in **Chester**, the county town with a fortress history. The largest fortified town of Roman Britain, in medieval times it was the centre of the Plantaganets' military campaigns against Wales, and boasts the most complete medieval and Roman city wall in Britain - two miles long with seven gates. Landmarks along the wall include the fifteenth-century King Charles Tower, from which

Charles I watched the defeat of the royalist side in the battle of Rowton Moor, and the Water Tower, which contains a display on the city's history. Other features of the city are the cathedral, containing architectural vestiges from the eleventh to the sixteenth centuries, including the intersecting stone arches of the 'crown of stone' and a cloistered garden; and the half-excavated Roman Amphitheatre, the largest in Britain, its estimated capacity of 7000 even greater than that in Caerleon.

Chester   **1**

National Grid Ref: SJ4066

|●| ◘ Faulkner Arms, The Plough, Miller's Kitchen Pub, King's Head, Spinning Wheel, Three Crowns, Chester Bells

(▲ 1m) *Chester Youth Hostel, Hough Green House, 40 Hough Green, Chester. CH4 8HD.*
Actual grid ref: SJ397651
Tel: **01244 680056**
Under 18: £6.55 **Adults:** £9.75
Evening Meals Available (6-7.30pm), Self-catering Facilities, Television, Games Room, Showers, Shop, Security Lockers, Laundry Facilities
Attractive house and mews 1 mile from the city centre, redecorated in keeping with Victorian origins. Comfortable accommodation, a good base for the city, good access to North Wales

(On route) *Pear Tree, 69 Hoole Road, Hoole, Chester, Cheshire, CH2 3NJ.*
Large comfortable Victorian house
Grades: AA 2 St
Tel: **01244 323260**
Rates fr: *£14.00-£16.00.*
Open: All Year
Beds: 2F 5D 5T 3S
Baths: 6 Ensuite 3 Shared
ㅎ ▣ 🗗 ✕ 🛒 ⓥ 🖭 ✿ ✀

(On route) *The Georgian House, 131 Boughton, Chester, Cheshire, CH3 5BH.*
Large Georgian town house; most rooms with view over river
Grades: ETB 2 Cr
Tel: **01244 312186**
Mr Chuter.
Rates fr: *£17.00-£20.00.*
Open: All Year (not Xmas)
Beds: 1F 4D 1T 1S
Baths: 7 Private
ㅎ (5) ▣ (7) 🗗 🛒 ⓥ

(1m) *Eversley Hotel, 9 Eversley Park, Chester, Cheshire, CH2 2AJ.*
Victorian residential hotel, bar, restaurant
Tel: **01244 373744**
Mr Povey.
Rates fr: *£21.50*-**£23.00**.
Open: All Year
Beds: 4F 3D 2T 2S
Baths: 9 Private 2 Shared
⚡ ⓟ (17) 🖵 ✕ ▥ Ⓥ

(1m) *Devonia, 33-35 Hoole Road, Chester, Cheshire, CH2 3NH.*
Large Victorian family-run guest house
Grades: ETB Listed, RAC Listed
Tel: **01244 322236**
Fax no: 01244 401511
Rates fr: *£15.00*-**£20.00**.
Open: All Year
Beds: 4F 3D 3T 1S
⚡ ⓟ (12) 🖵 🕇 ▥ Ⓥ

(1m) *Laurels, 14 Selkirk Road, Curzon Park, Chester, Cheshire, CH4 8AH.*
Private house, best residential area near racecourse
Tel: **01244 679682**
Mrs Roberts.
Rates fr: *£17.50*-**£18.00**.
Open: All Year (not Xmas)
Beds: 1F 1D 1S
Baths: 1 Private 2 Shared
⚡ ⓟ (3) 🖵 ▥

(1m) *Stone Villa, 3 Stone Place, Hoole, Chester, Cheshire, CH2 3NR.*
Accent on comfort and cleanliness
Grades: ETB 2 Cr, Comm
Tel: **01244 345014**
Mr Pow.
Rates fr: *£26.00*-**£32.00**.
Open: All Year (not Xmas)
Beds: 6D 2T 1S 1Triple
Baths: 10 Private
⚡ ⓟ (11) ✁ 🖵 ▥ Ⓥ ♦ ♪

(1m) *Castle House, 23 Castle Street, Chester, Cheshire, CH1 2DS.*
Tudor/Georgian house 1590 & 1738
Tel: **01244 350354**
Mr Marl.
Rates fr: *£21.00*-**£22.00**.
Open: All Year
Beds: 1F 1D 1T 2S
Baths: 3 Ensuite 1 Shared
⚡ ⓟ 🖵 🕇 ▥ Ⓥ

All rooms full and nowhere else to stay? Ask the owner if there's anywhere nearby

All details shown are as supplied by B&B owners in Autumn 1997.

(1m) *Grosvenor Place Guest House, 2-4 Grosvenor Place, Chester, Cheshire, CH1 2DE.*
City centre guest house
Tel: **01244 324455**
Mrs Wood.
Rates fr: *£16.00*-**£22.00**.
Open: All Year
Beds: 2F 2D 3T 3S
Baths: 4 Private 2 Shared
ⓟ 🖵 🕇 ▥ Ⓥ

(1m) *Ba Ba Guest House, 65 Hoole Road, Hoole, Chester, Cheshire, CH2 3NJ.*
Large Victorian family house
Tel: **01244 315047**
Mrs Smith.
Rates fr: *£15.00*-**£20.00**.
Open: All Year (not Xmas)
Beds: 3F 2D
Baths: 3 Private 2 Shared
⚡ ⓟ (5) 🖵 ▥ Ⓥ

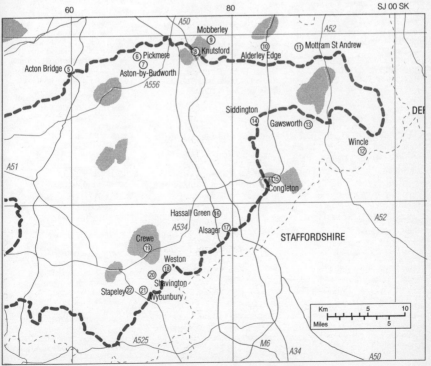

Littleton 2

National Grid Ref: SJ4466

¶¶ ⬛ The Plough

(0.5m) *Firbank, 64 Tarvin Road, Littleton, Chester, Cheshire, CH3 7DF.*
Traditional Victorian house, warm welcome, extensive gardens, two miles Chester
Tel: **01244 335644** Mrs Shambler.
Fax no: 01244 332068
Rates fr: *£18.00-£24.00.*
Open: All Year (not Xmas)
Beds: 2D **Baths:** 2 Ensuite
🄿 (2) ⌷ ⵀ 🏧.

Wervin 3

National Grid Ref: SJ4271

¶¶ ⬛ Wheatsheaf Hotel

(3m) *Wervin New Hall, Wervin, Chester, Cheshire, CH2 4BP.*
Tudor style mansion
Tel: **01244 372945** Mrs Warburton.
Rates fr: *£16.00-£17.00.*
Open: All Year (not Xmas)
Beds: 1F 1D 1T
Baths: 1 Private 2 Shared
🖢 (0) 🄿 (20) ⵘ⌷ ⵀ 🏧. 🗹 🛢 ⵌ

Guilden Sutton 4

National Grid Ref: SJ4468

¶¶ ⬛ Bird in Hand

(2m) *Garden Cottage, Guilden Sutton Lane, Guilden Sutton, Chester, Cheshire, CH3 7EX.*
Charming country cottage near city
Tel: **01244 300131**
Mrs Bennett.
Rates fr: *£15.00-£16.50.*
Open: All Year (not Xmas)
Beds: 1D 1T **Baths:** 1 Shared
🄿 (4) ⵘ⌷ 🏧. 🗹

Acton Bridge 5

National Grid Ref: SJ5975

(On route) *Horns Inn, Warrington Road, Acton Bridge, Little Leigh, Northwich, Cheshire, CW8 4QT.*
Traditional country pub, friendly atmosphere.
Tel: **01606 852192** Mr Redfern.
Rates fr: *£17.50-£25.00.*
Open: All Year
Beds: 1D 2T 1S **Baths:** 2 Shared
🖢 🄿 ⵘ⌷ ⵀ ✕ 🏧. 🗹

Pickmere 6

National Grid Ref: SJ6977

(2m) *Pickmere House, Park Lane, Pickmere, Knutsford, Cheshire, WA16 0JX.*
Highly acclaimed Listed Georgian house
Grades: ETB 2 Cr, AA 3 Q, RAC High Acclaim
Tel: **01565 733433** Mrs Brown.
Rates fr: *£19.50-£19.50.*
Open: All Year **Beds:** 4D 2T 3S
Baths: 6 Private 2 Shared
🖢 🄿 (10) ⵘ⌷ ⵀ ✕ 🏧. 🗹 🛢 ⵌ

Aston-by-Budworth 7

National Grid Ref: SJ6976

¶¶ ⬛ Red Lion, George & Dragon

(3m) *Clock Cottage, Hield Lane, Aston-by-Budworth, Northwich, Cheshire, CW9 6LP.*
Lovely C17th thatched country cottage, beautiful country garden, wooded countryside
Grades: ETB Listed, Approv
Tel: **01606 891271** Mrs Tanner-Betts.
Rates fr: *£17.50-£20.00.*
Open: All Year
Beds: 1T 2S **Baths:** 1 Shared
🖢 (2) 🄿 (6) ⵘ ✕ 🏧. 🖕 🗹

Chester to Knutsford

Attractions along the first stretch of the route after Chester include the Mouldsworth Motor Museum, a collection of vintage vehicles which, despite its name, also contains some early bicycles; and Delamere Forest Park, 4000 acres of woodland, with waymarked walks and cycling trails for if you fancy a diversion from the serious business of the cycleway itself. From here you strike out across the Cheshire Plain, and can admire the half-timbered cottages of the village of Great Budworth before reaching the town of **Knutsford**. *Canute's Ford*, where the Danish king crossed the Lily Stream in the early eleventh century, was important in medieval times for its market and coaching inns, but the modern town dates largely from the eighteenth century, and was the model for Elizabeth Gaskell's *Cranford* in the nineteenth. In more recent times, nearby Knutsford Heath was the scene of a memorable confrontation during the 1997 election campaign, between Martin Bell, who became Independent Member of Parliament, and Christine Hamilton, as she leapt heroically but vainly to the defence of her errant husband, Neil, the discredited sitting MP.

The Grid Reference beneath the location heading is for the village or town - *not* for individual houses, which are shown (where supplied) in each entry itself.

Knutsford 8

National Grid Ref: SJ7578

(0.5m) *Krakatoa, Manor Park South, Knutsford, Cheshire, WA16 8AG.*
Large private house
Tel: **01565 651157** Mrs Fisher.
Rates fr: *£18.00-£23.00.*
Open: All Year
Beds: 1D
Baths: 1 Private
🄿 (3) ⌷ ⵀ 🏧.

Mobberley 9

National Grid Ref: SJ7879

¶¶ ⬛ Bird In Hand

(2m) *Laburnum Cottage, Knutsford Road, Mobberley, Knutsford, Cheshire, WA16 7PU.*
Country house overlooking Tatton Park
Grades: ETB 2 Cr, High Comm, AA Prem, Select
Tel: **01565 872464** Mrs Foxwell.
Rates fr: *£21.00-£30.00.*
Open: All Year
Beds: 1D 2T 2S
Baths: 4 Private
🖢 🄿 (8) ⵘ⌷ 🏧. 🗹

Alderley Edge 10

National Grid Ref: SJ8478

¶¶ ⬛ Prospect House Hotel, Oakwood, Bird in Hand, Frozen Mop, Plough & Flail

(2m) *Trafford House Farm, Beswicks Lane, Row of Trees, Alderley Edge, Wilmslow, Cheshire, SK9 7SN.*
Spacious accommodation set in beautiful Cheshire countryside, with working stables
Tel: **01625 582160**
Mr & Mrs Blackmore.
Fax no: 01625 584968
Rates fr: *£15.00-£20.00.*
Open: All Year (not Xmas)
Beds: 1F 1T 1D **Baths:** 2 Shared
🖢 🄿 (10) ⵘ⌷ ⵀ ✕ 🏧. 🛢 ⵌ

Knutsford to Audlem

After Knutsford it's a gradual climb to Alderley Edge, a sandstone ridge inhabited by a legendary wizard, around **Macclesfield**, historically important for its silk production, and towards the edge of the **Peak District National Park**. Attractions along the way include two National Trust properties, a fifteenth-century water mill at Nether Alderley, and Hare Hill Gardens, a Victorian woodland garden and walled garden; and Prestbury, a village notable for its nineteenth-century weaver's cottages. A little way off the route is Tegg's Nose Country Park, where the gritstone hill provides a magnificent panorama in every direction, and then comes the most remote part of the cycleway, as you head towards the village of Wildboarclough inside the White Peak. After this the route takes you back down off the Peak; across the Macclesfield Canal you come to Galsworth Hall, a Tudor house set in beautiful grounds. Past Congleton and Alsager you come to Barthomley, another beautiful Cheshire village with half-timbered cottages and a seventeenth-century pub, the White Lion. The route bypasses Nantwich, famous for its timber-framed Tudor buildings and the fourteenth-century Church of St Mary, after Crewe, famous for its railway junction, and takes you to Audlem, which boasts another fourteenth-century church and stands upon the Shropshire Union Canal, with a succession of locks.

Mottram St Andrew   11

National Grid Ref: SJ8778

¶○¶ ◖ Bull's Head, Legh Arms

(1m) *Woodlands, Shaws Lane, Mottram St Andrew, Macclesfield, Cheshire, SK10 4RD.*
Luxury accommodation, beautiful location
Tel: **01625 828166** Mrs Bell.
Rates fr: *£18.00*-**£18.00**.
Open: All Year
Beds: 2D **Baths:** 1 Shared
❧ ▣ (4) ⛝ ⍩ ✕ 🎍 ♿ Ⓥ

(2m) *Goose Green Farm, Oak Road, Mottram St Andrew, Macclesfield, Cheshire, SK10 4RA.*
Quiet farmhouse with beautiful views
Grades: ETB 2 Cr, Comm
Tel: **01625 828814** Mrs Hatch.
Rates fr: *£18.00*-**£18.00**.
Open: All Year (not Xmas)
Beds: 1D 1T 2S
Baths: 1 Ensuite 1 Shared
❧ (5) ▣ (10) ✂ ⛝ 🎍 Ⓥ ✦

Wincle   12

National Grid Ref: SJ9566

¶○¶ ◖ Ship Inn

(1m) *Hill Top Farm, Wincle, Macclesfield, Cheshire, SK11 0QH.*
Peaceful and comfortable farmhouse accommodation
Tel: **01260 227257**
Mrs Brocklehurst.
Rates fr: *£17.00*-**£18.00**.
Open: All Year (not Xmas)
Beds: 1T 1S **Baths:** 1 Shared
❧ (3) ▣ (3) ✂ ⛝ ✕ 🎍 Ⓥ

The lowest *double* rate per person is shown in *italics*.

Gawsworth   13

National Grid Ref: SJ8969

(0.5m) *Rough Hey Farm, Leek Road, Gawsworth, Macclesfield, Cheshire, SK11 0JQ.*
Quiet, historic, modernised farmhouse
Grades: ETB 2 Cr, Comm
Tel: **01260 252296** Mrs Worth.
Rates fr: *£18.00*-**£18.00**.
Open: All Year (not Xmas)
Beds: 1D 1T 2S
Baths: 2 Private 1 Shared
❧ (3) ▣ (4) ✂ ⛝ 🎍 Ⓥ

Siddington   14

National Grid Ref: SJ8471

(1m) *Golden Cross Farm, Siddington, Macclesfield, Cheshire, SK11 9JP.*
Farmhouse in picturesque surroundings
Tel: **01260 224358**
Mrs Rush.
Rates fr: *£15.00*-**£15.00**.
Open: All Year (not Xmas)
Beds: 2D 2S
Baths: 2 Shared
❧ ▣ (4) ✂ ⛝ 🎍 Ⓥ

Congleton   15

National Grid Ref: SJ8663

¶○¶ ◖ Lamb Inn, Bull's Head Hotel, Brown Cow Inn, Edgerton Arms

(2m) *The Lamb Inn, 3 Blake St, Congleton, Cheshire, CW12 4DS.*
Central location. Convenient for Cheshire and SOT country houses and attractions
Tel: **01260 272731** Mr Kelly.
Rates fr: *£15.00*-**£16.00**.
Open: All Year
Beds: 1F 2D 2T 1S
Baths: 3 Private 1 Shared
❧ ▣ (20) ⛝ ⍩ ✕ 🎍 Ⓥ

(2m) *Loachbrook Farm, Sandbach Rd, Congleton, Cheshire, CW12 4TE.*
Actual grid ref: SJ833630
Beautiful C17th farmhouse, close to M6 and airport
Tel: **01260 273318**
Mrs Dale.
Rates fr: *£14.00*-**£16.00**.
Open: All Year (not Xmas)
Beds: 1D 2T 1S
Baths: 2 Shared
❧ (5) ▣ (6) ⛝ 🎍 Ⓥ

(2m) *Cuttleford Farm, Newcastle Road, Astbury, Congleton, Cheshire, CW12 4SD.*
160 acre mixed working farm
Grades: ETB 2 Cr
Tel: **01260 272499**
Mrs Downs.
Rates fr: *£14.00*-**£17.00**.
Open: All Year
Beds: 2D 1T
Baths: 1 Ensuite 1 Shared
❧ ▣ ⛝ ⍩ 🎍

(2m) *8 Cloud View, Congleton, Cheshire, CW12 3TP.*
Lovely family home, edge of countryside
Tel: **01260 276048**
Mrs Stewart.
Rates fr: *£13.50*-**£15.00**.
Open: All Year (not Xmas)
Beds: 1T 1S 1D
Baths: 1 Ensuite 1 Shared
❧ ▣ (1) ✂ ⛝ ✕ 🎍 Ⓥ

(2m) *Lion Swan Hotel, Swan Bank, Congleton, Cheshire, CW12 1JR.*
C16th hotel (former coaching inn)
Grades: ETB 4 Cr, AA 3 St, RAC 3 St
Tel: **01260 273115**
Mr Williams.
Fax no: 01260 299270
Rates fr: *£26.00*-**£31.00**.
Open: All Year
Beds: 1F 15D 1T 4S
Baths: 21 Private
❧ ▣ (40) ✂ ⛝ ⍩ ✕ 🎍 ♿ Ⓥ

Hassall Green 16

National Grid Ref: SJ7858

(2m) *Canal Centre & Village Store, Hassall Green, Sandbach, Cheshire, CW11 4TB.*
Actual grid ref: SJ780595
Grades: ETB Listed, Comm
Tel: **01270 762266**
Mr/Mrs Paine.
Rates fr: *£19.00-£19.00*.
Open: All Year
Beds: 1F 2D 2T 1S
Baths: 2 Ensuite 1 Private
🛇 🅿 (6) ❑ ⭐ ✕ 🎟 ⚓ 🎟 👜
C18th, family-run guesthouse, by the side of the Trent & Mersey Canal. Licensed restaurant, tearooms, giftshop, fishing, near J17 M6

Alsager 17

National Grid Ref: SJ7955

(0.5m) *The Limes, 32 Sandbach Road South, Alsager, Stoke on Trent. ST7 2LP.*
Detached, Victorian private house
Tel: **01270 874659**
Mrs Morgan.
Rates fr: *£14.00-£14.00*.
Open: All Year (not Xmas)
Beds: 1T 1S
🅿 (3) ⚡ 🎟.

Weston (Crewe) 18

National Grid Ref: SJ7352

(On route) *Snape Farm, Snape Lane, Weston (Crewe), Crewe, Cheshire, CW2 5NB.*
Warm comfortable Victorian farmhouse in quiet location
Grades: ETB 2 Cr, Comm
Tel: **01270 820208** (also fax no)
Mrs Williamson.
Rates fr: *£16.00-£18.00*.
Open: All Year (not Xmas)
Beds: 2T 1D
Baths: 1 Ensuite 1 Shared
🛇 🅿 (5) ❑ ⭐ ✕ 🎟 👜

Crewe 19

National Grid Ref: SJ7055

(3m) *Hunters Lodge Hotel, Sydney Road, Sydney, Crewe, Cheshire, CW1 1LU.*
Quiet country-style location. Sports complex.
Grades: AA 3 St
Tel: **01270 583440** Mr Panayi.
Rates fr: *£23.00-£26.00*.
Open: All Year
Beds: 1F 27D 4T 10S
Baths: 42 Private
🛇 🅿 (180) ❑ ✕ 🎟 ⚓ 👜

Shavington 20

National Grid Ref: SJ6951

(1m) *Oakland House, 252 Newcastle Road, Blakelow, Shavington, Nantwich, Cheshire, CW5 7ET.*
All home comforts, ideally situated
Grades: ETB 2 Cr, High Comm, AA 4 Q
Tel: **01270 67134**
Mr & Mrs Wetton.
Rates fr: *£16.00-£25.00*.
Open: All Year
Beds: 1F 2D 2T **Baths:** 5 Private
🛇 (14) 🅿 (10) ⚡ ❑ 🎟 ⚓

Wybunbury 21

National Grid Ref: SJ6949
🍴 🍺 Boar's Head, The Swan

(1m) *Lea Farm, Wrinehill Road, Wybunbury, Nantwich, Cheshire, CW5 7HS.*
Charming farmhouse set in landscaped gardens where peacocks roam
Grades: ETB 2 Cr, Comm
Tel: **01270 841429** Mrs Callwood.
Rates fr: *£15.00-£17.50*.
Open: All Year (not Xmas)
Beds: 1F 1D 1T
Baths: 2 Private 1 Shared
🛇 🅿 (22) ❑ ⭐ ✕ 👜

Stapeley 22

National Grid Ref: SJ6749
🍴 🍺 Lamb Hotel, Shroppie Fly

(2m) *York Cottage, 82 Broad Lane, Stapeley, Nantwich, Cheshire, CW5 7QL.*
Converted C19th country cottage, rural aspect - comfortable lounge, log fires - central heating
Grades: ETB Listed
Tel: **01270 628867** Mrs Winfield.
Rates fr: *£16.00-£17.00*.
Open: All Year (not Xmas)
Beds: 1D 1T 1S **Baths:** 1 Shared
🅿 (3) ❑ ⭐ 🎟. 👜

Hatton Heath 23

National Grid Ref: SJ4561
🍴 🍺 Grosvenor Arms

(2m) *Golborne Manor, Platts Lane, Hatton Heath, Chester, Cheshire, CH3 9AN.*
Victorian, luxury, country manor house
Grades: ETB Listed, High Comm
Tel: **01829 770310 / 0850 265425**
Mrs Ikin. Fax no: 01244 318084
Rates fr: *£25.00-£25.00*.
Open: All Year **Beds:** 1F 1T 1D
Baths: 2 Ensuite 1 Private
🛇 (Any) 🅿 (6) ⚡ ❑ 🎟 ⚓ 👜

Audlem to Chester

Two more villages worth a look along the route are Wrenbury and Marbury, before you arrive at **Malpas**, an historic market town with half-timbered buildings, Georgian houses and coaching inns. The town is also the place to sample the range of salty Cheshire cheeses, on sale everywhere. Notable places along the home strait of the cycleway are Stretton Mill, a working water mill that has been restored, and two castles - Peckforton Castle, built in the mid-nineteenth century medievalist revival for Lord Tollemache, and by contrast the ruins of the very genuinely medieval Beeston Castle, dating from the thirteenth century and set romantically against glorious views over the Cheshire Plain. From here you ride parallel to the Shropshire Union Canal back into **Chester**.

Higher Wych 24

National Grid Ref: SJ4943

(2m) *Mill House, Higher Wych, Malpas, Cheshire, SY14 7JR.*
Modernised mill house, rural setting
Grades: ETB 3 Cr, High Comm
Tel: **01948 780362** Mrs Smith.
Fax no: 01948 780566
Rates fr: *£16.00-£16.00*.
Open: All Year (not Xmas)
Beds: 1D 1T
Baths: 1 Private 1 Shared
🛇 🅿 (4) ✕ 🎟.

All details shown
are as supplied
by B&B owners in
Autumn 1997.

STILWELL'S BRITAIN BED & BREAKFAST

Bed & breakfast accommodation is a British institution. It's a great value alternative to expensive hotels and a world away from camping and caravanning. You may be touring, travelling or pursuing a hobby. You may just wish to get away from it all. Whatever the reason, the British bed & breakfast is the great value answer to all your accommodation needs.

There's such a wide range to choose from - private houses, country halls, farms, cottages, inns, small hotels and guest houses. Stilwell's Britain Bed & Breakfast 1998 publishes by far and away the most extensive list of bed & breakfasts available. The book is thus ideal for planning trips and short stays in every part of the country.

Arranged by country, county and location with local maps alongside, Stilwell's Britain Bed & Breakfast 1998 is the indispensable reference work for bed & breakfast accommodation in Britain.

- Plan your trips with no fuss!

- All official grades shown!

- Local maps - see where you want to stay at a glance!

- Pubs serving evening meals shown too!

- The largest choice ever - a massive 8,000 entries!

- Good value only - an average £17 to £18 a night!

- Handy size for easy packing!

Britain Bed & Breakfast is available from all good bookshops (ISBN 1-900861-02-X) or direct from Stilwell Publishing Ltd @ £9.95 plus £2 p&p (UK only).

Cumbria Cycleway

The **Cumbria Cycleway** is a mammoth 260-mile circular route around the perimeter of the County of Cumbria, from moorland and wooded river valleys inland to a long stretch along the coast, from Morecambe Bay to the Solway Firth. It completely avoids the Lakes (see the *CTC Dales Side to Side Tour* or the *Sustrans Sea to Sea* route for a route through the Lake District), and as such takes you to parts of the county not frequented by visitors. The route is clearly waymarked in both directions by brown 'Cumbria' direction signs with a cycle silhouette, and there is no designated start/finish. The description that follows takes the route clockwise from Carlisle.

A detailed **guide leaflet** to the cycleway route, which includes a list of cycle repair/hire shops on or near to the route, is available free from Cumbria County Council, Economy & Environment, Planning Division, County Offices, Kendal, Cumbria LA9 4RQ, tel 01539 773407; and a **guide book**, *The Cumbria Cycleway* by Roy Walker and Ron Jarvis (ISBN 1 852841 06 0) is published by Cicerone Press and available from the publishers at 2 Police Square, Milnthorpe, Cumbria LA7 7PY, tel 01539 562069, @ £5.99 (+75p p&p).

Maps: Ordnance Survey 1:50,000 Landranger series: 85, 86, 89, 90, 91, 96, 97, 98

The major **railway** termini are Carlisle, Oxenholme (near Kendal) and Penrith. There is also the famous scenic Leeds-Settle-Carlisle Railway, which stops at Garsdale, Kirkby Stephen and Appleby-in-Westmorland, and other local services.

Carlisle   1

National Grid Ref: NY3955

¶⊙ ⬛ Metal Bridge Inn

(▲ 0.5m) *University of Northumbria, The Old Brewery Residences, Bridge Lane, Caldewgate, Carlisle, Cumbria, CA2 5SR*.
Tel: **01228 597352**. After 6pm: **01228 59486**
Under 18: £10.00
Adults: £10.00
Self-catering Facilities, Showers, Laundry Facilities
Accommodation in an award-winning conversion of the former Theakston's brewery. Single study bedrooms with shared kitchen and bathroom in flats for upto 7 people

(0.5m) *Chatsworth Guest House, 22 Chatsworth Square, Carlisle, Cumbria, CA1 1HF*.
Grade II Listed city centre house overlooking gardens. Close to bus stations, rail and all amenities
Grades: ETB 2 Cr, Comm
Tel: **01228 24023** Mrs Irving.
Rates fr: *£14.00*-**£16.00**.
Open: All Year (not Xmas)
Beds: 2F 3T 2S
Baths: 2 Ensuite 1 Shared
⚡ (2) ⬜ ✕ ⬛ ⬩

(0.5m) *Howard Lodge, 90 Warwick Road, Carlisle, Cumbria, CA1 1JU*.
Actual grid ref: NY407558
Grades: ETB 1 Cr, Comm, AA 3 Q, Recomm
Tel: **01228 29842** Mr Hendrie.
Rates fr: *£15.00*-**£15.00**.
Open: All Year
Beds: 2F 1D 2T 1S
Baths: 6 Ensuite 1 Shared
⚡ ⚡ (6) ⬜ ✕ ⬛ Ⓥ
Large Victorian house on main road, 400 metres from city centre. Recently refurbished with ensuite facilities. Satellite TV and welcome tray in all rooms. Now with private parking

(0.25m) *Avondale, 3 St Aidans Road, Carlisle, Cumbria, CA1 1LT*.
Grades: ETB 2 Cr, High Comm, RAC Acclaim
Tel: **01228 23012** Mr & Mrs Hayes.
Rates fr: *£18.00*-**£20.00**.
Open: All Year (not Xmas)
Beds: 1D 2T
Baths: 1 Private 1 Shared
⚡ (3) ⬜ ✕ ⬛ Ⓥ
Attractive, comfortable Edwardian house in a quiet position, convenient for M6 (J43), city centre & amenities. Spacious well-furnished rooms. Most hospitable. Private parking

(0.25m) *Craighead, 6 Hartington Place, Carlisle, Cumbria, CA1 1HL*.
Actual grid ref: NY405559
Grades: ETB 2 Cr, Comm
Tel: **01228 596767** Mrs Smith.
Rates fr: *£15.50*-**£15.50**.
Open: All Year (not Xmas)
Beds: 1F 2D 1T 2S
Baths: 1 Ensuite 2 Shared
⚡ ⬜ ✝ ⬛ Ⓥ ⬩
Grade II Listed spacious Victorian town house with comfortable rooms and original features. CTV, tea/coffee tray - all rooms. Minutes walk city centre, bus & rail station and all amenities. Friendly personal service

(0.25m) *Cornerways Guest House, 107 Warwick Road, Carlisle, Cumbria, CA1 1EA*.
Large Victorian town house
Grades: ETB 1 Cr, Comm
Tel: **01228 21733** Mrs Fisher.
Rates fr: *£13.00*-**£14.00**.
Open: All Year (not Xmas)
Beds: 1F 2D 4T 3S
Baths: 2 Ensuite 2 Shared
⚡ ⚡ (5) ⬜ ✝ ✕ ⬛ Ⓥ ⬩

The lowest *double* rate per person is shown in *italics*.

(On route) *East View Guest House, 110 Warwick Road, Carlisle, Cumbria, CA1 1JU.*
Actual grid ref: NY407560
A warm welcome assured at this Victorian family-run guesthouse
Grades: ETB 1 Cr, Comm
Tel: 01228 22112 (also fax no)
Mrs MacKin.
Rates fr: *£16.00-£18.00.*
Open: All Year
Beds: 3F 3D 1T 1S
Baths: 8 Ensuite
⌖ �P (4) ⌧ ▥ ✦

(0.5m) *Courtfield Guest House, 169 Warwick Road, Carlisle, Cumbria, CA1 1LP.*
Short walk to historic city centre.
Close to M6, J43
Grades: ETB 3 Cr, High Comm
Tel: 01228 22767 Mrs Dawes.
Rates fr: *£17.50-£20.00.*
Open: All Year
Beds: 1F 2D 1T
Baths: 4 Private
⌖ �P (4) ⌧ 🛏 ✕ ▥ Ⓥ

(0.5m) *Langleigh House, 6 Howard Place, Carlisle, Cumbria, CA1 1HR.*
Comfortable home with Victorian furniture
Grades: ETB 2 Cr, High Comm, AA Listed
Tel: 01228 30440
Rates fr: *£20.00-£25.00.*
Open: All Year
Beds: 3D **Baths:** 3 Ensuite
⌖ �P (10) ⌧ ▥ & Ⓥ ✦

Carlisle

As a border city, **Carlisle**, the county town, was for centuries the focus of tribal struggles: the original settlement of Celtic Britons was subdued by the Roman Empire to build an outpost for the construction of Hadrian's Wall, and later attempts of Anglo-Saxons, Scots and Danes to prevail ended with the Norman takeover. However, the Scots never quite gave up, and captured the town for a brief period during the Jacobite rebellion of 1745. The notable remains of these struggles are the eleventh- to twelfth-century city walls and the Castle, built by the Norman King William Rufus, with many later additions, where Mary Queen of Scots was kept prisoner by Elizabeth I in 1568, and Scottish prisoners of war were accommodated after the crushing of the Jacobite rebellion. Carlisle Cathedral, built in red sandstone, was begun by the same king, completed by Henry I and desecrated by Cromwell's men five hundred years later. Two Romanesque arches remain from the original building, set against the Gothic East Window; there is also a treasury housing important objects from the city's ecclesiastical heritage.

(0.5m) *Marchmain Guest House, 151 Warwick Road, Carlisle, Cumbria, CA1 1LU.*
Comfortable accommodation with friendly atmosphere
Grades: ETB 1 Cr, Comm
Tel: 01228 29551 Mr Bertham.
Rates fr: *£16.00-£15.00.*
Open: All Year
Beds: 2F 2D 1T 1S
Baths: 1 Ensuite 2 Shared
⌖ ⅏ ⌧ ✕ ▥ Ⓥ

(0.5m) *7 Hether Drive, Lowry Hill, Carlisle, Cumbria, CA3 0ED.*
Bungalow ramped access. Wheel-in shower
Grades: ETB 1 Cr
Tel: 01228 27242 Mrs Young.
Rates fr: *£16.50-£18.50.*
Open: All Year **Beds:** 1F 1D 1T
Baths: 2 Private 1 Shared
⌖ (0) �P (2) ⌧ 🛏 ▥ & Ⓥ ✦

(0.5m) *Parkland Guest House, 136 Petteril Street, Carlisle, Cumbria, CA1 2AW.*
Good service guest house, Hadrian's Wall
Grades: ETB 3 Cr, Comm, AA 3 Q, Recomm
Tel: 01228 48331 (also fax no)
Mrs Murray.
Rates fr: *£15.00-£17.50.*
Open: All Year
Beds: 2F
⌖ ⅊ (3) ⅏ ⌧ 🛏 ✕ ▥ Ⓥ

(0.5m) *Howard House, 27 Howard Place, Carlisle, Cumbria, CA1 1HR.*
Elegant Victorian town house
Tel: 01228 29159 / 512550
Mrs Fisher.
Rates fr: *£15.00-£15.00.*
Open: All Year
Beds: 2F 3D 3T
Baths: 2 Private 2 Shared
⌖ ⌧ 🛏 ✕ ▥ Ⓥ 🛆 ✦

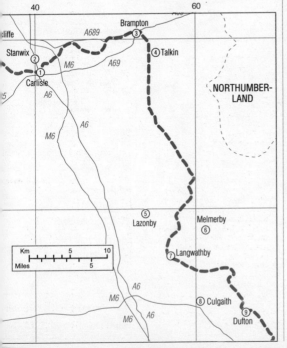

All rooms full and nowhere else to stay? Ask the owner if there's anywhere nearby

Stanwix 2

National Grid Ref: NY3957

(0.5m) *Angus Hotel, 14 Scotland Road, Stanwix, Carlisle, Cumbria, CA3 9DG.*
Actual grid ref: NY400571
Tel: **01228 523546**
Mr Webster.
Fax no: 01228 531895
Rates fr: £20.00-**£26.00**.
Open: All Year
Beds: 4F 3D 4T 3S
Baths: 11 Ensuite 3 Shared
ॐ ▣ (6) ⏣⏥□┢✕▥⦾Ⅵ⧫
Clean, Victorian town house, foundations on Hadrian's Wall. Excellent bistro local cheeses, reasonably priced. Secure garaging. Nearest to theatre, museum, castle. City centre 0.5 miles

Brampton 3

National Grid Ref: NY5360

⛌◀White Lion Hotel, Blacksmith Arms

(0.25m) *Beechwood, Capon Tree Road, Brampton, Cumbria, CA8 1QL.*
Detached house in own grounds
Grades: ETB Listed, Comm
Tel: **016977 2239** Mrs Clark.
Rates fr: £16.00-**£19.00**.
Open: All Year (not Xmas)
Beds: 1D 1T 1S **Baths:** 1 Shared
ॐ (2) ▣ (10) □▥Ⅵ

The *lowest* **single** rate *is shown in* **bold.**

(1m) *Cracrop Farm, Brampton, Cumbria, CA8 2BW.*
High standard farmhouse
Grades: ETB 3 St, High Comm, AA 4 Q, Select
Tel: **016977 48245**
Mrs Stobart.
Fax no: 016977 48333
Rates fr: £25.00-**£25.00**.
Open: All Year (not Xmas)
Beds: 1D 1T 1S
Baths: 3 Private
▣ (6) ⏣□✕▥, ⧫

Talkin 4

National Grid Ref: NY5457

(0.5m) *Hare & Hounds, Talkin, Brampton, Cumbria, CA8 1LE.*
Homely, friendly 200-year-old inn
Tel: **016977 3456**
Mr Goddard.
Rates fr: £10.00-**£15.00**.
Open: All Year
Beds: 1F 2D 2T 4S
Baths: 2 Ensuite 2 Shared
ॐ ▣ (20) ⏣□┢✕▥Ⅵ⬛

(0.5m) *Hullerbank, Talkin, Brampton, Cumbria, CA8 1LB.*
C17th farmhouse in quiet peaceful location
Tel: **016977 46668**
Mrs Stobbart.
Rates fr: £20.00-**£26.00**.
Open: All Year (not Xmas)
Beds: 1D 2T
Baths: 3 Private
ॐ (12) ▣ (6) ⏣□✕▥Ⅵ

Lazonby 5

National Grid Ref: NY5439

⛌◀Joiners Arms

(3m) *Banktop House, Lazonby, Penrith, Cumbria, CA10 1AQ.*
Early C17th yeoman farmer's residence
Grades: ETB 2 Cr, Comm
Tel: **01768 898268**
Mrs Carlyle.
Rates fr: £18.50-**£22.00**.
Open:
Beds: 1D 1T
Baths: 1 Ensuite 1 Private
ॐ (Any) ▣ (4) □Ⅵ

Melmerby 6

National Grid Ref: NY6137

⛌◀Shepherds Inn

(4m) *Gale Hall Farm, Melmerby, Penrith, Cumbria, CA10 1HN.*
Large comfortable farmhouse near Pennines and Lake District
Tel: **01768 881254**
Mrs Toppin.
Rates fr: £15.00-**£15.00**.
Open: Jun to Nov
Beds: 1F 1D 1S
Baths: 1 Shared
ॐ ▣ (3) □┢Ⅵ

Carlisle to the Eden Valley

Out of Carlisle you ride east, via Rickerby Park, to **Brampton**, within reach of a number of buildings of historic interest, including a section of Hadrian's Wall. Then it's south, passing Talkin Tarn Country Park, and down the foothills of the northern Pennines, through a string of villages whose names evidence this region's eclectic ancient history - Celtic (Castle Carrock, Cumrew), Anglo-Saxon (Newbiggin, Croglin), Scandinavian (Glassonby) - into the gentle Eden Valley. Here stand **Long Meg and Her Daughters**, a late neolithic stone circle - Long Meg herself stands 18 feet high and is named from her eerily humanoid profile. A little way off the route are the red sandstone town of **Penrith** and the ruins of Brougham Castle with its Britanno-Roman graveyard. **Appleby-in-Westmorland**, former county town of old Westmorland, has a castle with a Norman keep, a twelfth-century church and an annual gypsy Horse Fair. Crossing the Eden at Appleby, the route heads for **Kirkby Stephen**, where there is a thirteenth-century church. You now follow the Eden to its source on the edge of the **Yorkshire Dales National Park**, briefly leaving Cumbria.

Langwathby 7

National Grid Ref: NY5733

(1m) **Langstanes**, *Culgaith Road, Langwathby, Penrith, Cumbria, CA10 1NA.*
Actual grid ref: NY573336
Tel: **01768 881004** (also fax no)
Mr Granett.
Rates fr: £16.00-**£16.00**.
Open: All Year (not Xmas)
Beds: 1T 2D
Baths: 3 Ensuite
🅿 (3) 🛏 ▥ Ⅵ 🖤 ✦
Cumbrian sandstone house on edge of quiet village. All rooms centrally heated with beverage-making facilities & colour TV

Culgaith 8

National Grid Ref: NY6029
🍴 🍺 Black Swan

(2m) **Elm Tree Barn**, *Culgaith, Penrith, Cumbria, CA10 1QW.*
Tastefully converted C17th stone barn
Tel: **01768 88730** Mrs Wiedman.
Rates fr: £15.00-**£20.00**.
Open: All Year (not Xmas)
Beds: 1D 2T
Baths: 1 Ensuite 1 Shared
🛏 🅿 (4) ⅍ 🛏 ▥ Ⅵ 🖤 ✦

Bringing children with you? Always ask for any special rates.

Dufton 9

National Grid Ref: NY6825
🍴 🍺 Stag Inn

(▲On route) **Dufton Youth Hostel**, *Redstones, Dufton, Appleby-in-Westmorland, Cumbria, CA16 6DB.*
Actual grid ref: NY688251
Warden: Ms H Moore.
Tel: **017683 51236**
Under 18: £5.40
Adults: £8.00
Evening Meals Available (7pm), Family Bunk Rooms, Showers, Shop
Large stone-built house with log fire in attractive C18th village surrounded by fine scenery of the Eden Valley

(On route) **Dufton Hall Farm**, *Dufton, Appleby in Westmorland, Cumbria, CA16 6DD.*
C18th farmhouse in village centre, close to pub and shop
Grades: ETB 1 Cr, Approv
Tel: **017683 51573** Mrs Howe.
Rates fr: £18.00-**£20.00**.
Open: Mar to Oct
Beds: 1F 1D 1T
Baths: 2 Ensuite 1 Private
🛏 🅿 (4) ⅍ 🛏 🖤 ✦

(On route) **Ghyll View**, *Dufton, Appleby in Westmorland, Cumbria, CA16 6DF.*
Large Victorian private house
Tel: **017683 51855**
Mrs Hullock.
Rates fr: £17.00-**£17.00**.
Open: Easter to Oct
Beds: 3T 1S
Baths: 2 Shared
🅿 (4) 🛏 ✗

Appleby-in-Westmorland 10

National Grid Ref: NY6820
🍴 🍺 Royal Oak Inn

(0.25m) **Bongate House**, *Appleby-in-Westmorland, Cumbria, CA16 6UE.*
Actual grid ref: NY687202
Grades: ETB 3 Cr, Comm
Tel: **017683 51245** Mrs Dayson.
Fax no: 017683 51423
Rates fr: £17.50-**£17.50**.
Open: All Year (not Xmas)
Beds: 2F 3D 2T 1S
Baths: 5 Private
🛏 (7) 🅿 (8) 🛏 🛏 ✗ ▥ Ⅵ 🖤 ✦
Large Georgian guest house in an acre of secluded gardens. Taste good food in a relaxed atmosphere. Ideal base to tour Lakes, Dales and Borders

(0.25m) **Limnerslease**, *Bongate, Appleby-in-Westmorland, Cumbria, CA16 6UE.*
Family-run guest house 10 mins town centre
Tel: **017683 51578**
Mrs Coward.
Rates fr: £14.00.
Open: All Year (not Xmas)
Beds: 2D 1T
Baths: 1 Shared
🅿 (3) 🛏 ▥ Ⅵ 🖤 ✦

(0.25m) **Church View**, *Bongate, Appleby-in-Westmorland, Cumbria, CA16 6UN.*
Actual grid ref: NY689198
C18th Listed character house
Tel: **017683 51792** (also fax no)
Mrs Kemp.
Rates fr: £16.00-**£17.50**.
Open: All Year (not Xmas)
Beds: 1F 1D 1S
Baths: 1 Shared
🛏 (1) 🅿 (4) ⅍ 🛏 🛏 ▥ Ⅵ 🖤 ✦

(On route) **Weymyss House**, *48 Boroughgate, Appleby-in-Westmorland, Cumbria, CA16 6XG.*
Actual grid ref: NY684203
Georgian house in small country town
Tel: **017683 51494**
Mrs Hirst.
Rates fr: £15.00-**£15.00**.
Open: Easter to Nov
Beds: 1D 1T 1S
Baths: 2 Shared
🛏 🅿 (3) 🛏 ▥ Ⅵ ✦

(0.25m) **Howgill House**, *Bongate, Appleby-in-Westmorland, Cumbria, CA16 6UW.*
Private house set in large garden
Grades: ETB 1 Cr, Comm
Tel: **01768 351574 / 351240**
Mrs Pigney.
Rates fr: £13.00-**£14.50**.
Open: Easter to Oct
Beds: 2F 1T 1S
🛏 🅿 (6) 🛏 Ⅵ ✦

Colby   11

National Grid Ref: NY6620

🍴 🍺 New Inn, White Hart

(1m) *Nether Hoff*, Colby, Appleby in Westmorland, Cumbria, *CA16 6BD*.
Oak-beamed Westmorland stone farmhouse
Tel: **017683 52965** Mrs Thorburn.
Fax no: 017683 52902
Rates fr: *£17.50*-**£17.50**.
Open: All Year (not Xmas)
Beds: 1D 1T
Baths: 2 Private
🐾 🅿 (5) 🛏 ✕ 📖 Ⓥ

Drybeck   12

National Grid Ref: NY6615

(2m) *East View Farm*, Drybeck, Appleby In Westmorland, Cumbria, *CA16 6TF*.
Actual grid ref: NY666153
Comfortable traditional family farm. Hospitality assured. Bring your own wine
Tel: **017683 52079** Mrs Simpson.
Rates fr: *£15.00*-**£15.00**.
Open: All Year **Beds:** 1T 1D 1S
Baths: 1 Private 1 Shared
🐾 🅿 ⌿ 🛏 ✕ Ⓥ 🛆 ⚡

Soulby   13

National Grid Ref: NY7411

(On route) *Hutton Lodge*, Soulby, Kirkby Stephen, Cumbria, *CA17 4PL*.
Georgian house, tranquil riverside setting
Tel: **017683 71396** Mrs March.
Rates fr: *£16.50*-**£16.50**.
Open: All Year (not Xmas)
Beds: 1F 1T 1S **Baths:** 1 Shared
🐾 🅿 (3) 🛏 ✕ 📖 Ⓥ

Kirkby Stephen   14

National Grid Ref: NY7708

🍴 🍺 Pennine Hotel, Old Forge

(▲ On route) *Kirkby Stephen Youth Hostel*, Fletcher Hill, Market Street, Kirkby Stephen, Cumbria, *CA17 7QQ*.
Actual grid ref: NY774085
Warden: Ms C Seddon.
Tel: **017683 71793**
Under 18: £5.40 **Adults:** £8.00
Evening Meals Available (7pm), Family Bunk Rooms, Showers, Central Heating
Attractive converted chapel, just south of the town square in this interesting old market town in the Upper Eden Valley

The lowest *double* rate per person is shown in *italics*.

Eden Valley to Ulverston

From here it's through Garsdale to Sedbergh, and along the River Lune to **Kirkby Lonsdale**, where you can find the fourteenth-century stone Devil's Bridge, a thirteenth-century church and the famous view over the Lune Valley painted by Turner and idealised by Ruskin. Now you ride west along a stretch shared with the *Lancashire Cycleway*, to **Hutton Roof**, a hilltop hamlet commanding magnificent views, and then over Farleton Fell, and hit the coast at **Arnside**. You will now be at or near the coast for the rest of the way. Attractions along the next stretch include the Elizabethan Levens Hall, with the world-famous topiary gardens designed by Guillaume Beaumont (1694), a collection of Jacobean furniture and the earliest example of English patchwork. After Grange-over-Sands, **Cartmel** boasts two remainders of a twelfth-century priory which stood here until Henry VIII's Dissolution: St Mary's Church, with its many medieval tombs, and the Priory Gatehouse, now home to an art gallery. The next stage is through woodland via Cark and Greenodd to **Ulverston**, where three important figures from local history are represented in their different ways - the martial Sir John Barrow, secretary of the admiralty, by the Hoad Monument, fashioned after the design of the Eddystone Lighthouse, the pacific George Fox, the Quaker, whose home was Swarthmoor Hall, and the fantastic Stan Laurel, by the Laurel and Hardy Museum, attached to a cinema devoted to L & H's work.

(On route) *Jolly Farmers House*, 63 High Street, Kirkby Stephen, Cumbria, *CA17 4SH*.
Actual grid ref: NY774083
Grades: ETB 3 Cr, Comm
Tel: **017683 71063** (also fax no)
Mr Pepper.
Rates fr: *£16.00*-**£16.00**.
Open: All Year **Beds:** 2F 5T 1S
Baths: 5 Ensuite 3 Shared
🐾 🅿 (6) 🛏 ✕ 📖 Ⓥ 🛆 ⚡
Quality: Comfort: Right Price:
Something we believe in so come and relax in one of our spacious ensuite rooms. Home cooked food from £6.00

(On route) *The Old Court House*, High Street, Kirkby Stephen, Cumbria, *CA17 4SH*.
Actual grid ref: NY774083
Beautiful house, close to all amenities. Open fires, excellent breakfasts
Grades: ETB 2 Cr, High Comm
Tel: **017683 71061** (also fax no)
Mrs Claxton.
Rates fr: *£17.50*-**£20.00**.
Open: All Year
Beds: 1F 1D 1T **Baths:** 2 Private
🐾 (10) 🅿 (2) 🛏 📖 Ⓥ

(On route) *Claremont*, Nateby Rd, Kirkby Stephen, Cumbria, *CA17 4AJ*.
Actual grid ref: NY775083
Quiet, near town centre. Spacious rooms, excellent food, warm welcome
Tel: **017683 71787** Mrs Rennison.
Rates fr: *£14.00*.
Open: Easter to Oct
Beds: 1F 1T
Baths: 1 Ensuite 1 Shared
🐾 🅿 (2) 🛏 📖 Ⓥ 🛆 ⚡

(On route) *Lyndhurst*, 46 South Road, Kirkby Stephen, Cumbria, *CA17 4SN*.
Actual grid ref: NY772078
Delightful comfortable Victorian family home. A warm welcome. Excellent breakfast
Tel: **017683 71448** Mrs Bell.
Rates fr: *£15.00*-**£18.00**.
Open: Mar to Nov
Beds: 1D 2T
Baths: 1 Private 1 Shared
🐾 🅿 (3) ⌿ 🛏 ✕ 📖 Ⓥ 🛆 ⚡

(5m) *Cold Keld*, Fell End, Kirkby Stephen, Cumbria, *CA17 4LN*.
Farmhouse offering guided walking holidays
Tel: **015396 23273** (also fax no)
Mr & Mrs Trimmer.
Rates fr: *£16.00*-**£19.00**.
Open: All Year (not Xmas)
Beds: 1F 3D 1T
Baths: 5 Private
🐾 🅿 (12) ⌿ 🛏 🛏 📖 Ⓥ 🛆 ⚡

Outhgill   15

National Grid Ref: NY7801

(0.5m) *Ing Hill Lodge*, Outhgill, Mallerstang Dale, Kirkby Stephen, Cumbria, *CA17 4JT*.
Delightful Georgian country house, home cooking
Grades: ETB 2 Cr, Comm
Tel: **017683 71153** Mrs Sawyer.
Rates fr: *£20.00*-**£25.00**.
Open: All Year
Beds: 2D 1T
Baths: 3 Ensuite
🅿 (6) 🛏 🛏 ✕ 📖 🛆 ⚡

Sedbergh 16

National Grid Ref: SD6592

⌖⌖ ◁ Dalesman Inn, Red Lion

(On route) *Marshall House, Main Street, Sedbergh, Cumbria, LA10 5BL.*
Actual grid ref: SD658922
Tel: **015396 21053** Mrs Kerry.
Rates fr: £20.00-£28.00.
Open: All Year (not Xmas)
Beds: 1D 2T **Baths:** 3 Private
⪫ (12) ▣ (5) ⌗✕ ▥ & ⓥ ▯ ✦
Which? recommended town house situated under the magnificent Howgill Fells. Tastefully furnished rooms - 2 ground floor - log fires and large walled garden with stream

(On route) *Stable Antiques, 15 Back Lane, Sedbergh, Cumbria, LA10 5AQ.*
Actual grid ref: SD659921
C18th Wheelwright's cottage with wonderful views of Howgills
Tel: **015396 20251** Miss Thurlby.
Rates fr: £17.00-£17.00.
Open: All Year
Beds: 1D 1T **Baths:** 1 Shared
⪫ (10) ☆ ▥ ⓥ ▯ ✦

(On route) *Holmecroft, Station Rd, Sedbergh, Cumbria, LA10 5DW.*
Actual grid ref: SD650919
Detached Westmorland-style house enjoying superb views of Howgill Fells
Tel: **015396 20754** Mrs Sharrocks.
Rates fr: £17.00-£17.00.
Open: All Year (not Xmas)
Beds: 2D 1T **Baths:** 1 Shared
⪫ ▣ (6) ⅙ ⌗ ☆ ▥ ⓥ ▯ ✦

(0.5m) *Farfield Country Guest House, Garsdale Road, Garsdale, Sedbergh, Cumbria, LA10 5LP.*
Actual grid ref: SD677919
Beautiful Victorian house.
Outstanding views
Tel: **015396 20537** Mr & Mrs Clark.
Rates fr: £20.00-£22.00.
Open: All Year (not Xmas)
Beds: 1F 3D 2T 1S
Baths: 4 Ensuite 1 Private
⪫ ▣ (10) ⌗✕ ▥ ⓥ ▯

(On route) *Sun Lea, Joss Lane, Sedbergh, Cumbria, LA10 5AS.*
Actual grid ref: SD658922
Spacious Victorian family house
Grades: ETB Listed
Tel: **015396 20828** Mrs Ramsden.
Rates fr: £16.00-£16.00.
Open: All Year (not Xmas)
Beds: 2D 1T **Baths:** 2 Shared
⪫ ▣ (3) ⅙ ⌗ ▥ ⓥ ✦

(0.5m) *Randall Hill, Sedbergh, Cumbria, LA10 5HJ.*
Actual grid ref: SD649917
Country house in 3 acres
Tel: **015396 20633** Mrs Snow.
Rates fr: £15.00-£16.00.
Open: All Year
Beds: 1D 2T **Baths:** 1 Shared
⪫ ▣ (6) ⅙ ⌗ ☆ ▥ ⓥ ▯ ✦

(0.5m) *Turvey House, Sedbergh, Cumbria, LA10 5DJ.*
Stone-built large Victorian house
Grades: ETB Listed, Comm
Tel: **015396 20841**
Mr & Mrs Liddey-Smith.
Rates fr: £15.00.
Open: All Year
Beds: 1F 1D 1T **Baths:** 2 Shared
▣ (5) ⅙ ⌗ ▥ ⓥ ▯ ✦

Killington 17

National Grid Ref: SD6189

⌖⌖ ◁ The Head

(1m) *Killington Hall, Killington, Carnforth, Lancs, LA6 2HA.*
C16th hall, easy access to Lakes and Dales
Tel: **015396 20542**
Rates fr: £15.00-£15.00.
Open: Easter to October
Beds: 1T 1D
⪫ ▣ (4) ⅙ ⌗ ▥ ⓥ ✦

Kirkby Lonsdale 18

National Grid Ref: SD6178

⌖⌖ ◁ Lunesdale Arms Hotel, Snooty Fox

(1m) *Green Lane End Farm, Kirkby Lonsdale, Carnforth, Lancs, LA6 2PP.*
C17th farmhouse - working farm.
M6 2 miles
Tel: **01539 567236**
Mrs Nicholson.
Rates fr: £15.00-£17.00.
Open: Easter to Oct
Beds: 1D 1T
Baths: 1 Shared
⪫ ▣ (3) ⅙ ☆ ⓥ ✦

Pay B&Bs by cash or cheque and be prepared to pay up front.

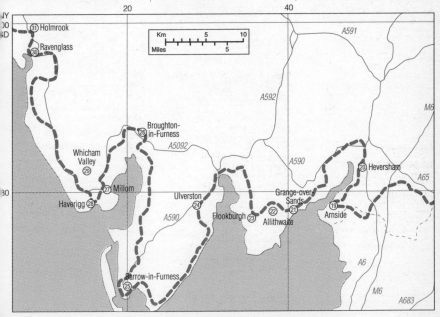

Ulverston to Ravenglass

The road out of Ulverston is largely alongside the beach, overlooking Morecambe Bay, scientifically important for the wading birds it supports. **Barrow-in-Furness** is the biggest town in Cumbria outside Carlisle, and sits at the opposite end of the cycleway and of the county, both in position and in character. This is the Furness Peninsula, the industrial powerhouse of old North Lancashire, the skyline dominated by the cranes of the shipyards. The town was built on the iron industry and is nowadays famous for Trident. The pre-industrial era is represented by Furness Abbey, the romantic sandstone ruin of a magnificent twelfth-century Cistercian foundation which was accorded the dubious honour of being the first large abbey earmarked for the scrapheap by Henry VIII. The next stage takes you north through several villages called Something-in-Furness and then off the Peninsula at **Duddon Bridge** and back into old Cumberland, as you follow the Duddon Estuary south along the opposite side to **Millom**. Then through a stretch of coast within the Lake District National Park by way of **Bootle** and **Waberthwaite** to **Ravenglass**, where if you wish you can take time out with a trip inland through Eskdale on the old narrow-gauge railway.

Arnside   19

National Grid Ref: SD4578

(▲ 0.25m) *Arnside Youth Hostel, Oakfield Lodge, Redhills Road, Arnside, Carnforth, Lancashire, LA5 0AT.*
Actual grid ref: SD452783
Tel: **01524 761781**
Under 18: £5.95
Adults: £8.80
Evening Meals Available (7pm), Television, Games Room, Showers, Laundry Facilities
A few minutes' walk from the shore with views across Morecambe Bay to the Lakeland Fells. A mellow stone house on the edge of a coastal village on the Kent estuary. RSPB reserve nearby

(On route) *Willowfield Hotel, The Promenade, Arnside, Carnforth, Lancs, LA5 0AD.*
Non-smokers' family-run hotel
Grades: ETB 3 Cr, Comm, AA 3 Q, RAC Listed
Tel: **01524 761354**
Mr Kerr.
Rates fr: £19.00-**£19.00**.
Open: All Year
Beds: 1F 4D 3T 2S
Baths: 7 Ensuite 2 Shared
🛏 🅿 (10) ⠵ ❏ ❦ ✕ ▥ Ⅴ ▮ ∦

Heversham   20

National Grid Ref: SD4983
🍴 🍷 Blue Bell Hotel

(0.5m) *Springlea, Heversham, Milnthorpe, Cumbria, LA7 7EE.*
Comfortable house overlooking restful countryside
Grades: AA 3 Q, Recomm
Tel: **015395 64026**
Mrs Green.
Rates fr: £15.00-**£18.50**.
Open: All Year
Beds: 1F 2D 1T
Baths: 2 Ensuite 1 Private
🛏 🅿 (3) ❏ ❦ ✕ ▥ Ⅴ ▮ ∦

Grange-over-Sands   21

National Grid Ref: SD4077
🍴 🍷 Hard Crag Hotel

(On route) *Grangeways, 6 Morecambe Bank, Grange-over-Sands, Cumbria, LA11 6DX.*
Excellent base for Lake District. Magnificent views overlooking Morecambe Bay
Grades: ETB 1 Cr, Comm
Tel: **015395 35329** Mrs Campbell.
Rates fr: £15.50-**£15.50**.
Open: Easter to Oct
Beds: 1F 1D 1T **Baths:** 1 Shared
🛏 (6) 🅿 (2) ⠵ ❏ ❦ ✕ ▥ Ⅴ ▮ ∦

(0.25m) *Hampsfell House Hotel, Hampsfell Road, Grange-over-Sands, Cumbria, LA11 6BG.*
Secluded hotel in own grounds
Grades: ETB 3 Cr, Comm
Tel: **015395 32567** Mr Sharrock.
Rates fr: £24.00-**£25.00**.
Open: All Year (not Xmas)
Beds: 1F 4D 4T
Baths: 9 Ensuite
🛏 🅿 (20) ⠵ ❏ ❦ ✕ ▥ Ⅴ

(0.25m) *Mayfields, 3 Mayfield Terrace, Kents Bank Road, Grange-over-Sands, Cumbria, LA11 7DW.*
Well-appointed charming Edwardian town house
Grades: ETB 3 Cr, Comm
Tel: **015395 34730** Mr Thorburn.
Rates fr: £20.00-**£18.50**.
Open: All Year (not Xmas)
Beds: 1D 1T 1S
Baths: 3 Ensuite 1 Shared
🛏 🅿 (3) ⠵ ❏ ✕ ▥ Ⅴ ▮

(0.25m) *Holme Lea Guest House, 90 Kentsford Road, Kents Bank, Grange-over-Sands, Cumbria, LA11 7BB.*
Victorian house overlooking bay
Tel: **015395 32545** Mrs Barton.
Rates fr: £17.00-**£17.00**.
Open: Mar to Oct
Beds: 1F 1D 1T 1S
Baths: 2 Ensuite 1 Shared
🛏 🅿 (4) ❏ ❦ ✕ ▥ Ⅴ ▮ ∦

Allithwaite   22

National Grid Ref: SD3876

(2m) *The Chateau, Flookbrook Road, Allithwaite, Grange-over-Sands, Cumbria, LA11 7JR.*
Comfortable, modern family home
Tel: **015395 32249**
Mr Robinson.
Rates fr: £13.50-**£13.50**.
Open: Feb to Nov
Beds: 1D 2T
Baths: 1 Ensuite 2 Shared
🛏 🅿 (4) ⠵ ❏ ❦ ✕ ▥ Ⅴ ▮ ∦

Flookburgh   23

National Grid Ref: SD3675
🍴 🍷 Rose & Crown

(0.5m) *Fieldhead Farm, Flookburgh, Grange-over-Sands, Cumbria, LA11 7LN.*
A C17th farmhouse on edge of ancient fishing village
Tel: **015395 58651**
Rates fr: £17.00-**£17.00**.
Open: All Year
Beds: 2D 1S
🛏 🅿 (2) ⠵ ❏ ✕ ▥ Ⅴ ▮ ∦

Ulverston   24

National Grid Ref: SD2878
🍴 🍷 Rose & Crown, Pier Castle, Farmers Arms

(On route) *Sefton House , Queen Street, Ulverston, Cumbria, LA12 7AF.*
Georgian town house in the centre of the busy market town of Ulverston
Tel: **01229 582190**
Mrs Glaister.
Fax no: 01229 581773
Rates fr: £20.00-**£22.50**.
Open: All Year (not Xmas)
Beds: 1F 2D
Baths: 3 Ensuite
🛏 🅿 (15) ❏ ✕ ▥ Ⅴ ▮ ∦

(0.25m) *Church Walk House,*
Church Walk, Ulverston, Cumbria,
LA12 7EW.
Actual grid ref: SD287785
Comfortable and homely Georgian
house, furnished with antiques
Grades: AA 3 Q
Tel: 01229 582211 Mr Chadderton.
Rates fr: £19.00-£17.50.
Open: All Year (not Xmas)
Beds: 1F 2D 1T 1S
Baths: 3 Private 1 Shared
🛇🗶🗘🏋🗶🔟🛇🔟📶

(0.25m) *Rock House, 1 Alexander*
Road, Ulverston, Cumbria,
LA12 0DE.
Actual grid ref: SD287779
Large well-established guest house,
centrally situated
Grades: ETB 1 Cr, Comm
Tel: 01229 586879 Mr Ramsay.
Rates fr: £17.00-£17.00.
Open: All Year (not Xmas)
Beds: 3F 1S
Baths: 1 Shared
🛇🗶🗘🗶🔟🛇🔟📶

The *lowest* **single**
rate *is shown in* **bold.**

NX 00 NY

Barrow-in-Furness   25

National Grid Ref: SD1969

🍴🍺 Brown Cow, White House

(On route) *Barrie House,*
179 Abbey Road, Barrow-in-
Furness, Cumbria, LA14 5JP.
Victorian home among trees and
roses, nearby lakes and sea
Tel: 01229 825507 (also fax no)
Mrs Maitland.
Rates fr: £15.00-£15.00.
Open: All Year
Beds: 1F 1D 2T 7S
Baths: 4 Private 3 Shared
🛇🗘🏋🗶🔟🛇

(On route) *Infield Hotel,* 276
Abbey Road, Barrow-in-Furness,
Cumbria, LA13 9JJ.
Hotel standards, guest house prices
Grades: ETB 2 Cr, Comm
Tel: 01229 831381 Mrs Parkin.
Rates fr: £16.00-£18.00.
Open: All Year
Beds: 3F 2D 2T 3S
Baths: 2 Private 2 Shared
🛇📶(9)🗶🗘🏋🗶🔟🛇

(On route) *White House Hotel,*
Abbey Road, Barrow-in-Furness,
Cumbria, LA13 8AE.
Always a friendly welcome here
Tel: 01229 827303 Parkin.
Fax no: 01229 835534
Rates fr: £17.00-£25.00.
Open: All Year
Beds: 1F 6T 3D 20S
Baths: 10 Ensuite 1 Private
4 Shared
🛇📶(40)🗶🗘🗶🔟📶

Broughton in Furness   26

National Grid Ref: SD2187

🍴🍺 Black Cock Inn

(On route) *Cobblers Cottage,*
Griffin Street, Broughton in
Furness, Cumbria, LA20 6HH.
Quaint C17th cottage
Tel: 01229 716413
Mr & Mrs Fletcher.
Rates fr: £17.50-£17.50.
Open: All Year (not Xmas)
Beds: 2D 1T
Baths: 1 Private 1 Shared
🛇🗶🗘🏋🔟

Millom   27

National Grid Ref: SD1780

🍴🍺 Station Hotel

(On route) *Fellview House, Bay*
View, Millom, Cumbria, LA18 5DF.
Large friendly family house
Tel: 01229 773325
Mrs Evison.
Rates fr: £15.00-£15.00.
Open: All Year (not Xmas)
Beds: 2T 1S
Baths: 2 Shared
🛇🗘🏋🗶🔟🛇

Haverigg   28

National Grid Ref: SD1578

🍴🍺 Harbour Hotel

(On route) *Dunelm Cottage, Main*
Street, Haverigg, Millom, Cumbria,
LA18 4EX.
Comfortable converted cottages.
Superior accomodation
Grades: AA 3 Q
Tel: 01229 770097
Mrs Fairless.
Rates fr: £18.50-£20.00.
Open: Feb to Dec
Beds: 1D 2T
Baths: 2 shared
🛇(5)📶🗘🏋🗶🔟🛇📶

Whicham Valley   29

National Grid Ref: SD1583

🍴🍺 Miners Arms

(0.5m) *Whicham Old School,*
Whicham Valley, Millom, Cumbria,
LA18 5LS.
Tastefully converted C16th village
school, 1 mile sea, lakes 30
minutes
Tel: 01229 773945
Mrs Woods.
Rates fr: £16.50-£16.50.
Open: All Year (not Xmas)
Beds: 2D 3T
Baths: 2 Ensuite 1 Private
🛇📶(4)🗘🏋🔟🛇📶

Ravenglass   30

National Grid Ref: SD0896

🍴🍺 Ratty Arms

(On route) *Muncaster Country*
Guest House, Ravenglass,
Cumbria, CA18 1RD.
Grades: RAC Listed
Tel: 01229 717693 (also fax no)
Mr Putnam.
Rates fr: £18.00-£18.00.
Open: All Year (not Xmas)
Beds: 1F 3D 2T 3S
Baths: 2 Ensuite 2 Shared
🛇📶(20)🗘🏋🗶🔟📶
Very comfortable licensed guest-
house with attractive garden
adjoining Muncaster Estate.
Convenient for miniature railway
and for walking in Eskdale and
Wasdale. Guided walking by
arrangement

(On route) *Eskmeals House,*
Eskmeal, Ravenglass, Cumbria,
CA19 5YA.
Listed secluded Georgian country
house
Tel: 01229 717151
Ms Stewart.
Rates fr: £15.00-£18.00.
Open: All Year
Beds: 1D 1T 1S
Baths: 2 Shared
🛇📶(6)🗘🏋🗶🔟🛇

(On route) *Muncaster Water Mill,*
Ravenglass, Cumbria, CA18 1ST.
Comfortable, welcoming C14th
working flour-mill
Tel: **01229 717232** Mr & Mrs Park.
Rates fr: *£17.00-£17.00*.
Open: All Year (not Xmas)
Beds: 1D 2T **Baths:** 2 Shared
ఈ ₽ (5) ⏚⏹ ⏰ ▥ ₺ ⓥ

Holmrook   31

National Grid Ref: SD0799

⏹ ☕ Lutwidge Arms, Horse &
Groom

(1m) *Hill Farm, Holmrook,*
Cumbria, CA19 1UG.
Comfortable farmhouse, excellent
views
Tel: **019467 24217** Mrs Leak.
Rates fr: *£13.50-£13.50*.
Open: All Year (not Xmas)
Beds: 2F 1D
Baths: 2 Shared
ఈ ₽ ⏹ ⏰ ▥ ⓥ ▪

(On route) *Low Holme, Drigg*
Road, Holmrook, Cumbria,
CA19 1YE.
Bungalow with views of fells
Tel: **019467 24219** Mrs Skeen.
Rates fr: *£11.00-£12.00*.
Open: All Year (not Xmas)
Beds: 1F
Baths: 1 Shared
ఈ ₽ (1) ⏚ ⏰ ▥

Egremont   32

National Grid Ref: NY0110

(0.5m) *Ghyll Farm Guest House,*
Egremont, Cumbria, CA22 2UA.
Large comfortable, clean friendly
farmhouse
Tel: **01946 822256** Mrs Holliday.
Rates fr: *£12.00-£12.00*.
Open: All Year (not Xmas)
Beds: 2F 2T
ఈ ₽ (8) ⏹ ✕ ▥

Cleator   33

National Grid Ref: NY0113

⏹ ☕ Grove Court Hotel

(2m) *Inglenook Cottage, 37 Main*
Street, Cleator, Cumbria, CA23 3BU.
Modernised clean, comfortable
cottage. Every facility
Tel: **01946 813156** Mrs Bradshaw.
Rates fr: *£14.50-£14.50*.
Open: All Year (not Xmas)
Beds: 1D 1T 1S
Baths: 1 Shared
ఈ ₽ (2) ⏹ ⏰ ▥ ▪ ⋏

St Bees   34

National Grid Ref: NX9711

⏹ ☕ Queens Head, Manor House,
Oddfellows

(0.5m) *Tomlin Guest House, 1*
Tomlin House, St Bees, Cumbria,
CA27 0EN.
Actual grid ref: NX963118
Comfortable Victorian house close
to beach and St Bees Head
Grades: ETB
Tel: **01946 822284** Mrs Whitehead.
Fax no: 01946 824243
Rates fr: *£14.00-£16.00*.
Open: All Year (not Xmas)
Beds: 1F 1D 2T
Baths: 2 Private 2 Shared
ఈ ₽ (2) ⏚⏹ ⏰ ▥ ⓥ ▪ ⋏

(1m) *Stonehouse Farm, Main*
Street, St Bees, Cumbria, CA27 0DE.
Actual grid ref: NX972119
Modern comfortable farmhouse,
centre village
Grades: ETB Listed, Approv
Tel: **01946 822224**
Mrs Smith.
Rates fr: *£16.00-£20.00*.
Open: All Year
Beds: 1F 2D 3T 1S
Baths: 4 Ensuite 2 Private
ఈ ₽ (10) ⏹ ⏰ ▥ ⓥ ▪ ⋏

(On route) *Outrigg House, St Bees,*
Cumbria, CA27 0AN.
Georgian guesthouse of unique
character located in village centre
Tel: **01946 822348**
Mrs Moffat.
Rates fr: *£15.00-£15.00*.
Open: All Year (not Xmas)
Beds: 1D 1T 1S
Baths: 1 Shared
ఈ ₽ (4) ⏚⏹ ⏰ ▥ ⓥ ▪ ⋏

(0.5m) *Fairladies Barn Guest*
House, Main Street, St Bees,
Cumbria, CA27 0AD.
Large converted barn, family-run
Tel: **01946 823864 / 822718**
Mrs Blakeley.
Rates fr: *£14.00-£14.00*.
Open: All Year
Beds: 1F 2D 4T 1S
Baths: 2 Shared
ఈ ₽ ⏹ ⏰ ▥ ⓥ

Sandwith   35

National Grid Ref: NX9614

⏹ ☕ Dog & Partridge, Lowther
Arms

(▲ 2m) *Tarn Flatt Camping*
Barn, Tarnflat Hall, Sandwith,
Whitehaven, Cumbria
Actual grid ref: NX947146
Adults: £3.35+
Situated on St Bees Head overlook-
ing Scottish coastline and the Isle
of Man. RSPB seabird reserve and
lighthouse nearby. ADVANCE
BOOKING ESSENTIAL

(1m) *Aikbank Cottage, Sandwith,*
Whitehaven, Cumbria, CA28 9UG.
Actual grid ref: NX964148
C17th Cottage and Post Office
Tel: **01946 695771**
Mrs Urwin.
Rates fr: *£15.00-£15.00*.
Open: All Year (not Xmas)
Beds: 1D 1S
Baths: 1 Shared
ఈ ₽ (2) ⏹ ⏰ ✕ ▥ ⓥ ▪ ⋏

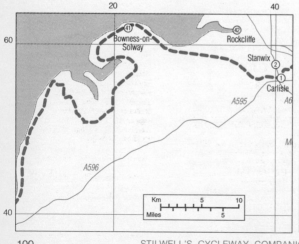

The Grid Reference
beneath the location
heading is for the
village or town - *not*
for individual houses,
which are shown
(where supplied) in
each entry itself.

Ravenglass to Carlisle

Sellafield will interest anyone on the nuclear trail from Barrow, and after **Egremont**, which offers the ruins of a Norman castle, the route passes **St Bees Head**, with its sandstone cliffs. The final stretch of coast, north-eastwards towards the Solway Firth, takes you through a series of towns reflecting the industrial history of the region: **Whitehaven** has been through a number of incarnations - harbour for St Bees Priory, major tobacco port, during which time the many Georgian buildings went up, and then coal and shipbuilding centre; **Workington** and **Maryport** are major nineteenth-century centres of the iron industry. A different side of Victoriana is reflected in **Silloth**, a planned town and resort. After this there is another Cistercian abbey at **Abbeytown** and then an idyllic section with magnificent views across the **Solway Firth**. Another historic site is the Roman fort at **Burgh-by-Sands**, before you cycle back into Carlisle.

Whitehaven 36

National Grid Ref: NX9718

(1m) *Corkickle Guest House,*
1 Corkickle, Whitehaven, Cumbria,
CA28 8AA.
Superb Georgian house.Residential licence. **Grades:** ETB 3 Cr, Comm
Tel: **01946 692073** (also fax no)
Mrs Pearson.
Rates fr: *£22.00-£24.50.*
Open: All Year (not Xmas/New Year)
Beds: 2D 2T 2S
Baths: 5 Ensuite 1 Private
🅿 (2) ⌨🗖📯✕🎦🆅🛈≠

(1m) *The Cross Georgian Guest House, Sneckyeat Rd, Hensingham, Whitehaven, Cumbria, CA28 8JQ.*
In private ground, spectacular views
Tel: **01946 63716** Mrs Bailey.
Rates fr: *£15.00-£15.00.*
Open: All Year **Beds:** 2T 2S
Baths: 2 Private 1 Shared
🛏🅿 (8) 🗖📯✕🎦🆅🛈

Workington 37

National Grid Ref: NX9927

🍽⌨ Traveller's Rest, Miners' Arms

(1m) *The Boston, 1 St Michael's Road, Workington, Cumbria, CA14 3EZ.*
Small guest house with big reputation. Ideal Lakes and sea
Grades: ETB Listed
Tel: **01900 603435**
Mrs A Clarke.
Rates fr: *£12.50-£16.00.*
Open: All Year
Beds: 1F 1D 2T 2S
Baths: 1 Private 1 Shared
🛏🅿 (3) 🗖🎦

(On route) *Sandmans Guest House, 123 John Street, Workington, Cumbria, CA14 3DD.*
Small, friendly guest house, home from home; easy access to Lakes
Tel: **01900 605763** Mrs McKenna.
Rates fr: *£12.50-£15.00.*
Open: All Year
Beds: 1F 3T
Baths: 1 Shared
🛏 (3) 🗖🎦🆅

(2m) *The Briery, Stainburn Road, Stainburn, Workington, Cumbria, CA14 4UJ.*
Friendly, family-run hotel
Tel: **01900 603395**
Mr Lavelle.
Rates fr: *£15.00-£20.00.*
Open: All Year
Beds: 4T 1S
🛏🅿 (60) 🗖📯✕🎦🛗🆅

Maryport 38

National Grid Ref: NY0336

🍽⌨ Stag Inn

(0.25m) *Ellenside Guest House, 17 Station Street, Maryport, Cumbria, CA15 6LS.*
Large Victorian comfortable house
Grades: ETB Listed
Tel: **01900 815440**
Mrs Kemp.
Rates fr: *£12.00-£12.00.*
Open: All Year
Beds: 1F 1D 1T 1S
Baths: 1 Shared
🛏🅿🗖🎦

Dearham 39

National Grid Ref: NY0736

(3m) *Old Mill Inn, Dearham, Maryport, Cumbria, CA15 7JP.*
Olde worlde family-run inn
Tel: **01900 813148**
Mrs Greenwood.
Rates fr: *£12.50-£16.00.*
Open: All Year
Beds: 1F 5D 1T
Baths: 2 Private 2 Shared
🛏 (1) 🅿 (60) 🗖📯✕🎦🆅

Crosscanonby 40

National Grid Ref: NY0739

🍽⌨ Stag Inn

(0.25m) *East Farm, Crosscanonby, Maryport, Cumbria, CA15 6SJ.*
Modernised comfortable farmhouse. Traditional breakfast, aquaria, leisure centre, beach nearby
Grades: ETB Listed, Comm
Tel: **01900 812153** Mrs Carruthers.
Rates fr: *£15.00-£15.00.*
Open: All Year (not Xmas)
Beds: 1F 1D **Baths:** 1 Shared
🛏 (2) 🅿 (2) 🗖🎦

Bowness-on-Solway 41

National Grid Ref: NY2262

🍽⌨ Highland Laddie

(On route) *The Old Rectory, Bowness-on-Solway, Carlisle, Cumbria, CA5 5AF.*
Actual grid ref: NY224626
Own grounds, birdwatching, quiet village at end of Hadrian's Wall
Grades: ETB 1 Cr
Tel: **016973 51055**
Mr & Mrs Knowles Wallsand.
Rates fr: *£15.00-£17.00.*
Open: All Year (not Xmas)
Beds: 3D 1S
Baths: 3 Ensuite 1 Shared
🅿⌨🗖✕🎦≠

(On route) *Maia Lodge, Bowness-on-Solway, Carlisle, Cumbria, CA5 5BH.*
Panoramic views of Solway Firth and Scottish Borders. End of Hadrian's Wall
Tel: **016973 51955** Mrs Chettle.
Rates fr: *£15.00-£20.00.*
Open: All Year (not Xmas)
Beds: 1F 1D 1T
Baths: 2 Shared
🛏 (5) 🅿 (4) ⌨🗖✕🎦🛈≠

Rockcliffe 42

National Grid Ref: NY3561

🍽⌨ Metal Bridge Inn

(5m) *Metal Bridge House, Metal Bridge, Rockcliffe, Carlisle, Cumbria, CA6 4HG.*
In country, close to M6/74
Grades: ETB 1 Cr, Comm
Tel: **01228 74695** Mr Rae.
Rates fr: *£14.00-£18.00.*
Open: All Year
Beds: 1D 2T **Baths:** 1 Shared
🛏🅿 (4) 🗖📯🎦

All rates are subject to alteration at the owners' discretion.

Essex Cycle Route

Essex provides good cycling country, as it is relatively flat, whilst offering a gentle agrarian beauty away from its ugly south end, which the cycle route avoids. The **Essex Cycle Route** consists of a large circuit around the interior of the county, with a 'spur' out east to the port of Harwich. Directed along quiet roads and not signposted, it is only a recommended tour, and you can devise your own alternatives at any point. The designated route can be cycled in either direction and you can start anywhere; for no particular reason, the description that follows takes the circuit clockwise from Coggeshall, east of Braintree, and finishes with the section to Harwich.

A detailed **guide booklet** to the cycleway route, which includes a list of cycle repair/hire shops on or near to the route, is available from Essex Tourism, Essex County Planning Department, County Hall, Chelmsford, Essex CM1 1LF, tel 01245 437548, @ £1.00 (inc p&p).

Maps: Ordnance Survey 1:50,000 Landranger series: 154, 155, 167, 168, 169

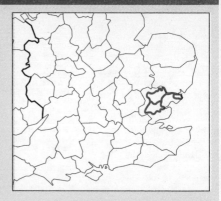

Essex is well-connected by **train** to London and to Eastern and Central England. Major railway termini are Chelmsford, Colchester and Harwich. London also connects to Stansted Airport, Stansted Mountfitchet, Elsenham, Newport and Audley End (for Saffron Walden). There are connections to many other places on or near the route.

Coggeshall to Maldon

Coggeshall is a medieval town on the banks of the Blackwater, one of Essex's major rivers, with the remains of a Cistercian Abbey nearby. In contrast with the Abbey ruins, there are two excellently preserved historic buildings: the Grange Barn is a 120-foot timber-framed barn constructed in 1140 to serve the Abbey, and is the oldest of its kind in Europe. It houses a display of historic farm wagons. Paycocke's is a merchant's house from the turn of the sixteenth century with rich panelling and wood carving, and a display of lace. On to **Cressing**, with more medieval timber-framed barns at nearby 'Cressing Temple', and **Terling**. From here there is an alternative route via **Pleshey**, where

you will find a Norman castle earthwork, and **Great Clanfield**, whose twelfth-century church is a Grade I Listed building with a mural of the Madonna and Child; connecting up to the eastern side of the circuit between Hatfield Broad Oak and Takeley. From Terling proceed to **Maldon**, on the Blackwater Estuary. This ancient town, with an attractive High Street, is famous for a battle fought here in 991, at which Viking invaders defeated the local East Saxons, told of in an early Anglo-Saxon poem, *The Battle of Maldon*. The millennium of the battle was commemorated by the *Maldon Embroidery*, made by local people in 1991. It celebrates the town's history and is on display in the Moot Hall. Also worth a look is the Hythe Quay with its Thames sailing barges.

Coggeshall   1

National Grid Ref: TL8522

|o| ♥The Woolpack

(0.25m) *White Heather Guest House,* 19 Colchester Road, *Coggeshall, Colchester, Essex, CO6 1RP.*
Actual grid ref: TL859228
Modern, family-run guesthouse
Grades: ETB Listed
Tel: **01376 563004** Mrs Shaw.
Rates fr: £20.00-£20.00.
Open: All Year **Beds:** 2D 1T 3S
Baths: 2 Ensuite 1 Shared
🄿 (8) ⏚ ⏛ ⏢ ⏣

Feering   2

National Grid Ref: TL8719

(2m) *The Old Anchor,* 132 Feering Hill, Feering, Colchester, Essex, *CO5 9PY.*
A large welcoming public house
Tel: **01376 570684**
Mr William Baldry.
Rates fr: £18.50-£18.50.
Open: All Year
Beds: 3D 3T 3S
Baths: 2 Shared
⏚ 🄿 (70) ⏛ ⏢ ⏣

Kelvedon   3

National Grid Ref: TL8518

|o| ♥The Sun

(4m) *Highfields Farm, Kelvedon, Colchester, Essex, CO5 9BJ.*
Timber-framed farmhouse set in quiet location in open countryside.
Convenient A12
Grades: ETB 2 Cr, Comm
Tel: **01376 570334** (also fax no)
Mrs Bunting.
Rates fr: £19.00-£20.00.
Open: All Year **Beds:** 3T
Baths: 2 Ensuite 1 Private
⏚ 🄿 (10) ⏛ ⏢ ⏣ ⏤ ⏥

Braintree 4

National Grid Ref: TL7623

(2m) *The Old House Guesthouse,*
11 Bradford Street, Braintree,
Essex, CM7 9AS.
Actual grid ref: TL760238
Family-run, C16th guest house
within walking distance town
centre
Grades: ETB 2 Cr, Comm
Tel: 01376 550457
Mrs Hughes.
Fax no: 01376 343863
Rates fr: *£17.00-***£22.00.**
Open: All Year
Beds: 2F 3D 1T
Baths: 4 Private 2 Shared
⌂ 🅿 (10) ⊬ ⌷ ✕ 📖 & � ♦

Felsted 5

National Grid Ref: TL6720

🍴 🍺 Flitch of Bacon, The
Chequers, The Swan, Yew Tree

(3m) *Yarrow, Felsted, Great*
Dunmow, Essex, CM6 3HD.
Actual grid ref: TL668206
Large Edwardian house in historic
village with beautiful countryside
views. No smoking in bedrooms
Grades: ETB 2 Cr, Comm
Tel: 01371 820878
Mr & Mrs Bellingham Smith.
Rates fr: *£16.00-***£17.00.**
Open: All Year
Beds: 2D 1T
Baths: 1 Ensuite 1 Shared
⌂ 🅿 (6) ⌷ 📖 ♦

(3m) *Potash Farm House,*
Causeway End Road, Cobblers
Green, Felsted, Great Dunmow,
Essex, CM6 3LX.
Half moated farmhouse, quietly
situated
Grades: ETB 1 Cr, Comm,
AA 4 Q
Tel: 01371 820510 (also fax no)
Mr & Mrs Smith.
Rates fr: *£17.00-***£20.00.**
Open: All Year
Beds: 1D 2T
Baths: 1 Shared
⌂ (5) ⊬ ⌷ 📖 ▽ ▮

Great Dunmow 6

National Grid Ref: TL6221

🍴 🍺 Kicking Dickey, Sailing Oak

(3m) *Mallards, Star Lane, Great*
Dunmow, Essex, CM6 1AY.
Modern farmhouse-style home, in
town
Grades: ETB 2 Cr
Tel: 01371 872641 Mrs Miller.
Rates fr: *£17.50-***£17.50.**
Open: All Year
Beds: 1D 1T
Baths: 2 Ensuite 1 Private
⌂ (0) 🅿 (10) ⌷ 🍴 📖 ▽

All rates are subject
to alteration at the
owners' discretion.

High season,
bank holidays and
special events mean
low availability
everywhere.

(4m) *Homelye Farm, Homelye*
Chase, Braintree Road, Great
Dunmow, Essex, CM6 3AW.
Motel-style chalets
Grades: ETB Listed
Tel: 01371 872127
Mrs Pickford.
Rates fr: *£20.00-***£20.00.**
Open: All Year
Beds: 1D 1T 1S
Baths: 3 Private
⌂ 🅿 (5) ⊬ ⌷ 📖

Margaret Roding 7

National Grid Ref: TL5912

(3m) *Greys, Ongar Road,*
Margaret Roding, Great Dunmow,
Essex, CM6 1QR.
Old beamed country cottage
Grades: ETB Listed, Comm
Tel: 01245 231509 Mrs Matthews.
Rates fr: *£19.00-***£20.00.**
Open: All Year (not Xmas)
Beds: 2D 1T
Baths: 1 Shared
⌂ (10) 🅿 (3) ⊬ 📖

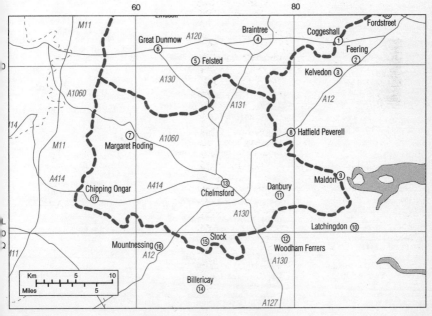

Hatfield Peverel 8

National Grid Ref: TL7811

¶❄ Square & Compasses, Cock Inn, William Boosey

(1m) *The Wick, Terling Hall Road, Hatfield Peverel, Chelmsford, Essex, CM3 2EZ.*
C16th farmhouse. Charming, comfortable. Large garden, duck pond and stream
Grades: ETB Listed, Comm
Tel: 01245 380705 Mrs Tritton.
Rates fr: *£20.00*-**£20.00**.
Open: All Year (not Xmas)
Beds: 2T
Baths: 1 Private 1 Shared
❄ (10) ᴾ (4) ☐ ★ ⅏ ♥

Maldon 9

National Grid Ref: TL8407

¶❄ Jolly Sailor, Hythe Quay

(0.25m) *Hillypool House, 14 North Street, Maldon, Essex, CM9 7HL.*
Comfortable family home near quay
Grades: ETB Listed, Comm
Tel: 01621 853885 (also fax no)
Mr & Mrs Knox.
Rates fr: *£17.50*-**£17.50**.
Open: All Year (not Xmas)
Beds: 1D 1T 1S **Baths:** 2 Shared
❄ ᴾ (3) ☐ ★ ✗ ⅏ ♥ ♠

Latchingdon 10

National Grid Ref: TL8800

¶❄ The Lion, Black Lion, The Huntsman

(2m) *Neptune Cafe Motel, Burnham Road, Latchingdon, Chelmsford, Essex, CM3 6EX.*
Motel set in village in Dengie Peninsula. Close boating & fishing areas. Large garden. Beautiful outlook
Grades: ETB Listed, Approv
Tel: 01621 740770 Mr Lloyd.
Rates fr: *£17.00*-**£24.00**.
Open: All Year (not Xmas)
Beds: 2F 6D 3T 4S
Baths: 10 Ensuite 1 Shared
❄ ᴾ (40) ⅄ ☐ ★ ⅏ ⅏ ♠ ♥ ♠

Danbury 11

National Grid Ref: TL7705

¶❄ The Bell, The Griffin

(2m) *Southways, Copt Hill, Danbury, Chelmsford, Essex, CM3 4NN.*
Quiet house in the country
Grades: ETB Listed
Tel: 01245 223428
Mrs Deavin.
Rates fr: *£16.00*-**£18.00**.
Open: All Year (not Xmas)
Beds: 2T
Baths: 1 Shared
❄ ᴾ (2) ☐ ★ ⅏.

(2m) *3 Millfields, Danbury, Chelmsford, Essex, CM3 4LE.*
Good quality, comfortable, quiet, friendly
Grades: ETB Listed
Tel: 01245 224946 Mrs Law.
Rates fr: *£18.00*-**£18.00**.
Open: All Year **Beds:** 1F 1D 1T
Baths: 1 Ensuite 1 Shared
❄ ᴾ (3) ⅄ ☐ ★ ⅏.

Woodham Ferrers 12

National Grid Ref: TQ7999

¶❄ The Bell

(2m) *Woolfes Cottage, The Street, Woodham Ferrers, Chelmsford, Essex, CM3 5RG.*
Large converted Victorian cottage
Tel: 01245 320037 Ms Oliver.
Rates fr: *£15.00*-**£18.00**.
Open: All Year
Beds: 1D 2T **Baths:** 1 Shared
❄ ᴾ (2) ⅄ ☐ ⅏ ♥

Chelmsford 13

National Grid Ref: TL7006

¶❄ The Ship

(5m) *Aarandale, 9 Roxwell Road, Chelmsford, Essex, CM1 2LY.*
Large Victorian house close to Chelmsford town centre and park
Tel: 01245 251713 Mrs Perera.
Rates fr: *£22.00*-**£22.00**.
Open: All Year (not Xmas)
Beds: 1D 4S
Baths: 1 Private 1 Shared
ᴾ (6) ☐ ✗ ⅏ ♥

Billericay 14

National Grid Ref: TQ6794

¶❄ King's Head, The Hoop

(2m) *Badgers Rest, 2 Mountview, Billericay, Essex, CM11 1HB.*
Modern detached house, excellent accommodation
Grades: ETB Listed, Comm
Tel: 01277 625384 / 0378 444169
Mr & Mrs Parker.
Fax no: 01277 633912
Rates fr: *£17.50*-**£20.00**.
Open: All Year
Beds: 1D 3S **Baths:** 2 Shared
❄ ᴾ (6) ⅄ ☐ ⅏ ♥

Stock 15

National Grid Ref: TQ6899

(0.5m) *Eibiswald, 85 Mill Road, Stock, Ingatestone, Essex, CM4 9LR.*
First class Anglo-Austrian hospitality
Tel: 01277 840631 Mrs Bates.
Rates fr: *£17.00*-**£24.00**.
Open: All Year (not Xmas)
Beds: 3D 3S
Baths: 1 Ensuite 1 Shared
❄ (10) ᴾ (4) ⅄ ☐ ⅏ ♥

Mountnessing 16

National Grid Ref: TQ6297

¶❄ George & Dragon

(2m) *Millers, Thoby Lane, Mountnessing, Brentwood, Essex, CM15 0TD.*
Beautiful comfortable house situated in farmland
Tel: 01277 354595 Mrs Stacey.
Rates fr: *£19.00*-**£27.00**.
Open: All Year
Beds: 3T
Baths: 1 Shared
❄ ᴾ (6) ⅄ ☐ ⅏.

Chipping Ongar 17

National Grid Ref: TL5503

¶❄ Black Bull, Green Man, Drill House

(1m) *Bumbles, Moreton Road, Chipping Ongar, Essex, CM5 0EZ.*
Actual grid ref: TL546052
Large, comfortable country cottage, centrally heated, also log fires in winter
Grades: ETB Listed, Comm
Tel: 01277 362695 Mrs Withey.
Fax no: 01277 365245
Rates fr: *£18.00*-**£18.00**.
Open: All Year (not Xmas)
Beds: 3T
Baths: 2 Shared
❄ (12) ᴾ (6) ⅄ ☐ ⅏ ♥ ♠ ✦

(2m) *Newhouse Farm, Mutton Row, Stanford Rivers, Chipping Ongar, Essex, CM5 9QH.*
Tudor farmhouse with disabled unit
Grades: ETB 1 Cr
Tel: 01277 362132
Mr & Mrs Martin.
Rates fr: *£16.00*-**£16.00**.
Open: All Year (not Xmas)
Beds: 1F 1D 4S
Baths: 1 Private 1 Shared
❄ ᴾ (50) ☐ ⅏ ♿ ♥ ♠

Henham 18

National Grid Ref: TL5428

¶❄ The Cock, The Crown, White Wall

(0.25m) *Bacons Cottage, Crow Street, Henham, Bishops Stortford, Herts, CM22 6AG.*
Picturesque village setting near Stansted Airport
Tel: 01279 850754 Mrs Philpot.
Rates fr: *£15.00*-**£16.00**.
Open: All Year (not Xmas)
Beds: 2D 1S
Baths: 1 Ensuite
ᴾ (1) ⅄ ☐ ★ ⅏.

The lowest *double* rate per person is shown in *italics*.

Maldon to Saffron Walden

From Maldon the route takes you south to **Purleigh**, where George Washington's great-grandfather was the local vicar, and then after East Hanningfield you can take a slight detour to the Royal Horticultural Society's Garden at Hyde Hall, a 24-acre hilltop garden with rose walks and waterfalls, as well as a small plant centre and a cafeteria. Around **Hanningfield Reservoir**, which offers sail-boarding, fishing and a nature trail, it's on to **Ingatestone**, where stands Ingatestone Hall, a redbrick Tudor mansion with 11 acres of grounds including a lake. On to the village of **Greensted**, where the Log Church is the oldest wooden church in the world, and then you turn north, through a string of medieval villages and near to the National Trust-owned **Hatfield Forest**, where there is a nature trail and lake. After this you pass close to **Stansted**

Airport, whose magnificent terminal building was designed by Norman Foster. You are now into the relative high ground of the chalk uplands of northwestern Essex. Between **Broxted** and **Thaxted** the route veers out into a loop that takes in the pretty villages of Clavering, Arkesden and Wendens Ambo and the town of **Saffron Walden**. Here you will find an art gallery, a museum, the Sun Inn, embellished with plasterwork decoration, and a maze on the town's common. Nearby stands **Audley End House**. This imposing mansion was built on the foundations of a Benedictine Abbey in the early seventeenth century for Thomas Howard, Lord Treasurer to King James I (who described it as 'too large for a King but might do for a Lord Treasurer'), but the interior was largely remodelled by Robert Adam in the eighteenth century. It has a splendid Renaissance facade and a garden landscaped by 'Capability' Brown.

Widdington 19
National Grid Ref: TL5331
|o| ◁ Fleur de Lys

(2m) *Pond Mead, Widdington, Saffron Walden, Essex, CB11 3SB*. Large converted farmhouse on edge of picturesque village
Grades: ETB 2 Cr, Approv
Tel: **01799 540201** Mr Geen.
Rates fr: *£17.00-£20.00*.
Open: All Year
Beds: 1F 1S
Baths: 1 Private
ঌ 🅿 (5) ◻ 🛏.

Ugley 20
National Grid Ref: TL5228
|o| ◁ Three Willows, The Chequers

(0.25m) *The Thatch, Cambridge Road, Ugley, Bishops Stortford, Herts, CM22 6HZ*. Convenient airport/M11. Warm, friendly atmosphere
Grades: ETB Listed, High Comm
Tel: **01799 543440**
Mrs Hawkes.
Rates fr: *£18.00-£20.00*.
Open: All Year (not Xmas)
Beds: 1F 2D 1T
Baths: 2 Ensuite 2 Shared
ঌ 🅿 (10) ◻ 🛏 🛏. 🆅

Pay B&Bs by cash or cheque and be prepared to pay up front.

Saffron Walden 21
National Grid Ref: TL5438
|o| ◁ The Crown, Eight Bells

(▲ 0.5m) *Saffron Walden Youth Hostel, 1 Myddylton Place, Saffron Walden, Essex, CB10 1BB*.
Actual grid ref: TL535386
Tel: **01799 523117**
Under 18: £5.40
Adults: £8.00
Evening Meals Available (7pm), Self-catering Facilities, Showers 500-year-old former maltings with oak beams and uneven floors, and courtyard garden, only 3 minutes' walk from historic town centre

(0.5m) *27 South Road, Saffron Walden, Essex, CB11 3DW*. Pretty, double-fronted Victorian cottage; short walk to town centre
Grades: ETB Listed
Tel: **01799 525425**
Mrs McBride.
Rates fr: *£18.00-£18.00*.
Open: All Year
Beds: 2T 1S
Baths: 1 Shared
ঌ ◻ 🛏.

(0.5m) *1 Gunters Cottages, Thaxted Road, Saffron Walden, Essex, CB10 2UT*. Quiet comfortable accommodation. Indoor heated swimming pool. Friendly welcome
Grades: ETB 2 Crown, Commended
Tel: **01799 522091**
Mrs Goddard.
Rates fr: *£18.00-£17.00*.
Open: All Year (not Xmas)
Beds: 2D 1S
Baths: 1 Private 1 Shared
🅿 (3) ⅍ ◻ 🛏.

(0.5m) *Ashleigh House, 7 Farmadine Grove, Saffron Walden, Essex, CB11 3DR*. Comfortable house in quiet location
Grades: ETB 2 Cr, Comm
Tel: **01799 513611**
Mrs Gilder.
Rates fr: *£15.00-£16.00*.
Open: All Year
Beds: 1D 1T 2S
Baths: 1 Private 1 Shared
(5) 🅿 (5) ⅍ ◻ 🛏. 🆅

(0.5m) *10 Victoria Avenue, Saffron Walden, Essex, CB11 3AE*. Friendly atmosphere, lockup for bicycles
Grades: ETB Listed
Tel: **01799 525923**
Mrs Gilder.
Rates fr: *£14.00-£14.00*.
Open: All Year
Beds: 1T 3S
Baths: 1 Shared
ঌ ⅍ ◻ 🛏. 🆅

Great Chesterford 22
National Grid Ref: TL5042
|o| ◁ Crown & Thistle, The Plough

(3m) *The Delles, Carmen Street, Great Chesterford, Saffron Walden, Essex, CB10 1NR*. Beautiful old farmhouse dating from 1520
Grades: ETB 2 Cr, High Comm
Tel: **01799 530256** (also fax no)
Mrs Chater.
Rates fr: *£21.00-£25.00*.
Open: All Year
Beds: 2D 1T
Baths: 1 Ensuite 2 Private
ঌ (2) 🅿 (5) ◻ 🛏 ✕ 🛏. 🆅 🏱

Essex Cycle Route

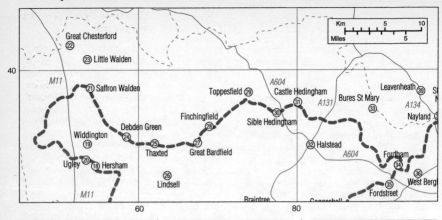

Little Walden 23

National Grid Ref: TL5441

¶ The Crown, Eight Bells

(2m) **Rowley Hill Lodge**, *Little Walden Road, Little Walden, Saffron Walden, Essex, CB10 1UZ.*
Attractive farm lodge with large secluded garden
Grades: ETB 2 Cr, Comm, AA 3 Q
Tel: 01799 525975 Mrs Haslam.
Fax no: 01799 516622
Rates fr: *£19.50-£25.00.*
Open: All Year (not Xmas)
Beds: 1D 1T **Baths:** 2 Private
🛇 🅿 (4) 🖵 ▥ Ⅴ ✓

Debden Green 24

National Grid Ref: TL5732

¶ White Hart

(1m) **Wigmores Farm**, *Debden Green, Saffron Walden, Essex, CB11 3LX.*
Situated in beautiful open countryside near Thaxted and Saffron Walden
Grades: ETB Listed, Comm
Tel: 01371 830050 Mrs Worth.
Rates fr: *£18.00-£20.00.*
Open: All Year
Beds: 2D 1T **Baths:** 2 Shared
🛇 🅿 (8) 🖵 � ✕ ▥ Ⅴ

Thaxted 25

National Grid Ref: TL6131

¶ The Swan, The Star, Rose & Crown

(0.25m) **Folly House**, *Watling Lane, Thaxted, Great Dunmow, Essex, CM6 2QY.*
Historic village, views, attentive service. Transfers to/from Stansted Airport available
Grades: ETB 2 Cr, Comm
Tel: 01371 830618 Mrs King.
Rates fr: *£20.00-£35.00.*
Open: All Year **Beds:** 2D 1T
Baths: 2 Private 1 Shared
🛇 🅿 (10) ✓ 🖵 ✕ ▥ Ⅴ

Lindsell 26

National Grid Ref: TL6427

(3m) **Cowels Cottage**, *Lindsell, Great Dunmow, Essex, CM6 3QG.*
Quiet rural situation. Handy Stansted Airport
Tel: **01371 870454** Mrs Gray.
Rates fr: *£18.00-£18.00.*
Open: All Year
Beds: 1D 2S
Baths: 1 Ensuite 2 Private
🅿 🖵 ▥ Ⅴ

Great Bardfield 27

National Grid Ref: TL6730

¶ The Vine

(On route) **Bucks House**, *Vine Street, Great Bardfield, Braintree, Essex, CM7 4SR.*
Beautiful C16th house, great breakfasts, warm welcome. Conservation village centre
Tel: **01371 810519** Mrs Turner.
Fax no: 01371 811175
Rates fr: *£17.50-£17.50.*
Open: All Year (not Xmas)
Beds: 1F 1 4D
Baths: 1Private 1Shared
🛇 ✓ 🖵 ♦ ▥ ▲ ♠

(0.25m) **Bell Cottage**, *Bell Lane, Great Bardfield, Braintree, Essex, CM7 4TH.*
Pretty C16th thatched cottage
Grades: ETB Listed
Tel: **01371 810149** (also fax no)
Mrs Mason.
Rates fr: *£16.00-£16.00.*
Open: All Year (not Xmas)
Beds: 1T 1S
Baths: 1 Shared
🛇 🖵 ♦ ▥ Ⅴ

The *lowest* single rate *is shown in* bold.

Finchingfield 28

National Grid Ref: TL6832

¶ The Fox

(0.25m) **Finchingfield House**, *Bardfield Road, Finchingfield, Braintree, Essex, CM7 4JS.*
Magnificent historic Tudor country house
Grades: ETB 2 Cr, Comm, AA 3 Q, RAC Listed
Tel: **01371 810289** (also fax no)
Mrs Patient.
Rates fr: *£20.00-£28.00.*
Open: All Year
Beds: 2D 1T
Baths: 1 Ensuite 1 Shared
🅿 (6) ✓ 🖵 ▥ Ⅴ

Toppesfield 29

National Grid Ref: TL7337

(2m) **Olivers Farm**, *Toppesfield, Halstead, Essex, CO9 4LS.*
C17th, quiet idyllic location
Tel: **01787 237642** Mrs Blackie.
Rates fr: *£18.00-£18.00.*
Open: All Year (not Xmas)
Beds: 2D 1T
Baths: 1 Ensuite 1 Shared
🛇 (10) 🅿 (4) ✓ 🖵

Sible Hedingham 30

National Grid Ref: TL7734

¶ The Swan, Sugar Loaves

(1m) **Hedingham Antiques**, *100 Swan Street, Sible Hedingham, Halstead, Essex, CO9 3HP.*
Large Victorian house/shop combined in centre village near pubs
Grades: ETB 1 Cr
Tel: **01787 460360** (also fax no)
Mrs Patterson.
Rates fr: *£17.50-£20.00.*
Open: All Year (not Xmas)
Beds: 1D 2T
Baths: 3 Private
🛇 🅿 (4) 🖵 ▥ Ⅴ

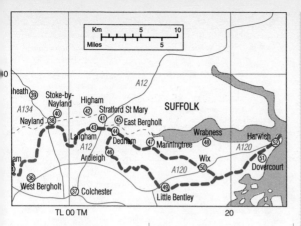

TL 00 TM   20

Saffron Walden to Fordham

Southeast of Saffron Walden you will find an interesting architecturally-eclectic church at **Debden**, before coming to **Thaxted**. Originating in Saxon times, the town has many medieval half-timbered buildings, including the Guildhall, which stands as evidence of the town's prosperity based historically on the cutlery industry. You are now on the long eastwards stretch of the route, which takes you through a series of attractive villages - Great Bardfield, Finchingfield and **Castle Hedingham**, where the well-preserved Norman castle keep is set in grounds with a formal canal and woodland walks. From here you continue east to **Fordham**, from where you can head south, cross the River Colne and proceed to **Coggeshall**; or continue into the eastern 'spur' to **Harwich**. A detour into **Colchester** will enable you to take in some of the rich store of architectural remains on offer in Britain's oldest town. (See under *Sustrans Hull to Harwich*.)

Castle Hedingham 31

National Grid Ref: TL7835

¶⊙¶ ◀ The Bell

(▲ 0.25m) *Castle Hedingham Youth Hostel, 7 Falcon Square, Castle Hedingham, Halstead, Essex, CO9 3BU.*
Actual grid ref: TL786355
Tel: 01787 460799
Under 18: £5.95
Adults: £8.80
Evening Meals Available (7pm), Self-catering Facilities, Showers
The Norman castle and half-timbered houses of Castle Hedingham add to the atmosphere of this hostel. 16th century building with modern annexe and large lawned garden.

(0.25m) *Pannells Ash Farm, Castle Hedingham, Halstead, Essex, CO9 3AD.*
Period furnished C15th farmhouse
Grades: ETB Listed, Comm
Tel: 01787 460364
Mrs Redgewell.
Rates fr: £15.50-**£16.50.**
Open: All Year (not Xmas)
Beds: 1F 1D 1T 1S
Baths: 1 Private 1 Shared
🛏 🅿 (6) ⊬ ⬜ 🎢 🕎 ✦

Halstead 32

National Grid Ref: TL8130

¶⊙¶ ◀ White Hart

(2m) *The Woodman Inn, Colchester Road, Halstead, Essex, CO9 2DY.*
Comfortable mock-Tudor public house
Tel: 01787 476218 (also fax no)
Mr Redsell.
Rates fr: £18.00-**£18.00.**
Open: All Year
Beds: 1F 1D 1T 1S
Baths: 1 Shared
🛏 🅿 (12) ⬜ ✕ 🎢

Bures St Mary 33

National Grid Ref: TL9034

(1m) *Queens House, Church Square, Bures St Mary, Suffolk, CO8 5AB.*
C16th country house, licensed restaurant
Grades: ETB 2 Cr
Tel: 01787 227760 Mrs Gordon.
Fax no: 01787 227903
Rates fr: £20.00-**£22.00.**
Open: All Year (not Xmas)
Beds: 1F 2D 2T
Baths: 4 Ensuite 1 Private
🛏 🅿 (2) ⬜ ✕ 🎢 🕎

Fordham 34

National Grid Ref: TL9228

(0.5m) *Kings Vineyard, Fordham, Colchester, Essex, CO6 3NY.*
Actual grid ref: TL9328
Warm hospitality, peaceful farmhouse, panoramic views
Grades: ETB 2 Cr, Comm
Tel: 01206 240377 Mrs Tweed.
Rates fr: £16.00-**£20.00.**
Open: All Year **Beds:** 1F 1D 1T
Baths: 1 Private 1 Shared
🛏 (1) 🅿 (6) ⬜ ✕ 🎢 🕎 🛊 ✦

Fordstreet 35

National Grid Ref: TL9226

¶⊙¶ ◀ Coopers' Arms, Queen's Head

(0.25m) *Old House, Fordstreet, Aldham, Colchester, Essex, CO6 3PH.*
Actual grid ref: TL920270
Fascinating Grade II b/w Tudor house with modern comforts, friendly atmosphere
Grades: ETB 1 Cr, Comm
Tel: 01206 240456 Mrs Mitchell.
Rates fr: £19.00-**£25.00.**
Open: All Year **Beds:** 1F 1T 1S
Baths: 1 Ensuite 2 Private
🛏 🅿 (8) ⬜ 🎢 🛊 ✦

West Bergholt 36

National Grid Ref: TL9627

¶⊙¶ ◀ White Hart, Treble Tile

(1m) *The Old Post House, 10 Colchester Road, West Bergholt, Colchester, Essex, CO6 3JG.*
Actual grid ref: TL9527
Large Victorian private house
Grades: ETB 2 Cr, Approv
Tel: 01206 240379 (also fax no)
Mrs Brown.
Rates fr: £16.00-**£20.00.**
Open: All Year (not Xmas)
Beds: 1F 1D 1T
Baths: 1 Ensuite 1 Shared
🛏 🅿 (3) ⬜ ✕ 🎢 🕎 🛊 ✦

The lowest *double* rate per person is shown in *italics*.

Colchester 37

National Grid Ref: TL9925

🍴 🍺 The Forresters, Rovers Tye, Siege House

(5m) *The Red House, 29 Wimpole Road, Colchester, Essex, CO1 2DL.*
Elegant, comfortable Victorian house. Short walk to town centre and stations
Tel: **01206 509005**
Mrs Harrington.
Rates fr: *£18.00-£20.00.*
Open: All Year
Beds: 1T 2D
Baths: 3 Ensuite
🛏 (2) 🗢 🖵 🗶 📖 Ⅴ 🛉

(5m) *St John's Guest House, 330 Ipswich Road, Colchester, Essex, CO4 4ET.*
Well situated close to town
Grades: ETB Listed
Tel: **01206 852288** Mrs Knight.
Rates fr: *£17.00-£25.00.*
Open: All Year
Beds: 1F 1D 2T 1S
Baths: 2 Ensuite 1 Shared
🛏 🖵 (10) 🗢 🖵 📖 Ⅴ

(5m) *The Old Manse, 15 Roman Road, Colchester, Essex, CO1 1UR.*
Quiet town centre location beside Castle Park. 3 minutes' walk to town
Grades: ETB Listed, AA 2 Q
Tel: **01206 545154** Ms Anderson.
Rates fr: *£18.00-£25.00.*
Open: All Year (not Xmas)
Beds: 1D 1T
Baths: 1 Private 2 Shared
🛏 (3) 🖵 (1) 🗢 🖵 📖 Ⅴ

(5m) *Globe Hotel, 71 North Station Road, Colchester, Essex, CO1 1RQ.*
Recently modernised Victorian pub/hotel
Tel: **01206 573881** Mr Higgins.
Rates fr: *£25.00-£30.00.*
Open: All Year
Beds: 3F 3D 3T 3S
Baths: 12 Private
🛏 🖵 🖵 🗶 📖 Ⅴ

(5m) *The Vines, 42 Military Road, Colchester, Essex, CO1 2AN.*
Large Georgian private house
Grades: ETB Listed
Tel: **01206 767301**
Rates fr: *£16.50-£19.00.*
Open: All Year **Beds:** 1D 1T
Baths: 1 Ensuite 1 Private
🛏 (0) 🖵 (1) 🗢 🖵 📖

Please don't camp

on *anyone's* land

without first obtaining

their permission.

Nayland 38

National Grid Ref: TL9734

🍴 🍺 White Hart, The Angel

(2m) *Gladwins Farm, Harpers Hill, Nayland, Colchester, Essex, CO6 4NU.*
Actual grid ref: TL961347
Suffolk farmhouse in Constable country. Indoor pool. Brochure
Grades: ETB 2 Cr, Comm
Tel: **01206 262261** Mrs Dossor.
Fax no: 01206 263001
Rates fr: *£26.00-£20.00.*
Open: All Year (not Xmas)
Beds: 2D 1T 1S
Baths: 3 Private 1 Shared
🛏 🖵 (12) 🖵 🗶 📖 Ⅴ 🛉

(1m) *Hill House, Gravel Hill, Nayland, Colchester, Essex, CO6 4JB.*
Actual grid ref: TL975345
C16th timber-framed "hall house"
Grades: ETB Listed, Comm
Tel: **01206 262782** Mrs Heigham.
Rates fr: *£19.00-£20.00.*
Open: All Year (not Xmas)
Beds: 1D 1T 1S
Baths: 1 Ensuite 1 Shared
🛏 (10) 🖵 (3) 🖵 📖 Ⅴ 🛉

Leavenheath 39

National Grid Ref: TL9536

(4m) *Leavenheath Farm, Locks Lane, Leavenheath, Colchester, Essex, CO6 4PF.*
Welcoming period farmhouse, in quiet setting
Grades: ETB Listed, High Comm
Tel: **01206 262322**
Mrs Warren Thomas.
Rates fr: *£18.00-£20.00.*
Open: All Year (not Xmas)
Beds: 1F 1D 2T 1S
Baths: 3 Ensuite 1 Private
🛏 (4) 🖵 (8) 🗢 🖵 🗶 📖 Ⅴ 🛉

Stoke-by-Nayland 40

National Grid Ref: TL9836

🍴 🍺 Black Horse, Angel Inn, Rose Inn

(3m) *Ryegate House, Stoke-by-Nayland, Colchester, Essex, CO6 4RA.*
Cheerful house in village setting
Grades: ETB 2 Cr, High Comm
Tel: **01206 263679** Mrs Geater.
Rates fr: *£18.50-£25.00.*
Open: All Year (not Xmas)
Beds: 2D 1T **Baths:** 3 Ensuite
🛏 (10) 🖵 (5) 🗢 🖵 📖

(3m) *Thorington Hall, Stoke-by-Nayland, Colchester, Essex, CO6 4SS.*
Beautiful C17th house, warm welcome
Grades: ETB Listed, Comm
Tel: **01206 337329** Mrs Wollaston.
Rates fr: *£20.00-£17.50.*
Open: Easter to Oct
Beds: 1F 2D 1T 1S
Baths: 3 Private 1 Shared
🛏 🖵 (4) 📖 Ⅴ

Stratford St Mary 41

National Grid Ref: TM0434

🍴 🍺 Marlborough Head, Sun Hotel, The Swan, Black Horse

(1m) *Teazles, Stratford St Mary, Colchester, Essex, CO7 6LU.*
Comfortable old merchant weaver's house
Tel: **01206 323148** Mrs Clover.
Rates fr: *£18.00-£18.00.*
Open: All Year
Beds: 1F 1D 1T 1S
Baths: 1 Ensuite 1 Shared
🛏 🖵 🗢 🖵 🗶 📖 Ⅴ 🛉

Higham 42

National Grid Ref: TM0335

(2m) *The Bauble, Higham, Colchester, Essex, CO7 6LA.*
Actual grid ref: TM031354
Peaceful old country home
Grades: ETB 2 Cr, High Comm, AA 4 Q, Recomm
Tel: **01206 337254** Mrs Watkins.
Fax no: 01206 337263
Rates fr: *£20.00-£22.00.*
Open: All Year
Beds: 2T 1S
Baths: 3 Ensuite
🛏 (12) 🖵 (5) 🗢 🖵 📖 Ⅴ 🛉

Langham 43

National Grid Ref: TM0233

🍴 🍺 Shepherd & Dog

(1m) *Oak Apple Farm, Greyhound Hill, Langham, Colchester, Essex, CO4 5QF.*
Actual grid ref: TM023320
Comfortable farmhouse with large attractive garden
Grades: ETB Listed
Tel: **01206 272234**
Mrs Helliwell.
Rates fr: *£18.50-£19.00.*
Open: All Year (not Xmas)
Beds: 2T 1S
Baths: 1 Shared
🛏 🖵 (6) 🖵 📖 Ⅴ 🛉

Dedham 44

National Grid Ref: TM0533

🍴 🍺 The Anchor, Marlborough Head, The Sun

(1m) *Mays Barn Farm, Mays Lane, Dedham, Colchester, Essex, CO7 6EW.*
Actual grid ref: TM0531
Secluded, comfortable old farmhouse
Grades: ETB 2 Cr, High Comm
Tel: **01206 323191**
Mrs Freeman.
Rates fr: *£19.00-£22.00.*
Open: All Year (not Xmas)
Beds: 1D 1T
Baths: 2 Private
🛏 (12) 🖵 (4) 🗢 🖵 📖 Ⅴ

East Bergholt 45

National Grid Ref: TM0735

⊮⊩ ◧ Red Lion, Carriers' Arms, King's Head

(2m) *Wren Cottage*, The St, East Bergholt, Colchester, Essex, CO7 6SE.
C16th cottage in middle of village, easy walk to Flatford, good pubs next to chemist
Grades: ETB Listed
Tel: **01206 298327**
Mrs Commercial.
Rates fr: *£20.00-£22.00*.
Open: Easter to Sep
Beds: 1F 1T **Baths:** 2 Ensuite
ঌ🅿🗔🛏🖾🆅

Ardleigh 46

National Grid Ref: TM0529

⊮⊩ ◧ Wooden Fender Inn

(On route) *Dundas Place*, Colchester Road, Ardleigh, Colchester, Essex, CO7 7NP.
Friendly, comfortable C17th cottage, pretty garden, Constable Country, convenient Harwich
Grades: ETB 2 Cr, Comm
Tel: **01206 230625** Mrs Le May.
Rates fr: *£17.00-£20.00*.
Open: All Year (not Xmas)
Beds: 1D 2T
Baths: 1 Ensuite 1 Shared
ঌ (12) 🅿 (3) ⅄🗔🛏🖾🆅

Manningtree 47

National Grid Ref: TM1031

⊮⊩ ◧ King's Arms, Village Maid

(0.5m) *Aldhams*, Bromley Road, Lawford, Manningtree, Essex, CO11 2NE.
Actual grid ref: TM098302
Grades: ETB 2 Cr, High Comm, AA 3 Q
Tel: **01206 393210** Mrs McEwen.
Fax no: 01255 870722
Rates fr: *£20.00-£25.00*.
Open: All Year (not Xmas)
Beds: 2D 1T 1S
Baths: 2 Private 1 Shared
ঌ🅿 (6) ⅄🗔🖾🆅⅍
Converted farmhouse in Lutyens style set in 3 acres and surrounded by fields. Wonderfully peaceful yet only a short drive to Harwich, Colchester and Dedham

Wrabness 48

National Grid Ref: TM1731

⊮⊩ ◧ Wheatsheaf Inn

(2m) *Dimbols Farm*, Station Road, Wrabness, Manningtree, Essex, CO11 2TH.
Actual grid ref: TM175313
Georgian farmhouse, peaceful environment, convenient for Beth Chatto's gardens
Grades: ETB 1 Cr, Comm
Tel: **01255 880328** (also fax no)
Mrs Macaulay.
Rates fr: *£15.00-£21.00*.
Open: All Year (not Xmas)
Beds: 1F 1D
Baths: 1 Shared
ঌ🅿 (4) ⅄🗔🖾🆅⅍

Little Bentley 49

National Grid Ref: TM1125

(On route) *Bentley Manor*, Little Bentley, Colchester, Essex, CO7 8SE.
C16th manor house
Tel: **01206 250622**
Mrs Dyson.
Rates fr: *£17.00-£22.00*.
Open: All Year (not Xmas)
Beds: 1F 1D 1T
ঌ🅿⅄🗔🖾

Wix 50

National Grid Ref: TM1628

⊮⊩ ◧ Village Maid

(1m) *Dairy House Farm*, Bradfield Road, Wix, Manningtree, Essex, CO11 2SR.
Spacious, quality rural accommodation. A really relaxing place to stay
Grades: ETB 2 Cr, High Comm
Tel: **01255 870322** Mrs Whitworth.
Fax no: 01255 870186
Rates fr: *£17.00-£22.00*.
Open: All Year (not Xmas)
Beds: 1D 2T
Baths: 2 Ensuite 1 Private
ঌ (10) 🅿 (10) 🗔🖾🆅🛆

(1m) *New Farm House*, Spinnells Lane, Wix, Manningtree, Essex, CO11 2UJ.
Country guesthouse with warmest welcome
Grades: ETB 3 Cr, Comm
Tel: **01255 870365** Mrs Mitchell.
Fax no: 01255 870837

Rates fr: *£21.00-£22.00*.
Open: All Year
Beds: 5F 1D 3T 3S
Baths: 7 Private 1 Shared
ঌ🅿 (20) 🗔🛏🗶🖾⅃🆅🛆⅍

Dovercourt 51

National Grid Ref: TM2531

(0.5m) *154 Fronks Road*, Dovercourt, Harwich, Essex, CO12 4EF.
Detached house in tree-lined boulevard
Tel: **01255 503081** (also fax no)
Mrs Cullen.
Rates fr: *£13.00-£15.00*.
Open: Dec to Jan
Beds: 1F 1T
Baths: 1 Shared
ঌ🅿 (4) ⅄🗔🖾

(0.5m) *Swyncombe Guest House*, 19 Cliff Road, Dovercourt, Harwich, Essex, CO12 3PP.
Warm family-run guest house
Tel: **01255 551245** Mr Cheney.
Rates fr: *£14.00-£14.00*.
Open: All Year (not Xmas)
Beds: 1F 1D 1S
Baths: 2 Shared
ঌ🅿🗔🛏🗶🖾🆅

Harwich 52

National Grid Ref: TM2431

⊮⊩ ◧ The Billy

(0.25m) *Reids of Harwich*, 3 West Street, Harwich, Essex, CO12 3DA.
Spacious Victorian property - historic location
Tel: **01255 506796** Mr Reid.
Rates fr: *£16.00-£16.00*.
Open: April to Oct
Beds: 1D 1T 1S
Baths: 2 Shared
ঌ (12) 🗔🖾🆅🛆⅍

(0.25m) *Queens Hotel*, 119 High Street, Dovercourt, Harwich, Essex, CO12 3AP.
Public house/hotel
Grades: ETB 1 Cr, Approv
Tel: **01255 502634** Mrs Skinner.
Rates fr: *£15.00-£15.00*.
Open: All Year
Beds: 1F 4T 2S
Baths: 2 Shared
ঌ🅿 (15) 🗔🗶🖾

Fordham to Harwich

The village of **Dedham** boasts an immaculate neo-classical row of houses, and a church where one of the pews is decorated in memory of the Apollo 11 moon landing. Just over the border in Suffolk, **Flatford Mill** has become dedicated to the memory of the painter John Constable, whose painting *The Hay Wain* featured the original mill, on the site of which the present Victorian building stands. The route to

Harwich runs along two alternative ways - the northern way goes through **Manningtree** and **Mistley**, the southern through **Ardleigh**, where there are a number of buildings of historic interest, and some other villages. The northern way is likely to be more crowded, particularly during summer. **Harwich** is a major ferry port to the European mainland, and can be used to link the Essex Cycle Route with Continental cycling tours.

Icknield Way

The great prehistoric track that runs from Dorset to The Wash along Southern England's chalk ridgeway is the most ancient road still in use in Europe. Although the name applied historically to the whole section from the Thames to the north coast of Norfolk, the present **Icknield Way** runs from the northern end of the Ridgeway National Trail in Buckinghamshire to the starting point, on Norfolk's southern border, of the Peddars Way, another National Trail. Passing through Buckinghamshire, Bedfordshire, Hertfordshire, Cambridgeshire, Essex and Suffolk, it is now a Regional Recreational Route created, primarily for walkers, by the Countryside Commission on the basis of work done by the Icknield Way Association. A little over 100 miles long, the route is waymarked by a distinctive flint axe emblem. **Note:** Cyclists should follow the route designed for horseriders. This frequently diverges from the walkers' route, which follows many footpaths open only to walkers. Wherever the two are different, follow the waymarks and signposts marked 'Riders' Route'.

Guides: *The Icknield Way Path – A Guide for Horseriders, Cyclists and Others* by Elizabeth Barrett (ISBN 0 951601 12 1), published by Wimpole Books and available from the publishers at Pip's Peace, Kenton, Stowmarket, Suffolk IP14 6JS, tel 01728 860429, @ £3.50 (+ 80p p&p), describes the riders' route, which cyclists should follow. This guide takes the route in reverse from the above description. It finishes at Luton, so you should also get hold of a copy of *The Icknield Way – A Walkers' Guide* (ISBN 0 952181 90 8), published by the Icknield Way Association and available from the Ramblers' Association National Office, 1/5 Wandsworth Road, London SW8 2XX, tel 0171 582 6878, @ £4.50 (+ 70p p&p). This guide has excellent material on the flora and fauna, archaeology and geology of the path.

Maps: Ordnance Survey 1:50,000 Landranger series: 144, 153, 154, 155, 165, 166

Trains: Tring, about 4 miles from Ivinghoe Beacon, is served by trains from London, as is Luton. Letchworth and Baldock are on the line between London and Cambridge. Newmarket is on the line between Cambridge and Ipswich. Thetford, about 6 miles from Knettishall Heath, is on the line between Cambridge and Norwich.

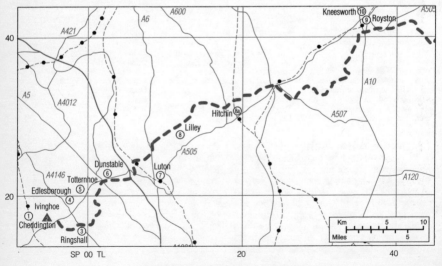

Cheddington 1

National Grid Ref: SP9217

¶ ◫ Carpenters' Arms

(0.5m) *Rose Cottage, 68 High Street, Cheddington, Leighton Buzzard, Beds, LU7 0RQ.*
Victorian house, garden N.G.S
Grades: ETB 1 Cr
Tel: 01296 668693
Mrs Jones.
Rates fr: *£18.00-£20.00.*
Open: All Year
Beds: 1D 1T 1S
Baths: 2 Shared
⊃ (11) ℙ (3) ✄ ⌺ ⊞ Ⓥ ⚡

All cycleways are
popular: you are
well-advised to
book ahead

Pay B&Bs by cash or
cheque and be prepared
to pay up front.

Ivinghoe 2

National Grid Ref: SP9416

(▲ 1m) *Ivinghoe Youth Hostel, The Old Brewery House, Ivinghoe, Leighton Buzzard, Bedfordshire, LU7 9EP.*
Actual grid ref: SP945161
Warden: A & G Fortune.
Tel: **01296 668251**
Under 18: £5.40
Adults: £8.00
Evening Meals Available (7pm),
Family Bunk Rooms, Showers,
Shop
Georgian mansion, once home of a local brewer, next to village church in Chilterns Area of Outstanding Natural Beauty

Ringshall 3

National Grid Ref: SP9814

¶ ◫ Bridgewater Arms

(1.5m) *12/13 Ringshall, Ringshall, Berkhamsted, Herts, HP4 1ND.*
200-year-old country cottage, home produce
Tel: **01442 843396** Mrs Martin.
Rates fr: *£13.00-£13.00.*
Open: All Year **Beds:** 1F 1T
Baths: 1 Private 1 Shared
⊃ (1 Month) ℙ ⌺ ⯒ ✗ ⊞ Ⓥ ⚑ ⚡

Edlesborough 4

National Grid Ref: SP9719

¶ ◫ The Bell, Golden Rule

(1m) *Ridgeway End, 5 Ivinghoe Way, Edlesborough, Dunstable, Beds, LU6 2EL.*
Bungalow set in quiet location
Tel: **01525 220405** Mrs Lloyd.
Rates fr: *£18.00-£18.00.*
Open: All Year (not Xmas)
Beds: 1F 1D 1T 1S
Baths: 1 Private 3 Shared
⊃ ℙ (3) ⌺ ⊞ Ⓥ ⚑ ⚡

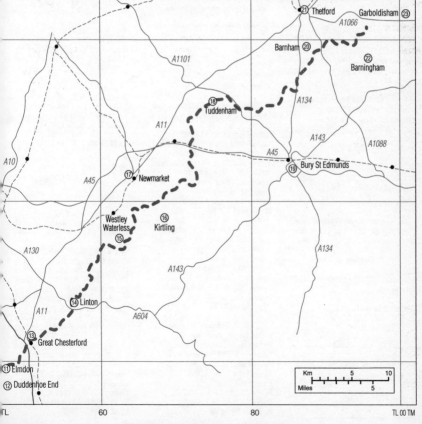

Ivinghoe Beacon to Baldock

The official start of the Icknield Way is at **Ivinghoe Beacon**, a hill with an ancient fort, which yields good views. Close by is Pitstone Windmill, the oldest in England (seventeenth century). Crossing into Bedfordshire, the route passes near **Whipsnade Wild Animal Park**, which you can tour by steam train, as well as on foot; and crosses the **Dustable Downs Country Park**, where there are several Neolithic burial mounds. From here you go through the towns of **Dunstable** and **Luton.** Luton Museum exhibits archaeological finds from the Icknield Way. Into Hertfordshire, and you reach **Telegraph Hill**, one of a series of such hills in a line from London to Great Yarmouth, named from the communication stations, which signalled using a system of shutters on the roof, of the Napoleonic Wars. The views from the hill are excellent. North of Tingley Wood is the Knocking Hoe long barrow, and a nearby National Nature Reserve. You head through the village of **Ickleford**, north of Hitchin, to reach **Letchworth**, an early 'garden city'. From here you pass to the north of **Baldock**, a town important in Iron Age and Roman times and developed by the Knights Templars. There are some fine Georgian buildings.

Totternhoe   5

National Grid Ref: SP9821

|○| ◖ Old Farm Inn

(0.5m) *Gower Cottage, 5 Brightwell Avenue, Totternhoe, Dunstable, Beds, LU6 1QT.*
Actual grid ref: SP994210
Executive style, country position. Close M1
Grades: ETB Listed, Recomm
Tel: 01582 601287 Mrs Mardell.
Rates fr: *£20.00-£20.25.*
Open: All Year (not Xmas)
Beds: 2D 1S
Baths: 1 Shared
🛏 🅿 (3) ⊬ 🗗 🎟 🛢 ⚡

Dunstable   6

National Grid Ref: TL0121

|○| ◖ Sugar Loaf

(1m) *Regent House Guest House, 79a High Street North, Dunstable, Beds, LU6 1JF.*
Located in town centre
Tel: 01582 660196
Mr Woodhouse.
Rates fr: *£15.00-£16.00.*
Open: All Year
Beds: 3T 2S
Baths: 2 Shared
🛏 🅿 (6) 🗗 ⌘ 🎟 🖩 🛢 ⚡

The lowest *double* rate per person is shown in *italics*.

Luton   7

National Grid Ref: TL0921

|○| ◖ O'Shea's, Barn Owl, Wigmore Arms

(1.25m) *Stockwood Hotel, 41-43 Stockwood Crescent, Luton, Beds, LU1 3SS.*
Actual grid ref: TL090206
Tudor-style town centre premises, near M1, airport, golf course
Tel: 01582 721000 Mr Blanchard.
Rates fr: *£20.00-£25.00.*
Open: All Year (not Xmas)
Beds: 1F 2D 6T 9S
Baths: 4 Private 3 Shared
🛏 🅿 (12) 🗗 ✕ 🎟.

(1.25m) *Belzayne, 70 Lalleford Road, Luton, Beds, LU2 9JH.*
Small, friendly guesthouse, convenient airport
Tel: 01582 736591 Mrs Bell.
Rates fr: *£11.00-£18.00.*
Open: All Year (not Xmas)
Beds: 1D 2T **Baths:** 2 Shared
🛏 (6) 🅿 (5) ✕ 🎟.

(1.25m) *Hill House, 93 London Road, Luton, Beds, LU1 3RG.*
In Luton, convenient for airport
Grades: ETB Listed
Tel: 01582 722725 Ms Stirling.
Rates fr: *£15.00-£20.00.*
Open: All Year
Beds: 2F 1D 1T 1S
Baths: 1 Ensuite 2 Shared
🛏 🅿 (5) 🗗 ⌘ 🎟.

All rates are subject to alteration at the owners' discretion.

(1.25m) *Spinner's , 46 Hill Rise, Sundon Park, Luton, Beds, LU3 3EE.*
Immaculate, comfortable, convenient M1/trains
Tel: 01582 508327 Mrs Spinner.
Rates fr: *£13.00-£13.00.*
Open: All Year (not Xmas)
Beds: 1T 1S
Baths: 1 Ensuite 1 Private
🛏 🅿 (2) ⊬ 🗗 🎟.

Lilley   8

National Grid Ref: TL1126

|○| ◖ Lilley Arms

(1m) *Lilley Arms, West Street, Lilley, Luton, Beds, LU2 8LN.*
Early C18th coaching inn
Tel: 01462 768371 Mrs Brown.
Rates fr: *£16.25-£18.50.*
Open: All Year
Beds: 1F 1D 1T
Baths: 2 Ensuite 1 Shared
🛏 🅿 ⊬ 🗗 ✕ 🎟 🖩 🛢 ⚡

Hitchin   8a

National Grid Ref: TL1930

(2m) *Long Ing, 64 Fishponds Road, Hitchin, Herts, SG5 1NU.*
Actual grid ref: TL182298
Edwardian house opposite swimming pool
Tel: 01462 458050 Mr Rollason.
Rates fr: *£15.00-£17.00.*
Open: All Year (not Xmas)
Beds: 1F 1T 1S **Baths:** 1 Shared
🛏 🗗 🎟. ⚡

(2m) *Ashford Guest House, 24 York Road, Hitchin, Herts, SG5 1XA.*
Large Victorian house
Tel: 01462 454183 Mr D'Angelo.
Rates fr: *£16.00-£16.00.*
Open: All Year **Beds:** 3T 2S
🛏 🅿 🗗 🎟.

Royston   9

National Grid Ref: TL3541

|○| ◖ Jockey Inn, White Bear Lodge

(0.25m) *Jockey Inn, 31-33 Baldock Street, Royston, Herts, SG8 5BD.*
Tel: 01763 243377 Mrs Critchell.
Rates fr: *£24.50-£24.50.*
Open: All Year (not Xmas)
Beds: 3T 1S **Baths:** 4 Ensuite
🛏 (8) 🅿 (10) 🗗 ✕ 🎟. 🖩
Traditional, friendly public house, real ales. Comfortable rooms, all ensuite with tea/coffee and cable TV. Hearty breakfast

(0.25m) *Greenlawns, 39 Market Hill, Royston, Herts, SG8 9JU.*
Large comfortable Victorian house
Tel: 01763 242619 Mrs Little.
Rates fr: *£18.00-£18.00.*
Open: All Year (not Xmas)
Beds: 1F 1D 1T **Baths:** 1 Shared
🛏 🅿 (3) ⊬ 🗗 🎟. 🖩

Kneesworth   10

National Grid Ref: TL3444

⚑ Queen Adelaide

(2.5m) *Fairhaven*, 102 Old North
Road, Kneesworth, Royston, Herts,
SG8 5JR.
Comfortable well-appointed
country home
Tel: **01763 249471**
Mrs Watson.
Rates fr: *£17.50*-**£17.50**.
Open: All Year (not Xmas)
Beds: 1D 1T 1S
Baths: 1 Shared
🛏 🅿 (3) ⚥ 🗖 ▥, Ⓥ

Elmdon   11

National Grid Ref: TL4639

(On route) *Elmdon Bury*, Elmdon,
Saffron Walden, Essex, *CB11 4NF*.
Actual grid ref: TL4640
Spacious comfortable renovated
Essex farmhouse
Grades: ETB 2 Cr, High Comm
Tel: **01763 838220** Mrs Pearson.
Fax no: 01763 838504
Rates fr: *£25.00*-**£30.00**.
Open: All Year (not Xmas)
Beds: 2D 1T
Baths: 3 Private
🛏 (10) 🅿 (12) ⚥ ✝ ✗ ▥, ✦

Duddenhoe End   12

National Grid Ref: TL4636

⚑ The Woopman

(1.5m) *Duddenhoe End Farm*,
Duddenhoe End, Saffron Walden,
Essex, *CB11 4UU*.
Delightful C17th farmhouse
Grades: ETB 2 Cr, Comm
Tel: **01763 838258**
Mrs Foster.
Rates fr: *£18.00*-**£22.00**.
Open: All Year (not Xmas)
Beds: 2D 1T
Baths: 3 Private
🛏 (12) 🅿 (3) ⚥ 🗖 ▥.

Great Chesterford   13

National Grid Ref: TL5042

⚑ Crown & Thistle, The Plough

(0.25m) *The Delles*, Carmen
Street, Great Chesterford, Saffron
Walden, Essex, *CB10 1NR*.
Beautiful old farmhouse dating
from 1520
Grades: ETB 2 Cr, High Comm
Tel: **01799 530256** (also fax no)
Mrs Chater.
Rates fr: *£21.00*-**£25.00**.
Open: All Year
Beds: 2D 1T
Baths: 1 Ensuite 2 Private
🛏 (2) 🅿 (5) 🗖 ✝ ✗ ▥, Ⓥ ♒

Linton   14

National Grid Ref: TL5646

⚑ The Crown, Dog & Duck

(On route) *Springfield House*, 14-
16 Horn Lane, Linton, Cambridge,
Cambs, *CB1 6HT*.
Peaceful, riverside Regency
residence with large garden in
historic village
Grades: ETB 2 Cr, Comm
Tel: **01223 891383**
Mrs Rossiter.
Rates fr: *£18.00*-**£20.00**.
Open: All Year
Beds: 2D
Baths: 1 Ensuite 1 Private
🛏 🅿 (4) ⚥ 🗖 ▥, Ⓥ ♒ ✦

(0.5m) *Linton Heights*,
36 Wheatsheaf Way, Linton,
Cambridge, Cambs, *CB1 6XB*.
Comfortable, friendly home,
sharing lounge
Tel: **01223 892516**
Mr & Mrs Peake.
Rates fr: *£15.00*-**£15.00**.
Open: All Year (not Xmas)
Beds: 1T 1S
Baths: 1 Shared
🛏 (6) 🅿 (2) ⚥ 🗖 ▥, ♒ ✦

Westley Waterless   15

National Grid Ref: TL6256

⚑ King's Head, Red Lion

(0.75m) *Westley House*, Westley
Waterless, Newmarket, Suffolk,
CB8 0RQ.
C18th Georgian country home,
quiet rural area 5 miles from
Newmarket
Grades: ETB Listed
Tel: **01638 508112** Mrs Galpin.
Fax no: 01638 508113
Rates fr: *£21.00*-**£22.00**.
Open: All Year
Beds: 2T 2S
Baths: 1 Private 1 Shared
🛏 (4) 🅿 (6) 🗖 ✝ ✗ ▥, Ⓥ ♒ ✦

Kirtling   16

National Grid Ref: TL6858

(2.75m) *Hill Farm Guest House*,
Kirtling, Newmarket, Suffolk,
CB8 9HQ.
Comfortable old farmhouse
Tel: **01638 730253** Mrs Benley.
Rates fr: *£20.00*-**£22.00**.
Open: All Year
Beds: 1D 1T 1S
Baths: 2 Ensuite
🅿 (4) 🗖 ✝ ✗ ▥, Ⓥ

Newmarket   17

National Grid Ref: TL6463

⚑ King's Head, Red Lion,
White Lion

(4.5m) *Falmouth House*,
Falmouth Avenue, Newmarket,
Suffolk, *CB8 0NB*.
Large, comfortable, modern,
detached house
Tel: **01638 660409**
Mrs Shaw.
Rates fr: *£19.00*-**£25.00**.
Open: All Year (not Xmas)
Beds: 1D 2T
Baths: 1 Shared
🛏 (10) 🅿 (6) 🗖 ✗ ▥, Ⓥ

Baldock to Gazeley

After **Ashwell**, an interesting village with a museum on local archaeological finds, the route enters Cambridgeshire and continues along Ashwell Street, a probably Roman road which may well be based on a stretch of the original Icknield Way, to reach **Melbourn**. Here you turn south before continuing eastwards to cross the River Cam into the northwestern corner of Essex, and the village of **Great Chesterford**, which was once a walled Roman town. Back in Cambridgeshire, the village of **Linton** has numerous sixteenth- and seventeenth-century houses, and a garden zoo. At **Balsham**, the county's highest point, there is a fascinating medieval church, which has a thirteenth-century bell tower, and a three-hundred-year-old musical manuscript on display. Crossing the ancient Fleam Dyke, you cycle up green hedged Fox Lane before wending your way through a string of villages to **Wooddition**, from where there are two routes to **Herringswell** in Suffolk. The northern alternative takes you via **Newmarket**, the famous horseracing centre, where you can visit the National Stud and the National Horseracing Museum, and **Chippenham**, with nearby Chippenham Park. The southern route leads over quieter roads through **Cheveley** and **Gazeley**, with its tower mill.

(4.5m) *29 Manderston Road,*
Newmarket, Suffolk, CB8 0NL.
B&B in historic Newmarket
Tel: **01638 603245** Marshall.
Rates fr: *£18.00.*
Open: All Year (not Xmas)
Beds: 1T 1S
⚡☐

Tuddenham   18

National Grid Ref: TL7371

🍴 ◧ White Hart

(0.25m) *Oakdene, Higham Road,*
Tuddenham, Bury St Edmunds,
Suffolk, IP28 6SG.
Very comfortable home from
home, ideally situated for
Newmarket Races
Grades: ETB Listed, Comm
Tel: **01638 718822** Mrs Titcombe.
Rates fr: *£16.50-£18.50.*
Open: All Year (not Xmas)
Beds: 2F 1T
Baths: 1 Ensuite 1 Shared
☺ ᴾ (3) ⚡☐✗🏠 ⓥ â ✦

Bury St Edmunds   19

National Grid Ref: TL8564

🍴 ◧ Masons' Arms, Pegotty's

(3m) *Ash Cottage, 59 Whiting*
Street, Bury St Edmunds, Suffolk,
IP33 1NP.
Listed Elizabethan town house in
ancient cathedral town
Tel: **01284 755098**
Mrs Barber-Lomax.
Rates fr: *£20.00-£28.00.*
Open: All Year
Beds: 1D 1T
Baths: 1 Ensuite 1 Private
☺ ☐🏠🏠 ⓥ

(3m) *Hilltop, 22 Bronyon Close,*
Bury St Edmunds, Suffolk, IP33 3XB.
Family home with ground floor
bedroom, quiet area
Grades: ETB Listed, Approv
Tel: **01284 767066** Mrs Hanson.
Rates fr: *£16.00-£16.00.*
Open: All Year (not Xmas)
Beds: 1F 1T 1S
Baths: 1 Private 1 Shared
☺ ᴾ (2) ☐🏠✗🏠 â✦

(3m) *Oak Cottage, 54 Guildhall*
Street, Bury St Edmunds, Suffolk,
IP33 1QF.
Listed Tudor cottage - town centre
- near theatre
Tel: **01284 762745 / 0467 303355**
Sheila Keeley.
Rates fr: *£13.00-£14.00.*
Open: All Year
Beds: 1F 1D 1T 1S
Baths: 1 Ensuite 1 Private 1 Shared
☺ ᴾ (1) ☐🏠✗🏠 ⓥ â✦

The lowest *double* rate per
person is shown in *italics*.

(3m) *The Leys, 113 Fornham*
Road, Bury St Edmunds, Suffolk,
IP32 6AT.
Large detached Victorian private
house
Tel: **01284 760225**
Mrs Lee.
Rates fr: *£17.00-£20.00.*
Open: All Year
Beds: 1F 1D 1T
Baths: 1 Private 1 Shared
☺ ᴾ (6) ⚡☐🏠

Barnham   20

National Grid Ref: TL8779

🍴 ◧ Grafton Arms

(0.5m) *East Farm, Barnham,*
Thetford, Norfolk, IP24 2PB.
Large, warm, comfortable farm
house
Grades: ETB 1 Cr, Comm
Tel: **01842 890231** Mrs Heading.
Rates fr: *£20.00-£23.00.*
Open: All Year (not Xmas)
Beds: 1D 1T
Baths: 2 Ensuite
☺ ᴾ (4) ☐ â✦

Thetford   21

National Grid Ref: TL8783

🍴 ◧ Black Horse, Anchor Hotel

(4m) *43 Magdalen Street,*
Thetford, Norfolk, IP24 2BP.
200-year-old cottage, near station
Tel: **01842 764564** Mrs Findlay.
Rates fr: *£17.00-£17.00.*
Open: All Year (not Xmas)
Beds: 2T 1S
Baths: 1 Shared
☐🏠 ✦

(4m) *The Wilderness, Earls Street,*
Thetford, Norfolk, IP24 2AF.
Tudor-style house, landscaped
garden
Tel: **01842 764646**
Mrs Pomorski.
Rates fr: *£17.00-£19.00.*
Open: All Year (not Xmas)
Beds: 3D 1S
Baths: 1 Shared
☺ (6) ᴾ (6) ⚡☐🏠 â✦

Barningham   22

National Grid Ref: TL9676

🍴 ◧ Royal George

(5m) *College House Farm,*
Bardwell Road, Barningham, Bury
St Edmunds, Suffolk, IP31 1DF.
Jacobean country house in four
acres. C17th Fison family home
Grades: ETB Listed, Comm
Tel: **01359 221512** (also fax no)
Mrs Brightwell.
Rates fr: *£22.00-£25.00.*
Open: All Year (not Xmas)
Beds: 2F 2D 1S
Baths: 1 Private 1 Shared
☺ (5) ᴾ (7) ⚡☐🏠& ⓥ

Gazeley to Knettishall Heath

You are now in the open
heath of **the Breckland**. The
way through Suffolk leads to
Icklingham, one of whose
two churches is medieval and
thatched and whose mill is
recorded in the Domesday
Book; nearby **West Stow
Country Park** has a
reconstructed Saxon village,
accurately based on
excavation work. The route
takes you around the west
and north of the **King's
Forest**, planted from 1935 to
celebrate the silver jubilee of
George V, to **Euston**, not the
London station but a village
close to Euston Hall, an
attractive eighteenth-century
house and grounds with
lakes, open to the public on
Thursdays. The earlier house
was a favourite haunt of the
seventeenth-century diarist
John Evelyn. From Euston it's
on to **Knettishall Heath
Country Park**, on the banks
of the Little Ouse.

Garboldisham   23

National Grid Ref: TM0081

🍴 ◧ The Fox, White Horse

(3.5m) *Ingleneuk Lodge, Hopton*
Road, Garboldisham, Diss,
Norfolk, IP22 2RQ.
Actual grid ref: TM002801
Spacious accommodation, 1.5 acres
in woodland setting, residents'
bar/lounge
Grades: ETB 2 Cr, Comm
Tel: **01953 681541**
Mr Boreham & Mrs B Fry.
Fax no: 01953 681633
Rates fr: *£25.50-£33.00.*
Open: All Year (not Xmas)
Beds: 1D 2T 1S **Baths:** 4 ensuite
☺ ᴾ (20) ☐🏠🏠&

(3.5m) *Swan House Bed and*
Breakfast, Hopton Road,
Garboldisham, Diss, Norfolk,
IP22 2RQ.
Comfortable C17th former
coaching house
Grades: ETB Listed, Comm
Tel: **01953 688221**
Miss May and Miss M Eldridge.
Rates fr: *£17.00-£22.00.*
Open: All Year (not Xmas)
Beds: 1D 1T 1S **Baths:** 1 Shared
☺ (12) ᴾ (6) ⚡☐🏠 ⓥ

STILWELL'S BRITAIN BED & BREAKFAST

Bed & breakfast accommodation is a British institution. It's a great value alternative to expensive hotels and a world away from camping and caravanning. You may be touring, travelling or pursuing a hobby. You may just wish to get away from it all. Whatever the reason, the British bed & breakfast is the great value answer to all your accommodation needs.

There's such a wide range to choose from - private houses, country halls, farms, cottages, inns, small hotels and guest houses. Stilwell's Britain Bed & Breakfast 1998 publishes by far and away the most extensive list of bed & breakfasts available. The book is thus ideal for planning trips and short stays in every part of the country.

Arranged by country, county and location with local maps alongside, Stilwell's Britain Bed & Breakfast 1998 is the indispensable reference work for bed & breakfast accommodation in Britain.

- **Plan your trips with no fuss!**

- **All official grades shown!**

- **Local maps - see where you want to stay at a glance!**

- **Pubs serving evening meals shown too!**

- **The largest choice ever - a massive 8,000 entries!**

- **Good value only - an average £17 to £18 a night!**

- **Handy size for easy packing!**

Britain Bed & Breakfast is available from all good bookshops
(ISBN 1-900861-02-X) or direct from Stilwell Publishing Ltd
@ £9.95 plus £2 p&p (UK only).

Lancashire Cycleway

At 250 miles, the **Lancashire Cycleway** is one of the longer county cycle routes, and really consists of two circular routes, around the northern and southern halves of the county, together forming a great figure of eight, linking up at the Ribble Valley town of Whalley. The north end of the northern circle links up with the *Cumbria Cycleway* - those with bags of energy and more time can undertake the two cycleways together to make a massive 500-mile tour of the beautiful northwest corner of England. The Lancashire route is signposted with blue cycle silhouette signs with a letter 'N' for the northern circle or 'S' for the southern circle, and can be cycled in either direction, but the County Council recommend cycling clockwise, to beat the prevailing southwesterly wind. The description that follows takes the route clockwise around the northern circle and then clockwise around the southern circle, starting and finishing both sections in Whalley.

A detailed **guide booklet** to the cycleway route is available free from the County Public Relations Officer, PO Box 78, County Hall, Preston PR1 8XJ, tel 01772 263521. In addition, over 200 attractions in the county are listed in a free leaflet, 'Great Days Out in Lancashire', available from the same address.

Maps: Ordnance Survey 1:50,000 Landranger series: 97, 98, 102, 103, 108, 109

Trains: Whalley is served by trains from Manchester and elsewhere. Numerous places on or near the route are served by the rail network.

Whalley   1

National Grid Ref: SD7336

(0.25m) Monk Hall, 78 Mitton Road, Whalley, Clitheroe, Lancs, *BB7 9JN*.
Small, friendly guest house
Grades: ETB 3 Cr, High Comm
Tel: **01254 822501** Hollin.
Rates fr: *£17.50*-£17.50.
Open: All Year
Beds: 2D 1T 1S
Baths: 4 Ensuite
🛇 🗇 ✕ 🎟 🛡

Hurst Green   2

National Grid Ref: SD6838

†○† 🍴 The Shireburn

(▲ 3m) Hurst Green Camping Barn, Greengore Farm, Hurst Green, Blackburn, Lancashire
Actual grid ref: SD674389
Tel: **01200 28366**
Adults: £3.35+
Simple barn, sleeps 12. Henry VII is reputed to have stayed at the hunting lodge at Greengore Farm. ADVANCE BOOKING ESSENTIAL

(3m) Shireburn Arms Hotel, Whalley Road, Hurst Green, Clitheroe, Lancs, *BB6 9QJ*.
C16th family-run hotel and Restaurant
Grades: ETB 4 Cr, Comm
Tel: **01254 826518** Alcock.
Fax no: 01254 826208
Rates fr: *£30.00*-£37.00.
Open: All Year
Beds: 1S 3F 8D 7T
Baths: 18 Private
🛇 🗇 (100) ⊭ 🗇 🎟 ✕ 🖩 ৬ 🛡

Ribchester   3

National Grid Ref: SD6435

†○† 🍴 Black Bull, White Bull, Hall's Arms

(1m) New House Farm, Preston Road, Ribchester, Preston, Lancs, *PR3 3XL*.
Old renovated farmhouse, rare breeds
Tel: **01254 878954** Bamber.
Rates fr: *£18.00*-£24.00.
Open: All Year
Beds: 1F 1D 1T
Baths: 3 Ensuite
🛇 (3) 🗇 (6) ⊭ 🗇 🖩 🛡 ✦

(1m) Smithy Farm, Huntingdon Hall Lane, Dutton, Ribchester, Preston, Lancs, *PR3 2ZT*.
Unspoilt countryside. 15 mins from M6. Friendly hospitality
Grades: ETB Listed
Tel: **01254 878250** Jackson.
Rates fr: *£12.50*-£18.00.
Open: All Year (not Xmas)
Beds: 1F 1D 1T **Baths:** 1 Shared
🛇 🗇 🗇 🎟 ✕ 🛡 ⋔ ✦

Longridge   4

National Grid Ref: SD6037

†○† 🍴 Alston Arms, Derby Arms

(0.25m) 14 Whittingham Road, Longridge, Preston, Lancs, *PR3 2AA*.
Homely, caring accommodation. Scenic area. Motorways accessibility. Sports, shopping, theatres
Tel: **01772 783992** Morley.
Rates fr: *£15.50*-£15.50.
Open: All Year
Beds: 1F 1T 1S **Baths:** 1 Shared
🛇 🗇 (3) 🗇 🖩 🛡

The lowest *double* rate per person is shown in *italics*.

(1m) *Jenkinsons Farmhouse,*
Longridge, Alston, Preston, Lancs,
PR3 3BD.
Old worlde farmhouse, outstanding
countryside
Grades: ETB 4Q, Select, AA 2A
Tel: 01772 782624 Ibison.
Rates fr: £20.00-£23.50.
Open: All Year (not Xmas)
Beds: 2D 3T 1S **Baths:** 4 Shared
🛇 (12) 🅿 (8) 🛏 🖺

Goosnargh 5

National Grid Ref: SD5536

🍽 🍺 Green Man

(On route) *Isles Field Barn, Syke*
House Lane, Goosnargh, Preston,
Lancs, PR3 2EN.
Spacious accommodation sur-
rounded by beautiful countryside.
Hearty breakfast. Friendly welcome
Tel: 01995 640398 Mr McHugh.
Rates fr: £17.00-£17.00.
Open: All Year **Beds:** 2F 1S
Baths: 2 Ensuite 1 Shared
🛇 🅿 (6) 🖵 🖺 🎥

Bilsborrow 6

National Grid Ref: SD5139

(0.25m) *Olde Duncombe House,*
Garstang Road, Bilsborrow,
Preston, Lancs, PR3 0RE.
Grades: ETB 3 Cr, High Comm
Tel: 01995 640336 Mr Bolton.
Rates fr: £22.50-£32.50.
Open: All Year
Beds: 2F 5D 2T 2S
Baths: 11 Private
🛇 🅿 (20) 🖵 🛏 🗙 🖺 ♿ 🎥
Traditional cottage-style family run
bed & breakfast offering a high
standard of accommodation. We
are situated alongside the tranquil
Lancaster canal. Ideal for business
people and toruists

All rates are subject
to alteration at the
owners' discretion.

(0.25m) *The Gables, Bilsborrow*
Lane, Bilsborrow, Preston, Lancs,
PR3 0RN.
A comfortable, friendly home
Tel: 01995 640683
Mrs Biscomb.
Rates fr: £15.00-£15.00.
Open: All Year (not Xmas)
Beds: 1D 1T 1S
Baths: 1 Shared
🅿 (5) ✂ 🖵 🖺

Barton 7

National Grid Ref: SD5137

🍽 🍺 Old Nell's

(2m) *Ratcliffe Farm, White Horse*
Lane, Barton, Preston, Lancs,
PR3 5AH.
Comfortable friendly farmhouse
Tel: 01995 640536 Worden.
Rates fr: £15.00-£15.00.
Open: All Year (not Xmas)
Beds: 1F 1D
Baths: 1 Shared
🛇 🅿 (4) 🖵 🎥

Bay Horse 8

National Grid Ref: SD4953

¶◎ ◖ Bay Horse Hotel

(0.5m) *Saltoke South, Bay Horse, Galgate, Lancaster. LA2 0HL.*
Family home in rural setting
Tel: **01524 752313**
Robin.
Rates fr: *£15.00-£20.00.*
Open: All Year (not Xmas)
Beds: 1F 1D 1T
🛇 🅿 (4) ✍ �...

(1m) *Stanley Lodge Farmhouse, Cockerham Road, Bay Horse, Lancaster. LA2 0HE.*
Farmhouse conveniently situated in rural area
Tel: **01524 791863**
Rates fr: *£16.00-£16.00.*
Open: All Year (not Xmas)
Beds: 1F 2D
Baths: 1 Shared
🛇 🅿 (4) ...

Quernmore 9

National Grid Ref: SD5160

(▲ 1m) *Quernmore Camping Barn, Brow Top Farm, Quernmore, Lancaster.*
Actual grid ref: SD528588
Tel: **Adults:** £3.35+
Self-catering Facilities, Parking
Superb remote location on an elevated hilltop with magnificent open views over Morecambe Bay and the Lake District Fells. No electricity: bring a torch. Farm cafe 1m. ADVANCE BOOKING ESSENTIAL

Bolton-le-Sands 10

National Grid Ref: SD4868

¶◎ ◖ Blue Anchor

(1m) *The Blue Anchor Hotel, Main Street, Bolton-le-Sands, Carnforth, Lancs, LA5 8DN.*
C18th coaching house. Ideally situated
Grades: ETB 3 Cr, Approv
Tel: **01524 823241**
Duncan.
Fax no: 01524 824745
Rates fr: *£20.00-£22.00.*
Open: All Year
Beds: 3D 1T
Baths: 4 Private

(1m) *Row-Bar, 4 Whin Grove, Bolton-le-Sands, Carnforth, Lancs, LA5 8DD.*
Friendly family-run private home
Tel: **01524 735369**
Udall.
Rates fr: *£15.00-£20.00.*
Open: All Year (not Xmas)
Beds: 1F 1D
Baths: 2 Ensuite

(1m) *Bankside Cottage, 21 Whin Grove, Bolton-le-Sands, Carnforth, Lancs, LA5 8DD.*
Canalside, village location, picturesque quiet
Tel: **01524 735078**
Addy.
Rates fr: *£15.00-£17.50.*
Open: All Year (not Xmas)
Beds: 3T
Baths: 2 Ensuite 1 Shared

All cycleways are popular: you are well-advised to book ahead

---

Carnforth 11

National Grid Ref: SD4970

¶◎ ◖ Bay Horse, Eagle's Head

(0.25m) *Capernwray House, Capernwray, Carnforth, Lancs, LA6 1AE.*
Grades: ETB 2 Cr, Comm
Tel: **01524 732363** (also fax no)
Mrs Smith.
Rates fr: *£21.00-£20.00.*
Open: All Year (not Xmas)
Beds: 2D 1T 1S
Baths: 3 Private
🛇 (5) 🅿 (8) ...
Beautiful country house. Panoramic views. Tastefully decorated throughout. No smoking. Close Lakes, Dales, Lancaster. Excellent stopover South - Scotland. Warm welcome our speciality! Phone for brochure

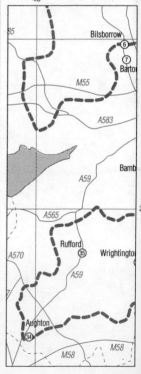

Whalley to Wrea Green

Whalley nestles in the beautiful Ribble Valley, where wooded lanes form the backdrop to countless picturesque villages. Traces of all aspects of the history of the Red Rose County can be found here - the ruined abbey recalling the Dissolution in the sixteenth century, the railway viaduct a reminder of the county's nineteenth-century history, when it was at the core of the Industrial Revolution. Proceeding west, the route hits the Ribble at **Ribchester**, where the Museum of Roman Antiquities tells of the town's history as a Roman fort, and the many weavers' cottages bear witness to Lancashire's historic textile industry. After the villages of **Inglewhite** and **Bilsborrow** you ride down into **the Fylde**, the plain of Western Lancashire north of the Ribble, and the old market town of **Kirkham**, another textile town which made sails for the Royal Navy. After the archetypal picturesque Fylde village of **Wrea Green**, you may wish to take a detour into the archetypal English seaside town of **Blackpool**, famous for its Pleasure Beach, Illuminations (during early autumn) and the Blackpool Tower, a halfsize copy of the more illustrious construction by Gustave Eiffel; as well as the baroque Grand Theatre and the Winter Gardens, scene of countless political party conferences.

(0.25m) *26 Victoria Street,*
Carnforth, Lancs, LA5 9ED.
Comfortable home, good food,
clean
Tel: **01524 732520** Dickinson.
Rates fr: £13.00-£14.00.
Open: All Year (not Xmas)
Beds: 1F 1D 1T **Baths:** 1 Shared
🅿 (2) 🖵 🎮 Ⓥ

Warton 12

National Grid Ref: SD5072
🍴 🍺 Country Hotel

(On route) *Cotestone Farm, Sand*
Lane, Warton, Carnforth, Lancs,
LA5 9NH.
Near Leighton Moss RSPB
Reserve, Lancaster/Morecambe,
Lakes & Dales
Tel: **01524 732418** Close.
Rates fr: £15.00-£16.00.
Open: All Year (not Xmas)
Beds: 1F 1D 1T 1S
Baths: 2 Shared
🐾 🅿 (3) 🖵 🍽 🎮 Ⓥ

(1m) *Kiln Croft, Main Street,*
Warton, Carnforth, Lancs, LA5 9NR.
Edwardian guest house and
restaurant
Tel: **01524 735788** Holmes.
Rates fr: £18.00-£22.00.
Open: All Year
Beds: 3F 1D **Baths:** 4 Ensuite
🐾 🅿 (8) 🖵 🍴 🍽 🎮 Ⓥ 🛈 ⚡

Silverdale 13

National Grid Ref: SD4675
🍴 🍺 Royal Hotel, Silverdale
Hotel.

(On route) *The Limes Village*
Guest House, 23 Stankelt Road,
Silverdale, Carnforth, Lancs,
LA5 0TF.
Exceptionally good food. Unspoilt
area. English Lake District,
Yorkshire Dales
Tel: **01524 701454** (also fax no)
Mrs Livesey.
Rates fr: £17.50-£24.50.
Open: All Year
Beds: 1F 1D 1T
Baths: 3 Private
🐾 🅿 (3) 🍽 🖵 🍽 🎮 Ⓥ ⚡

All rooms full and

nowhere else to stay?

Ask the owner if

there's anywhere

nearby

Arnside 14

National Grid Ref: SD4578

(⛺ 0.25m) *Arnside Youth Hostel,*
Oakfield Lodge, Redhills Road,
Arnside, Carnforth, Lancashire, LA5
0AT.
Actual grid ref: SD452783
Tel: **01524 761781**
Under 18: £5.95
Adults: £8.80
Evening Meals Available (7pm),
Television, Games Room,
Showers, Laundry Facilities
A few minutes' walk from the shore
with views across Morecambe Bay
to the Lakeland Fells. A mellow
stone house on the edge of a
coastal village on the Kent estuary.
RSPB reserve nearby

(On route) *Willowfield Hotel, The*
Promenade, Arnside, Carnforth,
Lancs, LA5 0AD.
Non-smokers' family-run hotel
Grades: ETB 3 Cr, Comm,
AA 3 Q, RAC Listed
Tel: **01524 761354**
Mr Kerr.
Rates fr: £19.00-£19.00.
Open: All Year
Beds: 1F 4D 3T 2S
Baths: 7 Ensuite 2 Shared
🐾 🅿 (10) 🍽 🖵 🍴 🍽 🎮 Ⓥ 🛈 ⚡

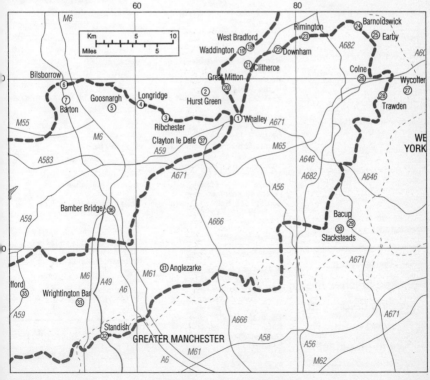

Kirkby Lonsdale 15

National Grid Ref: SD6178

⊪¶ ◖ Lunesdale Arms Hotel, Snooty Fox

(1m) *Green Lane End Farm,* *Kirkby Lonsdale, Carnforth, Lancs,* *LA6 2PP.*
C17th farmhouse - working farm.
M6 2 miles
Tel: **01539 567236**
Mrs Nicholson.
Rates fr: *£15.00-*£17.00.
Open: Easter to Oct
Beds: 1D 1T
Baths: 1 Shared
🛏 🅿 (3) ⊬ 🐾 Ⅴ ✦

Tunstall 16

National Grid Ref: SD6073

⊪¶ ◖ Lunesdale Arms

(1m) *Barnfield Farm, Tunstall,* *Kirkby Lonsdale, Carnforth, Lancs,* *LA6 2QF.*
Actual grid ref: SD607736
1702 family farmhouse on a 200 acre working farm
Tel: **01524 274284**
Mrs Stephenson.
Rates fr: *£15.00-*£16.00.
Open: All Year (not Xmas)
Beds: 1F 1D
Baths: 2 Shared
🛏 🅿 (2) ⊬ 🖵 🖢 Ⅴ 🍴 ✦

Slaidburn 17

National Grid Ref: SD7152

(▲ On route) *Slaidburn Youth* *Hostel, King's House, Slaidburn,* *Clitheroe, Lancashire, BB7 3ER.*
Actual grid ref: SD711523
Tel: **01200 446656. Advance** **bookings: 015242 41567**
Under 18: £4.00
Adults: £5.85
Self-catering Facilities, Showers, Shop
Basic village accommodation for *walkers and cyclists in the middle* *of the Forest of Bowland, at the* *centre of the picturesque village of* *Slaidburn. C17th former inn: basic* *facilities with an open fire and* *central heating*

Order your
packed lunches the
evening before you
need them.
Not at breakfast!

All details shown
are as supplied
by B&B owners in
Autumn 1997.

West Bradford 18

National Grid Ref: SD7444

⊪¶ ◖ Three Millstones

(On route) *Old Hall,* Back Lane, *West Bradford, Clitheroe, Lancs,* *BB7 4SN.*
Actual grid ref: SD745444
Spacious manor house in AONB
Tel: **01200 423282** Gretton.
Rates fr: *£15.00-*£17.00.
Open: All Year (not Xmas)
Beds: 1D 2T
Baths: 1 Private 1 Shared
🛏 🅿 (10) ⊬ 🖵 🐾 🖢 ✦

Waddington 19

National Grid Ref: SD7243

⊪¶ ◖ Lower Buck Inn, Waddington Arms

(On route) *Backfold Cottage,* The *Square, Waddington, Clitheroe,* *Lancs, BB7 3JA.*
Luxury mini country hotel
Tel: **01200 422367**
Mrs Forbes.
Rates fr: *£20.00-*£20.00.
Open: All Year
Beds: 1D 1T 1S
Baths: 3 Private
🛏 (10) 🅿 (10) 🖵 🐾 ✕ 🖢 Ⅴ 🍴 ✦

(0.25m) *Peter Barn Country* *House, Cross Lane, Waddington,* *Clitheroe, Lancs, BB7 3JH.*
Luxurious peaceful accommodation, beautiful garden
Grades: ETB Listed, High Comm
Tel: **01200 428585** Mrs Smith.
Rates fr: *£19.50-*£25.00.
Open: All Year (not Xmas)
Beds: 2D 1T **Baths:** 3 Private
🛏 (12) 🅿 (6) ⊬ 🖵 ✕ 🖢 Ⅴ

Great Mitton 20

National Grid Ref: SD7138

(0.25m) *Mitton Green Barn,* *Church Lane, Great Mitton,* *Clitheroe, Lancs, BB7 9PJ.*
Newly-converted barn offering luxury accommodation
Tel: **01254 826673** Hargreaves.
Rates fr: *£19.50-*£27.00.
Open: All Year
Beds: 2D 1T
Baths: 2 Private 1 Shared
🛏 🅿 (6) 🖵 🖢 Ⅴ

Wrea Green to the Lancaster Canal

Cycling north through the Fylde, you cross the River Wyre, and pass by the old marsh village of **Pilling** before crossing the **Lancaster Canal**. A possible detour here takes you to the lovely old port at **Glasson Dock**, from where you may wish to follow the River Lune Path north as an alternative to the designated route of the cycleway, rejoining it north of Lancaster. Either way, the county town is well worth a look. **Lancaster** boasts many elegant Georgian buildings, testament to its shadily prosperous period as a major port in the slave trade; the town's roots go back way beyond then to Roman Britain. Landmarks include Lancaster Castle, whose Norman keep overlooking the Lune presides over a crown court and the county's Shire Hall, the Priory Church of St Mary, a former Benedictine foundation notable for its Saxon doorway, the seventeenth-century Judges' Lodging (now a museum) and the grounds of the Ashton Memorial, sporting a butterfly and palm house.

Clitheroe 21

National Grid Ref: SD7441

⊪¶ ◖ Swan with Two Necks, Edisford Bridge Inn

(1m) *Selborne House,* Back *Commons, Clitheroe, Lancs,* *BB7 2DX.*
Quiet lane, short walk to town
Tel: **01200 423571 / 422236**
Barnes. Fax no: 01200 423571
Rates fr: *£15.00-*£17.50.
Open: All Year
Beds: 1F 2D 1T
Baths: 1 Private 1 Shared
🛏 🅿 (6) 🖵 🐾 ✕ 🖢 ♿ Ⅴ 🍴 ✦

The lowest *double* rate per
person is shown in *italics*.

> **All rooms full and**
> **nowhere else to stay?**
> **Ask the owner if**
> **there's anywhere**
> **nearby**

(1m) *Brooklands, 9 Pendle Road, Clitheroe, Lancs, BB7 1JQ.*
Actual grid ref: SD750414
Ribble Valley. Comfortable Victorian home
Grades: ETB Listed, Comm
Tel: 01200 422797 (also fax no) Lord.
Rates fr: *£16.00-£17.00.*
Open: All Year
Beds: 1D 2T
Baths: 1 Ensuite 2 Shared
ॐ ₽ (5) ⚘ ⊟ ₤ ✦

(1m) *Springfield Cottage, 18 Nelson Street, Low Moor, Clitheroe, Lancs, BB7 2NQ.*
Actual grid ref: SD730418
Home of character, Ribble Way
Tel: 01200 442237
Whitfield.
Rates fr: *£16.00-£16.00.*
Open: All Year
Beds: 1F 1D
Baths: 1 Shared
ॐ (0) ⊟ ⊞ ₤ ✦

Downham   22

National Grid Ref: SD7844

(▲ 0.5m) *Downham Camping Barn, Downland Estate, Downham, Clitheroe, Lancashire*
Actual grid ref: SD795445
Tel: 01200 28366
Adults: £3.35+
Simple barn, sleeps 12. Near the foot of Pandle Hill. ADVANCE BOOKING ESSENTIAL

Rimington   23

National Grid Ref: SD8045

⊪ ⊠ Asheton Arms, Moorcock Inn

(1m) *Wytha Farm, Rimington, Clitheroe, Lancs, BB7 4EQ.*
Working farmhouse with fantastic views
Tel: 01200 445295
Oliver.
Rates fr: *£13.50-£16.00.*
Open: All Year (not Xmas)
Beds: 1F 1D 1T
ॐ ₽ (3) ⊟ ⚘ ✕ ⊞ ₤ ✦

Barnoldswick   24

National Grid Ref: SD8746
⊪ ⊠ Fanny Grey

(0.25m) *Monks House, 5 Manchester Road, Barnoldswick, Colne, Lancs, BB8 5NZ.*
Centrally situated comfortable Georgian house
Tel: 01282 814423 Robinson.
Rates fr: *£16.00-£16.00.*
Open: All Year
Beds: 2T 2S
Baths: 2 Shared
ॐ ₽ ✕ ⊞ ₤ ✦

Earby   25

National Grid Ref: SD9046
⊪ ⊠ Red Lion

(▲ 2m) *Earby Youth Hostel, Glen Cottage, Birch Hall Lane, Earby, Colne, Lancashire, BB8 6JX.*
Actual grid ref: SD915468
Warden: Ms D Swift.
Tel: 01282 842349
Under 18: £4.95
Adults: £7.20
Family Bunk Rooms, Showers, Central Heating, Shop
Attractive cottage with own picturesque garden and waterfall, on NE outskirts of Earby

(1m) *Grange Fell, Skipton Road, Earby, Colne, Lancs, BB8 6JL.*
Apartment-style accommodation in Edwardian home
Tel: 01282 843621 Eden.
Rates fr: *£17.00-£19.00.*
Open: Easter to Oct
Beds: 1F
Baths: 1 Shared
ॐ ₽ ⊟ ⚘ ⊞ ₤

Colne   26

National Grid Ref: SD8940
⊪ ⊠ Alma Inn

(0.5m) *148 Keightley Road, Colne, Lancs, BB8 0PJ.*
Edwardian town house with many original features. Close to open countryside
Grades: ETB 2 Cr, High Comm
Tel: 01282 862002
Mrs Etherington.
Rates fr: *£16.00-£16.00.*
Open: Mar to Dec (not Xmas)
Beds: 2D 1S
Baths: 1 Private 1 Shared
ॐ (11) ₽ (1) ⊟ ⊞ ⊠

(1m) *Higher Wanless Farm, Red Lane, Colne, Lancs, BB8 7JP.*
Ideally situated, luxuriously furnished farmhouse
Grades: ETB 2 Cr, High Comm, AA 4 Q, Select
Tel: 01282 865301 Mitson.
Rates fr: *£19.00-£22.00.*
Open: Feb to Nov
Beds: 1F 1T
Baths: 1 Ensuite 1 Shared
ॐ (4) ₽ (4) ⊟ ✕ ⊞ ₤ ✦

> **High season,**
> **bank holidays and**
> **special events mean**
> **low availability**
> *everywhere.*

The Lancaster Canal to Whalley

From here you ride north through **Carnforth**, which offers railway enthusiasts the Steamtown Railway Museum, to the small coastal village of **Silverdale**, and then over the county boundary to **Arnside** in Cumbria; the headland between Silverdale and Arnside, overlooking Morecambe Bay, is a designated Area of Outstanding Natural Beauty. The next stretch, as far as Kirkby Lonsdale, is also part of the *Cumbria Cycleway*, and takes you over Farleton Fell to **Hutton Roof**, with its panoramic views. **Kirkby Lonsdale** is famous for the Devil's Bridge, as well as 'Ruskin's View', behind St Mary's Church. From here it is south through the wooded Lune Valley, and then the beautiful gritstone moorland of the **Forest of Bowland**, another designated Area of Outstanding Natural Beauty which belonged historically to the old rival, Yorkshire. The village of **Slaidburn** offers welcome refreshment at the thirteenth-century Hark and Bounty Inn; after this the route takes you through the old Ribble Valley villages of **Sawley**, with its twelfth-century abbey ruins, and **Waddington**, back to Whalley.

Wycoller   27
National Grid Ref: SD9339

(On route) *Wycoller Cottage,
Wycoller, Colne, Lancs, BB8 8SY.*
C17th cottage with exposed beams
Tel: **01282 867336** (also fax no)
Houlker.
Rates fr: *£20.00-£20.00*.
Open: All Year
Beds: 1D 1T 1S
Baths: 2 Private
🛏 🅿 (2) ⅍ 🗗 📖 Ⅴ

Trawden   28
National Grid Ref: SD9138
🍴 🍺 Sun Inn

(1m) *Middle Beardshaw Head
Farm, Trawden, Colne, Lancs,
BB8 8PP.*
C18th beamed farmhouse -
wonderful setting
Tel: **01282 865257** Mann.
Rates fr: *£17.50-£17.50*.
Open: All Year (not Xmas)
Beds: 1F 1D 2S
Baths: 1 Private 1 Shared
🛏 🅿 (10) 🗗 🐓 ✕ 📖 Ⅴ 🐴 ⅍

**Many rates vary
according to season -
the lowest only are
shown here**

**Please don't camp
on *anyone's* land
without first obtaining
their permission.**

Bacup   29
National Grid Ref: SD8622
🍴 🍺 Rose & Bowl

(3m) *Pasture Bottom Farm,
Bacup, Lancs, OL13 0UZ.*
Comfortable farmhouse bed &
breakfast in a quiet rural area on a
working beef farm
Grades: ETB 1 Cr, Approv
Tel: **01706 873790** (also fax no)
Isherwood.
Rates fr: *£13.50-£13.50*.
Open: All Year (not Xmas)
Beds: 2T **Baths:** 1 Shared
🛏 🅿 (4) ⅍ 🗗 🐓 ✕ 📖 🐴 ⅍

Stacksteads   30
National Grid Ref: SD8421

(2m) *Glen Heights, 190 Booth
Road, Stacksteads, Bacup, Lancs,
OL13 0TH.*
Comfortable family guest house
Tel: **01706 875459** Graham.
Rates fr: *£15.00-£18.50*.
Open: All Year
Beds: 1D 1T 1S
Baths: 1 Shared
🛏 (12) 🅿 (3) 🗗 ✕ 📖 Ⅴ

Anglezarke   31
National Grid Ref: SD6317
🍴 🍺 Bay Horse

(1m) *Jepsons Farm, Moor Road,
Anglezarke, Chorley, Lancs,
PR6 9DQ.*
Beautiful C17th stone farmhouse
Tel: **01257 481691** Hilton.
Rates fr: *£18.00-£18.00*.
Open: All Year (not Xmas)
Beds: 1F 1D 1T 1S
Baths: 2 Shared
🛏 🅿 (6) 🗗 ✕ 📖 Ⅴ

Standish   32
National Grid Ref: SD5610

(0.25m) *52 Bentham Road,
Standish, Wigan, Lancs, WN6 0ND.*
Large garden & sun lounge
Tel: **01257 422750**
Mrs Hutchinson.
Rates fr: *£10.00-£12.00*.
Open: All Year (not Xmas)
Beds: 1T **Baths:** 1 Private
🛏 🅿 (3) ⅍ 🗗 📖

Wrightington Bar   33
National Grid Ref: SD5313
🍴 🍺 Hind's Head

(2m) *95 Mossy Lea Road,
Wrightington Bar, Wigan, Lancs,
WN6 9RD.*
Modern bungalow near M6, J27
Tel: **01257 421929** Sutton.
Rates fr: *£12.00-£13.00*.
Open: All Year
Beds: 1D 2T **Baths:** 1 Shared
🛏 (2) 🅿 (6) ⅍ 🗗 📖

The Southern Circle

The northeastern half of the southern circle is a demanding up-and-down ride through the Lancashire Pennines. **Clitheroe** is a busy market town with a twelfth-century Castle keep. From here the route takes you around Pendle Hill; here in 1652 George Fox had the vision that led him to found the Society of Friends. **Downham** is an English village as archetypal as Castle Combe (see the *Wiltshire Cycleway*), but here church, pub, village green and stocks sit astride a hilltop. Now the route takes you to **Barnoldswick**, and around Colne, Nelson and Burnley - you are at the eastern end of Lancashire's central belt of industrial towns. Wycoller Country Park in the **Forest of Trawden** offers welcome respite; Towneley Hall, on the route around Burnley, is a fourteenth century house hosting an art gallery and museum with collections of eighteenth and nineteenth century paintings and decorative arts, and a natural history centre with an aquarium.

Now it's south, by Rawtenstall, Haslingden and Ramsbottom. The Peel Tower at **Holcombe** commemorates Sir Robert Peel; Turton Tower, by **Chapeltown**, is a medieval tower that was extended over the centuries into a country house: it has a local history museum and nine acres of woodland gardens. The next stretch descends off the West Pennine Moors onto the West Lancashire Plain, skirting the north of Greater Manchester and crossing the Leeds and Liverpool Canal a number of times. The beautiful Lever Park is on the edge of Lower Rivington Reservoir; Beacon Country Park, east of Skelmersdale, affords splendid views in all directions. The route now rounds **Ormskirk** and heads northwards, taking you near the Wildfowl and Wetland Centre at Martin Mere. The final stretch back into **Whalley** takes you south of Leyland and between Preston and Blackburn; attractions along the way include fifteenth-century houses at Rufford and Hoghton.

Aughton 34

National Grid Ref: SD3905

⊨◁ Derby Arms

(1m) *Thorn Tree Farm, Prescot Road, Aughton, Ormskirk, Lancs, L39 6RS.*
Farmhouse set in rural surroundings
Grades: ETB Listed, Comm
Tel: 01695 422109
R & W Pemberton.
Rates fr: *£20.00*-**£20.00**.
Open: All Year
Beds: 1F 1T1S
Baths: 1 Ensuite 2 Shared
⏰ (Any) ▣ (5) ⊬ ❑ ⌇ ▦ & ☑ ₤

The lowest *double* rate per person is shown in *italics*.

Rufford 35

National Grid Ref: SD4515

⊨◁ Rufford Arms Hotel, Bay Horse

(1m) *Rufford Arms Hotel, 380 Liverpool Road, Rufford, Ormskirk, Lancs, L40 1SG.*
Modern country hotel
Tel: 01704 822040 Lockwood.
Rates fr: *£17.50*-**£19.95**.
Open: All Year
Beds: 2F 15D **Baths:** 15 Private
⏰ ▣ (49) ❑ ⌇ ✕ ▦ & ☑ ₤

Bamber Bridge 36

National Grid Ref: SD5626

⊨◁ Hob Inn

(2m) *Anvil Guest House, 321 Station Road, Bamber Bridge, Preston, Lancs, PR5 6EE.*
Comfortable, friendly, near M6/J29, M61/J9
Tel: 01772 339022 Arkwright.
Rates fr: *£12.50*-**£14.00**.
Open: All Year (not Xmas)
Beds: 2F 1D 6T **Baths:** 2 Shared
❑ ▦

Clayton le Dale 37

National Grid Ref: SD6733

⊨◁ Royal Oak, Bay Horse

(0.5m) *2 Rose Cottage, Longsight Road (A59), Clayton le Dale, Blackburn, Lancs, BB1 9EX.*
Picturesque cottage, gateway to Ribble Valley. Comfortable, fully equipped rooms
Tel: 01254 813223
Adderley.
Fax no: 01254 813831
Rates fr: *£18.00*-**£21.00**.
Open: All Year
Beds: 1D 2T
Baths: 3 Private
⏰ ▣ (3) ❑ ⌇ ▦ ☑ ₤ ⚡

The *lowest* **single** rate *is shown in* **bold**.

Leicestershire County Cycle Route

The **Leicestershire County Cycle Route** is a 140-mile circular tour, which goes in an anticlockwise direction around the inside of the perimeter of most of Leicestershire, and through the middle of the County of Rutland, starting and finishing at Rutland Water. It is routed along quiet country lanes and tracks, almost completely avoiding main roads, through gentle terrain without rigorous climbs.

A detailed **guide leaflet** to the route is available from Leicestershire County Council, Countryside and Recreation Section, County Hall, tel 0116-265 7091. Cycle hire is available from Rutland Water Cycling at Whitwell and at Normanton, tel 01780 86705.

Maps: Ordnance Survey 1:50,000 Landranger series: 128, 129, 130, 140, 141

The major **railway** termini are at Oakham, Stamford, Melton Mowbray, Leicester, Loughborough, Hinckley and Market Harborough.

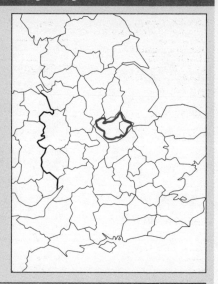

Rutland Water to Belvoir Castle

From Whitwell, on the banks of Rutland Water, you cycle north through the gentle Rutland countryside, and the villages of **Exton**, where the ruins of the early seventeenth-century Old Hall of Exton Park can be seen beyond the village church, Greetham and Thistleton. This stretch runs close to the Viking Way (see *Stilwell's National Trail Companion*), named from the history of this area as part of the Danelaw, ruled by the invaders that the kings of Wessex and England failed to keep at bay.

Through Thistleton Gap, where three counties meet, you take the Bronze Age track called Sewstern Lane into Leicestershire, and follow it north along the border with Lincolnshire before turning west towards **Buckminster**, and then north through a string of old farming villages to **Belvoir Castle**. On the site of a Norman castle, the present extravagant edifice was built in the mid-seventeenth century and rebuilt in 1816. It contains an impressive collection of tapestries and paintings, including Holbein's portrait of Henry VIII, and a garden with seventeenth-century sculptures.

Exton   1

National Grid Ref: SK9211
Yⁱⁱ ◖ Fox & Hounds

(0.25m) *Fox & Hounds, Exton, Oakham, Rutland, LE15 8AP.*
C17th inn
Grades: ETB Listed
Tel: **01572 812403** D Hillier.
Rates fr: *£18.00*-*£22.00.*
Open: All Year **Beds:** 1D 1T 1S
🛌 (8) 🅿 (2) ✕ 🎬 🗍

(0.25m) *Church Farmhouse, 5 Oakham Road, Exton, Oakham, Rutland, LE15 8AX.*
Listed homely farmhouse, beautiful village
Tel: **01572 813435** Mrs Hudson.
Rates fr: *£15.00*-*£15.00.*
Open: All Year
Beds: 1D 1T **Baths:** 1 Private
🛌 (5) 🅿 (2) ✑ 🖵 🎬 Ⅴ 🗍 ✦

Greetham   2

National Grid Ref: SK9214

(0.25m) *Priestwells, Main Street, Greetham, Oakham, Rutland, LE15 7HU.*
Modern house in peaceful surroundings
Tel: **01572 812660**
Mrs Wilson.
Rates fr: *£14.00*-*£14.00.*
Open: All Year
Beds: 1F 1D 1S
Baths: 2 Shared
🛌 🅿 (6) 🖵 🎬 🗍

The *lowest* **single** rate *is* shown in **bold.**

South Witham 3

National Grid Ref: SK9219

🍴 🍺 Black Bull, The Castle

(0.5m) *Rose Cottage, 7 High Street, South Witham, Grantham, Lincs, NG33 5QB.*
C18th stone cottage in 2 acres
Tel: **01572 767757**
Mrs Van Kimmenade.
Rates fr: *£15.50*-**£15.50**.
Open: All Year
Beds: 1T
Baths: 1 Private
🛇 🅿 □ ★ ✗ 💷 Ⅴ 🔒

Sproxton 4

National Grid Ref: SK8524

🍴 🍺 Crown Inn

(0.25m) *Appletree Cottage, Sproxton, Melton Mowbray, Leics, LE14 4QS.*
Self-catering (2 Keys, High Comm) also available
Tel: **01476 860435**
Mrs Slack.
Rates fr: *£18.00*-**£19.00**.
Open: All Year
Beds: 1D 1S
Baths: 1 Shared
🛇 🅿 (1) ⅙ □ 💷 Ⅴ

The lowest *double* rate per person is shown in *italics*.

Planning a longer stay? Always ask for any special rates.

Skillington 5

National Grid Ref: SK8925

(2m) *Beeches, Park Lane, Skillington, Grantham, Lincs, NG33 5HH.*
New bungalow, well appointed
Tel: **01476 860271** Mrs Black.
Rates fr: *£16.00*-**£16.00**.
Open: All Year (not Xmas)
Beds: 1D 1T 2S
Baths: 2 Private 1 Shared
🛇 (5) 🅿 (6) ⅙ □ ✗ 💷 🔒 ✦

Barkestone-le-Vale 6

National Grid Ref: SK7834

🍴 🍺 The Windmill, The Redmile

(1m) *Little Orchard, Chapel Street, Barkestone-le-Vale, Nottingham, Notts, NG13 0HE.*
Bungalow, picturesque village, near Belvoir Castle
Grades: ETB Listed, Comm
Tel: **01949 842698** Mrs Fisher.
Rates fr: *£15.00*-**£15.00**.
Open: All Year (not Xmas)
Beds: 1F 1D 1T 1S
Baths: 1 Shared
🛇 (3) 🅿 (4) □ ★ 💷 & Ⅴ ✦

Harby 7

National Grid Ref: SK7431

🍴 🍺 Peacock Inn, Red Lion, Martin's Arms

(0.25m) *Box House, Dickmans Lane, Harby, Melton Mowbray, Leics, LE14 4BG.*
Victorian farmhouse in the Vale of Belvoir
Tel: **01949 860248** Mrs Fox.
Rates fr: *£18.00*-**£20.00**.
Open: Mar to Nov
Beds: 1T **Baths:** 1 Ensuite
🅿 (1) ⅙ □ & Ⅴ ✦

Upper Broughton 8

National Grid Ref: SK6826

🍴 🍺 Golden Fleece, Crown Inn

(1m) *Sulney Fields, Colonels Lane, Upper Broughton, Melton Mowbray, Leics, LE14 3BD.*
Large country house, spectacular views
Tel: **01664 822204** (also fax no)
Mrs Dowson.
Rates fr: *£17.50*-**£20.00**.
Open: All Year (not Xmas)
Beds: 2D 2T 1S
Baths: 2 Private 2 Shared
🛇 🅿 (12) □ ★ ✗ 💷 Ⅴ ✦

Bringing children with you? Ask for any special rates.

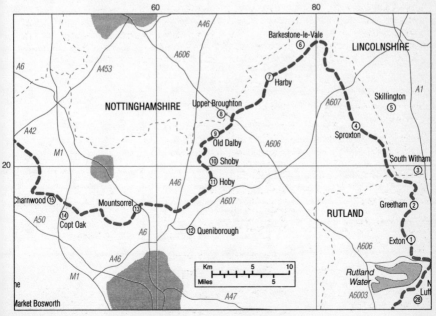

Old Dalby 9

National Grid Ref: SK6723

⑩ ⬛ Crown Inn, Red Lion

(1m) **Home Farm**, *Church Lane, Old Dalby, Melton Mowbray, Leics, LE14 3LB.*
Warm, comfortable, quiet Victorian farmhouse on edge of Doomsday village
Tel: **01664 822622** Mrs Anderson.
Fax no: 01664 823155
Rates fr: £20.00-£25.00.
Open: All Year
Beds: 1D 2T 2S
Baths: 4 Ensuite 1 Private
🅿 (5) ❑ ⌇ ▥ Ⓥ

Shoby 10

National Grid Ref: SK6820

⑩ ⬛ The Horse, The Stocks, The Crown

(2m) **Shoby Lodge Farm**, *Shoby, Melton Mowbray, Leics, LE14 3PF.*
Tel: **01664 812156** Mrs Lomas.
Rates fr: £15.00-£23.50.
Open: All Year (not Xmas)
Beds: 3D
Baths: 2 Ensuite 1 Shared
🛏 (14) 🅿 ❑ ▥ Ⓥ ♦ ⌇
Comfortable spacious farmhouse set in attractive gardens with beautiful views of surrounding countryside. Generous Aga cooked breakfast. Ideally situated for Leicestershire & Nottinghamshire

Hoby 11

National Grid Ref: SK6617

(On route) **Wreake Cottage**, *Lower Lane, Hoby, Melton Mowbray, Leics, LE14 3DT.*
Warm, welcoming cottage. Lovely views
Tel: **01664 434326**
Mrs Draper.
Rates fr: £15.00-£15.00.
Open: All Year (not Xmas)
Beds: 1T 1D
Baths: 1 Shared
🛏 🅿 (2) ❑ ⌇ ✕ ▥ Ⓥ ♦

Queniborough 12

National Grid Ref: SK6412

⑩ ⬛ Britannia Inn, Horse & Groom

(2m) **Three Ways Farm**, *Melton Road, Queniborough, Leicester, Leics, LE7 3FN.*
Actual grid ref: SK642129
Modern, comfortable, peaceful farm bungalow
Grades: ETB Listed, Comm
Tel: **0116 260 0472**
Mrs Clarke.
Rates fr: £16.00-£20.00.
Open: All Year (not Xmas)
Beds: 1D 1T 1S
Baths: 1 Shared
🛏 🅿 (20) ❑ ⌇ ▥ Ⓥ ♦ ⌇

The Grid Reference beneath the location heading is for the village or town - *not* for individual houses, which are shown (where supplied) in each entry itself.

Mountsorrel 13

National Grid Ref: SK5814

⑩ ⬛ Swan Inn, Stag & Pheasant

(0.25m) **Barley Loft Guest House**, *33a Hawcliffe Road, Mountsorrel, Loughborough, Leics, LE12 7AQ.*
Tel: **01509 413514**
Mrs Pegg.
Rates fr: £15.00-£16.00.
Open: All Year
Beds: 2F 3D 1S
Baths: 2 Shared
🛏 🅿 (12) ❑ ⌇ ✕ ▥ ♿ Ⓥ
Spacious bungalow, quiet rural location. Close A6 between Leicester and Loughborough. Outstanding riverside walking, local beauty spots. Traditional hearty breakfast. EM by arrangement. Suitable disabled

Belvoir Castle to Charnwood Forest

Shortly after Belvoir, the route turns southwestwards and runs parallel to the Grantham Canal as far as **Long Clawson**, where Stilton cheese is produced. From here you go on to **Old Dalby**, and then south to Hoby and along the River Wreake as far as **Ratcliffe** on the Wreake. From here, if you wish, you can take the substantial detour down the ancient Roman Fosse Way into **Leicester**, one of the major East Midlands cities, important in Roman times as a fort, and in the Danelaw period, and traditionally the home of King Lear. Nowadays it is a centre of Britain's Asian community. Notable sights are St Martin's Cathedral, originating from the eleventh century and modified in the Victorian period, St Nicholas' Church, whose nave is Saxon, and the half-timbered Guildhall. There are also Hindu, Jain and Sikh temples and various museums - the Leicestershire Museum and Art Gallery features a large German Expressionist collection and early twentieth-century British painting. From Ratcliffe the route goes through Sileby and crosses the River Soar into **Mountsorrel**. Then on to **Woodhouse Eaves**, a lovely old village built of the local slate. Here you will find Long Close, a 5-acre landscaped garden with wild flowers and shrubs. From here it's a short (if steepish) ride to Beacon Hill, a Bronze Age hill fort which yields magnificent views. You are now in **Charnwood Forest**, where the craggy hills and ferns make a landscape wilder than most of the county.

.25m) *The Swan Inn,*
oughborough Road, Mountsorrel,
oughborough, Leics, LE12 7AT.
17th riverside coaching inn
el: **0116 230 2340**
liss Gosnall.
ax no: 0116 237 6115
ates fr: *£16.00-£20.00.*
Open: All Year (not Xmas)
Beds: 1D 1T 1S **Baths:** 1 Shared
☆ �P (10) **🖵 ⊼ ✕ Ⅲ. Ⓥ**

'opt Oak   14

National Grid Ref: SK4813

▲ 1m) *Copt Oak Youth Hostel,*
Whitwick Road, Copt Oak,
Markfield, Leicestershire, LE67 9QB.
ctual grid ref: SK482129
el: **01530 242661**
Under 18: £4.45 **Adults:** £6.50
elf-catering Facilities, Showers,
ecurity Lockers
Converted shoolhouse in the hills
f northwest Leicestershire
roviding basic accommodation.
Charnwood Forest is nearby, with
uperb countryside for walking and
ycling

'aks in Charnwood   15

National Grid Ref: SK4716

🍺 Jolly Farmer

.5m) *St Josephs, Abbey Road,*
'aks in Charnwood, Coalville,
'eics, LE67 4UA.
Old country house, where hosts
velcome you to their home
'el: **01509 503943** Mrs Havers.
Rates fr: *£17.00-£17.00.*
Open: Easter to Oct
Beds: 1D 2T 2S
Baths: 2 Shared
☆ P (4) **🖵 Ⅲ. Ⓥ**

Charnwood Forest to Foxton

Cycling north out of Charnwood Forest, you come to **Breedon on the Hill**, where there is an iron age hill fort. A detour north from here will take you to the Donington Park motor racing circuit, which stages the British motorcycle Grand Prix every year and hosts an impressive collection of racing cars and motorcycles. Then it's southwest to **Staunton Harold**, with its rare Commonwealth period church. After a brief foray into Derbyshire, and the village of Smisby, you pass near to **Ashby-de-la-Zouch**, which has a striking castle, dating from Norman times to the fifteenth century and ruined in the Civil War, featuring an underground passageway for the non-claustrophobic. From here it's south through **Donisthorpe**, parallel to the River Mease through Measham, and southeastwards along the Ashby Canal from Shackerstone to **Market Bosworth**. From here it's on to Sutton Cheney, which is near to the site of the Battle of Bosworth Field, where the Wars of the Roses came to an end with the death of Richard III and the fall of the House of York at the hands of Henry VII, the first king in the Tudor line. There is a Country Park and Visitor Centre at the battlefield. Now it's on to Barwell and through **Burbage Common and Woods**, the remainder of the medieval Hinckley Forest, and then across the Fosse Way and east towards the locks on the Grand Union Canal at **Foxton**.

Order your

packed lunches the

evening before you

need them.

Not at breakfast!

Ashby de la Zouch   16

National Grid Ref: SK3516

(2m) *The Bungalow, 10 Trinity*
Close, Ashby de la Zouch,
Leicester, Leics, LE65 2GQ.
Private family home in quiet
cul-de-sac. Easy access to
motorways
Tel: **01530 560698** Ms Chapman.
Rates fr: *£15.00-£15.00.*
Open: All Year
Beds: 1T 1D **Baths:** 1 Shared
☆ P (2) **⊬ 🖵 ⊼ ✕ Ⅲ. Ⓥ**

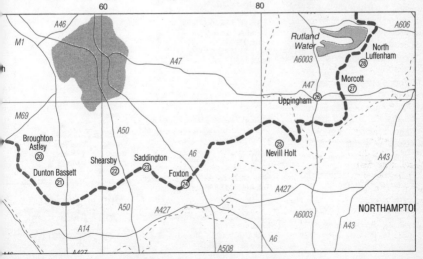

The lowest *double* rate per person is shown in *italics*.

Measham 17

National Grid Ref: SK3312

¶ ◫ The Swan

(0.25m) *Laurels Guest House, 17 Ashby Road, Measham, Swadlincote, Derbyshire, DE12 7JR.*
Modern guest house, rural pleasant surroundings
Grades: ETB 2 Cr
Tel: 01530 272567
Mrs Evans.
Rates fr: *£20.00*-**£18.00**.
Open: All Year
Beds: 1D 1T 1S
Baths: 2 Ensuite 1 Private
ඊ (1) ❒ (8) ⊬ ❏ Ⅲ, ▪

Congerstone 18

National Grid Ref: SK3605

¶ ◫ Rising Sun

(1m) *Church House Farm, Shadows Lane, Congerstone, Nuneaton, Warks, CV13 6NA.*
Spacious, comfortable, former farmhouse
Grades: ETB 2 Cr, Comm
Tel: 01827 880402
Mrs Martin.
Rates fr: *£17.00*-**£17.00**.
Open: All Year (not Xmas)
Beds: 1D 1T 1S
Baths: 1 Ensuite 1 Shared
ඊ (12) ❒ (6) ❏ Ⅲ, Ⅴ

The Country Code

Enjoy the countryside and respect its life and work

Guard against all risk of fire

Fasten all gates

Keep your dogs under close control

Keep to public paths across farmland

Use gates and stiles to cross fences, hedges and walls

Leave livestock, crops and machinery alone

Take your litter home

Help to keep all water clean

Protect wildlife, plants and trees

Take special care on country roads

Make no unnecessary noise

Market Bosworth 19

National Grid Ref: SK4003

(0.25m) *Bosworth Firs, Bosworth Road, Market Bosworth, Nuneaton, Warks, CV13 0DW.*
Comfortable, clean, friendly. Home cooking, varied menu. Attractive decor, furnishings
Grades: ETB 2 Cr, Comm
Tel: 01455 290727
Mrs Christian.
Rates fr: *£19.50*-**£19.50**.
Open: All Year
Beds: 2D 1T 2S
Baths: 1 Ensuite 2 Private 1 Shared
ඊ ❒ (6) ❏ ✗ Ⅲ, & Ⅴ ▪ ✦

Broughton Astley 20

National Grid Ref: SP5292

¶ ◫ White Horse, Bull's Head

(2m) *The Old Farm House, Old Mill Road, Broughton Astley, Leicester, Leics, LE9 6PQ.*
Quietly situated farmhouse in well served village, good local pubs/shops
Grades: ETB Listed
Tel: 01455 282254
Mrs Cornelius.
Rates fr: *£19.00*-**£19.00**.
Open: All Year
Beds: 2F 1T 1S
Baths: 2 Shared
ඊ ❒ (6) ⊬ ❏ ✗ Ⅲ, Ⅴ ▪ ✦

Dunton Bassett 21

National Grid Ref: SP5490

¶ ◫ Bassett Arms

(2m) *Ivydene Farmhouse, The Mount, Dunton Bassett, Lutterworth, Leics, LE17 5JL.*
Family farmhouse, warm welcome
Tel: 01455 202246
Mr Tebbutt.
Rates fr: *£15.00*-**£15.00**.
Open: All Year
Beds: 1D 1T 1S
Baths: 1 Private 1 Shared
ඊ ❏ ⊁ Ⅲ,

Shearsby 22

National Grid Ref: SP6290

(0.25m) *The Greenway, Knaptoft House Farm, Bruntingthorpe Road, Shearsby, Lutterworth, Leics, LE17 6PR.*
Spacious bungalow/farmhouse with lovely views
Grades: ETB 2 Cr, AA 4 Q, Select
Tel: 0116 247 8388 (also fax no)
Mr Hutchinson.
Rates fr: *£19.00*-**£24.00**.
Open: All Year (not Xmas)
Beds: 2D 1T
Baths: 2 Private 1 Shared
ඊ (6) ❒ (5) ❏ Ⅲ, Ⅴ

Foxton to Rutland Water

From here you proceed to **Hallaton**, a typical pretty English village with medieval church, pond and ancient pub on the village green. It is also the site, every Easter, of the centuries-old Hare Pie Scramble and Bottle-Kicking Contest, a permanent home fixture against the nearby village of Medbourne. Then the route takes you through Horninghold and around the **Eye Brook Reservoir**, an important wildfowl site. Back in Rutland, places of interest along the final stretch are the fourteenth-century Bede House at **Lyddington** and the circular maze at **Wing. Edith Weston**, on the southern side of Rutland Water provides access to sailing on England's largest lowland lake. Also available is trout fishing, and many other leisure activities. A detour to the western end of the lake takes you to the nature reserve, and it is not far to **Oakham**, Rutland's county town. **Normanton**, by Edith Weston, has a classical-style church which has now been converted into a museum and juts into the lake.

Saddington 23

National Grid Ref: SP6591

¶ ◫ Queen's Head

(1m) *Breach Farm, Shearsby Road, Saddington, Leicester, Leics, LE8 0QU.*
Modern, comfortable farmhouse with open views
Tel: 0116 240 2539 Mrs Thornton.
Rates fr: *£16.00*-**£17.00**.
Open: All Year (not Xmas)
Beds: 2D 1T **Baths:** 1 Shared
ඊ ❒ (4) ⊬ ❏ Ⅲ, Ⅴ

Bringing children with you? Always ask for any special rates.

Please don't camp on *anyone's* land without first obtaining their permission.

Foxton 24

National Grid Ref: SP7089

† Black Horse

(0.25m) *The Old Manse, Swingbridge Street, Foxton, Market Harborough, Leics, LE16 7RH.*
Period house in large gardens
Grades: ETB 2 Cr, High Comm
Tel: 01858 545456
Mrs Pickering.
Rates fr: £20.00-£25.00.
Open: All Year (not Xmas)
Beds: 1D 2T
Baths: 2 Ensuite
⊃ ₽ (5) ⊬ ⊡ ⊞

Nevill Holt 25

National Grid Ref: SP8193

† Nevill Arms

(2m) *Medbourne Grange, Nevill Holt, Medbourne, Market Harborough, Leics, LE16 8EF.*
Comfortable farmhouse with breathtaking views
Tel: 01858 565249 Mrs Beaty.
Fax no: 01858 565257
Rates fr: £17.00-£17.00.
Open: All Year (not Xmas)
Beds: 1D 1T 2S **Baths:** 2 Shared
⊃ ₽ (6) ⊬ ⊡ ✗ ⊞ ⊻ ✦

Uppingham 26

National Grid Ref: SP8699

† George & Dragon, White Hart

(2m) *8 Main Street, Uppingham, Oakham, Rutland, LE15 9HU.*
Modern country cottage in Rutland
Tel: 01572 747358 Mrs Warburton.
Rates fr: £15.00-£15.00.
Open: All Year (not Xmas)
Beds: 1D 1S **Baths:** 1 Shared
⊃ ₽ (2) ⊡ ⊁ ✗ ⊞ ⊻ ♠ ✦

Morcott 27

National Grid Ref: SK9200

† White Horse

(2m) *5 Church Lane, Morcott, Uppingham, Oakham, Rutland, LE15 9DH.*
Cosy home, well-kept garden
Tel: 01572 747829 Mrs Martin.
Rates fr: £15.00-£15.00.
Open: All Year
Beds: 1T 1D
Baths: 1 Shared
⊡ ⊁ ✗ ⊞ ⊻

North Luffenham 28

National Grid Ref: SK9303

(1m) *Pinfold House, 6 Pinfold Lane, North Luffenham, Oakham, Rutland, LE15 8LE.*
C18th cottage with large garden
Tel: 01780 720175 Mrs Cook.
Rates fr: £14.50-£16.00.
Open: All Year (not Xmas)
Beds: 2D 1T
Baths: 1 Shared
⊃ ₽ (4) ⊬ ⊡ ⊞ ⊻ ♠

Oxfordshire Cycleway

The **Oxfordshire Cycleway** is a circuit of the county, connected to Oxford, where it starts and finishes. It runs mainly along minor country roads and lanes, and takes in the whole range of the varied scenery Oxfordshire has to offer - the Cotswolds in the west, the Chilterns in the southeast and the Vale of the White Horse south of the Thames, where Britain's most ancient hillside carving lies close to the Ridgeway Path, the most ancient road still in use in Europe. The total distance around the circuit and into and out of Oxford is 178 miles, and the route is clearly signposted in both directions by blue Oxfordshire Cycleway direction signs with a cycle silhouette. The description which follows takes the circuit clockwise.

A detailed **guide booklet** to the cycleway route, which includes a list of cycle repair/hire shops on or near to the route, is available from Faith Cooke, Countryside Service, Department of Leisure and Arts, Oxfordshire County Council, Holton, Oxford OX33 1QQ, tel 01865 810226, @ £3.20 (+ 50p p&p).

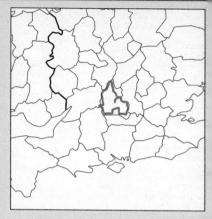

Maps: Ordnance Survey 1:50,000 Landranger series: 151, 163, 164, 165, 174, 175

Trains: Oxford, Didcot and Banbury are the main termini, with connections to other places on or near the route. Goring is a stop on the main line out of London.

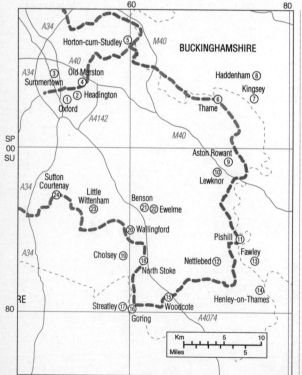

Oxford 1

National Grid Ref: SP5106

🍴 🍺 Duke of Monmouth, Carpenters' Arms, The Vine, Prince of Wales, The Tree, The Anchor, The Ox, Boundary House, White Horse, Eight Bells, Thatched Tavern

(▲ 1m) *Oxford Youth Hostel, 32 Jack Straw's Lane, Oxford. OX3 0DW.*
Actual grid ref: SP533074
Warden: Mr S Martin.
Tel: 01865 762997
Under 18: £6.55
Adults: £9.75
Evening Meals Available (6pm), Television, Games Room, Showers, Shop
Victorian mansion surrounded by trees in the conservation area of this historic university city

(1m) *Highfield West, 188 Cumnor Hill, Oxford. OX2 9PJ.*
Comfortable home in residential area, heated outdoor pool in season
Grades: ETB 2 Cr, High Comm
Tel: 01865 863007
Mr & Mrs Mitchell.
Rates fr: £20.00-£21.00.
Open: All Year (not Xmas)
Beds: 1F 1D 1T 2S
Baths: 3 Private 1 Shared
🛏 (3) 🅿 (5) ⚹ 🗖 🛉 🎱 Ⓥ

(1m) *Green Gables, 326 Abingdon Road, Oxford. OX1 4TE.*
Grades: ETB 2 Cr, Comm
Tel: 01865 725870 Mrs Ellis.
Fax no: 01865 753115
Rates fr: *£20.00*-**£25.00**.
Open: All Year (not Xmas/New Year)
Beds: 3F 4D 1T 1S
Baths: 6 Private 1 Shared
🛏 🅿 (8) 🗔 🛍 ♿ Ⓥ
Characterful, detached, Edwardian house shielded by trees. Bright spacious rooms with TV & beverage facilities. Ensuite rooms. 1.25 miles to city centre, on bus routes. Ample off-street parking

(1m) *Pine Castle Hotel, 290 Iffley Road, Oxford. OX4 4AE.*
Actual grid ref: SP528048
Close to shops, launderette, post office. Frequent buses. River walks nearby
Grades: ETB 3 Cr, High Comm
Tel: 01865 241497 / 728887
Mrs Morris.
Fax no: 01685 727230
Rates fr: *£28.00*-**£48.00**.
Open: All Year (not Xmas)
Beds: 1F 5D 2T **Baths:** 8 Ensuite
🛏 🅿 (4) 🗔 🛍 Ⓥ 🅰

(1m) *Gables Guest House, 6 Cumnor Hill, Oxford. OX2 9HA.*
Grades: ETB 2 Cr, High Comm
Tel: 01865 862153 Mrs Tompkins.
Fax no: 01865 864054
Rates fr: *£20.00*-**£24.00**.
Open: All Year (not Xmas)
Beds: 1F 2D 1T 2S
Baths: 5 Ensuite 1 Private
🛏 🅿 (6) ✔ 🗔 🛍 Ⓥ
Attractive detached house with beautiful garden, close to city centre, bus and railway stations. High quality rooms with satellite TV and direct dial telephones

(1m) *Combermere House, 11 Polstead Road, Oxford. OX2 6TW.*
Actual grid ref: SP507079
Quiet, tree-lined road, fifteen minutes walk centre and colleges
Grades: ETB Listed, Approv, AA Approv
Tel: 01865 556971 (also fax no)
Mr & Mrs Welding.
Rates fr: *£20.00*-**£24.00**.
Open: All Year **Beds:** 2F 1D 2T 4S
🛏 🅿 (3) 🗔 🐾 🛍 Ⓥ 🅰 ✎

(1m) *Sportsview Guest House, 106-110 Abingdon Road, Oxford. OX1 4PX.*
Family-run Victorian city centre establishment, ideally situated for visiting historic surrounding area
Grades: ETB 2 Cr, Approv
Tel: 01865 244268 Mrs Saini.
Fax no: 01865 249270
Rates fr: *£18.00*-**£26.00**.
Open: All Year (not Xmas)
Beds: 8F 3T 3D 6S
Baths: 9 Ensuite 5 Shared
🛏 (2) 🅿 (12) 🗔 🛍 Ⓥ

(1m) *58 St John Street, Oxford. OX1 2QR.*
Tall Victorian house
Tel: 01865 515454 Mrs Old.
Rates fr: *£18.00*-**£18.00**.
Open: All Year
Beds: 1F 1T 1S
Baths: 2 Shared
🛏 (12)

(1m) *Lakeside Guest House, 118 Abingdon Road, Oxford. OX1 4PZ.*
Edwardian house close to centre
Tel: 01865 244725
Mrs Shirley.
Rates fr: *£18.00*-**£25.00**.
Open: All Year
Beds: 2F 2D 1T
Baths: 2 Private 2 Shared
🛏 🅿 (6) ✔ 🗔 🐾 ✗ 🛍 ♿ Ⓥ

(1m) *5 Galley Field, Radley Road, Oxford. OX14 3RU.*
Detached 1960 house in quiet cul-de-sac
Tel: 01235 521088
Mrs Bird.
Rates fr: *£17.00*-**£20.00**.
Open: All Year
Beds: 3T **Baths:** 2 Shared
🛏 (12) 🅿 (2) ✔ 🗔 🛍

(1m) *Acorn Guest House, 260 Iffley Road, Oxford. OX4 1SE.*
Modern comfort in Victorian house
Grades: ETB Listed, AA Listed, RAC Listed
Tel: 01865 247998
Mrs Lewis.
Rates fr: *£17.00*-**£22.00**.
Open: All Year (not Xmas)
Beds: 3F 1T 2S
Baths: 2 Shared
🛏 🅿 (5) 🗔 🛍 Ⓥ

(1m) *Arden Lodge, 34 Sunderland Avenue, Oxford. OX2 8DX.*
Select, spacious, modern detached house
Grades: ETB Listed
Tel: 01865 552076
Mr & Mrs Price.
Rates fr: *£20.00*-**£25.00**.
Open: All Year
Beds: 1D 1T 1S **Baths:** 3 Private
🛏 🅿 (7) 🗔 🛍 Ⓥ

The lowest *double* rate per person is shown in *italics*.

Oxford

The city of **Oxford** is one of England's architectural treasure houses. The imposing facades, spires and 'quadrangles' (courtyards) of the colleges and other university buildings bear witness to centuries of conspicuous creation. But although the university is a dominant presence, Oxford is also an important commercial city, which has plenty of life of its own away from students and tourists. Of the colleges, Merton is the most beautiful - the Gothic college chapel and the library, which contains centuries-old globes and other trappings of Renaissance scholarship, stand on 'Mob Quad', built in the fourteenth century, which has the eerie atmosphere of a medieval time warp. Magdalen, with its secluded cloisters and the famous tower, is also well worth a visit. Christ Church is big and famous. Also worth a look are Trinity, where the college chapel, the first not built in the Gothic style, was designed by Wren, who also designed the Sheldonian Theatre; and St Catherine's, built in the 1960s in a unique and very distinctive style. Elsewhere, the University Museum is a Pre-Raphaelite gem, its interior constructed around intricate ironwork which plays visually on the dinosaur skeletons, surrounded by statues honouring notable figures of science and philosophy; the adjacent Pitt-Rivers Museum is a fantastic ethnographic collection best known for the shrunken heads from South America. The other major museum is the Ashmolean, the oldest museum in Britain, with a very impressive range of collections; and Christ Church has its own picture gallery, with a collection of Italian art. Away from the university, the city has many interesting pockets, not least the canalside backstreets of Jericho, famous for the Pre-Raphaelite St Barnabas' Church; and don't leave Oxford without trying one or two of its many excellent pubs.

(1m) *The Garden House, 10 Red Copse Lane, Oxford. OX1 5ER.*
Peaceful, quite residential area
Grades: ETB 2 Cr, Comm
Tel: 01865 739006
Mrs Morrison.
Rates fr: *£20.00*-£25.00.
Open: All Year
Beds: 2T
Baths: 2 Private
🖵 🛏 🛲 🌢

(1m) *Cornerways Guest House, 282 Abingdon Road, Oxford. OX1 4TA.*
Friendly establishment near city centre
Grades: ETB 2 Cr, Comm
Tel: 01865 240135
Mrs Jeakings.
Rates fr: *£21.00*-£26.00.
Open: All Year (not Xmas)
Beds: 1F 1D 1T 1S
🛏 🅿 (2) 🖵 🛲

(1m) *Guest House, 103-105 Woodstock Road, Oxford. OX2 6HL.*
5 mins walk to city centre
Grades: ETB 2 Cr
Tel: 01865 552579 Mr Pal.
Fax no: 01865 311244
Rates fr: *£20.00*-£25.00.
Open: All Year
Beds: 2F 3D 4T 4S
Baths: 4 Ensuite 4 Shared
🛏 (1) 🅿 (12) 🖵 🛲 🛲 & �V

(1m) *Ascot Guest House, 283 Iffley Road, Oxford. OX4 4AQ.*
Comfortable Victorian house: pretty rooms
Tel: 01865 240259 Miss Hall.
Rates fr: *£19.00*-£28.00.
Open: All Year
Beds: 2F 2D 2T 1S
Baths: 7 Ensuite
🛏 🅿 (2) 🖵 🛲 �V

Headington 2

National Grid Ref: SP5407

🍽 🍺 White Horse

(1m) *Sandfield House, 19 London Road, Headington, Oxford, Oxon, OX3 7RE.*
Close hospitals, Oxford Brookes University, M40
Grades: ETB 2 Cr, Comm
Tel: 01865 762406 (also fax no)
Mrs Anderson.
Rates fr: *£24.00*-£30.00.
Open: All Year (not Xmas)
Beds: 2D 2S
Baths: 3 Ensuite 1 Private
🛏 🅿 (5) 🖵 🛲 �V

The *lowest* **single** rate *is shown in* **bold.**

Oxford to Wallingford

When you've had your fill of **Oxford**, the cycleway commences with a leisurely stretch linking you to the county circuit at **Horton-cum-Studley**, where you turn southeast, to reach **Worminghall** in Buckinghamshire. A short detour from here will bring you to Waterperry Gardens, an 83-acre herbaceous and alpine centre with a Saxon church and a gallery which exhibits and sells paintings, ceramics and textiles. From Worminghall it's not far to the pretty small town of **Thame**. From here you head south and after Sydenham and Kingston Blount up into the beautiful wooded countryside of the **Chiltern Hills**. An attraction along this stretch of the way is Stonor Park. This beautiful house in a picturesque setting was built over centuries and is the ancestral home of a Catholic family and a notable centre of resistance to protestant domination: the martyr Edmund Campion received sanctuary here before being captured and hanged in 1581. There is a fine art collection including paintings by Tintoretto and Caracci. From here it is on to the village of **Bix**. The Fox pub is recommended. From here a detour is possible to **Henley-on-Thames**, famous for rowing, and with a wide Georgian High Street. From Bix it's on to **Goring**, at the southwestern end of the Chiltern range. From here there is an alternative route (best attempted only on an all terrain bicycle) along the ancient **Ridgeway Path**, from which you can link up to the *Round Berkshire Cycle Route*. From Goring you go north, parallel to the Thames, to Crowmarsh Gifford, where you cross the river into the small town of **Wallingford**.

Summertown 3

National Grid Ref: SP5108

🍽 🍺 King's Arms, Dew Drop Inn

(1.5m) *Adam's Guest House, 302 Banbury Road, Summertown, Oxford. OX2 7ED.*
B&B close to city centre
Tel: 01865 56118
Mr Strange.
Rates fr: *£19.00*-£25.00.
Open: All Year
Beds: 2F 2D 2T
Baths: 3 Shared
🛏 (5) 🖵 🛲 �V 🌢

Old Marston 4

National Grid Ref: SP5208

🍽 🍺 Victoria Arms

(0.5m) *The Bungalow, Cherwell Farm, Mill Lane, Old Marston, Oxford, Oxon, OX3 0QF.*
Modern bungalow set in five acres; open countryside
Grades: ETB Listed
Tel: 01865 557171
Burdon.
Rates fr: *£19.00*-£25.00.
Open: Mar to Oct
Beds: 2T 2D
Baths: 2 Ensuite 1 Shared
🛏 (5) 🅿 (6) 🖵 🛲 &

Horton-cum-Studley 5

National Grid Ref: SP5912

(0.25m) *Kings Arms Hotel, Horton-cum-Studley, Oxford. OX33 1AY.*
Actual grid ref: SP6012
Friendly, relaxed country village hotel, serving good food and real ales
Grades: ETB 3 Cr, Comm
Tel: 01865 351235
Mr Balfour-Morrison.
Fax no: 01865 351721
Rates fr: *£27.50*-£35.00.
Open: All Year
Beds: 1F 5D 2T 2S
Baths: 10 Ensuite
🛏 (4) 🅿 (20) 🖵 ✕ 🛲 �V 🌢

Thame 6

National Grid Ref: SP7005

🍽 🍺 Royal Oak

(0.25m) *Vine Cottage, Moreton, Thame, Oxon, OX9 2HX.*
Novelist's enchanting cottage near Oxford
Tel: 01844 216910
Ms Blumenthal.
Rates fr: *£20.00*-£18.50.
Open: All Year (not Xmas)
Beds: 1D 1S
Baths: 1 Shared
🛏 (10) 🅿 (6) 🖵 🛲 🌢

Kingsey 7

National Grid Ref: SP7406

|⚬| ◖ Three Horseshoes

(1m) *Foxhill, Kingsey, Aylesbury, Bucks, HP17 8LZ.*
Large, comfortable C17th farm-house
Grades: AA Listed, 3 Q
Tel: 01844 291650 Mr Hooper.
Rates fr: *£19.00-£23.00.*
Open: Feb to Nov
Beds: 1D 2T
Baths: 1 Shared
🛏 (5) 🅿 (20) ⅍ 🗗 🛏 📖 ☑

Haddenham 8

National Grid Ref: SP7408

(2m) *Haydon House, 54 Churchway, Haddenham, Aylesbury, Bucks, HP17 8HA.*
Large Victorian private house
Tel: 01844 291067 Mrs Wright.
Rates fr: *£16.00-£16.00.*
Open: All Year (not Xmas)
Beds: 1T 1D 2S
Baths: 2 Shared
🛏 🅿 (5) ⅍ 🗗 🛏 📖

Aston Rowant 9

National Grid Ref: SU7298

|⚬| ◖ Old Leatherne Bottle

(0.75m) *Libra, Chinnor Road, Aston Rowant, Chinnor, Oxford. OX9 5SH.*
Actual grid ref: SU728985
Comfortable, family-run detached house
Tel: 01844 351856 Mrs Trotman.
Rates fr: *£17.00-£18.00.*
Open: All Year (not Xmas)
Beds: 2T
Baths: 1 Shared
🛏 (8) 🅿 (4) ⅍ 🗗 🛏 ✕ 📖 ☑ ♿ ⅍

Lewknor 10

National Grid Ref: SU7197

(2m) *Peel Guest House, London Road, Lewknor, Watlington, Oxon, OX9 5SA.*
Detached house overlooking Chiltern escarpment
Tel: 01844 351310 Ms Hunt.
Rates fr: *£18.00-£20.00.*
Open: All Year (not Xmas)
Beds: 5T 1S
Baths: 3 Private 1 Shared
🛏 (10) 🅿 (7) 🗗 📖 ☑ ♿ ⅍

Bringing children with you? Always ask for any special rates.

Pishill 11

National Grid Ref: SU7289

|⚬| ◖ Crown Inn

(0.5m) *Bank Farm, Pishill, Henley-on-Thames, Oxon, RG9 6HJ.*
Actual grid ref: SU724898
Quiet comfortable farmhouse, beautiful countryside
Grades: ETB Listed, Approv
Tel: 01491 638601 Mrs Lakey.
Rates fr: *£15.00-£12.00.*
Open: All Year
Beds: 1F 1S
Baths: 1 Ensuite 1 Shared
🛏 🅿 (10) 🗗 🛏 📖 ♿ ⅍

Nettlebed 12

National Grid Ref: SU6986

|⚬| ◖ Crown Inn

(2m) *Park Corner Farm House, Nettlebed, Henley-on-Thames, Oxon, RG9 6DX.*
Queen Anne brick-and-flint farmhouse
Tel: 01491 641450 Mrs Rutter.
Rates fr: *£16.00-£18.00.*
Open: All Year (not Xmas)
Beds: 2T
Baths: 1 Shared
🛏 🅿 ⅍ 🛏 📖 ⅍

Fawley 13

National Grid Ref: SU7586

|⚬| ◖ Walnut Tree, Golden Ball

(1.5m) *Jacksons, Fawley Bottom, Fawley, Henley-on-Thames, Oxon, RG9 6JJ.*
Actual grid ref: SU748870
Comfortable farmhouse in rural location, with warm welcome, good food
Tel: 01491 575330
Mrs Brook.
Rates fr: *£17.50-£17.50.*
Open: All Year (not Xmas)
Beds: 1F 1T
Baths: 1 Shared
🛏 🅿 🗗 🛏 ✕ 📖 ☑ ♿ ⅍

Henley-on-Thames 14

National Grid Ref: SU7682

|⚬| ◖ The Anchor, Ye Olde Bell, Bottle & Glass, Walnut Tree

(2m) *Lenwade, 3 Western Road, Henley-on-Thames, Oxon, RG9 1JL.*
Beautiful Victorian family home, convenient river, restaurants, public transport
Grades: ETB 2 Cr, High Comm, AA 4 Q
Tel: 01491 573468 (also fax no)
Mrs Williams.
Rates fr: *£20.00-£28.00.*
Open: All Year
Beds: 1D 2T
Baths: 2 Private 2 Shared
🛏 🅿 (2) 🗗 🛏 📖 ☑ ⅍

The Grid Reference beneath the location heading is for the village or town - *not* for individual houses, which are shown (where supplied) in each entry itself.

(2m) *Ledard, Rotherfield Road, Henley-on-Thames, Oxon, RG9 1NN.*
Actual grid ref: SU761814
Elegant, well-appointed Victorian house, convenient for town and countryside
Tel: 01491 575611
Mrs Howard.
Rates fr: *£18.00-£18.00.*
Open: All Year (not Xmas)
Beds: 1F 1D
Baths: 1 Private
🛏 🅿 (4) 🗗 📖 ♿ ⅍

(2m) *4 Coldharbour Close, Henley-on-Thames, Oxon, RG9 1QP.*
Quiet bungalow in large garden
Tel: 01491 575297 (also fax no)
Mrs Bower.
Rates fr: *£17.00-£20.00.*
Open: Easter to Nov
Beds: 1F 1T
Baths: 1 Private 1 Shared
🛏 🅿 (2) ⅍ 🗗 ✕ 📖 ☑

(2m) *Amervyn House, 4 St Marks Road, Henley-on-Thames, Oxon, RG9 1LJ.*
Comfortable Victorian house very close to town, river and railway station
Grades: ETB 1 Cr, Comm
Tel: 01491 575331
Mrs Ely.
Fax no: 01491 411747
Rates fr: *£23.50-£27.00.*
Open: All Year (not Xmas)
Beds: 1D 1T 1S
Baths: 1 Ensuite 1 Shared
🛏 (12) 🗗 🛏 📖

(2m) *New Lodge, Henley Park, Henley-on-Thames, Oxon, RG9 6HU.*
Actual grid ref: SU758847
Small Victorian lodge cottage
Grades: ETB 1 Cr, Comm
Tel: 01491 576340 (also fax no)
Mrs Warner.
Rates fr: *£16.50-£22.00.*
Open: All Year
Beds: 2D
Baths: 2 Private
🛏 🅿 (7) ⅍ 🗗 📖 ♿ ☑ ♿ ⅍

The lowest *double* rate per person is shown in *italics*.

(2m) *The Laurels, 107 St Marks Road, Henley-on-Thames, Oxon, RG9 1LP*.
Large, comfortable house in quiet location
Tel: **01491 572982** Mrs Bridekirk.
Rates fr: *£20.00*-£25.00.
Open: All Year
Beds: 1F 1D 1T
Baths: 1 Private 1 Shared
🛏 🅿 (2) 🛏 🛒 ⚘

(2m) *43 Valley Road, Henley-on-Thames, Oxon, RG9 1RL*.
Modern 3 storey town house
Tel: **01491 573545** Mrs Williams.
Rates fr: *£17.00*-£17.00.
Open: All Year (not Xmas)
Beds: 1T 2S **Baths:** 1 Shared
🛏 (10) 🅿 (2) 🛒 🛒

(2m) *Old Bell House, Northfield End, Henley-on-Thames, Oxon, RG9 2JG*.
Large attractive Georgian town house
Tel: **01491 574350** Mrs Duckett.
Fax no: 01491 571544
Rates fr: *£20.00*-£20.00.
Open: All Year
Beds: 1F 1T
Baths: 2 Private
🛏 🅿 (2) 🛒 🛒 ⚘

(2m) *Alftrudis, 8 Norman Avenue, Henley-on-Thames, Oxon, RG9 1SG*.
Victorian house in town centre
Grades: ETB 1 Cr, High Comm
Tel: **01491 573099** Mrs Lambert.
Rates fr: *£20.00*-£30.00.
Open: All Year
Beds: 2D 1T
Baths: 2 Ensuite 1 Private
🛏 (8) 🅿 (2) 🛒 🛒

(2m) *11 Western Road, Henley-on-Thames, Oxon, RG9 1JL*.
Comfortable, well-situated detached house
Tel: **01491 572066**
Mrs Smith.
Rates fr: *£17.50*-£30.00.
Open: All Year (not Xmas)
Beds: 1D 1S
Baths: 1 Shared
🛏 🅿 (1) 🛒 🛒

Woodcote   15

National Grid Ref: SU6481

🍴 🍺 Red Lion, White Lion, Highwayman

(0.25m) *Hedges, South Stoke Road, Woodcote, Reading, Berks, RG8 0PL*.
Peaceful rural situation. Historic area of Outstanding Natural Beauty
Grades: ETB 2 Cr, Comm
Tel: **01491 680461**
Mrs Howard-Allen.
Rates fr: *£16.00*-£16.00.
Open: All Year (not Xmas)
Beds: 2T 2S
Baths: 2 Shared
🛏 (2) 🅿 (4) 🛒 🛒 🛒

Goring   16

National Grid Ref: SU6081

🍴 🍺 Catherine Wheel, John Barley Corn, Miller of Mansfield

(0.5m) *14 Mountfield, Wallingford Road, Goring, Reading, Berks, RG8 0BE*.
Modern home in riverside village
Tel: **01491 872029**
Mrs Ewen.
Rates fr: *£17.50*-£20.00.
Open: All Year
Beds: 1D 1T 1S
Baths: 1 Shared
🛏 🅿 (4) 🛒 🛒 ✕ 🛒 🛒 ⚘

Streatley   17

National Grid Ref: SU5980

(🔺 1m) *Streatley-on-Thames Youth Hostel, Hill House, Reading Road, Streatley, Reading, Berkshire, RG8 9JJ*.
Actual grid ref: SU591806
Warden: Mr A Wilson.
Tel: **01491 872278**
Under 18: £6.55
Adults: £9.75
Evening Meals Available (7pm), Family Bunk Rooms, Television, Showers, Shop
Homely Victorian family house, completely refurbished, in a beautiful riverside village

North Stoke   18

National Grid Ref: SU6186

🍴 🍺 Perch & Pike

(0.5m) *The Old Farm House, North Stoke, Wallingford, Oxon, OX10 6BL*.
Actual grid ref: SU610862
C17th flint farmhouse and garden in quiet Thameside village
Tel: **01491 837079**
Mrs Lucey.
Rates fr: *£20.00*-£20.00.
Open: All Year
Beds: 2T 1S
Baths: 1 Shared
🅿 (4) 🛒 🛒 🛒 🛒 ⚘

(0.25m) *Footpath Cottage, The Street, North Stoke, Wallingford, Oxon, OX10 6BJ*.
C18th cottage, exquisite village
Tel: **01491 839763**
Mrs Tanner.
Rates fr: *£17.00*-£18.00.
Open: All Year
Beds: 2D 1S
Baths: 1 Private 1 Shared
🛏 🛒 🛒 ✕ 🛒 Ⓥ 🛒 ⚘

Wallingford to Lechlade

From here the route takes you west and close to **Didcot**, where there is a railway museum. Between Appelford and Culham you can make a detour to the pretty town of **Abingdon**. There are scant remains of the Benedictine abbey which went the way of all the others under Henry VIII, but there is an impressive Perpendicular church, St Helen's, the seventeenth-century County Hall and many streets with seventeenth- and eighteenth-century houses. Westwards to **Wantage**, birthplace of Alfred the Great, whose statue stands imposingly over the town square. Further westwards, the route passes close to the world-famous prehistoric White Horse

hillside carving. By far the oldest of England's chalk carvings, the figure captures in huge bold lines the movement of a galloping horse. The earthworks of Uffington Castle, a fort from the same era, stand atop the hill. From here, where the Ridgeway alternative rejoins the main route, it's north to **Uffington**, and on to **Faringdon**. A short stretch west to Coleshill and then north to **Buscot** brings you close to Buscot Park, a National Trust property with painted pannels and stained glass by Edward Burne-Jones. Just over the border in Gloucestershire is the village of **Lechlade**, built of Cotswold limestone and boasting a church, St Lawrence's, whose spire is celebrated in a poem by Shelley. The village is the highest navigable point of the Thames.

Please don't camp on *anyone's* land without first obtaining their permission.

Cholsey 19

National Grid Ref: SU5886

†◑ ◁ Red Lion, Walnut Tree

(1m) *Old Blackalls, Old Blackalls Drive, Cholsey, Wallingford, Oxon, OX10 9HD.*
Friendly, family house in rural position
Tel: **01491 652864**
Mrs Robson.
Rates fr: *£17.50-£17.50*.
Open: All Year (not Xmas)
Beds: 1D
Baths: 1 Ensuite
🛏 🅿 (5) ⅍ 🗖 ✕ 🕮 ₺ 🖾 ⚡

Wallingford 20

National Grid Ref: SU6089

†◑ ◁ Bell Inn, Queen's Head, Six Bells, Chillingford Bridge Hotel

(0.25m) *Little Gables,*
166 Crowmarsh Hill, Wallingford, Oxford. OX10 8BG.
Delightfully large, private house
Grades: ETB 2 Cr, Comm
Tel: **01491 837834** (also fax no)
Mrs Reeves.
Rates fr: *£22.50-£30.00*.
Open: All Year
Beds: 2F 1D 1T 1S
Baths: 2 Ensuite 2 Private
🛏 🅿 ⅍ 🗖 🕮 ₺ 🖾 ⚡

(1m) *North Farm, Shillingford Hill, Wallingford, Oxon, OX10 8ND.*
Actual grid ref: SU586924
Quiet farmhouse near River Thames
Grades: ETB 2 Cr, High Comm
Tel: **01865 858406**
Mrs Warburton.
Fax no: 01865 858519
Rates fr: *£22.00-£25.00*.
Open: All Year (not Xmas)
Beds: 1D 1T
Baths: 2 Private
🛏 (8) 🅿 ⅍ 🗖 ✕ 🕮 🖾 🖾 ⚡

(0.5m) *The Nook, 2 Thames Street, Wallingford, Oxon, OX10 0BH.*
Character house close to river/town
Tel: **01491 834214**
Mrs Colclough.
Rates fr: *£19.00-£28.00*.
Open: All Year
Beds: 1D 2T
Baths: 1 Shared
🛏 🅿 🗖 🕮 🖾 🖾

(0.5m) *3 Aston Close, Wallingford, Oxon, OX10 9AY.*
Modern, quiet private house
Tel: **01491 836434** Mrs Holmes.
Rates fr: *£15.00-£17.50*.
Open: All Year (not Xmas)
Beds: 1D 1T
Baths: 1 Private 1 Shared
🛏 (5) 🅿 (3) ⅍ 🗖 🕮

Benson 21

National Grid Ref: SU6191

†◑ ◁ Three Horseshoes

(2m) *Fyfield Manor, Brook Street, Benson, Wallingford, Oxon, OX10 6HA.*
C12th manor house. Large, comfortable period bedrooms with ensuite facilities
Tel: **01491 835184** Mrs Brown.
Fax no: 01491 825635
Rates fr: *£22.50-£30.00*.
Open: All Year (not Xmas)
Beds: 1F 1D 1T
Baths: 2 Ensuite 1 Private
🛏 (10) 🅿 (10) ⅍ 🗖 🕮 🖾 🖾 ⚡

Planning a longer stay? Always ask for any special rates.

Ewelme 22

National Grid Ref: SU6491

(3m) *May's Farm, Turner's Court, Ewelme, Wallingford, Oxon, OX10 6QF.*
Working stock farm, fabulous views. Quiet
Tel: **01491 641294**
Mrs Passmore.
Rates fr: *£17.50-£18.00*.
Open: All Year (not Xmas)
Beds: 1D 1T
Baths: 1 Private 1 Shared
🛏 (10) 🅿 🗖 🖙 🕮 🖾 🖾 ⚡

Little Wittenham 23

National Grid Ref: SU5693

†◑ ◁ The Vine, The Plough

(2m) *Rooks Orchard, Little Wittenham, Abingdon, Oxon, OX14 4QY.*
Actual grid ref: SU563927
C17th Listed house, beams, inglenooks
Grades: ETB 2 Cr, High Comm
Tel: **01865 407765**
Mrs Welfare.
Rates fr: *£19.00-£24.00*.
Open: All Year (not Xmas)
Beds: 1D 1T
Baths: 1 Ensuite 1 Private
🛏 🅿 (4) ⅍ 🗖 🖙 ✕ 🕮 🖾 🖾 ⚡

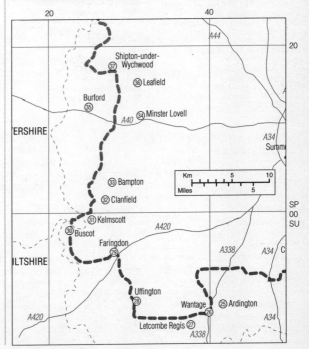

Sutton Courtenay 24

National Grid Ref: SU5093

iol ⊄ George & Dragon, The Fish

(0.25m) *Bekynton House, 7 The Green, Sutton Courtenay, Abingdon, Oxon, OX14 4AE.*
Period house on village green near River Thames. Walled garden
Tel: **01235 848630** Ms Cornwall.
Fax no: 01235 848436
Rates fr: *£20.00-£25.00*.
Open: All Year (not Xmas)
Beds: 1D 1T 1S **Baths:** 2 Shared
ॐ ₽ (2) ⊬ ⌷ ✕ Ⅲ ⓥ â ✦

Ardington 25

National Grid Ref: SU4387

iol ⊄ Boar's Head

(2m) *Orpwood House, Ardington, Wantage, Oxon, OX12 8PN.*
Spacious farmhouse in picturesque downland village. Swimming pool in summer
Tel: **01235 833300** Mrs Haigh.
Fax no: 01235 820950
Rates fr: *£19.50-£19.50*.
Open: All Year (not Xmas)
Beds: 1F 2T 1S
Baths: 1 Private 2 Shared
ॐ ₽ (15) ⊬ ⌷ ✕ Ⅲ ⓥ â ✦

Wantage 26

National Grid Ref: SU4087

iol ⊄ Bell Inn

(0.25m) *The Bell Inn, 38 Market Place, Wantage, Oxon, OX12 8AH.*
C16th market town inn serving home cooked food in friendly atmosphere
Tel: **01235 763718** (also fax no)
Mrs Williams.
Rates fr: *£17.50-£17.50*.
Open: All Year
Beds: 2F 3D 3T 5S
Baths: 7 Ensuite 2 Shared
ॐ ⌷ ✝ ✕ Ⅲ ⓥ

(0.25m) *Ormond Guest House, 23 Ormond Road, Wantage, Oxon, OX12 8EG.*
Victorian house near town centre
Tel: **01235 762409**
Mr & Mrs Mudway.
Rates fr: *£18.00-£20.00*.
Open: All Year
Beds: 2F 4T
Baths: 3 Private 2 Shared
ॐ ₽ (8) ⌷ ✝ Ⅲ ⓥ

Letcombe Regis 27

National Grid Ref: SU3886

iol ⊄ The Sparrow, The Lamb

(0.5m) *Quince Cottage, Letcombe Regis, Wantage, Oxon, OX12 9J.*
Spacious C18th thatched house
Tel: **01235 763652**
Mrs Boden.
Rates fr: *£17.00-£17.50*.
Open: All Year
Beds: 1T 1S
Baths: 1 Private
ॐ (1) ₽ (2) ⊬ ⌷ ✝ Ⅲ ⓥ â ✦

Uffington 28

National Grid Ref: SU3089

iol ⊄ Fox & Hounds, White Horse

(1m) *Sower Hill Farm, Uffington, Faringdon, Oxon, SN7 7QH.*
Actual grid ref: SU3087
Modern farmhouse and stables with brilliant views: ideal walkers, riders
Tel: **01367 820758**
Mrs Cox.
Rates fr: *£18.00-£18.00*.
Open: All Year (not Xmas)
Beds: 1D 1T 1S
Baths: 2 Shared
₽ (6) ⊬ ⌷ Ⅲ â ✦

(0.25m) *Norton House, Broad Street, Uffington, Faringdon, Oxon, SN7 7RA.*
Actual grid ref: SU305895
Friendly C18th family home in centre of quiet, pretty village
Tel: **01367 820230** (also fax no)
Mrs Oberman.
Rates fr: *£17.00-£18.00*.
Open: All Year
Beds: 1F 1D 1S
Baths: 2 Private
ॐ ₽ (3) ⊬ ⌷ ✝ Ⅲ ⓥ â ✦

(0.25m) *The Craven, Uffington, Faringdon, Oxon, SN7 7RD.*
C17th thatched, beamed farmhouse/hotel
Tel: **01367 820449** Mrs Wadsworth.
Rates fr: *£20.00-£25.00*.
Open: All Year
Beds: 1F 3D 2T 2S
Baths: 2 Private 2 Shared
ॐ ₽ (9) ⌷ ✝ ✕ Ⅲ ⓑ ⓥ â ✦

Faringdon 29

National Grid Ref: SU2895

iol ⊄ Fox & Hounds

(1m) *Bowling Green Farm, Stanford Road, Faringdon, Oxon, SN7 8EZ.*
Attractive C18th period farmhouse
Grades: ETB 2 Cr
Tel: **01367 240229** Mr Barnard.
Rates fr: *£20.00-£25.00*.
Open: All Year
Beds: 2F
Baths: 2 Ensuite
ॐ ₽ (6) ⌷ Ⅲ ⓥ

From Lechlade through the Cotswolds

Back in Oxfordshire, **Kelmscott Manor** (open Wednesdays, April-September), a classic Elizabethan manor, was home to the founder of the Arts and Crafts movement, socialist William Morris, for the last twenty-five years of his life. The house sports decor by Morris' friends in the Pre-Raphaelite movement, including Edward Burne-Jones (who worked on Buscot Park whilst staying here) and Dante Gabriel Rossetti, who had an affair with Morris' wife, Jane. From here you ride north; a detour westwards from Shilton will take you to the Cotswold Wildlife Park. On to **Swinbrook**, on the banks of the Windrush, where the church boasts the Tudor and Stuart Fettiplace

Monuments. A short detour leads to **Burford,** another beautiful village of Cotswold stone with an impressive sloping High Street lined by fourteenth- to sixteenth-century houses. The most interesting feature of the large parish church is tucked away high up in the rafters - a small statue of a pagan deity by a craftsman hedging his bets for the hereafter. The churchyard was the scene in the seventeenth century of the martyrdom of Levellers in Cromwell's army, members of a radical democratic movement shot for refusing to fight in Ireland. North of Swinbrook you come into the ancient **Wychwood** region. You are now in true Cotswold country, where you remain for most of the remaining distance - this lengthy stretch of the cycleway affords the most picturesque landscape.

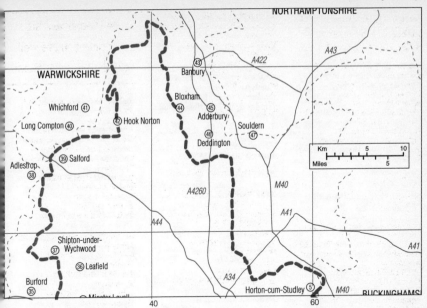

Buscot 30

National Grid Ref: SU2397

¶⁰¹ ⊄ Trout Inn

(0.25m) *Apple Tree House,*
Buscot, Faringdon, Oxon, SN7 8DA.
Listed property - National Trust
village
Grades: ETB 2 Cr
Tel: **01367 252592** Mrs Reay.
Rates fr: *£17.00-£22.00.*
Open: All Year
Beds: 2D 1T
Baths: 1 Ensuite 2 Shared
🛏 🅿 (8) 🖵 🎟 🗹 ▮

Kelmscott 31

National Grid Ref: SU2599

(0.5m) *The Plough Inn, Kelmscott,*
Lechlade, Glos, GL7 3HG.
Actual grid ref: SU249992
Comfortable, well appointed inn
Tel: **01367 253543** Mr Pardoe.
Fax no: 01367 252514
Rates fr: *£25.00-£30.00.*
Open: All Year
Beds: 1F 4D 3T
Baths: 8 Private
🛏 🅿 (12) 🖵 🎟 ✕ 🎟 🗹 ▮ ⚲

Bringing children with
you? Always ask for
any special rates.

All rates are subject
to alteration at the
owners' discretion.

Clanfield 32

National Grid Ref: SP2801

¶⁰¹ ⊄ Clanfield Tavern

(2m) *The Granary, Clanfield,*
Bampton, Oxon, OX18 2SH.
Actual grid ref: SP284018
Ground-floor twin ensuite, others
upstairs. Near Thames, Cotswolds,
Oxford
Grades: ETB 2 Cr, Comm
Tel: **01367 810266**
Mrs Payne.
Rates fr: *£17.00-£17.00.*
Open: All Year (not Xmas)
Beds: 1D 1T 1S
Baths: 1 Private 1 Shared
🅿 (4) ⚲ 🖵 🎟 ⚲

(2m) *Chestnut Grove,*
Clanfield, Bampton, Oxon,
OX18 2RG.
Modern, newly-built house
Tel: **01367 810249**
Miss Pocock.
Rates fr: *£15.00-£15.00.*
Open: All Year
Beds: 1D 2S
Baths: 2 Private
🛏 🅿 (3) ⚲ 🖵 🎟 ▮ ⚲

Bampton 33

National Grid Ref: SP3103

(3m) *Morar, Weald Street,*
Bampton, Oxon, OX18 2HL.
Actual grid ref: SP312026
Grades: ETB 2 Cr, High Comm
Tel: **01993 850162**
Ms Rouse.
Fax no: 01993 851738
Rates fr: *£21.50-£21.50.*
Open: March to Dec
Beds: 2D 1T
Baths: 2 Ensuite 1 Private
🛏 (6) 🅿 (5) ⚲ 🖵 ✕ 🎟 🗹 ⚲
Wake to the smell of homemade
bread, look out over rolling fields.
Enjoy hearty breakfasts plus
homemade preserves. Bicycles
garaged: boots dried: thermos filled
free

(3m) *Elephant & Castle, Bridge*
Street, Bampton, Oxon,
OX18 2HA.
Olde worlde country pub
Tel: **01993 850316**
Mrs Rainey.
Rates fr: *£15.00-£20.00.*
Open: All Year
Beds: 1D 2T
Baths: 3 Ensuite
🛏 (12) 🅿 (20) 🖵 ✕ 🎟 🗹 ▮ ⚲

All cycleways are
popular: you are well-
advised to book ahead

From the Cotswolds to Oxford

The northernmost point of the route is **Hornton**, from where you turn southwards and head to **Broughton**, where stands Broughton Castle, an Elizabethan mansion surrounded by a moat. It contains splendid pannelling, fireplaces and plaster ceilings. Inhabited by a Parliamentarian in the Civil War, it was captured by the Royalists after the Battle of Edgehill, a few miles away in Warwickshire. There is a display of Civil War arms and armour. From here you can make a detour to visit **Banbury**, the main town of Northern Oxfordshire. The Victorian market cross stands on the site of a medieval original. After Broughton you head south into the **Cherwell Valley**. A detour from **Upper Heyford** leads to Rousham House, a seventeenth-century mansion which served as a Royalist garrison during the Civil War. It has the only surviving landscape garden by William Kent. From Upper Heyford it's an easy ride to Horton-cum-Studley to complete the county circuit, and you can return to Oxford by the route along which you left.

(3m) *Romany Inn, Bridge Street, Bampton, Oxon, OX18 2HA.*
Grades: ETB 2 Cr, Approv
Tel: **01993 850237** Mr Booth.
Fax no: 01993 852133
Rates fr: *£17.50*-**£22.50**.
Open: All Year
Beds: 3F 4D 2T 1S
Baths: 10 Private
🛇 🅿 (7) 🖵 🕯 ✕ 🛏 ⬟
C19th Georgian building. Chef proprietor. Inn & restaurant, Good Beer Guide, Good Pub Guide. Quiet village location - brochures

The lowest *double* rate per person is shown in *italics*.

Minster Lovell   34

National Grid Ref: SP3110

🍴 🍺 White Hart, Old Swan

(3m) *Hill Grove Farm, Minster Lovell, Witney, Oxon, OX8 5NA.*
Comfortable farmhouse overlooking Windrush River
Grades: ETB 2 Cr, High Comm, AA 3 Q
Tel: **01993 703120**
Mrs Brown.
Fax no: 01993 700528
Rates fr: *£19.00*-**£18.00**.
Open: All Year (not Xmas)
Beds: 1D 1T
Baths: 1 Ensuite 1 Private
🛇 🅿 (6) ✂ 🖵 🛏

Burford   35

National Grid Ref: SP2512

🍴 🍺 The Mermaid, Cotswold Arms, Royal Oak

(2m) *Highway Hotel, Inc Burford Needlecraft, 117 High Street, Burford, Oxon, OX18 4RG.*
Guest house built in 1520, perfectly situated base for Cotswolds
Grades: ETB 2 Cr
Tel: **01993 822136** (also fax no)
Mr Cohen.
Rates fr: *£20.00*-**£30.00**.
Open: All Year
Beds: 2F 7D 2T
Baths: 9 Private 1 Shared
🛇 🖵 🕯 🛏 ⬟ 🗹 ✦

(2m) *Providence Cottage, 26 High Street, Burford, Oxon, OX18 4RR.*
Elegant C15th traditional stone cottage
Grades: ETB 2 Cr, High Comm
Tel: **01993 823310**
Mrs Theodorou.
Rates fr: *£20.00*.
Open: All Year (not Xmas)
Beds: 1D 1T
Baths: 1 Ensuite 1 Private
🛇 (14) ✂ 🖵 🛏 🗹

Leafield   36

National Grid Ref: SP3115

🍴 🍺 The Spindleberry, Royal Oak, The Fox

(2m) *Greenside Cottage, The Ridings, Leafield, Witney, Oxon, OX8 5NN.*
Stone cottage on Cotswold village green. Lovely garden
Grades: ETB 2 Cr, Comm
Tel: **01993 878368** (also fax no)
Mrs Martin-Doyle.
Rates fr: *£18.00*-**£18.00**.
Open: All Year
Beds: 1D 1T 1S
Baths: 1 Ensuite 1 Private
🛇 (7) 🅿 (3) ✂ 🖵 🛏 🗹

(2m) *Langley Farm, Leafield, Witney, Oxon, OX8 5QD.*
Formerly royal hunting lodge. Ideal for touring from peaceful surroundings
Tel: **01993 878686** Mrs Greves.
Rates fr: *£14.00*-**£28.00**.
Open: May to Oct
Beds: 2D 1T
Baths: 1 Private 1 Shared
🛇 (8) 🅿 (8) 🖵 🕯 🛏

(2m) *Pond View, 10 Fairspear Road, Leafield, Witney, Oxon, OX8 5NT.*
Quiet house with lovely views
Grades: ETB Listed commended
Tel: **01993 878133** Mrs Wiggins.
Rates fr: *£16.00*-**£16.00**.
Open: All Year
Beds: 1D 1T 2S
Baths: 1En -suite 2 Shared
🛇 🅿 (3) 🖵 🛏 🗹

Shipton-under-Wychwood   37

National Grid Ref: SP2717

🍴 🍺 Shaven Crown, Lamb Inn

(0.5m) *6 Courtlands Road, Shipton-under-Wychwood, Chipping Norton, Oxon, OX7 6DF.*
Friendly, quiet, comfortable house/garden
Grades: ETB Listed, Comm
Tel: **01993 830551**
Mr & Mrs Fletcher.
Rates fr: *£17.50*-**£20.00**.
Open: All Year **Beds:** 2D 1T
Baths: 2 Ensuite 1 Private
🅿 (3) ✂ 🖵 🛏 🗹 ♿ ✦

Adlestrop   38

National Grid Ref: SP2427

🍴 🍺 Fox Inn

(1m) *Honeybrook Cottage, 2 Main Street, Adlestrop, Moreton in Marsh, Glos, GL56 0YN.*
Tranquil village setting, fine views
Tel: **01608 658884** (also fax no)
Mrs Warrick.
Rates fr: *£18.50*-**£22.00**.
Open: Feb - Nov
Beds: 1D 1T
Baths: 1 Ensuite 1 Private
🛇 (12) 🅿 (2) ✂ 🖵 🛏 🗹 ✦

Salford   39

National Grid Ref: SP2828

🍴 🍺 Black Horse, Red Lion

(1m) *Kingsmoor Cottage, Chapel Lane, Salford, Chipping Norton, Oxon, OX7 5YN.*
Quiet Cotswold village, traditional comfort
Tel: **01608 643276** Mrs Barnard.
Rates fr: *£14.00*-**£14.00**.
Open: All Year
Beds: 1T **Baths:** 1 Shared
🛇 🅿 (1) 🖵 🛏 🛏

Long Compton 40

National Grid Ref: SP2832

¶◑ ◖ Red Lion, Gate Hangs High.
Fox & Hounds

(1.5m) *Archways, Crockwell Street, Long Compton, Shipston on Stour, Warks, CV36 5JN.*
Charming C17th Cotswold cottage midway Oxford Stratford - ideal for Cotswolds
Grades: ETB 1 Cr, Comm
Tel: **01608 684358**
Mrs Cunnington.
Rates fr: *£16.00-£17.00.*
Open: All Year (not Xmas)
Beds: 2D 1T
Baths: 2 Shared
ॐ ₽ (4) ◻ ▥ ▮ ◈

Whichford 41

National Grid Ref: SP3134

¶◑ ◖ The Gate

(3m) *Ascott House Farm, Whichford, Long Compton, Shipston on Stour, Warks, CV36 5PP.*
Cotswold farmhouse, area of natural beauty
Grades: ETB 2 Cr
Tel: **01608 684655** (also fax no)
Mrs Haines.
Rates fr: *£16.00-£18.00.*
Open: All Year
Beds: 1F 1D 1T
Baths: 2 Ensuite 1 Shared
ॐ ₽ (12) ◻ ☆ ▥ Ⓥ ◈

Hook Norton 42

National Grid Ref: SP3533

(0.25m) *Pear Tree Inn, Scotland End, Hook Norton, Banbury, Oxon, OX15 5NU.*
Quiet country pub near brewery
Grades: ETB 2 Cr, Comm
Tel: **01608 737482** Mrs Tindsley.
Rates fr: *£17.50-£20.00.*
Open: All Year (not Xmas)
Beds: 1D
Baths: 1 Private
ॐ ₽ (15) ◻ ☆ ✕ ▥ Ⓥ

Banbury 43

National Grid Ref: SP4540

¶◑ ◖ Swan Inn

(1.5m) *Belmont Guest House, 34 Crouch Street, Banbury, Oxon, OX16 9PR.*
Tel: **01295 262308** Mr Raby.
Rates fr: *£17.50-£24.00.*
Open: All Year (not Xmas)
Beds: 1F 2D 3T 2S
Baths: 5 Private 1 Shared
ॐ (10) ₽ (6) ◻ ✕ ▥ ₺ Ⓥ ◈
Large Victorian house (detached). Family run business, mainly ensuite bedrooms, clean and comfortable. Within walking distance of town amenities, many restaurants

Bloxham 44

National Grid Ref: SP4236

¶◑ ◖ Red Lion, Joiners' Arms

(0.25m) *The Knoll Guest House, Little Bridge Road, Bloxham, Banbury, Oxon, OX15 4PU.*
Lovely Geogian private village house. **Grades:** ETB Listed
Tel: **01295 720843** Mr Woodward.
Fax no: 01295 721764
Rates fr: *£17.50-£20.00.*
Open: All Year (not Xmas)
Beds: 2D 1T 1S
Baths: 2 Ensuite 2 Shared
₽ (Yes) ✄ ◻ ☆ ▥ Ⓥ

Adderbury 45

National Grid Ref: SP4735

(3m) *Morgans Orchard Restaurant, 9 Twyford Gardens, Twyford, Adderbury, Banbury, Oxon, OX17 3JA.*
Licensed French restaurant with rooms
Tel: **01295 812047** Mr Morgan.
Rates fr: *£18.00-£19.50.*
Open: All Year
Beds: 1D 3T 1S
Baths: 1 Private 4 Shared
ॐ ₽ ◻ ☆ ✕ ▥ Ⓥ ▮

Deddington 46

National Grid Ref: SP4631

¶◑ ◖ Black Boy, The Unicorn

(2m) *Hillbarn, Milton Gated Road, Deddington, Banbury, Oxon, OX15 0TS.*
Peaceful farmhouse accommodation. Beautiful views. Convenient Stratford, Warwick, Oxford, Cotswolds
Grades: ETB Listed, Comm
Tel: **01869 338631**
Mrs White.
Rates fr: *£18.00-£20.00.*
Open: All Year
Beds: 1F 1D 1T
Baths: 1 Shared
ॐ ₽ (6) ◻ ▥ ₺ Ⓥ

Souldern 47

National Grid Ref: SP5231

¶◑ ◖ The Fox

(2m) *The Fox Inn, Souldern, Bicester, Oxon, OX6 9JN.*
C18th stone village inn
Tel: **01869 345284**
Mr MacKay.
Fax no: 01869 345667
Rates fr: *£16.00-£19.50.*
Open: All Year
Beds: 1T 3D
Baths: 2 Ensuite 1 Shared
ॐ ₽ (10) ◻ ☆ ✕ ▥ Ⓥ

(2m) *Towerfields, Tusmore Road, Souldern, Bicester, Oxon, OX6 9HY.*
Renovated farmhouse, smallholding, rare breeds
Grades: ETB 2 Cr, Comm
Tel: **01869 346554**
Mrs Hamilton Gould.
Fax no: 01869 345157
Rates fr: *£24.00-£24.00.*
Open: All Year (not Xmas)
Beds: 1D 1T 1S
Baths: 3 Ensuite
ॐ ₽ (4) ✄ ◻ ☆ ✕ ▥ ₺

South Downs Way

At 96 miles, this route is shorter than many featured in this book. However, designed as a National Trail for walkers, it is routed mainly along a chalk track, which can get muddy, and involves a considerable amount of climbing, so should only really be undertaken on an all terrain bicycle. It runs west along the ridge of the great chalk escarpment of the South Downs, from Eastbourne in East Sussex to Winchester in Hampshire. The views from the path, southwards out to sea and northwards over the Sussex Weald, are stunning.

The route is waymarked along its whole length by the National Trail acorn symbol, and, by virtue of the fact that these walking routes are long-established by comparison with Britain's still relatively nascent cycleways, is very well served by thoroughgoing **guide books**. You will find everything you need (including mapping) in the *National Trail Guide - South Downs Way* by Paul Millmore (ISBN 1 85410 099 8), published by Aurum Press in association with the Countryside Commission and Ordnance Survey @ £10.99. This book includes a list of cycle repair/hire shops on or near to the route; and a general list of facilities available at locations along the way.

Other guides are *Along the South Downs Way to Winchester* by the Society of Sussex Downsmen, available from the RA's National Office at 1/5 Wandsworth Road, London SW8 2XX, tel 0171-582 6878, @ £5.00 (+£1.00 p&p);

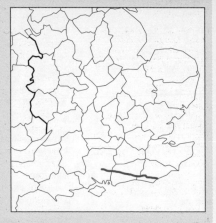

A Guide to the South Downs Way by Miles Jebb (ISBN 09 471170 4), published by Constable & Co Ltd @ £10.95;

and *South Downs Way & The Downs Link* by Kev Reynolds (ISBN 1 85284 023 4), published by Cicerone Press and available from the publishers at 2 Police Square, Milnthorpe, Cumbria LA7 7PY, tel 01539 562069, @ £5.99 (+75p p&p).

Maps: Ordnance Survey 1:50,000 Landranger series: 185, 197, 198, 199

Trains: Services from London go to Eastbourne, Lewes and Brighton (all from Victoria) and to Petersfield and Winchester (from Waterloo). Many other places along or near to the route are covered by local services.

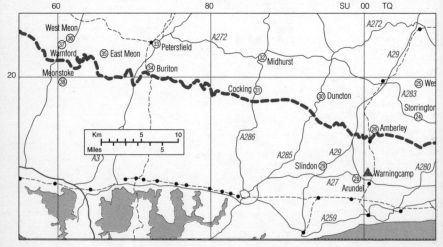

Eastbourne 1

National Grid Ref: TQ5900

¹⁰¹ ◀ The Marine, The Lamb, The Terminus, Pilot & Shipping

(▲ On route) *Eastbourne Youth Hostel, East Dean Road, Eastbourne, East Sussex, BN20 8ES.*
Actual grid ref: TQ588990
Warden: Mr & Mrs P & A Haugrik.
Tel: **01323 721081**
Under 18: £5.40
Adults: £8.00
Family Bunk Rooms, Showers, Central Heating, Shop
Former golf clubhouse on South Downs, 450ft above sea level with sweeping views across Eastbourne & Pevensey Bay

(2m) *Camberley Hotel, 27-29 Elms Avenue, Eastbourne, E. Sussex, BN21 3DN.*
Tel: **01323 723789**
Rates fr: *£15.50*-**£15.50.**
Open: March to Oct
Beds: 4F 3T 3D 2S
Baths: 7 Ensuite 2 Shared
🐾 🄿 (3) 🖵 ✕ Ⓥ 🛆 ⚡
Situated in a pleasant avenue close to town centre, sea front and all amenites. Licensed, ensuite, teamaking, colour TV in bedrooms. English breakfast

(2m) *Arden Hotel, 17 Burlington Place, Eastbourne, E. Sussex, BN21 4AR.*
Non-smoking, Victorian, family-run hotel
Tel: **01323 639639**
Mr Jones.
Rates fr: *£20.00*-**£20.00.**
Open: All Year (not Xmas)
Beds: 2F 5D 5T 2S
Baths: 9 Private 1 Shared
🐾 🄿 (4) ⊬ 🖵 🖿 Ⓥ 🛆

(1m) *Edelweiss Hotel, 10-12 Elms Avenue, Eastbourne, E. Sussex, BN21 3DN.*
Grades: ETB 2 Cr, Comm
Tel: **01323 732071** (also fax no)
Mr & Mrs Butler.
Rates fr: *£15.00*-**£15.00.**
Open: All Year
Beds: 1F 6D 5T 2S
Baths: 3 Private 4 Shared
🐾 🖵 ✕ 🖿 Ⓥ 🛆
Small family-run hotel set in picturesque avenue close to seafront. Rooms with TV & teamaking. Guests' lounge, bar, evening meals available. Excellent value

(2m) *Marwood House, 122/123 Royal Parade, Eastbourne, E. Sussex, BN22 7JY.*
Seafront guest house. Unrestricted parking, home cooking, open all year
Tel: **01323 730791**
Rates fr: *£15.00*-**£15.00.**
Open: All Year (not Xmas)
Beds: 2T 3D 2S **Baths:** 1 Ensuite
🐾 (7) ⊬ 🖵 🛏 ✕ 🖿 🛆 Ⓥ

The lowest *double* rate per person is shown in *italics.*

Eastbourne to Alfriston

Eastbourne is a typical English seaside resort, with a three-mile seafront and a Victorian pier. One feature worth a mention is the Trower Gallery and Museum, which exhibits contemporary art. The initial stretch of the way skirts Paradise Wood and climbs gently to the top of the Downs, continuing to the village of **Jevington**. (The alternative route over Beachy Head and the Seven Sisters is for walkers only and cannot be cycled.) A little way off the path beyond Jevington, the Lullington Heath National Nature Reserve can be reached by a bridleway. At **Wilmington**, a little way off the route, stands a ruined Benedictine priory and a twelfth-century church, but more renowned is the ancient hillside carving, the Long Man. This massive representation of a figure bearing a staff in each hand had long faded until the Victorian restoration. It is likely they modified the image so as not to offend the sensibilities of the period (compare the Cerne Giant in Dorset), and as such it was not so much a restoration as a desecration, which begs the question, why did they bother restoring it at all? Close by lies the old smuggling village of **Alfriston** with a number of centuries-old inns and an untouched fourteenth-century church known as 'the cathedral of the Downs', and beyond it the noted viewpoint at Firle Beacon.

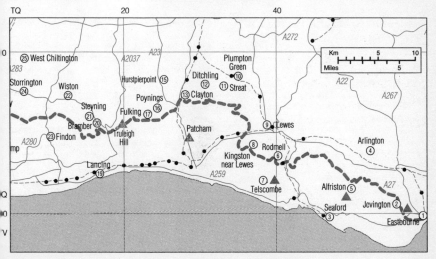

All rooms full and nowhere else to stay? Ask the owner if there's anywhere nearby

---

(0.75m) *Southcroft Private Hotel,*
15 South Cliff Avenue, Eastbourne,
E. Sussex, BN20 7AH.
Actual grid ref: TV609979
Elegant Edwardian town house
Grades: ETB 3 Cr, Comm
Tel: **01323 729071** Mr Ellis.
Rates fr: *£21.00-£21.00*.
Open: All Year (not Xmas)
Beds: 3D 2T 1S
Baths: 6 Ensuite
⊁ ❏ ✕ Ⅲ & Ⅴ ⋒ ⊬

(0.5m) *Cherry Tree Hotel,*
15 Silverdale Road, Eastbourne,
E. Sussex, BN20 7AJ.
Small family-run quality hotel
Grades: ETB 3 Cr, High Comm
Tel: **01323 722406** Mr Clarke.
Fax no: 01323 648838
Rates fr: *£24.00-£24.00*.
Open: All Year
Beds: 2F 3D 3T 2S
Baths: 10 Private
⇄ (7) ❏ ✕ Ⅲ. Ⅴ ⋒ ⊬

Pay B&Bs by cash or cheque and be prepared to pay up front.

(0.5m) *Seagulls Guest House,*
12 South Cliff Avenue, Eastbourne,
E. Sussex, South Downs Way,
BN20 7AH.
Edwardian, welcoming, near sea &
South Downs
Tel: **01323 737831** Mrs Rogers.
Rates fr: *£18.00-£17.50*.
Open: All Year
Beds: 3D 2T 1S
Baths: 2 Ensuite 2 Shared
⇄ (4) ⊬ ❏ ✕ Ⅲ. Ⅴ ⊬

(2.5m) *Bay Lodge Hotel,*
61 62 Royal Parade, Eastbourne,
E. Sussex, BN20 7AQ.
Small seafront Victorian hotel
Grades: ETB 3 Cr, Comm
Tel: **01323 732515** Mr Hunt.
Fax no: 01323 735009
Rates fr: *£19.00-£19.00*.
Open: Mar to Oct
Beds: 5D 4T 3S
Baths: 9 Ensuite
⇄ (7) ₽ ❏ ✕ Ⅲ. Ⅴ ⋒

(1m) *Pevensey Lodge,* *27 Pevensey*
Road, Eastbourne, E. Sussex,
BN21 3HR.
Family-run licensed guest house
Grades: ETB 2 Cr Comm
Tel: **01323 649539** Mrs Chapman.
Rates fr: *£16.00-£16.00*.
Open: Feb to Nov
Beds: 2F 1D 1T 2S
Baths: 6 Private
⇄ (3) ❏ ✕ Ⅲ. ⋒

(1m) *Gladwyn Hotel,*
16 Blackwater Road, Eastbourne,
E. Sussex, BN21 4JD.
Family-run, homely, comfortable
hotel
Tel: **01323 733142**
Mr Williams.
Rates fr: *£15.75-£15.75*.
Open: All Year
Beds: 2F 3D 5T 2S
Baths: 9 Private
⇄ ₽ ❏ ┢ ✕ ⋒

(1m) *Heatherdene Hotel,*
26-28 Elms Avenue, Eastbourne,
E. Sussex, BN21 3DN.
Licensed hotel close to seafront &
town centre
Grades: ETB 2 Cr
Tel: **01323 723598** Mrs Mockford.
Fax no: 01323 722338
Rates fr: *£16.00-£16.00*.
Open: All Year
Beds: 1F 3D 8T 3S
Baths: 5 Private 4 Shared
⇄ ❏ ┢ ✕ Ⅲ. & Ⅴ

(2m) *Courtlands Hotel,* *68 Royal*
Parade, Eastbourne, E. Sussex,
BN22 7AQ.
Seafront position, business/touring
base
Grades: ETB 2 Cr, RAC Listed,
Acclaim
Tel: **01323 721068**
Rates fr: *£17.00-£17.00*.
Open: All Year
Beds: 3F 2D 1T 2S
Baths: 3 Ensuite 1 Private
⇄ ₽ (2) ❏ ✕ Ⅴ ⋒ ⊬

(2 m) *Adrian House Hotel,*
24 Selwyn Road, Eastbourne,
E. Sussex, BN21 2LR.
Family-run hotel. Quiet area
Grades: ETB 3 Cr
Tel: **01323 720372**
Mr & Mrs Miles.
Rates fr: *£17.00-£17.00*.
Open: All Year
Beds: 1F 5D 1T 3S
Baths: 5 Private 2 Shared
⇄ ₽ (10) ❏ ┢ ✕ Ⅲ. Ⅴ

All cycleways are popular: you are well-advised to book ahead

---

Alfriston to Ditchling Beacon

After crossing one of the many English rivers called Ouse into the village of **Southease**, whose church has a circular Saxon tower, a short detour will take you into the pretty town of **Lewes,** site of the 1264 Battle of Lewes between Henry III and Simon de Montfort, and the burning of the Protestant Lewes Martyrs in 1556. Here in the eighteenth century lived the great progressive writer Thomas Paine. Predominantly Georgian, there are older parts including the Norman castle. Several miles after Southease you come to **Ditchling Beacon**, site of an Iron Age fort and close to a Sussex Wildlife Trust nature reserve. A short detour north leads to **Ditchling**, where you will find a house that belonged to Anne of Cleves, who was, for six months in 1540, the

fourth wife of Henry VIII, who fell in love with Holbein's portrait of her only to be disappointed with the real thing. I can't imagine she was less disappointed herself, but at least she fared better than Anne Boleyn and Catherine Howard, in that she came out of it with her neck intact (and, indeed, outlived Henry by ten years and Catherine Parr, his last wife, by nine). A longer detour south will take you into **Brighton**, the hippest town on the South Coast, with a strong arts scene including a major festival in May, and a thriving gay community. The town is famous for the Brighton Pavilion, an extravagant Oriental-Gothic construction built for the Prince Regent by John Nash; also on offer are the Palace Pier and the impressive Sea Life Centre; and the Brighton Museum and Art Gallery houses an interestingly eclectic collection.

The lowest *double* rate per person is shown in *italics*.

(0.5m) *Cuckmere House,* 20 South Cliff Avenue, Eastbourne, E. Sussex, BN20 7AH.
Warm, friendly and comfortable
Tel: **01323 720492**
Mr Dent.
Rates fr: *£19.00*-**£19.00**.
Open: All Year
Beds: 3D 2T 1S
Baths: 6 Private
⌂✕🖾🗹

Jevington 2
National Grid Ref: TQ5601

(0.25m) *Ash Farm,* Filching, Jevington, Polegate, E. Sussex, BN26 5QA.
Actual grid ref: TQ565029
150-year-old Downland farmhouse
Tel: **01323 487335**
Mr Steer.
Fax no: 01323 484474
Rates fr: *£16.50*-**£18.50**.
Open: All Year
Beds: 1F 1D 1T
Baths: 2 Private 1 Shared
🛏🅿(20)✍⌂🛏✕🖾🗹🕯✦

Seaford 3
National Grid Ref: TV4898

(3m) *Silverdale,* 21 Sutton Park Road, Seaford, E. Sussex, BN25 1RH.
Outstanding hospitality & service
Grades: ETB 3 Cr, Comm
Tel: **01323 491849**
Mr Cowdrey.
Fax no: 01323 891131
Rates fr: *£13.00*-**£15.00**.
Open: All Year
Beds: 3F 4D 4T 1S
Baths: 5 Private 3 Shared
🛏🅿(6)⌂🛏✕🖾🛇🗹🕯

The Grid Reference beneath the location heading is for the village or town - *not* for individual houses, which are shown (where supplied) in each entry itself.

Arlington 4
National Grid Ref: TQ5407
🍴🍺Old Oak, Yew Tree

(2.5m) *Bates Green,* Arlington, Polegate, E. Sussex, BN26 6SH.
Actual grid ref: TQ553077
Tile-hung farmhouse, plantsmans' tranquil garden
Grades: AA 5 Q
Tel: **01323 482039** (also fax no)
Mrs McCutchan.
Rates fr: *£22.00*-**£30.00**.
Open: All Year (not Xmas)
Beds: 1D 2T
Baths: 3 Private
🅿(3)✍⌂🖾🗹🕯✦

Alfriston 5
National Grid Ref: TQ5103
🍴🍺Market Cross, George Inn, Smugglers Inn, Wingrove Inn

(▲2.5m) *Alfriston Youth Hostel,* Frog Firle, Alfriston, Polegate, East Sussex, BN26 5TT.
Actual grid ref: TQ518019
Warden: Ms W Nicholls.
Tel: **01323 870423**
Under 18: £5.95 **Adults:** £8.80
Evening Meals Available (6.30pm), Family Bunk Rooms, Television, Showers, Central Heating, Shop
A comfortable Sussex country house dating from 1530, set in Cuckmere Valley with views over river and Litlington

(On route) *Pleasant Rise Farm,* Alfriston, Polegate, E. Sussex, BN26 5TN.
Very quiet, beautiful house - lovely views
Tel: **01323 870545** Mrs Savage.
Rates fr: *£18.50*-**£18.50**.
Open: All Year (not Xmas)
Beds: 2D 1T 1S
Baths: 2 Private
🛏(7)🅿(4)✍⌂🖾🗹🕯✦

(0.5m) *Winton Street Farm Cottage,* Winton Street, Alfriston, Polegate, E. Sussex, BN26 5UH.
Actual grid ref: TQ522038
Comfy beds, substantial breakfasts
Tel: **01323 870118** Mrs Fitch.
Rates fr: *£15.00*-**£15.00**.
Open: All Year
Beds: 1F 1D 1T 1S
Baths: 2 Shared
🛏(5)🅿(2)✍⌂🛏🖾🗹🕯✦

Rodmell 6
National Grid Ref: TQ4105

(On route) *Barn House,* Rodmell, Lewes, E. Sussex, BN7 3HE.
Converted C18th barn
Tel: **01273 477865** Mr Fraser.
Rates fr: *£20.00*-**£25.00**.
Open: Mar to Jan
Beds: 4D 3T 1S **Baths:** 8 Private
🛏🅿(10)✍⌂✕🖾🗹🕯✦

High season, bank holidays and special events mean low availability *everywhere*.

(On route) *Bankside,* Rodmell, Lewes, E. Sussex, BN7 3EZ.
Actual grid ref: TQ410198
Comfortable, converted cart lodge
Tel: **01273 477058**
Mrs Burnaby Davies.
Rates fr: *£16.50*-**£20.00**.
Open: All Year (not Xmas)
Beds: 1F
Baths: 1 Private
🛏⌂🖾🗹🕯✦

Telscombe 7
National Grid Ref: TQ4003

(▲1.5m) *Telscombe Youth Hostel,* Bank Cottages, Telscombe, Lewes, East Sussex, BN7 3HZ.
Actual grid ref: TQ405033
Tel: **01273 301357**
Under 18: £4.95
Adults: £7.20
Self-catering Facilities, Family Bunk Rooms, Showers, Shop, No Smoking
Three 200-year-old cottages combined into one hostel, next to the Norman church in a small unspoilt village in Sussex Downs AONB

The Country Code
Enjoy the countryside and respect its life and work
Guard against all risk of fire
Fasten all gates
Keep your dogs under close control
Keep to public paths across farmland
Use gates and stiles to cross fences, hedges and walls
Leave livestock, crops and machinery alone
Take your litter home
Help to keep all water clean
Protect wildlife, plants and trees
Take special care on country roads
Make no unnecessary noise

Kingston near Lewes   8

National Grid Ref: TQ3908

|O| ⫷ Juggs

(0.25m) *Nightingales, The Avenue, Kingston near Lewes, Lewes, E. Sussex, BN7 3LL.*
Actual grid ref: TQ389083
Marvellous breakfast, lovely garden, quiet. Meet Ben, our black labrador!
Grades: AA 4 Q, Select
Tel: **01273 475673** (also fax no)
Mr Hudson.
Rates fr: *£22.50*-**£20.00**.
Open: All Year
Beds: 1D 1T
Baths: 1 Ensuite 1 Private
⛵ 🄿 (2) ⊬ ⌷ ⵗ ⊞ 🅚 🅥 ≟ ✦

Lewes   9

National Grid Ref: TQ4110

|O| ⫷ Royal Oak, Pelham Arms, Cock Inn, Steward's Enquiry

(2m) *Millers, 134 High Street, Lewes, E. Sussex, BN7 1XS.*
Actual grid ref: TQ411100
Attractive C16th town house
Tel: **01273 475631** Mrs Tammar.
Fax no: 01273 486226
Rates fr: *£25.00*-**£45.00**.
Open: All Year (not Xmas)
Beds: 2D
Baths: 2 Ensuite
⊬ ⌷ ⊞

(3m) *Crink House, Barcombe Mills, Lewes, E. Sussex, BN8 5BJ.*
Victorian farmhouse with panoramic views. Welcoming rural family home
Tel: **01273 400625**
Mrs Gaydon.
Rates fr: *£21.00*-**£28.00**.
Open: All Year (not Xmas)
Beds: 2D 1T
Baths: 3 Ensuite
⛵ 🄿 (10) ⊬ ⌷ ⊞ 🅥

(1.5m) *Castle Banks Cottage, Castle Bank, Lewes, E. Sussex, BN7 1UZ.*
Beamed cottage, pretty garden, quiet lane. Close castle, shops, restaurants
Tel: **01273 476291** (also fax no)
Mrs Wigglesworth.
Rates fr: *£20.00*-**£20.00**.
Open: All Year
Beds: 1T 1S
Baths: 1 Shared
⛵ ⊬ ⊞ 🅥 ✦

All rates are subject to alteration at the owners' discretion.

The lowest double *rate per person is shown in* italics.

(2m) *Felix Gallery, 2 Sun Street, Lewes, E. Sussex, BN7 2QB.*
Modernised period house, town centre
Tel: **01273 472668** Mrs Whitehead.
Rates fr: *£19.00*-**£25.00**.
Open: All Year
Beds: 1T 1S **Baths:** 1 Shared
⛵ (8) ⌷ ⊞ 🅥 ✦

(0.25m) *Grey Tiles, 12 Gundreda Road, Lewes, E. Sussex, BN7 1PX.*
Quiet location, excellent facilities, special rates for longer stays
Tel: **01273 471805** Mr Fuller.
Rates fr: *£19.00.*
Open: All Year
Beds: 1T **Baths:** 1 Private
⛵ (7) 🄿 (3) ⊬ ⌷ ⊞ 🅥 ✦

(1m) *Hillside, Rotten Row, Lewes, E. Sussex, BN7 1TN.*
Central, beautiful views, quiet road
Tel: **01273 473120** Miss Hollins.
Rates fr: *£21.00*-**£20.00**.
Open: All Year
Beds: 1D 1T 1S **Baths:** 1 Ensuite
⛵ (1) 🄿 (3) ⊬ ⌷ ⊞ 🅥 ✦

(2m) *European House, 7 Dorset Road, Lewes, E. Sussex, BN7 1TH.*
Conveniently situated in quiet road
Tel: **01273 476703**
Mr & Mrs Smith.
Rates fr: *£15.00*-**£15.00**.
Open: All Year
Beds: 1T 2S
⛵ (12) 🄿 (0) ⌷ ⊞

(1.5m) *Ousedale House, Offham, Lewes, E. Sussex, BN7 3QF.*
Victorian country house
Tel: **01273 478680**
Mr & Mrs Gough.
Fax no: 01273 486510
Rates fr: *£22.00*-**£24.00**.
Open: All Year **Beds:** 1F 1D 1T
Baths: 2 Ensuite 1 Private
🄿 (17) ⊬ ⌷ ⵗ ⊞ 🅥 ≟ ✦

Plumpton Green   10

National Grid Ref: TQ3616

|O| ⫷ Winning Post, Half Moon

(3m) *Farthings, Station Road, Plumpton Green, Lewes, E. Sussex, BN7 3BY.*
Actual grid ref: TQ365172
Chalet bungalow in village setting
Tel: **01273 890415** Mrs Baker.
Rates fr: *£18.50*-**£20.00**.
Open: All Year (not Xmas)
Beds: 2D 1T
Baths: 1 Ensuite 1 Shared
⛵ (11) 🄿 (5) ⊬ ⌷ ⵗ ✕ ⊞ ≟ ✦

Streat   11

National Grid Ref: TQ3515

(1.5m) *North Acres, Streat, Hassocks, W. Sussex, BN6 8RX.*
Large, quiet Victorian country house
Tel: **01273 890278**
Mr & Mrs Eastwood.
Rates fr: *£15.00*-**£15.00**.
Open: All Year (not Xmas)
Beds: 1F 2T
Baths: 2 Shared
⛵ 🄿 ⊬ ⌷ ⊞ ≟ ✦

Ditchling   12

National Grid Ref: TQ3215

|O| ⫷ White Horse, Blacksmiths' Arms

(1.75m) *Longcroft, Beacon Road, Ditchling, Hassocks, W. Sussex, BN6 8UZ.*
Actual grid ref: GR326147
Beautiful South Downs country house
Tel: **01273 842740**
Mr & Mrs Scull.
Rates fr: *£22.50*-**£28.00**.
Open: All Year
Beds: 2D 1T
Baths: 2 Ensuite 1 Private
⛵ (7) 🄿 (10) ⊬ ⌷ ✕ ⊞ 🅥 ≟ ✦

Clayton   13

National Grid Ref: TQ3014

|O| ⫷ Jack & Jill

(0.25m) *Dower Cottage, Underhill Lane, Clayton, Hassocks, W. Sussex, BN6 9PL.*
Actual grid ref: TQ309136
Tel: **01273 843363**
Mrs Bailey.
Fax no: 01273 846836
Rates fr: *£20.00*-**£25.00**.
Open: All Year (not Xmas)
Beds: 1F 3D 1T 1S
Baths: 2 Ensuite 1 Shared
⛵ 🄿 (8) ⊬ ⌷ ⊞ 🅥 ≟ ✦
Lovely country house in peaceful location near South Downs Way, wonderful views from all rooms. Guest library. Brighton 15 minutes. Gatwick & Newhaven within 30 minutes

Order your packed lunches the *evening before* you need them. Not at breakfast!

Patcham 14

National Grid Ref: TQ3008

(▲ 3.5m) *Brighton Youth Hostel, Patcham Place, London Road, Patcham, Brighton, East Sussex, BN1 8YD.*
Actual grid ref: TQ300088
Warden: Mrs S Vanossi.
Tel: **01273 556196**
Under 18: £6.55
Adults: £9.75
Evening Meals Available (7pm), Family Bunk Rooms, Television, Games Room, Showers, Shop, Security Lockers, Parking
Splendid country house with Queen Anne front, on the edge of Brighton and the South Downs

Hurstpierpoint 15

National Grid Ref: TQ2816

¶ ◀ New Inn

(2.5m) *Wickham Place, Wickham Drive, Hurstpierpoint, Hassocks, W. Sussex, BN6 9AP.*
Ideally situated in a pretty village
Tel: **01273 832172**
Mrs Moore.
Rates fr: *£18.50*-**£22.00.**
Open: All Year (not Xmas)
Beds: 1D 2T
Baths: 1 Shared
 ⌂ ▣ (5) ⚡ ⌷ ⊶ ▦.

Poynings 16

National Grid Ref: TQ2612

(0.25m) *Manor Farm, Poynings, Brighton, E. Sussex, BN45 7AG.*
Comfortable farmhouse on working farm
Tel: **01273 857371** (also fax no)
Mrs Revell.
Rates fr: *£22.00*-**£25.00.**
Open: Mar to Dec
Beds: 1D 2T
Baths: All Ensuite
 ⌂ (8) ▣ (6) ⚡ ⌷ ✕ ▦. ▮ ⚡

Fulking 17

National Grid Ref: TQ2411

¶ ◀ Shepherd & Dog, Royal Oak

(1.75m) *Downers Vineyard, Clappers Lane, Fulking, Henfield, W. Sussex, BN5 9NH.*
Actual grid ref: TQ247128
Panoramic views, Brighton 8 miles, Gatwick 23 miles, South Downs Way nearby
Grades: ETB Listed
Tel: **01273 857484**
Mrs Downer.
Fax no: 01273 857068
Rates fr: *£17.00*-**£20.00.**
Open: All Year (not Xmas)
Beds: 1D 1T
Baths: 2 Shared
▣ (6) ⌷ ⊶ ▦. ⚡

All details shown are as supplied by B&B owners in Autumn 1997.

Truleigh Hill 18

National Grid Ref: TQ2210

(▲ On route) *Truleigh Hill Youth Hostel, Tottington Barn, Truleigh Hill, Shoreham-by-Sea, West Sussex, BN43 5FB.*
Actual grid ref: TQ220105
Warden: Mr A Harris.
Tel: **01903 813419**
Under 18: £5.95 **Adults:** £8.80
Evening Meals Available (7pm), Family Bunk Rooms, Television, Showers, Shop
Modern hostel in the Sussex Downs AONB with conservation project and old dew pond in grounds

---

Pay B&Bs by cash or cheque and be prepared to pay up front.

Lancing 19

National Grid Ref: TQ1804

(3m) *The Moorings, 71 Brighton Road, Lancing, W. Sussex, BN15 8RB.*
1930s house on seafront
Tel: **01903 755944** Mr Stuart.
Rates fr: *£15.00*-**£15.00.**
Open: All Year (not Xmas)
Beds: 1F 1D 1T 1S
Baths: 1 Shared
 ⌂ ▣ ⌷ ⊶ ▦. ♡ ⚡

All cycleways are popular: you are well-advised to book ahead

---

Bramber 20

National Grid Ref: TQ1810

¶ ◀ Castle Hotel

(1m) *Castle Hotel, The Street, Bramber, Steyning, W. Sussex, BN44 3WE.*
Actual grid ref: TQ189106
Spacious, characterful, romantic, friendly inn
Tel: **01903 812102** Mrs Mitchell.
Fax no: 01903 816711
Rates fr: *£17.00*-**£22.00.**
Open: All Year **Beds:** 2F 4D 2T
Baths: 6 Ensuite 4 Shared
 ⌂ ▣ (20) ⚡ ⌷ ⊶ ✕ ▦. ▮ ⚡

Ditchling Beacon to Buriton

After Ditchling Beacon you cross into West Sussex and come to **Pyecombe**, before passing Devil's Dyke, a deep valley formed in the Ice Age with an Iron Age fort, en route to **Upper Beeding**, with the Saxon Botolphs Church and a ruined Norman castle at Bramber nearby. A little after this the route joins the road between Worthing and Steyning and juts north before leaving the road and passing close to another Iron Age hill fort, Chanctonbury Ring, which is topped with a coronet of trees. Past Washington, the route leads to the village of **Amberley**, which has a twin-towered castle gatehouse and a number of attractive pubs, before passing between two chalk pits. The village hosts the Chalk Pits Museum, including a narrow-gauge quarry railway. After Amberley and **Houghton**, a detour along a bridleway is possible to **Bignor**, where there is a Roman villa with mosaic floors on show. The way now crosses Stane Street, the Roman route from London to Chichester, and there are magnificent views southwards to Chichester Cathedral and the sea. The next stretch is a long wooded section of the Downs, which takes you to **Cocking**, over **Pen Hill**, around **Beacon Hill** and on to **Harting Hill**, before crossing the border into Hampshire. Queen Elizabeth Country Park, by **Buriton**, is a beautiful woodland area which has an ancient farm with a reconstruction Iron Age settlement.

Steyning 21

National Grid Ref: TQ1711

🍴 🍺 Star Inn

(0.75m) **5 Coxham Lane**, *Steyning, W. Sussex, BN44 3LG.*
Comfortable house in quiet lane
Tel: **01903 812286** Mrs Morrow.
Rates fr: *£15.00*-**£15.00**.
Open: All Year (not Xmas)
Beds: 2T 1S
Baths: 1 Shared
🅿 (4) 🐾 📺, Ⅵ ⓐ ✦

(1m) **Milestones**, *25 High Street, Steyning, W. Sussex, BN44 3YE.*
Located on edge of South Downs
Tel: **01903 812338** Mrs Wood.
Rates fr: *£20.00*-**£18.00**.
Open: All Year (not Xmas)
Beds: 1D 1T 1S
Baths: 3 Private
🅿 (1) ⊬ 🖵 ✗ 📺, Ⅵ ⓐ

(1.25m) **The Old Museum House**, *93 High Street, Steyning, W. Sussex, BN44 3RE.*
Comfortable Georgian house, home produce
Tel: **01903 812317** Mrs Dawson.
Rates fr: *£17.00*-**£20.00**.
Open: All Year (not Xmas)
Beds: 1D 1T
Baths: 2 Shared
🅿 (3) ⊬ 🖵 📺, Ⅵ ✦

Wiston 22

National Grid Ref: TQ1414

(1m) **Buncton Manor Farm**, *Steyning Road, Wiston, Steyning, W. Sussex, BN44 3DD.*
Actual grid ref: TQ146136
C15th farmhouse on working farm
Tel: **01903 812736**
Mrs Rowland.
Rates fr: *£19.00*-**£23.00**.
Open: All Year
Beds: 1F 1T
Baths: 1 Shared
🛏 🅿 (6) 🖵 ✗ 📺, Ⅵ ⓐ ✦

Findon 23

National Grid Ref: TQ1208

🍴 🍺 Village House Hotel

(2.5m) **Racehorse Cottage**, *Nepcote, Findon, Worthing, W Sussex, BN14 0SN.*
Actual grid ref: TQ128083
Comfortable cottage under Cissbury Ring
Tel: **01903 873783** Mr Lloyd.
Rates fr: *£16.00*-**£20.00**.
Open: All Year (not Xmas)
Beds: 2T **Baths:** 1 Shared
🛏 (5) 🅿 (2) 🖵 🐾 ✗ 📺, Ⅵ ✦

(2m) **Findon Tower**, *Cross Lane, Findon, Worthing, W Sussex, BN14 0UG.*
Actual grid ref: TQ123083
Elegant Edwardian country house
Grades: ETB 2 Cr, Comm
Tel: **01903 873870**
Mr & Mrs Smith.
Rates fr: *£17.50*-**£25.00**.
Open: All Year (not Xmas)
Beds: 2D 1T
Baths: 2 Ensuite 1 Private
🛏 🅿 (10) ⊬ 🐾 📺, Ⅵ ⓐ ✦

Storrington 24

National Grid Ref: TQ0814

🍴 🍺 Frankland Arms, Anchor Inn, Old Forge, Bridge Inn

(1.5m) **Willow Tree Cottage**, *Washington Road, Storrington, Pulborough, W. Sussex, RH20 4AF.*
Actual grid ref: TQ104134
Tel: **01903 740835** Mrs Smith.
Fax no: 01903 262277
Rates fr: *£20.00*-**£20.00**.
Open: All Year (not Xmas)
Beds: 2D 1T
Baths: 4 Private
🛏 🅿 (10) ⊬ 🖵 🐾 📺, Ⅵ ⓐ ✦
Welcoming, friendly, quiet. All rooms ensuite. Colour TV, tea-making facilities. Situated at foot of Sussex Downs. Arundel, Worthing 10 minutes. Children & dogs welcome

(1.75m) **No 1, Lime Chase (Off Fryern Road)**, *Storrington, Pulborough, W. Sussex, RH20 4LX.*
Actual grid ref: TQ089147
Secluded luxury in Area of Outstanding Natural Beauty
Grades: ETB Listed, High Comm
Tel: **01903 740437** (also fax no)
Mrs Warton.
Rates fr: *£20.00*-**£20.00**.
Open: All Year (not Xmas)
Beds: 1F 1T 1S
Baths: 1 Ensuite 1 Shared
🛏 (10) 🅿 (5) ⊬ 🖵 📺, 🖐 Ⅵ ⓐ ✦

(2.25m) **Oakfield House**, *Merrywood Lane, Thakeham, Storrington, Pulborough, W. Sussex, RH20 3HD.*
Actual grid ref: TQ1015
Modern, comfortable, delightful countryside home
Tel: **01903 740843**
Mrs Arter.
Rates fr: *£18.00*-**£17.00**.
Open: All Year (not Xmas)
Beds: 1D 2S
Baths: 1 Private 1 Shared
🅿 (3) ⊬ 🖵 📺, Ⅵ ⓐ ✦

West Chiltington 25

National Grid Ref: TQ0918

🍴 🍺 Queen's Head, Elephant & Castle

(3m) **New House Farm**, *Broadford Bridge Road, West Chiltington, Pulborough, W. Sussex, RH20 2LA.*
Actual grid ref: TQ089184
Grades: ETB 2 Cr, Comm
Tel: **01798 812215**
Ms Steele.
Rates fr: *£20.00*-**£25.00**.
Open: Jan to Nov
Beds: 1D 2T
Baths: 3 Private
🛏 (10) 🅿 (6) 🖵 📺.
Comfortable beamed farmhouse with log fires in winter. Many places of historical interest nearby. Nearest coast 10 miles (Worthing) 35 mins drive Gatwick. Off road parking

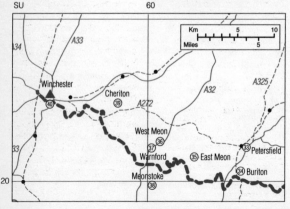

The Grid Reference beneath the location heading is for the village or town - *not* for individual houses, which are shown (where supplied) in each entry itself.

Amberley 26

National Grid Ref: TQ0313

¶ ◀ The Sportsman, Black Horse

(0.75m) *Woodybanks, Crossgates, Amberley, Arundel, W. Sussex, BN18 9NR.*
Actual grid ref: TQ041136
Nestling in the South Downs, panoramic views across Wildbrooks
Tel: 01798 831295 Mrs Hardy.
Rates fr: *£16.50-£20.00.*
Open: All Year (not Xmas)
Beds: 1T 1D
🛏 🅿 (3) ⊬ ♐ 🕮 ♿ Ⓥ 🛆 ⚡

(1m) *Bacons, Amberley, Arundel, W. Sussex, BN18 9NJ.*
Pretty old cottage
Tel: 01798 831234 Mrs Jollands.
Rates fr: *£17.00-£17.00.*
Open: All Year (not Xmas)
Beds: 2T **Baths:** 1 Shared
🛏 🕮

Warningcamp 27

National Grid Ref: TQ0306

(🔺 3.5m) *Arundel Youth Hostel, Warningcamp, Arundel, West Sussex, BN18 9QY.*
Actual grid ref: TQ032076
Warden: Mr M Hiles.
Tel: 0101903 882204
Under 18: £5.95 **Adults:** £8.80
Evening Meals Available (7pm), Family Bunk Rooms, Television, Games Room, Showers, Shop
Georgian building 1.5 miles from ancient town of Arundel, dominated by its castle & the South Downs

Arundel 28

National Grid Ref: TQ0106

¶ ◀ Six Bells, White Hart, The Spur, Plough & Sail

(3m) *Bridge House, 18 Queen Street, Arundel, W. Sussex, BN18 9JG.*
Actual grid ref: TQ020069
C18th family-run guest house
Grades: ETB 3 Cr, Comm
Tel: 01903 882142
Freecall: 0500 323224
Mr Hutchinson.
Fax no: 01903 883600
Rates fr: *£15.00-£20.00.*
Open: All Year (not Xmas)
Beds: 6F 9D 2T 2S
Baths: 15 Private 4 Shared
🛏 🅿 (10) 🞐 ♐ ✕ 🕮 Ⓥ 🛆 ⚡

All cycleways are popular: you are well-advised to book ahead

---

Many rates vary according to season - the lowest only are shown here

---

(3m) *Portreeves Acre, The Causeway, Arundel, W. Sussex, BN18 9JL.*
Actual grid ref: TQ0207
Modern house beside River Arun
Tel: 01903 883277 Mr Rogers.
Rates fr: *£18.00-£20.00.*
Open: All Year (not Xmas)
Beds: 2D 1T
Baths: 3 Private
🛏 (8) 🅿 (7) 🞐 ♐ 🕮 Ⓥ ⚡

Slindon 29

National Grid Ref: SU9608

¶ ◀ Newburgh Arms, The Spur

(2.75m) *Mill Lane House, Mill Lane, Slindon, Arundel, W. Sussex, BN18 0RP.*
Actual grid ref: SU964084
House & Coach House, quiet location. Superb views to coast
Grades: ETB 2 Cr, Comm
Tel: 01243 814440 Mrs Fuente.
Rates fr: *£20.00-£26.00.*
Open: All Year
Beds: 2F 2D 2T 1S
Baths: 7 Ensuite
🛏 🅿 (7) 🞐 ♐ ✕ 🕮 ♿ Ⓥ 🛆 ⚡

Duncton 30

National Grid Ref: SU9517

¶ ◀ The Cricketers, The Forresters

(1.5m) *Drifters, Duncton, Petworth, W. Sussex, GU28 0JZ.*
Lovely, friendly modern house. Welcome to a comfortable friendly house overlooking countryside
Tel: 01798 342706 Mrs Folkes.
Rates fr: *£17.00-£21.00.*
Open: All Year
Beds: 1D 2T 1S
Baths: 1 Ensuite 1 Shared
🅿 (3) ⊬ ♐ ✕ 🕮 🛆 ⚡

Cocking 31

National Grid Ref: SU8717

(0.25m) *Cocking Village Tea Rooms, Chichester Road, Cocking, Midhurst, W. Sussex, GU29 0HN.*
1815 house with tea garden
Tel: 01730 813336 Mrs Thomas.
Rates fr: *£18.00-£24.00.*
Open: All Year (not Xmas)
Beds: 2D 1T
Baths: 1 Shared
🛏 🅿 (5) 🕮 🛆 ⚡

Midhurst 32

National Grid Ref: SU8821

¶ ◀ Crown Inn

(3m) *The Crown Inn, Edinburgh Square, Midhurst, W. Sussex, GU29 9NL.*
Actual grid ref: SU887215
C16th free house, real ales, log fires. home cooked food
Grades: ETB Listed
Tel: 01730 813462 Mr Stevens.
Rates fr: *£15.00-£17.50.*
Open: All Year
Beds: 1D 1T 1S **Baths:** 1 Shared
⊬ 🞐 ♐ ✕ 🕮 Ⓥ 🛆 ⚡

The lowest *double* rate per person is shown in *italics.*

Buriton to Winchester

The meandering path through Hampshire takes you on from **Butser Hill** to **Old Winchester Hill**, where there is an Iron Age fort, a nature reserve and a viewpoint from which you can see to the Isle of Wight in clear weather. After Exton you climb towards another **Beacon Hill**, with superb views over the Meon Valley. The final stretch leads to **Telegraph Hill** and Chilcomb, with its early Saxon church, and into **Winchester**. The ancient capital of the kingdom of Wessex, the end of Saxon hegemony was confirmed here by the coronation of Norman King William the Conqueror, whose son William Rufus is buried in the cathedral, as is Jane Austen. Built over centuries, the cathedral is a hotch-potch of Norman, Gothic and Perpendicular. The city goes back further, evidenced by the Iron Age fort overlooking it and a remaining part of the Roman wall. Other sights include Wolvesey Castle and the City and Westgate Museums.

Petersfield 33

National Grid Ref: SU7423

|O| ⌕ Five Bells, Good Intent

(4m) *Ridgefield, Station Road, Petersfield, Hants, GU32 3DE.*
Actual grid ref: SU743237
Friendly family atmosphere, near town & station; Portsmouth ferries: 20 mins drive
Tel: 01730 261402 Mrs West.
Rates fr: *£18.00*-**£18.00**.
Open: All Year (not Xmas)
Beds: 1D 2T
Baths: 2 Shared
⌂ ℙ (4) ⌀ ⌂ ▥ ⌖ Ⓥ ⌀

(4m) *Heath Farmhouse, Sussex Road, Petersfield, Hants, GU31 4HU.*
Actual grid ref: SU7522
Pretty Georgian farmhouse, lovely views, quiet surroundings, near town
Grades: ETB 2 Cr, Comm
Tel: 01730 264709
Mrs Scurfield.
Rates fr: *£17.00*-**£20.00**.
Open: All Year (not Xmas)
Beds: 1D 1T
Baths: 1 Ensuite 1 Shared
⌂ ℙ (4) ⌂ ▥ Ⓥ ⌀

Buriton 34

National Grid Ref: SU7320

(0.25m) *Pilmead House, North Lane, Buriton, Petersfield, Hants, GU31 5RS.*
Stone-built Victorian family house
Tel: 01730 266795 Mrs Moss.
Rates fr: *£18.50*-**£20.00**.
Open: All Year
Beds: 1D 1T
⌂ ℙ (3) ⌀ ⌂ ⌂ ✕ ▥ Ⓥ ⌀ ⌀

East Meon 35

National Grid Ref: SU6822

|O| ⌕ Old George, Issac Walton, Thomas Lord

(On route) *Coombe Cross House, Coombe Road, East Meon, Petersfield, Hants, GU32 1HQ.*
Actual grid ref: SU667210
Good walks around area, fishing, good golf courses, riding
Grades: ETB Listed
Tel: 01730 823298 Mrs Bulmer.
Fax no: 01730 823515
Rates fr: *£25.00*-**£30.00**.
Open: All Year (not Xmas)
Beds: 1D 2T
Baths: 2 Private 1 Shared
⌂ (8) ℙ (12) ⌂ ✕ ▥ Ⓥ ⌀ ⌀

The lowest *double* rate per person is shown in *italics*.

Please respect a B&B's wishes regarding children, animals & smoking.

(0.75m) *Drayton Cottage, East Meon, Petersfield, Hants, GU32 1PW.*
Actual grid ref: SU669232
Beamed cottage overlooking River Meon
Grades: ETB Listed, High Comm
Tel: 01730 823472 Mrs Rockett.
Rates fr: *£20.00*-**£22.00**.
Open: All Year
Beds: 1T 1D
Baths: 1 Ensuite 1 Private
⌂ (9) ℙ (3) ⌂ ✕ ▥ Ⓥ ⌀ ⌀

West Meon 36

National Grid Ref: SU6424

|O| ⌕ Thomas Lord Inn, Red Lion, The Shire

(2.25m) *Brocklands Farm, West Meon, Petersfield, Hants, GU32 1JN.*
Actual grid ref: SU639237
Secluded modern farmhouse in Meon Valley. Traditionally furnished. Outstanding views
Grades: ETB Listed, Comm
Tel: 01730 829228 Mrs Wilson.
Rates fr: *£18.00*-**£18.00**.
Open: All Year (not Xmas)
Beds: 2D 1T
Baths: 2 Shared
ℙ (6) ⌀ ⌂ ⌂ ▥ Ⓥ ⌀ ⌀

(1.5m) *The Court House, West Meon, Petersfield, Hants, GU32 1JG.*
Old manor house in beautiful village. Countryside walks. Family atmosphere
Grades: ETB Listed
Tel: 01730 829336 Mrs Traill.
Rates fr: *£15.00*-**£20.00**.
Open: All Year
Beds: 1F 1T 2D 1S
Baths: 3 Shared
⌂ ℙ (8) ⌂ ⌂ ✕ ▥ Ⓥ ⌀ ⌀

Warnford 37

National Grid Ref: SU6223

|O| ⌕ George & Falcon

(1m) *Hayden Barn Cottage, Warnford, Southampton, Hants, SO32 3LF.*
Actual grid ref: SU634229
Real hospitality and comfort, surrounded by beautiful garden and countryside
Grades: ETB 2 Cr, High Comm
Tel: 01730 829454 Mrs Broadbent.
Rates fr: *£20.00*-**£19.00**.
Open: Mar to Jan
Beds: 2T
Baths: 1 Ensuite 1 Private
⌂ ℙ (5) ⌀ ⌂ ▥ Ⓥ ⌀ ⌀

Meonstoke 38

National Grid Ref: SU6119

|O| ⌕ The Shoe, Buck's Head

(On route) *Harvestgate Farm, Stocks Lane, Meonstoke, Southampton, Hants, SO32 3NQ.*
Actual grid ref: SU627201
Modernised farmhouse in beautiful countryside
Tel: 01489 877675
Mrs Allan.
Rates fr: *£20.00*-**£20.00**.
Open: Apr to Sep
Beds: 1D 1T
Baths: 2 Ensuite
⌂ (15) ℙ (5) ⌀ ⌂ ▥ ⌖ Ⓥ

Cheriton 39

National Grid Ref: SU5828

(2.5m) *Brandy Lea, Cheriton, Alresford, Hants, SO24 0QQ.*
Friendly semi-detached next to pub
Tel: 01962 771534
Mrs Hoskings.
Rates fr: *£13.50*-**£13.50**.
Open: All Year
Beds: 1T
Baths: 1 Private
⌂ ℙ ⌂ ⌂ ▥

Winchester 40

National Grid Ref: SU4829

|O| ⌕ Bell Inn, Wykeham Arms, Roebuck Inn, King's Head, White Horse, The Queen, King Alfred, Willow Tree, Fox & Hounds, Cart & Horses, Stanmore Hotel

(▲ On route) *Winchester Youth Hostel, The City Mill, 1 Water Lane, Winchester, Hampshire, SO23 8EJ.*
Actual grid ref: SU486293
Warden: Mr L Garvin.
Tel: **01962 853723**
Under 18: £5.95
Adults: £8.80
Evening Meals Available (7pm), Family Bunk Rooms, Showers, No Smoking
Charming C18th watermill (NT) straddling the River Itchen at East End of King Alfred's capital

(1m) *5 Ranelagh Road, Winchester, Hants, SO23 9TA.*
Actual grid ref: SU476287
Grades: ETB 2 Cr, Comm
Tel: **01962 869555**
Mr Farrell.
Rates fr: *£17.00*-**£18.00**.
Open: All Year (not Xmas)
Beds: 1F 1D 1T 1S
Baths: 2 Private 2 Shared
⌂ (5) ℙ (1) ⌀ ⌂ ▥ ⌀
Turn of the century Victorian villa, furnished in that style. We are close to the Cathedral and like to share our love of Winchester with our guests

(1m) *85 Christchurch Road,*
Winchester, Hants, so23 9QY.
Actual grid ref: SU473282
Comfortable detached Victorian
family house. Convenient base for
Hampshire sightseeing
Grades: ETB 2 Cr, Comm
Tel: 01962 868661 (also fax no)
Mrs Fetherston-Dilke.
Rates fr: *£21.00-£20.00.*
Open: All Year (not Xmas)
Beds: 1D 1T 1S
Baths: 2 Ensuite 1 Shared
🛏 🅿 (3) 🚫🚪 🏞 Ⅴ ✦

(1.5m) *54 St Cross Road,*
Winchester, Hants, so23 9PS.
Victorian family house, near water
meadows
Grades: ETB Listed, Comm
Tel: 01962 852073 (also fax no)
Mrs Blockley.
Rates fr: *£18.50-£20.00.*
Open: All Year
Beds: 1D 1T 1S **Baths:** 1 Shared
🛏 (5) 🅿 (2) 🚫🚪 🏞

Bringing children with you? Always ask for any special rates.

(1.5m) *Sycamores, 4 Bereweeke*
Close, Winchester, Hants, so22 6AR.
Actual grid ref: SU472304
Convenient but peaceful location
about 2km/1m north-west of city
centre
Grades: ETB Listed, Comm
Tel: 01962 867242 Mrs Edwards.
Fax no: 01962 620300
Rates fr: *£18.00.* **Open:** All Year
Beds: 2D 1T **Baths:** 3 Private
🅿 (3) 🚫🚪 🏞 Ⅴ

(1m) *32 Hyde Street, Winchester,*
Hants, so23 7DX.
Actual grid ref: SU481301
Attractive C18th town house, close
to city centre
Grades: ETB 1 Cr, Approv
Tel: 01962 851621 Mrs Tisdall.
Rates fr: *£16.00-£19.00.*
Open: All Year (not Xmas)
Beds: 1F 1D **Baths:** 1 Shared
🛏 🚫🚪 🏞

(3m) *The Lilacs, 1 Harestock*
Close, Off Andover Road North,
Winchester, Hants, so23 6NP.
Actual grid ref: SU468321
Attractive Georgian-style family
home. **Tel: 01962 884122** Mrs Pell.
Rates fr: *£16.00-£19.00.*
Open: All Year (not Xmas)
Beds: 1F 1D 1T
Baths: 1 Private 1 Shared
🛏 🅿 (2) 🚫🚪 🐾 🏞 Ⅴ ⚓ ✦

All cycleways are popular: you are well-advised to book ahead

---

(On route) *Brambles, Northbrook*
Avenue, Winchester, Hants,
so23 0JW.
Actual grid ref: SU492294
Delightful self-contained studio flat
Grades: ETB Listed, High Comm
Tel: 01962 856387 Mrs Meadows.
Rates fr: *£18.00-£25.00.*
Open: All Year
Beds: 1F **Baths:** 1 Private
🛏 🅿 (2) 🚫🚪 🏞 Ⅴ ⚓ ✦

(1m) *Dellbrook, Hubert Road,*
St Cross, Winchester, Hants,
so23 9RG.
Actual grid ref: SU474278
Spacious welcoming Edwardian
family home
Grades: ETB 2 Cr, Comm
Tel: 01962 865093 (also fax no)
Mrs Leonard.
Rates fr: *£19.00-£26.00.*
Open: All Year
Beds: 1F 2T
Baths: 2 Ensuite 1 Shared
🛏 🅿 (4) 🚪 🐾 ✗ 🏞 Ⅴ ✦

Surrey Cycleway

At 86 miles, the **Surrey Cycleway** is the shortest featured in this book. It is in fact a circular tour of the southeast of the county, over the chalk escarpment that is the North Downs and then through the southern woodlands - steering well clear of London. The route runs anticlockwise and is signposted by brown Surrey Cycleway direction signs with a cycle silhouette; the description that follows starts and finishes at Boxhill and Westhumble Railway Station.

A detailed **guide leaflet** to the cycleway route, which includes a list of cycle repair/hire shops on or near to the route, is available free from the County Cycling Officer, Surrey County Council, County Hall, Kingston-upon-Thames KT1 2DN, tel 0181-541 8044.

Maps: Ordnance Survey 1:50,000 Landranger series: 186, 187

Surrey is well-connected by **train** to London and everywhere else in the Southeast. Trains to Boxhill and Westhumble, as well as many other locations, connect to Clapham Junction.

Westhumble   1

National Grid Ref: TQ1651

¶⌖ ◧ Stepping Stones

(0.25m) *Treetops*, *Pilgrims Way, Westhumble, Dorking, Surrey, RH5 6AP*.
Quiet, friendly, detached house overlooking Boxhill
Grades: ETB Listed
Tel: 01306 883905 Miss Wood.
Rates fr: *£17.50*-**£25.00**.
Open: All Year (not Xmas)
Beds: 1D **Baths:** 1 Shared
🄿⌅◻✕🞔.Ⅴ♦⚡

Dorking   2

National Grid Ref: TQ1649

¶⌖ ◧ King William, The Bush, King's Arms, Old School House

(1m) *The Waltons*, *5 Rose Hill, Dorking, Surrey, RH4 2EG*.
Listed house in conservation area. Beautiful views and friendly atmosphere
Grades: ETB Listed
Tel: 01306 883127 Mrs Walton.
Rates fr: *£17.50*-**£20.00**.
Open: All Year
Beds: 2F 1D 1T **Baths:** 3 Shared
🗢🄿(3)⌅◻🞔✕🞔.Ⅴ♦⚡

The lowest *double* rate per person is shown in *italics*.

(1m) *Shrub Hill*, *3 Calvert Road, Dorking, Surrey, RH4 1LT*.
Actual grid ref: TQ167504
Convenient, comfortable, quiet family home, 400 yards to main line station
Tel: 01306 885229
Mrs Scott Kerr.
Rates fr: *£22.00*-**£22.00**.
Open: All Year (not Xmas)
Beds: 1T 1S 1D
Baths: 1 Shared 1 Ensuite
🗢(5)🄿(2)⌅◻🞔🞔.Ⅴ

(1m) *Highbank*, *1 Townfield Road, Dorking, Surrey, RH4 2HX*.
Family home - central - lovely views
Tel: 01306 888135
Mrs Paul.
Rates fr: *£20.00*-**£20.00**.
Open: All Year
Beds: 1T 1S
Baths: 1 Private 1 Shared
◻🞔.

(1m) *Torridon Guest House*, *Longfield Road, Dorking, Surrey, RH4 3DF*.
Large chalet bungalow - quiet location
Grades: ETB Listed, Comm
Tel: 01306 883724
Mrs Short.
Fax no: 01306 880759
Rates fr: *£18.00*-**£22.00**.
Open: All Year
Beds: 1D 1T 1S
Baths: 1 Shared
🗢🄿(2)⌅◻🞔✕🞔.♿Ⅴ⚡

Westcott   3

National Grid Ref: TQ1448

¶⌖ ◧ The Crown, Prince of Wales, Wotton Hatch

(0.5m) *The Dene*, *Hole Hill, Westcott, Dorking, Surrey, RH4 3LS*.
Actual grid ref: TQ136491
Large country house in seven acres
Tel: 01306 885595 Mrs King.
Rates fr: *£15.00*-**£20.00**.
Open: All Year (not Xmas)
Beds: 1F 1D 2T
Baths: 2 Shared
🗢🄿(10)◻🞔✕🞔.♦⚡

Abinger Hammer   4

National Grid Ref: TQ0947

¶⌖ ◧ Wootton Hatch

(0.25m) *Crossways Farm*, *Raikes Lane, Abinger Hammer, Dorking, Surrey, RH5 6PZ*.
Listed C17th farmhouse
Tel: 01306 730173 Mrs Hughes.
Rates fr: *£17.00*-**£21.00**.
Open: Mar to Nov
Beds: 1F 1D 1T
Baths: 1 Private 1 Shared
🗢🄿(3)⌅◻🞔.♦⚡

Bringing children with you? Always ask for any special rates.

Abinger Common 5

National Grid Ref: TQ1145

⚲ ◐ Stephan Langton

(2m) *Leylands Farm*, *Sheephouse Lane, Abinger Common, Dorking, Surrey, RH5 6JU.*
Actual grid ref: TQ132456
Self-contained annexe of period farmhouse
Grades: ETB Listed, High Comm
Tel: **01306 730115** Mrs Eshelby.
Fax no: 01306 881287
Rates fr: *£20.00-***£35.00**.
Open: All Year (not Xmas)
Beds: 2F
Baths: 1 Ensuite
🛏 🅿 (4) �🖉 ⛌ 🖴

Holmbury St Mary 6

National Grid Ref: TQ1144

⚲ ◐ Royal Oak, Parrot Inn, The Volunteer

(▲ 2m) *Holmbury St Mary Youth Hostel, Radnor Lane, Holmbury St Mary, Dorking, Surrey, RH5 6NW.*
Actual grid ref: TQ104450
Warden: Mr G Jervis.
Tel: **01306 730777**
Under 18: £5.95 **Adults:** £8.80
Evening Meals Available (7pm),
Self-catering Facilities, Family
Bunk Rooms, Grounds Available
for Games, Showers, Parking,
Camping Facilities, No Smoking
*Set in its own 5000 acres of wood-
land grounds, this purpose-built
hostel offers tranquil beauty among
the Surrey Hills*

(2m) *Woodhill Cottage, Holmbury
St Mary, Dorking, Surrey, RH5 6NL.*
Actual grid ref: TQ108453
Comfortable country family home
Tel: **01306 730498** Mrs McCann.
Rates fr: *£17.00-***£20.00**.
Open: All Year
Beds: 1F 1D 1T
Baths: 1 Ensuite 2 Shared
🛏 🅿 (3) �🖉 ⭐ ✕ 🖴 Ⓥ ⚘

Westhumble to Bramley

The first part of the route takes you to **Ranmore Common**; nearby stands **Polesden Lacey**, an elegant Regency house with a collection of furniture, silverware, porcelain and paintings amassed in Edwardian times and a country estate with landscaped walks. Cycling around the White Downs and Hackhurst Downs, you come to **Shere**, an old village whose name means 'clear stream', from the brook that runs through it, and then **Wonersh** and **Bramley**. A detour north will take you to **Guildford**, the county town, noted for its cobbled High Street with Georgian architecture, as well as one or two older buildings - the Guildhall dates from Tudor times but has a Restoration facade with a gilded clock dated 1683. Also on the High Street is Guildford House Gallery, a restored seventeenth-century house displaying pictures and craftwork. There is also a small ruined Norman castle, and the red-brick cathedral dating from 1954. Just outside Guildford to the east is Clandon Park, a house dating from c1730 whose grand Palladian exterior contrasts with the Baroque ceiling of the Marble Hall.

All rooms full and nowhere else to stay? Ask the owner if there's anywhere nearby

(2m) *Bulmer Farm, Holmbury
St Mary, Dorking, Surrey, RH5 6LG.*
Actual grid ref: TQ114441
Quiet modernised C17th
farmhouse/barn
Grades: ETB 2 Cr, Comm
Tel: **01306 730210** Mrs Hill.
Rates fr: *£18.00-£19.00*.
Open: All Year
Beds: 3D 5T
Baths: 5 Private 2 Shared
🛏 (12) 🅿 (12) ⭐ 🖉 ⛌ ⭐ 🖴 ⚘ Ⓥ ⚘

Shere 7

National Grid Ref: TQ0747

⚲ ◐ White Horse, Prince of Wales, The Compasses

(0.5m) *Lockhurst Hatch Farm,
Lockhurst Hatch Lane, Shere,
Guildford, Surrey, GU5 9JN.*
Actual grid ref: TQ067449
Listed farmhouse set in own
secluded valley in Surrey Hills
Tel: **01483 202689** Mrs Gellatley.
Rates fr: *£18.00-£22.00*.
Open: All Year (not Xmas)
Beds: 1F 1T **Baths:** 1 Shared
🛏 🅿 ⛌ 🖉 ✕ ⚘ ⚘

The *lowest* **single** rate *is shown in* **bold**.

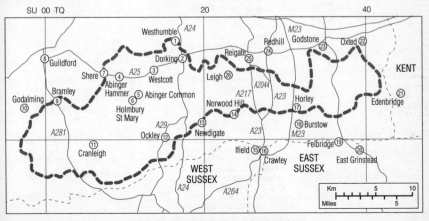

(On route) **Manor Cottage**, *Shere, Guildford, Surrey, GU5 9JE.*
C16th cottage in beautiful village
Grades: ETB Listed
Tel: 01483 202979 Mrs James.
Rates fr: *£16.00*-**£18.00**.
Open: Easter to Oct
Beds: 1D 1S
Baths: 1 Shared
🛏 (6) �P 🖾 V ✦

(On route) **Cherry Trees**, *Gomshall, Shere, Guildford, Surrey, GU5 9HE.*
Actual grid ref: TQ072487
Quiet comfortable home, beautiful garden set in lovely old village
Tel: 01483 202288 Mrs Warren.
Rates fr: *£19.50*-**£19.50**.
Open: Jan to Nov
Beds: 1D 2T 1S
Baths: 2 Private 1 Shared
🛏 P (4) 🖾 ☐ 🖾 ▪ ✦

Guildford   8

National Grid Ref: SU9949

🍴 🍺 King's Head, Jolly Farmer

(3m) **Atkinsons Guest House**, *129 Stoke Road, Guildford, Surrey, GU1 1ET.*
Tel: 01483 38260 Mrs Atkinson.
Rates fr: *£18.50*-**£22.00**.
Open: All Year
Beds: 1F 1D 1T 1S
Baths: 2 Ensuite 1 Shared
🛏 (6) P (2) ☐ 🖾.
Small comfortable family-run guest house close to town centre & all local amenities. All rooms with colour TV, hairdriers etc. Some ensuites available

(3m) **Weybrook House**, *113 Stoke Road, Guildford, Surrey, GU1 1ET.*
Actual grid ref: SU998504
Quiet family B&B. Main road, town centre, near stations.
Delicious breakfast
Tel: 01483 302394
Mr & Mrs Bourne.
Rates fr: *£16.00*-**£22.00**.
Open: All Year (not Xmas)
Beds: 1F 1D 1S **Baths:** 2 Shared
🛏 ☐ 🖾 🖾 V ▪ ✦

The Grid Reference beneath the location heading is for the village or town - *not* for individual houses, which are shown (where supplied) in each entry itself.

Pay B&Bs by cash or cheque and be prepared to pay up front.

(3m) **Greyfriars**, *Castle Hill, Guildford, Surrey, GU1 3SY.*
Large Victorian private house in conservation area
Tel: 01483 61795 Mr Parsons.
Rates fr: *£15.00*-**£15.00**.
Open: All Year
Beds: 1F 1D 2T 2S
Baths: 3 Shared
🛏 P (4) ☐ 🖾 V ▪ ✦

(3m) **Westbury Cottage**, *Waterden Road, Guildford, Surrey, GU1 2AN.*
Cottage-style house in large secluded garden
Grades: ETB Listed
Tel: 01483 822602 Mrs Smythe.
Rates fr: *£20.00*-**£22.00**.
Open: All Year (not Xmas)
Beds: 1D 2T
Baths: 1 Shared
🛏 (12) P (3) 🖾 ☐ 🖾.

(3m) **Cobbity**, *87 Wodeland Avenue, Guildford, Surrey, GU2 5LA.*
Superbly situated Edwardian town house
Tel: 01483 61209
Mr & Mrs Nossiter.
Rates fr: *£15.00*-**£18.00**.
Open: All Year
Beds: 2T 1S
Baths: 1 Shared
🛏 P (2) 🖾 ☐ 🐾 🖾.

Bramley   9

National Grid Ref: TQ0044

🍴 🍺 Jolly Farmer

(1m) **Beevers Farm**, *Chinthurst Lane, Bramley, Guildford, Surrey, GU5 0DR.*
Modern comfortable farmhouse
Grades: ETB Listed
Tel: 01483 898764 Mr Cook.
Rates fr: *£14.00*-**£20.00**.
Open: Easter to Nov
Beds: 1F 2T
Baths: 1 Private 1 Shared
🛏 P (10) 🖾 ☐ 🖾 ▪ ✦

Godalming   10

National Grid Ref: SU9643

(1m) **Meads Hotel**, *65 Meadrow, Godalming, Surrey, GU7 3HS.*
Charming elegant & comfortable hotel
Grades: ETB Listed, AA Listed
Tel: 01483 421800
Mr Smith.
Rates fr: *£21.00*-**£26.00**.
Open: All Year
Beds: 3F 4D 3T 5S
Baths: 6 Private 3 Shared
🛏 P ☐ 🐾 🖾.

Cranleigh   11

National Grid Ref: TQ0638

🍴 🍺 The Wheatsheaf

(2m) **Dalkeith**, *Horsham Road, Cranleigh, Surrey, GU6 8DW.*
Guests' comments: Unbeatable, Gold star
Tel: 01483 272730 (also fax no)
Mrs Addison.
Rates fr: *£20.00*-**£25.00**.
Open: All Year
Beds: 2D 1T
Baths: 1 Shared
🛏 P (6) 🖾 ☐ 🖾.

Ockley   12

National Grid Ref: TQ1439

🍴 🍺 Scarlett Arms

(1m) **Hazels**, *Walliswood, Ockley, Dorking, Surrey, RH5 5PL.*
Separate suite - off the beaten track - beautiful country garden
Tel: 01306 627228 Mrs Floud.
Rates fr: *£20.00*-**£25.00**.
Open: All Year
Beds: 1F
Baths: 1 Ensuite
🛏 P (2) 🖾 ☐ 🖾 V

Newdigate   13

National Grid Ref: TQ1942

🍴 🍺 Surrey Oaks, Six Bells

(1m) **Sturtwood Farm**, *Partridge Lane, Newdigate, Dorking, Surrey, RH5 5EE.*
Comfortable, friendly farmhouse
Grades: ETB 2 Cr, Comm
Tel: 01306 631308
Mrs MacKinnon.
Fax no: 01306 631908
Rates fr: *£17.50*-**£20.00**.
Open: All Year (not Xmas)
Beds: 1T 1S 1D
Baths: 1 Ensuite 1 Shared
🛏 P (10) 🖾 ☐ 🐾 ✕ 🖾 V

Norwood Hill   14

National Grid Ref: TQ2443

🍴 🍺 Fox Revived

(1m) **Latchetts Cottage**, *Ricketts Wood Road, Norwood Hill, Horley, Surrey, RH6 0ET.*
Cosy country cottage
Grades: ETB Listed
Tel: 01293 862831 Mrs Lees.
Rates fr: *£18.50*-**£20.00**.
Open: All Year (not Xmas)
Beds: 2D 1S
Baths: 1 Shared
🛏 P (5) 🖾 ☐ 🖾 V

The lowest *double* rate per person is shown in *italics*.

Ifield 15

National Grid Ref: TQ2537

|●| ◖ The Gate

(2m) *Waterhall Country House,*
Prestwood Lane, Ifield Wood,
Ifield, Crawley, W Sussex, RH11 0LA.
Luxury accommodation in open
countryside
Grades: ETB 2 Cr, Comm
Tel: 01293 520002
Mr & Mrs Dawson.
Fax no: 01293 539905
Rates fr: £20.00-£25.00.
Open: All Year (not Xmas)
Beds: 1F 2D 2T 1S
Baths: 6 Ensuite
⛺ 🅿 ⊬ 🛏 🖳 ↺

Crawley 16

National Grid Ref: TQ2537

|●| ◖ Royal Oak, The Greyhound

(3m) *Brooklyn Manor Hotel,*
Bonnetts Lane, Crawley, W.
Sussex, RH11 0NY.
Ideal location for Gatwick
overnight stopover. Courtesy
transport & holiday parking
Grades: ETB 2 Cr, Comm
Tel: 01293 546024 Mr Davis.
Fax no: 01293 510366
Rates fr: £19.50-£27.00.
Open: All Year (not Xmas)
Beds: 2F 4D 4T 1S
Baths: 4 Private 3 Shared
⛺ 🅿 (100) 🛏 🖳

Horley 17

National Grid Ref: TQ2843

|●| ◖ Ye Olde Six Bells, Game
Bird, The Foresters, Air Balloon

(0.5m) *Rosemead Guest House,*
19 Church Road, Horley, Surrey,
RH6 7EY.
Small guest house, convenient
Gatwick airport 5 mins
Grades: ETB Listed, Comm,
AA 3 Q
Tel: 01293 784965 / 430546
Mr Wood. Fax no: 01293 430547
Rates fr: £19.00-£25.00.
Open: All Year (not Xmas)
Beds: 1F 2D 1T 2S
Baths: 2 Private 2 Shared
⛺ 🅿 (8) ⊬ 🛏 🕿 🖳

(0.5m) *Melville Lodge Guest*
House, 15 Brighton Road, Horley,
Surrey, RH6 7HH.
Family-run Edwardian guest house
Grades: ETB 2 Cr, Approv
RAC Listed
Tel: 01293 784951
Mrs Brooks.
Fax no: 01293 785669
Rates fr: £17.50-£20.00.
Open: All Year
Beds: 1F 3D 2T 1S
Baths: 3 Ensuite 2 Shared
⛺ (1) 🅿 🛏 🕿 🖳 ↺

All paths are popular: you are well-advised to book ahead

(0.5m) *Yew Tree, 31 Massetts*
Road, Horley, Surrey, RH6 7DQ.
5 minutes taxi Gatwick Airport,
near town centre & rail station
Grades: ETB Listed
Tel: 01293 785855 Mr Stroud.
Rates fr: £15.00-£15.00.
Open: All Year **Beds:** 1F 2D 1T 2S
Baths: 2 Shared
⛺ (1) 🅿 (10) 🛏 🖳

(0.5m) *Berrens Guest House,*
62 Massetts Road, Horley, Surrey,
RH6 7DS.
Five minutes' drive to airport
Grades: ETB Listed
Tel: 01293 786125 (also fax no)
Mr Worham.
Rates fr: £17.00-£22.00.
Open: All Year **Beds:** 1F 1D 1T 2S
Baths: 2 Shared
⛺ 🅿 ⊬ 🛏 🖳

(0.25m) *Prinsted Guest House,*
Oldfield Road, Horley, Surrey,
RH6 7EP.
Superior Victorian house in quiet
situation, ideal for Gatwick airport
Grades: ETB Listed, Comm
Tel: 01293 785233 Mrs Kendall.
Fax no: 01293 820624
Rates fr: £18.50-£30.00.
Open: All Year (not Xmas)
Beds: 1F 3D 2T 2S
Baths: 6 Ensuite 1 Shared
⛺ 🅿 ⊬ 🛏 🖳 ✦

(0.5m) *Copperwood Guest House,*
Massetts Road, Horley, Surrey,
RH6 7DJ.
Gatwick Airport 5 minutes
Grades: ETB 2 Cr, Comm
Tel: 01293 783388
Mrs Hooks.
Fax no: 01293 420156
Rates fr: £18.00-£26.00.
Open: All Year
Beds: 1F 1D 1T 2S
Baths: 1 Private 2 Shared
⛺ 🅿 (5) ⊬ 🛏 🖳 Ⓥ

(0.5m) *Oakdene Guest House,*
32 Massetts Road, Horley, Surrey,
RH6 7DS.
Large Victorian guest house
Grades: ETB Listed
Tel: 01293 772047
Mr Ali.
Fax no: 01293 771586
Rates fr: £19.00-£25.00.
Open: All Year (not Xmas)
Beds: 1F 1D 1T 3S
Baths: 2 Shared
⛺ 🅿 (10) ⊬ 🛏 🖳 ↺

(0.5m) *Chalet Guest House,*
77 Massetts Road, Horley, Surrey,
RH6 7EB.
Modern. Close town - Gatwick
Airport
Grades: ETB 2 Cr, Comm,
AA 3 Q, RAC Acclaim
Tel: 01293 821666
Mr Shortland.
Fax no: 01293 821619
Rates fr: £22.00-£26.00.
Open: All Year (not Xmas)
Beds: 1F 1D 1T 4S
Baths: 5 Private 1 Shared
⛺ 🅿 (12) ⊬ 🛏 🖳

Bramley to Westhumble

From Bramley it's southwest to **Godalming**, and then around Hydon Heath to **Dunsfold** and east, crossing the Wey and Arun Canal, to Alfold Crossways and then **Ellen's Green**. Shortly after here there is a link to Leith Hill, the highest point in Southeast England. Back on the route and cycling east, you are now in the lush woodland of the south of the county. Near to **Ockley** are nature reserves at Wallis Wood and Vann Lake, and the Hannah Peschar Sculpture Garden, an open-air gallery which features annual exhibitions of contemporary sculpture, both figurative and abstract and in all materials. Then it's east through a string of villages and small towns whose medieval names bespeak the era when this whole region was covered by trees - **Newdigate** ('Gate near a new wood'), **Horley** ('Woodland clearing in a horn of land'), **Lingfield** ('Wood-dwellers' field') - to the eastern end of the route at **Haxted Mill**, a working mill with old-world milling machinery, which hosts, from Easter to mid-September, a museum of the history of milling. The next stretch takes you via **Bletcingley** to **Outwood**, with another mill and nearby Outwood Common, and then by way of Woodhatch, Reigate Heath, Betchworth and Brockham back into the vicinity of **Box Hill**, which it is worth climbing for the magnificent view, and to the station at Westhumble.

All details shown
are as supplied
by B&B owners in
Autumn 1997.

(0.5m) *The Corner House,*
72 Massetts Road, Horley, Surrey,
RH6 7ED.
Quality accommodation, Gatwick 5
minutes
Grades: ETB 2 Cr
Tel: **01293 784574** Mrs Smith.
Rates fr: *£18.00-£23.00.*
Open: All Year
Beds: 3F 3D 2T 5S
Baths: 4 Private 3 Shared
ờ 🅿 (30) ⵣ ⵟ ✕ ⵎ 🆅

(0.5m) *Felcourt Guest House,*
79 Massetts Road, Horley, Surrey,
RH6 7EB.
Airport 3 minutes, close to town
Grades: ETB Listed
Tel: **01293 782651 / 776255**
Mr Ahmed. Fax no: 01293 782651
Rates fr: *£15.00-£18.00.*
Open: All Year
Beds: 3F 4D 2T 2S
Baths: 4 Private 3 Shared
ờ 🅿 (12) ⵣ ⵟ ⵠ ✕ ⵎ ⵄ 🆅 ⵙ

(0.5m) *Southbourne Guest House,*
34 Massetts Road, Horley, Surrey,
RH6 7DS.
Popular Victorian house near
Gatwick
Tel: **01293 771991** Mrs Castellari.
Rates fr: *£17.00-£18.00.*
Open: All Year (not Xmas)
Beds: 1F 2D 2T 1S
Baths: 1 Ensuite 1 Private 1 Shared
ờ 🅿 (20) ⵟ ⵟ ⵎ 🆅

Burstow   18

National Grid Ref: TQ3041

(1m) *Burstow Park, Antlands*
Lane, Burstow, Horley, Surrey,
RH6 9TF.
Converted farmhouse, now family
home
Tel: **01293 785936** Mrs Puttock.
Fax no: 01293 774694
Rates fr: *£18.00-£18.00.*
Open: All Year
Beds: 2T 1S **Baths:** 1 Shared
ờ 🅿 (10) ⵣ ⵎ

Many rates vary
according to season -
the lowest only are
shown here

Felbridge   19

National Grid Ref: TQ3639

(2m) *Toads Croak House, 30*
Copthorne Road, Felbridge, East
Grinstead, W Sussex, RH19 2NS.
Quiet, beautiful house, gardens.
Non-smoking
Tel: **01342 328524**
Rates fr: *£16.50-£17.00.*
Open: All Year
Beds: 1F 1T 1D 1S
Baths: 2 Ensuite 1 Shared
ờ 🅿 (7) ⵣ ⵟ ⵎ 🆅

East Grinstead   20

National Grid Ref: TQ3938
🍴 ⵛ Ship Inn

(3m) *Brentridge, 24 Portland*
Road, East Grinstead, W. Sussex,
RH19 4EA.
Beautiful garden, central and quiet.
Close to Gatwick, M25 & south
coast
Tel: **01342 322004**
Mrs Greenwood.
Fax no: 01342 324145
Rates fr: *£16.00-£20.00.*
Open: All Year
Beds: 1D 1T 1S
Baths: 2 Shared
ờ 🅿 (2) ⵣ ⵟ ⵎ ⵠ

(3m) *Ship Inn, Ship Street, East*
Grinstead, W. Sussex, RH19 4EG.
Very friendly, family-run freehouse
Tel: **01342 323197 / 312089**
Mr Connor.
Rates fr: *£17.50-£20.00.*
Open: All Year
Beds: 7T
Baths: 2 Ensuite 1 Shared
ờ 🅿 (12) ⵟ ⵟ ✕ ⵎ

(3m) *Cranston House, Cranston*
Road, East Grinstead, W. Sussex,
RH19 3HW.
House with parking near Gatwick
Tel: **01342 323609**
Mr Linacre.
Rates fr: *£16.00-£20.00.*
Open: All Year
Beds: 1F 1T 1S
Baths: 1 Ensuite 1 Shared
ờ (6) 🅿 (4) ⵣ ⵟ ✕ ⵎ 🆅

Edenbridge   21

National Grid Ref: TQ4446
🍴 ⵛ The Four Elms

(3m) *Knowlands, Four Elms,*
Edenbridge, Kent, TN8 6NA.
Actual grid ref: TQ469478
Spacious Edwardian private
country house, non-smoking
Tel: **01732 700314** (also fax no)
Mr & Mrs Haviland.
Rates fr: *£27.50-£35.00.*
Open: All Year (not Xmas)
Beds: 2D 1S
🅿 (3) ⵣ ⵟ ✕ ⵎ 🆅 ⵙ ⵠ

Please don't camp
on *anyone's* land
without first obtaining
their permission.

Oxted   22

National Grid Ref: TQ3852
🍴 ⵛ The George, Royal Oak

(1m) *Pinehurst Grange Guest*
House, East Hill (Part of A25),
Oxted, Surrey, RH8 9AE.
Actual grid ref: TQ393525
Comfortable Victorian ex-
farmhouse with traditional service
and relaxed friendly atmosphere
Tel: **01883 716413**
Mr Rodgers.
Rates fr: *£19.50-£24.00.*
Open: All Year (not Xmas/
New Year)
Beds: 1D 1T 1S
Baths: 1 Shared
ờ (5) 🅿 (3) ⵣ ⵟ ⵎ ⵙ ⵠ

(0.5m) *Old Forge House, Merle*
Common, Oxted, Surrey, RH8 0JB.
Actual grid ref: TQ416493
Comfortable home in rural
surroundings
Tel: **01883 715969**
Mrs Mills.
Rates fr: *£16.00-£18.00.*
Open: All Year (not Xmas)
Beds: 1D 1T 1S
Baths: 1 Shared
ờ 🅿 (3) ⵟ ⵟ ⵎ 🆅 ⵙ ⵠ

(1m) *The Croft, Quarry Road,*
Oxted, Surrey, RH8 9HE.
Actual grid ref: TQ393521
Substantial Edwardian house -
peaceful location
Tel: **01883 713605**
Mrs Todd.
Rates fr: *£19.50-£21.00.*
Open: All Year
Beds: 1F 1T 1D
Baths: 1 Shared
ờ (5) 🅿 (8) ⵣ ⵟ ⵎ ⵙ

Order your
packed lunches the
evening before you
need them.
Not at breakfast!

Godstone 23

National Grid Ref: TQ3551

|●| ◁| Coach House

(0.25m) **Godstone Hotel**, *The Green, Godstone, Surrey*, *RH9 8DT*.
C16th coaching house, original timbers, inglenook fireplaces
Tel: **01883 742461** (also fax no)
Mr Howe.
Rates fr: *£22.50-£32.00*.
Open: All Year
Beds: 1F 5D 2T **Baths:** 8 Private
🛏 🅿 🗆 🛏 ✕ 🏢 Ⓥ 🛈 ✓

Redhill 24

National Grid Ref: TQ2750

|●| ◁| The Sun, The Abbott, Home Cottage, The Toby

(1m) **Lynwood Guest House**, *50 London Rd, Redhill, Surrey*, *RH1 1LN*.
Actual grid ref: TQ280511
Large Victorian modernised house
Tel: **01737 766894** Mrs Rao.
Rates fr: *£20.00-£26.00*.
Open: All Year
Beds: 4F 1D 2T 2S
Baths: 3 Ensuite 1 Shared
🛏 🅿 (7) 🗆 🏢 ✓

(1m) **Arun Lodge Guest House**, *37 Redstone Hill, Redhill, Surrey*, *RH1 4AW*.
Beautifully decorated Edwardian house, set just 2 minutes' walk Redhill centre
Grades: ETB Listed
Tel: **01737 761933** (also fax no)
Ms Metcalfe.
Rates fr: *£22.00-£26.00*.
Open: All Year
Beds: 1F 1D 1T 1S
Baths: 2 Ensuite 1 Shared
🛏 🅿 (8) 🗆 🏢 ⅙ ✓

Reigate 25

National Grid Ref: TQ2649

(1m) **Norfolk Lodge Hotel**, *23-25 London Road, Reigate, Surrey*, *RH2 9PY*.
Very comfortable, licensed family hotel
Tel: **01737 248702**
Mr Bowley.
Rates fr: *£15.00-£24.00*.
Open: All Year
Beds: 3F 2D 5T 6S
Baths: 2 Shared
🛏 🅿 (50) 🗆 🛏

Leigh 26

National Grid Ref: TQ2246

(1m) **Barn Cottage**, *Church Road, Leigh, Reigate, Surrey*, *RH2 8RF*.
Converted C17th barn, beautiful gardens with swimming pool 100 yards from pub
Grades: ETB Listed
Tel: **01306 611347**
Mrs Comer.
Rates fr: *£22.00-£25.00*.
Open: All Year
Beds: 1D 1T
Baths: 2 Shared
🛏 🅿 (3) 🗆 ✕ 🏢 Ⓥ 🛈 ✓

High season,
bank holidays and
special events mean
low availability
everywhere.

Wiltshire Cycleway

The **Wiltshire Cycleway** is a 160-mile circular tour of the County of Wiltshire, which takes you from rolling hills to the Salisbury Plain, from prehistoric chalk hillside carvings and Stonehenge to old English villages and towns - Salisbury, Marlborough, Malmesbury and close to Bath, across the border in Somerset. It is signposted in both directions by blue Wiltshire Cycleway direction signs with a cycle silhouette, but is designed to be cycled anticlockwise. NB: There are a number of alternative routes, for which the signposts feature coloured spots; for the route featured in this book follow the plain blue signs.

A detailed **guide leaflet** to the cycleway route is available free from the Director of Environmental Services, Wiltshire County Council, County Hall, Trowbridge, Wiltshire BA14 8JD, tel 01225 713349. A separate factsheet on cycle repair/hire shops is also available free from the same address. In addition, a free Wiltshire information pack on attractions in the county is available from Dept 368, Wiltshire Tourism, 1 Upcott Avenue, Barnstaple, Devon EX31 1HN, tel 01271 329522.

Maps: Ordnance Survey 1:50,000 Landranger series: 172, 173, 174, 183, 184

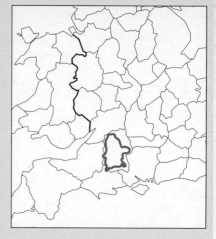

Trains: Bath, Chippenham and Swindon are on the main London (Paddington)-Bristol railway line. Frome, Westbury, Pewsey and Great Bedwyn are on the main London (Paddington)-Penzance line. Salisbury, Tisbury and Gillingham are on the line that runs between London Waterloo and Exeter. Bath, Bradford-on-Avon, Trowbridge, Westbury, Warminster and Salisbury are on the Bristol-Southampton line.

Malmesbury   1

National Grid Ref: ST9387

⏚ ⬛ Suffolk Arms, Whole Hog, Duke of York, King's Arms, Horse & Groom, The Wheatsheaf, Plough Inn, Old Inn

(0.25m) **Bremilham House,** *Bremilham Road, Malmesbury, Wilts, SN16 0DQ.*
Tel: **01666 822680** Mrs Ball.
Rates fr: *£16.00*-**£18.50.**
Open: All Year
Beds: 2D 1T
Baths: 2 Shared
⏚ ▣ (3) ⬚ ⊀ ✕ ▥ 🖤 ᵛ ♠ ✓
Delightful Edwardian cottage in historic Malmesbury. Central for Bath, Cheltenham, Salisbury & the glorious Cotswolds. Traditional English breakfast. Delicious home cooked evening meals. Quiet location

---

The lowest *double* rate per person is shown in *italics*.

The *lowest* **single** rate *is shown in* **bold.**

(0.25m) **Whychurch Farm,** *Malmesbury, Wilts, SN16 9JL.*
C17th farmhouse, central for Bath/Cotswolds
Grades: ETB Listed, Comm
Tel: **01666 822156**
Mr & Mrs Weaver.
Rates fr: *£15.00*-**£17.50.**
Open: All Year (not Xmas)
Beds: 1D 1T
Baths: 2 Ensuite 2 Shared
⏚ ▣ (8) ⊀ ⬚ ✕ ▥ & ᵛ

Yatton Keynell   2

National Grid Ref: ST8676

⏚ ⬛ Bell Inn, Salutation Inn

(0.25m) **Mermaids Barn,** *Yatton Keynell, Chippenham, Wilts, SN14 7BA.*
Modernised, quiet country property
Tel: **01249 782326** (also fax no)
Mrs Doughty.
Rates fr: *£16.50*-**£20.00.**
Open: All Year Beds: 1T Baths: 1 Private
⏚ ▣ (3) ⊀ ⬚ ▥ & ᵛ

(1m) **Oakfield Farm,** *Easton Piercy Lane, Yatton Keynell, Chippenham, Wilts, SN14 6JU.*
Modern farmhouse. Quiet, beautiful location
Grades: ETB Listed, Comm
Tel: **01249 782355** Mrs Read.
Rates fr: *£17.50*-**£20.00.**
Open: Mar to Oct
Beds: 1F 1D 1T
Baths: 1 Private 1 Shared
⏚ ▣ (10) ⊀ ⬚ ▥ ᵛ

Biddestone   3

National Grid Ref: ST8673

⏚ ⬛ White Horse, Biddestone Arms

(On route) **Home Farm,** *Biddestone, Chippenham, Wilts, SN14 7DQ.*
Working farm in picturesque village
Grades: ETB 2 Cr, Comm, AA 3 Q, Recomm
Tel: **01249 714475** (also fax no)
Mr & Mrs Smith.
Rates fr: *£17.50*-**£20.00.**
Open: All Year Beds: 1F 1D 1S
Baths: 2 Ensuite 1 Private
⏚ ▣ (4) ⊀ ⬚ ▥ ᵛ ♠ ✓

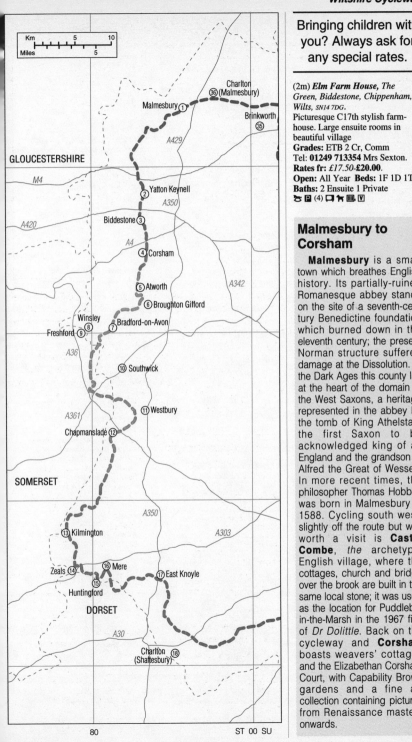

ST 00 SU

Bringing children with you? Always ask for any special rates.

(2m) *Elm Farm House, The Green, Biddestone, Chippenham, Wilts, SN14 7DG.*
Picturesque C17th stylish farm-house. Large ensuite rooms in beautiful village
Grades: ETB 2 Cr, Comm
Tel: **01249 713354** Mrs Sexton.
Rates fr: *£17.50-£20.00.*
Open: All Year **Beds:** 1F 1D 1T
Baths: 2 Ensuite 1 Private
⌂ ℗ (4) ⊡ ⊀ ⊞ Ⅴ

Malmesbury to Corsham

Malmesbury is a small town which breathes English history. Its partially-ruined Romanesque abbey stands on the site of a seventh-century Benedictine foundation which burned down in the eleventh century; the present Norman structure suffered damage at the Dissolution. In the Dark Ages this county lay at the heart of the domain of the West Saxons, a heritage represented in the abbey by the tomb of King Athelstan, the first Saxon to be acknowledged king of all England and the grandson of Alfred the Great of Wessex. In more recent times, the philosopher Thomas Hobbes was born in Malmesbury in 1588. Cycling south west, slightly off the route but well worth a visit is **Castle Combe**, *the* archetypal English village, where the cottages, church and bridge over the brook are built in the same local stone; it was used as the location for Puddleby-in-the-Marsh in the 1967 film of *Dr Dolittle*. Back on the cycleway and **Corsham** boasts weavers' cottages and the Elizabethan Corsham Court, with Capability Brown gardens and a fine art collection containing pictures from Renaissance masters onwards.

Corsham 4

National Grid Ref: ST8670

¶⚫ White Horse Inn, Hare & Hounds

(0.25m) *Bellwood, 45 Pickwick, Corsham, Wilts, SN13 0HX.*
Actual grid ref: ST863706
Charming 1708 cottage (adjacent to owners), pubs nearby, Bath 8 miles
Tel: **01249 713434** Mrs Elliott.
Rates fr: *£16.50-£18.00.*
Open: All Year
Beds: 2T 1S
Baths: 1 Prvate 1 Shared
🛏 🅿 (5) ⚡ 🗲 ⛉ 🖿 Ⅵ ♦ ✦

(0.25m) *Halfway Firs, 5 Halfway Firs, Corsham, Wilts, SN13 0PJ.*
Comfortable converted farm cottage. Tel: **01225 810552**
Mr & Mrs Fisher.
Rates fr: *£16.00-£16.00.*
Open: All Year (not Xmas)
Beds: 1F 1D 1S
Baths: 1 Shared
🛏 (8) 🅿 (3) 🗲 ⚡ 🖿

(0.25m) *75 High Street, Corsham, Wilts, SN13 0HA.*
Listed C18th stone house
Grades: ETB Listed, Comm
Tel: **01249 713366** Mrs Rodger.
Rates fr: *£16.00-£18.00.*
Open: All Year
Beds: 1F 1D 1T
Baths: 1 Shared
🛏 ⚡ 🖿 Ⅵ

(1m) *Pickwick Lodge Farm, Corsham, Wilts, SN13 0PS.*
Spacious well-furnished farmhouse, half mile off A4
Tel: **01249 712207** Mrs Stafford.
Fax no: 01249 701904
Rates fr: *£17.00-£22.00.*
Open: All Year (not Xmas)
Beds: 2D 1T
Baths: 1 Ensuite 1 Private 1 Shared
🛏 🅿 (4) 🗲 ⚡ 🖿 Ⅵ

Atworth 5

National Grid Ref: ST8665

¶⚫ The Forresters

(1m) *Church Farm, Atworth, Melksham, Wilts, SN12 8JA.*
Working dairy farm, large garden
Tel: **01225 702215** Mrs Hole.
Rates fr: *£15.00-£18.00.*
Open: Easter to Oct
Beds: 1F 1D
Baths: 1 Shared
🛏 🅿 (4) ⚡ Ⅵ

Broughton Gifford 6

National Grid Ref: ST8763

¶⚫ Bell on the Common

(1m) *Frying Pan Farm, Broughton Gifford, Melksham, Wilts, SN12 8LL.*
Comfortable C17th farmhouse
Grades: ETB 2 Cr, Comm
Tel: **01225 702343**
Mrs Pullen.
Rates fr: *£17.00-£18.00.*
Open: All Year (not Xmas)
Beds: 1D 1T
Baths: 1 Ensuite 1 Shared
🛏 (2) 🅿 (3) 🗲 ⚡ 🖿 Ⅵ

Bradford-on-Avon 7

National Grid Ref: ST8261

¶⚫ Seven Stars, Barge Inn, Cross Guns, King's Arms, Bear Inn, The Beehive

(0.25m) *Great Ashley House, Ashley Lane, Bradford-on-Avon, Wilts, BA15 2PP.*
Quiet country house. Pool table. Jacuzzi
Tel: **01225 863381**
Mrs Rawlings.
Rates fr: *£15.00-£15.00.*
Open: All Year (not Xmas)
Beds: 2D 1T **Baths:** 1 Shared
🛏 (Any) 🅿 (3) 🗲 ⚡ 🖿 Ⅵ ✦

(0.25m) *The Locks, 265 Trowbridge Road, Bradford-on-Avon, Wilts, BA15 1UA.*
Private house alongside restored canal
Tel: **01225 863358**
Mrs Benjamin.
Rates fr: *£15.00-£15.00.*
Open: All Year
Beds: 1F 2T
Baths: 1 Ensuite 1 Shared
🛏 🅿 (4) 🗲 ⚡ 🖿 Ⅵ ✦

(0.25m) *Avonvilla, Avoncliff, Bradford-on-Avon, Wilts, BA15 2HD.*
River & canalside private fishing
Tel: **01225 863867**
Mrs Mumford.
Rates fr: *£15.00-£15.00.*
Open: All Year
Beds: 1D 1T 1S
Baths: 1 Private 1 Shared
🛏 (5) 🅿 (3) 🗲 ⚡ 🖿 Ⅵ

(0.25m) *The Barge Inn, 17 Frome Road, Bradford-on-Avon, Wilts, BA15 2EA.*
Grade II Listed building
Tel: **01225 863403**
Ms Maytom-Jones.
Rates fr: *£22.50-£22.50.*
Open: All Year
Beds: 2D 1T
Baths: 1 Private 1 Shared
🛏 (0) 🅿 (40) ⚡ 🗲 ✕ 🖿 Ⅵ ♦ ✦

(0.25m) *Fern Cottage, 74 Monkton Farleigh, Bradford-on-Avon, Wilts, BA15 2QJ.*
C17th cottage in conservation village
Grades: ETB 2 Cr, High Comm, AA Prem, Select, RAC High Acclaim
Tel: **01225 859412**
Mrs Valentine.
Fax no: 01225 859018
Rates fr: *£25.00-£30.00.*
Open: All Year
Beds: 1F 2D
Baths: 2 Ensuite 1 Private
🛏 🅿 (5) 🗲 ⚡ 🖿 Ⅵ

Corsham to Salisbury

Bradford on Avon, another quaint English town, centres on an arched stone bridge over the Avon, and also features a tithe barn and the ancient Saxon Church of St Laurence. From here you may wish to take a detour to **Bath**, which is possible to reach by bicycle along the towpath of the Kennet and Avon Canal (see the *Sustrans* West Country Way). South of Bradford-on-Avon you pass the ruins of Farleigh Castle and you can find Iford Manor and its famous landscaped garden with the mediterranean plants, by Harold Peto. The next stretch takes in a piece of Wiltshire's famous prehistory, as you pass the renowned Westbury White Horse hillside carving - you are now at the west side of Salisbury Plain.

This pocket of the county contains a clutch of stately piles - **Longleat** boasts the bizarre combination of a splendid renaissance manor and a theme park with only one obvious feature in common with the house: its sheer scale - based on an African safari park, it offers a variety of other attractions including the world's longest maze. **Stourhead**, although built on a comparable scale, is more restrained in every respect. Dating from the eighteenth century, the Palladian mansion is accompanied by a famous landscaped garden, whose carefully-orchestrated classical harmony is mirrored in a lake; also here is King Alfred's Tower, a folly offering impressive views. **Stourton House Gardens**, nearby, have a collection of unusual plants. From here it is a beautiful ride around the West Wiltshire Downs towards Salisbury.

(0.25m) *Bear Inn, 26 Silver Street, Bradford-on-Avon, Wilts, BA15 1JY.*
Town centre, Napoleonic traditional inn
Tel: **01225 866632** Mr Borland.
Rates fr: *£19.00*-**£28.00.**
Open: All Year
Beds: 1F 1D **Baths:** 2 Private
⌂ ❑ ✕ ▥ �

Winsley 8

National Grid Ref: ST7961

|●| ◖ Seven Stars

(1m) *Serendipity, 19f Bradford Road, Winsley, Bradford-on-Avon, Wilts, BA15 2HW.*
Beautiful bungalow, between Bath & Bradford-on-Avon
Grades: ETB Listed, 3Q
Tel: **01225 722380** Mrs Shepherd.
Rates fr: *£18.00*-**£25.00.**
Open: All Year **Beds:** 1F 1D 1S
Baths: 2 Ensuite 1 Private
⌂ 🅿 (5) ⊁ ❑ ▥ & 🔲 ⓐ ✦

Freshford 9

National Grid Ref: ST7860

|●| ◖ The Inn, Old Coaching Inn

(1m) *Long Acre, 17 Staples Hill, Freshford, Bath. BA3 6EL.*
Magnificent southerly views, own 3 acres
Tel: **01225 723254** Mrs Cameron.
Rates fr: *£16.00*-**£18.00.**
Open: All Year **Beds:** 2D 1T
Baths: 2 Ensuite 1 Shared
❑ ⓗ ▥ 🔲

Southwick 10

National Grid Ref: ST8355

|●| ◖ Hungerford Arms

(2m) *Brooksfield House, Vaggs Hill, Southwick, Trowbridge, Wilts, BA14 9NA.*
Delightful converted country barn
Grades: ETB Listed, 2 Cr, High Comm
Tel: **01373 830615** Mrs Parry.
Rates fr: *£20.00*-**£15.00.**
Open: All Year (not Xmas)
Beds: 2D 1T
Baths: 1 Ensuite 1 Private 1 Shared
⌂ 🅿 (20) ❑ ▥ 🔲

Westbury 11

National Grid Ref: ST8650

|●| ◖ Royal Oak, Full Moon, Kicking Donkey

(2m) *Glenmore Farm, The Ham, Westbury, Wilts, BA13 4HQ.*
Actual grid ref: ST865526
Comfortable friendly farmhouse
Tel: **01373 865022** Mrs Painter.
Rates fr: *£17.50*-**£20.00.**
Open: All Year **Beds:** 1F 1T
Baths: 1 Ensuite 1 Private
⌂ 🅿 (20) ❑ ✕ ▥ 🔲

(1m) *Brokerswood House, Brokerswood, Westbury, Wilts, BA13 4EH.*
Situated in woodland park
Tel: **01373 823428** Mrs Phillips.
Rates fr: *£14.00*-**£14.00.**
Open: All Year (not Xmas)
Beds: 1F 1T 1S **Baths:** 2 Ensuite
⌂ (1) 🅿 (6) ❑ ⓗ

Chapmanslade 12

National Grid Ref: ST8348

(1m) *Spinney Farmhouse, Thoulstone, Chapmanslade, Westbury, Wilts, BA13 4AQ.*
In heart of Wiltshire countryside.
Easy reach of Bath, Longleat
Tel: **01373 832412** Mrs Hoskins.
Rates fr: *£16.00*-**£17.00.**
Open: All Year
Beds: 1F 1D 1T **Baths:** 2 Shared
⌂ 🅿 (8) ❑ ⓗ ✕ ▥ ⓐ ✦

Kilmington 13

National Grid Ref: ST7736

|●| ◖ Spread Eagle

(0.25m) *The Red Lion Inn, On B3092 (Mere to Frome road), Kilmington, Warminster, Wilts, BA12 6RP.*
Actual grid ref: ST786354
C15th traditional country inn, comfortable accommodation. 1 mile NT Stourhead Gardens
Tel: **01985 844263** Mr Gibbs.
Rates fr: *£15.00*-**£20.00.**
Open: All Year
Beds: 1D 1T **Baths:** 1 Shared
⌂ (4) 🅿 (25) ⓗ ▥ 🔲

Zeals 14

National Grid Ref: ST7731

|●| ◖ White Lion

(0.25m) *Cornerways Cottage, Zeals, Longcross, Warminster, Wilts, BA12 6LL.*
Grades: ETB 2 Cr, Comm
Tel: **01747 840477** (also fax no)
Mrs Snook.
Rates fr: *£17.50*-**£25.00.**
Open: All Year (not Xmas/New Year)
Beds: 2D 1T
Baths: 2 Ensuite 1 Private
⌂ (8) 🅿 (6) ⊁ ❑ ✕ ▥ 🔲 ⓐ ✦
Cornerways is a C18th cottage offering a high standard of accommodation with a lovely 'cottagey' feel, complemented by excellent breakfasts in the old dining room. Stourhead 2 miles, Longleat 4 miles

---

The lowest *double* rate per person is shown in *italics*.

Please don't camp on *anyone's* land without first obtaining their permission.

Huntingford 15

National Grid Ref: ST8029

|●| ◖ Dolphin Inn

(0.25m) *Huntingford Oak, Huntingford, Gillingham, Dorset, SP8 5QH.*
Modern house on working farm
Grades: ETB 2 Cr, High Comm
Tel: **01747 860574**
Mrs James.
Rates fr: *£19.00*-**£21.00.**
Open: All Year (not Xmas)
Beds: 1F 1D 1T
Baths: 3 Private
⌂ 🅿 (15) ❑ ▥ & 🔲

Mere 16

National Grid Ref: ST8132

|●| ◖ Talbot Inn, Butt & Sherry, Ship Hotel

(0.5m) *Downleaze, North Street, Mere, Warminster, Wilts, BA12 6HH.*
Comfortable in quiet area
Grades: ETB Listed
Tel: **01747 860876**
Mrs Lampard.
Rates fr: *£15.00*-**£17.00.**
Open: All Year (not Xmas)
Beds: 1D 1T
Baths: 1 Shared
⌂ 🅿 (3) ❑ ▥

(0.5m) *Norwood House, Mere, Warminster, Wilts, BA12 6LA.*
Large family house, rural setting
Tel: **01747 860992** (also fax no)
Mrs Tillbrook.
Rates fr: *£15.00*-**£17.00.**
Open: All Year
Beds: 1F **Baths:** 1 Ensuite
⌂ 🅿 (3) ❑ ▥

East Knoyle 17

National Grid Ref: ST8830

(0.25m) *Swainscombe, The Green, East Knoyle, Salisbury, Wilts, SP3 6BN.*
Beautiful period thatched country house
Tel: **01747 830224** (also fax no)
Mrs Orman.
Rates fr: *£19.00*-**£22.50.**
Open: All Year (not Xmas)
Beds: 2D 1T 2S
Baths: 1 Ensuite 2 Private 1 Shared
⌂ (10) 🅿 (6) ⊁ ❑ ⓗ ✕ ▥ 🔲 ⓐ ✦

Salisbury to Amesbury

Wilton House, just before Salisbury, dates mainly from the seventeenth century, when Inigo Jones rebuilt it after a fire, and includes a fantastic collection of paintings and landscaped parkland with an old English rose garden. **Salisbury** is an historic city most famous for its cathedral, whose 404-foot spire is the tallest in England, and which is also notable for the chapter house, the vaulted cloisters and the library, which contains one of only four existing original copies of the Magna Carta. The secluded Cathedral Close leads into the narrow medieval city streets. Cycling north, **Old Sarum** is the site of an Iron Age fort, and was settled by Romans, Saxons and Normans, and was the original site of the cathedral before it was transferred (including the fabric) to Salisbury. **Amesbury** is where to make the detour to **Stonehenge**, the world-renowned prehistoric enigma at the heart of Salisbury Plain. In fact the remains of several different constructions separated by hundreds of years, the site seems to have been a centre of religious devotion for centuries. The stones of the earlier circle were hewn from a quarry in Wales and transported; the later circle is remarkable for the sheer size of the megaliths, and their construction into sets of two uprights crossed by a lintel.

Charlton (Shaftesbury) 18

National Grid Ref: ST9022

|O| ◀ The Talbot, Grove Arms,

(1m) *Charnwood Cottage*, *Charlton, Shaftesbury, Dorset, SP7 9LZ.*
Actual grid ref: ST902226
C17th thatched cottage with lovely garden. Good base for touring
Tel: **01747 828310** Mrs Morgan.
Rates fr: *£16.00*-**£20.00**.
Open: All Year (not Xmas)
Beds: 1F 1D **Baths:** 1 Shared
🛏 (5) 🅿 (2) 🖵 🛏 🛋.

Coombe Bissett 19

National Grid Ref: SU1026

|O| ◀ Fox & Goose

(2m) *Swaynes Firs Farm*, *Grimsdyke, Coombe Bissett, Salisbury, Wilts, SP5 5RF.*
Grades: ETB 1 Cr, Approv
Tel: **01725 519240** Mr Shering.
Rates fr: *£20.00*-**£20.00**.
Open: All Year (not Xmas)
Beds: 1F 2T **Baths:** 3 Private
🛏 🅿 (6) 🖵 🛏 🛋.
Spacious farmhouse on working farm with horses, cattle, poultry, geese & duck ponds. All rooms ensuite with colour TV & nice views

(2m) *Cross Farm, Coombe Bissett, Salisbury, Wilts, SP5 4LY.*
Comfortable farmhouse on working farm. Tel: **01722 718293** Mrs Kittermaster.
Rates fr: *£18.00*-**£18.00**.
Open: All Year
Beds: 1F 1T 1S **Baths:** 2 Shared
🛏 🅿 (4) 🖵 🛏 🛋. 🅅 ✔

(1m) *Two Bridges, Homington Road, Coombe Bissett, Salisbury, Wilts, SP5 4LR.*
Riverside home in pretty village
Grades: ETB 2 Cr, Comb
Tel: **01722 718531** Mrs Germain.
Rates fr: *£19.00*-**£25.00**.
Open: All Year (not Xmas)
Beds: 2T
Baths: 1 Ensuite 1 Private
🛏 (5) 🅿 (2) ✔ 🖵 🛋.

Salisbury 20

National Grid Ref: SU1430

|O| ◀ Fox & Goose Inn, George & Dragon, Avon Inn, Bell Inn, Castle Inn, Haunch of Venison

(▲ 0.25m) *Salisbury Youth Hostel, Milford Hill House, Milford Hill, Salisbury, Wiltshire, SP1 2QW.*
Actual grid ref: SU149299
Tel: **01722 327572**
Under 18: £6.55 **Adults:** £9.75
Evening Meals Available (5.30-8pm), Television, Laundry Facilities, Camping Facilities
200-year-old listed building in secluded grounds only a few minutes from the city centre. Enjoy the relaxed atmosphere of the hostel and the well-tended grounds which include a fine old Cedar tree

(0.25m) *48 Wyndham Road, Salisbury, Wilts, SP1 3AB.*
Tastefully restored Edwardian family home. **Grades:** ETB Listed, Comm
Tel: **01722 327757**
Mrs Jukes.
Rates fr: *£16.00*-**£18.00**.
Open: All Year **Beds:** 2D 1T
Baths: 1 Ensuite 1 Shared
🛏 ✔ 🖵 🛋. 🅅

(0.25m) *The Gallery, 36 Wyndham Road, Salisbury, Wilts, SP1 3AB.*
Grades: ETB Listed, Comm
Tel: **01722 324586 / 500956**
Mrs Musslewhite.
Fax no: 01722 324586
Rates fr: *£16.50*-**£23.00**.
Open: All Year
Beds: 1D 2T **Baths:** 3 Ensuite
🛏 (12) ✔ 🖵 🛋. 🅅
Experience our warm hospitality & delicious breakfasts in a non-smoking environment. Well-situated for exploring Salisbury & the many attractions in the area

(0.25m) *Cricket Field Cottage House, Wilton Road, Salisbury, Wilts, SP2 7NS.*
C19th cottage with pavilion annexe. Situated on cricket field
Grades: ETB 3 Cr, High Comm, AA 4 Q select, RAC Acclaim
Tel: **01722 322595** (also fax no)
Mrs James.
Rates fr: *£22.00*-**£32.00**.
Open: All Year
Beds: 4F 5D 2T 3S
Baths: 14 Ensuite
🅿 (14) ✔ 🖵 🗙 🛋. 👶 🅅 🍴

(0.25m) *Rokeby Guest House, 3 Wain-A-Long Road, Salisbury, Wilts, SP1 1LJ.*
Grades: ETB 3 Cr, Comm
Tel: **01722 329800** (also fax no)
Mrs Rogers.
Rates fr: *£20.00*-**£30.00**.
Open: All Year
Beds: 5F 1D 3T
Baths: 5 Ensuite 2 Private 2 Shared
🅿 (7) 🖵 🗙 🛋. 🅅 🍴 🍴 ✔
Beautiful, nostalgic Edwardian guest house quietly situated 10 minutes' walk city/cathedral. Large landscaped gardens with summerhouse, ornamental pond/fountain. Gymnasium, elegant conservatory, licensed restaurant. Brochure available

(0.25m) *The Old Bakery, 35 Bedwin Street, Salisbury, Wilts, SP1 3UT.*
C15th house - cosy oak-beamed bedrooms - city centre location
Grades: ETB 1 Cr, Comm
Tel: **01722 320100**
Mr & Mrs Bunce.
Rates fr: *£17.00*-**£18.00**.
Open: All Year (not Xmas)
Beds: 1F 1D 1T 1S
Baths: 2 Private 1 Shared
🖵 🛋. 🅅

(0.25m) *Michaelmas Cottage, 1 Guilder Lane, Salisbury, Wilts, SP1 1HW.*
Delightful town centre cottage. 400 years of charm & character
Grades: ETB Listed, Comm
Tel: **01722 329580** Mrs Robinson.
Rates fr: *£14.00*.
Open: Easter to Oct
Beds: 1D
Baths: 1 Shared (hostess only)
✔ 🖵 🅅

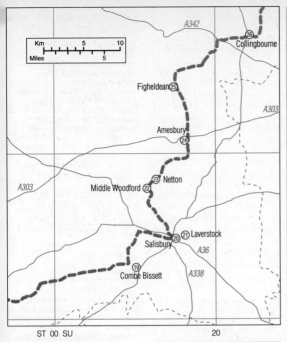

ST 00 SU   20

(0.25m) *Gerrans House, 91 Castle
Road, Salisbury, Wilts, SP1 3RW.*
Comfortable detached house,
private facilities
Grades: ETB 2 Cr, High Comm,
AA 4 Q, Select
Tel: **01722 334394** Mrs Robins.
Rates fr: *£18.00-£25.00.*
Open: Easter to Nov
Beds: 1D 1T **Baths:** 2 Ensuite
🛇 (7) ◻ (2) ⚡◻ ▥.

(0.25m) *Leenas Guest House,
50 Castle Road, Salisbury, Wilts,
SP1 3RL.*
Attractive & comfortable family
house
Tel: **01722 335419** Mrs Street.
Rates fr: *£18.50-£19.00.*
Open: All Year
Beds: 1F 2D 2T 1S
Baths: 5 Ensuite 1 Shared
🛇 ◻ (6) ◻ ▥.

(0.25m) *Hillside, 72 St Marks
Avenue, Salisbury, Wilts, SP1 3DW.*
Comfortable home in secluded
surroundings
Tel: **01722 335474** Mrs Browning.
Rates fr: *£16.00-£16.00.*
Open: All Year (not Xmas)
Beds: 1D 1T **Baths:** 2 Shared
🛇 (7) ◻ (4) ◻ ⚡ ▥. ▾

**Bringing children with
you? Always ask for
any special rates.**

**Pay B&Bs by cash or
cheque and be prepared
to pay up front.**

(0.25m) *The Bell Inn, Warminster
Road, Salisbury, Wilts, SP2 0QD.*
Main road. Village pub
Grades: ETB 2 Cr
Tel: **01722 743336** Mr Elmer.
Rates fr: *£18.00-£20.00.*
Open: All Year
Beds: 1D 1T 1S **Baths:** 3 Private
🛇 (10) ◻ (50) ⚡◻✕ ▥. ▾

(0.25m) *Richburn Guest House,
23-35 Estcourt Road, Salisbury,
Wilts, SP1 3AP.*
Comfortable, homely, Victorian
house
Grades: ETB 2 Cr, Approv,
AA 1 Q, RAC Listed
Tel: **01722 325189** Mrs Loader.
Rates fr: *£15.00-£17.50.*
Open: All Year (not Xmas)
Beds: 2F 4D 2T 2S
Baths: 2 Private 2 Shared
🛇 ◻ (10) ⚡◻ ▥. ▾

(0.25m) *Beulah, 144 Britford
Lane, Salisbury, Wilts, SP2 8AL.*
Bungalow at end of cul-de-sac
Grades: ETB Listed
Tel: **01722 333517** Mr & Mrs Bath.
Rates fr: *£15.00-£15.00.*
Open: All Year
Beds: 1F 1S **Baths:** 1 Shared
🛇 (2) ◻ (4) ⚡◻ ▥. ▪

(0.25m) *Clovelly Guest House,
17-19 Mill Road, Salisbury, Wilts,
SP2 7RT.*
Warm welcome in historic
Salisbury
Grades: ETB Listed, Comm,
AA 3 Q
Tel: **01722 322055**
Rates fr: *£20.00-£21.00.*
Open: All Year
Beds: 2F 2D 4T 6S
Baths: 6 Private 7 Shared
🛇 ◻ (14) ⚡◻ ★ ▥. ▾ ▪

(0.25m) *20 Queens Road,
Salisbury, Wilts, SP1 3AJ.*
Private house, 10 mins from town
Tel: **01722 336024**
Mrs Jerred.
Rates fr: *£12.00-£12.00.*
Open: Easter to Oct
Beds: 1T 1S
Baths: 1 Shared
🛇 (5) ◻ ▥.

Laverstock   21

National Grid Ref: SU1530

🍴 🍺 Duck Inn

(1m) *Pasket House, 57 Church Rd,
Laverstock, Salisbury, Wilts, SP1 1QY.*
Spacious, detached, quiet comfort-
able house
Grades: ETB 2 Cr
Tel: **01722 327651**
Mrs Naish.
Rates fr: *£15.00-£18.00.*
Open: All Year (not Xmas)
Beds: 1D 2T
Baths: 3 Private
🛇 (3) ◻ (4) ⚡◻ ▥. ▾

Middle Woodford   22

National Grid Ref: SU1136

🍴 🍺 The Wheatsheaf, Bridge Inn

(0.5m) *Great Croft, Middle
Woodford, Salisbury, Wilts, SP4 6NR.*
Situated between Salisbury &
Stonehenge
Tel: **01722 782357**
Mrs Cates.
Rates fr: *£16.00-£20.00.*
Open: All Year (not Xmas)
Beds: 1T
Baths: 1 Ensuite
🛇 ◻ (2) ⚡◻ ▥. ▾

Netton   23

National Grid Ref: SU1336

🍴 🍺 Black Horse

(0.25m) *The Old Bakery, Netton,
Salisbury, Wilts, SP4 6AW.*
Pleasantly modernised, former
village bakery
Grades: ETB 1 Cr, Comm
Tel: **01722 782351** Mrs Dunlop.
Rates fr: *£15.00-£15.00.*
Open: All Year (not Xmas)
Beds: 1D 1T 1S **Baths:** 1 Shared
🛇 (5) ◻ (3) ◻ ★ ▥.

ST 00 SU   20

(0.25m) *Thorntons, Netton,*
Salisbury, Wilts, SP4 6AW.
Friendly comfortable quiet village
house
Grades: ETB Listed, Approv
Tel: **01722 782535** Mrs Bridger.
Rates fr: *£15.50-£16.50.*
Open: All Year (not Xmas)
Beds: 1F 1D **Baths:** 2 Shared
🛏 🅿 (3) ⌿ 🖵 ✕ 🛏 🖳 & Ⅴ ▯

(0.25m) *Avonbank, Netton,*
Salisbury, Wilts, SP4 6AW.
Comfortable friendly, in small
village
Tel: **01722 782331** Mrs Vincent.
Rates fr: *£16.00-£20.00.*
Open: All Year (not Xmas)
Beds: 1D 3T
Baths: 1 Ensuite 2 Shared
🛏 🅿 (3) ⌿ 🖵 ✕ 🖳 & Ⅴ

Amesbury   24

National Grid Ref: SU1541

🍴 🍺 New Inn, Antrobus Arms

(0.5m) *Mandalay Guest House,*
15 Stonehenge Road, Amesbury,
Salisbury, Wilts, SP4 7BA.
Elegantly furnished, ensuite bed-
rooms
Grades: ETB 1 Cr, High Comm
Tel: **01980 623733** Mr Courtney.
Fax no: 01980 626642
Rates fr: *£19.00-£28.00.*
Open: All Year
Beds: 1F 1D 2T 1S **Baths:** 5 Private
🛏 🅿 (5) ⌿ 🖵 🖳

(0.5m) *Church Cottage, Church*
Street, Amesbury, Salisbury, Wilts,
SP4 7EY.
Beautiful bedrooms with
ensuite/private bathrooms
Grades: ETB 1 Cr, High Comm
Tel: **01980 624650**
Mr & Mrs Jeffrey.
Rates fr: *£19.00-£29.00.*
Open: All Year (not Xmas)
Beds: 3D
Baths: 3 Private
🛏 (10) ⌿ 🖵 🖳 Ⅴ ▯

Figheldean   25

National Grid Ref: SU1547

🍴 🍺 Dog & Gun

(0.25m) *Vale House, Figheldean,*
Salisbury, Wilts, SP4 8JJ.
Comfortable family house. Centre
village. **Grades:** ETB 2 Cr, Comm
Tel: **01980 670713**
Mrs Strefford.
Rates fr: *£14.50-£14.50.*
Open: All Year (not Xmas)
Beds: 2T 1S
Baths: 1 Ensuite 1 Shared
🛏 🅿 (3) 🖵 🖳 Ⅴ

___

All cycleways are
popular: you are well-
advised to book ahead

Collingbourne Ducis   26

National Grid Ref: SU2453

🍴 🍺 The Shears, School House

(1m) *Hougoumont Farm,*
Collingbourne Ducis,
Marlborough, Wilts, SN8 3ET.
Spacious, comfortable & peaceful
Tel: **01264 850260** Mrs Carter.
Rates fr: *£16.00-£16.00.*
Open: All Year (not Xmas)
Beds: 2D 2T **Baths:** 2 Shared
🛏 🖵 🖳 ⌿

(1m) *Manor Farm, Collingbourne*
Ducis, Marlborough, Wilts, SN8 3SD.
Comfortable farmhouse with
period character
Tel: **01264 850251** Mrs May.
Rates fr: *£17.50-£15.00.*
Open: All Year **Beds:** 2T 1S
Baths: 1 Ensuite 1 Shared
🛏 🅿 (50) ⌿ 🖵 🛏 🖳 ▯ ♠ ⌿

West Grafton   27

National Grid Ref: SU2460

(2m) *Mayfield, West Grafton,*
Marlborough, Wilts, SN8 3BY.
Delightful C15th thatched manor
house surrounded by large peaceful
gardens
Grades: ETB Listed, High Comm
AA 5 Q, Premier Select
Tel: **01672 810339** Mrs Orssich.
Rates fr: *£24.00-£30.00.*
Open: All Year (not Xmas)
Beds: 1T 2D **Baths:** 3 Ensuite
🛏 🅿 (6) 🖵 🖳 & Ⅴ ▯ ⌿

Ramsbury   28

National Grid Ref: SU2771

🍴 🍺 The Raven, The Lamb on the
Strand, George & Dragon

(On route) *Marridge Hill House,*
Ramsbury, Marlborough, Wilts,
SN8 2HG.
Comfortable, relaxed home with
warm welcome
Tel: **01672 520237** Mrs Davies.
Fax no: 01672 520053
Rates fr: *£17.00-£22.00.*
Open: All Year (not Xmas)
Beds: 3T
Baths: 1 Ensuite 1 Shared
🛏 (5) 🅿 (6) ⌿ 🖵 🛏 🖳 Ⅴ

Mildenhall   29

National Grid Ref: SU2070

🍴 🍺 The Horseshoe

(0.25m) *Watersedge, Werg Lane,*
Mildenhall, Marlborough, Wilts,
SN8 2LY.
Riverside position in beautiful
Kennet Valley
Tel: **01672 511590** Mrs Hodder.
Rates fr: *£16.50-£17.00.*
Open: All Year (not Xmas)
Beds: 1D 1S **Baths:** 1 Shared
🛏 (11) 🅿 (3) 🖵 🛏 🖳

Marlborough 30

National Grid Ref: SU1869

🍴 🍺 The Sun, Oddfellows Arms, The Bear, Wellington Arms, Roebuck Inn

(0.25m) *Redlands, Elcot Lane, Marlborough, Wilts, SN8 2BA.*
Warm welcome, rural views, excellent food
Grades: ETB 2 Cr, Comm, AA 4 Q
Tel: 01672 515477 (also fax no)
Mrs Camm.
Rates fr: *£17.50-£25.00.*
Open: All Year (not Xmas)
Beds: 2D 1T
Baths: 1 Ensuite 1 Shared
🛇 🅿 (4) ⊬⌷🗶 🎟. 🎟 🛊

(0.25m) *Kennet Beeches, 54 George Lane, Marlborough, Wilts, SN8 4BY.*
Comfortable modern house, riverside garden
Grades: ETB Listed
Tel: 01672 512579
Mr & Mrs Young.
Rates fr: *£16.00-£16.00.*
Open: All Year
Beds: 2T 1S
Baths: 1 Shared
🅿 (2) ⊬ 🎟. 🎟 ✦

(0.25m) *Cartref, 63 George Lane, Marlborough, Wilts, SN8 4BY.*
Actual grid ref: SU1969
Family home near country town
Grades: ETB Listed, Comm
Tel: 01672 512771 Mrs Harrison.
Rates fr: *£16.00-£16.00.*
Open: All Year (not Xmas)
Beds: 1F 1D 1T
Baths: 1 Shared
🛇 (1) 🅿 (2) 🎟 🎟. 🎟 🛊 ✦

(0.25m) *5 Reeds Ground, London Road, Marlborough, Wilts, SN8 2AW.*
Modern clean comfortable private house
Tel: 01672 513926 Mrs Waite.
Rates fr: *£16.00-£20.00.*
Open: All Year (not Xmas)
Beds: 1D
Baths: 1 Private
🅿 (2) ⊬⌷ 🎟. 🛊 ✦

Manton 31

National Grid Ref: SU1768

🍴 🍺 Oddfellows' Arms

(1m) *Sunrise Farm, Manton, Marlborough, Wilts, SN8 4HL.*
Actual grid ref: SU168682
Quietly situated, restful home, panoramic views
Tel: 01672 512878 (also fax no)
Mrs Couzens.
Rates fr: *£16.00-£20.00.*
Open: Easter to Sep
Beds: 1D 2T
Baths: 1 Private 1 Shared
🅿 (4) ⊬⌷ 🎟. 🎟 🛊

All rates are subject to alteration at the owners' discretion.

Broad Hinton 32

National Grid Ref: SU1076

🍴 🍺 Crown Inn

(On route) *Damar Guest House, Post Office Lane, Broad Hinton, Swindon, Wilts, SN4 9PB.*
Large modern house, lovely views
Tel: 01793 731442 Mrs Baker.
Rates fr: *£15.00-£17.50.*
Open: All Year (not Xmas)
Beds: 1F 1T 1S **Baths:** 1 Shared
🛇 (8) 🅿 (5) ⊬⌷ 🎟. 🎟 🛊 ✦

Uffcott 33

National Grid Ref: SU1278

🍴 🍺 Crown Inn, Bell Inn

(1m) *Uffcott House, Uffcott, Swindon, Wilts, SN4 9NB.*
Actual grid ref: SU126775
Spacious period farmhouse, superb views
Tel: 01793 731207 (also fax no)
Mr & Mrs Hussey.
Rates fr: *£17.00-£24.00.*
Open: All Year (not Xmas)
Beds: 1D 2T
Baths: 1 Private 1 Shared
🛇 (8) 🅿 (6) ⊬⌷ 🎟. ✦

Broad Town 34

National Grid Ref: SU0977

(2m) *Little Cotmarsh Farm, Broad Town, Wootton Bassett, Swindon, Wilts, SN4 7RA.*
Actual grid ref: SU0979
Superb accommodation in peaceful hamlet
Tel: 01793 731322 Mrs Richards.
Rates fr: *£16.00-£16.00.*
Open: All Year (not Xmas)
Beds: 1F 1D 1T
Baths: 1 Private 2 Shared
🛇 🅿 (10) ⊬⌷ 🎟. 🛊 ✦

Brinkworth 35

National Grid Ref: SU0184

🍴 🍺 Three Crowns

(2m) *B & B, Bella Pais, Barnes Green, Brinkworth, Chippenham, Wilts, SN15 5AG.*
Comfortable friendly village house
Grades: ETB Listed, Comm
Tel: 01666 510204 Mrs Bennett.
Fax no: 01666 510520
Rates fr: *£15.00-£15.00.*
Open: All Year (not Xmas)
Beds: 2D 1S **Baths:** 1 Shared
🛇 🅿 (4) ⊬⌷ 🎟 🗶 🎟. 🎟 🛊

Amesbury to Malmesbury

The cycleway now heads north up the east side of Salisbury Plain, through the Vale of Pewsey, back across the Kennet and Avon Canal and into the Marlborough Downs. **Marlborough** has the widest high street in England, with a fine display of Georgian buildings and half-timbered cottages. Back up into the Downs, and a worthwhile detour would be south along **the Ridgeway** National Trail to Avebury, another important prehistoric site. Here stands a stone circle far wider than Stonehenge, though the stones are much smaller and not so consummately finished. Nearby are Silbury Hill, Europe's largest man-made prehistoric mound, and West Kennet Long Barrow, a burial complex dating from the fourth millennium BC. This is probably best attempted only on an all terrain bicycle. Close to the junction of the cycleway with the Ridgeway is **Hackpen Hill**, where you will find another white horse hillside carving and a panoramic viewpoint over Swindon to the Thames Valley. From here it's off the Downs into the final stretch to Malmesbury.

Charlton (Malmesbury)36

National Grid Ref: ST9589

🍴 🍺 Horse & Groom

(1m) *Stonehill Farm, Charlton, Malmesbury, Wilts, SN16 9DY.*
Welcoming, comfortable beds, delicious breakfasts
Grades: ETB Listed, Comm, AA 2 Q
Tel: 01666 823310 (also fax no)
Mr & Mrs Edwards.
Rates fr: *£17.50-£18.00.*
Open: All Year **Beds:** 1D 2T
Baths: 1 Private 1 Shared
🛇 🅿 (4) ⌷ 🎟 🎟. ✦

Yorkshire Dales Cycleway

The Yorkshire Dales National Park, the heart of the Pennines, is one of England's most beautiful areas, with rolling moors forming the backdrop to gentle river valleys. The **Yorkshire Dales Cycleway** is a 131-mile tour of the Dales, starting and finishing at Skipton. The route is directed along quiet roads, but some sections are very up-and-down, so a reasonably resilient bike (and cyclist!) is necessary. The cycleway is signposted by rectangular blue direction signs with a cycle silhouette.

A detailed **guide** to the cycleway route (6 route cards), which includes a list of cycle repair/hire shops on or near to the route, is available from the Yorkshire Dales National Park Authority, Cragg Hill Road, Horton-in-Ribblesdale, Settle, North Yorkshire BD24 0HN, tel 01729 860481, @ £2 (+50p p&p).

Maps: Ordnance Survey 1:50,000 Landranger series: 98, 99, 103, 104

Trains: Skipton, Settle & Dent are served by the famous scenic Leeds-Settle-Carlisle Railway.

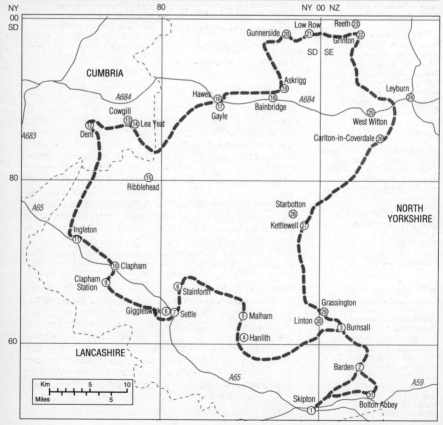

Skipton 1

National Grid Ref: SD9851

¶ ☜ Elm Tree, Slater's Arms

(0.25m) *Highfield Hotel,*
58 Keighley Road, Skipton,
N. Yorks, BD23 2NB.
Friendly town hotel, luxury ensuite
accommodation, centrally heated,
bar, restaurant
Grades: ETB 3 Cr, Approv,
AA 3 Q, RAC Acclaim
Tel: 01756 793182 (also fax no)
Rates fr: £18.50-**£18.50.**
Open: All Year (not Xmas)
Beds: 2F 1T 5D 2S
Baths: 10 Ensuite
☒ ☐ ☐ ✕ ▥ â

(5m) *Low Skibeden Farmhouse,*
Skibeden Road, Skipton, N. Yorks,
BD23 6AB.
A peaceful location with lovely
gardens & panoramic countryside
views
Grades: ETB 2 Cr, Comm
Tel: 01756 793849 / 0411 275683
Mrs Simpson.
Fax no: 01756 793804
Rates fr: £16.00-**£30.00.**
Open: All Year **Beds:** 3F 1D 1T
Baths: 3 Ensuite 2 Shared
☒ (12) ☐ (5) ⟀ ☐ ▥ ⩔

(0.25m) *Syke House, 103 Raikes*
Road, Skipton, N. Yorks, BD23 1LS.
Set in quiet residential area
Tel: 01756 793460 Mrs Lambert.
Rates fr: £15.00-**£17.50.**
Open: All Year (not Xmas)
Beds: 1T 1D
Baths: 1 Ensuite 1 Shared
☒ (0) ☐ (2) ⟀ ☐ ✕ ▥ Ⓥ

Barden 2

National Grid Ref: SE0557

(0.25m) *Howgill Lodge, Barden,*
Skipton, N. Yorks, BD23 6DJ.
Actual grid ref: SE065593
Converted C17th barn, magnificent
views
Tel: 01756 720655 Mrs Foster.
Rates fr: £26.00-**£32.00.**
Open: All Year
Beds: 1F 2D 1T
Baths: 4 Ensuite
☒ ☐ (6) ☐ ▥ â ⩔

Burnsall 3

National Grid Ref: SE0361

(1m) *Holly Tree Farm, Thorpe,*
Burnsall, Skipton, N. Yorks,
BD23 6BJ.
Actual grid ref: SE014617
Quiet, homely Dales sheep farm
Tel: 01756 720604 Mrs Hall.
Rates fr: £17.00-**£17.00.**
Open: All Year
Beds: 1D 1S
Baths: 1 Shared
⟀ ☐

(On route) *Red Lion Hotel,*
Burnsall, Skipton, N. Yorks,
BD23 6BU.
Actual grid ref: SE033612
C16th ferryman's inn on River
Wharfe
Grades: AA 2 St, RAC 2 St
Tel: 01756 720204 Mrs Grayshon.
Fax no: 01756 720292
Rates fr: £32.00-**£32.00.**
Open: All Year
Beds: 2F 4D 4T 1S
Baths: 12 Ensuite
☒ ☐ (40) ☐ ✕ ▥ Ⓥ â ⩔

Hanlith 4

National Grid Ref: SD9061

¶ ☜ The Buck

(0.5m) *Coachmans Cottage,*
Hanlith, Malham, Skipton,
N. Yorks, BD23 4BP.
Tranquil C17th cottage, every
comfort
Tel: 01729 830538 Mrs Jenkins.
Rates fr: £21.00-**£25.00.**
Open: All Year (not Xmas)
Beds: 2D 1T **Baths:** 3 Private
☒ (10) ☐ (3) ⟀ ☐ ▥ â ⩔

Pay B&Bs by cash or
cheque and be prepared
to pay up front.

Malham 5

National Grid Ref: SD9062

¶ ☜ Lister's Arms, Buck Hotel

(▲ 0.25m) *Malham Youth Hostel,*
John Dower Memorial Hostel,
Malham, Skipton, North Yorkshire,
BD23 4DE.
Actual grid ref: SD901629
Warden: M & C Peryer.
Tel: 01729 830321
Under 18: £6.55
Adults: £9.75
Evening Meals Available (7pm),
Family Bunk Rooms, Television,
Showers, Shop
Superbly located purpose-built
hostel close to centre of
picturesque Malham village

(1m) *Miresfield Farm, Malham,*
Skipton, N. Yorks, BD23 4DA.
Grades: ETB 3 Cr, Comm
Tel: 01729 830414
Mrs Sharp.
Rates fr: £20.00-**£30.00.**
Open: All Year
Beds: 2F 6D 6T 1S
Baths: 12 Private 2 Shared
☒ ☐ ☐ ☆ ✕ ▥ ⅙ Ⓥ â ⩔
Listed farmhouse in landscaped
garden. All home cooking. Two
well furnished lounges with TV &
log fires. Groups catered for

Skipton to Ingleton

Skipton, one of the important market towns of the region,
traces its roots to an ancient Anglo-Saxon settlement - its name
means 'sheep farm'. Skipton Castle is one of the best-
preserved medieval castles in Britain; at the centre stands a
single yew tree planted in 1659. Also here are Holy Trinity
Church, notable for the fifteenth-century bossed roof, and a
museum of Craven, the North Yorkshire district in which the
town lies. Out of Skipton the route heads northeast into
Wharfedale. Here you will find the fifteenth-century Barden
Tower, looking out across Barden Moor, before heading on to
Appletreewick and the picturesque village of **Burnsall**. Then
it's west through the beautiful limestone scenery of the
Southern Dales into **Malhamdale**, where stand Malham Cove, a
breathtaking 300-foot-high limestone natural amphitheatre, and
the deep ravine of Gordale Scar. Close by you can find Janet's
Foss, a waterfall with overhanging trees. The route passes to
the south of **Malham Tarn**, an upland lake with a nature reserve
protecting many species of waterfowl, and takes you westwards around the imposing mass of **Fountains Fell** and into
Ribblesdale. Here you cycle south alongside the famous
Leeds-Settle-Carlisle Railway line, through the typically pretty
Dales villages of Stainforth and Langcliffe into **Settle**. From here
it's northwest to **Clapham**, continuing to Ingleton with
Ingleborough, one of the so-called Three Peaks, on your right:
remains of a Celtic settlement can be found at the gritstone
summit by anyone wishing to take time out and make the climb.

(On route) *Sparth House Hotel,*
Malham, Skipton, N. Yorks,
BD23 4DA.
Tel: **01729 830315**
Mr & Mrs Oates.
Fax no: 01729 830672
Rates fr: £18.50-£22.00.
Open: All Year
Beds: 6D 3T 1S
Baths: 7 Ensuite 3 Shared
🛏 🅿 (4) ☐ ✕ Ⅲ & Ⅴ
Small family-run country house
hotel in picturesque traditional
Dales village. Licensed bar,
comfortable accommodation,
superb food. Super value, half
board breaks all year

(On route) *Beck Hall,* *Malham,*
Skipton, N. Yorks, *BD23 4DJ.*
Set in riverside garden
Tel: **01729 830332**
Mr & Mrs Boatwright.
Rates fr: £15.00-£18.50.
Open: All Year (not Xmas)
Beds: 2F 8D 2T 1S
Baths: 11 Private 4 Shared
🛏 🅿 (30) ☗ ✕ Ⅲ Ⅴ

Stainforth   6

National Grid Ref: SD8267

(▲ 0.25m) *Stainforth Youth*
Hostel, Taitlands, Stainforth,
Settle, North Yorkshire, BD24 9PA.
Actual grid ref: SD821668
Warden: D & D McGuinness.
Tel: **01729 823577**
Under 18: £5.40 **Adults:** £8.00
Evening Meals Available (7pm),
Family Bunk Rooms, Television,
Showers, Shop
Victorian Listed building with fine
interior, set in extensive grounds
with grazing paddock. Discount
taxi service to/from Horton
available

Settle   7

National Grid Ref: SD8163
🍴 🍺 Black Horse

(On route) *Langcliffe Lodge,*
Langcliffe Road, Settle, N. Yorks,
BD24 9LT.
Attractive cosy Victorian country
lodge
Tel: **01729 823362** Mrs Westall.
Rates fr: £18.50-£20.00.
Open: All Year
Beds: 2D 1T
Baths: 3 Ensuite
🛏 🅿 (4) ⅍ ☐ ☗ ✕ Ⅲ & Ⅴ ▮ ⅍

(0.25m) *Liverpool House, Chapel*
Square, Settle, N. Yorks, BD24 9HR.
Mid C18th town house
Tel: **01729 822247** Mrs Duerden.
Rates fr: £16.00-£16.00.
Open: All Year
Beds: 2D 3T 3S
Baths: 2 Shared
🛏 🅿 (8) ⅍ ☐ Ⅲ ▮ ⅍

Giggleswick   8

National Grid Ref: SD8164

(0.5m) *The Black Horse Hotel,*
Church Street, Giggleswick, Settle,
N. Yorks, BD24 0BJ.
C16th coaching inn, log fire, real
ales, good food
Grades: ETB 3 Cr
Tel: **01729 822506**
Mr & Mrs Starkey.
Rates fr: £20.00-£25.00.
Open: All Year (not Xmas)
Beds: 1F 2T
Baths: 3 Ensuite
🛏 🅿 (20) ☗ ☗ ✕ Ⅲ Ⅴ ▮

(0.5m) *Yorkshire Dales Field*
Centre, Church Street,
Giggleswick, Settle, N. Yorks,
BD24 0BE.
Famous for cooking, groups only
Tel: **01729 824180** Mrs Barbour.
Rates fr: £8.50-£8.50.
Open: All Year
Beds: 6F 2S
Baths: 5 Shared
🛏 🅿 (7) ⅍ ☐ ☗ ✕ Ⅲ Ⅴ ▮ ⅍

Clapham Station   9

National Grid Ref: SD7367

(0.25m) *Flying Horseshoe Hotel,*
Clapham Station, Clapham,
Lancaster. LA2 8ES.
Idyllic spot - panoramic views
Tel: **015242 51229**
Mr & Mrs Harris.
Rates fr: £20.00-£25.00.
Open: All Year
Beds: 3D 1T
Baths: 4 Ensuite
🛏 🅿 (40) ☐ ☗ ✕ Ⅲ Ⅴ

Clapham   10

National Grid Ref: SD7469
🍴 🍺 Goat Gap Inn

(0.25m) *Goat Gap Inn, Newby,*
Clapham, Lancaster. LA2 8JB.
Goat Gap Inn, famous C17th
hostelry
Tel: **015242 41230**
Mr & Mrs Willis.
Rates fr: £24.00-£35.00.
Open: All Year
Beds: 1F 4D 1T
Baths: 4 Ensuite 2 Shared
🛏 🅿 (80) ☐ ☗ ✕ Ⅲ Ⅴ ▮ ⅍

Pay B&Bs by
cash or cheque and
be prepared to
pay up front.

Ingleton   11

National Grid Ref: SD6973
🍴 🍺 Bridge Hotel, Craven Heifer,
Marton Arms, Wheatsheaf Hotel

(▲ 0.25m) *Ingleton Youth Hostel,*
Greta Tower, Sammy Lane,
Ingleton, Carnforth, Lancashire,
LA6 3EG.
Actual grid ref: SD695733
Tel: **015242 41444**
Under 18: £4.95 **Adults:** £7.20
Evening Meals Available (7pm),
Self-catering Facilities, Showers,
In a location ideal for families,
adjacent to the National Park and
with an outdoor swimming pool
nearby, the hostel is also popular
with walkers and a centre for
climbing, caving and exploring the
Dales

(1m) *Gatehouse Farm, Far West*
House, Ingleton, Carnforth, Lancs,
LA6 3NR.
Working farm, home cooking, in
Yorkshire Dale National Park
Grades: ETB 2 Cr, Comm
Tel: **015242 41458 / 41307**
Mrs Lund.
Rates fr: £18.00-£20.00.
Open: All Year (not Xmas)
Beds: 1F 1D 1T
Baths: 3 Ensuite
🛏 🅿 (4) ⅍ ☐ ☗ ✕ Ⅲ Ⅴ ▮

(0.25m) *Springfield Hotel, Main*
Street, Ingleton, Carnforth, Lancs,
LA6 3HJ.
Victorian villa in own grounds.
Central Lakes and Dales. Private
fishing, home cooking, panoramic
views
Grades: ETB 3 Cr, Comm
Tel: **015242 41280** Mr Thornton.
Rates fr: £22.00-£22.00.
Open: All Year (not Xmas)
Beds: 1F 3D 1T
Baths: 5 Private 1 Shared
🛏 🅿 (12) ☐ ☗ ✕ Ⅲ Ⅴ ▮ ⅍

(0.25m) *Riversmeet, Garden*
Holme, Ingleton, Carnforth, Lancs,
LA6 3ES.
Modern, quiet private house
Tel: **015242 42118** Mrs Kirkbride.
Rates fr: £15.00-£19.00.
Open: All Year (not Xmas)
Beds: 1D
Baths: 1 Ensuite
🛏 🅿 (4) ☐ ☗ Ⅲ Ⅴ

(0.25m) *Ingleborough View Guest*
House, Main Street, Ingleton,
Carnforth, Lancs, LA6 3HH.
Picturesque riverside location.
excellent accommodation
Grades: ETB 2 Cr, High Comm
Tel: **015242 41523**
Mrs Brown.
Rates fr: £18.00-£25.00.
Open: All Year (not Xmas)
Beds: 1F 2D 1T
Baths: 2 Ensuite 2 Private
🛏 🅿 (4) ☐ ☗ Ⅲ Ⅴ ▮ ⅍

Dent   12

National Grid Ref: SD7086

¶¶ ◀ Sun Inn, George & Dragon

(On route) *Stone Close Tea Shop,
Main Street, Dent, Sedbergh,
Cumbria, LA10 5QL.*
Actual grid ref: SD705868
C17th oak-beamed, stone-flagged
tea-shop
Tel: 015396 25231 Mr Rushton.
Fax no: 01539 726567
Rates fr: *£14.75-£18.75.*
Open: Jan to Dec
Beds: 1F 1D 1S **Baths:** 1 Shared
♿ ⅊ ⊁ 🛏 ▥ ⓘ ⊛

(0.25m) *Dent Stores, Dent,
Sedbergh, Cumbria, LA10 5QL.*
Village centre, friendly family
house
Tel: 015396 25209 Mrs Smith.
Rates fr: *£16.00-£16.00.*
Open: All Year (not Xmas)
Beds: 2D 1T 1S **Baths:** 1 Shared
♿ ⅊ (3) ⊡ 🛏 ▥ ⓘ ⊛

(2m) *Rash House, Dent Foot,
Dent, Sedbergh, Cumbria, LA10 5SU.*
Actual grid ref: SD6690
C18th farmhouse
Tel: 015396 20113 (also fax no)
Mrs Hunter.
Rates fr: *£16.00-£18.00.*
Open: All Year (not Xmas)
Beds: 1F 1D
Baths: 1 Shared
♿ ⅊ (2) ⊡ 🛏 ✕ ▥ ⓘ ⊛

(0.25m) *Smithy Fold, Whernside
Manor, Dent, Sedbergh, Cumbria,
LA10 5RE.*
Actual grid ref: SD725859
Small C18th country house
Tel: 015396 25368 Mrs Cheetham.
Rates fr: *£15.00-£15.00.*
Open: All Year (not Xmas)
Beds: 1F 1D 1T **Baths:** 1 Shared
♿ ⅊ (6) ⊡ 🛏 ✕ ▥ ⓘ ⊛

(0.25m) *Slack Cottage, Dent,
Sedbergh, Cumbria, LA10 5QU.*
Actual grid ref: SD716859
Comfortable old cottage
Tel: 015396 25439 Mrs Gunson.
Rates fr: *£13.00-£13.00.*
Open: All Year (not Xmas)
Beds: 1D 1S **Baths:** 1 Shared
♿ ⅊ ⅊ 🛏 ▥ ⓘ ⊛

Cowgill   13

National Grid Ref: SD7587

¶¶ ◀ Sportsman Inn

(0.25m) *The Sportsman's Inn,
Cowgill, Dent, Sedbergh,
LA10 5RG.*
300-year-old Dales inn, Listed
building
Tel: 015396 25282 Mrs Martin.
Rates fr: *£20.00.*
Open: All Year
Beds: 1F 3D 2T **Baths:** 3 Shared
♿ ⅊ (10) 🛏 ✕ ▥ ⓘ

(0.25m) *Scow Cottage, Cowgill,
Dent, Sedbergh, Cumbria, LA10 5RN.*
Actual grid ref: SD774853
Attractive, comfortable 250-year-
old Dales farmhouse
Tel: 015396 25445 Mrs Ferguson.
Rates fr: *£16.00-£19.00.*
Open: All Year
Beds: 1D 1T
Baths: 1 Shared
♿ (12) ⅊ (4) ⅊ 🛏 ✕ ▥ ⓘ ⊛

Lea Yeat   14

National Grid Ref: SD7686

(0.25m) *River View, Lea Yeat,
Cowgill, Sedbergh, Cumbria,
LA10 5RF.*
Actual grid ref: SD761869
Converted Quaker meeting house
Tel: 015396 25592
Mr & Mrs Playfoot.
Rates fr: *£15.00-£15.00.*
Open: All Year (not Xmas)
Beds: 1D 1T **Baths:** 1 Shared
♿ (12) ⅊ (2) ⅊ ⊡ ▥ ⓘ ⊛

All cycleways are
popular: you are well-
advised to book ahead

Ribblehead   15

National Grid Ref: SD7880

¶¶ ◀ Station Inn

(3m) *Gearstones Farm,
Ribblehead, Ingleton, Carnforth,
Lancs, LA6 3AS.*
Old Dales farm cottage
Tel: 015242 41405 Mrs Timmins.
Rates fr: *£14.00-£14.00.*
Open: Easter to Oct
Beds: 1F 1D 1T
Baths: 1 Shared
♿ ⅊ ✕ ▥ ⓘ ⊛

Hawes   16

National Grid Ref: SD8789

¶¶ ◀ White Hart Inn, Board Hotel,
Fountain Hotel, Crown Hotel

(▲0.25m) *Hawes Youth Hostel,
Lancaster Terrace, Hawes, North
Yorkshire, DL8 3LQ.*
Actual grid ref: SD867897
Warden: C & P Harman.
Tel: 01969 667368
Under 18: £5.95 **Adults:** £8.80
Evening meals Available (7pm),
Family Bunk Rooms, Television,
Games Room, Showers, Shop
*Friendly and attractively
refurbished purpose-built hostel
overlooking Hawes and
Wensleydale beyond*

Ingleton to Redmire

From Ingleton you head north through **Kingsdale**, and cross into Cumbria with **Whernside**, another of the Three Peaks, towering to your right and **Gragareth** to the left - you are now in **Deepdale**, one of the most scenic parts of the cycleway. Deepdale leads into **Dentdale**, which shelters the picturesque village of **Dent**, with its cobbled streets. From Dent it's east to **Cowgill** and then across the Leeds-Settle-Carlisle Railway line and back into North Yorkshire. Here you cycle northeast through **Widdale**, with Widdale Fell on the left, to **Hawes**, the main market town of **Wensleydale**, renowned for its eponymous cheese. Worth a visit here is the Dales Countryside Museum, tracing the history of many local industries. There is also a National Park Information Centre. A little to the north of the town is Hardaw Force, the highest above-ground single-drop waterfall in England, and further along the same detour you can find the Buttertubs, a striking group of natural wells. From Hawes you head east through Wensleydale along the banks of the River Ure to **Askrigg**, and then north, climbing steeply across the heather moorland of Askrigg Common, before descending into **Swaledale**, one of the most idyllically beautiful (famous for its distinctive breed of sheep). This rugged landscape, marked by the famous Dales dry stone walls, forms the backdrop for a string of pretty villages before you head south at **Grinton**, climbing over Grinton Moor and then descending back into Wensleydale at the village of **Redmire**. Close to here stands Bolton Castle, dating from 1379, where Mary, Queen of Scots was imprisoned in the late sixteenth century.

(0.25m) *Tarney Fors, Hawes,*
N. Yorks, DL8 3LS.
Grades: ETB 3 Cr, Comm
Tel: 01969 667475 Mrs Harpley.
Rates fr: *£24.00*-**£38.00**.
Open: Mar to Nov
Beds: 3D
Baths: 3 Private
🄿 ⍨ 🗖 ✕ 🖬 Ⓥ ♦
Beautiful ex-farmhouse in idyllic
location for walking, cycling,
touring. Good food, wonderful
breakfasts, off road parking,
licensed. 1.5 miles west of Hawes.

(0.25m) *Ebor House, Burtersett*
Road, Hawes, N. Yorks, DL8 3NT.
Actual grid ref: SD876897
Family-run, central, friendly. Ideal
base for touring the Dales
Grades: ETB 3 Cr, Comm
Tel: 01969 667337 (also fax no)
Mrs Clark.
Rates fr: *£17.00*-**£17.00**.
Open: All Year (not Xmas)
Beds: 2D 1T 1S
Baths: 2 Private 1 Shared
🄿 🄿 (4) ⍨ 🗖 🖬 🖬 Ⓥ ♦

(On route) *Old Station House,*
Hawes, N. Yorks, DL8 3NL.
Actual grid ref: SD875898
Grades: ETB 2 Cr, High Comm
Tel: 01969 667785
Mr & Mrs Watkinson.
Rates fr: *£20.00*-**£28.00**.
Open: All Year (not Xmas/New
Year)
Beds: 1D 2T
Baths: 2 Ensuite 1 Private
🄿 (4) ⍨ 🗖 🖬 ᏸ ♦
Former stationmaster's house with
large garden. Comfortable lounge
with large selection of books and
maps. Open fire. Friendly
welcome; free supper drinks served
in lounge

(0.25m) *Steppe Haugh Guest*
House, Townhead, Hawes, N.
Yorks, DL8 3RH.
C17th house offering a wealth of
character and atmosphere
Grades: ETB 2 Cr, Comm
Tel: 01969 667645 Mrs Grattan.
Rates fr: *£17.00*-**£19.00**.
Open: All Year
Beds: 4D 1T 1S
Baths: 2 Ensuite 2 Shared
ᏸ (7) 🄿 (6) 🗖 ᕁ ✕ 🖬 Ⓥ

(0.25m) *Board Hotel, Market*
Place, Hawes, N. Yorks, DL8 3RQ.
A friendly traditional Dales pub
Grades: ETB 2 Cr, Comm
Tel: 01969 667223 Mr Barron.
Rates fr: *£20.00*-**£20.00**.
Open: All Year
Beds: 2D 1T **Baths:** 3 Private
ᏸ 🄿 🗖 ✕ 🖬 Ⓥ ᏸ

The lowest *double* rate per
person is shown in *italics*.

(0.25m) *Halfway House, Hawes,*
N. Yorks, DL8 3LL.
Actual grid ref: SD865902
Small homely Dales farmhouse
Tel: 01969 667442 Mrs Guy.
Rates fr: *£16.00*-**£20.00**.
Open: Easter to Nov
Beds: 1D 1T **Baths:** 1 Shared
ᏸ 🄿 (4) ⍨ 🗖 Ⓥ ♦

(0.25m) *Pry House, Hawes,*
N. Yorks, DL8 3LP.
Actual grid ref: SD8691
Working farm in Herriot country
Tel: 01969 667241 Mrs Fawcett.
Rates fr: *£15.00*-**£16.00**.
Open: Easter to Nov
Beds: 1F 2D
Baths: 1 Shared
ᏸ 🄿 (3) ⍨ 🗖 🖬 Ⓥ ♦

(0.25m) *The Green Dragon Inn,*
Hardraw, Hawes, N. Yorks, DL8 3.
Olde worlde inn/hotel, fully mod-
ernised
Tel: 01969 667392 Mr Stead.
Rates fr: *£17.00*-**£18.00**.
Open: All Year (not Xmas)
Beds: 1F 11D 1T 3S
Baths: 16 Private
ᏸ 🄿 🄿 ᕁ ✕ 🖬 Ⓥ ᏸ ♦

(0.25m) *Cocketts Hotel &*
Restaurant, Market Place, Hawes,
N. Yorks, DL8 3RD.
C17th old Quaker meeting house
Grades: ETB 3 Cr, High Comm,
AA 2 St
Tel: 01969 667312 Mr Bedford.
Rates fr: *£22.00*-**£30.00**.
Open: All Year (not Xmas)
Beds: 6D 2T
Baths: 8 Ensuite
ᏸ (10) 🄿 ⍨ 🗖 ✕ 🖬 ᏸ Ⓥ ᏸ ♦

Gayle   17
National Grid Ref

🍴 ⌖ Board Hotel, Fountain Hotel,
Crown Hotel

(0.5m) *Gayle Laithe, Gayle,*
Hawes, N. Yorks, DL8 3RR.
Modern, comfortable, converted
barn
Tel: 01969 667397
Mrs McGregor.
Rates fr: *£16.00*-**£16.00**.
Open: Easter to Nov
Beds: 1D 1T 1S
Baths: 1 Shared
ᏸ 🄿 (2) 🗖 🖬 Ⓥ ᏸ

(0.5m) *East House, Gayle, Hawes,*
N. Yorks, DL8 3RZ.
Actual grid ref: SD871892
Spacious comfortable country
house
Grades: ETB 2 Cr, Comm
Tel: 01969 667405
Mrs Ward.
Rates fr: *£16.00*-**£16.00**.
Open: Easter to October
Beds: 1F 1T 1D 1S
Baths: 1 Ensuite 1 Shared
ᏸ (5) 🄿 (3) 🗖 🖬 Ⓥ ᏸ ♦

(0.5m) *Ivy House, Gayle, Hawes,*
N. Yorks, DL8 3RZ.
Quiet, comfortable house, beautiful
views
Tel: 01969 667476
Mrs Chapman.
Rates fr: *£13.00*-**£14.00**.
Open: All Year (not Xmas)
Beds: 1F 1D
Baths: 1 Shared
🄿 ⍨ 🗖 ᕁ 🖬 ♦

(0.5m) *Rookhurst Hotel, West*
End, Gayle, Hawes, N. Yorks,
DL8 3RT.
Family-run hotel beside Pennine
Way
Grades: AA 2 St
Tel: 01969 667454 (also fax no)
Mrs VanDerSteen.
Rates fr: *£30.00*-**£30.00**.
Open: Feb to Dec
Beds: 4D 1T
Baths: 5 Private
ᏸ (12) 🄿 (10) ⍨ 🗖 ✕ 🖬 Ⓥ ᏸ ♦

Bainbridge   18
National Grid Ref: SD9390

(1m) *High Force Farm,*
Bainbridge, Leyburn, N. Yorks,
DL8 3DL.
Warm welcome, relaxed
atmosphere
Tel: 01969 650379
Mrs Iveson.
Rates fr: *£13.00*.
Open: Jan to Nov
Beds: 1F 1D
Baths: 2 Shared
ᏸ (5) 🄿 (2) 🖬

(0.5m) *Rose & Crown Hotel,*
Bainbridge, Wensleydale, Leyburn,
N. Yorks, DL8 3EE.
500 year-old coaching inn
Grades: ETB 4 Cr, Comm,
AA 2 St, RAC 2 St
Tel: 01969 650225
Mr Collins.
Fax no: 01969 650735
Rates fr: *£26.30*-**£30.00**.
Open: All Year
Beds: 1F 9D 2T
Baths: 12 Private
ᏸ 🄿 (65) 🗖 ᕁ ✕ 🖬 Ⓥ ᏸ ♦

Askrigg   19
National Grid Ref: SD9491

🍴 ⌖ Crown Inn

(0.5m) *Whitfield, Helm, Askrigg,*
Leyburn, N. Yorks, DI8 3JF.
Tranquil environment with spectac-
ular views
Grades: ETB 2 Cr, Comm
Tel: 01969 650565 (also fax no)
Mr Empsall.
Rates fr: *£18.00*-**£18.00**.
Open: All Year (not Xmas)
Beds: 1T
Baths: 1 Ensuite 1 Shared
ᏸ 🄿 (2) ⍨ 🗖 ᕁ 🖬 Ⓥ ♦

(0.25m) *Milton House, Askrigg, Leyburn, N. Yorks, DL8 3HJ.*
Lovely comfortable family home situated in beautiful open countryside. Private parking
Grades: ETB 2 Cr, Comm
Tel: 01969 650217 Mrs Percival.
Rates fr: *£18.00.*
Open: All Year (not Xmas)
Beds: 3D
Baths: 3 Private
🛏 (10) 🅿 (3) ♁ ⽹ ✕ ▥ Ⓥ ⓐ ⼳

(0.25m) *Thornsgill House, Moor Road, Askrigg, Leyburn, N. Yorks, DL8 3HH.*
A warm welcome awaits you
Grades: ETB 2 Cr, High Comm
Tel: 01969 650617 Mrs Gilyeat.
Rates fr: *£21.00.*
Open: All Year
Beds: 2D 1T
Baths: 3 Private
🛏 (10) 🅿 (3) ⼳ ♁ ⽹ ✕ ▥ Ⓥ ⓐ

(0.25m) *Lucys House, Askrigg, Leyburn, N. Yorks, DL8 3HT.*
C17th cottage. Lovely views & garden
Tel: 01969 650586 Mrs Hartley.
Rates fr: *£17.00-£17.00.*
Open: All Year (not Xmas)
Beds: 1T
Baths: 1 Private
⼳ ♁ ⽹ ✕ ▥ Ⓥ

Gunnerside   20

National Grid Ref: SD9598
🍴 🍺 Farmers' Arms

(0.25m) *Oxnop Hall, Low Oxnop, Gunnerside, Richmond, N. Yorks, DL11 6JJ.*
Oxnop Hall is in an environmentally sensitive area. Stone walls and barns
Grades: ETB 3 Cr, Comm
Tel: 01748 886253 Mrs Porter.
Rates fr: *£23.00-£23.00.*
Open: All Year (not Xmas)
Beds: 1F 3D 1T 1S
Baths: 6 Private
🛏 (7) 🅿 (6) ⼳ ✕ ▥ ⓐ ⼳

(0.25m) *Rogans Country House, Gunnerside, Richmond, N. Yorks, DL11 6JW.*
Actual grid ref: SD940977
Exceptional accommodation for the discerning
Tel: 01748 886414 Mrs Trafford.
Rates fr: *£22.00-£25.00.*
Open: All Year (not Xmas)
Beds: 2D 1T
Baths: 3 Private
🛏 🅿 (6) ⼳ ♁ ⽹ ▥ ⓐ ⼳

The *lowest* single rate *is shown in* bold.

Low Row   21

National Grid Ref: SD9897
🍴 🍺 Punch Bowl Inn

(▲ 0.25m) *Low Row Camping Barn, Low Whita Farm, Low Row, Richmond, North Yorkshire,*
Actual grid ref: SE003983
Warden: Mr & Mrs Clarkson.
Tel: 01629 825850 (Northern Regional Office) Adults: £3.35+
Simple barn, sleeps 15. Heart of the fantastic Dales. ADVANCE BOOKING ESSENTIAL

(0.5m) *Glory Be, Blades, Low Row, Richmond, N. Yorks, DL11 6PS.*
Actual grid ref: SD980985
Peaceful, luxurious, magnificent views
Tel: 01748 886361 Mrs Jutsum.
Rates fr: *£19.00-£24.00.*
Open: All Year (not Xmas)
Beds: 1T 1S
Baths: 1 Ensuite 1 Shared
🛏 🅿 (4) ⼳ ♁ ✕ ▥ Ⓥ ⓐ ⼳

(0.5m) *Punch Bowl Inn, Low Row, Richmond, N. Yorks, DL11 6PF.*
Actual grid ref: SD987984
Informal, hospitable C17th inn
Tel: 01748 886233 Mr Roe.
Rates fr: *£15.00-£19.00.*
Open: All Year **Beds:** 4F 3D 5T 2S
Baths: 5 Private
🛏 🅿 ♁ ✕ ▥ Ⓥ ⓐ ⼳

Grinton   22

National Grid Ref: SE0498

(▲ 0.25m) *Grinton Lodge Youth Hostel, Grinton, Richmond, North Yorkshire, DL11 6HS.*
Actual grid ref: SE048975
Warden: D & V Lawson.
Tel: 01748 884206
Under 18: £5.40 **Adults:** £8.00
Evening Meals Available (7pm), Family Bunk Rooms, Television, Games Room, Showers, Central Heating, Shop, Parking
Originally built as a shooting lodge, high on the moors above Grinton village, with great views of Swaledale & Arkengarthdale

Reeth   23

National Grid Ref: SE0499
🍴 🍺 King's Arms Hotel, Bridge Inn, Black Bull, Buck Hotel

(0.5m) *Springfield House, Quaker Close, Reeth, Richmond, N. Yorks, DL11 6UY.*
Actual grid ref: SE039993
Stone built, beautiful gardens, superb views. Hearty breakfasts, wonderful walks
Grades: ETB Listed, Comm
Tel: 01748 884634 Mrs Guy.
Rates fr: *£16.00-£16.00.*
Open: All Year (not Xmas)
Beds: 1D 1T 1S **Baths:** 1 Shared
🛏 (9) 🅿 (5) ⼳ ♁ ▥ Ⓥ ⓐ ⼳

Redmire to Skipton

From Redmire it's east to **Wensley**, which gave the Dale its name, from where anyone interested can make a detour to see the imposing ruins of Middleham Castle, dating from 1170, for a short time the home of Richard III. At Wensley you cross the Ure and begin the climb southwards through **Coverdale**, the meadows at the bottom giving way to windswept fells. A steep descent to the Park Gill Beck stream leads to the village of **Kettlewell**. From here you cycle south through Upper Wharfedale, below Kilnsey Crag, a great limestone overhang, and through Grass Wood, a swathe of ancient woodland which is now an important conservation area, to **Grassington**, a village with a Georgian cobbled central square, on the site of a seventh-century settlement. Here you will find the Upper Wharfedale Museum. Now it's downdale back to Burnsall, and retracing your tyre-tracks to Appletreewick and Barden Tower you go on to **Bolton Abbey**. Here stand the ruins of Bolton Priory, a twelfth-century Augustinian foundation which fell victim to the Dissolution, one of the sites in the North of England painted by Turner and hyperbolised by Ruskin. From here you return to Skipton.

(0.5m) *2 Bridge Terrace, Reeth, Richmond, N. Yorks, DL11 6TP.*
Actual grid ref: SD041991
A welcoming, friendly home
Tel: 01748 884572
Mrs Davies.
Rates fr: *£14.50-£17.00.*
Open: Easter to Oct
Beds: 1D 1T
Baths: 1 Shared
🛏 ⼳ ▥ Ⓥ ⓐ ⼳

(0.5m) *Arkle House*, Mill Lane, Reeth, Richmond, N. Yorks, *DL11 6SJ.*
Actual grid ref: SE038994
Large Georgian private house
Tel: **01748 884815** Mr Simpson.
Rates fr: *£15.00*-**£20.00**.
Open: All Year (not Xmas)
Beds: 1F 1T 1D
Baths: 2 Ensuite 1 Shared
ᗡ (11) ▣ (3) ⌷ 📻 Ⓥ 🛉 ≁

(0.5m) *The Black Bull*, Reeth, Richmond, N. Yorks, *DL11 6SZ.*
In Yorkshire Dales National Park, overlooking village green
Tel: **01748 884213** Mrs Sykes.
Rates fr: *£16.00*-**£16.00**.
Open: All Year
Beds: 3F 5D 1T 1S
Baths: 3 Private 3 Shared
ᗡ ⌷ 📻 ✕ 📻 Ⓥ 🛉 ≁

Leyburn   24

National Grid Ref: SE1190

⑪ ◤ Sandpiper Inn, Golden Lion, Bolton Arms

(2m) *Secret Garden House*, Grove Square, Leyburn, N. Yorks, *DL8 5AE.*
Secluded walled garden & conservatory. Filmed in Herriot series. Ideal for walking & touring
Grades: ETB 3 Cr, Comm
Tel: **01969 623589** Mr Digges.
Rates fr: *£20.00*-**£20.00**.
Open: All Year (not Xmas)
Beds: 2D 2T
Baths: 4 Ensuite
ᗡ (10) ▣ (12) ⌷ 📻 ✕ 📻 Ⓥ

(2m) *Wensley House*, Grove Square, Leyburn, N. Yorks, *DL8 5AG.*
Converted terraced Georgian stone farmhouse
Tel: **01969 623792** Mr Mitchell.
Rates fr: *£14.00*-**£14.00**.
Open: All Year (not Xmas)
Beds: 2D 1T **Baths:** 1 Shared
ᗡ ⅄ ⌷ 📻 📻 Ⓥ 🛉

West Witton   25

National Grid Ref: SE0688

(2m) *The Old Vicarage*, West Witton, Leyburn, N. Yorks, *DL8 4LX.*
Comfortable Georgian house, lovely views
Tel: **01969 622108** Mrs Coates.
Rates fr: *£18.00*-**£22.00**.
Open: Easter to Oct
Beds: 2D 1T
Baths: 2 Ensuite 1 Private
▣ (6) ⌷ 📻 📻

The lowest *double* rate per person is shown in *italics*.

Carlton-in-Coverdale   26

National Grid Ref: SE0684

(On route) *Abbots Thorn*, Carlton-in-Coverdale, Leyburn, N. Yorks, *DL8 4AY.*
Comfortable, traditional Yorkshire Dales cottage
Tel: **01969 640620**
Mrs Lashmar.
Rates fr: *£16.00*-**£16.00**.
Open: Jan to Dec
Beds: 2D 1T
Baths: 2 Ensuite
ᗡ (12) ⅄ ⌷ 📻 ✕ 📻 Ⓥ 🛉 ≁

Kettlewell   27

National Grid Ref: SD9772

⑪ ◤ Race Horses, The Bluebell, Fox & Hounds, King's Head

(▲ 0.25m) *Kettlewell Youth Hostel*, Whernside House, Kettlewell, Skipton, North Yorkshire, *BD23 5QU.*
Actual grid ref: SD970724
Warden: Mr G Chamberlain.
Tel: **01756 760232**
Under 18: £5.95
Adults: £8.80
Evening Meals Available (7pm), Family Bunk Rooms, Television, Showers, Shop
Large house right in the middle of pretty Wharfedale village of Kettlewell, ideal for families and small groups

(0.25m) *Langcliffe House*, Kettlewell, Skipton, N. Yorks, *BD23 5RJ.*
Grades: ETB 4 Cr, Comm, AA 4 Q, RAC High Acclaim
Tel: **01756 760243**
Mr Elliott.
Rates fr: *£30.00*-**£40.00**.
Open: All Year
Beds: 1F 2T 2D
Baths: 5 Ensuite
ᗡ ▣ ⌷ 📻 📻 ♿ Ⓥ 🛉 ≁
Kettlewell in Upper Wharfedale. Traditional stone house with beautiful gardens. Ensuite bedrooms. Elegant lounge with log fire. Conservatory restaurant serving superb food in a panoramic setting

(0.25m) *Chestnut Cottage*, Kettlewell, Skipton, N. Yorks, *BD23 5RL.*
Delightful country cottage. Beautiful gardens, leading down to village stream
Tel: **01969 622092**
Mrs Lofthouse.
Rates fr: *£18.50*-**£18.50**.
Open: All Year
Beds: 1D 2T
Baths: 2 Shared
ᗡ ▣ (3) ⌷ 📻

(0.25m) *The Elms*, Middle Lane, Kettlewell, Skipton, N. Yorks, *BD23 5QX.*
Grades: ETB 2 Cr, High Comm
Tel: **01756 760224** Mr Cuthbert.
Fax no: 01756 760380
Rates fr: *£21.00*-**£29.00**.
Open: All Year (not Xmas)
Beds: 2D 1T
Baths: 3 Ensuite
▣ (3) ⅄ ⌷ 📻 Ⓥ ≁
Warm friendly accommodation in our roomy Victorian home, with a secluded garden, in this typical Yorkshire Dales village. Panoramic views across & up Upper Wharfedale

(0.25m) *Lynburn*, Kettlewell, Skipton, N. Yorks, *BD23 5RF.*
Comfortable Dales cottage, superb position
Tel: **01756 760803**
Mrs Thornborrow.
Rates fr: *£18.00*-**£25.00**.
Open: Easter to Oct
Beds: 1D 1T
Baths: 1 Shared
▣ (2) ⌷ 📻 Ⓥ 🛉 ≁

(1m) *High Fold*, Kettlewell, Skipton, N. Yorks, *BD23 5RJ.*
Dales barn recently converted to high standard
Grades: ETB 3 Cr, Deluxe
Tel: **01756 760390** Mr Earnshaw.
Rates fr: *£25.00*-**£30.00**.
Open: Feb to Dec
Beds: 1F 2D 1T
Baths: 4 Ensuite
ᗡ (2) ▣ (4) ⌷ 📻 ✕ 📻 ♿ Ⓥ 🛉 ≁

(1m) *Fold Farm*, Kettlewell, Skipton, N. Yorks, *BD23 5RH.*
C15th farmhouse in quiet location
Tel: **01756 760886** Mrs Lambert.
Rates fr: *£18.00*-**£25.00**.
Open: Easter to Oct
Beds: 2D 1T
Baths: 3 Private
ᗡ (10) ▣ (10) ⅄ ⌷ 📻 Ⓥ

Starbotton   28

National Grid Ref: SD9574

⑪ ◤ The Fox

(2m) *Fox & Hounds Inn*, Starbotton, Skipton, N. Yorks, *BD23 5HY.*
Traditional cosy Dales inn
Tel: **01756 760269**
Mr & Mrs McFadyen.
Fax no: 01756 760862
Rates fr: *£22.00*-**£30.00**.
Open: Mid-Feb to Dec
Beds: 1D 1T **Baths:** 2 Private
▣ (10) ⌷ 📻 ✕ 📻 Ⓥ 🛉

All cycleways are popular: you are well-advised to book ahead

(2m) *Hill Top Country Guest House,* Starbotton, Skipton, N. Yorks, *BD23 5HY*.
C17th Listed farmhouse
Grades: ETB 2 Cr, High Comm, AA 5 Q, Prem Select
Tel: 01756 760321 Mr Rathmell.
Rates fr: *£25.00-£32.00*.
Open: Easter to Nov
Beds: 1F 3D 1T
Baths: 5 Ensuite
🛏 (6) ▣ (6) ⌷ ✕ ⊞, Ⅴ ✦ ⚡

Grassington 29

National Grid Ref: SE0064

🍴 🍺 Black Horse, Devonshire Hotel, The Forresters, Old Hall Inn

(0.25m) *Grassington Lodge, 8 Wood Lane,* Grassington, Skipton, N. Yorks, *BD23 5LU*.
Grades: ETB 2 Cr
Tel: 01756 752518 (also fax no)
Mr & Mrs Wade.
Rates fr: *£16.00-£22.00*.
Open: All Year
Beds: 5D 4T
Baths: 6 Ensuite 2 Shared
🛏 ▣ (9) ⌷ ✕ ⊞, Ⅴ ✦ ⚡
Family-run Victorian guest house enjoying quiet position in own grounds - 100 metres from Grassington village square in the heart of the Yorkshire Dales. Lock-up cycle shed and private car park

(0.25m) *Springroyd House, 8a Station Road,* Grassington, Skipton, N. Yorks, *BD23 5NQ*.
Actual grid ref: SD980631
Conveniently situated, friendly family home
Tel: 01756 752473 Mr Berry.
Rates fr: *£16.50-£20.00*.
Open: All Year
Beds: 1D 1T
Baths: 2 Shared
🛏 (5) ▣ (2) ⌷ ⌷ ⊞, ⊞, Ⅴ ✦ ⚡

(0.25m) *Mayfield Bed & Breakfast,* Low Mill Lane, Grassington, Skipton, N. Yorks, *BD23 5BX*.
Actual grid ref: SE000635
Riverside Dales long house. Guest rooms overlook fells and river
Tel: 01756 753052
Mr & Mrs Trewartha.
Rates fr: *£18.00-£20.00*.
Open: All Year
Beds: 1F 1T 1D
Baths: 1 Ensuite 1 Shared
🛏 ▣ (10) ⌷ 🐾 ⊞, Ⅴ ✦ ⚡

(0.25m) *Burtree Cottage,* Hebden Road, Grassington, Skipton, N. Yorks, *BD23 5LH*.
Old stone cottage, lovely garden
Tel: 01756 752442 Mrs Marsden.
Rates fr: *£15.00-£20.00*.
Open: Easter to Oct
Beds: 1D 1T
Baths: 1 Shared
🛏 (10) ▣ (3) ⌷ ⊞, Ⅴ ✦ ⚡

(0.25m) *Town Head Guest House, 1 Low Lane,* Grassington, Skipton, N. Yorks, *BD23 5AU*.
Modern comfortable guest house
Grades: ETB 2 Cr, Comm
Tel: 01756 752811 Mrs Lister.
Rates fr: *£21.00-£30.00*.
Open: All Year (not Xmas)
Beds: 3D 1T **Baths:** 4 Ensuite
🛏 (7) ▣ (3) ⌷ ⊞, ⚑

(0.25m) *3 Wharfeside Avenue,* Grassington, Skipton, N. Yorks, *BD23 5BS*.
Large, comfortable, warm family house
Grades: ETB 2 Cr
Tel: 01756 752115
Mr & Mrs Cahill.
Rates fr: *£18.00-£18.00*.
Open: Easter to Nov
Beds: 1F 1T 1S **Baths:** 1 Private
🛏 ▣ (3) ⌷ ⊞, Ⅴ ✦ ⚡

(0.25m) *Ashfield House Hotel,* Grassington, Skipton, N. Yorks, *BD23 5AE*.
Quality C17th private hotel
Grades: ETB 3 Cr, High Comm, AA 4 Q, Select
Tel: 01756 752584 (also fax no)
Mr & Mrs Harrison.
Rates fr: *£25.00-£25.00*.
Open: Feb to Dec
Beds: 4D 3T
Baths: 6 Ensuite 1 Private
🛏 (5) ▣ (7) ⌷ ✕ ⊞, Ⅴ ⚡

Linton 30

National Grid Ref: SD9962

(▲0.5m) *Linton Youth Hostel,* The Old Rectory, Linton, Skipton, North Yorkshire, *BD23 5HH*.
Actual grid ref: SD998627
Warden: Mr R Suddaby.
Tel: 01756 752400
Under 18: £5.95 **Adults:** £8.80
Evening Meals Available (7pm), Family Bunk Rooms, Showers, Parking
C17th former rectory in own grounds, across the stream from the village green, in one of Wharfedale's most picturesque and unspoilt villages

Bolton Abbey 31

National Grid Ref: SE0753

(1m) *Hesketh Farm Cottage,* Bolton Abbey, Skipton, N. Yorks, *BD23 6HA*.
Large working hill/sheep farm cottage
Tel: 01756 710332 Mrs Heseltine.
Rates fr: *£15.00-£20.00*.
Open: 1st May to 1st Nov.
Beds: 1D 1T
Baths: 1 Ensuite 1 Shared
🛏 ▣ (6) ⌷ ⊞, ⚡

CTC Circular Tour of East Anglia

The **Circular Tour of East Anglia** is a huge 336-mile route prepared by the Cyclists' Touring Club, which follows a circle around the whole of East Anglia, as well as straying briefly across the Stour into northern Essex. Starting and finishing in Cambridge, you will follow quiet roads through some of the region's most scenic country, including the North Nofolk Coast, the Broads, Dunwich on the Suffolk Heritage Coast and Constable's Dedham Vale. This is excellent cycling country, where you will not be troubled by steep ascents.

A **guide** pamphlet to the route is available from the Cyclists' Touring Club. You have to be a member to get it. Contact them at Cotterell House, 69 Meadrow, Godalming, Surrey GU7 3HS, tel 01483 417217, fax 01483 426994, e-mail cycling@ctc.org.uk.

Maps: Ordnance Survey 1:50,000 Landranger series: 132, 133, 134, 143, 144, 154, 155, 156, 168, 169

Trains: Cambridge, King's Lynn, Norwich and Ipswich are all main line termini; there are connecting services to many other places on or near the route.

Cambridge   1
National Grid Ref: TL4658

|●| ◖ The Unicorn, Old Spring, Milton Arms, Robin Hood, The Crown, George Inn, Sweeney Todd, Master Mariner, Red Bull, Hat & Feathers, Milton Arms, Haymakers, Traveller's Rest, Issac Newton, Clarendon Arms

(▲ 0.5m) *Cambridge Youth Hostel,* 97 Tenison Road, Cambridge. *CB1 2DN.*
Actual grid ref: TL460575
Tel: **01223 354601**
Under 18: £7.30 **Adults:** £10.70
Evening Meals Available (6-7.30pm), Self-catering Facilities, Games Room, Showers, Laundry Facilities, Licensed Premises
A Victorian town house with modern facilities, just minutes from the train station and only 15 mins walk or a short bus ride from the town centre

(0.5m) *Home From Home,* 39 Milton Road, Cambridge. *CB4 1XA.*
Grades: ETB 1 Cr, Comm
Tel: **01223 323555 / 0589 990698**
Mrs Fasano. Fax no: 01223 323555
Rates fr: *£18.00*-**£25.00.**
Open: All Year
Beds: 2D 1T
Baths: 2 Ensuite 1 Private
☺ ℙ (3) ⊬ ☐ ▥, Ⓥ
Very comfortable spacious family home, ideally located for river and colleges. All rooms with own facilities providing home from home hospitality and excellent breakfasts

(0.5m) *Victoria B&B,* 57 Arbury Road, Cambridge. *CB4 2JB.*
Tel: **01223 350086** Mrs Fasano.
Fax no: 01223 565660
Rates fr: *£19.00*-**£25.00.**
Open: All Year
Beds: 1D 2T
Baths: 2 Ensuite 1 Private
☺ ℙ (1) ⊬ ☐ ▥, Ⓥ
Situated just 1.5 miles from Cambridge city centre, with ensuite or private facilities, television, tea and coffee and a warm welcome to all guests

(0.5m) *70 Girton Road,* Cambridge. *CB3 0LN.*
Lovely outlook opposite college playing field. Just off A14. Golf nearby
Tel: **01223 276277** Mrs Barnes.
Rates fr: *£16.00*-**£17.00.**
Open: All Year
Beds: 1D 1T 2S
☺ (6) ℙ (2) ⊬ ☐ ▥, Ⓥ ▮

(0.5m) *Tudor Cottage,* 292 Histon Road, Cambridge. *CB4 3HF.*
Comfortable friendly private home
Tel: **01223 565212** Mrs Celentano.
Fax no: 01223 565660
Rates fr: *£19.00*-**£25.00.**
Open: All Year
Beds: 1T **Baths:** 1 Ensuite
☺ ℙ (2) ⊬ ☐ ▥, Ⓥ

The *lowest* single rate *is shown* in bold.

(0.5m) *Ashtrees Guest House,* 128 Perne Road, Cambridge, Cambs, *CB1 3RR.*
Comfortable suburban residence with garden
Grades: ETB Listed, Comm
Tel: **01223 411233**
Mrs Hill.
Rates fr: *£18.00*-**£19.00.**
Open: Mid Jan to Xmas
Beds: 1F 3D 1T 2S
Baths: 1 Private 6 Shared
☺ ℙ (6) ⊬ ☐ ✕ ▥.

(0.5m) *Cristinas Guest House,* 47 St Andrews Road, Cambridge. *CB4 1DL.*
15 minutes' walk from city centre
Grades: ETB 2 Cr, Comm
Tel: **01223 365855**
Mrs Celentano.
Fax no: 01223 365855 / 327700
Rates fr: *£21.00*-**£24.00.**
Open: All Year (not Xmas)
Beds: 1F 7T 1S
Baths: 7 Ensuite 2 Shared
☺ ℙ (8) ☐ ▥, Ⓥ

(1m) *53 Eltisley Avenue,* Cambridge. *CB3 9JQ.*
Close to city centre - university departments - Grantchester meadows - quiet area
Grades: ETB Listed
Tel: **01223 560466**
Mrs Dathan.
Rates fr: *£19.00*-**£20.00.**
Open: All Year (not Xmas)
Beds: 1F 1D 1S
Baths: 1 Shared
☺ ⊬ ☐ ▥, Ⓥ

Cambridge

The historic university city of **Cambridge**, where the River Cam winds between colleges and green spaces, offers a wealth of glories to the exploring visitor. The colleges are, by and large, bigger and richer than those in Oxford - the wealth of Trinity, for example, is legendary, and shows from the moment you enter the resplendent Great Court, whose Tudor Gothic buildings form the largest courtyard of its kind in the world. The college's Wren Library houses an important manuscript collection. Cambridge's most renowned building is the chapel at King's College, built during the latter part of the fifteenth century. One of the most splendid examples of English Perpendicular architecture, this is the largest edifice in the world with a fan-vaulted ceiling. The chapel choir is world famous; the massive organ dates originally from the reign of James II. The two parts of Queen's College are connected by the Mathematical Bridge, an eighteenth-century experiment which was meant to be kept in place purely by the forces the many wooden beams exerted on each other. This worked fine for a hundred years until some wise guy decided to take it apart and put it back together again - the nuts and bolts bear witness to the failure of the second half of that plan. The superb Fitzwilliam Museum includes Egyptian and Greek antiquities and a gallery of European art including a substantial nineteenth- and twentieth-century British collection. The other gallery well worth a look is the wonderful Kettle's Yard, where the mostly early twentieth-century art is set amid a living space with ceramics and other crafts. The Botanic Garden has a magnificent water garden and winter garden and is an excellent place for pre- or post-cycle tour relaxation.

(1.5m) *Arbury Lodge, 82 Arbury Road, Cambridge. CB4 2JE.*
Comfortably furnished. Good parking. Easy access to A14 and city centre. **Grades:** ETB Listed, Comm
Tel: **01223 364319** Mrs Celentano.
Fax no: 01223 566988
Rates fr: *£19.00*-**£22.00.**
Open: All Year
Beds: 1F 2D 1T 1S
Baths: 2 Ensuite 1 Private 1 Shared
🛏 🅿 (8) 🖵 📖 Ⓥ

(0.5m) *Avimore Guest House, 310 Cherry Hinton Road, Cambridge. CB1 4AU.*
Warm, friendly, family-run guest house. Good breakfast. Private parking
Grades: ETB 2 Cr, AA 2 Q
Tel: **01223 410956** Gawthrop.
Rates fr: *£20.00*-**£20.00.**
Open: All Year (not Xmas)
Beds: 1F 2T 2D 2S
Baths: 3 Ensuite 3 Private 3 Shared
🛏 (2) 🅿 (8) ⊬ 🖵 📖 ♿ Ⓥ

(0.5m) *Leverton House, 732 Newmarket Road, Cambridge. CB5 8RS.*
Comfortable friendly family house very close to airport. Private facilities
Tel: **01223 292094** Mrs Ison.
Rates fr: *£17.00*-**£22.00.**
Open: All Year
Beds: 1T 1S **Baths:** 1 Private
🛏 🅿 ⊬ 🖵 ✕ 📖 Ⓥ

(0.5m) *Bon Accord House, 20 St Margarets Square, Off Cherry Hinton Road, Cambridge, Cambs, CB1 4AP.*
Actual grid ref: TL469565
Non-smokers only. Quiet situation
Grades: ETB Listed
Tel: **01223 411188** Mrs Northrop.
Rates fr: *£18.00*-**£21.00.**
Open: All Year (not Xmas)
Beds: 3D 1T 5S
Baths: 1 Private 2 Shared
🅿 (9) ⊬ 🖵 📖 Ⓥ

(0.5m) *Double Two, 22 St Margarets Road, Cambridge. CB3 0LT.*
Quiet, comfortable friendly home, with attractive garden, convenient A14/M11
Tel: **01223 276103** (also fax no) Mrs Noble.
Rates fr: *£19.00*-**£25.00.**
Open: All Year (not Xmas)
Beds: 1D 2T
Baths: 2 Private 1 Shared
🛏 🅿 (1) ⊬ 🖵 ♛ 📖 Ⓥ

(0.5m) *264 Hills Road, Cambridge. CB2 2QE.*
Elegant new accommodation in Cambridge, on bus route to city centre
Grades: ETB 1 Cr, High Comm
Tel: **01223 248369**
Mrs Owen. Fax no: 01223 441276
Rates fr: *£27.50*-**£35.00.**
Open: All Year
Beds: 1D **Baths:** 1 Private
🛏 🅿 (2) ⊬ 🖵 ♛ 📖

(0.25m) *39 Trumpington Street, Cambridge. CB2 1QY.*
Old town centre college house
Tel: **01223 355439** Mrs Rowell.
Rates fr: *£20.00*-**£21.00.**
Open: All Year (not Xmas)
Beds: 1D 1T 4S **Baths:** 2 Shared
🛏 (6) 🅿 (1) ⊬ 🖵 ♛ 📖 Ⓥ

(0.5m) *El Shaddai, 41 Warkworth Street, Cambridge, Cambs, CB1 1EG.*
Centrally located, large quiet house
Tel: **01223 327978** Mrs Droy.
Fax no: 01223 501024
Rates fr: *£18.00*-**£20.00.**
Open: All Year
Beds: 1F 2D 1T 1S
Baths: 1 Private 1 Shared
🛏 🅿 ⊬ 🖵 📖

The lowest *double* rate per person is shown in *italics.*

Histon 2

National Grid Ref: TL4363

(0.25m) *Wynwyck, 55 Narrow Lane, Histon, Cambridge. CB4 4HD.*
Modern, comfortable, quiet, peaceful. Ideal for Cambridge and East Anglia
Tel: **01223 232496**
Mrs Torrens.
Rates fr: *£23.00-£26.00.*
Open: All Year (not Xmas)
Beds: 1F 1D 2T
Baths: 2 Ensuite 1 Shared
🛏 🅿 (4) 🗲 🛏 🖳 🎛

Wilburton 3

National Grid Ref: TL4874

(1m) *Sharps Farm, Twenty Pence Road, Wilburton, Ely, Cambs, CB6 3PX.*
Comfortable countryside location, warm welcome
Grades: ETB 1 Cr
Tel: **01353 740360**
Mrs Peck.
Rates fr: *£17.00-£20.00.*
Open: All Year
Beds: 2F 1D 1T 1S
Baths: 1 Private
🛏 🅿 (10) 🗲 🛏 🗙 🖳 🖒 🎛 ⓘ ✦

Stretham 4

National Grid Ref: TL5074

🍴 🗨 Red Lion

(2m) *Bridge House, Green End, Stretham, Ely, Cambs, CB4 4EA.*
Period farmhouse: river frontage in 13 acres. Relaxed atmosphere. Wonderful walks
Tel: **01353 649212**
Mr & Mrs Whitmore.
Rates fr: *£17.50-£22.50.*
Open: All Year (not Xmas)
Beds: 1F 1T 1D
Baths: 3 Ensuite
🛏 🅿 🗲 🛏 🛏 🖳 🖒 🎛

Ely 5

National Grid Ref: TL5480

🍴 🗨 The Crown, The Highflyer, Red Lion, The Boathouse, Cutter Inn

(0.25m) *Cathedral House, 17 St Mary's Street, Ely, Cambs, CB7 4ER.*
Tel: **01353 662124** (also fax no)
Mr & Mrs Farndale.
Rates fr: *£25.00-£35.00.*
Open: All Year (not Xmas)
Beds: 2D 1T
Baths: 3 Ensuite
🛏 🅿 (3) 🗲 🛏 🖳 🎛
A Grade II Listed house, within the shadow of the cathedral and close to museums, restaurants, shops etc. All rooms overlook delightful walled garden. Ely is an ideal base to tour East Anglia

(0.25m) *The Nyton Hotel, 7 Barton Road, Ely, Cambs, CB7 4HZ.*
Quiet residential hotel. Ample parking. Ensuite rooms. Fully licensed restaurant Close city centre.
Grades: ETB 3 Cr
Tel: **01353 662459**
Mr Setchell.
Fax no: 01353 666217
Rates fr: *£25.00-£33.00.*
Open: All Year
Beds: 3F 3D 2T 2S
Baths: 10 Ensuite
🛏 🅿 🗔 🛏 🗙 🖳 🖒 🎛

(0.25m) *82 Broad Street, Ely, Cambs, CB7 4BE.*
Comfortable, convenient, converted Victorian house walking distance Cathedral, station, river
Tel: **01353 667609**
Mr & Mrs Hull.
Rates fr: *£15.00-£15.00.*
Open: All Year (not Xmas)
Beds: 1D 1T
Baths: 2 Shared
🛏 🅿 🗲 🛏 🖳 🎛 ⓘ

(0.25m) *84 Broad Street, Ely, Cambs, CB7 4BE.*
Private cottage near river/cathedral
Tel: **01353 666862** Mrs Collins.
Rates fr: *£14.00-£14.00.*
Open: All Year
Beds: 1F 1D
Baths: 1 Shared
🛏 🗲 🛏 🖳 🎛 ⓘ ✦

(0.25m) *Annesdale Lodge, 8 Annesdale, Ely, Cambs, CB7 4BN.*
Riverside accommodation near railway station
Tel: **01353 667533**
Mr & Mrs Drage.
Rates fr: *£20.00-£35.00.*
Open: All Year
Beds: 2D
Baths: 2 Private
🛏 🅿 (2) 🗲 🛏 🛏 🎛

Queen Adelaide 6

National Grid Ref: TL5580

🍴 🗨 The Highflyer

(2m) *Greenways, Prickwillow Road, Queen Adelaide, Ely, Cambs, CB7 4TZ.*
Comfortable modern ground floor accommodation, 1.5 miles from Ely
Tel: **01353 666706**
Mr Dunlop-Hill.
Rates fr: *£19.00-£20.00.*
Open: All Year
Beds: 1F 1D 1T 1S
Baths: 2 Ensuite 2 Shared
🛏 🅿 (6) 🗔 🛏 🖳 🖒 ⓘ ✦

The *lowest* **single** rate *is shown in* **bold.**

Little Downham 7

National Grid Ref: TL5283

🍴 🗨 The Anchor, The Plough

(2m) *Bury House, 11 Main Street, Little Downham, Ely, Cambs, CB6 2ST.*
Actual grid ref: TL526841
Comfortable friendly home
Tel: **01353 699386 / 698766**
Mrs Ambrose.
Rates fr: *£18.00-£18.00.*
Open: All Year (not Xmas)
Beds: 1F 1D 1T
Baths: 2 Shared
🛏 🅿 (2) 🗲 🗔 🗙 🖳 🎛 ⓘ ✦

Littleport 8

National Grid Ref: TL5686

🍴 🗨 Black Horse, The Crown

(0.25m) *50 High Street, Littleport, Ely, Cambs, CB6 1HE.*
Large converted bungalow
Tel: **01353 861059**
Mr & Mrs Bowditch.
Rates fr: *£17.50-£20.00.*
Open: All Year (not Xmas)
Beds: 1F 1D 1T 2S
Baths: 5 Ensuite
🛏 (2) 🅿 (6) 🗲 🛏 🗙 🖳 🖒 🎛

(0.25m) *The Laurels, 104 Victoria Street, Littleport, Ely, Cambs, CB6 1LZ.*
Hospitality - comfort - excellent breakfast - parking
Tel: **01353 861972 / 01850 199299**
Mrs Sicard.
Rates fr: *£18.00-£36.00.*
Open: All Year (not Xmas)
Beds: 1D 2T
Baths: 3 Ensuite
🅿 (4) 🗲 🗔 🖳 🎛

Downham Market 9

National Grid Ref: TF6103

🍴 🗨 Crown Hotel

(0.25m) *Park House, 74 London Road, Downham Market, Norfolk, PE38 9AT.*
Welcoming 1833 farmhouse in town
Tel: **01366 387035** Mrs Johnson.
Rates fr: *£14.00-£15.00.*
Open: All Year (not Xmas)
Beds: 1F 1D 1T **Baths:** 1 Shared
🛏 🅿 (6) 🗔 🛏 🖳

(0.25m) *The Dial House, 12 Railway Road, Downham Market, Norfolk, PE38 9EB.*
Comfortable C18th family home
Grades: ETB 3 Cr, Comm, AA 3 Q
Tel: **01366 388358** Mrs Murray.
Fax no: 01366 384844
Rates fr: *£16.00-£22.00.*
Open: All Year **Beds:** 1D 2T
Baths: 2 Ensuite 1 Shared
🅿 (6) 🗲 🗔 🛏 🗙 🎛

Cambridge to King's Lynn

Heading north out of Cambridge through **Histon** and **Cottenham**, the route strikes out into **the Fens**, the low-lying country of northern Cambridgeshire and southern Lincolnshire which, before it was drained in the seventeenth century, was inhospitable marshland. For miles before you reach **Ely**, the cathedral tower rises before you. Standing atop the Isle of Ely, a piece of hardly high ground amid the Fens, this beautiful town has many Georgian houses as well as the magnificent Romanesque cathedral. On the site of a seventh-century abbey founded by St Ethelreda, the present building was put up by the Normans between 1071 and 1189, in thanksgiving for the defeat of Hereward the Wake, leader of a band of Anglo-Saxons holding out against the invasion. The gothic Octagon and lantern tower (a construction formally unique in England which splendidly reflects the evening sun), constructed in the fourteenth century after the central tower collapsed, is striking against the earlier style of the taller West Tower. From the same period dates the Lady Chapel, a building renowned among musicians for its exquisite acoustic. From Ely it's northwards through Littleport and into Norfolk, following the Ouse to **Downham Market** and on to **King's Lynn**, which lies a short way upstream from where the Ouse flows into the Wash. There is much to see here: St George's Guildhall, one of England's largest, dates from the fifteenth century and now houses an arts centre and a restaurant, the Customs House at Purfleet Quay is a small seventeenth-century Palladian building, and St Margaret's church boasts two impressive Flemish brasses. The Old Gaol House holds a display of treasures from the town's past; the True's Yard museum offers a glimpse of life in the old fishing community through two tiny preserved cottages.

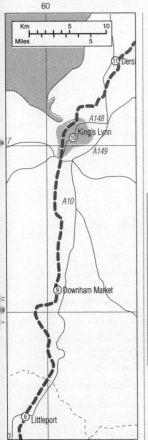

King's Lynn   10

National Grid Ref: TF6120

¶❦ The Wild Fowler, Lord Kelvin

(▲ 1m) *King's Lynn Youth Hostel,* Thoresby College, College Lane, King's Lynn, Norfolk, *PE30 1JB.*
Actual grid ref: TF616199
Tel: 01553 772461
Under 18: £5.40 **Adults:** £8.00
Self-catering Facilities, Showers
Traditional hostel in a wing of the 500-year-old Chantry college building in the historic part of King's Lynn. Discover heritage buildings and museums and other attractions in the varied West Norfolk countryside

(1m) *Guanock Hotel, Southgates, London Road, King's Lynn, Norfolk, PE30 5JG.*
Grades: ETB Listed, AA Listed, RAC Listed
Tel: 01553 772959 (also fax no)
Mr Parchment.
Rates fr: *£17.00-£21.00.*
Open: All Year
Beds: 5F 4D 3T 5S
Baths: 5 Shared
🛏 (1) 🅿 (12) 🛏✗ 🎱 Ⓥ ▮
Warm friendly hotel noted for cleanliness and good food. Close to town centre and all industrial estates, adjacent to historic Southgates, near Sandringham House

Pay B&Bs by cash or cheque and be prepared to pay up front.

All cycleways are popular: you are well-advised to book ahead

(1m) *Havana Guest House,* 117 Gaywood Road, King's Lynn, Norfolk, *PE30 2PU.*
Large Victorian house, comfort-able, well-appointed bedrooms, ample parking
Grades: ETB 2 Cr, Comm, AA 3 Q, RAC Acclaim
Tel: 01553 772 331
Mr & Mrs Breed.
Rates fr: *£15.00-£17.00.*
Open: All Year (not Xmas)
Beds: 1F 2D 3T 1S
Baths: 4 Private 1 Shared
🛏 (2) 🅿 (8) ⌀✗ 🎱 Ⓥ ▮

(1m) *Maranatha Guest House,* 115 Gaywood Road, King's Lynn, Norfolk, *PE30 2PU.*
Large Victorian guesthouse with garden, parking
Grades: ETB 2 Cr, Approv
Tel: 01553 774596 Mr Bastone.
Rates fr: *£14.00-£17.00.*
Open: All Year
Beds: 2F 2D 2T 3S
Baths: 2 Ensuite 1 Private
🛏 🅿 (8) 🛏🛏✗ 🎱 Ⓥ

(1m) *Flints Hotel,* 73 Norfolk St, King's Lynn, Norfolk, *PE30 1AD.*
Modern hotel
Grades: ETB Listed, Approv
Tel: 01553 769400 Mr Flint.
Rates fr: *£18.00-£18.00.*
Open: All Year
Beds: 1F 1D 1T 1S
🛏 (1) 🅿 (7) 🛏✗ 🎱 Ⓥ

(1m) *Fairlight Lodge,* 79 *Goodwins Road, King's Lynn, Norfolk, PE30 5PE.*
Lovely Victorian home, warm welcome
Grades: ETB 2 Cr, High Comm, AA 4 Q
Tel: 01553 762234 Mrs Rowe.
Fax no: 01553 770280
Rates fr: *£16.00-£20.00.*
Open: All Year (not Xmas)
Beds: 2D 3T 2S
Baths: 4 Ensuite 2 Shared
🛇 🅿 (6) 🛏 🖰 Ⅷ Ⅵ

Dersingham 11

National Grid Ref: TF6830
🍴 🍺 The Feathers

(0.5m) *Meadow Vale,* 63 *Manor Road, Dersingham, Kings Lynn, Norfolk, PE31 6LH.*
Modern comfortable house, friendly atmosphere
Grades: ETB Listed, Comm
Tel: 01485 540769 Mrs Williams.
Rates fr: *£15.00-£15.00.*
Open: Easter to Oct
Beds: 1D 1T 1S **Baths:** 1 Shared
🛇 (8) 🅿 (4) ⅙ 🖵 Ⅷ

(0.5m) *The White House,* 44 *Hunstanton Road, Dersingham, Kings Lynn, Norfolk, PE31 6HQ.*
Comfortable, warm welcome, good breakfast
Tel: 01485 541895
Ms Nightingale.
Rates fr: *£15.50-£15.50.*
Open: All Year
Beds: 2D 2T 1S
Baths: 1 Private 2 Shared
🛇 🅿 (5) 🖵 🛏 Ⅷ 🕭 Ⅵ

Docking 12

National Grid Ref: TF7637
🍴 🍺

(0.25m) *Haddin, Ringstead Road, Docking, Kings Lynn, Norfolk, PE31 8PL.*
Dormer bungalow in large garden
Tel: 01485 518701 Mr Thomas.
Rates fr: *£15.00-£15.00.*
Open: All Year (not Xmas)
Beds: 2T **Baths:** 1 Shared
🅿 (3) ⅙ 🖵 ✕ Ⅷ

Choseley 13

National Grid Ref: TF7540

(2m) *Choseley Farmhouse, Choseley, Docking, Kings Lynn, Norfolk, PE31 8PQ.*
Actual grid ref: TF755408
C16th Listed farmhouse with Tudor chimneys
Tel: 01485 512331
Major & Mrs Hutchinson.
Rates fr: *£15.00-£15.00.*
Open: Easter to Oct
Beds: 1D 1T **Baths:** 1 Shared
🅿 (6) ✦

Brancaster 14

National Grid Ref: TF7743
🍴 🍺 Ship Hotel

(2m) *The Old Bakery, Main Road, Brancaster, Kings Lynn, Norfolk, PE31 8AZ.*
Delightful converted old bakery and cottage set in grounds of one acre
Tel: 01485 210501
Mrs Townshend.
Rates fr: *£18.00-£22.50.*
Open: All Year (not Xmas)
Beds: 1F 2D 1S
Baths: 2 Ensuite 2 Shared
🛇 🅿 (3) 🖵 Ⅷ 🕭 ✦

Burnham Market 15

National Grid Ref: TF8342
🍴 🍺 Hoste Arms, The Fishes

(On route) *Millwood, Herrings Lane, Burnham Market, Kings Lynn, Norfolk, PE31 8DW.*
Actual grid ref: TF8343
Peaceful, luxurious, coastal country house
Grades: ETB Listed, High Comm
Tel: 01328 730152 Mrs Leftley.
Fax no: 01328 730158
Rates fr: *£25.00-£30.00.*
Open: All Year (not Xmas)
Beds: 1D 1T
Baths: 2 Ensuite
🛇 (8) 🅿 (4) ⅙ 🖵 🛏 Ⅷ

Burnham Overy 16

National Grid Ref: TF8442
🍴 🍺 The Hero

(0.5m) *Ostrich House, Burnham Overy, Kings Lynn, Norfolk, PE31 8HU.*
Actual grid ref: TF842429
300-year-old Listed end-of-terrace cottage
Grades: ETB Listed
Tel: 01328 738517 Mrs O'Connor.
Rates fr: *£16.00-£16.00.*
Open: All Year (not Xmas)
Beds: 1D 1T 1S **Baths:** 2 Shared
🅿 (3) 🖵 Ⅷ 🕭 ✦

Burnham Overy Staithe 17

National Grid Ref: TF8444

(1.5m) *Domville Guest House, Glebe Lane, Burnham Overy Staithe, Kings Lynn, Norfolk, PE31 8JQ.*
Quietly situated, family-run guest house
Grades: ETB 1 Cr, Comm
Tel: 01328 738298 Mrs Smith.
Rates fr: *£17.00-£17.00.*
Open: All Year (not Xmas)
Beds: 2D 2T 4S
Baths: 2 Private 2 Shared
🛇 (6) 🅿 (10) ⅙ 🖵 ✕ Ⅵ 🕭 ✦

Wells-next-the-Sea 18

National Grid Ref: TF9143
🍴 🍺 Lifeboat Inn, Three Horseshoes, Crown Hotel

(0.25m) *The Cobblers Guest House, Standard Road, Wells-next-the-Sea, Norfolk, NR23 1JU.*
Actual grid ref: TF918435
Tel: 01328 710155 (also fax no)
Mr & Mrs Stew.
Rates fr: *£13.00-£17.00.*
Open: All Year
Beds: 2F 1T 3D 2S
Baths: 3 Ensuite 2 Shared
🛇 (5) 🅿 (8) 🖵 ✕ Ⅷ Ⅵ ✦
Family-run guest house set close to the harbour in Wells. Comfortable guest lounge and conservatory. Private, secluded garden and off-street parking

(0.25m) *Mill House, Northfield Lane, Wells-next-the-Sea, Norfolk, NR23 1JZ.*
Actual grid ref: TF918435
Mill House: a former mill-owner's house in secluded gardens
Tel: 01328 710739 Mr Downey.
Rates fr: *£17.00-£17.50.*
Open: All Year
Beds: 1F 3D 2T 2S
Baths: 6 Ensuite 2 Private
🛇 (8) 🅿 (10) 🖵 🛏 ✕ Ⅷ 🕭 ✦

(On route) *The Warren, Warham Road, Wells-next-the-Sea, Norfolk, NR23 1NE.*
Comfortable bungalow in quiet location. 10 minutes' walk from all amenities
Grades: ETB Listed
Tel: 01328 710273 Mrs Wickens.
Rates fr: *£18.00-£20.00.*
Open: All Year (not Xmas)
Beds: 1D 1T
Baths: 1 Ensuite 1 Private
🅿 (2) ⅙ 🖵 🛏 Ⅷ Ⅵ

(On route) *The Normans Guest House, Invaders Court, Standard Road, Wells-next-the-Sea, Norfolk, NR23 1JW.*
Actual grid ref: TF917435
Elegant Georgian house within courtyard. Some rooms overlook saltmarshes
Tel: 01328 710657
Mrs MacDonald.
Fax no: 01328 710468
Rates fr: *£23.50-£30.00.*
Open: All Year (not Xmas)
Beds: 6D 1T **Baths:** 7 Ensuite
🅿 (10) ⅙ 🖵 🛏 Ⅷ ✦

(0.25m) *St Heliers Guest House, Station Road, Wells-next-the-Sea, Norfolk, NR23 1EA.*
Large Georgian house, centrally located
Tel: 01328 710361 (also fax no)
Mrs Kerr.
Rates fr: *£16.00-£20.00.*
Open: All Year
Beds: 1F 1D 1T **Baths:** 2 Shared
🅿 (5) ⅙ 🖵 Ⅷ Ⅵ 🕭 ✦

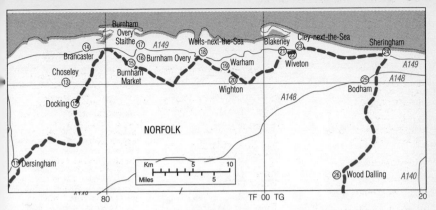

(0.25m) *East House, East Quay, Wells-next-the-Sea, Norfolk, NR23 1LE.*
Actual grid ref: TF921437
Old house overlooking coastal marsh
Tel: **01328 710408** Mrs Scott.
Rates fr: *£20.00*-**£25.00**.
Open: All Year (not Xmas)
Beds: 2T
Baths: 2 Ensuite
🛇 (7) 🅿 (2) ⌷ 🎟 🖽 ⊬

(0.25m) *Greengates, Stiffkey Road, Wells-next-the-Sea, Norfolk, NR23 1QB.*
Actual grid ref: TF9243
Cottage with views over marshes
Tel: **01328 711040** Mrs Jarvis.
Rates fr: *£16.00*-**£20.00**.
Open: All Year (not Xmas)
Beds: 1T 1D **Baths:** 2 Private
🅿 (2) ⌷ 🖽.

(0.25m) *Brooklands, 31 Burnt Street, Wells-next-the-Sea, Norfolk, NR23 1HP.*
Charming beamed 200-year-old house
Tel: **01328 710768** Mrs Wykes.
Rates fr: *£15.00*-**£18.00**.
Open: Apr to Oct
Beds: 1F 1D
Baths: 1 Shared
🛇 (7) 🅿 (2) ⊬⌷ 🎟 🖽.

(0.25m) *Eastdene Guest House, Northfield Lane, Wells-next-the-Sea, Norfolk, NR23 1LH.*
Comfortable guest house
Tel: **01328 710381** Mrs Court.
Rates fr: *£18.00*-**£20.00**.
Open: All Year
Beds: 1D 2T 1S
Baths: 3 Private 1 Shared
🛇 (9) 🅿 (5) ⊬⌷ 🎟 ✕ 🖽 Ⅴ ⚲ ⊬

All rates are subject to alteration at the owners' discretion.

(0.25m) *Hideaway, Red Lion Yard, Wells-next-the-Sea, Norfolk, NR23 1AX.*
Actual grid ref: TF924344
Annexe on to private house
Grades: ETB 2 Cr, Comm
Tel: **01328 710524** Miss Higgs.
Rates fr: *£17.00*-**£20.00**.
Open: Jan to Nov
Beds: 1D 2T **Baths:** 3 Ensuite
🅿 (3) ⌷ 🎟 ✕ 🖽 Ⅴ ⚲ ⊬

(0.25m) *West End House, Dogger Lane, Wells-next-the-Sea, Norfolk, NR23 1BE.*
Small friendly guest house
Tel: **01328 711190** Mr Cox.
Rates fr: *£14.00*-**£14.00**.
Open: All Year **Beds:** 1F 1T 1D 1S
Baths: 2 Shared
🛇 🅿 (4) ⌷ 🎟 🖽 Ⅴ

Warham   19
National Grid Ref: TF9441

(On route) *The Three Horseshoes / The Old Post Office, 69 Bridge Street, Warham, Wells-next-the-Sea, Norfolk, NR23 1NL.*
Dream country cottage
Tel: **01328 710547** Mr Salmon.
Rates fr: *£20.00*-**£20.00**.
Open: All Year (not Xmas)
Beds: 3D 1S
Baths: 1 Private 1 Shared
🛇 (14) 🅿 (20) ⌷ 🎟 ✕ 🖽 Ⅴ ⚲ ⊬

The lowest *double* rate per person is shown in *italics*.

King's Lynn to the North Norfolk Coast

Attractions on the route northeast out of King's Lynn include **Castle Rising**, where the impressively well-preserved twelfth-century keep is surrounded by a large earthwork, and the village has a group of seventeenth-century almshouses. A little way further on stands **Sandringham House**, a private country retreat of the Royal family (but open to the public) built in the late nineteenth century in the neo-Jacobean style, set in sixty acres of pretty grounds. The next stretch takes you to **Docking**, in the relative high ground of western Norfolk, and then on to the **North Norfolk Coast**, where you pass through a series of attractive villages and small towns - **Brancaster Staithe**, **Wells-next-the-Sea**, **Blakeney**, **Cley-next-the-Sea** and **Sheringham**, many of which contain old cottages built of local flint. This is a designated Area of Outstanding Natural Beauty - a very apt description (although a despicable bureaucratic term) of a stretch of coastline with dunes, sandbanks and salt marshes which supports a huge array of wildlife (especially birds) in its many nature reserves. **Burnham Thorpe** is the birthplace of Horatio Nelson, and boasts the Lord Nelson pub, where he had his last meal before setting out on the campaign from which he would not return. **Cley Marshes** is Britain's oldest nature reserve, sheltering a great variety of wading birds; from Blakeney you can take a boat trip to see the seals at Blakeney Point.

Wighton 20

National Grid Ref: TF9439

Sandpiper Inn

(1.5m) ***The Carpenters' Arms,*** *57 High Street, Wighton, Wells-next-the-Sea, Norfolk,* NR23 1PF.
Actual grid ref: TF942397
Tel: **01328 820752**
Mrs Marsh.
Rates fr: *£17.50*-**£25.00**.
Open: All Year
Beds: 1D 2T
Baths: 1 Shared
(7) (30)
This traditional village inn set in the River Stiffkey valley offers peace and quiet along with delicious home-cooked food and excellent ales

Blakeney 21

National Grid Ref: TG0243

King's Arms, White Horse

(0.25m) ***Springers,*** *55 New Road, Off Coast Road, Blakeney, Holt, Norfolk,* NR25 7PA.
Actual grid ref: TG029435
Non-smoking, with warm welcome
Tel: **01263 740103**
Mrs Buckey.
Rates fr: *£17.50*-**£21.00**.
Open: All Year
Beds: 1T
Baths: 1 Ensuite
(6)

(On route) ***Dallinga,*** *71 Morston Road, Blakeney, Holt, Norfolk,* NR25 7BD.
Modern deluxe, ensuite
Tel: **01263 740943**
Mr & Mrs Ward.
Rates fr: *£15.00*-**£20.00**.
Open: All Year
Beds: 1D 1T
Baths: 2 Ensuite
(13) (6)

(On route) ***Bramble Lodge,*** *3 Morston Road, Blakeney, Holt, Norfolk,* NR25 7PF.
Accommodation of a high standard
Tel: **01263 740191** (also fax no)
Mrs Gray.
Rates fr: *£18.00*-**£23.00**.
Open: All Year (not Xmas)
Beds: 1D 2T
Baths: 3 Ensuite
(3)

Planning a longer stay? Always ask for any special rates.

Wiveton 22

National Grid Ref: TG0442

The Bell

(0.25m) ***Flintstones Guest House,*** *Wiveton, Holt, Norfolk,* NR25 7TL.
Actual grid ref: TG0443
Situated in peaceful, picturesque village
Grades: ETB Listed, Comm, AA 3 Q, RAC Acclaim
Tel: **01263 740337** Mr Ormerod.
Rates fr: *£17.00*-**£22.00**.
Open: All Year (not Xmas)
Beds: 3F 1D 1S
Baths: 5 Private
(5)

(0.25m) ***Rosemeade,*** *The Street, Wiveton, Holt, Norfolk,* NR25 7TH.
Tranquil 1930s bungalow, plus chalet
Tel: **01263 740747** Mrs Sayers.
Rates fr: *£15.00*-**£18.00**.
Open: All Year (not Xmas)
Beds: 2D 1T
Baths: 2 Shared

Cley-next-the-Sea 23

National Grid Ref: TG0443

George & Dragon

(On route) ***The George & Dragon,*** *Cley-next-the-Sea, Holt, Norfolk,* NR25 7RN.
Actual grid ref: TG047439
Centrally-heated, comfortable Edwardian inn
Grades: ETB 3 Cr, Comm
Tel: **01263 740652** Mr Sewell.
Fax no: 01263 741275
Rates fr: *£20.00*-**£35.00**.
Open: All Year (not Xmas)
Beds: 1F 4D 2T 1S
Baths: 6 Private 1 Shared
(30)

(On route) ***Cley Windmill,*** *Cley-next-the-Sea, Holt, Norfolk,* NR25 7NN.
Actual grid ref: TG045441
Comfortable guest house with stunning views
Tel: **01263 740209** (also fax no)
Mr Buisseret.
Rates fr: *£25.00*-**£30.00**.
Open: All Year
Beds: 5D 3T
Baths: 6 Private 1 Shared
(6)

(On route) ***Marshlands,*** *High Street, Cley-next-the-Sea, Holt, Norfolk,* NR25 7RB.
Actual grid ref: TG045438
Victorian old town hall house
Tel: **01263 740284**
Mr & Mrs Kinsella.
Rates fr: *£15.00*-**£25.00**.
Open: All Year (not Xmas)
Beds: 1D 2T
Baths: 2 Ensuite 1 Private
(5)

All cycleways are popular: you are well-advised to book ahead

Sheringham 24

National Grid Ref: TG1543

The Crown, Windham Arms, Red Lion, Two Lifeboats

(▲ 0.25m) ***Sheringham Youth Hostel,*** *1 Cremer's Drift, Sheringham, Norfolk,* NR26 8BJ.
Actual grid ref: TG159428
Warden: Ms J Cooper.
Tel: **01263 823215**
Under 18: £6.55 **Adults:** £9.75
Evening Meals Available (7pm), Family Bunk Rooms, Television, Games Room, Showers, Shop
Victorian building with modern annexe & facilities for disabled. Wide sandy beaches, good bird-watching & a seal colony on this coast

(0.25m) ***Holly Cottage,*** *14a The Rise, Sheringham, Norfolk,* NR26 8QB.
Award-winning luxury ensuites, short walk sea. Warm Christian welcome
Tel: **01263 822807** Mrs Perkins.
Rates fr: *£15.00*-**£18.00**.
Open: All Year (not Xmas)
Beds: 2F/D
Baths: 2 Ensuite
(3)

(0.25m) ***Beeston Hills Lodge,*** *64 Cliff Road, Sheringham, Norfolk,* NR26 8BJ.
Edwardian lodge, superb sea views. Stephen Spender, poet, lived here
Tel: **01263 821900** (also fax no)
Rowan.
Rates fr: *£16.50*-**£24.00**.
Open:
Beds: 1F 1D 1S
Baths: 1 Private 1 Shared
(5)

(0.25m) ***The Bay-Leaf Guest House,*** *10 St Peters Road, Sheringham, Norfolk,* NR26 8QY.
Charming Victorian licensed guesthouse, nestled between steam railway and sea
Grades: ETB 1 Cr, Comm
Tel: **01263 823779** Mr Pigott.
Rates fr: *£17.00*-**£17.00**.
Open: All Year
Beds: 4F 1D 2T **Baths:** 7 Ensuite
(4)

The *lowest* **single** rate *is shown in* **bold.**

(0.25m) *Camberley Guest House,* 62 Cliff Road, Sheringham, Norfolk, NR26 8BJ.
Comfortable spacious, ideally situated, quiet. Slipway to beach immediately opposite
Grades: ETB 2 Cr, Comm
Tel: 01263 823101
Mr & Mrs Simmons.
Rates fr: £18.00-**£18.00**.
Open: All Year (not Xmas)
Beds: 2F 2D 2T
Baths: 6 Private
🅿 (8) 🖵 🖩 ♣

(0.25m) *The Old Vicarage,* Sheringham, Norfolk, NR26 8NH.
Attractive turn-of-century house. Lovely pine staircase
Tel: 01263 822627 Mrs O'Connor.
Rates fr: £21.00.
Open: All Year (not Xmas)
Beds: 1F 1D 1T
Baths: 3 Ensuite
🅿 (5) 🖵 🖈 ✕ 🖩 🎝 ♣

(0.25m) *Sans Souci,* 19 Waterbank Road, Sheringham, Norfolk, NR26 8RB.
Charming Victorian guest house
Tel: 01263 824436 Mrs Majewski.
Rates fr: £15.00-**£15.00**.
Open: Easter to Oct
Beds: 1D 1T 1S
Baths: 1 Shared
🅂 🅿 (3) 🖵 🖈 🖩

(0.25m) *Wykeham Guest House,* Morley Road North, Sheringham, Norfolk, NR26 8JB.
Quiet family home, centrally located
Tel: 01263 823818 Mrs Meakin.
Rates fr: £16.50-**£16.50**.
Open: Apr to Oct
Beds: 1F 1D 1T 1S
Baths: 1 Private 1 Shared
🅂 🅿 (6) 🖵 🖩 🗓 ♣

(0.25m) *Montague Lodge,* 1 Montague Road, Sheringham, Norfolk, NR26 8LN.
Large house in quiet road
Tel: 01263 822267 Mrs Childs.
Rates fr: £15.50-**£15.50**.
Open: All Year
Beds: 2F 3D 2T 2S
Baths: 3 Private 2 Shared
🅂 (10) 🅿 🖵 🖈 ✕ 🖩 🎝 🗓

Bodham 25

National Grid Ref: TG1240
🍴 🍺 Wheatsheaf, Red Lion

(0.5m) *The Old Foundry House,* The Street, Bodham, Holt, Norfolk, NR25 6NP.
Converted 250-year-old foundry
Tel: 01263 588449
Mr & Mrs Gimbrere.
Rates fr: £16.00-**£18.00**.
Open: All Year
Beds: 1D 1T
Baths: 1 Shared
🅂 🅿 🖵 🖩 🗓

Wood Dalling 26

National Grid Ref: TG0927
🍴 🍺 Earl Arms

(3m) *Westwood Barn,* Wood Dalling, Norwich. NR11 6SW.
Outstanding accommodation, idyllic countryside location for Norwich, Broads, coastal resorts
Grades: ETB 2 Cr, High Comm
Tel: 01263 584108 Mrs Westwood.
Rates fr: £22.00-**£32.00**.
Open: All Year
Beds: 2D 1T
Baths: 3 Private
🅂 (12) 🅿 (6) ⚡ 🖵 ✕ 🖩 🎝 🗓

Cawston 27

National Grid Ref: TG1323

(2m) *Grey Gables Hotel,* Norwich Road, Cawston, Norwich. NR10 4EY.
Former rectory in rural setting
Tel: 01603 871259 Mr Snaith.
Rates fr: £21.00-**£21.00**.
Open: All Year (not Xmas)
Beds: 1F 4D 2T 2S
Baths: 7 Private 1 Shared
🅂 🅿 (15) 🖵 🖈 ✕ 🖩 🗓

Wymondham 28

National Grid Ref: TG1101
🍴 🍺 Three Boars, The Pelican, Crossed Keys

(1m) *Willow Farm,* Wattlefield, Wymondham, Norfolk, NR18 9PA.
Peaceful farmhouse, relaxed atmosphere
Grades: ETB Listed, Comm
Tel: 01953 604679 Mrs Highton.
Rates fr: £18.00-**£18.00**.
Open: All Year (not Xmas)
Beds: 1D 1T 1S
Baths: 2 Shared
🅂 🅿 🖵 🖈 🖩 🗓

(0.25 milesm) *Turret House,* 27 Middleton Street, Wymondham, Norfolk, NR18 0AB.
Large central Victorian private house
Tel: 01953 603462 (also fax no)
Mrs Morgan.
Rates fr: £15.00-**£15.00**.
Open: All Year (not Xmas)
Beds: 1F 1T
Baths: 1 Shared
🅂 🅿 (2) ⚡ 🖵 🖈 🖩

Please respect a B&B's wishes regarding children, animals & smoking.

Norwich 29

National Grid Ref: TG2308
🍴 🍺 King's Head, Coach & Horses, The Pickwick, The Black Horse, The Mitre

(🔺 1m) *Norwich Youth Hostel,* 112 Turner Road, Norwich, Norfolk, NR2 4HB.
Actual grid ref: TG213095
Tel: 01603 627647
Under 18: £5.95 **Adults:** £8.80
Evening Meals Available (6.30-7.15pm), Self-catering Facilities, Television, Showers
In quiet suburban street outside the city centre, a good place for exploring Norwich. Within easy reach of East Anglian countryside, from seaside to the Broads

(1m) *Earlham Guest House,* 147 Earlham Road, Norwich. NR2 3RG.
Grades: ETB 2 Cr, Comm, AA 3 Q
Tel: 01603 454169 (also fax no)
Mr & Mrs Wright.
Rates fr: £17.00-**£20.00**.
Open: All Year
Beds: 2F 1T 2D 2S
Baths: 2 Ensuite 2 Shared
🅂 ⚡ 🖵 🖩 🗓
Susan and Derek Wright offer welcoming and friendly hospitality with comfortable and modern facilities close historic Norwich centre and University. Non-smoking. Visa, Mastercard

(1m) *Chiltern House,* 2 Trafford Road, Norwich. NR1 2QW.
Good home cooking. 5 minutes city centre. Celia & Ken Harrison welcome you all year round
Grades: ETB Listed
Tel: 01603 663033 Mrs Harrison.
Rates fr: £17.00-**£17.00**.
Open: All Year **Beds:** 1F 1D 5S
Baths: 1 Ensuite 1 Shared
🅂 🖵 ✕ 🖩 🎝 🗓

(1m) *Edmar Lodge,* 64 Earlham Road, Norwich. NR2 3DF.
A real home from home. Come and be spoilt!
Grades: ETB 2 Cr, Comm
Tel: 01603 615599 Mrs Lovatt.
Fax no: 01603 632977
Rates fr: £16.50-**£23.00**.
Open: All Year
Beds: 2F 1D 1T 1S
Baths: 3 Private 2 Shared
🅂 🅿 (6) 🖵 🖩 🗓

(1m) *Trebeigh House,* 16 Brabazon Road, Hellesdon, Norwich. NR6 6SY.
Friendly comfortable, quiet private house. Convenient airport and tourist attractions
Tel: 01603 429056 Mrs Jope.
Fax no: 01603 414247
Rates fr: £16.00-**£17.00**.
Open: All Year (not Xmas)
Beds: 1D 1T **Baths:** 1 Shared
🅂 🅿 (2) ⚡ 🖵 🖩 🗓 🍴

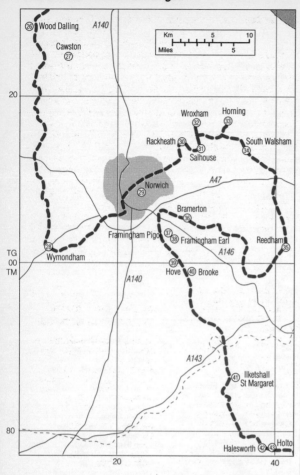

(1m) *30 St Stephens Road*,
Norwich. *NR1 3RA*.
Beautifully restored Victorian
Listed house
Tel: **01603 760238** Mrs Middleton.
Rates fr: *£15.00*-**£22.00**.
Open: All Year (not Xmas)
Beds: 2D
Baths: 1 Shared
🛇 🅿 (1) 🛌 🖵 🎞️

Rackheath   30

National Grid Ref: TG2813

🍴 🍺 Green Man

(2m) *Barn Court*, Back Lane,
Rackheath, Norwich. NR13 6NN.
Traditional Norfolk barn
conversion
Grades: ETB Listed, Comm
Tel: **01603 782536** (also fax no)
Mrs Simpson.
Rates fr: *£18.00*-**£18.00**.
Open: All Year (not Xmas)
Beds: 2D 1T
Baths: 1 Ensuite 2 Shared
🛇 🅿 (3) 🖵 🛌 ✗ 🎞️ Ⓥ 🍴

(2m) *Manor Barn House*, Back
Lane, Rackheath, Norwich.
NR13 6NN.
Traditional C17th Norfolk barn,
exposed beams
Grades: ETB 2 Cr, Comm
Tel: **01603 783543**
Mrs Lebbell.
Rates fr: *£17.00*-**£18.00**.
Open: All Year
Beds: 3D 2T 1S
Baths: 5 Ensuite 1 Private
🛇 (3) 🅿 (6) 🖵 🛌 🎞️ ♿

Salhouse   31

National Grid Ref: TG3114

🍴 🍺 Bell Inn

(On route) *Brooksbank*, Lower
Street, Salhouse, Norwich.
NR13 6RW.
C18th house in heart of Broads
Grades: ETB 2 Cr, Comm
Tel: **01603 720420** Mr & Mrs Coe.
Rates fr: *£17.00*-**£20.00**.
Open: All Year
Beds: 2D 1T
Baths: 3 Private
🅿 (4) 🛌 🖵 🛌 🎞️

Wroxham   32

National Grid Ref: TG3017

🍴 🍺 Broads Hotel

(0.25m) *The Mount*, 93 Norwich
Road, Wroxham, Norwich. NR12 8RX.
Delightful Broads guesthouse
Grades: ETB 2 Cr, Comm
Tel: **01603 783909** Mrs Leeming.
Rates fr: *£18.00*-**£22.00**.
Open: All Year (not Xmas)
Beds: 2D 1T
Baths: 1 Ensuite 2 Shared
🅿 (3) 🛌 🖵 🎞️ Ⓥ

(1m) *Rosedale*, 145 Earlham Road,
Norwich. NR2 3RG.
Comfortable, friendly, family guest
house
Grades: ETB Listed, Approv
Tel: **01603 453743**
Mrs Curtis.
Fax no: 01603 408473
Rates fr: *£16.50*-**£16.00**.
Open: All Year (not Xmas)
Beds: 1F 1D 3T 3S
Baths: 2 Shared
🛇 (4) 🅿 (1) 🖵 🎞️ Ⓥ

(1m) *Alpha Hotel*, 82 Unthank
Road, Norwich. NR2 2RW.
Comfortable Victorian rectory with
character
Grades: ETB 2 Cr
Tel: **01603 621105** (also fax no)
Mr Downton.
Rates fr: *£20.00*-**£22.00**.
Open: All Year (not Xmas)
Beds: 6D 6T 9S
Baths: 10 Ensuite 4 Shared
🛇 (10) 🅿 (16) 🛌 🖵 🎞️

(1m) *The Sycamores*, 59 Aylsham
Road, Norwich. NR3 2HF.
Comfortable, modern, private
house
Grades: ETB Listed, Comm
Tel: **01603 665798** Mrs Adams.
Rates fr: *£16.00*-**£16.00**.
Open: Mar to Dec **Beds:** 1F 1D
Baths: 1 Ensuite 1 Private
🛇 (3) 🅿 (2) 🛌 🖵 🎞️ Ⓥ

(1m) *Butterfield Hotel*, 4 Stracey
Road, Norwich. NR1 1EZ.
Large Victorian private house
Grades: ETB Listed
Tel: **01603 661008 / 624041**
Rates fr: *£34.00*-**£17.00**.
Open: All Year (not Xmas)
Beds: 4F 4D 4S
Baths: 4 Ensuite 2 Shared
🛇 🅿 🖵 🛌 ✗ 🎞️ ♿

The *lowest* **single**
rate *is shown in* **bold.**

The North Norfolk Coast to the Broads

At **Sheringham** the route turns sharply south and heads inland over the flat farmlands of northeastern Norfolk, via **Reepham**, eventually arriving at **Wymondham**. Here you will find grand Georgian facades, older half-timbered buildings, and an abbey ruined in the Dissolution. From Wymondham it's northeast into **Norwich**. The capital of East Anglia was economically important for centuries before the Industrial Revolution; the city bears traces of every period of English history. Tombland is the old Saxon market place, close to the picturesque half-timbered houses of Elm Hill. The Norman keep of Norwich Castle, dating from the twelfth century, ranks with the Tower of London as England's best surviving Norman fortification. The city's cathedral is also a Norman foundation, with later additions - the vaulted roof, with illustratively carved bosses,

and the spire (the tallest in England after Salisbury) date from the fifteenth century. The most important modern building is the Sainsbury Centre for the Visual Arts, designed in the 1970s by Norman Foster, which houses a brilliant display in which central figures of western modern art (Picasso, Modigliani, Giacometti) share space with African, Pacific and Native American exhibits. The next part of the tour is a circular exploration of the **Norfolk Broads National Park**, from **Wroxham**, **Ranworth** and **Acle** to **Reedham** and **Loddon**. Widened stretches of the Rivers Bure, Ant, Thurne, Yare and Waveney form one of Europe's most important wetlands, a massive haven for wildlife, particularly birds. For those with an iterest in conservation the Broadland Conservation Centre at Ranworth is a must. This village also has a church, St Helen's, which has a medieval painted screen and a fourteenth-century illuminated manuscript, as well as a tower which yields spectacular Broadland views.

Horning 33

National Grid Ref: TG3417

†○| ◖ Ferry Pub

(3m) *Keppelgate, Upper Street, Horning, Norwich. NR12 8NG.*
Open countryside near Broads coast
Tel: **01692 630610** Mrs Freeman.
Rates fr: *£15.00*-**£18.00**.
Open: All Year (not Xmas)
Beds: 1F 1D 1T
Baths: 1 Ensuite 1 Shared
Ö (3) ⓟ (4) ⌨ ⚌ & Ⅴ

South Walsham 34

National Grid Ref: TG3613

†○| ◖ Ship Inn, King's Arms

(1m) *Old Hall Farm, South Walsham, Norwich. NR13 6DT.*
Thatched farmhouse in Broadland village. **Grades:** ETB 2 Cr
Tel: **01603 270271** Mrs Dewing.
Rates fr: *£15.00*-**£20.00**.
Open: Easter to Oct **Beds:** 2D 1T
Baths: 1 Ensuite 2 Shared
ⓟ (4) ⌯ ⌨ ⚌ Ⅴ ▮

Reedham 35

National Grid Ref: TG4201

†○| ◖ Railway Tavern, Ferry Inn

(On route) *The Railway Tavern, 17 The Havaker, Reedham, Norwich. NR13 3HG.*
Norfolk Broads - free house - CAMRA
Grades: ETB Listed, Comm
Tel: **01493 700340** (also fax no)
Mrs Swan.
Rates fr: *£25.00*-**£30.00**.
Open: All Year
Beds: 1F 1D 1T **Baths:** 3 Ensuite
Ö ⓟ (8) ⌯ ⌨ ⌇ ✕ ⚌ & Ⅴ ▮ ⌀

(On route) *Briars, Riverside, Reedham, Norwich. NR13 3TF.*
Grades: ETB 2 Cr, Comm
Tel: **01493 700054** (also fax no)
Mr Monk.
Rates fr: *£23.75*-**£34.00**.
Open: All Year (not Xmas)
Beds: 3D
Baths: 3 Ensuite
Ö ⓟ (6) ⌨ ⌇ ✕ ⚌ Ⅴ ▮
This welcoming home has a wonderful location with a residents' lounge and balcony overlooking the River Yare. Ensuite, pine furnished, comfortable bedrooms. Tearoom adjoining

(On route) *The Old Post Office, 26 The Hills, Reedham, Norwich. NR13 3AR.*
Self-contained converted village post office. Outdoor, heated swimming pool. Lovely gardens
Grades: ETB Listed, Comm
Tel: **01493 701262** Mrs Blanche.
Fax no: 01493 701635
Rates fr: *£20.00*-**£30.00**.
Open: All Year
Beds: 1D
Baths: 1 Ensuite
Ö ⓟ ⌨ ⚌

Bramerton 36

National Grid Ref: TG2905

†○| ◖ Woods End Tavern

(0.25m) *Rolling Acre, Woods End, Bramerton, Norwich. NR14 7ED.*
Comfortable period country house.
Quiet, fine view
Tel: **01508 538529** Mrs Barton.
Rates fr: *£17.50*-**£19.00**.
Open: All Year
Beds: 1F 1D
Baths: 1 Ensuite 1 Shared
Ö (12) ⓟ (6) ⌨ ⌇ ⚌ Ⅴ

Framingham Pigot 37

National Grid Ref: TG2703

†○| ◖ Railway Tavern, The Gull

(0.5m) *The Old Rectory, Rectory Lane, Framingham Pigot, Norwich. NR14 7QQ.*
Friendly comfortable Victorian Rectory. Large garden. 10 mins Norwich centre
Grades: ETB Listed
Tel: **01508 493082**
Mrs Thurman.
Rates fr: *£19.00*-**£19.00**.
Open: All Year (not Xmas)
Beds: 1F 1D 1T
Baths: 2 Ensuite 1 Shared
Ö ⓟ (6) ⌇ ⌨ ⚌ ⌀

Framingham Earl 38

National Grid Ref: TG2702

(1m) *Oakfield, Yelverton Road, Framingham Earl, Norwich. NR14 7SD.*
Peaceful, superior accommodation, excellent breakfast
Grades: ETB Listed, High Comm
Tel: **01508 492605** Mrs Thompson.
Rates fr: *£16.00*-**£17.00**.
Open: All Year (not Xmas)
Beds: 1D 1T 1S
Baths: 1 Private 1 Shared
Ö (12) ⓟ (4) ⌇ ⌨ ⚌

All rates are subject
to alteration at the
owners' discretion.

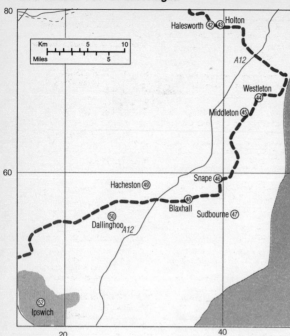

Halesworth ㊷㊸ Holton

A12

Westleton ㊹

Middleton ㊺

60

Hacheston ㊾   Snape ㊻

㊽

Blaxhall   Sudbourne ㊼

㊿
Dallinghoo *A12*

52
Ipswich

20   40

Km   5   10
Miles   5

Howe — 39

National Grid Ref: TG2700

🍴 🍺 Wildebeest Arms

(1m) *Church Farm House, Howe, Norwich. NR15 1HD.*
Peaceful C16th farmhouse 6 miles Norwich
Grades: ETB 2 Cr
Tel: **01508 550565** Ms Michie.
Rates fr: *£18.00*-**£18.00**.
Open: All Year **Beds:** 2D 1T
Baths: 1 Ensuite 1 Private
🛏 🅿 (6) ⅓ 🗗 🕻 🛏 🎦 🆅

Brooke — 40

National Grid Ref: TM2899

🍴 🍺 The Dove

(1m) *Welbeck House, Brooke, Norwich. NR15 1AT.*
Peaceful pinkwashed 1680 former farmhouse. Reduced rates over 3 days
Tel: **01508 550292** (also fax no)
Mrs Vivian-Neal.
Rates fr: *£18.00*-**£16.00**.
Open: All Year (not Xmas)
Beds: 1D 1T 1S
Baths: 1 Shared
🛏 (10) 🅿 (6) ⅓ 🗗 🕻 🗙 🎦 🆅 ⚡

The lowest *double* rate per
person is shown in *italics*.

The *lowest* **single**

rate *is shown in* **bold.**

Ilketshall St Margaret — 41

National Grid Ref: TM3585

🍴 🍺 Rumburgh Buck

(1m) *Shoo-Devil Farmhouse, Ilketshall St Margaret, Bungay, Suffolk, NR35 1QU.*
Comfortable, secluded thatched C16th farmhouse
Grades: ETB 2 Cr, Comm
Tel: **01986 781303** Mrs Lewis.
Rates fr: *£17.50*-**£20.00**.
Open: Easter to Oct
Beds: 1D 1T
Baths: 2 Ensuite
🅿 (6) ⅓ 🗗 🗙 🎦 🆅

Halesworth — 42

National Grid Ref: TM3877

🍴 🍺 Queen's Head

(0.5m) *Fen Way, School Lane, Halesworth, Suffolk, IP19 8BW.*
Bungalow set in peaceful meadowland
Tel: **01986 873574** Mrs George.
Rates fr: *£14.00*-**£16.00**.
Open: All Year
Beds: 2D 1T **Baths:** 1 Shared
🛏 (5) 🅿 (5) ⅓ 🗗 🗙 🎦

Holton — 43

National Grid Ref: TM4077

(0.25m) *Gavelcroft, Harrisons Lane, Holton, Halesworth, Suffolk, IP19 8LY.*
Listed C16th farmhouse in tranquil surroundings
Tel: **01986 873117**
Mrs Hart.
Rates fr: *£18.00*-**£22.00**.
Open: All Year (not Xmas)
Beds: 1F 1T
Baths: 2 Private
🛏 🅿 (8) ⅓ 🗗 🕻 🗙 🎦 �ⅅ 🆅

Westleton — 44

National Grid Ref: TM4469

🍴 🍺 White Horse, The Crown

(0.25m) *Barn Cottage, Mill Street, Westleton, Saxmundham, Suffolk, IP17 3BD.*
Interesting cottage home, residents' lounge. Close RSPB Minsmere
Tel: **01728 648437**
Mr & Mrs Allen.
Rates fr: *£17.00*-**£17.00**.
Open: All Year (not Xmas)
Beds: 1D 2T
Baths: 2 Shared
🛏 🅿 (3) 🗗 🎦 🆅 ⚡

Middleton — 45

National Grid Ref: TM4367

🍴 🍺 Middleton Bell

(0.25m) *Rose Villa, The Street, Middleton, Saxmundham, Suffolk, IP17 3NJ.*
Private house, close to Minsmere
Tel: **01728 648489** Mrs Crowden.
Rates fr: *£15.00*-**£13.00**.
Open: All Year
Beds: 1D 1T
Baths: 1 Shared
🅿 (3) 🗗 🎦

Snape — 46

National Grid Ref: TM3959

🍴 🍺 Golden Key, The Crown

(0.25m) *Flemings Lodge, Gromford Lane, Snape, Saxmundham, Suffolk, IP17 1RG.*
Modern bungalow, overlooking open farmland
Grades: ETB Listed, Comm
Tel: **01728 688502**
Mrs Edwards.
Rates fr: *£18.00*-**£25.00**.
Open: All Year (not Xmas)
Beds: 1D 1T
Baths: 1 Shared
🅿 (3) ⅓ 🗗 🎦 🆅

Sudbourne 47

National Grid Ref: TM4153

¶❶ Fisize Inn

(3m) *Long Meadow, Gorse Lane,
Sudbourne, Woodbridge, Suffolk,
IP12 2BD*.
Quiet traditonal bungalow, show
garden. Very quiet rural location
Grades: ETB Listed, Comm
Tel: 01394 450269
Mrs Wood.
Rates fr: *£15.00*-**£15.00**.
Open: All Year (not Xmas)
Beds: 1D 1T 1S
Baths: 1 Private 1 Shared
🛏 (12) ❷ (4) ⊁☐🔭🎢

Blaxhall 48

National Grid Ref: TM3656

(▲0.25m) *Blaxhall Youth Hostel,
Heath Walk, Blaxhall, Woodbridge,
Suffolk, IP12 2EA*.
Actual grid ref: TM369570
Tel: 01728 688206
Under 18: £5.40
Adults: £8.00
Evening Meals Available (7pm),
Self-catering Facilities, Showers,
Security Lockers
*Traditional hostel, once a village
school, offering modest accommo-
dation. RSPB reserves of Minsmere
and Havergate nearby. Snape
Maltings concert hall 2m*

Hacheston 49

National Grid Ref: TM3059

¶❶ White Horse

(2m) *Cherry Tree House,
Hacheston, Woodbridge, Suffolk,
IP13 0DR*.
Large C17th farmhouse, large
garden
Tel: 01728 746371
Mrs Hall.
Rates fr: *£15.00*-**£16.00**.
Open: All Year
Beds: 1F 1T 2S
Baths: 2 Shared
🛏 ❷ (3) ☐✗🎢🎬⊁

Dallinghoo 50

National Grid Ref: TM2655

¶❶ Three Tuns, The Castle

(1m) *Old Rectory, Dallinghoo,
Woodbridge, Suffolk, IP13 0LA*.
Restful rural retreat, regularly
revisited. Guest rooms have
southerly views
Grades: ETB Listed, Comm
Tel: 01473 737700
Mrs Quinlan.
Rates fr: *£15.00*.
Open: All Year (not Xmas)
Beds: 1D 1T
Baths: 1 Private 1 Shared
🛏 ❷ (6) ⊁🎬🎬

Sproughton 51

National Grid Ref: TM1244

¶❶ Royal George, The Beagle,
Wild Man

(On route) *Finjaro Guest House,
Valley Farm Drive, Hadleigh
Road, Sproughton, Ipswich,
Suffolk, IP8 3EL*.
Set in countryside, Constable
Country location. 2 miles from
Ipswich
Grades: ETB 1 Cr, Comm
Tel: 01473 652581 (also fax no)
Mrs Finbow.
Rates fr: *£17.50*-**£18.00**.
Open: All Year (not Xmas)
Beds: 2D 1T 1S **Baths:** 2 Shared
🛏 (5) ❷ (8) ⊁☐✗🎬🎬

Ipswich 52

National Grid Ref: TM1644

¶❶ Westerfield Swan, The
Greyhound, The Ram, White Horse

(3m) *Orwell View, 24 Vermont
Road, Ipswich, Suffolk, IP4 2SR*.
Peaceful, close to centre, easy
parking
Tel: 01473 211451 Mrs Carroll.
Rates fr: *£12.50*-**£12.50**.
Open: All Year (not Xmas)
Beds: 1T 1S **Baths:** 1 Shared
❷ (4) ☐🎢✗🎬🎬🖊

(3m) *Maple House,
114 Westerfield Road, Ipswich,
Suffolk, IP4 2XW*.
Attractive private house near park
Tel: 01473 253797
Mrs Seal.
Rates fr: *£25.00*-**£15.00**.
Open: All Year (not Xmas)
Beds: 1D 1S
Baths: 1 Shared
❷ (3) ⊁☐🎢✗🎬♿⊁

(3m) *107 Hatfield Road, Ipswich,
Suffolk, IP3 9AG*.
Large Victorian guest house,
modern facilities
Tel: 01473 723172
Mrs Debenham.
Fax no: 01473 270876
Rates fr: *£14.00*-**£15.00**.
Open: All Year
Beds: 1D 2T
Baths: 1 Private 2 Shared
🛏 ❷ ☐🎢✗🎬♿🎬

(3m) *Craigerne, Cauldwell
Avenue, Ipswich, Suffolk, IP4 4DZ*.
Tastefully restored Victorian,
gardens, parking
Tel: 01473 718200
Mrs Krotunas.
Rates fr: *£15.00*-**£15.00**.
Open: All Year (not Xmas)
Beds: 1D 1T 3S
Baths: 3 Ensuite 1 Shared
❷ (10) ☐✗🎬🎬

The Broads to Cambridge

The route out of the Broads takes you back close to the southeastern corner of Norwich before heading south to where you cross the Waveney and enter Suffolk at **Bungay**. From here it's on, through **Halesworth**, to **Dunwich** on the Suffolk Heritage Coast. A small village is all that now remains of the ancient seat of the Kings of East Anglia - the 'lost city' has gradually been given up, over the centuries, to the sea: the last of its twelve churches fell over the cliffs in 1919, and its remains can sometimes be seen at low tide. The story is told by the local museum, and there are maps and prints of the old city in the Ship Inn. From Dunwich you head south into Benjamin Britten country, and **Snape**, where the Maltings concert hall hosts every June the major performances of the Aldeburgh Festival, founded in 1948 by Britten, one of the most important British composers of this century. From Snape the route takes you inland west to **Wickham Market**, an attractive small town, before skirting Ipswich and heading south into Constable country. **East Bergholt** was Constable's birthplace, and it's a brief jaunt to **Flatford**, where his painting *The Hay Wain* featured the original mill, on the site of which the present Victorian building stands, and then on to **Dedham**, which boasts an immaculate neo-classical row of houses. From here you cycle close to the Stour through Stratford St Mary, Higham, Stoke-by-Nayland and Nayland to **Bures**, where you cross the river into Essex and continue to **Castle Hedingham**, where you can find a well-preserved Norman keep and the Colne Valley steam railway centre. The final stretch northeastwards leads back to Cambridge.

(3m) *Lochiel Guest House, 216 Felixstowe Road, Ipswich, Suffolk, IP3 9AE.*
Large Victorian detached house
Tel: **01473 727775** Mrs McEvoy.
Rates fr: *£14.00-£14.00.*
Open: All Year
Beds: 1F 1D 3T 4S
Baths: 3 Private
🛇 🖵 🖵 ⋔ ✕ 🖿.

(3m) *Mount Pleasant,*
103 Anglesea Road, Ipswich, Suffolk, IP1 3PJ.
Tranquil, elegant Victorian town house
Tel: **01473 251601**
Rates fr: *£21.00-£27.00.*
Open: All Year (not Xmas)
Beds: 2D 1T 1S
Baths: 3 Ensuite 1 Private
🛇 (8) 🅿 (4) 🖵 🖿.

(3m) *Bridge Guest House,*
4 Ancaster Road, Ipswich, Suffolk, IP1 9AA.
Family-run guest house, close town centre
Tel: **01473 601760**
Mr Pelletier.
Rates fr: *£14.00-£18.00.*
Open: All Year
Beds: 3F 6D 7S
Baths: 5 Private 3 Shared
🛇 🅿 (12) 🖵 ⋔ 🖿. 🅅

Copdock 53

National Grid Ref: TM1141

🍴 🍺 Brook Inn

(0.25m) *Westhill, Elm Lane, Copdock, Ipswich, Suffolk, IP6 3ET.*
Attractive rural Georgian private house
Grades: ETB Listed Comm
Tel: **01473 730259** (also fax no)
Mrs Winship.
Rates fr: *£17.50-£17.50.*
Open: All Year (not Xmas)
Beds: 2T 1S
Baths: 1 Shared
🛇 (10) 🅿 (4) ⅍ 🖵 ⋔ 🖿.

East Bergholt 54

National Grid Ref: TM0735

🍴 🍺 Red Lion, Carriers' Arms, King's Head

(On route) *Wren Cottage, The Street, East Bergholt, Colchester, Essex, CO7 6SE.*
C16th cottage in middle of village, easy walk to Flatford, good pubs, next to chemist
Grades: ETB Listed
Tel: **01206 298327**
Mrs Commercial.
Rates fr: *£20.00-£22.00.*
Open: Easter to Sep
Beds: 1F 1T
Baths: 2 Ensuite
🛇 🅿 🖵 ⋔ 🖿. 🅅

Dedham 55

National Grid Ref: TM0533

🍴 🍺 The Anchor, Marlborough Head, The Sun

(1m) *Mays Barn Farm, Mays Lane, Dedham, Colchester, Essex, CO7 6EW.*
Actual grid ref: TM0531
Secluded, comfortable old farmhouse
Grades: ETB 2 Cr, High Comm
Tel: **01206 323191**
Mrs Freeman.
Rates fr: *£19.00-£22.00.*
Open: All Year (not Xmas)
Beds: 1D 1T
Baths: 2 Private
🛇 (12) 🅿 (4) ⅍ 🖵 🖿. 🅅

Langham 56

National Grid Ref: TM0233

🍴 🍺 Shepherd & Dog

(2m) *Oak Apple Farm, Greyhound Hill, Langham, Colchester, Essex, CO4 5QF.*
Actual grid ref: TM023320
Comfortable farmhouse with large attractive garden
Grades: ETB Listed
Tel: **01206 272234**
Mrs Helliwell.
Rates fr: *£18.50-£19.00.*
Open: All Year (not Xmas)
Beds: 2T 1S
Baths: 1 Shared
🛇 🅿 (6) 🖵 🖿. 🅅 🛇 ✦

Stratford St Mary 57

National Grid Ref: TM0434

🍴 🍺 Marlborough Head, Sun Hotel, The Swan, Black Horse

(0.25m) *Teazles, Stratford St Mary, Colchester, Essex, CO7 6LU.*
Comfortable old merchant weaver's house
Tel: **01206 323148** Mrs Clover.
Rates fr: *£18.00-£18.00.*
Open: All Year
Beds: 1F 1D 1T 1S
Baths: 1 Ensuite 1 Shared
🛇 🅿 ⅍ 🖵 ⋔ 🖿. 🅅 🛇 ✦

Higham 58

National Grid Ref: TM0335

(On route) *The Bauble, Higham, Colchester, Essex, CO7 6LA.*
Actual grid ref: TM031354
Peaceful old country home
Grades: ETB 2 Cr, High Comm, AA 4 Q, Recomm
Tel: **01206 337254** Mrs Watkins.
Fax no: 01206 337263
Rates fr: *£20.00-£22.00.*
Open: All Year
Beds: 2T 1S
Baths: 3 Ensuite
🛇 (12) 🅿 (5) ⅍ 🖵 🖿. 🅅 🛇 ✦

Stoke-by-Nayland 59

National Grid Ref: TL9836

🍴 🍺 Black Horse, Angel Inn, Rose Inn

(0.25m) *Ryegate House, Stoke-by-Nayland, Colchester, Essex, CO6 4RA.*
Cheerful house in village setting
Grades: ETB 2 Cr, High Comm
Tel: **01206 263679**
Mr & Mrs Geater.
Rates fr: *£18.50-£25.00.*
Open: All Year (not Xmas)
Beds: 2D 1T
Baths: 3 Ensuite
🛇 (10) 🅿 (5) ⅍ 🖵 ⋔ 🖿.

(0.25m) *Thorington Hall, Stoke-by-Nayland, Colchester, Essex, CO6 4SS.*
Beautiful C17th house, warm welcome
Grades: ETB Listed, Comm
Tel: **01206 337329** Mrs Wollaston.
Rates fr: *£20.00-£17.50.*
Open: Easter to Oct
Beds: 1F 2D 1T 1S
Baths: 3 Private 1 Shared
🛇 🅿 (4) ⋔ 🅅

Nayland 60

National Grid Ref: TL9734

🍴 🍺 White Hart, The Angel

(1m) *Gladwins Farm, Harpers Hill, Nayland, Colchester, Essex, CO6 4NU.*
Actual grid ref: TL961347
Suffolk farmhouse in Constable country. Indoor pool. Brochure
Grades: ETB 2 Cr, Comm
Tel: **01206 262261** Mrs Dossor.
Fax no: 01206 263001
Rates fr: *£26.00-£20.00.*
Open: All Year (not Xmas)
Beds: 2D 1T 1S
Baths: 3 Private 1 Shared
🛇 🅿 (12) 🖵 ⋔ ✕ 🖿. 🅅 🛇 ✦

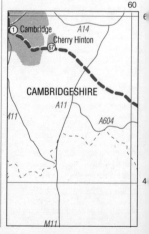

(0.25m) *Hill House, Gravel Hill, Nayland, Colchester, Essex,* CO6 4JB.
Actual grid ref: TL975345
C16th timber-framed "hall house"
Grades: ETB Listed, Comm
Tel: **01206 262782**
Mrs Heigham.
Rates fr: *£19.00*-**£20.00**.
Open: All Year (not Xmas)
Beds: 1D 1T 1S
Baths: 1 Ensuite 1 Shared
🛏 (10) 🅿 (3) ◻ 🎔 🖥 ☑ ⓘ ⚡

Leavenheath 61

National Grid Ref: TL9536

(3m) *Leavenheath Farm, Locks Lane, Leavenheath, Colchester, Essex,* CO6 4PF.
Welcoming period farmhouse, in quiet setting
Grades: ETB Listed, High Comm
Tel: **01206 262322**
Mrs Warren Thomas.
Rates fr: *£18.00*-**£20.00**.
Open: All Year (not Xmas)
Beds: 1F 1D 2T 1S
Baths: 3 Ensuite 1 Private
🛏 (4) 🅿 (8) ⬠ ◻ 🎔 ✗ 🖥 ☑ ⚡

Bures St Mary 62

National Grid Ref: TL9034

(0.25m) *Queens House, Church Square, Bures St Mary, Suffolk,* CO8 5AB.
C16th country house, licensed restaurant
Grades: ETB 2 Cr
Tel: **01787 227760**
Mrs Gordon.
Fax no: 01787 227903
Rates fr: *£20.00*-**£22.00**.
Open: All Year (not Xmas)
Beds: 1F 2D 2T
Baths: 4 Ensuite 1 Private
🛏 🅿 (2) ◻ ✗ 🖥 ☑

Castle Hedingham 63

National Grid Ref: TL7835
🍽 ⬠ The Bell

(▲ 0.25m) *Castle Hedingham Youth Hostel, 7 Falcon Square, Castle Hedingham, Halstead, Essex,* CO9 3BU.
Actual grid ref: TL786355
Tel: **01787 460799**
Under 18: £5.95 **Adults:** £8.80
Evening Meals Available (7pm), Self-catering Facilities, Showers
The Norman castle and half-timbered houses of Castle Hedingham add to the atmosphere of this hostel. 16th century building with modern annexe and large lawned garden

(0.25m) *Pannells Ash Farm, Castle Hedingham, Halstead, Essex,* CO9 3AD.
Period furnished C15th farmhouse
Grades: ETB Listed, Comm
Tel: **01787 460364** Mrs Redgewell.
Rates fr: *£15.50*-**£16.50**.
Open: All Year (not Xmas)
Beds: 1F 1D 1T 1S
Baths: 1 Private 1 Shared
🛏 🅿 (6) ⬠ ◻ 🖥 ☑ ⚡

Sible Hedingham 64

National Grid Ref: TL7734
🍽 ⬠ The Swan, Sugar Loaves

(1m) *Hedingham Antiques, 100 Swan Street, Sible Hedingham, Halstead, Essex,* CO9 3HP.
Large Victorian house/shop combined in centre village near pubs
Grades: ETB 1 Cr
Tel: **01787 460360** (also fax no)
Mrs Patterson.
Rates fr: *£17.50*-**£20.00**.
Open: All Year (not Xmas)
Beds: 1D 2T **Baths:** 3 Private
🛏 🅿 (4) ◻ 🖥 ☑

Toppesfield 65

National Grid Ref: TL7337

(1m) *Olivers Farm, Toppesfield, Halstead, Essex,* CO9 4LS.
C17th, quiet idyllic location
Tel: **01787 237642** Mrs Blackie.
Rates fr: *£18.00*-**£18.00**.
Open: All Year (not Xmas)
Beds: 2D 1T
Baths: 1 Ensuite 1 Shared
🛏 (10) 🅿 (4) ⬠ ◻

Steeple Bumpstead 66

National Grid Ref: TL6841

(0.25m) *Yew Tree House, 15 Chapel Street, Steeple Bumpstead, Haverhill, Suffolk,* CB9 7DQ.
Victorian home offering superior accommodation
Grades: ETB 1 Cr, Comm
Tel: **01440 730364** (also fax no)
Mrs Stirling.
Rates fr: *£18.00*-**£17.00**.
Open: All Year **Beds:** 1D 1T 1S
Baths: 2 Ensuite 1 Shared
🛏 (2) 🅿 (2) ⬠ ◻ ✗ 🖥 ☑ ⓘ

Cherry Hinton 67

National Grid Ref: TL4856
🍽 ⬠ Robin Hood

(0.25m) *Hamden Guest House, 89 High Street, Cherry Hinton, Cambridge.* CB1 4LU.
Grades: ETB Listed, Comm, AA 2 Q
Tel: **01223 413263** Mr Casciano.
Fax no: 01223 245960
Rates fr: *£22.50*-**£28.00**.
Open: All Year
Beds: 1F 2D 1T 2S **Baths:** 6 Ensuite
🛏 (10) 🅿 (7) ◻ 🖥
Comfortable bedrooms with private facilities, situated on the outskirts of Cambridge within short distance of city centre, local shops, pubs & restaurant within walking distance

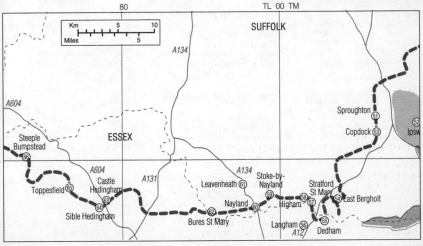

CTC Circular Tour of South Devon

The **Circular Tour of South Devon is** a 192-mile route put together by the Cyclists' Touring Club which covers some of Devon's most magnificent coutryside, from the beautiful South Coast to the wild open expanse of Dartmoor, starting and finishing at Exeter, and passing through Plymouth, one of the West Country's most important cities. The route also takes in the southeastern corner of Cornwall, as far as the eastern edge of Bodmin Moor and Whitsand Bay in the south. So long as you take care not to gorge yourself on clotted cream, the tour will be an experience to relish.

A **guide** pamphlet to the route is available from the Cyclists' Touring Club. You have to be a member to get it. Contact them at Cotterell House, 69 Meadrow, Godalming, Surrey GU7 3HS, tel 01483 417217, fax 01483 426994, e-mail cycling@ctc.org.uk.

Maps: Ordnance Survey 1:50,000 Landranger series: 191, 192, 201, 202

Trains: Exeter and Plymouth are major termini in the Intercity network. Liskeard, Torquay and Paignton are also served by trains.

Exeter   1

National Grid Ref: SX9192

|●| ◧ Nutwell Lodge, Mill-on-the-Exe, The Papermakers, Chaucer's Inn, Seven Stars, The Admiral, Bystock Hotel, The Imperial, White Horse Inn, George & Dragon, Puffing Billy

(▲ 0.5m) *Exeter Youth Hostel,*
47 Countess Wear Road, Exeter,
Devon, EX2 6LR.
Actual grid ref: SX941897
Tel: **01392 873329**
Under 18: £6.55
Adults: £9.75
Evening Meals Available (6.30-7.30pm), Self-catering Facilities, Television, Showers, Security Lockers, Laundry Facilities, Camping Facilities
A comfortable hostel with modern facilities on the outskirts of the city

(0.5m) *St Davids Guest House,*
89 St Davids Hill, Exeter, Devon,
EX4 4DW.
Tel: **01392 434737** (also fax no)
Mr & Mrs Morris.
Rates fr: *£15.00-£15.00.*
Open: All Year
Beds: 1F 1D 1T 2S
Baths: 4 Ensuite 1 Private
🛏 🅿 (4) 🖵 🏂 🛏 ☑
Stations and city centre 10 minutes' walk. Comfortable warm and friendly. All modern facilities. Excellent English breakfast or Continental alternative included

(0.5m) *The Grange, Stoke Hill,*
Exeter, Devon, EX4 7JH.
Country house in private grounds
Grades: ETB 2 Cr, Comm
Tel: **01392 259723**
Mr Dudley.
Rates fr: *£15.00-£20.00.*
Open: All Year
Beds: 2D 2T
Baths: 4 Ensuite
🛏 🅿 (8) 💤 🖵 🛏

(0.5m) *Raffles, 11 Blackall Road,*
Exeter, Devon, EX4 4HD.
Attractive Victorian town house close to city centre
Grades: ETB 3 Cr, Comm
Tel: **01392 270200**
Mr Hyde.
Rates fr: *£22.00-£30.00.*
Open: All Year
Beds: 2F 2D 1T 2S
Baths: 7 Private
🛏 🅿 (4) 🖵 🏂 🗙 🛏 ☑

(On route) *Clock Tower Hotel,*
16 New North Road, Exeter,
Devon, EX4 4HF.
Central, few minutes level walk cathedral, shops and station. Award winning patio garden. Request brochure
Tel: **01392 424545**
Mrs Blackshaw.
Fax no: 01392 218445
Rates fr: *£13.50-£17.00.*
Open: All Year
Beds: 2F 6D 5T 3S
Baths: 8 Private 3 Shared
🛏 🖵 🏂 🛏 ☑ ✦

(0.5m) *Meads Guest House, 2 St*
Davids Hill, Exeter, Devon, EX4 3RG.
Attractive, comfortable accommodation near Cathedral
Tel: **01392 274886** Mr Bodemeaid.
Rates fr: *£16.00-£16.00.*
Open: All Year **Beds:** 2D 1T 1S
Baths: 2 Private 2 Shared
🛏 🅿 🖵 🗙 🛏 ☑ 🍷

(0.5m) *Hillcrest Corner,*
1 Hillcrest Park, Exeter, Devon,
EX4 4SH.
Vegetarian, adjacent university, quiet, views
Tel: **01392 77443** Mr & Mrs Bligh.
Rates fr: *£14.50-£14.50.*
Open: All Year (not Xmas)
Beds: 1D 1T 1S **Baths:** 1 Shared
🛏 🅿 (2) 💤 🖵 🗙 🛏 ☑ ✦

(0.5m) *Claremont, 36 Wonford*
Road, Exeter, Devon, EX2 4LD.
Clean, quiet, near city centre
Tel: **01392 274699** Mrs Self.
Rates fr: *£19.00-£26.00.*
Open: All Year
Beds: 1F 1D 1T **Baths:** 3 Private
🛏 (5) 🅿 (1) 💤 🖵 🛏 ☑

(0.5m) *Park View Hotel, 8 Howell*
Road, Exeter, Devon, EX4 4LG.
Family-run hotel overlooking park
Grades: ETB 2 Cr, Comm,
AA 3 Q, RAC Acclaim
Tel: **01392 71772** Mrs Batho.
Rates fr: *£17.50-£20.00.*
Open: All Year (not Xmas)
Beds: 2F 7D 3T 3S
Baths: 10 Ensuite 2 Shared
🛏 🅿 (6) 🖵 🏂 🛏 & 🍷 ✦

Exeter to Postbridge

Exeter, the Roman outpost for the southwestern extremity of conquered Britain, is today the county town of Devon and a city rich in architectural heritage. Its chief glory is the cathedral, one of the group of magnificent Gothic constructions in the English West Country - the ornately-carved west front is a gallery of sculpture comparable to that at Wells. The vault is the longest continuous Gothic ceiling in the world. Exeter's Guildhall is the oldest still-used municipal building in Britain, originating in the twelfth century but dominated by the Renaissance portico. The city also hosts a Maritime Museum, which reflects Devon's seafaring heritage, although the range is international. Out of Exeter you head west to Longdown and Dunsford, where the route strikes out into **Dartmoor National Park.** In the vicinity of **Drewsteignton** you will find Castle Drogo, a twentieth-century mock-medieval fortification designed by Lutyens and built from the local granite, commanding breathtaking views of the Teign Gorge; and Fingal's Bridge, a beauty spot by a stream with a pub called The Angler's Rest. Then it's on to the quaint Devon town of **Chagford**, an old stannary town with a fifteenth-century church. From here you head towards the heart of Dartmoor, a beautiful wilderness of heather-clad desolation grazed by Dartmoor Ponies which have been here for thousands of years, the bleak setting for Conan Doyle's *Hound of the Baskervilles.* This great elevation of the granite batholith that is Devon and Cornwall is scattered with impressively complete remains of prehistoric settlements, and inscribed by countless streams and rivers which flow down off it in all directions. The B3212 road takes you to the Warren House Inn, where you can find rest and refreshment amid the desolate landscape.

(0.5m) *Janbri Guest House, 102 Alphington Road, Exeter, Devon, EX2 8HZ.*
Large Victorian private house
Tel: **01392 77346** Mr Prest.
Rates fr: *£14.00-*£15.00.
Open: All Year **Beds:** 2F 2T 1S
🛏🅿🍳🛅✕🖵Ⅴ⚓

(0.5m) *Killarney Guest House, Alphington Street, Exeter, Devon, EX2 8AT.*
Comfortable, friendly, family guest house
Tel: **01392 76932** Mrs Flint.
Rates fr: *£14.00-*£15.00.
Open: All Year (not Xmas)
Beds: 1F 3D 2T 3S
Baths: 3 Shared
🛏🅿✂🛅🛅🖵Ⅴ

(0.5m) *Crossmead, Dunsford Hill, Exeter, Devon, EX4 1TF.*
Comfortable rooms within tranquil grounds
Tel: **01392 422 594** Mrs Snow.
Rates fr: *£12.50-*£12.50.
Open: All Year
Beds: 1F 24D 15T 54S
Baths: 26 Ensuite 63 Shared
🛏 (0) 🅿 (110) 🛅✕🖵Ⅴ

(0.5m) *Cyrnea, 73 Howell Road, Exeter, Devon, EX4 4LZ.*
'Home from home', excellent value
Tel: **01392 438386** (also fax no)
Mrs Budge.
Rates fr: *£13.00-*£13.00.
Open: All Year **Beds:** 1F 3D 2T 2S
Baths: 1 Ensuite 3 Shared
🛏🅿 (2) 🛅🖵Ⅴ

(0.5m) *Oakcliffe Hotel, 73 St Davids Hill, Exeter, Devon, EX4 4DW.*
Comfortable family-run guest house
Tel: **01392 58288** Mrs Kenshole.
Rates fr: *£13.00-*£16.00.
Open: All Year (not Xmas)
Beds: 1F 2D 2T 2S
Baths: 1 Ensuite 3 Private 3 Shared
🛏🅿🍳🛅🖵Ⅴ

The lowest *double* rate per person is shown in *italics.*

---

60   80

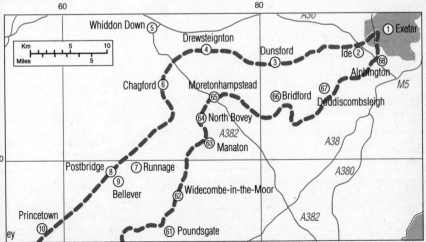

Ide 2

National Grid Ref: SX9090

❦ ⊄ The Huntsman

(1m) *Drakes Farm House, Ide, Exeter, Devon, EX2 9RQ.*
Characterful house, coffee/tea making facilities
Tel: **01392 256814 / 495564**
Fax no: 01392 256814
Rates fr: *£15.00-£17.50.*
Open: All Year
Beds: 1F 1D 1T
Baths: 2 Ensuite 1 Private
❦ 🅿 (6) ⅏ 🗖 ▥.

Dunsford 3

National Grid Ref: SX8189

❦ ⊄ The Lamb

(▲ 0.5m) *Steps Bridge Youth Hostel, Steps Bridge, Dunsford, Exeter, Devon, EX6 7EQ.*
Actual grid ref: SX802882
Tel: **01647 252435**
Under 18: £4.95
Adults: £7.20
Self-catering Facilities, Showers
A back-to-nature haven of peace and tranquillity in secluded woodland. This small self-catering hostel with modest facilities has a friendly atmosphere and overlooks the beautiful Teign Valley

(0.5m) *Steps Bridge Inn, Dunsford, Exeter, Devon, EX6 7EG.*
On the banks of the Teign
Tel: **01647 252313** Mrs Woodford.
Rates fr: *£15.00-£17.00.*
Open: Easter to Sept
Beds: 4D 3T **Baths:** 7 Private
❦ 🅿 (30) ❦ ▥. ▥

(1m) *Upperton Farm, Dunsford, Exeter, Devon, EX6 7AQ.*
Large 400-year-old farmhouse
Grades: ETB 1 Cr, Comm
Tel: **01647 24311**
Mrs & Mrs Tripp.
Rates fr: *£15.00-£15.00.*
Open: Mar to Oct **Beds:** 3D
❦ 🅿 ⅏ 🗖 ✕ ▥

Drewsteignton 4

National Grid Ref: SX7390

❦ ⊄ Drewe Arms, Old Inn

(On route) *The Old Inn Restaurant, The Square, Drewsteignton, Exeter, Devon, EX6 6QR.*
Actual grid ref: SX736909
Former C18th inn. Very comfortable accommodation, picturesque village, glorious countryside. 3 nights less 10%
Tel: **01647 281276** Mrs Gribble.
Rates fr: *£22.50-£27.50.*
Open: Jan to Dec **Beds:** 2D 1T
Baths: 1 Ensuite 1 Private
1 Shared
❦ (3) 🅿 (3) 🗖 ❦ ✕ ▥ ⅋ ⅌

Planning a longer stay? Always ask for any special rates.

(On route) *The Old Rectory, Drewsteignton, Exeter, Devon, EX6 6QT.*
Actual grid ref: SX737908
Georgian house in two acres
Tel: **01647 281269** Mrs Emanuel.
Rates fr: *£18.00-£25.00.*
Open: All Year (not Xmas)
Beds: 2D 1T
Baths: 1 Private 1 Shared
❦ 🅿 (3) ⅏ ✕ ▥. ▥ ⅌

Whiddon Down 5

National Grid Ref: SX6892

❦ ⊄ Post Inn

(2m) *Tor View, Whiddon Down, Okehampton, Devon, EX20 2PR.*
Beautiful location, edge of Dartmoor
Tel: **01647 231447** Mrs Knox.
Fax no: 01647 231623
Rates fr: *£16.00-£16.00.*
Open: Easter to Nov
Beds: 1D 1T
Baths: 1 Shared
❦ 🅿 (2) ⅏ 🗖 ▥. ▥ ⅋ ⅌

20   40   60

60

Km 5 10
Miles 5

Chagford 6

National Grid Ref: SX7087

†⊙† 🍺 Ring O' Bells, Bullers Arms, Sandy Park Inn

(0.25m) *St Johns West, Chagford, Newton Abbot, Devon, TQ13 8HJ.*
Actual grid ref: SX690889
Stunning granite house overlooking Dartmoor
Tel: **01647 432468**
Mr & Mrs West.
Rates fr: *£22.50*-**£25.00**.
Open: All Year
Beds: 1F 1D 1T 1S
Baths: 2 Ensuite
🛇 (12) 🅿 (6) ⊬🖵 🛏 ✗ Ⅲ. Ⅴ

(On route) *Glendarah House, Lower Street, Chagford, Newton Abbot, Devon, TQ13 8BZ.*
Actual grid ref: SX703879
Spacious Victorian house, peaceful location 5 minutes' walk village centre
Grades: ETB 2 Cr, High Comm
Tel: **01647 433270** Mrs Bellenger.
Fax no: 01647 433483
Rates fr: *£22.50*-**£25.00**.
Open: All Year (not Xmas)
Beds: 3D 3T
Baths: 6 Ensuite
🛇 (10) 🅿 (7) ⊬🖵 Ⅲ. 🖪 ⊬

(0.25m) *Lower Jurston, Chagford, Newton Abbot, Devon, TQ13 8EQ.*
One of Devon's last unspoilt medieval farmsteads
Tel: **01647 433443** Mrs Evans.
Rates fr: *£20.00*-**£20.00**.
Open: All Year (not Xmas)
Beds: 1D 1T 1S
Baths: 1 Ensuite 1 Private 1 Shared
🅿 (4) ⊬🖵 Ⅲ. Ⅴ

(0.25m) *Lawn House, 24 Mill Street, Chagford, Newton Abbot, Devon, TQ13 7AW.*
C18th thatched house, centre of Chagford
Tel: **01647 433329** Mrs Law.
Rates fr: *£18.00*-**£25.00**.
Open: Easter to Oct
Beds: 1F 2D
🛇 (8) ⊬🖵 🛏 Ⅲ. 🖪 🛈

(1m) *Yellam Farm, Chagford, Newton Abbot, Devon, TQ13 8JH.*
Actual grid ref: SX7186
Country house B&B in 170 acres
Tel: **01647 432211**
Mrs Prysor-Jones.
Rates fr: *£17.95*-**£17.95**.
Open: All Year (not Xmas)
Beds: 2D 1T
Baths: 2 Shared
🛇 🅿 🖵 🛏 Ⅲ. 🖪 🛈 ⊬

The *lowest* single rate *is shown in* bold.

Postbridge to Gunnislake

At Postbridge, the famous clapper bridge dates from the thirteenth century; the huge granite slabs astride the East Dart River seem to have grown there. After a brief wooded stretch and then more open moorland you reach Two Bridges, before heading on to **Princetown**. Here stands, most famously, Dartmoor Prison, built originally for POWs of the Napoleonic War. The town itself is the largest on Dartmoor, and the highest substantial human settlement in England. The main National Park Information Centre is located here. Then it's on to Yelverton, where you leave the National Park. The route now leads to Buckland Abbey, a Cistercian monastery later inhabited by Sir Francis Drake, now housing a Drake display. From here it's on to Buckland Monachorum and then westwards across the River Tavy at Denham Bridge, from where you can make a detour to Morwellham Quay, a museum of the local copper-mining community and Industrial Revolution theme village.

The lowest *double* rate per person is shown in *italics*.

Runnage 7

National Grid Ref: SX6679

(🔺 1m) *Runnage Camping Barn, Runnage, Yelverton, Devon*
Actual grid ref: SX667792
Tel: **01271 24420 Adults:** £3.35+
Evening Meals Available, Showers
Simple barn on a working farm, sleeps upto 15. ADVANCE BOOKING ESSENTIAL

Postbridge 8

National Grid Ref: SX6579

†⊙† 🍺 Old Inn, Warren House Inn

(0.5m) *Higher Lydgate Farm, Postbridge, Yelverton, Devon, PL20 6TJ.*
Actual grid ref: SX652788
Working farm close river/village in centre of spectacular Dartmoor
Tel: **01822 880274**
Mrs Greatrex.
Rates fr: *£18.00*-**£20.00**.
Beds: 1F 1T 1D
Baths: 1 Ensuite 1 Private
🛇 🅿 (6) ⊬🖵 🛏 Ⅲ. 🖪 ⊬

(1m) *Headland Warren Farm, Postbridge, Yelverton, Devon, PL20 6TB.*
Open moorland setting. Total peace and seclusion. Walking, riding, birdwatching
Grades: ETB 3 Cr
Tel: **01822 880206** Miss Wynne.
Rates fr: *£20.00*-**£20.00**.
Open: Easter to Nov
Beds: 2T 1D **Baths:** 2 Ensuite
🛇 🅿 (4) ⊬🖵 🛏 ✗ Ⅲ. 🖪 🛈 ⊬

(On route) *Hartyland, Postbridge, Yelverton, Devon, PL20 6SZ.*
Large, warm, comfortable Dartmoor house, direct access to open moorland
Tel: **01822 880210**
Mr & Mrs Bishop.
Rates fr: *£18.00*-**£18.00**.
Open: All Year (not Xmas)
Beds: 1F 2T 1S
Baths: 2 Shared
🛇 🅿 (4) 🖵 🛏 ✗ Ⅲ. 🖪 🛈 ⊬

Bellever 9

National Grid Ref: SX6577

(🔺 1m) *Bellever Youth Hostel, Bellever, Postbridge, Yelverton, Devon, PL20 6TU.*
Actual grid ref: SX654773
Warden: Mr I Harris.
Tel: **01822 880227**
Under 18: £5.95
Adults: £8.80
Evening Meals Available (7pm), Self-catering Facilities, Family Bunk Rooms, Grounds Available for Games, Parking, No Smoking
Recently refurbished converted barn, idyllically situated at the heart of Dartmoor National Park

Princetown 10

National Grid Ref: SX5873

†⊙† 🍺 Railway Inn

(0.25m) *The Railway Inn, Two Bridges Road, Princetown, Yelverton, Devon, PL20 6QS.*
A Dartmoor village inn
Tel: **01822 890232**
Mr Uren.
Rates fr: *£15.50*-**£17.50**.
Open: All Year
Beds: 1F 2D 2T
Baths: 1 Shared
🛇 🅿 (20) ✗ Ⅲ. 🖪

Sampford Spiney 11

National Grid Ref: SX5372

🍴 🍺 Walkhampton Inn

(3m) *Eggworthy Farm*, *Sampford Spiney, Yelverton, Devon, PL20 6LJ*.
Relaxing Dartmoor farmhouse, quiet location
Grades: ETB 1 Cr, Comm
Tel: 01822 852142 Mrs Landick.
Rates fr: *£16.00-£17.00*.
Open: All Year
Beds: 2D 1S **Baths:** 1 Shared
🛇 ₽ (6) ☐ 🏅 🎟 🍴

Meavy 12

National Grid Ref: SX5467

🍴 🍺 The Oaks

(2m) *Greenwell Farm*, *Meavy, Yelverton, Devon, PL20 6PY*.
Welcoming family family farmhouse on Dartmoor
Grades: ETB 3 Cr, Comm
Tel: 01822 853563 (also fax no)
Mrs Cole.
Rates fr: *£20.00-£25.00*.
Open: All Year (not Xmas)
Beds: 2D 1T
Baths: 2 Ensuite 1 Private
🛇 ₽ (8) ☐ ✗ 🎟 🞖 🍴 ♦

Yelverton 13

National Grid Ref: SX5267

🍴 🍺 Rock Inn

(0.25m) *The Rosemont*,
Greenbank Terrace, Yelverton, Devon, PL20 6DR.
Large Victorian house within Dartmoor National Park. Historic Plymouth 9 miles
Grades: ETB Listed, Comm
Tel: 01822 852175 Mrs Eastaugh.
Rates fr: *£18.00-£21.00*.
Open: All Year **Beds:** 2F 3D 2T 2S
Baths: 4 Ensuite 2 Shared
🛇 ₽ ☐ 🏅 🎟.

(0.25m) *Waverley Guest House*,
5 Greenbank Terrace, Yelverton, Devon, PL20 6DR.
Family-run Victorian guest house
Grades: ETB 2 Cr, Comm
Tel: 01822 854617 (also fax no)
Mrs Gent. **Rates fr:** *£19.00-£19.00*.
Open: All Year
Beds: 2F 1D 1T 1S
Baths: 5 Private
🛇 ₽ (4) ☐ 🏅 🎟 🞖 🍴

(1m) *Peek Hill Farm*, *Yelverton, Yelverton, Devon, PL20 6PD*.
Comfortable, easy-going, working farmhouse
Grades: ETB 2 Cr, Comm
Tel: 01822 854408 (also fax no)
Mrs Colton.
Rates fr: *£17.00-£20.00*.
Open: All Year (not Xmas)
Beds: 1F 1D **Baths:** 2 Ensuite
🛇 ₽ (6) 🞖 ☐ 🏅 ✗ 🎟 🞖 🍴 ♦

Horrabridge 14

National Grid Ref: SX5169

🍴 🍺 Leaping Salmon, London Inn

(2m) *Dunridge*, *Horrabridge, Yelverton, Devon, PL20 7QT*.
Tel: **01822 855131** (also fax no)
Mrs Neenan.
Rates fr: *£18.00-£20.00*.
Open: All Year
Beds: 1F 1D
Baths: 1 Shared
🛇 ₽ (10) 🞖 🎟 🞖
Country house in idyllic grounds within Dartmoor National Park. Elegant but homely. Wonderfully tranquil setting. Both open moor and village pubs and shops close by

(2m) *The Old Mine House*,
Sortridge, Horrabridge, Yelverton, Devon, PL20 7UA.
Actual grid ref: SX510707
Fascinating house; idyllic grounds! Hospitable cycling/walking photo-journalist owner. WELCOME!
Tel: **01822 855586**
Mr Robinson.
Rates fr: *£16.00-£16.00*.
Open: All Year
Beds: 1F 2T 2D
Baths: 2 Shared

Clearbrook 15

National Grid Ref: SX5265

(2m) *Rosehill*, *Clearbrook, Yelverton, Devon, PL20 6JD*.
Village house, edge of Dartmoor
Tel: **01822 852130** Mrs Wing.
Rates fr: *£14.00-£14.00*.
Open: All Year (not Xmas)
Beds: 2D 1T
Baths: 1 Private
🛇 (5) ₽ (6) 🞖 ☐ ✗ 🎟 🞖

Milton Combe 16

National Grid Ref: SX4865

(▲ 1m) *Lopwell Camping Barn*,
Lopwell, Milton Combe, Yelverton, Devon
Actual grid ref: SX475650
Adults: £3.35+
Self-catering Facilities, Showers
Converted barn on the banks of the River Tamar on the edge of Dartmoor. ADVANCE BOOKING ESSENTIAL

(1m) *Blowiscombe Barton*, *Milton Combe, Yelverton, Devon, PL20 6HR*.
Modernised secluded farmhouse. Swimming pool
Grades: ETB 3 Cr, Comm
Tel: **01822 854853**
Mrs Fisk.
Rates fr: *£17.50-£22.00*.
Open: All Year (not Xmas)
Beds: 2D 1T
Baths: 3 Private
🛇 ₽ (6) ☐ ✗ 🎟 🞖

Gulworthy 17

National Grid Ref: SX4572

(2m) *Rubbytown Farm*,
Gulworthy, Tavistock, Devon, PL19 8PA.
Charming C17th farmhouse, wonderful views
Grades: ETB 2 Cr, High Comm
Tel: **01822 832493** Mrs Steer.
Rates fr: *£18.00*.
Open: All Year (not Xmas)
Beds: 3T **Baths:** 3 Ensuite
🛇 (5) ₽ (6) ☐ ✗ 🎟 🞖

Tavistock 18

National Grid Ref: SX4874

🍴 🍺 Elephant's Nest, Cornish Arms, Carpenters' Arms, Ordulph Arms, Blacksmiths' Arms, Trout & Tipple

(3m) *Kingfisher Cottage*, *Mount Tavy Road, Vigo Bridge, Tavistock, Devon, PL19 9JB*.
Riverside accommodation in characterful cottage near town and beautiful Dartmoor
Grades: ETB 2 Cr, Comm
Tel: **01822 613801** Mrs Toland.
Rates fr: *£15.00-£18.00*.
Open: All Year
Beds: 2D 1T
Baths: 1 Ensuite 1 Shared
🛇 ₽ (4) 🞖 ☐ 🏅 🎟 🞖 🍴 ♦

(3m) *April Cottage*, *Mount Tavy Road, Vigo Bridge, Tavistock, Devon, PL19 9JB*.
On fringe of Dartmoor, C19th stone-built cottage in picturesque riverbank location. Ideal touring base
Grades: ETB 2 Cr, Comm
Tel: **01822 613280**
Mrs Bacon.
Rates fr: *£16.00-£18.00*.
Open: All Year (not Xmas)
Beds: 2D 1T **Baths:** 3 Ensuite
🛇 (1) ₽ (5) 🞖 ☐ 🏅 🎟 🞖 🍴 ♦

(4m) *Hele Farm*, *Tavistock, Devon, PL19 8PA*.
Welcome in Listed 1780 farmhouse
Grades: ETB 2 Cr
Tel: **01822 833084** Mrs Steer.
Rates fr: *£16.00-£20.00*.
Open: Easter to Nov
Beds: 2D
Baths: 2 Private
🛇 ₽ (4) 🞖 ☐ 🏅 🎟 🞖 ♦

(3m) *Eko Brae*, *4 Bedford Villas, Springhill, Tavistock, Devon, PL19 8LA*.
Georgian villa overlooking Tavistock
Grades: ETB 2 Cr, Comm
Tel: **01822 614028** Mrs Rodgers.
Rates fr: *£19.00-£16.00*.
Open: All Year (not Xmas)
Beds: 3F 1D 1S
Baths: 3 Ensuite 2 Shared
🛇 ₽ (6) ☐ 🏅 🎟 🞖

(3m) *Westward, 15 Plymouth Road, Tavistock, Devon, L19 8AU.*
Listed Victorian house in centre of small historic town with charm
Grades: ETB 2 Cr, Comm
Tel: **01822 612094**
Ms Parkin.
Rates fr: *£13.00*-**£13.00**.
Open: All Year (not Xmas)
Beds: 1F 1D 1S
Baths: 1 Ensuite 1 Shared
🛏 🅿 (3) ❏ ☇ ▥ ▥

(3m) *Arandor, Violet Road, Mount Tavy Road, Tavistock, Devon, PL19 9JD.*
Attractive house with extensive views
Grades: ETB 2 Cr, High Comm
Tel: **01822 613070**
Mrs Heard.
Rates fr: *£16.50*-**£25.00**.
Open: All Year (not Xmas)
Beds: 1D 2T
Baths: 1 Private 1 Shared
🛏 (9) 🅿 (4) ❏ ▥ ▥

Gunnislake 19

National Grid Ref: SX4371

(0.25m) *Sandhill House, Tavistock Road, Gunnislake, Cornwall, PL18 9DR.*
Regency country manor house
Tel: **01822 832442**
Mrs Collins.
Rates fr: *£18.00*-**£20.00**.
Open: Easter to Nov
Beds: 4D 2T
Baths: 5 Private 1 Shared
🛏 (12) 🅿 (12) ⅍ ❏ ✕ ▥ ▥ ⌾ ⚡

Harrowbarrow 20

National Grid Ref: SX3969

(1m) *The Divot, Harrowbarrow, Callington, Cornwall, PL17 8JJ.*
Close National Trust, golf. Quiet
Tel: **01579 350910**
Mr & Mrs Griffiths.
Rates fr: *£15.00*-**£15.00**.
Open: All Year
Beds: 1T
🅿 (1) ❏ ▥

Downgate 21

National Grid Ref: SX3672

(0.5m) *Niggles Nook Guest House, Sandercock Close, Downgate, Callington, Cornwall, PL17 8JS.*
Ideal for family holidays
Tel: **01579 370813**
Mrs Bartlett.
Rates fr: *£13.00*-**£13.00**.
Open: All Year
Beds: 2D 1T
Baths: 1 Shared
🛏 🅿 (4) ⅍ ❏ ✕ ▥ ▥ ⌾ ⚡

Callington 22

National Grid Ref: SX3669

🍽 🍺 Coachmakers' Arms, Who'd Have Thought It
(1.5m) *Dozmary, Tors View Close, Tavistock Road, Callington, Cornwall, PL17 7DY.*
Spacious dormer bungalow in quiet cul-de-sac
Grades: ETB 1 Cr, Comm, AA 3 Q, Recomm
Tel: **01579 383677** Mrs Wills.
Rates fr: *£16.00*-**£18.00**.
Open: All Year (not Xmas)
Beds: 1F 1D 1T
Baths: 2 Ensuite 1 Private
🛏 🅿 (4) ⅍ ❏ ▥ ▥

(2m) *Dupath Farm, Callington, Cornwall, PL17 8AD.*
Spacious 200-year-old farmhouse
Tel: **01579 382197**
Mrs Coombe.
Rates fr: *£15.00*-**£15.00**.
Open: All Year
Beds: 1F 1D
Baths: 2 Private
🛏 🅿 (6) ⅍ ❏ ▥

Stoke Climsland 23

National Grid Ref: SX3674

(2m) *Penpill Farmhouse, Stoke Climsland, Callington, Cornwall, PL17 8QE.*
Georgian farmhouse, gardens, home cooking
Grades: ETB 2 Cr
Tel: **01579 370540**
Mr & Mrs Rae.
Rates fr: *£18.00*-**£20.00**.
Open: All Year
Beds: 2F 3D 2T
Baths: 7 Private
🛏 🅿 ❏ ✕ ▥ ▥

Merrymeet 24

National Grid Ref: SX2765

🍽 🍺 Butchers' Arms

(1.5m) *Homer House, Merrymeet, Liskeard, Cornwall, PL14 3LS.*
Beautiful converted farmhouse
Tel: **01579 345378** Mrs Beer.
Rates fr: *£15.00*-**£20.00**.
Open: All Year
Beds: 2D 1T
Baths: 3 Private
🛏 (5) 🅿 (6) ⅍ ❏ ▥ ⅍ ▥

Liskeard 25

National Grid Ref: SX2564

🍽 🍺 Fountain Hotel, Stag Inn

(0.5m) *Hyvue House, Barras Cross, Liskeard, Cornwall, PL14 6BN.*
Tel: **01579 348175** Mrs Demmer.
Rates fr: *£17.50*-**£17.50**.
Open: All Year (not Xmas)
Beds: 2D 1T
Baths: 3 Private
🅿 (6) ⅍ ❏ ▥ ▥
Family-run exclusively for non-smokers on outskirts of town overlooking Bodmin Moor. We pride ourselves on providing excellent food and comfort. Private parking

(0.5m) *Elnor Guest House, 1 Russell Street, Liskeard, Cornwall, PL14 4BP.*
Friendly, family guest house
Grades: ETB 2 Cr, Comm, AA 3 Q
Tel: **01579 342472**
Mrs Strudwick.
Fax no: 01579 345673
Rates fr: *£16.50*-**£16.50**.
Open: All Year (not Xmas)
Beds: 2F 2D 1T 4S
Baths: 7 Private 2 Shared
🛏 🅿 (6) ❏ ✕ ▥

Gunnislake to Kingsand

The route now takes you to the River Tamar and across one of Europe's most ancient boundaries, into Cornwall, at Gunnislake. A very worthwhile detour south from here leads to Cotehele, a superlatively well-preserved Tudor manor house, set around three courtyards with an impressive hall hung with tapestries. The estate is set in an idyllic wooded corner of the Tamar Valley and contains richly planted gardens. From Gunnislake it's west through a series of Cornish villages to Henwood, on the edge of Bodmin Moor, which has a landscape like Dartmoor in miniature. From here you head south across the moor, passing close to a number of prehistoric sites, notably the 'Hurlers' stone circle, to St Cleer, named after one of Cornwall's Celtic Saints, before reaching **Liskeard.** From here the route wends its way to the South Coast at Seaton, from where the next stretch runs above the sandy beaches of Whitsand Bay into the Rame Peninsula, to Kingsand, on Cawsand Bay, and through Mount Edgcumbe Country Park, where you will find an eighteenth-century landscaped garden with follies and forts and wild fallow deer.

(0.5m) *Hotel Nebula*, 27 Higher Lux Street, Liskeard, Cornwall, *PL14 3JU*.
Comfortable Grade II Listed hotel
Tel: **01579 343989** Mr Rogers.
Rates fr: *£23.00*-**£23.00**.
Open: All Year
Beds: 2F 1D 2T 1S
Baths: 6 Private
♿ 🅿 (22) ❒ ✕ 🖿 Ⓥ

Menheniot 26

National Grid Ref: SX2862

(0.5m) *Trewint Farm*, Menheniot, Liskeard, Cornwall, *PL14 3RE*.
C17th comfortable farmhouse, working farm
Grades: ETB 2 Cr, Comm, RAC Listed
Tel: **01579 347155** Mrs Rowe.
Fax no: 01579 341155
Rates fr: *£16.00*-**£20.00**.
Open: All Year (not Xmas)
Beds: 1F 2D
Baths: 3 Ensuite
♿ 🅿 (6) ❒ ✕ Ⓥ

Widegates 27

National Grid Ref: SX2857

🍽 🍺 Copley Arms

(2m) *Coombe Farm*, Widegates, Looe, Cornwall, *PL13 1QN*.
Lovely country house in wonderful setting
Grades: ETB 3 Cr, High Comm, AA 5 Q, Prem Select, RAC High Acclaim
Tel: **01503 240223** Mr Low.
Fax no: 01503 240895
Rates fr: *£23.00*-**£23.00**.
Open: Mar to Nov
Beds: 4F 3D 3T
Baths: 10 Private
♿ (5) 🅿 (20) ⅃ ❒ 🍴 ✕ 🖿 ⅙ Ⓥ ♠ ⚶

(2m) *Treveria Farm*, Widegates, Looe, Cornwall, *PL13 1QR*.
Delightful manor house, rural views
Grades: ETB 2 Cr, Comm
Tel: **01503 240237** (also fax no) Mrs Kitto.
Rates fr: *£18.00*-**£25.00**.
Open: Easter to Oct
Beds: 3D
Baths: 3 Private
🅿 (3) ⅃ ❒ 🖿 Ⓥ

(2m) *Polgover Farm*, Widegates, Looe, Cornwall, *PL13 1PY*.
Attractive, peaceful, C16th manor house
Grades: ETB Listed
Tel: **01503 240248** Mrs Wills.
Rates fr: *£14.00*.
Open: Easter to Oct
Beds: 1F 1D 1T
♿ 🅿 🖿 Ⓥ

Downderry 28

National Grid Ref: SX3254

🍽 🍺 Smugglers Inn

(0.25m) *Cair*, Deviock, Downderry, Torpoint, Cornwall, *PL11 3DN*.
Old farmhouse, large gardens, overlooking sea
Tel: **01503 250320** Mrs Connell.
Fax no: 01503 250272
Rates fr: *£16.00*-**£16.00**.
Open: Easter to Oct
Beds: 1F 1D 1T
Baths: 3 Ensuite
♿ 🅿 ⅃ 🖿 ⚶

Crafthole 29

National Grid Ref: SX3654

🍽 🍺 Finnygook Inn

(0.25m) *The Bungalow*, Cliff Road, Crafthole, Torpoint, Cornwall, *PL11 3BY*.
Homely hospitality in superb setting
Tel: **01503 230334** Mrs Harvey.
Rates fr: *£15.00*-**£15.00**.
Open: April to Oct
Beds: 1D 1T
Baths: 1 Shared
🅿 ⅃ ❒ Ⓥ ♠ ⚶

Kingsand 30

National Grid Ref: SX4350

🍽 🍺 Halfway House Inn

(0.25m) *The Halfway House Inn*, Fore Street, Kingsand, Cawsand Bay, Torpoint, Cornwall, *PL10 1NA*.
Actual grid ref: SX435505
Family-run, coastal inn with fish speciality restaurant
Grades: ETB 3 Cr, High Comm
Tel: **01752 822279** Mr Riggs.
Fax no: 01752 823146
Rates fr: *£22.00*-**£22.00**.
Open: All Year
Beds: 1F 3D 1S
Baths: 5 Private
♿ 🅿 (200) ❒ 🍴 ✕ 🖿 Ⓥ ♠ ⚶

(0.25m) *Algoma*, The Green, Kingsand, Cawsand Bay, Cornwall, *PL10 1NH*.
Actual grid ref: SX434506
Spacious C18th house. Sea views overlooking bay, close to all amenities
Tel: **01752 822706** Mr Ogilvie.
Fax no: 01752 822657
Rates fr: *£18.50*-**£25.00**.
Open: All Year (not Xmas)
Beds: 1F 1D
Baths: 2 Ensuite
♿ ❒ 🖿 ♠ ⚶

All cycleways are popular: you are well-advised to book ahead

(0.25m) *Clarendon*, Garrett Street, Cawsand, Kingsand, Torpoint, Cornwall, *PL10 1PD*.
18th Century seafront village property
Tel: **01752 823460** Mrs Goodwright.
Rates fr: *£14.00*-**£14.00**.
Open: All Year (not Xmas)
Beds: 1D 1T 1S
Baths: 1 Shared
♿ (5) 🖿

(0.25m) *The Haven*, Market Street, Kingsand, Torpoint, Cornwall, *PL10 1ND*.
Beautiful old house overlooking sea
Tel: **01752 823860** Mrs Taylor.
Rates fr: *£16.00*-**£16.00**.
Open: All Year (not Xmas)
Beds: 1D 1T 1S **Baths:** 1 Shared
♿ ⅙ ❒ 🖿 Ⓥ ♠ ⚶

(0.25m) *Cliff House*, Devon Port Hill, Kingsand, Torpoint, Cornwall, *PL10 1NT*.
Grade II Listed house in Rame Peninsula conservation area. Lovely sea views
Tel: **01752 823110** Mrs Heasman.
Rates fr: *£20.00*-**£25.00**.
Open: All Year
Beds: 2D 1T
Baths: 3 Ensuite
♿ 🅿 (2) ⅙ ❒ ✕ 🖿 Ⓥ

Mount Edgcumbe 31

National Grid Ref: SX4552

(0.25m) *Friary Manor Hotel*, Maker Heights, Mount Edgcumbe, Millbrook, Torpoint, Cornwall, *PL10 1JB*.
Actual grid ref: SX435517
C18th manor house in secluded location above Cawsand Bay
Grades: ETB 3 Cr, Comm
Tel: **01752 822112** Mr & Mrs Wood.
Fax no: 01752 822804
Rates fr: *£22.50*-**£29.00**.
Open: All Year
Beds: 3F 3D 3T 2S
Baths: 6 Ensuite 1 Private
♿ 🅿 (25) ❒ 🍴 ✕ 🖿 Ⓥ ♠ ⚶

Planning a longer stay? Always ask for any special rates.

Plymouth 32

National Grid Ref: SX4756

🍴 🍺 Town House, Yard Arm, The Hoe, Mount Pleasant, Odd Wheel, Eddystone Inn, West Hoe, Frog & Frigate, The Waterfront, The Walrus

(▲ 0.5m) *Plymouth Youth Hostel,*
Belmont House, Devonport Road,
Stoke, Plymouth, Devon, PL3 4DW.
Actual grid ref: SX461555
Warden: Ms B Cambridge.
Tel: **01752 562189**
Under 18: £6.55
Adults: £9.75
Evening Meals Available (7pm),
Family Bunk Rooms, Television,
Games Room, Showers, Shop
Classical Grecian-style house built
in 1820 for a wealthy banker, set in
own grounds, within easy walking
distance of the city centre

(1m) *Hotspur Guest House,*
108 North Road East, Plymouth,
Devon, PL4 6AW.
Grades: ETB 1 Cr, Approv
Tel: **01752 663928**
Taylor.
Fax no: 01752 261493
Rates fr: £13.50-£14.50.
Open: All Year (not Xmas)
Beds: 5F 2T 1D 3S
🛇🚪📺🛏✕▦Ⓥⓘ
Victorian property less than 7 min-
utes' walk to city centre, bus/rail
stations, historic Hoe/Barbican 10
minutes' walk. Ideal touring centre
for Dartmoor and the South West

(1m) *Teviot Guest House,*
20 North Road East, Plymouth,
Devon, PL4 6AS.
Early Victorian town house
offering quality and comfort,
central location
Tel: **01752 262656**
Mrs Fisher.
Fax no: 01752 251660
Rates fr: £17.00-£20.00.
Open: All Year (not Xmas)
Beds: 2F 2D 1T 1S
Baths: 2 Ensuite 3 Private
1 Shared
🛇(7)🅿(2)⚲📺▦Ⓥⓘ⚲

(1m) *Rusty Anchor, 30 Grand*
Parade, West Hoe, Plymouth,
Devon, PL1 3DJ.
Tel: **01752 663924** (also fax no)
Ms Turner.
Rates fr: £12.50-£12.50.
Open: All Year
Beds: 4F 1D 2T 2S
Baths: 3 Ensuite 2 Private 2
Shared
🛇🚪📺✕▦Ⓥⓘ⚲
Situated on the sea front, walking
distance city centre, Hoe. Excellent
reputation for cleanliness, friendly
atmosphere and good food.
Holiday or business, all are wel-
come in our family-run restaurant

Kingsand to Salcombe

The Cremyll to Stonehouse ferry takes you across the Tamar Estuary back into Devon and the city of **Plymouth**, one of Britain's most important maritime cities. Plymouth Hoe, the historic promenade from which the city spreads out, gives magnificent views across Plymouth Sound, also at times catching strong winds. Here in 1588, having caught wind of the approaching Spanish Armada whilst in the middle of a game of bowls, Sir Francis Drake declared, "There is plenty of time to win this game and to thrash the Spaniards too". Allegedly. Close by are the Barbican, whose Tudor and Jacobean buildings form the heart of old Plymouth, with the Mayflower Steps from which the Pilgrim Fathers set sail; and the Royal Citadel, a fortification built during the Restoration to keep this Parliamentarian town in check. Heading east out of Plymouth, the route takes you down the east side of the Yealm Estuary to Newton Ferrers and Noss Mayo, and back onto the South Coast; before again heading inland and through a string of villages of the picturesque South Hams district, to **Salcombe**.

(1m) *Sea Breezes, 28 Grand*
Parade, West Hoe, Plymouth,
Devon, PL1 3DJ.
Actual grid ref: SX483538
Tel: **01752 667205** (also fax no)
Mr & Mrs Lake.
Rates fr: £16.00-£16.00.
Open: All Year
Beds: 3F 2D 2T 1S
Baths: 2 Ensuite 2 Private
2 Shared
🛇🚪📺✕▦Ⓥⓘ
A warm welcome assured in our
elegant Victorian town-house on
sea front. Theatres, shopping
centre, historic Hoe and Barbican
close by. Ideal touring centre for
South West Peninsula

(1m) *Trillium House Hotel,*
4 Alfred Street, The Hoe, Plymouth,
Devon, PL1 2RP.
Comfortable, central Hoe, Barbican
Tel: **01752 670452**
Mrs Cross.
Fax no: 01752 600085
Rates fr: £17.00-£20.00.
Open: All Year
Beds: 2F 1D 2T 2S
Baths: 4 Private 1 Shared
🛇🅿(3)🚪✕▦Ⓥⓘ⚲

(1m) *Allington House, 6 St James*
Place East, The Hoe, Plymouth,
Devon, PL1 3AS.
Tel: **01752 221435**
Mrs Budziak.
Rates fr: £16.00-£20.00.
Open: All Year
Beds: 4D 1T 1S
Baths: 3 Ensuite 1 Shared
🅿(2)🚪📺Ⓥ
Victorian town house in secluded
square. On Plymouth Hoe, close to
historic Barbican and city centre,
South-West Way and continental
Ferries. Comfort and excellent
breakfast

(1m) *Mountbatten Hotel,*
52 Exmouth Road, Stoke,
Plymouth, Devon, PL4 4QH.
Grades: ETB 3 Cr, Comm
Tel: **01752 563843** Mr Hendy.
Fax no: 01752 606014
Rates fr: £17.50-£18.00.
Open: All Year
Beds: 3F 6D 2T 4S
Baths: 7 Ensuite 2 Shared
🛇🅿(4)🚪📺✕▦Ⓥⓘ
Small licensed Victorian hotel,
quiet cul-de-sac overlooking park-
land. Easy reach city centre /
ferryport, good access Cornwall.
Secure parking, well appointed
rooms, phones, CTVs. Extensive
menus

(1m) *The Dudley, 42 Sutherland*
Road, Mutley, Plymouth, Devon,
PL4 6BN.
Actual grid ref: SX484555
Charming Victorian town house.
Good breakfasts and comfortable,
homely accommodation
Grades: ETB 3 Cr, Comm
Tel: **01752 668322**
Mr Punter & Miss A Hayes.
Fax no: 01752 673763
Rates fr: £15.00-£17.00.
Open: All Year
Beds: 2F 2T 1D 2S
Baths: 6 Ensuite 1 Shared
🛇🅿(3)🚪📺✕▦Ⓥⓘ⚲

(1m) *Osmond Guest House,*
42 Pier Street, West Hoe,
Plymouth, Devon, PL1 3BT.
Seafront Edwardian house.
Walking distance to all attractions
Grades: ETB 2 Cr, High Comm
Tel: **01752 229705**
Mrs Richards.
Rates fr: £15.00-£16.00.
Open: All Year (not Xmas)
Beds: 1F 2D 2T 1S
Baths: 2 Private 2 Shared
🛇🅿(2)🚪📺▦♿ⓘ⚲

All rooms full and
nowhere else to stay?
Ask the owner if
there's anywhere
nearby

(1m) *Berkeleys Of St James,*
4 St James Place East, The Hoe,
Plymouth, Devon, PL1 3AS.
Large Victorian town house
Grades: ETB 2 Cr, Comm
Tel: 01752 221654
Mrs Coon.
Rates fr: *£17.50-£21.00.*
Open: All Year
Beds: 1F 1D 2T 1S
Baths: All Ensuite
🛏 🅿 (2) 🍴 🗖 🛏 🏠 ⚗ ♿ 📺 🛈 ✤

(1m) *Sunray Hotel, 3/5 Alfred*
Street, The Hoe, Plymouth, Devon,
PL1 2RP.
Large Victorian centrally located
hotel
Tel: 01752 669113
Mr Sutton.
Fax no: 01752 268969
Rates fr: *£18.00-£18.50.*
Open: All Year
Beds: 3F 10D 3T 3S
Baths: 16 Ensuite
🅿 (6) 🗖 🏠 🛈 ✤

(1m) *Sydney Guest House,*
181 North Road West, Plymouth,
Devon, PL1 5DE.
Imposing Sea Captain's house in
picturesque East Neuk
Grades: ETB 3 Cr, High Comm
Tel: 01752 266541
Mrs Puckey.
Fax no: 01333 310573
Rates fr: *£26.50-£35.00.*
Open: All Year
Beds: 2F 2D 2T 2S
Baths: 2 Private
🛏 🗖 🍴 🏠 📺

(1m) *The Churston, 1 Apsley*
Road, Plymouth, Devon, PL4 6PJ.
Arrive guests. Depart friends
Tel: 01752 664850
Mr Tiley.
Rates fr: *£16.00-£16.00.*
Open: All Year (not Xmas)
Beds: 1F 2D 2T 3S
Baths: 2 Private 2 Shared
🗖 🍴 🏠 ⚗ 🛈

(1m) *Olivers Hotel & Restaurant,*
33 Sutherland Road, Plymouth,
Devon, PL4 6BN.
Actual grid ref: SX481555
Former Victorian merchant's house
Grades: ETB 3 Cr, Comm
Tel: 01752 663923
Mrs Purser.
Rates fr: *£21.00-£19.00.*
Open: All Year (not Xmas)
Beds: 1F 2D 1T 2S
Baths: 4 Ensuite 1 Shared
🛏 (12) 🅿 (2) 🗖 🍴 🏠 📺

(1m) *Avalon Guest House, 167*
Citadel Road, The Hoe, Plymouth,
Devon, PL1 2HU.
Comfortable, family-run guest
house
Tel: 01752 668127 Mrs Wright.
Rates fr: *£15.00-£16.00.*
Open:
Beds: 1F 2D 1T 2S
Baths: 1 Ensuite 3 Private 1
Shared
🛏 🗖 🏠 📺

Turnchapel   33
National Grid Ref: SX4952

(2m) *Boringdon Arms, Boringdon*
Terrace, Turnchapel, Plymouth,
Devon, PL9 9TQ.
Award-winning real ale pub
Grades: ETB Listed
Tel: 01752 402053 Mrs Rayne.
Rates fr: *£15.00-£20.00.*
Open: All Year
Beds: 2F 2D 2T
Baths: 1 Ensuite 1 Shared
🛏 🅿 🍴 🍴 🗖 🛈

Many rates vary
according to season -
the lowest only are
shown here

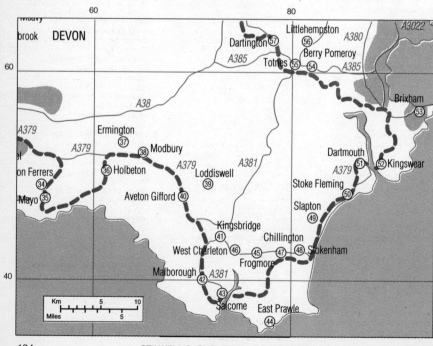

Newton Ferrers 34

National Grid Ref: SX5448

¶¶ ⌘ Old Ship, Dolphin Inn, Swan Inn

(0.25m) *Crown Yealm, Bridgend Hill, Newton Ferrers, Plymouth, Devon, PL8 1AW.*
Actual grid ref: SX5447
Grades: ETB Listed
Tel: **01752 872365** (also fax no)
Mrs Johnson.
Rates fr: *£17.00-£21.00*.
Open: All Year
Beds: 1F 1D 1T
Baths: 1 Ensuite 1 Shared
🛇 🅿 (9) 🛏 🖤 ⬛ 🛆
Beautiful riverside country house. All guest rooms overlook garden to water's edge. Comfortable beds, good breakfasts, private off road parking. Between Dartmoor and South Devon Coast on River Yealm Estuary

(0.25m) *Melbury, Church Park Road, Newton Ferrers, Plymouth, Devon, PL8 1AZ.*
South-facing comfortable bungalow. "Sense & Sensibility" filmed in locality
Tel: **01752 872755** Mrs Hemming.
Rates fr: *£15.00-£17.00*.
Open: All Year **Beds:** 2D 2T
Baths: 2 Ensuite 1 Shared
🛇 🛏 🖤 ⬛ 🅥 🛆

(0.25m) *Maywood Cottage, Bridgend, Newton Ferrers, Plymouth, Devon, PL8 1AW.*
Modernised cottage in estuary village
Tel: **01752 872372** Mrs Cross.
Rates fr: *£15.00-£17.00*.
Open: All Year **Beds:** 1F 2T
Baths: 1 Ensuite 1 Private
🛇 🅿 (2) 🛏 🖤 ⬛ 🅥

Noss Mayo 35

National Grid Ref: SX5447

¶¶ ⌘ Old Ship Inn, Swan Inn

(0.25m) *Rowden House, Stoke Road, Noss Mayo, Plymouth, Devon, PL8 1JG.*
Actual grid ref: SX555472
Victorian farmhouse with lovely garden in peaceful rural setting
Tel: **01752 872153** Mrs Hill.
Rates fr: *£17.50-£17.50*.
Open: Apr to Oct
Beds: 1F 1T
Baths: 1 Private
🛇 🅿 (3) 🛏 ⬛ 🛆

(0.25m) *Higher Shippen, Worswell Barton Fr., Noss Mayo, Plymouth, Devon, PL8 1HB.*
5 mins from coastal path
Tel: **01752 872977** (also fax no)
Mrs Rogers.
Rates fr: *£16.50-£16.50*.
Open: All Year **Beds:** 1D
🛇 🅥 ⬛ 🛆

Holbeton 36

National Grid Ref: SX6150

(0.25m) *The Mildmay Colours Inn, Holbeton, Plymouth, Devon, PL8 1NA.*
Traditional village inn with brewery
Tel: **01752 830248** Mrs Martin.
Rates fr: *£20.00-£20.00*.
Open: All Year
Beds: 1F 1D 6T
Baths: 8 Private
🛇 🅿 (25) 🛏 🖤 ⬛ 🅥

Ermington 37

National Grid Ref: SX6453

¶¶ ⌘ First & Last

(1m) *Waye Farm, The Grange, Ermington, Ivybridge, Devon, PL21 9NU.*
Peaceful, idyllically situated, high standard
Tel: **01752 830427**
Mr & Mrs Livermore.
Rates fr: *£16.00-£22.00*.
Open: All Year
Beds: 1D 1T
Baths: 2 Ensuite
🛇 🅿 (4) 🛏 🅥 🛆

Modbury 38

National Grid Ref: SX6551

¶¶ ⌘ First & Last, Mildmay Colours

(0.25m) *Goutsford, Modbury, Ivybridge, Devon, PL21 9NY.*
Private cottage in peaceful woodland setting
Tel: **01548 830633** Mrs Ewen.
Rates fr: *£17.00-£20.00*.
Open: All Year (not Xmas)
Beds: 1D 2T
Baths: 3 Private
🛇 (10) 🅿 (4) 🖤 🛏 ⬛

Loddiswell 39

National Grid Ref: SX7148

(2m) *Riverleigh, Topsham Bridge, Loddiswell, Kingsbridge, Devon, TQ7 4DR.*
C18th cottage with gardens & woodlands
Tel: **01548 550372** Mrs Betts.
Rates fr: *£15.00-£17.50*.
Open: Apr to Sept
Beds: 1F 1T
Baths: 1 Ensuite 1 Shared
🛇 (1) 🅿 (2) 🛏 🖤 ⬛ 🅥

All rates are subject to alteration at the owners' discretion.

Aveton Gifford 40

National Grid Ref: SX6947

¶¶ ⌘ Sloop Inn, Churchhouse Inn

(On route) *Court Barton Farmhouse, Aveton Gifford, Kingsbridge, Devon, TQ7 4LE.*
Grades: ETB 2 Cr, High Comm
Tel: **01548 550312** (also fax no)
Mrs Balkwill.
Rates fr: *£20.00-£20.00*.
Open: All Year (not Xmas)
Beds: 2F 2D 2T 1S
Baths: 6 Ensuite 1 Shared
🛇 🅿 (10) 🛏 ⬛ 🅥 🛆 🛆
Delightful C16th farmhouse, peacefully set in colourful gardens 100 yds from village. Ensuite bedrooms. Perfect centre for coast and moors. You'll love our scrumptious breakfasts!!

(0.25m) *Marsh Mills, Aveton Gifford, Kingsbridge, Devon, TQ7 4JW.*
Georgian millhouse, now a smallholding, peaceful and secluded. Ample parking
Tel: **01548 550549** (also fax no)
Mrs Newsham.
Rates fr: *£15.00-£15.00*.
Open: All Year
Beds: 1D 1T 1S
Baths: 2 Ensuite 1 Shared
🛇 (6) 🅿 (6) 🛏 🛆 🛆

Kingsbridge 41

National Grid Ref: SX7344

¶¶ ⌘ Dolphin Inn, Church House Inn, Crabshell Inn, The Globe

(1m) *Rockwood Hotel, Embankment Road, Kingsbridge, Devon, TQ7 1JZ.*
Completely refurbished hotel
Tel: **01548 852480**
Rates fr: *£20.00-£25.00*.
Open: All Year
Beds: 5D 2T 1S
Baths: 8 Private
🛇 🅿 🛏 🖤 ⬛ 🅥

(2m) *Centry Farm, Kingsbridge, Devon, TQ7 2HF.*
Extremely comfortable farmhouse, beautiful setting
Tel: **01548 852037**
Mrs Lidstone.
Rates fr: *£16.00-£22.00*.
Open: Easter to Oct
Beds: 1D 1T
Baths: 2 Ensuite
🅿 (8) 🗡 🛏

(1m) *Riverside House, Kingsbridge, Devon, TQ7 2NR.*
Comfortable converted village cottage
Tel: **01548 531617** (also fax no)
Mr & Mrs Parrish.
Rates fr: *£15.00-£15.00*.
Open: Easter to Oct
Beds: 1T
🗡 🛏 ⬛

Malborough 42

National Grid Ref: SX7039

🍴🍺 Royal Oak, Old Inn, Lodge Hotel

(0.25m) *Bolberry View, 5 Well Hill Close, Malborough, Kingsbridge, Devon, TQ7 3SS.*
Lovely views, quiet, near Salcombe
Tel: **01548 560793** Mrs Hilditch.
Rates fr: £13.50-£15.00.
Open: All Year (not Xmas)
Beds: 1D 1T **Baths:** 1 Shared
🛏 (3) 🅿 (2) 🍴🐾🍺

(0.25m) *Higher Collaton House, Collaton, Malborough, Kingsbridge, Devon, TQ7 3D.*
Idyllic, peaceful, relax in luxury
Tel: **01548 560826** Mrs Hernaiz.
Rates fr: £16.00-£15.00.
Open: Easter to Mid Oct
Beds: 2D 1T 1S
Baths: 2 Ensuite 2 Private
🛏 (7) 🅿 (4) ⊬🖵 Ⅴ

Salcombe 43

National Grid Ref: SX7339
🍴🍺 The Fortescue

(0.25m) *Widdecombe, Herbert Road, Salcombe, Devon, TQ8 8HN.*
Country style home, panoramic views
Tel: **01548 842127**
Mrs MacDonald.
Rates fr: £18.50-£19.50.
Open: All Year **Beds:** 1F 1D 1T
Baths: 2 Ensuite 1 Private
🛏 (5) 🅿 (2) ⊬🖵 Ⅴ

(0.25m) *Dell House, Dell Court, Onslow Road, Salcombe, Devon, TQ8 8BW.*
Actual grid ref: SX735391
Large family home. 8 mins walk from town
Tel: **01548 843215** Mrs Pritchard.
Rates fr: £13.50-£18.50.
Open: Feb to Nov
Beds: 1F 1D 1T **Baths:** 2 Shared
🛏 🅿 (3) 🖵 🖵 Ⅴ

(0.25m) *Torre View Hotel, Devon Road, Salcombe, Devon, TQ8 8HJ.*
Actual grid ref: SX7439
Cosy licensed hotel, excellent views
Grades: ETB 3 Cr, Comm
Tel: **01548 842633** (also fax no)
Mrs Bouttle.
Rates fr: £24.00-£27.00.
Open: March to Oct.
Beds: 1F 4D 2T 1S
Baths: 8 Private
🛏 (4) 🅿 (5) ⊬🖵✕🖵 ▮

Pay B&Bs by cash or cheque and be prepared to pay up front.

(0.25m) *Suncroft, Fortescue Road, Salcombe, Devon, TQ8 8AP.*
Spacious home spectacular coastal views
Tel: **01548 843975** Mr Sherlock.
Rates fr: £20.00-£30.00.
Open: All Year (not Xmas)
Beds: 3D
Baths: 1 Ensuite 1 Shared
🛏 🅿 (3) 🖵 🖵 Ⅴ

(0.25m) *Lyndhurst Hotel, Bonaventure Road, Salcombe, Devon, TQ8 8BG.*
Edwardian harbour-master's residence
Grades: ETB 3 Cr, Comm, AA 4 Q, Select, RAC High Acclaim
Tel: **01548 842481** (also fax no)
Mr & Mrs Towner.
Rates fr: £20.00-£20.00.
Open: Feb to Oct
Beds: 1F 3D 4T
Baths: 8 Private
🛏 (5) 🅿 (4) ⊬🖵✕🖵 Ⅴ ▮ ✦

East Prawle 44

National Grid Ref: SX7836
🍴🍺 The Freebooter, Millbrook Inn, Pig's Nose Inn

(2m) *Hines Hill, East Prawle, Kingsbridge, Devon, TQ7 2BZ.*
Actual grid ref: SX784363
Tel: **01548 511263** (also fax no)
Mrs Morris.
Rates fr: £22.00-£26.50.
Open: Mar to Oct
Beds: 2D 1T **Baths:** 3 Ensuite
🛏 (12) 🅿 (8) ⊬🖵🐾🖵 Ⅴ ▮
Breathtaking panorama of Devon's southernmost coast from tranquil clifftop gardens, overlooking sandy beaches, coastal path, near Salcombe. Generous imaginative cooking, considerate hospitality. Sea views from every elegantly furnished room

(2m) *Stures Court, East Prawle, Kingsbridge, Devon, TQ7 2BY.*
C17th thatched cottage, C20th comfort
Grades: ETB Listed, High Comm
Tel: **01548 511261** Miss Benson.
Rates fr: £15.00-£15.00.
Open: All Year
Beds: 2D 2S **Baths:** 1 Shared
🛏 (7) ⊬🖵🖵 Ⅴ ▮ ✦

(2m) *The Forge on the Green, East Prawle, Kingsbridge, Devon, TQ7 2BU.*
Grades: ETB 2 Cr, High Comm
Tel: **01548 511210** (also fax no)
Rates fr: £20.00-£25.00.
Open: All Year **Beds:** 2D
Baths: 1 Ensuite 1 Private
🅿 ⊬🖵🐾🖵 Ⅴ
Acclaimed luxury cottage with picturesque views from Prawle Green to the sea. Ensuite spa bath plus all facilities. Fabulous buffet breakfast. Gourmet dinners by arrangement

Order your packed lunches the *evening before* you need them. Not at breakfast!

Frogmore 45

National Grid Ref: SX7742

(1m) *The Globe Inn, Frogmore, Kingsbridge, Devon, TQ7 2NR.*
Delightful, friendly creekside inn, ideal base for all holiday activites. Bar meals available
Grades: ETB 2 Cr, Comm
Tel: **01548 531351** (also fax no)
Mr & Mrs Johnston.
Rates fr: £17.00-£20.00.
Open: All Year
Beds: 2F 3D 1T
Baths: 3 Private 2 Shared
🛏 🅿 (20) 🖵🐾✕🖵 Ⅴ

West Charleton 46

National Grid Ref: SX7542
🍴🍺 Ashburton Arms, Globe Inn

(2m) *West Charleton Grange, West Charleton, Kingsbridge, Devon, TQ7 2AD.*
Actual grid ref: SX750430
Tel: **01548 531779**
Mr & Mrs Fowles.
Fax no: 01548 531100
Rates fr: £20.00-£25.00.
Open: Feb to Oct
Beds: 1D 1T
Baths: 1 Ensuite 1 Private
🛏 (10) 🅿 (14) ⊬🖵🖵 ✦
Old rectory, in 11 acre secluded valley. Wildlife lake. Approached down 0.25 mile private drive. Superb 30ft indoor heated pool. Games room. Large guest breakfast room/lounge

The Grid Reference beneath the location heading is for the village or town - *not* for individual houses, which are shown (where supplied) in each entry itself.

Chillington   47

National Grid Ref: SX7942

🍴 🍺 Church House Inn, Chilllington Inn

(0.25m) *The Chillington Inn, Chillington, Kingsbridge, Devon, TQ7 2J.*
Tel: **01548 580244**
Mr & Mrs Starr.
Rates fr: *£19.50-£25.00.*
Open: All Year **Beds:** 1F 2D
Baths: 1 Ensuite 2 Private
🛏 🍴 🖵 🐾 🛆 🍽 🎫 🖩 🛆 ⚡
Small friendly village pub, circa 1600. Beams, open fires. Central South Hams (between Salcombe/Dartmouth) Two miles to magnificent coast/beaches. Excellent food/beer/accommodation

(0.25m) *Coleridge, Chillington, Kingsbridge, Devon, TQ7 2JG.*
Georgian farmhouse on working farm
Grades: ETB Listed
Tel: **01548 580274** Mrs Darke.
Rates fr: *£15.00-£15.00.*
Open: May to Oct
Beds: 1F 1T
Baths: 1 Private 1 Shared
🛏 (3) 🅿 (2) 🍴 🖵

Stokenham   48

National Grid Ref: SX8042

🍴 🍺 Tradesman's Arms, Church House Inn, Globe Inn

(On route) *Woodland View, Kiln Lane, Stokenham, Kingsbridge, Devon, TQ7 2SQ.*
Modern comfortable, quiet guest house
Grades: ETB 2 Cr, Comm
Tel: **01548 580542** Mrs Cadman.
Rates fr: *£15.15-£16.50.*
Open: Easter to end-Sept
Beds: 2D 2T 1S
Baths: 2 Ensuite 2 Private
🛏 (0) 🅿 (8) 🖵 🐾 🖩 ♿

Slapton   49

National Grid Ref: SX8245

🍴 🍺 Queen's Arms, Tower Inn

(1m) *Start House, Start, Slapton, Kingsbridge, Devon, TQ7 2QD.*
Actual grid ref: SX809448
Grades: ETB 2 Cr, Comm
Tel: **01548 580254** Mrs Ashby.
Rates fr: *£19.00-£17.00.*
Open: All Year (not Xmas)
Beds: 2D 1T 1S
Baths: 2 Private 1 Shared
🛏 🅿 (4) 🍴 🖵 🐾 🛆 🍽 🖩 🎫 ⚡
Situated in quiet hamlet 1 mile from Slapton. Comfortable Georgian house overlooking beautiful valley. 2 acre attractive partly-terraced garden. Ideal for wildlife and walking

(0.5m) *Old Walls, Slapton, Kingsbridge, Devon, TQ7 2QN.*
Actual grid ref: SX822449
Listed C18th house in beautiful village near sea, Nature Reserve
Tel: **01548 580516** Mrs Mercer.
Rates fr: *£16.00-£16.00.*
Open: All Year (not Xmas)
Beds: 3F
Baths: 1 Ensuite 1 Private 1 Shared
🛏 🍴 🖵 🐾 🖩 🎫 🛆 ⚡

Stoke Fleming   50

National Grid Ref: SX8648

🍴 🍺 Green Dragon, Endsleigh Hotel, Fleming's

(0.25m) *Southfield House, Stoke Fleming, Dartmouth, Devon, TQ6 0NR.*
Very warm welcome in elegant Georgian house
Tel: **01803 770359**
Mrs Nixon.
Rates fr: *£16.00-£20.00.*
Open: All Year (not Xmas)
Beds: 1D 2T
Baths: 2 Ensuite 1 Private
🅿 (3) 🍴 🖵 🖩 🎫 🛆 ⚡

Dartmouth   51

National Grid Ref: SX8751

🍴 🍺 Royal Castle Hotel, Seale Arms, Cherub Inn, Seven Stars, The Dolphin, The Windjammer, Market House, The Castle

(0.25m) *The Captain's House, 18 Clarence Street, Dartmouth, Devon, TQ6 9NW.*
Tel: **01803 832133** Mr Jestico.
Rates fr: *£20.00-£30.00.*
Open: Mar to Oct
Beds: 1F 2D 1T 1S
Baths: 5 Ensuite
🍴 🖵 🖩 ⚡
Georgian Listed house built 1730. Quiet street close town/river. All rooms TV, radio, tea/coffee, fridge, hairdryer, etc. Choice breakfasts with homemade produce

(0.25m) *79 Victoria Road, Dartmouth, Devon, TQ6 9RX.*
The Cedars, level location, near town centre, friendly welcome
Tel: **01803 834421**
Rates fr: *£15.00-£15.00.*
Open: All Year (not Xmas)
Beds: 2F 1D 1S **Baths:** 1 Shared
🛏 🍴 🐾 🖩 🛆 ⚡

(0.25m) *Valley House, 46 Victoria Road, Dartmouth, Devon, TQ6.*
Comfortable small friendly guest house
Tel: **01803 834045** Mr & Mrs Ellis.
Rates fr: *£19.50-£25.00.*
Open: All Year (not Xmas)
Beds: 2D 2T
Baths: 4 Ensuite
🅿 (4) 🍴 🍽 🖩 🎫 ⚡

Please don't camp on *anyone's* land without first obtaining their permission.

(0.25m) *Victoria Cote, 105 Victoria Road, Dartmouth, Devon, TQ6 9DY.*
Detached, comfortable, Victorian house 5 minutes' stroll from town centre
Tel: **01803 832997** Mr Fell.
Rates fr: *£20.00-£25.00.*
Open: All Year (not Xmas)
Beds: 3D **Baths:** 3 Private
🛏 🅿 (5) 🍴 🐾 🍽 🖩 🎫

Salcombe to Totnes

Here you take the ferry across the Kingsbridge Estuary and head due east until you hit the coast again at Torcross, where the route takes you alongside the sandy beach of Start Bay as far as Strete Gate, from where you climb through the village of Strete and head on to the wooded cliffs above the beautiful Blackpool Sands, and through Stoke Fleming to **Dartmouth**. Here you can see the Butterwalk, a row of seventeenth-century timber-framed houses, the small maritime museum and the crumbling medieval Cherub Inn. Dartmouth Castle was built in the late fifteenth century, one of the first in England designed for artillery. Take a ferry across the Dart Estuary - from here you more-or-less closely follow the Dart upstream to Dartmeet, on the moor, the confluence of the East and West Dart rivers. Through Galmpton and Stoke Gabriel you reach **Totnes**, a well-endowed market town with many Elizabethan buildings, an eleventh-century guildhall and a Norman castle.

80

(0.25m) *Brenec House, 73 South Ford Road, Dartmouth, Devon, TQ6 9QT.*
Pleasant, comfortable small guest house
Tel: **01803 834788**
Mr & Mrs Culley.
Rates fr: *£16.00*-**£14.00**.
Open: All Year (not Xmas)
Beds: 1F 1D 1S **Baths:** 1 Shared
🛇 🄿 🖵 🛒 💷 🗎 ✦

(0.25m) *Ford House, 44 Victoria Road, Dartmouth, Devon, TQ6 9DX.*
Guest House in beautiful Devon
Grades: ETB 3 Cr, High Comm, AA 5 Q, RAC High Acclaim
Tel: **01803 834047** (also fax no)
Mr Turner.
Rates fr: *£25.00*-**£35.00**.
Open: March to October
Beds: 2T 2D
Baths: 3Ensuite 1Private
🛇 🄿 (All) 🖵 🛒 ✕ 💷 🗎

(0.25m) *Boringdon House, 1 Church Road, Dartmouth, Devon, TQ6 9HQ.*
Spacious, welcoming, elegant Georgian house
Grades: ETB 2 Cr, High Comm
Tel: **01803 832235**
Mr Green.
Rates fr: *£22.50*-**£38.00**.
Open: Mar to Dec
Beds: 1D 2T
Baths: 3 Ensuite
🄿 (4) 🖵 💷

(0.25m) *Three Feathers, 51 Victoria Road, Dartmouth, Devon, TQ6 9RX.*
Early Victorian town house
Tel: **01803 834694**
Mrs George.
Rates fr: *£14.50*-**£16.50**.
Open: All Year (not Xmas)
Beds: 4F 1T
Baths: 3 Ensuite 1 Shared
🛇 🄿 🖵 🛒 💷 💷 ✦

(0.25m) *Britannia, 19 Clarence Street, Dartmouth, Devon, TQ6 9NW.*
B&B in picturesque South Devon
Tel: **01803 833069** Mrs Dash.
Rates fr: *£17.00*-**£17.00**.
Open: All Year (not Xmas)
Beds: 1F 1T 1S
Baths: 1 Private 1 Shared
🛇 (1) 🖵 🛒 💷 💷 ✦

(0.25m) *75 Victoria Road, Dartmouth, Devon, TQ6 9RX.*
Large Victorian house
Tel: **01803 833415** Mr Bruckner.
Rates fr: *£14.00*-**£15.00**.
Open: Easter to Jan
Beds: 2F 1D 1T 1S
Baths: 2 Shared
🛇 🖵 💷 ✦

Pay B&Bs by cash or cheque and be prepared to pay up front.

(0.25m) *Regency House, 30 Newcomen Rd, Dartmouth, Devon, TQ6 9BN.*
Actual grid ref: SX879510
Overlooking the beautiful River Dart
Tel: **01803 832714**
Mrs Shalders.
Rates fr: *£22.00*.
Open: All Year (not Xmas)
Beds: 1F 2D **Baths:** 3 Ensuite
🛇 ✕ 🖵 💷 & 💷 ✦

(0.25m) *Townstal Farm House, Townstal Road, Dartmouth, Devon, TQ6 9HY.*
Charming family-run C16th farmhouse
Grades: ETB 3 Cr, Comm, AA 3 Q, Recomm
Tel: **01803 832300**
Mr Edge.
Rates fr: *£22.50*-**£20.00**.
Open: All Year
Beds: 5F 9D 2T 1S
Baths: 14 Ensuite 3 Shared
🛇 🄿 (18) 🖵 🛒 ✕ 💷 & 💷 🗎

(0.25m) *Oaklands, 6 Vicarage Hill, Dartmouth, Devon, TQ6 9EW.*
Victorian house with southerly aspect
Tel: **01803 833274**
Mrs MacVitie.
Rates fr: *£17.50*-**£20.00**.
Open: Easter to Dec
Beds: 1F 2T
Baths: 1 Ensuite 1 Shared
🛇 🄿 (2) 🖵 💷

Kingswear   52

National Grid Ref: SX8851

(0.5m) *Carlton House, Higher Street, Kingswear, Dartmouth, Devon, TQ6 0AG.*
Magnificent views over Dartmouth Harbour
Tel: **01803 752244**
Mr & Mrs Congdon.
Rates fr: *£14.00*-**£15.00**.
Open: All Year
Beds: 2F 2D 1T 1S
Baths: 2 Shared
🛇 🖵 🛒 ✕ 💷 💷 🗎 ✦

Brixham   53

National Grid Ref: SX9255

🍴 🍺 Smugglers' Haunt Hotel, Blue Anchor, Berry Head Hotel, Weary Ploughman

(1m) *Sampford House, 57-59 King Street, Brixham, Devon, TQ5 9TH.*
Superb view over harbour and Torbay. A distinct nautical flavour
Tel: **01803 857761**
Boulton.
Rates fr: *£16.00*-**£25.00**.
Open: All Year
Beds: 5D
Baths: 4 Ensuite 1 Private
🛇 🄿 (2) 🖵 🛒 ✕ 💷 🗎 ✦

(1m) *Mimosa Cottage,*
75 New Road, Brixham, Devon,
TQ5 8NL.
Spacious, well-furnished Georgian house
Tel: **01803 855719** Mr Kershaw.
Rates fr: *£14.00*-**£15.00.**
Open: All Year (not Xmas)
Beds: 2D 1T 1S
Baths: 2 Private 1 Shared
⛺ (2) **P** (4) ⌨ ⌂ ▥ Ⓥ ✦

(1m) *Smugglers Haunt Hotel,* &
Restaurant, Church Hill, Brixham,
Devon, TQ5 8HH.
Friendly, private 300-year-old hotel
Tel: **01803 853050**
Mr Hudson.
Rates fr: *£14.00*-**£18.00.**
Open: All Year
Beds: 2F 7D 4T 4S
Baths: 5 Private 4 Shared
⛺⌨⌂✗▥ⓘ⛾

(1m) *Melville Hotel,* 45 New Road,
Brixham, Devon, TQ5 8NL.
Victorian house full of charm,
character
Tel: **01803 852033**
Mr & Mrs Hancock.
Rates fr: *£13.50*-**£14.50.**
Open: Mar to Dec
Beds: 3F 2D 2T 2S
Baths: 2 Ensuite 2 Shared
⛺ **P** (9) ⌨✗Ⓥⓘ✦

Berry Pomeroy   54

National Grid Ref: SX8261

🍴 ◧ Pig & Whistle, Kingsbridge Inn

(1m) *Berry Farm,* Berry Pomeroy,
Totnes, Devon, TQ9 6LG.
Welcome, spacious, clean and comfortable
Grades: ETB Listed, Comm
Tel: **01803 863231**
Mrs Nicholls.
Rates fr: *£16.00*-**£18.00.**
Open: All Year (not Xmas)
Beds: 1F 1D 1T
Baths: 1 Shared
⛺ (3) **P** (4) ✍⌨✗Ⓥ✦

Totnes   55

National Grid Ref: SX8060

🍴 ◧ Church House Inn, Tally Ho Inn, Kingsbridge Inn

(0.25m) *Great Court Farm,*
Weston Lane, Totnes, Devon,
TQ9 6LB.
Victorian farmhouse, spacious comfortable rooms. Good home cooking, friendly atmosphere
Grades: ETB 1 Cr, High Comm
Tel: **01803 862326**
Mrs Hooper.
Rates fr: *£16.00*-**£17.00.**
Open: All Year
Beds: 1F 1D 1T
Baths: 1 Ensuite 2 Shared
⛺ **P** (3) ✍⌨✗▥Ⓥ✦

(0.25m) *2 Antrim Terrace,* Totnes,
Devon, TQ9 5QA.
Spacious elegant Edwardian house overlooking Norman castle near town centre
Tel: **01803 862638**
Mrs Allen.
Rates fr: *£16.00*-**£16.00.**
Open: All Year **Beds:** 1D 1T 2S
Baths: 1 Ensuite 2 Shared
✍⌨▥Ⓥ

(0.25m) *Lower Blakemore Farm,*
HR. Plymouth Road, Totnes,
Devon, TQ9 6DN.
Comfortable farmhouse on working farm
Grades: ETB 2 Cr
Tel: **01803 863718**
Mrs Anning.
Rates fr: *£14.00*-**£14.00.**
Open: All Year
Beds: 1F 1T
Baths: 2 Ensuite
⛺ **P** (6) ✍⌨✗▥Ⓥ

(0.25m) *Royal Seven Stars Hotel,*
The Plains, Totnes, Devon, TQ9 5DD.
Former coaching inn, c1660
Grades: ETB 3 Cr, AA 2 St,
RAC 2 St
Tel: **01803 862125**
Mr Stone.
Rates fr: *£27.00*-**£40.00.**
Open: All Year
Beds: 2F 12D 3T 1S
Baths: 12 Private 3 Shared
⛺ **P** (20) ⌨⌂✗▥

Littlehempston   56

National Grid Ref: SX8162

(2m) *Buckyette Farm,*
Littlehempston, Totnes, Devon,
TQ9 6ND.
Victorian farm house in Dart Valley
Tel: **01803 762638**
Mrs Miller.
Rates fr: *£17.50*-**£17.50.**
Open: Mar to Oct
Beds: 4F 1D 1T
Baths: 6 Ensuite
⛺ **P** (8) ⌨♿Ⓥ

Dartington   57

National Grid Ref: SX7862

(▲ 0.25m) *Dartington Youth
Hostel,* Lownard, Dartington,
Totnes, Devon, TQ9 6JJ.
Actual grid ref: SX782622
Tel: **01803 862303**
Under 18: £5.40
Adults: £8.00
Self-catering Facilities, Showers
A small traditional cottage-style hostel with a wooden cabin annexe containing the bunkrooms, in a peaceful village setting complete with babbling brook and colourful gardens. An ideal base for exploring the South Hams countryside

The lowest *double* rate per person is shown in *italics*.

Buckfast   58

National Grid Ref: SX7367

🍴 ◧ Abbey Inn

(0.25m) *Leat House,* Grange
Road, Buckfast, Buckfastleigh,
Devon, TQ11 0EH.
Modern house near Abbey & Moors
Tel: **01364 642129** (also fax no)
Mrs Nesbitt.
Rates fr: *£20.00*-**£20.00.**
Open: All Year (not Xmas)
Beds: 1D 1T 1S
Baths: 1 Ensuite 1 Shared
P (4) ⌨▥Ⓥ✦

Totnes to Exeter

From **Totnes** it's on to **Dartington**; Dartington Hall has 25 acres of gardens and a fourteenth-century timbered Great Hall where concerts are held. You reach the edge of the moor at **Buckfastleigh**; Buckfast Abbey, a working Benedictine monastery founded in the late nineteenth century, stands on the site of an eleventh-century foundation which fell victim, like all the others, to Henry VIII. From Buckfastleigh you head back up onto Dartmoor, turning north at Dartmeet to reach **Widecombe in the Moor**, renowned from the folk song about its fair: you can find the grave of Tom Cobbleigh at the fourteenth-century granite church, known as 'the cathedral of the moor', which is also noted for its painted rood screen. The road north takes you through the attractive villages of **North Bovey** and **Moretonhampstead**, then east through **Bridford** and Christow and off the moor at Lower Ashton. From here you head northeastwards through Shillingford St George and Shillingford Abbot back into **Exeter**.

Scorriton 59

National Grid Ref: SX7068

(0.25m) *Scorriton Down Farm*,
Scorriton, Buckfastleigh, Devon,
TQ11 0JB.
Dartmoor farmhouse with
panoramic views
Tel: **01364 644236**
Mrs Batt.
Rates fr: *£15.00*-**£15.00**.
Open: All Year (not Xmas)
Beds: 1F 1D 1T
Baths: 1 Private
🛏 🅿 (6) 🗔 🛏 ✗ 🎹 Ⅴ

Holne 60

National Grid Ref: SX7069

🍴 🍺 Church House Inn,
Tradesman's Arms

(On route) *Middle Leat*, Holne,
Ashburton, Newton Abbot, Devon,
TQ13 7SJ.
Actual grid ref: SX707695
Comfortable accommodation,
wonderful views, set in 3 acres.
Vegetarians welcome
Tel: **01364 631413**
Mrs Torr.
Rates fr: *£15.00*-**£17.50**.
Open: All Year
Beds: 1F 1D
Baths: 1 Private
🛏 🅿 🔗 🗔 🛦 Ⅴ ♦ ⚡

(1m) *Middle Stoke Farm*, Holne,
Ashburton, Devon, TQ13 7SS.
Lovely peaceful location on
Dartmoor
Tel: **01364 631444**
Miss Neal.
Rates fr: *£16.00*-**£16.00**.
Open: All Year (not Xmas)
Beds: 1D
Baths: 1 Private
🛏 🅿 (2) 🔗 🗔 🛏 🎹 ♦ ⚡

(1m) *Wellpritton Farm*, Holne,
Ashburton, Newton Abbot, Devon,
TQ13 7RX.
Farmhouse, farmfood, lovely
setting
Grades: ETB 2 Cr, High Recomm
Tel: **01364 631273**
Ms Gifford.
Rates fr: *£18.00*-**£18.00**.
Open: All Year
Beds: 2F 1T 1D 1S
Baths: 5 Ensuite
🛏 🅿 (10) 🗔 🛏 ✗ 🎹 Ⅴ ♦ ⚡

**Always telephone
to get directions to
the B&B - you will
save time!**

(0.25m) *Hunters Reach*,
Michelcombe Lane, Holne, Newton
Abbot, Devon, TQ13 7WR.
Actual grid ref: SX703693
Modern comfortable bungalow.
Peaceful location
Tel: **01364 631300**
Mr & Mrs Dance.
Rates fr: *£14.00*-**£15.00**.
Open: All Year (not Xmas)
Beds: 2D 1S
Baths: 1 Shared
🛏 🅿 (4) 🔗 🗔 🛏 🎹

(0.5m) *Mill Leat Farm*, Holne,
Ashburton, Newton Abbot, Devon,
TQ13 7RZ.
Actual grid ref: SX713685
Off the beaten track
Grades: ETB 1 Cr, Approv
Tel: **01364 631283**
Mrs Cleave.
Rates fr: *£16.00*-**£18.00**.
Open: All Year (not Xmas)
Beds: 2F
Baths: 1 Ensuite 1 Shared
🛏 🅿 (2) 🗔 🛏 ✗ Ⅴ ♦ ⚡

(0.25m) *Hazelwood*, Holne,
Newton Abbot, Devon, TQ13 7SJ.
Actual grid ref: SX706694
Panoramic views, personal service,
homemade bread
Tel: **01364 631235**
Mrs Mortimore.
Rates fr: *£16.00*-**£16.00**.
Open: All Year (not Xmas)
Beds: 1D 1S
🛏 🅿 🔗 🗔 🛏 ✗ 🎹 ♿ Ⅴ ♦ ⚡

Poundsgate 61

National Grid Ref: SX7072

🍴 🍺 Tavistock Inn

(1m) *Lower Aish Guest House*,
Poundsgate, Ashburton, Newton
Abbot, Devon, TQ13 7NY.
C17th house on Dartmoor
Tel: **01364 631229**
Mrs Wilkinson.
Rates fr: *£15.00*-**£18.00**.
Open: Easter to Oct
Beds: 1F 3D
🛏 🅿 (8) 🗔 🛏 🎹 ⚡

Widecombe in the Moor 62

National Grid Ref: SX7176

🍴 🍺 The Old Inn

(1m) *Ley Farm*, Widecombe in the
Moor, Newton Abbot, Devon,
TQ13 7TR.
Quality C15th thatched Devon
longhouse. Spectacular setting,
excellent cuisine
Tel: **01364 621331**
Mrs Tame.
Rates fr: *£16.00*-**£24.00**.
Open: Easter to Nov
Beds: 1F 1D 1T
Baths: 1 Ensuite 1 Shared
🛏 (6) 🅿 🔗 🛏 ✗ 🎹 Ⅴ ♦ ⚡

Manaton 63

National Grid Ref: SX7581

(▲ 2m) *Great Houndtor Camping*
Barn, Great Houndtor, Manaton,
Lustleigh, Newton Abbot, Devon,
Actual grid ref: SX749795
Adults: £3.35+
Showers
Restored house on the eastern edge
of Dartmoor near Manaton.
ADVANCE BOOKING
ESSENTIAL

North Bovey 64

National Grid Ref: SX7383

(On route) *Gatehouse*, North
Bovey, Moretonhampstead, Devon,
TQ13 8RB.
Beautiful medieval Devon
longhouse
Grades: AA 5 Q
Tel: **01647 440479** Mrs Williams.
Rates fr: *£24.00*-**£29.00**.
Open: All Year
Beds: 3D
Baths: 3 Private
🅿 (3) 🔗 🗔 🛏 ✗ 🎹 Ⅴ

Moretonhampstead 65

National Grid Ref: SX7586

🍴 🍺 London Inn, White Hart

(1m) *Great Sloncombe Farm*,
Moretonhampstead, Devon,
TQ13 8QF.
C13th Dartmoor farmhouse
Grades: ETB 3 Cr, High Comm,
AA 4 Q
Tel: **01647 440595** (also fax no)
Mrs Merchant.
Rates fr: *£20.00*-**£20.00**.
Open: All Year
Beds: 2D 1T
Baths: 3 Private 1 Shared
🛏 (8) 🅿 (3) 🔗 🗔 🛏 ✗ 🎹 Ⅴ ♦ ⚡

(0.25m) *Yarningale*, Exeter Road,
Moretonhampstead, Newton Abbot,
Devon, TQ13 8QA.
Secluded property with stunning
views
Grades: ETB 2 Cr
Tel: **01647 440560** (also fax no)
Mrs Radcliffe.
Rates fr: *£15.00*-**£15.00**.
Open: All Year
Beds: 2F
Baths: 2 Ensuite
🛏 🅿 (3) 🔗 🗔 🛏 ✗ 🎹 Ⅴ ♦ ⚡

**Please respect
a B&B's wishes
regarding children,
animals & smoking.**

(0.25m) *Wray Barton Manor, Moretonhampstead, Newton Abbot, Devon, TQ13 8SE*.
Elegant, peaceful Victorian manor house
Tel: **01647 440467**
Mrs Pollard.
Rates fr: *£17.00*-**£17.00**.
Open: Easter to Oct
Beds: 3D 2T
Baths: 3 Private 2 Shared
ॐ 🄿 ⊬ 🗗 ⴕ 🕮 🆅

Bridford 66

National Grid Ref: SX8186

⑩ ◫ Bridford Inn

(On route) *Horse-Engine House, Lowton Farm, Bridford, Exeter, Devon, EX6 7EN*.
Secluded converted horse-engine house
Tel: **01647 252209** Mr Joslin.
Rates fr: *£13.50*-**£15.50**.
Open: All Year
Beds: 1D 1T
ॐ 🄿 (4) ⊬ 🗗 ✕ 🕮 🆅

Doddiscombsleigh 67

National Grid Ref: SX8586

⑩ ◫ Nobody Inn

(2m) *Whitemoor Farm, Doddiscombsleigh, Exeter, Devon, EX6 7PU*.
Grades: ETB 1 Cr, Approv, AA 2 Q
Tel: **01647 252423**
Rates fr: *£17.50*-**£18.00**.
Open: All Year (not Xmas)
Beds: 1T 1D 2S
Baths: 1 Shared
ॐ 🄿 (6) ⊬ 🗗 ⴕ ✕ 🕮 🆅 ✧
C16th thatched farmhouse surrounded by garden and farmyard in Area of Outstanding Natural Beauty - oak beams and doors. Log fires in winter. Home produce

The *lowest* **single** rate *is shown in* **bold.**

Planning a longer stay? Always ask for any special rates.

Alphington 68

National Grid Ref: SX9189

⑩ ◫ The Admiral

(0.25m) *The Old Mill, Mill Lane, Alphington, Exeter, Devon, EX2 8SG*.
Bicycles garaged. Fresh farm breakfast. Large garden.
Recommended worldwide!
Tel: **01392 259977** (also fax no)
Mrs Marchant.
Rates fr: *£10.00*-**£10.00**.
Open: All Year
Beds: 2F 1D 1T 1S
Baths: 1 Private 1 Shared
ॐ 🄿 (8) ⊬ 🗗 🕮 ♿ 🆅 ▮ ✧

CTC Dales Side to Side Cycle Tour

The **Dales Side to Side Cycle Tour** is a crossing of the North of England from coast to coast through Cumbria and North Yorkshire, designed by the Cyclists' Touring Club for energetic cylists who like a challenge - some steep climbing is involved. It links three National Parks - from Seascale on the West Coast, the route commences with a jaunt through the southern Lake District, crosses the Pennines through the Yorkshire Dales and finally takes you across the North York Moors, ending at Robin Hood's Bay. As such it is an ideal way to experience the full range of landscape the North has to offer.

A **guide** pamphlet to the route is available from the Cyclists' Touring Club. You have to be a member to get it. Contact them at Cotterell House, 69 Meadrow, Godalming, Surrey GU7 3HS, tel 01483 417217, fax 01483 426994, e-mail cycling@ctc.org.uk.

Maps: Ordnance Survey 1:50,000 Landranger series: 89, 90, 91, 93, 94, 97, 98, 99, 100

Trains: Seascale is on the line that runs up the Cumbrian west coast between Lancaster and Carlisle. Kendal connects via Oxenholme to the Intercity network. Kirkby Stephen is on the famous scenic Leeds-Settle-Carlisle Railway. Thirsk is on the main London-Edinburgh Intercity line. Several places on the route through the North York Moors are on the branch line that runs from Middlesbrough to Whitby via Battersby.

Wellington   1

National Grid Ref: NY0804

(▲ 0.25m) *Mill House Camping Barn, Wellington, Gosforth, Seascale, Cumbria*
Actual grid ref: NY080044
Adults: £3.35+
On a large working farm in a secluded valley well placed for climbing and fell-walking. ADVANCE BOOKING ESSENTIAL

Nether Wasdale   2

National Grid Ref: NY1204

(▲ 1m) *Wastwater Youth Hostel, Wasdale Hall, Nether Wasdale, Seascale, Cumbria, CA20 1ET.*
Actual grid ref: NY145045
Tel: 019467 26222
Under 18: £5.95 **Adults:** £8.80
Evening Meals Available (7pm), Self-catering Facilities, Games Room, Showers
Lovely National Trust half-timbered house dating from 1829, furnished in period style with many original features. Grounds extend down to the slopes of Wastwater, the deepest lake in England

(On route) *Low Wood Hall Hotel, Nether Wasdale, Seascale, Cumbria, CA20 1ET.*
Victorian country house hotel
Grades: ETB 4 Cr, Comm
Tel: 019467 26289
Mr Brassington.
Rates fr: *£28.50*-£35.00.
Open: All Year (not Xmas)
Beds: 4F 6D 7T 1S
Baths: 13 Ensuite 1 Private
🛇 🅿 (24) ❑ ✕ ▥ Ⓥ ⋔ ⚡

Irton   3

National Grid Ref: NY1000

(2m) *Cookson Place Farm, Irton, Holmrook, Cumbria, CA19 1YQ.*
Comfortable farmhouse in quiet area
Tel: 01946 724286 Mrs Crayston.
Rates fr: *£13.00*-£13.00.
Open: All Year
Beds: 1D 1T
Baths: 1 Shared
🅿 ⚡ ❑ ▥ Ⓥ

The lowest *double* rate per person is shown in *italics*.

Eskdale Green   4

National Grid Ref: NY1400
🍴 🍺 King George IV Inn

(On route) *The Ferns, Eskdale Green, Holmrook, Cumbria, CA19 1UA.*
Victorian residence of considerable character
Tel: 019467 23217 Mrs Prestwood.
Rates fr: *£16.50*-£18.00.
Open: All Year **Beds:** 1F 1D 1T
Baths: 1 Ensuite 2 Shared
🛇 (0) 🅿 (4) ❑ ⋔ ▥ Ⓥ ⋔ ⚡

Boot   5

National Grid Ref: NY1701

(▲ 0.25m) *Eskdale Youth Hostel, Boot, Holmrook, Cumbria, CA19 1TH.*
Actual grid ref: NY195010
Tel: 019467 23219
Under 18: £5.95 **Adults:** £8.80
Evening Meals Available (7pm), Self-catering Facilities, Games Room, Showers, Laundry Facilities
Purpose-built hostel in extensive grounds set amid the quieter south west Lakeland fells. Popular with families. Low level paths and high level ridge walks with fine views attract walkers of all abilities

Seascale to Hawkshead

Starting from the seaside village of **Seascale**, the route enters the **Lake District** at Gosforth, and wends its way between the Cumbrian Mountains. Gouged into shape by glaciers during the Ice Age, these peaks offer the most dramatic scenery in England, hurled up towards the heavens from the dales and deep lakes that plunge down below them. From **Nether Wasdale**, the route passes through woodland into Eskdale. With the central mass of **Sca Fell** towering away to the left and Harter Fell to the right, you reach the first major challenge of the route as you tackle the steep climb and drop of **Hardknott Pass**. Then after the relative ease of the Duddon Valley, the Wrynose Pass takes you to Three Shire Stone, erstwhile meeting point of the old counties of Cumberland, Westmorland

and Lancashire. From here you descend steeply to Fell Foot, and reach the delightful miniature lake of Little Langdale Tarn. Out of here flows the River Brathay which eventually winds up flowing into the north end of Windermere. You cycle past a waterfall before reaching **Skelwith Bridge**, and the more dramatic Skelwith Force. From here you head south to **Hawkshead**, where Wordsworth went to school. The school can be visited, as can the Beatrix Potter Gallery, celebrating another local notable. The church is also interesting - although built in the fifteenth century, it is designed after the Romanesque style. For anyone of artistic bent with time available, a detour into nearby **Grizedale Forest** is well worthwhile: this large tract of woodland contains numerous sculptures by artists who have been coming here for twenty years.

Elterwater 6

National Grid Ref: NY3204

|◎| ◫ Britannia Inn

(▲ 1m) *Elterwater (Langdale) Youth Hostel*, Elterwater, Ambleside, Cumbria, *LA22 9HX*.
Actual grid ref: NY327046
Tel: **015394 37245**
Under 18: £5.40
Adults: £8.00
Evening Meals Available (7pm), Self-catering Facilities, Showers *Converted farmhouse and barn on the edge of the hamlet of Elterwater. Close to the fells at the head of Langdale, at the heart of classic Lakeland scenery - a favourite with walkers and climbers*

(1m) *Britannia Inn*, Elterwater, Langdale, Ambleside, Cumbria, *LA22 9HP*.
Traditional Lakeland inn overlooking village green. Cosy bars with log fires
Grades: ETB 3 Cr, Comm
Tel: **015394 37210** Fax no: 015394 37311
Rates fr: *£19.00*-**£19.00**.
Open: All Year (not Xmas)
Beds: 3T 9D 1S
Baths: 9 Ensuite 1 Private 1 Shared
🐾 🖵 🛏 ✕ 🎞 Ⅴ 👜 ✦

The *lowest* single rate *is shown in* bold.

All cycleways are popular: you are well-advised to book ahead

(1m) *Barnhowe*, Elterwater, Ambleside, Cumbria, *LA22 9HU*.
Homemade bread. Quiet beautiful location. Super walking
Grades: ETB 1 Cr, Comm
Tel: **015394 37346**
Mr & Mrs Riley.
Rates fr: *£16.00*-**£16.00**.
Open: Feb to Nov
Beds: 1D 1T 1S
Baths: 1 Shared
🐾 🅿 (7) ⅙ 🖵 🎞 Ⅴ ✦

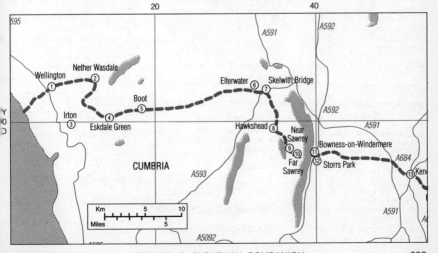

Hawkshead to Keld

From Hawkshead you cycle down the east side of **Esthwaite Water** and through **Near Sawrey** - where you can find Hill Top, the home of Beatrix Potter - and **Far Sawrey** to the banks of **Windermere**, the largest lake in England. Here you take the ferry to the east bank, just south of **Bowness-on-Windermere**, where the Windermere Steamboat Museum includes the oldest mechanically-powered boat in the world, 'Dolly', built in 1850. The route now takes you east through **Crook**, and out of the National Park, into **Kendal**, an historic town built in grey limestone, where there is plenty to see if you have time to stop. Abbot Hall, a Georgian building of 1759, houses two museums - an Art Gallery with works of Turner, Ruskin and local artists, as well as a display of Lancastrian Gillows furniture; and the Museum of Lakeland Life and Industry. The ruined Kendal Castle sits atop a hill. And don't forget to stock up on Kendal mint cake for the rest of the way. From here you go east and into the **Yorkshire Dales National Park**, shortly arriving at **Sedbergh**, where you will find a National Park Information Centre. Now it's northeastwards through the Rawthey Valley and over Ash Fell to arrive at **Kirkby Stephen** in the Eden Valley, and then southeast over Nateby Common into North Yorkshire and through Birkdale Common down to **Keld**. This vicinity is notable for the 'laithes', ancient barns which are all around.

Skelwith Bridge 7

National Grid Ref: NY3403

¶◀ Skelwith Bridge Hotel

(0.25m) *Greenbank, Skelwith Bridge, Ambleside, Cumbria, LA22 9NW.*
Actual grid ref: NY345033
Country comfort; home-baked bread!
Grades: ETB 2 Cr, High Comm
Tel: **015394 33236**
Mr Green.
Rates fr: *£19.00-£24.00.*
Open: All Year
Beds: 2D 1T
Baths: 3 Ensuite
ॐ (8) ▣ (5) ⅍ ⌷ 🎟 Ⓥ ᵢ ⋆

Hawkshead 8

National Grid Ref: SD3597

¶◀ Drunken Duck Inn, Outgate Inn

(▲0.25m) *Hawkshead Youth Hostel, Esthwaite Lodge, Hawkshead, Ambleside, Cumbria, LA22 0QD.*
Actual grid ref: SD354966
Tel: **015394 36293**
Under 18: £6.55 Adults: £9.75
Evening Meals Available (7pm), Self-catering Facilities, Television, Games Room, Showers, Laundry Facilities, Licensed Premises
Handsome regency mansion in wooded grounds overlooking Esthwaite Water. The separate courtyard contains excellent family accommodation

(0.25m) *Borwick Lodge, Hawkshead, Ambleside, Cumbria, LA22 0PU.*
Grades: ETB 2 Cr, Highly Commended
Tel: **015394 36332** (also fax no)
Mr & Mrs Haskell.
Rates fr: *£19.00-£19.00.*
Open: All Year
Beds: 1F 4D 1T
Baths: all Ensuite
ॐ (8) ▣ (8) ⅍ ⌷ 🎟 Ⓥ ᵢ ⋆
Award-Winning 'Accommodation of the Highest Standards'. A rather special C17th country house with magnificent panoramic views. Quietly secluded yet ideally placed in the heart of the Lakes and close to restaurants and inns. Beautiful bedrooms, all ensuite. Also 'Special Occasions' and 'Romantic Breaks' king-size four poster rooms. Totally non-smoking

(0.25m) *Betty Fold Guest House, Hawkshead Hill, Hawkshead, Ambleside, Cumbria, LA22 0PS.*
Large private house
Grades: ETB 2 Cr, High Comm
Tel: **015394 36611** Mr Marsden.
Rates fr: *£18.00-£24.00.*
Open: All Year
Beds: 1F 1D 1T Baths: 3 Private
ॐ ▣ (8) ⌷ ✕ 🎟 Ⓥ ᵢ ⋆

Near Sawrey 9

National Grid Ref: SD3795

¶◀ Tower Bank Arms

(On route) *High Green Gate Guest House, Near Sawrey, Ambleside, Cumbria, LA22 0LF.*
Converted C18th farmhouse in Beatrix Potter's village
Grades: ETB 2 Cr
Tel: **015394 36296** Miss Fletcher.
Rates fr: *£20.00-£23.00.*
Open: Apr to Oct
Beds: 4F 1D
Baths: 3 Private 1 Shared
ॐ ▣ (6) ⌷ 🛏 ✕ 🎟 Ⓥ

(On route) *Beechmount, Near Sawrey, Ambleside, Cumbria, LA22 0JZ.*
Fabulous views. Breakfast brochure available
Grades: ETB 2 Cr
Tel: **015394 36356**
Mrs Siddall.
Rates fr: *£19.50-£21.00.*
Open: All Year
Beds: 3D
Baths: 3 Private
ॐ ▣ (3) ⌷ 🛏 🎟 Ⓥ

(On route) *Buckle Yeat Guest House, Near Sawrey, Hawkshead, Ambleside, Cumbria, LA22 0LF.*
Traditional & picturesque Lakeland cottage
Tel: **015394 36446** (also fax no)
Mr Kirby.
Rates fr: *£20.00-£20.00.*
Open: All Year
Beds: 1F 4D 1T 1S
Baths: 6 Ensuite 1 Private
ॐ ▣ (8) ⌷ 🛏 🎟 Ⓥ

Far Sawrey 10

National Grid Ref: SD3895

¶◀ Sawrey Hotel, Tower Bank Arms

(On route) *West Vale Country Guest House, Far Sawrey, Ambleside, Cumbria, LA22 0LQ.*
Peaceful, private, family-run accommodation overlooking open countryside. Home cooking
Grades: ETB 3 Cr, High Comm, RAC High Acclaim
Tel: **015394 42817**
Mrs Forbes.
Rates fr: *£23.00-£23.00.*
Open: Mar to Oct
Beds: 1F 4D 2T
Baths: 6 Ensuite 1 Private
ॐ (7) ▣ (7) ⌷ ✕ 🎟 Ⓥ ᵢ ⋆

(On route) *Sawrey Hotel*, *Far Sawrey, Ambleside, Cumbria, LA22 0LQ*.
C18th country inn
Grades: ETB 3 Cr, Comm
Tel: **015394 43425** (also fax no)
Mr Brayshaw.
Rates fr: *£23.00-£23.00*.
Open: All Year (not Xmas)
Beds: 6F 7D 5T 4S
Baths: 18 Private 1 Shared
☎ ₽ (30) ⌂ ⵟ ✕ ▥ Ⓥ ♿

Bowness-on-Windermere11

National Grid Ref: SD4097

🍽 ⛊ Hole in' t' Wall, Greys Inn, Village Inn, Royal Oak, John Peel

(0.5m) *The Poplars*, *Lake Road, Bowness-on-Windermere, Windermere, CumbriaCumbria, LA23 2EQ*.
Grades: ETB 2 Cr, Comm
Tel: **015394 42325** (also fax no)
Mr & Mrs Riggs.
Rates fr: *£19.50-£19.50*.
Open: Feb to Dec
Beds: 4D 2T 1S
Baths: 6 Ensuite 1 Private
☎ (5) ₽ (7) ⌂ ⵟ ✕ ▥ Ⓥ ♿
Ideally situated midway between Bowness & Windermere. Superior ensuite accommodation coupled with the finest cuisine. Unique friendly atmosphere. Ideal base for walkers, golfers, fishing & cycling

All rooms full and nowhere else to stay? Ask the owner if there's anywhere nearby

All rates are subject to alteration at the owners' discretion.

(0.5m) *Fairfield Hotel*, *Brantfell Road, Bowness-on-Windermere, Windermere, Cumbria, LA23 3AE*.
Actual grid ref: SD967404
Grades: ETB 3 Cr, Comm
Tel: **015394 46565** (also fax no)
Mr & Mrs Hood.
Rates fr: *£23.00-£33.00*.
Open: Feb to Oct
Beds: 2F 5D 1T 1S
Baths: 8 Ensuite 1 Private
☎ ₽ (12) ⅍ ✕ ▥ ♿ ✓
Small friendly family-run hotel in Bowness at the end of the Dales Way. Ensuite rooms with colour TVs. Leisure facilities. Ideal venue to end your walk. Private car park

(0.5m) *Cranleigh Hotel*, *Kendal Road, Bowness-on-Windermere, Windermere, Cumbria, LA23 3EW*.
Close to lake, with free use of private leisure centre
Grades: ETB 3 Cr, Comm
Tel: **015394 43293**
Mr Wigglesworth.
Rates fr: *£18.00-£18.00*.
Open: All Year
Beds: 3F 9D 3T **Baths:** 15 Private
☎ ₽ ⅍ ⌂ ✕ ▥ Ⓥ ♿ ✓

(0.5m) *Brooklands*, *Ferry View, Bowness-on-Windermere, Windermere, Cumbria, LA23 3JB*.
Delightful Lakeland stone guest house in rural position. 15 minutes' walk lake
Grades: ETB 2 Cr, Comm, AA 3 Q
Tel: **015394 42344** Renwick.
Rates fr: *£16.00-£16.00*.
Open: All Year (not Xmas)
Beds: 3F 2D 1T 1S
Baths: 5 Ensuite 2 Private
☎ ₽ (6) ⌂ ⵟ ▥ ♿ ✓

(0.5m) *Lingwood*, *Birkett Hill, Bowness-on-Windermere, Windermere, Cumbria, LA23 3EZ*.
Actual grid ref: SD403964
Friendly, comfortable, family guest house
Grades: ETB 2 Cr, Comm
Tel: **015394 44680**
Mr & Mrs Atkinsin.
Rates fr: *£19.00-£22.00*.
Open: All Year
Beds: 3F 3D
Baths: 4 Ensuite 2 Private
☎ ₽ (6) ⌂ ▥ ✓

(0.5m) *Above The Bay*, *Brackenfield, Bowness-on-Windermere, Windermere, Cumbria, LA23 3HL*.
Close to village centre. Free leisure club membership. Ample parking
Tel: **015394 88658** Mr Bell.
Fax no: 015394 48007
Rates fr: *£17.50-£20.00*.
Open: All Year
Beds: 1F 2D 1T 1S
Baths: 5 Private
☎ (11) ₽ (10) ⅍ ⌂ ⵟ ▥ ♿ Ⓥ ♿ ✓

(0.5m) *Virginia Cottage*, *Kendal Road, Bowness-on-Windermere, Windermere, Cumbria, LA23 3EJ*.
C18th cottage in heart of Bowness village, close lake, shops, restaurants. Leisure facilities, private parking
Grades: ETB 2 Cr, Comm
Tel: **015394 44891** Mr Tyler.
Rates fr: *£15.00-£20.00*.
Open: All Year **Beds:** 2F 9D
Baths: 5 Private 3 Shared
☎ ₽ (9) ⌂ ⵟ ▥ Ⓥ ♿ ✓

Bringing children with you? Always ask for any special rates.

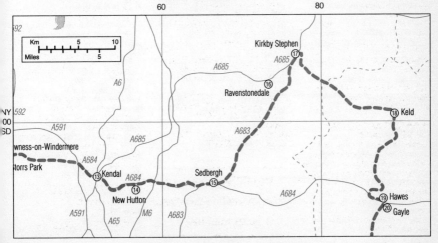

(0.5m) **Bay House Lake View,**
*Guest House, Fallbarrow Road,
Bowness-on-Windermere,
Windermere, Cumbria, LA23 3DJ.*
Informal, fun & friendly guest
house
Grades: ETB Listed
Tel: 015394 43383 Mrs Large.
Rates fr: *£14.50-***£15.20.**
Open: All Year
Beds: 2F 3D 1T **Baths:** 2 Shared
🛇 🅿 (4) 🖵 ⅍ ✕ 🎟, Ⅴ ♦ ⁄

(0.5m) **Holmlea,** *Kendal Road,
Bowness-on-Windermere,
Windermere, Cumbria, LA23 3EW.*
Friendly, close to lake & amenites
Grades: ETB 2 Cr, Comm, RAC
Listed
Tel: 015394 42597 Mrs Goodacre.
Rates fr: *£16.50-***£16.50.**
Open: All Year **Beds:** 3D 1T 2S
Baths: 4 Private 2 Shared
🛇 🅿 (7) 🖵 ✕ 🎟, Ⅴ ♦ ⁄

(0.5m) **Holly Cottages,** *Rayrigg
Road, Bowness-on-Windermere,
Windermere, Cumbria, LA23 3BZ.*
Actual grid ref: SD404972
Centre of Bowness-on-Windermere
Tel: 015394 44250 Mr Bebbington.
Rates fr: *£17.50-***£17.50.**
Open: All Year
Beds: 2F 6D 1T 1S
Baths: 6 Private 1 Shared
🛇 🅿 (9) ⁄ 🖵 ⅍ 🎟, Ⅴ ♦ ⁄

(0.5m) **Albert Hotel,** *Queens
Square, Bowness-on-Windermere,
Windermere, Cumbria, LA23 3BY.*
Friendly Victorian inn &
bunkhouse
Tel: 015394 43241 Mr Taylor.
Rates fr: *£17.50-***£25.00.**
Open: All Year
Beds: 3F 3D
Baths: 6 Ensuite
🛇 (1) 🖵 ⅍ ✕ 🎟, Ⅴ ♦ ⁄

(0.5m) **Thornleigh,** *Thornbarrow
Road, Bowness-on-Windermere,
Windermere, Cumbria, LA23 2EW.*
Comfortable, friendly, Lakeland
stone house
Grades: ETB 2 Cr
Tel: 015394 44203 Mr Stone.
Rates fr: *£15.00-***£15.00.**
Open: All Year
Beds: 1T 1D 2F 1S
Baths: 3 Ensuite
🛇 (3) 🅿 (6) ⁄ 🖵 ⅍ 🎟, Ⅴ ♦

Storrs Park   12

National Grid Ref: SD4096

(0.25m) **Beech Tops,** *Meadowcroft
Lane, Storrs Park, Bowness-on-
Windermere, Cumbria, LA23 3JJ.*
Spacious bedroom suites in modern
house, woodland setting near lake
Tel: 015394 45453
Mrs Lewthwaite.
Rates fr: *£17.50-***£25.00.**
Open: Mar to Nov
Beds: 2F **Baths:** 2 Ensuite
🛇 (3) 🅿 (4) ⁄ 🖵 🎟, Ⅴ ♦ ⁄

Kendal   13

National Grid Ref: SD5192

🍴 🍺 Crown Inn, Hare & Hounds,
Kendal Arms, Wheatsheaf,
Gateway Hotel, Union Tavern,
Ring O' Bells, Jolly Anglers

(▲ 0.5m) **Kendal Youth Hostel,**
*118 Highgate, Kendal, Cumbria,
LA9 4HE.*
Actual grid ref: SD515924
Warden: Mr Butcher.
Tel: 01539 724066
Under 18: £5.95 **Adults:** £8.80
Evening Meals Available (7pm),
Self-catering Facilities, Shop,
Parking
*Converted Georgian town house,
adjoining Brewery Arts Centre, in
a prime position in the centre of
Kendal*

(0.5m) **Bridge House,** *65 Castle
Street, Kendal, Cumbria, LA9 7AD.*
Actual grid ref: SD5293
Beautiful Georgian Listed building.
Free Kendal Cake for
cyclists/walkers
Grades: ETB 1 Cr
Tel: 01539 722041 Mrs Brindley.
Rates fr: *£16.00-***£20.00.**
Open: All Year
Beds: 1F 1T
Baths: 1 Shared
🛇 ⁄ 🖵 ⅍ 🎟, Ⅴ ♦ ⁄

(0.5m) **Olde Peat Cotes,** *Sampool
Lane, Levens, Kendal, Cumbria,
LA8 8EH.*
Grades: ETB Listed
Tel: 015395 60096 Mrs Parsons.
Rates fr: *£10.00-***£10.00.**
Open: All Year (not Xmas)
Beds: 1F 1T
Baths: 1 Shared
🛇 🅿 (2) ⁄ 🖵 ⅍ 🎟, & Ⅴ
Homely, modern bungalow,
suitable wheelchairs. Ideal stopover
south to Scotland. Edge of Lake
District. Beautiful rural setting.
Salmon fishing available. Personal
service. Children welcome

(0.5m) **Newlands Guest House,**
*37 Milnthorpe Road, Kendal,
Cumbria, LA9 5QG.*
Actual grid ref: SD515916
Comfortable, friendly Victorian
house. Quality breakfast with
homemade marmalade
Grades: ETB 2 Cr, Comm
Tel: 01539 725340 Mrs Horsley.
Rates fr: *£16.00-***£16.00.**
Open: All Year (not Xmas)
Beds: 1F 2D 1T 1S
Baths: 2 Private 1 Shared
🛇 🅿 (5) 🖵 ⅍ 🎟, Ⅴ ♦ ⁄

**Planning a longer
stay? Always ask for
any special rates.**

(0.5m) **Hillside Guest House,**
*4 Beast Banks, Kendal, Cumbria,
LA9 4JW.*
Large Victorian guest house, town
centre. Ideal for Lake District and
Yorkshire Dales
Grades: ETB 2 Cr, Comm
Tel: 01539 722836
Mrs Denison.
Rates fr: *£19.00-***£16.00.**
Open: All Year
Beds: 4D 3S
Baths: 5 Ensuite 4 Private
🛇 (4) 🅿 (4) 🖵 ⅍ 🎟, ⁄

(0.5m) **Sundial House,** *51
Milnthorpe Road, Kendal,
Cumbria, LA9 5EQ.*
Actual grid ref: SD515916
A quality guest house at the gate-
way to the Lakes
Tel: 01539 724468 Mrs Bowker.
Rates fr: *£16.00-***£16.00.**
Open: All Year
Beds: 1F 3D 2T 1S
Baths: 1 Ensuite 3 Shared
🛇 🅿 (8) 🖵 ⅍ 🎟, Ⅴ ♦ ⁄

(0.5m) **Fairways,** *102 Windermere
Road, Kendal, Cumbria, LA9 5EZ.*
Victorian guest house, ensuite
rooms. TV, tea/coffee. Lovely
views
Grades: ETB 2 Cr, Comm
Tel: 01539 725564 Mrs Paylor.
Rates fr: *£17.00-***£18.00.**
Open: All Year
Beds: 1F 2D
Baths: 3 Ensuite
🛇 (2) 🅿 (4) ⁄ 🖵 🎟, Ⅴ ⁄

(0.5m) **Sonata,** *19 Burnside Road,
Kendal, Cumbria, LA9 4RL.*
Actual grid ref: SD513933
Friendly family-run guest house
Grades: ETB Listed, Comm
Tel: 01539 732290
Mr Wilkinson.
Rates fr: *£16.50-***£19.00.**
Open: All Year
Beds: 1F 2D 1T 1S
Baths: 2 Ensuite 3 Shared
🛇 🖵 ⅍ ✕ 🎟, Ⅴ ♦ ⁄

(0.5m) **Birslack Grange,** *Hutton
Lane, Levens, Kendal, Cumbria,
LA8 8PA.*
Peaceful, secluded, converted
farmhouse
Grades: AA 3 Q
Tel: 015395 60989
Mrs Carrington-Birch.
Rates fr: *£16.00-***£18.50.**
Open: All Year
Beds: 1F 3T 1S
Baths: 3 Private
🛇 🅿 (6) ⁄ 🖵 ⅍ ✕ 🎟, & Ⅴ ♦ ⁄

(0.5m) **Fell View,** *100 Windermere
Road, Kendal, Cumbria, LA9 5EZ.*
Friendly Victorian guest house
Grades: ETB 2 Cr, Comm
Tel: 01539 728431 Mrs Bousfield.
Rates fr: *£17.50.*
Beds: 1T 2D
Baths: 2 Ensuite
🛇 (12) 🅿 (3) ⁄ 🖵 🎟, Ⅴ

(0.5m) *Park Lea, 15 Sunnyside, Kendal, Cumbria, LA9 7DJ.*
Actual grid ref: SD519924
Comfortable Victorian house overlooking parkland
Grades: ETB 2 Cr, Comm
Tel: **01539 740986** Mr Bunney.
Rates fr: *£17.00-£17.00*.
Open: All Year (not Xmas)
Beds: 2D 1T
Baths: 2 Ensuite 1 Private
🅿 (2) ⛬ 🏠 🖿 Ⅴ ✦

(1m) *Garnette House Farm, Kendal, Kendal, Cumbria, LA9 5SF.*
Actual grid ref: SD500959
C15th farmhouse near village
Grades: ETB 2 Cr, Comm,
AA 3 Q, RAC Acclaim
Tel: **01539 724542** Mrs Beaty.
Rates fr: *£16.00*.
Open: All Year (not Xmas)
Beds: 2F 3D 1T
Baths: 3 Private
⛬ 🅿 (6) ⛬ ✗ Ⅴ

(1m) *Natland Mill Beck Farm, Kendal, Cumbria, LA9 7LH.*
Lake District. On working dairy farm. Hospitality recommended in C17th old farmhouse
Grades: AA 3 Q
Tel: **01539 721122**
Mrs Gardner.
Rates fr: *£15.00-£16.00*.
Open: Easter to Oct
Beds: 1D 1T 1S
Baths: 1 Ensuite 1 Private 1 Shared
⛬ 🅿 (3) 🖿 Ⅴ ▮

(0.5m) *Brantholme, 7 Sedbergh Road, Kendal, Cumbria, LA9 6AD.*
Family-run guest house. Victorian house in large private garden.
Grades: ETB Listed
Tel: **01539 722340**
Mrs Bigland.
Rates fr: *£18.00-£25.00*.
Open: Feb to Nov
Beds: 3T
Baths: 2 Ensuite 1 Private
⛬ 🅿 (5) ✗ Ⅴ ▮ ✦

(0.5m) *West Mount, 39 Milnthorpe Road, Kendal, Cumbria, LA9 5QG.*
Outskirts of historic market town
Tel: **01539 724621**
Mr Keep.
Rates fr: *£16.00-£16.00*.
Open: All Year
Beds: 1F 2D
⛬ (1) 🅿 (3) ⛬ ✗ 🖿 Ⅴ

(0.5m) *9-11 Sandes Avenue, Kendal, Cumbria, LA9 4LL.*
Two Victorian houses, tastefully converted
Grades: AA 1 Q, Recomm, RAC Acclaim
Tel: **01539 724028**
Mr & Mrs Martindale.
Rates fr: *£21.00-£28.00*.
Open: All Year
Beds: 1F 4D 3S
Baths: 8 Private
⛬ (8) 🅿 (6) 🖿 Ⅴ

(0.5m) *7 Thorny Hills, Kendal, Cumbria, LA9 7AL.*
Quiet, unspoilt Georgian town house
Tel: **01539 720207** Mrs Jowett.
Rates fr: *£17.00-£19.00*.
Open: Jan to Nov
Beds: 2D 1T
Baths: 3 Ensuite
⛬ ⛬ 🖿 ✗ 🖿 Ⅴ

New Hutton　　　14
National Grid Ref: SD5691
🍴 🍺 Station Inn

(1m) *Cragg Farm, New Hutton, Kendal, Cumbria, LA8 0BA.*
C17th farmhouse, tastefully modernised, 3 miles M6, J37
Grades: ETB Listed, Comm
Tel: **01539 721760**
Mrs Knowles.
Rates fr: *£15.50-£16.50*.
Open: Mar to Oct
Beds: 1F 1D 1S
Baths: 1 Shared
⛬ 🅿 (3) ⛬ ⛬ 🖿 Ⅴ

(0.5m) *Borrans, New Hutton, Kendal, Cumbria, LA8 0AT.*
B&B in 1729 house
Tel: **01539 722969**
Ms Ellis.
Rates fr: *£15.00-£15.00*.
Open: Easter to Oct
Beds: 4D 1S
Baths: 2 Shared
⛬ (1) 🅿 (8) ⛬ 🖿 Ⅴ

Sedbergh　　　15
National Grid Ref: SD6592
🍴 🍺 Dalesman Inn, Red Lion

(On route) *Marshall House, Main Street, Sedbergh, Cumbria, LA10 5BL.*
Actual grid ref: SD658922
Tel: **015396 21053**
Mrs Kerry.
Rates fr: *£20.00-£28.00*.
Open: All Year (not Xmas)
Beds: 1D 2T
Baths: 3 Private
⛬ (12) 🅿 (5) ⛬ ✗ 🖿 ♿ Ⅴ ▮ ✦
Which? recommended town house situated under the magnificent Howgill Fells. Tastefully furnished rooms - 2 ground floor - log fires and large walled garden with stream

(On route) *Stable Antiques, 15 Back Lane, Sedbergh, Cumbria, LA10 5AQ.*
Actual grid ref: SD659921
C18th Wheelwright's cottage with wonderful views of Howgills
Tel: **015396 20251**
Miss Thurlby.
Rates fr: *£17.00-£17.00*.
Open: All Year
Beds: 1D 1T
Baths: 1 Shared
⛬ (10) 🏠 🖿 Ⅴ ▮ ✦

(On route) *Holmecroft, Station Road, Sedbergh, Cumbria, LA10 5DW.*
Actual grid ref: SD650919
Detached Westmorland-style house enjoying superb views of Howgill Fells
Tel: **015396 20754**
Mrs Sharrocks.
Rates fr: *£17.00-£17.00*.
Open: All Year (not Xmas)
Beds: 2D 1T
Baths: 1 Shared
⛬ 🅿 (6) ⛬ 🏠 🖿 Ⅴ ▮ ✦

(0.5m) *Farfield Country Guest House, Garsdale Road, Garsdale, Sedbergh, Cumbria, LA10 5LP.*
Actual grid ref: SD677919
Beautiful Victorian house. Outstanding views
Tel: **015396 20537**
Mr & Mrs clark.
Rates fr: *£20.00-£22.00*.
Open: All Year (not Xmas)
Beds: 1F 3D 2T 1S
Baths: 4 Ensuite 1 Private
⛬ 🅿 (10) ⛬ ✗ 🖿 Ⅴ ▮

(On route) *Sun Lea, Joss Lane, Sedbergh, Cumbria, LA10 5AS.*
Actual grid ref: SD658922
Spacious Victorian family house
Grades: ETB Listed
Tel: **015396 20828**
Mr & Mrs Ramsden.
Rates fr: *£16.00-£16.00*.
Open: All Year (not Xmas)
Beds: 2D 1T
Baths: 2 Shared
⛬ 🅿 (3) ⛬ 🖿 Ⅴ ▮ ✦

(0.5m) *Randall Hill, Sedbergh, Cumbria, LA10 5HJ.*
Actual grid ref: SD649917
Country house in 3 acres
Tel: **015396 20633**
Mrs Snow.
Rates fr: *£15.00-£16.00*.
Open: All Year
Beds: 1D 2T
Baths: 1 Shared
⛬ 🅿 (6) ⛬ 🏠 🖿 Ⅴ ▮

The Grid Reference beneath the location heading is for the village or town - *not* for individual houses, which are shown (where supplied) in each entry itself.

(0.5m) *Turvey House, Sedbergh, Cumbria, LA10 5DJ*.
Stone-built large Victorian house
Grades: ETB Listed, Comm
Tel: 015396 20841
Mr & Mrs Liddey-Smith.
Rates fr: *£15.00*. **Open:** All Year
Beds: 1F 1D 1T **Baths:** 2 Shared
🅿 (5) ⚴ ☐ 🛏 Ⅴ 🛆 ⚡

Ravenstonedale 16

National Grid Ref: NY7203

🍴 ⚑ King's Head

(1.5m) *The Book House, Grey Garth, Ravenstonedale, Kirkby Stephen, Cumbria, CA17 4NQ*.
Secondhand bookshop in former vicarage
Tel: 015396 23634 Mrs Irwin.
Fax no: 015396 23434
Rates fr: *£14.50-£14.50*.
Open: All Year (not Xmas)
Beds: 1F 1T 1S **Baths:** 1 Shared
☎ 🅿 (4) ☐ 🛏 Ⅴ

Kirkby Stephen 17

National Grid Ref: NY7708

🍴 ⚑ Pennine Hotel, Old Forge

(⚠ On route) *Kirkby Stephen Youth Hostel, Fletcher Hill, Market Street, Kirkby Stephen, Cumbria, CA17 7QQ*.
Actual grid ref: NY774085
Warden: Ms C Seddon.
Tel: **017683 71793**
Under 18: £5.40 **Adults:** £8.00
Evening Meals Available (7pm),
Family Bunk Rooms, Showers,
Central Heating
Attractive converted chapel, just south of the town square in this interesting old market town in the Upper Eden Valley

(On route) *Jolly Farmers House, 63 High Street, Kirkby Stephen, Cumbria, CA17 4SH*.
Actual grid ref: NY774083
Grades: ETB 3 Cr, Comm
Tel: 017683 71063 (also fax no)
Mr Pepper.
Rates fr: *£16.00-£16.00*.
Open: All Year
Beds: 2F 5T 1S
Baths: 5 Ensuite 3 Shared
☎ 🅿 (6) ☐ 🛏 ✕ 🛆 Ⅴ 🛆 ⚡
Quality: Comfort: Right Price:
Something we believe in so come
and relax in one of our spacious
ensuite rooms. Home cooked food
from £6.00

(On route) *The Old Court House, High Street, Kirkby Stephen, Cumbria, CA17 4SH*.
Actual grid ref: NY774083
Beautiful house, close to all amenities. Open fires, excellent breakfasts
Grades: ETB 2 Cr, High Comm
Tel: 017683 71061 (also fax no)
Mrs Claxton.
Rates fr: *£17.50-£20.00*.
Open: All Year
Beds: 1F 1D 1T
Baths: 2 Private
☎ (10) 🅿 (2) ☐ 🛏 🛆 Ⅴ

(On route) *Claremont, Nateby Road, Kirkby Stephen, Cumbria, CA17 4AJ*.
Actual grid ref: NY775083
Quiet, near town centre. Spacious rooms, excellent food, warm welcome
Tel: **017683 71787**
Mrs Rennison.
Rates fr: *£14.00*.
Open: Easter to Oct
Beds: 1F 1T
Baths: 1 Ensuite 1 Shared
☎ 🅿 (2) ☐ 🛏 🛆 Ⅴ 🛆 ⚡

(On route) *Lyndhurst, 46 South Road, Kirkby Stephen, Cumbria, CA17 4SN*.
Actual grid ref: NY772078
Delightful comfortable Victorian family home. A warm welcome.
Excellent breakfast
Tel: **017683 71448** Mrs Bell.
Rates fr: *£15.00-£18.00*.
Open: Mar to Nov
Beds: 1D 2T
Baths: 1 Private 1 Shared
☎ 🅿 (3) ⚴ ☐ ✕ 🛆 Ⅴ 🛆 ⚡

(5m) *Cold Keld, Fell End, Kirkby Stephen, Cumbria, CA17 4LN*.
Farmhouse offering guided walking holidays
Tel: **015396 23273** (also fax no)
Mr & Mrs Trimmer.
Rates fr: *£16.00-£19.00*.
Open: All Year (not Xmas)
Beds: 1F 3D 1T
Baths: 5 Private
☎ 🅿 (12) ⚴ ☐ 🛏 🛆 Ⅴ 🛆 ⚡

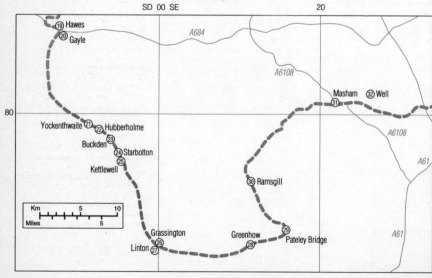

Keld to Masham

From Keld you head on to **Thwaite** in Swaledale, and then past the Buttertubs, a series of deeply-eroded potholes, climbing over Stags Fell down to High Shaw, where Hardraw Force is the highest above-ground single-drop waterfall in England. **Hawes** is the main town of Wensleydale (as in the cheese). Worth a visit here is the Dales Countryside Museum, tracing the history of many local industries. There is also a National Park Information Centre. The route south through the centre of the Dales involves a great deal of up-and-down, leading over Langstrothdale Chase to **Kettlewell** in Wharfedale, and then below Kilnsey Crag, a great limestone overhang, and through Grass Wood, a swathe of ancient woodland which is now an important conservation area, to **Grassington**, a village with a Georgian cobbled central square. Here you will find the Upper Wharfedale Museum. Then it's east to **Hebden**, and on to the edge of the National Park where the impressive Stump Cross Caverns are well worth a look. Pateley Bridge is in Nidderdale, actually outside the National Park but lovely nonetheless. Now you head northwest through the dale to **Lofthouse** and then northeast to **Masham**, where real ale enthusiasts can take a tour of the Theakston's brewery.

Keld 18

National Grid Ref: NY8901

⚑ Tan Hill Inn

(▲ 0.25m) **Keld Youth Hostel,** *Keld Lodge, Keld, Upper Swaledale, Richmond, North Yorkshire, DL11 6LL.*
Actual grid ref: NY891009
Warden: Mr L Roe.
Tel: **01748 886259**
Under 18: £4.95 **Adults:** £7.20
Evening Meals Available (7pm), Family Bunk Rooms, Television, Showers, Central Heating, Shop *Former shooting lodge located at the head of Swaledale, surrounded by moorland & waterfalls*

The lowest *double* rate per person is shown in *italics*.

Many rates vary according to season - the lowest only are shown here

(1m) **Frith Lodge,** *Keld, Richmond, N. Yorks, DL11 6EB.*
Actual grid ref: NY891031
Family-run farmhouse accommodation
Tel: **01748 886489**
Mrs Pepper.
Rates fr: *£15.00*-**£15.00**.
Open: All Year
Beds: 2T
Baths: 1 Shared

Hawes 19

National Grid Ref: SD8789

⚑ White Hart Inn, Board Hotel, Fountain Hotel, Crown Hotel

(▲ 0.25m) **Hawes Youth Hostel,** *Lancaster Terrace, Hawes, North Yorkshire, DL8 3LQ.*
Actual grid ref: SD867897
Warden: C & P Harman.
Tel: **01969 667368**
Under 18: £5.95
Adults: £8.80
Evening Meals Available (7pm), Family Bunk Rooms, Television, Games Room, Showers, Shop *Friendly and attractively refurbished purpose-built hostel overlooking Hawes and Wensleydale beyond*

(0.25m) **Tarney Fors,** *Hawes, N. Yorks, DL8 3LS.*
Grades: ETB 3 Cr, Comm
Tel: **01969 667475**
Mrs Harpley.
Rates fr: *£24.00*-**£38.00**.
Open: Mar to Nov
Beds: 3D
Baths: 3 Private
Beautiful ex-farmhouse in idyllic location for walking, cycling, touring. Good food, wonderful breakfasts, off road parking, licensed. 1.5 miles west of Hawes.

(0.25m) **Ebor House,** *Burtersett Road, Hawes, N. Yorks, DL8 3NT.*
Actual grid ref: SD876897
Family-run, central, friendly. Ideal base for touring the Dales
Grades: ETB 2 Cr, Comm
Tel: **01969 667337** (also fax no)
Mrs Clark.
Rates fr: *£17.00*-**£17.00**.
Open: All Year (not Xmas)
Beds: 2D 1T 1S
Baths: 2 Private 1 Shared

(0.25m) *Old Station House,* Hawes, N. Yorks, *DL8 3NL.*
Actual grid ref: SD875898
Grades: ETB 2 Cr, High Comm
Tel: 01969 667785
Mr & Mrs Watkinson.
Rates fr: *£20.00*-**£28.00.**
Open: All Year (not Xmas/New Year)
Beds: 1D 2T
Baths: 2 Ensuite 1 Private
🅿 (4) ⅍ 🖵 🛋 ♿ ⓘ ✦
Former stationmaster's house with large garden. Comfortable lounge with large selection of books and maps. Open fire. Friendly welcome; free supper drinks served in lounge

(0.25m) *Steppe Haugh Guest House,* Townhead, Hawes, N. Yorks, *DL8 3RH.*
C17th house offering a wealth of character and atmosphere
Grades: ETB 2 Cr, Comm
Tel: 01969 667645 Mrs Grattan.
Rates fr: *£17.00*-**£19.00.**
Open: All Year
Beds: 4D 1T 1S
Baths: 2 Ensuite 2 Shared
🛏 (7) 🅿 (6) ⅍ 🕭 🗙 🖳 Ⓥ

(0.25m) *Board Hotel,* Market Place, Hawes, N. Yorks, *DL8 3RQ.*
A friendly traditional Dales pub
Grades: ETB 2 Cr, Comm
Tel: 01969 667223 Mr Barron.
Rates fr: *£20.00*-**£20.00.**
Open: All Year
Beds: 2D 1T
Baths: 3 Private
🛏 🅿 🖵 🗙 🖳 Ⓥ ⓘ

(0.25m) *Halfway House,* Hawes, N. Yorks, *DL8 3LL.*
Actual grid ref: SD865902
Small homely Dales farmhouse
Tel: 01969 667442 Mrs Guy.
Rates fr: *£16.00*-**£20.00.**
Open: Easter to Nov
Beds: 1D 1T
Baths: 1 Shared
🛏 🅿 (4) ⅍ 🖵 Ⓥ ✦

(0.25m) *Pry House,* Hawes, N. Yorks, *DL8 3LP.*
Actual grid ref: SD8691
Working farm in Herriot country
Tel: 01969 667241
Mrs Fawcett.
Rates fr: *£15.00*-**£16.00.**
Open: Easter to Nov
Beds: 1F 2D
Baths: 1 Shared
🛏 🅿 (3) ⅍ 🖵 🖳 Ⓥ ⓘ ✦

(0.25m) *The Green Dragon Inn,* Hardraw, Hawes, N. Yorks, *DL8 3.*
Olde worlde inn/hotel, fully modernised
Tel: 01969 667392
Mr Stead.
Rates fr: *£17.00*-**£18.00.**
Open: All Year (not Xmas)
Beds: 1F 11D 1T 3S
Baths: 16 Private
🛏 🅿 🖵 🕭 🗙 🖳 Ⓥ ⓘ ✦

(0.25m) *Cocketts Hotel & Restaurant,* Market Place, Hawes, N. Yorks, *DL8 3RD.*
C17th old Quaker meeting house
Grades: ETB 3 Cr, High Comm, AA 2 St
Tel: 01969 667312 Mr Bedford.
Rates fr: *£22.00*-**£30.00.**
Open: All Year (not Xmas)
Beds: 6D 2T
Baths: 8 Ensuite
🛏 (10) 🅿 ⅍ 🖵 🗙 🖳 ♿ Ⓥ ⓘ ✦

Gayle 20
National Grid Ref:

🍴 ◫ Board Hotel, Fountain Hotel, Crown Hotel

(0.25m) *Gayle Laithe,* Gayle, Hawes, N. Yorks, *DL8 3RR.*
Modern, comfortable, converted barn
Tel: 01969 667397 Mrs McGregor.
Rates fr: *£16.00*-**£16.00.**
Open: Easter to Nov
Beds: 1D 1T 1S
Baths: 1 Shared
🛏 🅿 (2) 🖵 🖳 Ⓥ ⓘ

(0.25m) *East House,* Gayle, Hawes, N. Yorks, *DL8 3RZ.*
Actual grid ref: SD871892
Spacious comfortable country house
Grades: ETB 2 Cr, Comm
Tel: 01969 667405 Mrs Ward.
Rates fr: *£16.00*-**£16.00.**
Open: Easter to October
Beds: 1F 1T 1D 1S
Baths: 1 Ensuite 1 Shared
🛏 (5) 🅿 (3) 🖵 🖳 Ⓥ ⓘ ✦

(0.25m) *Ivy House,* Gayle, Hawes, N. Yorks, *DL8 3RZ.*
Quiet, comfortable house, beautiful views
Tel: 01969 667476 Mrs Chapman.
Rates fr: *£13.00*-**£14.00.**
Open: All Year (not Xmas)
Beds: 1F 1D
Baths: 1 Shared
🅿 ⅍ 🖵 🕭 🖳 ✦

(0.25m) *Rookhurst Hotel,* West End, Gayle, Hawes, N. Yorks, *DL8 3RT.*
Family-run hotel beside Pennine Way
Grades: AA 2 St
Tel: 01969 667454 (also fax no) Mrs Van Der Steen.
Rates fr: *£30.00*-**£30.00.**
Open: Feb to Dec
Beds: 4D 1T **Baths:** 5 Private
🛏 (12) 🅿 (10) ⅍ 🖵 🗙 🖳 Ⓥ ⓘ ✦

Planning a longer stay? Always ask for any special rates.

The lowest *double* rate per person is shown in *italics.*

Yockenthwaite 21
National Grid Ref: SD9079

🍴 ◫ George Inn

(On route) *Low Raisgill Cottage,* Yockenthwaite, Hubberholme, Skipton, N. Yorks, *BD23 5JQ.*
Actual grid ref: SD906786
Quietly situated in unspoilt Longshortdale
Tel: 01756 760351
Mrs Middleton.
Rates fr: *£17.00*-**£17.00.**
Open: All Year
Beds: 1F 1D 1T
Baths: 3 Private
🅿 🖵 🗙 🖳 Ⓥ ⓘ ✦

Hubberholme 22
National Grid Ref: SD9278

(0.25m) *The George Inn,* Hubberholme, Skipton, N. Yorks, *BD23 5JE.*
An original & unspoilt C16th Dales country inn
Grades: RAC Listed
Tel: 01756 760223 (also fax no)
Mr Lanchbury.
Rates fr: *£18.50*-**£25.00.**
Open: All Year
Beds: 4D 3T
Baths: 4 Ensuite 3 Shared
🛏 (8) ⅍ 🖵 🗙 🖳 Ⓥ ⓘ ✦

(0.5m) *Church Farm,* Hubberholme, Skipton, N. Yorks, *BD23 5JE.*
Actual grid ref: SD935773
Comfortable farmhouse Bed & Breakfast
Tel: 01756 760240 Mrs Huck.
Rates fr: *£15.00*-**£15.00.**
Open: All Year
Beds: 1F 1T
Baths: 1 Shared
🛏 🅿 🖵 🖳 Ⓥ ⓘ ✦

Buckden 23
National Grid Ref: SD9477

🍴 ◫ Buck Inn

(On route) *West Winds Cottage,* Buckden, Skipton, N. Yorks, *BD23 5JA.*
Country cottage accommodation in quiet village, ideally situated for walkers
Tel: 01765 760883
Miss Thornborrow.
Rates fr: *£15.00*-**£17.00.**
Open: All Year (not Xmas)
Beds: 1T 2D
Baths: 1 Shared
🛏 (10) ⅍ 🖳 Ⓥ ⓘ

Starbotton 24

National Grid Ref: SD9574

|o| ◖ The Fox

(On route) *Fox & Hounds Inn,
Starbotton, Skipton, N. Yorks,
BD23 5HY.*
Traditional cosy Dales inn
Tel: **01756 760269**
Mr & Mrs McFadyen.
Fax no: 01756 760862
Rates fr: £22.00-**£30.00**.
Open: Mid-Feb to Dec
Beds: 1D 1T
Baths: 2 Private
🅿 (10) ⬛ ⊁ ✕ ▥ Ⅴ ♦

(On route) *Hill Top Country Guest
House, Starbotton, Skipton, N.
Yorks, BD23 5HY.*
C17th Listed farmhouse
Grades: ETB 2 Cr, High Comm,
AA 5 Q, Prem Select
Tel: **01756 760321** Mr Rathmell.
Rates fr: £25.00-**£32.00**.
Open: Easter to Nov
Beds: 1F 3D 1T **Baths:** 5 Ensuite
🖏 (6) 🅿 (6) ⬛ ✕ ▥ Ⅴ ♦ ✦

Kettlewell 25

National Grid Ref: SD9772

|o| ◖ Race Horses, The Bluebell,
Fox & Hounds, King's Head

(▲ 0.25m) *Kettlewell Youth
Hostel, Whernside House,
Kettlewell, Skipton, North
Yorkshire, BD23 5QU.*
Actual grid ref: SD970724
Warden: Mr G Chamberlain.
Tel: **01756 760232**
Under 18: £5.95 **Adults:** £8.80
Evening Meals Available (7pm),
Family Bunk Rooms, Television,
Showers, Shop
*Large house right in the middle of
pretty Wharfedale village of
Kettlewell, ideal for families and
small groups*

(0.25m) *Langcliffe House,
Kettlewell, Skipton, N. Yorks,
BD23 5RJ.*
Grades: ETB 4 Cr, Comm,
AA 4 Q, RAC High Acclaim
Tel: **01756 760243** Mr Elliott.
Rates fr: £30.00-**£40.00**.
Open: All Year
Beds: 1F 2T 2D
Baths: 5 Ensuite
🖏 🅿 ⬛ ⊁ ✕ ▥ & Ⅴ ♦ ✦
Kettlewell in Upper Wharfedale.
Traditional stone house with beau-
tiful gardens. Ensuite bedrooms.
Elegant lounge with log fire.
Conservatory restaurant serving
superb food in a panoramic setting

**The *lowest* single
rate *is shown in* bold.**

**All rates are subject
to alteration at the
owners' discretion.**

(0.25m) *The Elms, Middle Lane,
Kettlewell, Skipton, N. Yorks,
BD23 5QX.*
Grades: ETB 2 Cr, High Comm
Tel: **01756 760224**
Mr Cuthbert.
Fax no: 01756 760380
Rates fr: £21.00-**£29.00**.
Open: All Year (not Xmas)
Beds: 2D 1T
Baths: 3 Ensuite
🅿 (3) ⊁ ⬛ ▥ Ⅴ ✦
Warm friendly accommodation in
our roomy Victorian home, with a
secluded garden, in this typical
Yorkshire Dales village. Panoramic
views across & up Upper
Wharfedale

(0.25m) *Chestnut Cottage,
Kettlewell, Skipton, N. Yorks,
BD23 5RL.*
Delightful country cottage.
Beautiful gardens, leading down to
village stream
Tel: **01969 622092**
Mrs Lofthouse.
Rates fr: £18.50-**£18.50**.
Open: All Year
Beds: 1D 2T
Baths: 2 Shared
🖏 🅿 (3) ⬛ ▥.

(0.25m) *Lynburn, Kettlewell,
Skipton, N. Yorks, BD23 5RF.*
Comfortable Dales cottage, superb
position
Tel: **01756 760803**
Mrs Thornborrow.
Rates fr: £18.00-**£25.00**.
Open: Easter to Oct
Beds: 1D 1T
Baths: 1 Shared
🅿 (2) ⬛ ▥ ♦ ✦

(1m) *High Fold, Kettlewell,
Skipton, N. Yorks, BD23 5RJ.*
Dales barn recently converted to
high standard
Grades: ETB 3 Cr, Deluxe
Tel: **01756 760390** Mr Earnshaw.
Rates fr: £25.00-**£30.00**.
Open: Feb to Dec
Beds: 1F 2D 1T
Baths: 4 Ensuite
🖏 (2) 🅿 (4) ⬛ ⊁ ✕ ▥ & Ⅴ ♦ ✦

(1m) *Fold Farm, Kettlewell,
Skipton, N. Yorks, BD23 5RH.*
C15th farmhouse in quiet location
Tel: **01756 760886** Mrs Lambert.
Rates fr: £18.00-**£25.00**.
Open: Easter to Oct
Beds: 2D 1T
Baths: 3 Private
🖏 (10) 🅿 (10) ⊁ ⬛ ▥ Ⅴ

Grassington 26

National Grid Ref: SE0064

|o| ◖ Black Horse, Devonshire
Hotel, The Forresters, Old Hall Inn

(0.25m) *Grassington Lodge, 8
Wood Lane, Grassington, Skipton,
N. Yorks, BD23 5LU.*
Grades: ETB 2 Cr
Tel: **01756 752518** (also fax no)
Mr & Mrs Wade.
Rates fr: £16.00-**£22.00**.
Open: All Year
Beds: 5D 4T
Baths: 6 Ensuite 2 Shared
🖏 🅿 (9) ⬛ ⊁ ✕ ▥ Ⅴ ♦ ✦
Family-run Victorian guest house
enjoying quiet position in own
grounds - 100 metres from
Grassington village square in the
heart of the Yorkshire Dales. Lock-
up cycle shed and private car park

(0.25m) *Springroyd House,
8a Station Road, Grassington,
Skipton, N. Yorks, BD23 5NQ.*
Actual grid ref: SD980631
Conveniently situated, friendly
family home
Tel: **01756 752473** Mr Berry.
Rates fr: £16.50-**£20.00**.
Open: All Year
Beds: 1D 1T
Baths: 2 Shared
🖏 (5) 🅿 (2) ⊁ ⬛ ⊁ ▥ Ⅴ ♦ ✦

(0.25m) *Mayfield Bed &
Breakfast, Low Mill Lane,
Grassington, Skipton, N. Yorks,
BD23 5BX.*
Actual grid ref: SE000635
Riverside Dales long house. Guest
rooms overlook fells and river
Tel: **01756 753052**
Mr & Mrs Trewartha.
Rates fr: £18.00-**£20.00**.
Open: All Year
Beds: 1F 1T 1D
Baths: 1 Ensuite 1 Shared
🖏 🅿 (10) ⊁ ⊁ ▥ Ⅴ ♦ ✦

(0.25m) *Burtree Cottage, Hebden
Road, Grassington, Skipton, N.
Yorks, BD23 5LH.*
Old stone cottage, lovely garden
Tel: **01756 752442**
Mrs Marsden.
Rates fr: £15.00-**£20.00**.
Open: Easter to Oct
Beds: 1D 1T
Baths: 1 Shared
🖏 (10) 🅿 (3) ⊁ ⬛ ▥ Ⅴ ✦

(0.25m) *Town Head Guest House,
1 Low Lane, Grassington, Skipton,
N. Yorks, BD23 5AU.*
Modern comfortable guest house
Grades: ETB 2 Cr, Comm
Tel: **01756 752811**
Mrs Lister.
Rates fr: £21.00-**£30.00**.
Open: All Year (not Xmas)
Beds: 3D 1T
Baths: 4 Ensuite
🖏 (7) 🅿 (3) ⊁ ⬛ ▥ ♦

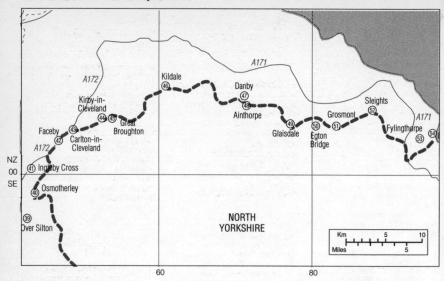

(0.25m) *3 Wharfeside Avenue, Grassington, Skipton, N. Yorks, BD23 5BS.*
Large, comfortable, warm family house
Grades: ETB 2 Cr
Tel: 01756 752115
Mr & Mrs Cahill.
Rates fr: *£18.00-£18.00.*
Open: Easter to Nov
Beds: 1F 1T 1S
Baths: 1 Private
🛇 🅿 (3) ⏚⏛ 🖵 ▥ ▣ ▮ ✦

(0.25m) *Ashfield House Hotel, Grassington, Skipton, N. Yorks, BD23 5AE.*
Quality C17th private hotel
Grades: ETB 3 Cr, High Comm, AA 4 Q, Select
Tel: 01756 752584 (also fax no)
Mr & Mrs Harrison.
Rates fr: *£25.00-£25.00.*
Open: Feb to Dec
Beds: 4D 3T
Baths: 6 Ensuite 1 Private
🛇 (5) 🅿 (7) ⏚⏛ 🖵 ✗ ▥ ▣ ✦

Linton   27

National Grid Ref: SD9962

(▲ On route) *Linton Youth Hostel, The Old Rectory, Linton, Skipton, North Yorkshire, BD23 5HH.*
Actual grid ref: SD998627
Warden: Mr R Suddaby.
Tel: 01756 752400
Under 18: £5.95 **Adults:** £8.80
Evening Meals Available (7pm), Family Bunk Rooms, Showers, Parking
C17th former rectory in own grounds, across the stream from the village green, in one of Wharfedale's most picturesque and unspoilt villages

Greenhow   28

National Grid Ref: SE1164

🍴 🍺 Miners' Arms

(0.25m) *Mole End, Greenhow, Pateley Bridge, Harrogate, N. Yorks, HG3 5JQ.*
Comfortable stone-built private house
Tel: 01423 712565
Mr & Mrs Knowles.
Rates fr: *£16.00-£20.00.*
Open: All Year
Beds: 1D 2T
Baths: 1 Private 1 Shared
🛇 (12) 🅿 (5) 🖵 🛏 ▥ ▣ ▮ ✦

Pateley Bridge   29

National Grid Ref: SE1565

(0.25m) *Woodlands, Bewerley, Pateley Bridge, Harrogate, N. Yorks, HG3 5HS.*
Comfortable Victorian house. Wonderful views
Tel: 01423 711175 Mrs Shaw.
Rates fr: *£18.00-£25.00.*
Open: All Year (not Xmas)
Beds: 1D 1T
Baths: 2 Private
🛇 🅿 (2) ⏚⏛ 🖵 🛏 ▥ ▣

(0.25m) *Grassfields Country Hotel, Wath Road, Pateley Bridge, Harrogate, N. Yorks, HG3 5HL.*
Georgian mansion in private grounds set in Area of Outstanding Natural Beauty
Grades: ETB 3 Cr, Comm, AA 2 St
Tel: 01423 711412
Mrs Garforth.
Rates fr: *£19.00-£25.00.*
Open: All Year
Beds: 2F 2D 4T 1S
Baths: 9 Ensuite
🛇 🅿 (20) 🖵 🛏 ✗ ▥ ▣

Ramsgill   30

National Grid Ref: SE1171

🍴 🍺 Yorke Arms

(On route) *Longside House, Ramsgill, Pateley Bridge, N. Yorks, HG3 5RH.*
Grades: ETB Listed
Tel: 01423 755207 Mrs Crosse.
Rates fr: *£22.00-£26.00.*
Open: Mar to Nov
Beds: 1F 1D 1T
Baths: 2 Ensuite 1 Private
🛇 🅿 (4) 🖵 ▥ ▣
Former shooting lodge 6 miles from Pateley Bridge on the 53 miles Nidderdale Way. AONB. Superb views towards Gouthwaite Reservoir & its bird sanctuary

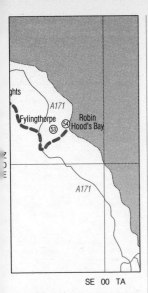

SE 00 TA

Masham 31

National Grid Ref: SE2280

(0.25m) *Bank Villa Guest House,
Masham, Ripon, N. Yorks, HG4 4DB.*
Stone-built Georgian house
Tel: **01765 689605** Mr Gill.
Rates fr: *£19.00-£28.00.*
Open: Easter to Oct
Beds: 3D 3T **Baths:** 1 Shared
🛇 (5) ⅃ ⬜ ⴕ ✗ ⅲ Ⓥ

**Please don't camp
on *anyone's* land
without first obtaining
their permission.**

Well 32

National Grid Ref: SE2682

⦿ ⬛ Freemasons' Arms, Boot &
Shoe

(1m) *Upsland Farm, Lime Lane,
Well, Bedale, N. Yorks, DL8 2PA.*
Moated site, lovely farmhouse.
Brass beds
Grades: ETB 2 Cr, High Comm
Tel: **01845 567709**
Mrs Hodgson.
Rates fr: *£20.00-£22.00.*
Open: All Year (not Xmas)
Beds: 3F
Baths: 3 Ensuite
🛇 🅿 (4) ⅃ ⬜ ⴕ ✗ ⅲ Ⓥ ⓘ ⅃

Carlton Miniott 33

National Grid Ref: SE3981

⦿ ⬛ Dog & Gun

(1m) *Carlton House Farm,
Carlton Miniott, Thirsk, N. Yorks,
YO7 4NJ.*
A warm Yorkshire welcome awaits
you in our comfortable farmhouse
home
Tel: **01845 524139**
Mrs Lee.
Rates fr: *£15.00-£20.00.*
Open: All Year
Beds: 2D
Baths: 1 Shared
🛇 (10) 🅿 (2) ⬜ ⅲ ⓘ

(1m) *Grove Farm, Carlton Miniott,
Thirsk, N. Yorks, YO7 4NJ.*
Very comfortable bungalow over-
looking farmland. Near local pub
Tel: **01845 524257**
Mrs Corner.
Rates fr: *£12.50-£15.00.*
Open: All Year
Beds: 1D
Baths: 1 Shared
🛇 🅿 (6) ⅃ ⬜ ⴕ ⅲ ⅗ Ⓥ ⓘ ⅃

Sowerby 34

National Grid Ref: SE4281

⦿ ⬛ Shepherd's Table

(0.25m) *The Old Manor House,
27 Front Street, Sowerby, Thirsk,
N. Yorks, YO7 1JQ.*
Restored C15th manor house.
Guest suites overlooking gardens
or village green
Grades: ETB 4 Cr, Comm
Tel: **01845 526642**
Mr Jackson.
Fax no: 01845 526568
Rates fr: *£20.00-£35.00.*
Open: All Year (not Xmas)
Beds: 1F 1D
Baths: 2 Ensuite
🅿 ⅃ ⬜ ⅲ ⓘ ⅃

South Kilvington 35

National Grid Ref: SE4282

⦿ ⬛ Old Oak Tree

(1.5m) *Thornborough House
Farm, South Kilvington, Thirsk,
N. Yorks, YO7 2NP.*
A warm welcome awaits in our
comfortable 200 year old farm-
house
Grades: ETB 2 Cr
Tel: **01845 522103** (also fax no)
Mrs Williamson.
Rates fr: *£14.00-£14.00.*
Open: All Year
Beds: 1D 1T 1S
Baths: 3 Private
🛇 🅿 (4) ⅃ ⬜ ⴕ ✗ ⅲ Ⓥ

**High season,
bank holidays and
special events mean
low availability
*everywhere.***

Masham to Robin Hood's Bay

The next stretch leads to **Thirsk**, the setting for James Herriot's books, and then on to **Boltby**, below the steep escarpment of the Hambleton Hills. Here you enter the **North York Moors National Park**, the largest expanse of heather moorland in England, offering, through-out, magnificent views for miles around. From Boltby it's a fairly tough ride across country to **Osmotherley**. Near here stand the ruins of Mount Grace Priory, the best-preserved Carthusian monastery in England. This order practised the most spartan regime of them all, inhabiting solitary cells, with a vow of silence. These stark walls are surrounded by the most magnificent woodland. From here you descend to Swainby and cycle through a string of villages to **Great Broughton**, and then on to **Battersby** and **Kildale**. From here you head east to Commondale and on to **Danby**, where you will find the fourteenth-century Danby Castle and the Moors Centre, the National Park's main information point, housed in an eighteenth-century manor. You now head east through another Eskdale, an idyllically beautiful stretch of the route, as far as **Sleights**. Now you climb through **Ugglebarnby** into the final stretch, which takes you eventually down off the coastal plateau to the sea at **Robin Hood's Bay**. Here the village hides houses and pubs in its many cobbled nooks.

Thirsk   36

National Grid Ref:

🍴 🍺 Old Oak Tree, Golden Fleece, Darrowby Inn, Black Swan, Carpenters' Arms, Sheppards Table

(0.25m) *Doxford House, 73 Front Street, Sowerby, Thirsk, N. Yorks, YO7 1JP*.
Attractive Georgian house over-looking village green. Ideal centre for touring
Grades: ETB 2 Cr, Approv
Tel: 01845 523238 Mrs Proudley.
Rates fr: *£16.00*-£21.00.
Open: All Year (not Xmas)
Beds: 2F 1D 1T
Baths: 4 Ensuite
🛏 🅿 (4) 🍴 🗙 🔚 🛁 ⚘ ⓥ

(0.25m) *Lavender House, 27 Kirkgate, Thirsk, N. Yorks, YO7 1PL*.
Welcoming, comfortable house. Good base for Dales and Moors
Grades: ETB 1 Cr, Comm
Tel: 01845 522224 Mrs Dodds.
Rates fr: *£14.50*-£14.50.
Open: All Year (not Xmas)
Beds: 2F 1S **Baths:** 2 Shared
🛏 🅿 (3) 🍴 🗙 🔚 ⓥ ⚘

(On route) *Brook House, Ingramgate, Thirsk, N. Yorks, YO7 1DD*.
Large private Victorian house set in two acres of gardens
Tel: 01845 522240 Mrs McLauchlan.
Fax no: 01845 523133
Rates fr: *£16.00*-£23.00.
Open: All Year (not Xmas)
Beds: 2D 1T **Baths:** 1 Shared
🛏 🅿 (6) 🗙 🔚 🔙

(0.25m) *8a The Conifers, Ingramgate, Thirsk, N. Yorks, YO7 1DD*.
Large Victorian dower house
Tel: 01845 522179 Mrs Lee.
Rates fr: *£13.50*-£13.50.
Open: All Year
Beds: 1F 1D 1S
Baths: 1 Shared
🛏 🅿 (3) 🗙 🔚 🔙

(0.25m) *Three Tuns Hotel, Market Place, Thirsk, N. Yorks, YO7 1LH*.
Family-run Georgian coaching inn
Grades: ETB 3 Cr, Approv
Tel: 01845 523124 Mrs Robinson.
Rates fr: *£22.50*-£30.00.
Open: All Year
Beds: 3F 6D 2T
Baths: 11 Private
🛏 🅿 (50) 🗙 🗙 🔚 ⓥ ⚘

Pay B&Bs by cash or cheque and be prepared to pay up front.

The lowest *double* rate per person is shown in *italics*.

Sutton-under-Whitestonecliffe   37

National Grid Ref: SE4883

🍴 🍺 Hambleton Inn, Whitestonecliffe Inn

(2m) *High Cleaves, Sutton-under-Whitestonecliffe, Thirsk, N. Yorks, YO7 2QD*.
Magnificent views of York Vale
Tel: 01845 597612 (also fax no) Mrs Haggas.
Rates fr: *£25.00*-£35.00.
Open: All Year
Beds: 1F 1D
Baths: 2 Ensuite
🛏 🅿 (20) 🗙 🔙

Boltby   38

National Grid Ref: SE4986

🍴 🍺 Carpenters' Arms

(0.25m) *Town Pasture Farm, Boltby, Thirsk, N. Yorks, YO7 2DY*.
Actual grid ref: SE494866
Comfortable farmhouse in beautiful village. Central for York/Dales/E Coast
Grades: ETB 2 Cr, Comm
Tel: 01845 537298 Mrs Fountain.
Rates fr: *£16.50*-£17.50.
Open: All Year
Beds: 1F 1T
Baths: 2 Ensuite
🛏 🅿 (3) 🗙 🗙 🔚 ⓥ ⚘

Over Silton   39

National Grid Ref: SE4593

🍴 🍺 Gold Cup Inn

(2m) *Moorfields Farm, Over Silton, Thirsk, N. Yorks, YO7 2LJ*.
Actual grid ref: SE451932
Yorkshire stone farm house close to North York Moors
Tel: 01609 883351 Mrs Goodwin.
Rates fr: *£13.50*-£13.50.
Open: All Year
Beds: 1D 1S
Baths: 1 Shared
🅿 (4) 🗙 🗙 🗙 🔚 ⓥ

(2m) *Thistle Garth, Over Silton, Thirsk, N. Yorks, YO7 2LJ*.
Actual grid ref: SE452932
Large family country house
Tel: 01609 883495 Mrs Martin.
Rates fr: *£14.00*-£14.00.
Open: All Year (not Xmas)
Beds: 2D 1T
Baths: 1 Shared
🛏 (10) 🅿 (4) 🗙 🔚 ⓥ ⚘

Osmotherley   40

National Grid Ref: SE4597

🍴 🍺 Golden Lion, Queen Catherine Hotel

(▲ On route) *Osmotherley Youth Hostel, Cote Ghyll, Osmotherley, Northallerton, North Yorkshire, DL6 3AH*.
Actual grid ref: SE461981
Warden: Ms H Ward.
Tel: 01609 883575
Under 18: £5.95 **Adults:** £8.80
Evening Meals Available (7pm), Family Bunk Rooms, Television, Games Room, Showers, Shop
Surrounded by woodland, the youth hostel is fully modernised with excellent facilities, right on the edge of the North York Moors National Park

(On route) *Quintana House, Back Lane, Osmotherley, Northallerton, N. Yorks, DL6 3BJ*.
Actual grid ref: SE457974
Detached stone cottage with locking stone garage in National Park
Grades: ETB Listed, Comm
Tel: 01609 883258 Dr Bainbridge.
Rates fr: *£18.00*.
Open: All Year (not Xmas)
Beds: 1D 1T
Baths: 1 Shared
🛏 (12) 🅿 (1) 🗙 🗙 🔚 ⓥ ⚘ ⚘

(On route) *Foxton Mill, Osmotherley, Northallerton, N. Yorks, DL6 3PZ*.
Actual grid ref: SE452965
Converted C17th corn mill
Tel: 01609 883377 Mrs Russell.
Rates fr: *£20.00*-£20.00.
Open: All Year (not Xmas)
Beds: 1D 1T
Baths: 1 Private 1 Shared
🛏 (10) 🅿 (6) 🗙 🗙 🗙 🔚 ⓥ ⚘ ⚘

Ingleby Cross   41

National Grid Ref: NZ4500

🍴 🍺 Black Horse, Blue Bell Inn

(2m) *North York Moors Adventure Ctr, Park House, Ingleby Cross, Northallerton, N. Yorks, DL6 3PE*.
Actual grid ref: NZ453995
Comfortable sandstone farmhouse in woodland
Tel: 01609 882571 Mr Bennett.
Rates fr: *£14.00*-£14.00.
Open: All Year (not Xmas)
Beds: 2F 1D 1T 2S
Baths: 2 Shared
🛏 (1) 🅿 (10) 🗙 🗙 🗙 🔚 ⓥ ⚘

(2m) *Blue Bell Inn, Ingleby Cross, Northallerton, N. Yorks, DL6 3NF*.
Friendly village inn
Tel: 01609 882272 Mrs Kinsella.
Rates fr: *£15.00*-£15.00.
Open: All Year
Beds: 1D 4T **Baths:** 5 Ensuite
🛏 🅿 (20) 🗙 ⓥ ⚘ ⚘

Faceby 42

National Grid Ref: NZ4903

(0.25m) *Four Wynds, Whorl Hill, Faceby, Middlesbrough. TS9 7BZ.*
Actual grid ref: NZ487033
Modern, comfortable farmhouse - ideally situated
Tel: **01642 701315** Mr Barnfather.
Rates fr: *£15.00-£15.00.*
Open: All Year
Beds: 1F 1D 1T
Baths: 1 Ensuite 1 Shared
🛇 🅿 (8) ⌿ 🗙 ⏳ ♥ 🕮 ⓥ 🛉 ⚡

Carlton-in-Cleveland 43

National Grid Ref: NZ5004

(0.25m) *The Blackwell Ox, Carlton-in-Cleveland, Stokesley, Middlesbrough. TS9 7DJ.*
Comfortable, family-run, traditional country inn
Tel: **01642 712287**
Mr & Mrs Burton.
Rates fr: *£19.00-£28.50.*
Open: All Year (not Xmas)
Beds: 2F
Baths: 2 Private
🛇 🅿 (50) ⌿ 🗙 ⏳ 🕮 ⓥ

Kirby-in-Cleveland 44

National Grid Ref: NZ5208

(1m) *Dromonby Hall Farm, Busby Lane, Kirby-in-Cleveland, Stokesley, Middlesbrough. TS9 7AP.*
Spacious modern farmhouse
Tel: **01642 712312** Mrs Weighell.
Rates fr: *£15.00-£17.50.*
Open: All Year (not Xmas)
Beds: 1D 2T
Baths: 1 Shared
🛇 (2) 🅿 (6) ⌿ 🗙 🕮 🛉 ⚡

Great Broughton 45

National Grid Ref: NZ5406

🍴 🍺 Bay Horse, Jet Miners, The Wainstones

(0.25m) *Red Hall, Great Broughton, Middlesbrough, N. Yorks, TS9 7ET.*
Actual grid ref: NZ560068
Grades: AA 4 Q
Tel: **01642 712300** (also fax no)
Mrs Richmond.
Rates fr: *£27.50-£30.00.*
Open: All Year
Beds: 1F 2D
Baths: 3 Ensuite
🛇 🅿 (10) ⌿ 🗙 ♥ 🕮 ⓥ 🛉 ⚡
Welcoming, elegant C17th Grade II Listed country house, combining complete modernisation, antique furnishings, walled garden, drinks licence, exquisite views, set in tranquil meadowland on fringe of North York Moors National Park. Ideal walking & touring base and for North Yorkshire Coast. Stabling, tennis

(0.25m) *The Hollies, 98 High Street, Great Broughton, Middlesbrough, N. Yorks, TS9 7HA.*
Actual grid ref: NZ551059
Set in picturesque village close to national park, Captain Cook country
Tel: **01642 710592** (also fax no)
Mrs Scott.
Rates fr: *£15.00-£15.00.*
Open: All Year
Beds: 1F 1D
Baths: 1 Shared
🛇 🅿 (2) ⌿ 🗙 ♥ 🕮 ⓥ 🛉 ⚡

(0.25m) *Ingle Hill, Ingleby Road, Great Broughton, Middlesbrough, N. Yorks, TS9 7ER.*
Actual grid ref: NZ548063
Spectacular views. North Yorkshire moors. Warm welcome. Transport to walks
Tel: **01642 712449**
Mrs Sutcliffe.
Rates fr: *£16.00-£17.50.*
Open: All Year (not Xmas)
Beds: 1F 2D 1T
Baths: 2 Private 1 Shared
🛇 (2) 🅿 (3) ⌿ 🗙 ♥ 🕮 ⓥ 🛉 ⚡

(0.25m) *Hilton House, 52 High Street, Great Broughton, Stokesley, N. Yorks, TS9 7EG.*
Actual grid ref: NZ546063
Walkers' haven in delightful 200-year-old former village bakehouse
Tel: **01642 712526**
Mrs Mead.
Rates fr: *£18.00-£18.00.*
Open: All Year (not Xmas)
Beds: 1D 2T
Baths: 2 Ensuite 1 Shared
🛇 🅿 (3) ⌿ 🗙 ⓥ 🛉 ⚡

Kildale 46

National Grid Ref: NZ6009

(🔺 0.25m) *Kildale Camping Barn, Park Farm, Kildale, Whitby, North Yorkshire*
Actual grid ref: NZ602085
Warden: Mr & Mrs Cook.
Tel: **01629 825650**
Adults: £3.35+
Simple barn, sleeps 12. A Listed building, superbly located on the North York Moors. ADVANCE BOOKING ESSENTIAL

Danby 47

National Grid Ref: NZ7008

🍴 🍺 Duke of Wellington, Moorlands Hotel

(0.25m) *Sycamore House, Danby, Whitby, N. Yorks, YO21 2NW.*
C17th farmhouse. Stunning views
Tel: **01287 660125**
Mr Lowson.
Rates fr: *£16.00-£16.00.*
Open: All Year (not Xmas)
Beds: 1F 1D 1T 1S
Baths: 2 Shared
🛇 🅿 (6) ⌿ 🗙 🗙 🕮 ⓥ 🛉 ⚡

The *lowest* **single** rate *is shown in* **bold.**

(1m) *Botton Grove Farm, Danby Head, Danby, Whitby, N. Yorks, YO21 2NH.*
Stunning scenery. Large, comfortable, stone-built farmhouse. Working sheep farm
Tel: **01287 660284**
Mrs Tait.
Rates fr: *£15.00-£15.00.*
Open: May to Feb
Beds: 1D 1T 2S
Baths: 1 Shared
🛇 🅿 (3) 🗙 ♥ 🕮 ⓥ 🛉 ⚡

Ainthorpe 48

National Grid Ref:

🍴 🍺 Fox & Hounds Inn

(0.25m) *Fox & Hounds Inn, Ainthorpe, Danby, Whitby, N. Yorks, YO21 2LD.*
C16th coaching inn
Tel: **01287 660218**
Mrs Dickinson.
Rates fr: *£18.00-£20.00.*
Open: All Year
Beds: 2F 4D 2T 1S
Baths: 2 Shared
🛇 🅿 (40) 🗙 🕮 ⓥ 🛉 ⚡

Glaisdale 49

National Grid Ref: NZ7603

🍴 🍺 Angler's Rest

(On route) *Arncliffe Arms Hotel, Glaisdale, Whitby, N. Yorks, YO21 2QL.*
Actual grid ref: NZ782055
Tel: **01947 897209**
Mr Westwood.
Rates fr: *£15.00-£15.00.*
Open: All Year
Beds: 1F 2D 2T 1S
Baths: 2 Shared
🛇 🅿 ⌿ ♥ 🗙 🕮 ⓥ 🛉 ⚡
Curry lovers - a must. Romantic area along River Esk close to 'Beggars Bridge', 1 min from railway station. Entertainment if required. Car park Coast to Coast Packhorse drop off / pick up point

(1m) *Red House Farm, Glaisdale, Whitby, N. Yorks, YO21 2PZ.*
Actual grid ref: NZ772049
Listed Georgian farmhouse, tastefully refurbished. Walks from doorstep. Friendly animals
Tel: **01947 897242** (also fax no)
Mr Spashett.
Rates fr: *£20.00-£20.00.*
Open: All Year
Beds: 1F 2D 1T
Baths: 4 Private 1 Shared
🛇 🅿 (4) ⌿ 🗙 ♥ 🕮 ⓥ 🛉 ⚡

(1m) **Hollins Farm**, Glaisdale, Whitby, N. Yorks, YO21 2PZ.
Actual grid ref: NZ753042
Comfortable farmhouse B&B; bedrooms have tea/coffee, H&C, TV, sitting room, conservatory
Tel: **01947 897516**
Mrs Mortimer.
Rates fr: £15.00-£13.00.
Open: All Year (not Xmas)
Beds: 1F 1D 1T 1S
🛏 🅿 🛒 🍴 Ⓥ ✦

(1m) **Egton Banks Farm**, Glaisdale, Whitby, N. Yorks, YO21 2QP.
Lovely old farmhouse in secluded valley, pretty decor. Warm welcome
Grades: ETB 1 Cr, Comm
Tel: **01947 897289**
Richardson.
Rates fr: £15.00-£16.00.
Open: Easter to October
Beds: 1F 1T 1D
🛏 (1) 🅿 (6) ⚿ 🗆 ✗ 🖿 Ⓥ ♿ ✦

(0.25m) **The Grange**, Glaisdale, Whitby, N. Yorks, YO21 2QW.
Country manor house
Tel: **01947 897241** Mrs Kelly.
Rates fr: £16.00-£16.00.
Open: Feb to Nov
Beds: 2D 1T
Baths: 1 Ensuite 2 Private 1 Shared
🛏 (10) 🅿 (6) 🗆 🍴 ✗ 🖿 Ⓥ

(0.25m) **Sycamore Dell**, Glaisdale, Whitby, N. Yorks, YO21 2PZ.
Actual grid ref: NZ769047
Comfortable converted C17th barn
Tel: **01947 897345**
Mr & Mrs Hogben.
Rates fr: £15.00-£15.00.
Open: Mar to Oct
Beds: 1F 2D 2S
Baths: 1 Shared
🛏 (11) 🅿 (3) ⚿ 🗆 🖿 ♿ ✦

(On route) **The Railway Station**, Glaisdale, Whitby, N. Yorks, YO21 2QL.
Working railway station, Esk Valley
Tel: **01947 897533**
Messrs Silkstone.
Rates fr: £15.00.
Open: All Year (not Xmas)
Beds: 1T
Baths: 1 Ensuite
🅿 (2) 🗆 ✗ 🖿 Ⓥ

Egton Bridge   50

National Grid Ref: NZ8005

(1m) **Postgate Inn**, Egton Bridge, Whitby, N. Yorks, YO21 1UX.
As seen in 'Heartbeat' on TV!
Tel: **01947 895241**
Mr Mead.
Rates fr: £18.00-£18.00.
Open: All Year
Beds: 1F 4D 1T 1S
Baths: 1 Private 2 Shared
🛏 🅿 🗆 🍴 ✗ 🖿 Ⓥ ♿

(1m) **Horseshoe Hotel**, Egton Bridge, Whitby, N. Yorks, YO21 1XE.
Comfortable, family-run riverside hotel
Tel: **01947 895245**
Mr & Mrs Mullins.
Rates fr: £19.00-£26.00.
Open: All Year (not Xmas)
Beds: 4D 2T
Baths: 3 Private 3 Shared
🛏 🅿 🗆 ✗ 🖿 Ⓥ ♿

Grosmont   51

National Grid Ref: NZ8205

🍽 🍺 The Wheatsheaf, The Horseshoe

(On route) **Eskdale**, Grosmont, Whitby, N. Yorks, YO22 5PT.
Actual grid ref: NZ825054
Detached Georgian house
Grades: ETB Listed, Comm
Tel: **01947 895385** Mrs Counsell.
Rates fr: £16.00-£16.00.
Open: Easter to Nov
Beds: 2D 2S
Baths: 1 Shared
🛏 🅿 (4) 🗆 🍴 🖿 Ⓥ ♿ ✦

(On route) **Woodside**, Front Street, Grosmont, Whitby, N. Yorks, YO22 5PF.
Actual grid ref: NZ830052
Friendly family home. Delightful views
Tel: **01947 895205** Mrs Beesley.
Rates fr: £16.00-£20.00.
Open: March to Nov
Beds: 2T
Baths: 1 Shared
🛏 🅿 (2) ⚿ 🗆 🍴 🖿 Ⓥ ♿ ✦

Sleights   52

National Grid Ref: NZ8607

🍽 🍺 Shepherd's Purse, The Plough, Granby Inn

(0.25m) **Ryedale House**, 154-8 Coach Road, Sleights, Whitby, N. Yorks, YO22 5EQ.
Tel: **01947 810534** Mrs Beale.
Rates fr: £17.50.
Open: Mar to Oct
Beds: 2D 1T **Baths:** 3 Private
🅿 (3) ⚿ 🗆 🖿 Ⓥ
National Park 'Heartbeat' country 3.5 miles Whitby. Relaxing house with high standards, private facilities. garden, magnificent views, extensive traditional/vegetarian menu. Non smokers only. No pets

(0.25m) **Inkwells Guest House**, 1 Eskdaleside, Sleights, Whitby, N. Yorks, YO22 5EP.
Actual grid ref: NZ865068
Stone-built converted village school
Tel: **01947 810959** (also fax no)
Mrs Thompson.
Rates fr: £16.50-£16.50.
Open: All Year
Beds: 2D 1T 1S **Baths:** 1 Shared
🛏 (5) 🅿 (3) ⚿ 🗆 🍴 🖿 Ⓥ ✦

(0.25m) **Inkwells Guest House**, 1 Eskdaleside, Sleights, Whitby, N. Yorks.
Actual grid ref: NZ865068
Stone-built converted village school
Tel: **01947 810959** (also fax no)
Mrs Thompson.
Rates fr: £16.50-£16.50.
Open: All Year
Beds: 2D 1T 1S
Baths: 1 Shared
🛏 (5) 🅿 (3) ⚿ 🗆 🍴 🖿 Ⓥ ✦

(0.25m) **Fernbank**, 11 Carr Hill Lane, Sleights, Whitby, N. Yorks, YO21 1RS.
Large family home, superb surroundings
Tel: **01947 811320** Mrs Grindle.
Rates fr: £15.00-£20.00.
Open: All Year (not Xmas)
Beds: 2D
Baths: 2 Ensuite
🅿 (2) ⚿ 🗆 🖿.

Fylingthorpe   53

National Grid Ref: NZ9404

🍽 🍺 Fylingdale Inn

(2m) **Croft Farm**, Fylingthorpe, Whitby, N. Yorks, YO22 4PW.
Farmhouse & cottage. Panoramic views
Grades: ETB Listed, High Comm
Tel: **01947 880231**
Mrs Featherstone.
Rates fr: £17.50-£17.50.
Open: Easter to Oct
Beds: 1F 1D 1S
Baths: 1 Private 1 Shared
🛏 (5) 🅿 (4) ⚿ 🗆 🖿 Ⓥ ♿ ✦

Robin Hood's Bay   54

National Grid Ref: NZ9504

🍽 🍺 Bay Hotel, Dolphin Inn, Flyingdale Inn, Grosvenor Hotel, Victoria Hotel

(1m) **The White Owl**, Station Road, Robin Hood's Bay, Whitby, N. Yorks, YO22 4RL.
Large interesting private house, central location but near cliff edge
Tel: **01947 880879**
Mr & Mrs Higgins.
Rates fr: £17.00-£17.00.
Open: All Year
Beds: 1F 1D 1T
Baths: 3 Private
🛏 🅿 (3) 🗆 🍴 🖿 Ⓥ ♿ ✦

(1m) **Victoria Hotel**, Robin Hood's Bay, Whitby, N. Yorks, YO22 4RL.
Victorian hotel overlooking sea. Ideal centre for walking holiday
Grades: ETB 2 Cr, Comm
Tel: **01947 880205**
Mr Gibson.
Rates fr: £28.00-£25.00.
Open: All Year (not Xmas)
Beds: 2F 6D 2T 1S
Baths: 9 Ensuite 2 Shared
🛏 🅿 (14) ✗ 🖿 Ⓥ ♿ ✦

(1m) *Gilders Green, Raw, Robin Hood's Bay, Whitby, N. Yorks, YO22 4PP*.
C17th farm cottage on working sheep farm. Bedtime drink
Rates fr: *£15.00-£16.00*.
Open: Easter to Oct
Beds: 1F
Baths: 1 Shared
⛺ 🅿 🗕 ⵍ

(1m) *Meadowfield, Mount Pleasant North, Robin Hood's Bay, Whitby, N. Yorks, YO22 4RE*.
Victorian house, in quiet road. Clean, comfortable, plenty of food
Tel: **01947 880564** Mrs Luker.
Rates fr: *£14.50-£20.00*.
Open: All Year
Beds: 2D 2T 1S
Baths: 1 Private 1 Shared
ⵍ 🗕 🖳 Ⓥ 🔋 ⵍ

Pay B&Bs by
cash or cheque and
be prepared to
pay up front.

(1m) *Rosegarth, Thorpe Lane, Robin Hood's Bay, Whitby, N. Yorks, YO22 4RN*.
Friendly home. Ideal touring area for moor and coastal villages
Tel: **01947 880578** Mrs Stubbs.
Rates fr: *£16.00-£17.00*.
Open: Easter to Nov
Beds: 1D 1T 1S   **Baths:** 1 Shared
⛺ (11) 🅿 (4) 🗕 ⵍ 🖳 ⵍ

(1m) *Moor View House, Robin Hood's Bay, Whitby, N. Yorks, YO22 4RA*.
Double-fronted villa overlooking countryside
Tel: **01947 880576**
Mrs Eatough.
Rates fr: *£17.00*.
Open: Easter to Oct
Beds: 1F 3D 2T
Baths: 1 Ensuite 3 Shared
⛺ 🅿 (y) ✕ 🖳

(1m) *Muir Lea Stores, Robin Hood's Bay, Whitby, N. Yorks, YO22 4SF*.
Actual grid ref: NZ952052
C18th smugglers' retreat
Tel: **01947 880316**
Mrs Leaf.
Rates fr: *£15.00-£17.00*.
Open: All Year
Beds: 4D
🗕 ⵍ 🖳 ⵍ

(1m) *Devon House, Station Road, Robin Hood's Bay, Whitby, N. Yorks, YO22 4RL*.
Actual grid ref: NZ952054
Modern, clean, comfortable Victorian house
Tel: **01947 880197** Mrs Duncalfe.
Rates fr: *£15.00-£20.00*.
Open: All Year (not Xmas)
Beds: 1F 1D 1T 1S
Baths: 2 Shared
⛺ 🅿 ⵍ 🗕 🖳 Ⓥ 🔋 ⵍ

(1m) *Wayfarer, Robin Hood's Bay, Whitby, N. Yorks, YO22 4RL*.
Actual grid ref: NZ952067
Cliff top at finish of Dales Side to Side Cycle Tour
Tel: **01947 880240** Mrs Gray.
Rates fr: *£14.00-£16.00*.
Open: All Year
Beds: 1F 4D 2T 1S
Baths: 3 Ensuite 2 Shared
⛺ 🅿 (5) 🗕 ⵍ 🖳 🔋 ⵍ

All details shown
are as supplied
by B&B owners in
Autumn 1997.

CTC Western Isles Cycle Tour

The **Western Isles Cycle Tour** is a 200-mile tour designed by the Cyclists' Touring Club over the undulating terrain of the great, remote archipelago off Scotland's north west coast, the Scottish heartland of Gaelic language and culture. Starting at **Stornoway** on the Isle of Lewis, you will tour **North Lewis** before heading south through **Harris** and catching the ferry to the diminutive island of **Berneray**, and then to **North Uist**. Having travelled from the northern to the southern end of the road which links North Uist, **Benbecula** and **South Uist**, you take the ferry to **Barra** for a tour around that island. For most of the route you will be on the islands' main roads, but in this sparsey populated region, traffic is very light – any difficulty you encounter is more likely to be due to strong winds in an austere landscape that is virtually without trees. Outside Stornoway road signs are in Gaelic only – you are advised to equip yourself with a bilingual map before beginning the tour. You are advised also to avoid arriving at or departing from accommodation in Lewis, Harris, North Uist and Benbecula on a Sunday.

A **guide** pamphlet to the route is available from the Cyclists' Touring Club. You must become a member to get it. Contact them at Cotterell House, 69 Meadrow, Godalming, Surrey GU7 3HS, tel 01483 417217, fax 01483 426994, e-mail cycling@ctc.org.uk.

Maps: Ordnance Survey 1:50,000 Landranger series: 8, 14, 18, 22, 31. Place names on these maps are in Gaelic only: it is probably a good idea to get hold of a bilingual map also – these are available from Tourist Information Centres in the Western Isles if you have not got one before you arrive.

Tourist information centres: Stornoway, 01851 703088. **Tarbert**, 01859 502011 (Easter to Oct). **Lochmaddy**, 01876 500321 (Easter to Oct). **Lochboisdale**, 01878 700286 (Easter to Oct).

Transport: Ferry crossings connect Stornoway with Ullapool; Tarbert and Lochmaddy with Uig on the Isle of Ske; and Lochboisdale and Castlebay with Oban. Ullapool can be reached by bus from Inverness – you will need to book in advance to take bicycles on the bus; Oban by rail from Glasgow Queen Street and Edinburgh.

Lewis Stornoway   1

National Grid Ref: NB4232

¦●¦ ◗■ Caledonia Hotel, Seaforth Hotel, County Hotel

(On route) **Arnside**, 12 Churchill Drive, Stornoway, Isle of Lewis, HS1 2NP.
Friendly accommodation. Backpackers welcome; 5 - 10 mins' walk from ferry. Town centre 5 mins
Tel: **01851 704893** Mrs Campbell.
Rates fr: *£14.00*-**£14.00**.
Open: All Year (not Xmas)
Beds: 1T **Baths:** 1 Shared
🛏 🅿 (1) 🖵 📖 📋 🋠 ✦

The lowest *double* rate per person is shown in *italics*.

The *lowest* **single** rate *is shown in* **bold.**

(0.25m) **13 Garden Road**, Stornoway, Isle of Lewis, HS1 2QJ.
5 minutes from ferry, comfortable family home
Tel: **01851 705315** Mrs Carmichael.
Rates fr: *£15.00*-**£15.00**.
Open: All Year (not Xmas)
Beds: 1F
🛏 🖵 🋠 📖

(0.25m) **7 Garden Road**, Stornoway, Isle of Lewis, HS1 2QN.
Very comfortable family home
Tel: **01851 702768** Mrs Scott.
Rates fr: *£15.00*-**£15.00**.
Open: Easter to 1st Oct
Beds: 1D 1T **Baths:** 2 Shared
✄ 🖵 📖 📋

Lewis Newmarket   2

National Grid Ref: NB4235

(0.25m) **Lathamor**, Bakers Road, Newmarket, Isle of Lewis. HS2 0EA.
Spacious family home with panoramic views
Grades: ETB Listed, Comm
Tel: **01851 706093** (also fax no)
Mrs Ferguson.
Rates fr: *£15.00*-**£15.00**.
Open: All Year
Beds: 1F 1D 1T 1S
Baths: 2 Shared
🛏 🅿 (4) 🖵 🋠 ✕ 📖 📋 🟊 ✦

Bringing children with you? Always ask for any special rates.

Stornoway to Harris

Stornoway, where you begin, is the only substantial town in the islands – make sure you get any necessities here before setting off. North Lewis consists mainly of the Black Moor peat bog, from which islanders have for centuries made a living by cutting peat, which forms due to a high degree of acidity in the soil and is used as fuel. The first stretch of the way leads to **Port of Ness** at the northern end of the archipelago, where stands the Butt of Lewis Lighthouse. If you can only imagine this phrase spoken in soft tones by a voice with a Home Counties accent, you've been listening to the shipping forecast on Radio 4. Below the lighthouse large colonies of sea birds nest on the cliffs; you may also spot seals.

Heading back down the west coast, at **Arnol** you will find the Arnol Blackhouse Museum. Blackhouses were traditional croft homesteads blackened by soot from the peat fire burning in the centre; this preserved and restored example shows what island life was like until less than fifty years ago. **Carloway** is situated on the banks of an idyllic loch, and has gorgeous views of the mountains to the south; here Carloway Broch, an excellently preserved Pictish fort, rises from an outcrop. The **Callanish** Standing Stones, dating from around 2000 BC in Neolithic times, occupy a stunning setting against the backdrop of East Loch Roag. After returning to Stornoway you head out over the more mountainous terrain of South Lewis, through **Balallan** and Aribruach.

Lewis Laxdale 3

National Grid Ref: NB4234

(0.25m) *2 Laxdale, Laxdale, Isle of Lewis.* HS2 0DS.
100-year-old house, remodernised
Tel: **01851 702975**
Mrs MacKenzie.
Rates fr: *£14.00-£14.00.*
Open: Easter to Nov
Beds: 1F 2T
Baths: 2 Shared
⛄ (1) 🅿 (5) 🗖 🖰 ✕ 🎹 Ⅴ

Lewis Barvas (Barabhas) 4

National Grid Ref: NB3649

(0.25m) *Rockvilla, Barvas (Barabhas), Isle of Lewis.* HS2 0QN.
Scotland B&B. Quiet location overlooking fields on to the sea
Grades: ETB 2 Cr, Comm
Tel: **01851 840286** Mrs MacDonald.
Rates fr: *£15.00-£15.00.*
Open: All Year
Beds: 1F 1T 1D 1S
Baths: 1 Ensuite 1 Private 1 Shared
⛄ 🅿 ✍ 🗖 🖰 ✕ 🎹 Ⅴ ♠ ✦

Lewis South Galson (Gabhsann) 5

National Grid Ref: NB4358

(1m) *Galson Farm Guest House, Gabhsunn Bho Dheas, South Galson (Gabhsann), Isle of Lewis.* HS2 0SH.
Luxuriously restored C18th farmhouse, 18-acre working croft
Tel: **01851 850492** Mr Russell.
Rates fr: *£24.00-£29.00.*
Open: All Year
Beds: 1D 2T
Baths: 3 Private 1 Shared
⛄ 🅿 (8) ✍ 🗖 🖰 ✕ 🎹 Ⅴ

Lewis Port of Ness (Port Nis) 6

National Grid Ref: NB5363

(0.25m) *Cliff House, Port of Ness (Port Nis), Isle of Lewis.* HS2 0XA.
Cliff house above sandy beach
Tel: **01851 810278** Mrs Morrison.
Rates fr: *£16.00-£16.00.*
Open: Easter to Oct
Beds: 1D 2T **Baths:** 1 Shared
⛄ 🅿 🗖 🖰 ✕ 🎹 Ⅴ

(0.25m) *Harbour View Guest House, Port of Ness (Port Nis), Isle of Lewis.* HS2 0XA.
Characterful accommodation in beautiful location
Grades: ETB 1 Cr, Comm
Tel: **01851 810735**
Mr & Mrs Barber.
Rates fr: *£17.00-£17.00.*
Open: All Year (not Xmas)
Beds: 1D 1T **Baths:** 1 Shared
⛄ (8) 🅿 (3) ✍ 🗖 ✕ 🎹 Ⅴ ♠

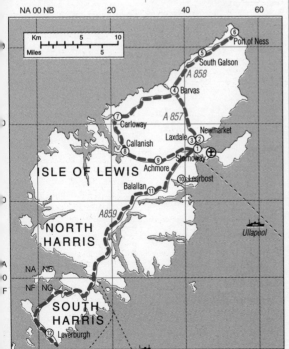

All cycleways are popular: you are well-advised to book ahead

Through Harris to Leverburgh

Really part of the same island as Lewis, but psychologically separated by the mountains between, Harris offers the Western Isles' most breathtaking scenery. You enter Harris as you cross the Vigadale River where it flows into sensational Loch Seaforth, after which the road winds its way below the Clisham, the islands' highest peak at 2619 feet. At the isthmus of **Tarbert** you pass from North Harris into South Harris, where the road down the west coast is a treat – magnificent beaches against the backdrop of vast tracts of *machair* (dunes covered with grass and wild flowers), with the most stunning views across to the mountains of North Harris. The end of the road is Rodel, where sixteenth-century St Clement's Church is the historic burial place of the MacLeods of Harris. Abandoned after the reformation, it feels like a time warp in this most Protestant of places. From here you double back to **Leverburgh** to get the boat.

(0.25m) *Eisdean, 12 Fivepenny, Port of Ness (Port Nis), Isle of Lewis. HS2 0XG.*
Modern comfortable crofthouse, coastal location
Grades: ETB Comm. Listed
Tel: **01851 810240** Ms Macleod.
Fax no: 01851 810488
Rates fr: *£17.00-£17.00*.
Open: All Year
Beds: 1F 1T 1S
Baths: 1 Shared
ᵺ ₽ (4) ⛺ ⊁ ✕ ▥ Ⓥ ♠ ⚡

Pay B&Bs by cash or cheque and be prepared to pay up front.

All cycleways are popular: you are well-advised to book ahead

---

Lewis Carloway   7

National Grid Ref: NB2042

(▲ 1m) *Garenin Youth Hostel, Carloway, Isle of Lewis, HS2 9AL.*
Actual grid ref: NB193442
Under 18: £3.85 **Adults:** £4.65
Self-catering Facilities
Old blackhouse restored by the Garenin Trust, in a village set in a peaceful bay on the rugged west coast of Lewis. No advance bookings accepted

Lewis Callanish (Calanis) 8

National Grid Ref: NB2133

(0.25m) *Eshcol Guest House, 21 Breascleit, Callanish (Calanis), Isle of Lewis. HS2 9ED.*
Ensuite facilities. Callanish Stones nearby
Grades: ETB Listed, 3 Cr, High Comm
Tel: **01851 621357**
Mrs MacArthur.
Rates fr: *£25.00-£27.00*.
Open: Mar to Oct
Beds: 1D 2T **Baths:** 3 Private
ᵺ (7) ₽ (12) ⊁ ⛺ ⛅ ✕ ▥ Ⓥ ♠

Lewis Achmore (Achamor) 9

National Grid Ref: NB3128

(0.25m) *Lochview, 35b Achmore, Achmore (Achamor), Lochs, Isle of Lewis. HS2 9DU.*
Ideally situated for touring island
Grades: ETB 1 Cr, Comm
Tel: **01851 860205**
Mrs Golder.
Rates fr: *£15.00-£15.00*.
Open: All Year (not Xmas)
Beds: 2D 1T
ᵺ ₽ (6) ⛺ ⛅ ✕ ▥ Ⓥ

Lewis Leurbost (Liurbost) 10

National Grid Ref: NB3725

(2m) *Glen House, 77 Liurbost, Lochs, Leurbost (Liurbost), Isle of Lewis. HS2 9NL.*
Tel: **01851 860241** Mrs Reid.
Rates fr: *£18.50-£18.50*.
Open: All Year
Beds: 1T 1D **Baths:** 1 Private
ᵺ ₽ ⛺ ✕ ▥ ⅙ Ⓥ ♠ ⚡
Quiet country residence overlooking scenic sea loch, offering high standard of accommodation & food & guest lounge

---

Lewis
Balallan (Baile Ailein) 11

National Grid Ref: NB2920

(0.25m) *Penamber, 55 Balallan, Balallan (Baile Ailein), Lochs, Isle of Lewis. HS2 9PT.*
Ideal base Harris/Lewis, fly fishing
Tel: **01851 830351**
Mrs Smith.
Rates fr: *£14.00*.
Open: Apr to Oct
Beds: 1D 1T
Baths: 1 Ensuite 1 Shared
ᵺ ₽ (4) ⛺ ⛅ ✕ ▥ Ⓥ ♠ ⚡

(0.25m) *Clearview, 44 Balallan, Balallan (Baile Ailein), Isle of Lewis. HS2 9PT.*
Modern bungalow in elevated location
Grades: ETB 1 Cr, Comm
Tel: **01851 830472**
Mr & Mrs Mackay.
Rates fr: *£15.00-£15.00*.
Open: All Year (not Xmas)
Beds: 1F 1D
Baths: 1 Shared
ᵺ ₽ (6) ⅙ ⛺ ✕ ▥.

Harris Leverburgh   12

National Grid Ref: NG0186

(0.25m) *Caberfeidh House, Leverburgh, Isle of Harris, HS5 3TL.*
Large house in village centre
Grades: ETB 2 Cr, Comm
Tel: **01895 520276**
Mrs MacKenzie.
Rates fr: *£15.00-£15.00*.
Open: All Year
Beds: 1F 1D 1T
Baths: 1 Private 1 Shared
ᵺ ₽ ⅙ ⛺ ✕ ▥ Ⓥ ♠ ⚡

(0.25m) *St Kilda House, Leverburgh, Isle of Harris, HS5 3UB.*
Former C19th schoolhouse, overlooking sea
Grades: ETB 3 Cr, High Comm
Tel: **01859 520419** Miss Massey.
Rates fr: *£25.00-£35.00*.
Open: All Year
Beds: 1D 1T
Baths: 2 Ensuite
ᵺ (10) ₽ ⅙ ⛺ ✕ ▥ Ⓥ ♠

Isle of Berneray   13

National Grid Ref: NF9282

(▲ On route) *Berneray Youth Hostel, Isle of Berneray, North Uist, HS6 5BQ.*
Actual grid ref: NF932814
Under 18: £3.85
Adults: £4.65
Self-catering Facilities
On beach overlooking the Sound of Harris. No advance bookings accepted

---

North Uist Lochmaddy 14

National Grid Ref: NF9168

(▲ 0.25m) *Lochmaddy Youth Hostel, Ostram House, Lochmaddy, North Uist, HS6 5AE.*
Actual grid ref: NF918687
Tel: 01876 500368
Under 18: £4.95
Adults: £6.10
Self-catering Facilities
Sea bathing, archaeological excavations, Highland Games, local history and birdwatching are among the attractions of North Uist

North Uist
Carinish (Cairinis) 15

National Grid Ref: NF8259

†◯ ◁ Westford Inn, Langash Lodge Hotel

(0.25m) *Bonnieview, 19 Cairinis, Carinish (Cairinis), Lochmaddy, Isle of North Uist, HS6 5HN.*
Comfortable crofthouse with lovely views and Highland cattle, bike hire
Grades: ETB 3 Cr, High Comm
Tel: 01876 580211
Mrs Morrison.
Rates fr: *£18.00-£22.00.*
Open: All Year
Beds: 2D **Baths:** 2 Ensuite
🅿 ⅍ ▭ ✕ ▥ Ⅴ ▯

Benbecula Creagorry
(Creag Ghoraidh) 16

National Grid Ref: NF7948

†◯ ◁ Dark Island Hotel, Orosay Inn

(0.25m) *Dunfarquhar, Creag Ghoraidh, Creagorry (Creag Ghoraidh), Isle of Benbecula. HS7 5PY.*
Comfortable croft house
Tel: 01870 602227
Mrs MacSween.
Rates fr: *£16.00-£16.00.*
Open: All Year (not Xmas)
Beds: 3F 1T **Baths:** 1 Shared
🐾 (7) 🅿 (12) ▭ ✕ ▥ Ⅴ ⅙

South Uist Howmore 17

National Grid Ref: NF7536

(▲ 0.5m) *Howmore Youth Hostel, Howmore, South Uist, HS8 5SH.*
Actual grid ref: NF757265
Under 18: £3.85
Adults: £4.65
Self-catering Facilities
Small crofthouse, handy for the magnificent, peaceful island beaches. Good hillwalking. Loch Druidibeg nature reserve is near the hostel. No advance bookings accepted

Leverburgh to Lochboisdale

Benbecula is the psychological dividing line between North and South in the Western Isles chain: Lewis, Harris and North Uist are Great Britain's most fervently Protestant region (don't expect lively pubs, nor to shop or sail on a Sunday); in the Catholic islands of South Uist and Barra, the flavour of life is more relaxed. North Uist and Benbecula are low-lying islands almost swamped by lochs; at **Lochmaddy** on North Uist the Taigh Chearsabhagh museum and arts centre, with a cafe upstairs, occupies a converted eighteenth-century house. A small granite statue of *Our Lady of the Isles* at the roadside below Rueval Hill marks your arrival on South Uist. The road takes you through the rich *machair* landscape behind the seamless sandy beach of the island's west side. Towards the south of the island, the route passes close to a cairn that marks the birthplace of Flora MacDonald, the local heroine who helped 'Bonnie' Prince Charles Edward Stuart escape from Benbecula to Skye after his final defeat at Culloden, at the hands of the Duke of Cumberland, the end of the Jacobite Rebellion. The road culminates at **Lochboisdale** for the ferry.

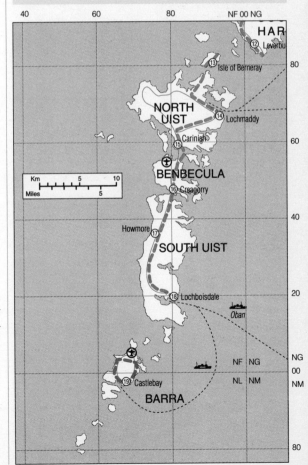

The Isle of Barra

This wonderful little island is a microcosm of the Western Isles, with fine sandy beaches, *machair*, mountains, lochans and Neolithic remains packed within its circumference. The ferry arrives at the diminutive town of Castlebay, where twelfth-century Kisimul Castle (restored earlier this century), the ancestral seat of the MacNeil clan, sits on a rocky islet in the bay. The A888 road will take you around a complete circuit of the island, with superb views on all sides.

South Uist Lochboisdale 18

National Grid Ref: NF7919

†○† ◫ Borrodale Hotel, Lochboisdale Hotel

(0.25m) ***Brae Lea House,*** *Lasgair, Lochboisdale, Isle of South Uist, HS8 5TH.*
Modern bungalow, near ferry terminal
Grades: ETB 3 Cr, Comm
Tel: 01878 700497 (also fax no)
Mrs Murray.
Rates fr: *£22.50-***£25.00**.
Open: All Year **Beds:** 1F 2T 2D 1S
Baths: 6 Ensuite
ॐ ▣ ☐ ㄱ Ⅲ ᵶ Ⅴ ᵢ ⁄

(0.25m) ***Kilchoan Bay,*** *445 Loch Baghasdail, Lochboisdale, Isle of South Uist, HS8 5TN.*
Comfortable, renovated croft house
Tel: 01878 700517 Mrs MacDonald.
Rates fr: *£14.00-***£14.00**.
Open: All Year
Beds: 1D 1T **Baths:** 2 Shared
ॐ ▣ ☐ ㄱ Ⅲ Ⅴ

Barra Castlebay 19

National Grid Ref: NL6698

†○† ◫ Craigard Hotel

(0.25m) ***Grianamul,*** *Bagh a Chasteil, Castlebay, Isle of Barra, HS9 5XD.*
Recently refurbished, near ferry
Tel: 01871 810416
Mrs MacNeil.
Rates fr: *£18.00-***£18.00**.
Open: All Year (not Xmas)
Beds: 1F 1D 1T
Baths: 3 Ensuite
ॐ ▣ ⅃ ☐ Ⅲ.

(0.5m) ***123 Craigston,*** *Castlebay, Isle of Barra, HS9 5UP.*
Good Scottish cooking, comfortable accommodation
Tel: 01871 810688 Mrs Maclean.
Rates fr: *£15.00-***£15.00**.
Open: All Year
Beds: 1F 2T 1D
Baths: 1 Ensuite 2 Shared
ॐ ▣ ☐ ㄱ ✕ Ⅲ. Ⅴ ᵢ ⁄

Sustrans
ROUTES FOR PEOPLE

Sustrans is a charity which for two decades has created traffic free paths for walkers, cyclists and people with disabilities. In 1995 the Millennium Commission awarded Sustrans £42.5 million towards the development of an 8,000-mile National Cycle Network.

National Cycle Network

The National Cycle Network offers a genuine alternative to the motor car by running through towns and cities, and linking urban centres to the countryside with high quality, signposted routes. It will pass within 2 miles of over 20 million people and is scheduled for completion in 2005, with 3,000 miles to be completed by June 2000.

Safe Routes to Schools

This project, which will develop networks of walking and cycling routes around schools, has been so successful that it has inspired many similar initiatives. Sustrans produce a range of materials to help you get a scheme off the ground in your area.

Sustrans Information Service

Sustrans publish and stock a range of maps, leaflets, information sheets and technical publications. For a free catalogue with further information about Sustrans and the National Cycle Network, and details on how to become a supporter, please contact the Sustrans Information Service, PO Box 21, Bristol BS99 2HA, tel 0117-929 0888, or surf the Web and visit us at **www.sustrans.org.uk**.

CTC
Cycling for All

The CTC is the biggest, longest established and most influential British cycling organisation. No one else can claim to be as important to individual cyclists or to the whole field of on- and off-road cycling as the CTC.

The CTC was formed in 1878. Cycling was in its infancy, was a pastime for the wealthy, and the CTC fought to defend cyclists' rights in Edwardian Britain.

More than 100 years later, we're still supporting our 60,000 members and affiliates and working relentlessly to see that on-road cyclists have safe, scenic and civilised roads to ride on, and off-road cyclists have their rights of way kept open. Our members are commuter cyclists, committed long-distance tourists, addicted mountain bikers, mums with cycle-carried kids in child-seats on the pillion, increasing numbers of road-racers, recumbent enthusiasts - they all cycle, and they all recognise that CTC membership is essential to their day-to-day peace of mind, crucial to lobbying for better facilities for cyclists throughout Britain.

Why join? If you ride a bike, you're not immortal, and can't defy gravity, you need CTC membership.

Contact us at CTC, Cotterell House, 69 Meadrow, Godalming, Surrey GU7 3HS, tel 01483 417217, fax 01483 426994, e-mail **cycling@ctc.org.uk**. Visit us on the Web at **www.ctc.org.uk**.

NOT LISTED IN STILWELL'S?

Do you know of a B&B that should be listed in these pages, but isn't? Use this form to recommend the B&B, telling us briefly why you think it merits inclusion.

I nominate the following B&B for inclusion in next year's edition of Stilwell's Britain: Bed & Breakfast/Cycleway Companion.

B&B Owner's Name ....

B&B Address ....

....

B&B Tel No ....

Reasons for Nomination ....

....

....

Nominated by ....

Nominee's Address ....

Send this form to:
Britain: B&B, Stilwell Publishing Ltd, The Courtyard,
59 Charlotte Road, Shoreditch, London, EC2A 3QT.

NOT LISTED IN STILWELL'S?

Do you know of a B&B that should be listed in these pages, but isn't? Use this form to recommend the B&B, telling us briefly why you think it merits inclusion.

I nominate the following B&B for inclusion in next year's edition of Stilwell's Britain: Bed & Breakfast/Cycleway Companion.

B&B Owner's Name ....

B&B Address ....

....

B&B Tel No ....

Reasons for Nomination ....

....

....

Nominated by ....

Nominee's Address ....

Send this form to:
**Britain: B&B, Stilwell Publishing Ltd, The Courtyard,
59 Charlotte Road, Shoreditch, London, EC2A 3QT.**

NOT LISTED IN STILWELL'S?

Do you know of a B&B that should be listed in these pages, but isn't? Use this form to recommend the B&B, telling us briefly why you think it merits inclusion.

I nominate the following B&B for inclusion in next year's edition of Stilwell's Britain: Bed & Breakfast/Cycleway Companion.

B&B Owner's Name ....

B&B Address ....

....

B&B Tel No ....

Reasons for Nomination ....

....

....

Nominated by ....

Nominee's Address ....

Send this form to:
**Britain: B&B, Stilwell Publishing Ltd, The Courtyard,
59 Charlotte Road, Shoreditch, London, EC2A 3QT.**

NOT LISTED IN STILWELL'S?

Do you know of a B&B that should be listed in these pages, but isn't? Use this form to recommend the B&B, telling us briefly why you think it merits inclusion.

I nominate the following B&B for inclusion in next year's edition of Stilwell's Britain: Bed & Breakfast/Cycleway Companion.

B&B Owner's Name ....

B&B Address ....

....

B&B Tel No ....

Reasons for Nomination ....

....

....

Nominated by ....

Nominee's Address ....

Send this form to:
Britain: B&B, Stilwell Publishing Ltd, The Courtyard,
59 Charlotte Road, Shoreditch, London, EC2A 3QT.

ORDER A COPY FOR A FRIEND OR COLLEAGUE

Yes, I wish to order a copy of

( ) **Stilwell's Directory: Britain - Bed & Breakfast 1998 @ £11.95 (inc. £2 p&p)**

( ) **Stilwell's Directory: Ireland - Bed & Breakfast 1998 @ £7.95 (inc. £1 p&p)**

( ) **Stilwell's National Trail Companion 1998 @ £10.95 (inc. £1 p&p)**

( ) **Stilwell's Cycleway Companion 1998 @ £10.95 (inc. £1 p&p)**

Sterling or EC currency cheques only please, made payable to Stilwell Publishing Ltd. Please send me my copy within 21 days of receipt of this order.

Name ....

Address ....

....

.... Postcode ....

Tel No ....

Please send this order form, accompanied by your payment, to:
Copy Sales, Stilwell Publishing Ltd, The Courtyard, 59 Charlotte Road, Shoreditch, London, EC2A 3QT.

Please debit my credit/payment card (Visa/Mastercard only).

Card No. .... Expiry date ..../........./........

Signature ....

If different from above please state card-holder name exactly as it appears on the card, followed by card-holder address.

ORDER A COPY FOR A FRIEND OR COLLEAGUE

Yes, I wish to order a copy of

( ) **Stilwell's Directory: Britain - Bed & Breakfast 1998 @ £11.95 (inc. £2 p&p)**

( ) **Stilwell's Directory: Ireland - Bed & Breakfast 1998 @ £7.95 (inc. £1 p&p)**

( ) **Stilwell's National Trail Companion 1998 @ £10.95 (inc. £1 p&p)**

( ) **Stilwell's Cycleway Companion 1998 @ £10.95 (inc. £1 p&p)**

Sterling or EC currency cheques only please, made payable to Stilwell Publishing Ltd. Please send me my copy within 21 days of receipt of this order.

Name ....

Address ....

....

.... Postcode ....

Tel No ....

Please send this order form, accompanied by your payment, to:
Copy Sales, Stilwell Publishing Ltd, The Courtyard, 59 Charlotte Road, Shoreditch, London, EC2A 3QT.

Please debit my credit/payment card (Visa/Mastercard only).

Card No. .... Expiry date ..../......./........

Signature ....

If different from above please state card-holder name exactly as it appears on the card, followed by card-holder address.